ROUTLEDGE LIBRARY EDITIONS:
POLITICAL THOUGHT AND POLITICAL
PHILOSOPHY

Volume 42

THE PROBLEM OF FEDERALISM

THE PROBLEM OF FEDERALISM
A Study in the History of Political Theory - Volume One

SOBEI MOGI

LONDON AND NEW YORK

First published in 1931 by George Allen & Unwin Ltd.

This edition first published in 2020
by Routledge
2 Park Square, Milton Park, Abingdon, Oxon OX14 4RN

and by Routledge
52 Vanderbilt Avenue, New York, NY 10017

Routledge is an imprint of the Taylor & Francis Group, an informa business

© 1931 Sobei Mogi

All rights reserved. No part of this book may be reprinted or reproduced or utilised in any form or by any electronic, mechanical, or other means, now known or hereafter invented, including photocopying and recording, or in any information storage or retrieval system, without permission in writing from the publishers.

Trademark notice: Product or corporate names may be trademarks or registered trademarks, and are used only for identification and explanation without intent to infringe.

British Library Cataloguing in Publication Data
A catalogue record for this book is available from the British Library

ISBN: 978-0-367-21961-1 (Set)
ISBN: 978-0-429-35434-2 (Set) (ebk)
ISBN: 978-0-367-22241-3 (Volume 42) (hbk)
ISBN: 978-0-429-27402-2 (Volume 42) (ebk)

Publisher's Note
The publisher has gone to great lengths to ensure the quality of this reprint but points out that some imperfections in the original copies may be apparent.

Disclaimer
The publisher has made every effort to trace copyright holders and would welcome correspondence from those they have been unable to trace.

THE PROBLEM OF FEDERALISM

A STUDY IN THE HISTORY OF
POLITICAL THEORY

by

SOBEI MOGI

With a Preface by
PROFESSOR HAROLD J. LASKI

VOLUME ONE

LONDON
GEORGE ALLEN & UNWIN LTD
MUSEUM STREET

FIRST PUBLISHED IN 1931

All rights reserved
PRINTED IN GREAT BRITAIN BY
UNWIN BROTHERS LTD., WOKING

TO
PROFESSOR HAROLD J. LASKI

PREFACE

It is not often that a student learned in the ways of oriental civilisation has sought technically to appraise the drift of Western ideas. I venture to think that Mr. Mogi's discussion of modern federalism will be found interesting if only because it reveals the impact of peculiarly Western conceptions upon a mind to which they have come with the full force of novelty. Mr. Mogi has traversed ground which it is unlikely any scholar will travel again, at least in quite the same way. His report upon the nature of the territory he has crossed has value because it indicates to other scholars the rich materials which await detailed investigation.

During the course of his work Mr. Mogi has often remarked to me upon the paucity of books dealing with the theme he has been studying. Englishmen, notably, have done all too little for the historical study of political ideas. Few even of our own classical texts have been really well edited; many of them are unavailable to the average reader; and some of the most seminal works of continental thinkers remain practically unknown in this country. If Mr. Mogi's book draws attention to the need for further work in this field, I am certain he will feel himself amply repaid.

Perhaps I ought to add that Mr. Mogi's method of investigation and his scheme of values are both his own. In discussing the work with him in the last few years, I have been astonished at the decisiveness of his own judgment and the ease with which he has moved amidst alien literatures. He has paid European civilisation a great compliment by his intense and patient interest in its political philosophy. I hope that his ardent toil will meet with the recognition it deserves.

HAROLD J. LASKI

NOTE

The present work is an attempt at a comprehensive and critical survey of the historical development and practical application of the idea of federalism as a form of state organisation—an ideal federal form which in the author's judgment must be adopted more and more as real democracy progresses, and the functions which the state is called on to perform increase accordingly.

The literature of the subject is extensive, and I hope that the present survey will be useful to students of a political problem of great complexity, the solution of which is of vital importance for the reason indicated.

I must express my sincere thanks to Professor Harold J. Laski, my teacher, who inspired me to take up the study of political science during my work at the London School of Economics and Political Science. I must also thank him and Mr. and Mrs. Percy Ashley for kindly reading my manuscripts and proofs in the course of publication.

SOBEI MOGI

LONDON
September, 1931

"Le vingtième siècle ouvrira l'ère des fédérations, ou l'humanité recommencera un purgatoire de mille ans.

"Le vrai problème à résoudre n'est pas en réalité le problème politique, c'est le problème économique."
P. J. Proudhon.
Du Principe Fédératif.

"We are in the midst of a new movement for the conquest of self-government."
Harold J. Laski.
The Pluralistic State.

CONTENTS

	PAGE
PREFACE (Professor Harold J. Laski)	7
AUTHOR'S NOTE	9

PART I

THE HISTORY OF AMERICAN FEDERAL IDEAS

CHAPTER I

DEVELOPMENT OF FEDERAL IDEAS BEFORE THE EIGHTEENTH CENTURY   21

§ 1. Modern federalism—Origin of the federal idea—Grecian federalism—Aristotle—Polybius and Strabo—Rise of the Roman Empire—Engelbert von Volkerdorf—Dante—Bartolus—Rise of the territorial state and conception of sovereignty—Jean Bodin—Johannes Althusius—Hoenonius, Casmannus and Christoph Besold—Ludolph Hugo—Hugo Grotius—Pufendorf

§ 2. Influence of the seventeenth and eighteenth centuries on modern federalism—Hobbes—John Locke—Montesquieu—J. J. Rousseau—Kant's international federalism

CHAPTER II

DEVELOPMENT OF THE IDEAS OF MODERN FEDERALISM IN THE UNITED STATES OF AMERICA   42

§ 1. Underlying idea of federalism in America—Harrington, Algernon Sydney, John Locke—Conditions of early American colonies—Puritanism and colonial politics—Roger Williams and John Cotton—Thomas Hooker—Mayflower Covenant and Quaker Communities—Discontent with England—Revolution—Declaration of Independence—Formation of American Confederation—Constitution of 1787

CHAPTER III

IDEAS OF THE FEDERALISTS   50

§ 1. Outline of the federal theory of Hamilton, Madison and Jay

§ 2. Nature of the federal state—The fundamental principles—Republican form of government—Its legislative, executive and judicial system—Standardisation of the form of government—Majority rule—Executive efficiency—Interrelation of authority—The organisation of federal assemblies—Distribution of powers—Main principle

CHAPTER IV

THE FEDERALISM OF JEFFERSON   PAGE 72

§ 1. Comparison of Jefferson and Hamilton—Jefferson's republicanism and his theory of constitution—Jeffersonian democracy and sovereignty—Decentralisation and federalism—Amendment of constitution—Main principle

CHAPTER V

THE FEDERAL IDEAS OF DE TOCQUEVILLE   86

§ 1. Development of the American federal state—General political idea—The conception of sovereignty—Principle of federalism—Relation of federal and individual states—Characteristics of federalism—Republicanism and federalism—Organs of the federal state—Federalism and democracy

CHAPTER VI

DEVELOPMENT OF FEDERAL IDEAS IN THE UNITED STATES OF AMERICA FROM KENT TO CALHOUN AND WEBSTER   97

§ 1. Federal ideas from 1800 to 1861—Chief Justice Marshall—James Kent—Joseph Story—Madison's later views

§ 2. The federal idea of St. George Tucker—Of William Rawle

§ 3. John Calhoun—Conception of sovereignty—Of federalism—Theory of nullification and secession

§ 4. Daniel Webster—Conception of sovereignty—Federalism, constitutionalism and theory of nullification

CHAPTER VII

DEVELOPMENT OF FEDERAL IDEAS, 1866–1900   122

§ 1. The general development of the federal state before and after the Civil War—Rise of a new federal idea—Francis Lieber—Theory of the state—Conception of sovereignty—Federalism—Historical survey of the federal State—Idea of secession—Constitutionalism and federalism

§ 2. Political and economic condition of the United States after the Civil War—Austinian theory of state and conception of sovereignty—Austinian principle of federalism—Political and federal principle of O. Brownson—of Joel Tiffany and John N. Pomeroy—of John C. Hurd

§ 3. Federal theory of J. A. Jameson—of T. Woolsey—of John W. Burgess

§ 4. Survey of later nineteenth century federal ideas

CONTENTS

CHAPTER VIII

BRYCE'S THEORY OF FEDERALISM   162

§ 1. Rise of American nationalism—Idea of the federal state of America—System of the federal state—Conception of sovereignty and distribution of powers—Nullification and secession—Federal state, legislative, executive and judicature—Merits and demerits of federalism

CHAPTER IX

DEVELOPMENT OF AMERICAN FEDERAL IDEAS FROM THE BEGINNING OF THE TWENTIETH CENTURY TO THE PRESENT DAY   177

§ 1. Political and economic conditions of America in 1900

§ 2. Woodrow Wilson

§ 3. A. L. Lowell—W. W. Willoughby—Willoughby's theory of federalism—German influence of federalism

§ 4. German legal conception of federalism on the theory of Willoughby and his followers—Merriam—Dunning—H. J. Ford

§ 5. Rise of pragmatic philosophy—William James—Roscoe Pound—John Dewey's pragmatic logic—Views of Croly and Lippman—Charles Beard's federalism—F. J. Goodnow on public administration—Present-day American federalism—Contrasting views of W. Thompson and H. P. Judson—Pragmatic theory of the pluralistic state

PART II

THE HISTORY OF BRITISH FEDERAL IDEAS

CHAPTER I

DEVELOPMENT OF BRITISH FEDERAL IDEAS FROM THE SEVENTEENTH CENTURY UP TO THE PRESENT DAY   207

§ 1. Formation of the United Kingdom—John Locke—David Hume's utilitarianism and federalism

§ 2. Colonial development of the British Empire—David Hume—Adam Smith—Edmund Burke—Bentham and James Mill

§ 3. Development of federalism in Canada—Report of Lord Durham—Problem of union between Lower and Upper Canada—Statesmanship of Earl Grey and Elgin's Viceroyship—Formation of responsible government—Quebec Resolution of 1864—Canadian federalism—The federal ideal of John MacDonald—The British North America Act—Earl of Carnarvon on the Canadian federal constitution

§ 4. Colonial development of the British Empire—Rise of Imperial federalism—Godley, Sir Julius Vogel and Joseph Howe—Edward Jenkins—Goldwin Smith on imperial federation—Sir Robert Rogers

—Disraeli's view of imperial unity—Sir F. E. Young—S. W. Kelsey—Forster—Formation of the Imperial Federation League—C. C. Cunningham—N. D. Davis on representative councils—John Morley—Seeley—F. P. Labillière—Gladstone's attitude towards imperial federation in 1893—Activities of the Imperial Federation League up to 1911

§ 5. Formation of the Colonial Conference of 1887—Lord Haldane's view on the federal constitutions in the Empire—Rise of the Australian federal commonwealth—Report on trade and plantation—Establishment of responsible government of New Zealand in 1854—in the Australian colonies in 1850—Australian inter-colonial federation mooted—Attempted tariff agreement between New South Wales and Victoria—Suggestion of inter-colonial free trade—Repeal of Australian Colonial Duties Act—Charles Gavan Duffy's Royal Commission—Inter-colonial Conference of 1881—Draft federal constitution of Sir Henry Parkes—Convention of the colonies of Australia in 1883—Australian movement towards federation—Meeting of representatives of the colonies in 1890—National Australian Convention in 1891—Conference of Australian Prime Ministers in 1895—Convention of 1897—Australian Federation Bill of 1900—Nature of Australian federalism—Joseph Chamberlain

§ 6. Formation of the Union of South Africa—Imperial federalism of Baron Felix von Oppenheimer—Imperial Conference of 1911—Asquith's views—Devolution—T. A. Spalding's idea on devolution—The majority and minority reports on devolution—The Webbs' ideal socialist commonwealth—The functional guild state of G. D. H. Cole—Laski's view of devolution—Finer's functional representation—Committee system of Parliament—Murray MacDonald's view of devolution—Dicey's unwritten constitution of the Imperial Conference—Federal India

CHAPTER II

MODERN FEDERAL IDEAS IN GREAT BRITAIN   277

§ 1. Jeremy Bentham
§ 2. John Austin
§ 3. John Stuart Mill
§ 4. Edward A. Freeman
§ 5. James Bryce—Henry Sidgwick—Dicey
§ 6. Rise of the pluralist theory of the state—Otto Gierke's *Genossenschaftstheorie* and Maitland's pluralist legal theory—Frederick W. Maitland's theory of personality of organised groups—The conception of the right and duty bearing unit—John N. Figgis's conception of Church in the modern state—Guild socialist state of A. J. Penty and S. G. Hobson—G. D. H. Cole's view of pluralist state—The Webbs' pluralist socialist commonwealth—Ernest Barker's discredited state—Laski's pluralist theory of the state—Laski's pragmatic utilitarianism and federalism

PART III

THE HISTORY OF GERMAN FEDERAL IDEAS

CHAPTER I

PAGE

DEVELOPMENT OF FEDERAL IDEAS FROM HUGO AND PUFENDORF TO GEORG WAITZ ... 327

§ 1. Grecian federalism—Federal idea in the Roman Empire—Feudalism and federalism—Formation of the United Netherlands in 1579—Johannes Althusius—Hugo Grotius and Pufendorf—Ludolph Hugo—The development of the federal idea from American federalists to Georg Waitz

§ 2. Mediaeval Germanic communities—The Reformation—Rise of the German territorial states—Kammeralists and Frederick the Great—The Napoleonic invasion of German Empire—Destruction of German feudalism—Formation of the *Rheinbund* in 1806—Frederick the Great's ideal of *Fürstenbund*—Rise of German nationalism—The philosophy of Kant and Hegel—Savigny's historical legalism—Stahl's religious interpretation of jurisprudence—German legal philosophy—The Confederation of 1815—The Frankfurt liberalism of 1848 and American federalism—Rise of the *Staatslehre*—Juristic theory of unions of states—General survey of German federalism

§ 3. The federal ideas of Ludolph Hugo—Pufendorf—J. J. Moser—Johann Stephen Pütter—Häberlein and Leist—Publicists in the early nineteenth century—International federalism of Montesquieu, Wolff, Kant and Spinoza—Influence of *Rheinbund* on federal idea—The federal conceptions of K. S. Zachariä—Günther Heinrich von Berg—W. J. Behr—J. L. Klüber—Heeren and J. F. Fries—Friedrich W. Tittmann

§ 4. Rise of liberalism—Schurig's *Fürstenbund*—Federal idea of Friedrich von Gagern—P. A. Pfizer—Carl Welcker—Influence of the French Revolution of 1848 on German federal development—Revision of Swiss Constitution—Federal conceptions of Kasimir Pfyffer and Troxler—Ludwig Snell—Frankfurt National Assembly

§ 5. The federal idea of J. K. Bluntschli—Heinrich A. Zachariä——J. Stahl and Radowitz

CHAPTER II

DEVELOPMENT OF FEDERAL IDEAS FROM GEORG WAITZ TO MAX SEYDEL ... 369

§ 1. Georg Waitz—Political idea—Theory of state—Conception of sovereignty—The union of states—Theory of federal state

§ 2. German federal idea after Waitz—Federal conception of Hermann Schulze—Rise of the *Herrschaftstheorie*—C. F. Gerber's federal conception—H. Ahren's philosophical theory of federalism—Robert von Mohl's juristic theory of federalism—The federal idea of H. von Treitschke—Rüttimann—H. A. Zachariä—Pözl—Heinrich Escher—Heinrich Zöpfl—Otto Mejer—Carl von Kaltenborn—Joseph Held—Philosophical federalism of A. Trendelenburg—J. Blumer

§ 3. The contrasting views of von Mohl and Georg Meyer—Rise of the theory of *Competenz-Competenz*—Federal idea of Böhlau—Rönne—G. Meyer—Robert von Mohl's theory of federal state—Comparison of von Mohl and G. Meyer—Federal conception of F. von Martitz—G. Meyer—von Mohl—L. Auerbach—Joseph Held—Max Seydel

CHAPTER III

DEVELOPMENT OF FEDERAL IDEAS FROM MAX SEYDEL TO SIEGFRIED BRIE   418

§ 1. Federal idea of Max Seydel—Albert Haenel

§ 2. The federal theory of Paul Laband—Phillip Zorn—Constantinus Bake—Bluntschli's later federal view

§ 3. Georg Jellinek—Theory of union of the state—Theory of the state conception of sovereignty

§ 4. Jellinek's division of the union of the states—Historical-political unions—Colony—Incorporation—Personal union—Unorganised unions—Community of states and system of states—State treaty—Treaty occupation and subordination of a state in administration—Alliance—Protection guarantee and perpetual neutrality—*Staatenstaat*

§ 5. Organised unions—International administrative unions—Confederation—Real union

§ 6. Jellinek's theory of the federal state—Principle of federalism

§ 7. Heinrich Rosin—Theory of state and conception of sovereignty—Federalism

§ 8. Siegfried Brie—Theory of state—Conception of sovereignty—Theory of the union of states—Unorganised state association

§ 9. Brie's theory of permanent organised association of states—Confederation and federal state

§ 10. G. Meyer's theory—Theory and conception of state sovereignty—G. Meyer's later view of the federal state

INDEX   589

PART I
THE HISTORY OF AMERICAN FEDERAL IDEAS

CHAPTER I

DEVELOPMENT OF FEDERAL IDEAS BEFORE THE EIGHTEENTH CENTURY

§ 1

The idea of federalism in the modern sense can hardly have reached any political thinkers till the time when the American constitution was drawn up.

The constitution of 1787 in the United States of America was influenced chiefly by political expediency, rather than by any political legacy of federal doctrine from Europe. The federal idea, which federal authority infused into the individual life of the members of the states as the standard of the nation without their governmental agency, was first shown to us by the formulated policy of the American federalists. In order to realise a true federalism, we must look at the idea in its germ as well as in its development, and must trace federal principles from their birth.

The first glimpse of the federal principle was about the third century B.C. (281–146), in Greece.[1] There is, however, no sufficiently clear description of federalism in Greek political thought even though the first confederacy in history was the Achaean League. There were problems of practical politics; how, for instance, to unite several city states at particular times for special purposes. The association of the Amphictyonic Council was merely a voluntary association of city states for specific purposes under the oath of the Temple of Delphos. However freely deputies were appointed by the citizens, and whatever authority was vested in the council, its aims were limited to the common welfare and the declaration or cessation of war.

The power of the elaborate city state, which was based upon absolute sovereignty, was so strong that powerful members, instead of being kept in due subordination, could tyrannise over the weak.

[1] Before the Grecian Age there were crude types of federations. The government of the Israelites was a federation held together by no political authority, but by the unity of race and faith, and founded, not on physical force, but on a voluntary covenant. The principle of self-government was carried out not only in each tribe, but in every group of at least one hundred and twenty families; and there was neither privilege of rank nor inequality before the law.

The Achaean League, in the strict sense of confederation, was a perfect union on paper and in theory, but the members of the League held independent political power in various forms of government and no direct contact between the populace and the Senate was permitted.

The Abbé de Mably remarked of Greece that "the popular government, which was so tempestuous elsewhere, caused no disorders in the members of the Achaean Republic, because it was there tempered by the general authority and law of confederacy."

It was only when the Romans were summoned to aid Achaia against Macedonian aggression that internal dissensions broke out. These dissensions, fostered by the Romans, soon led to the destruction of "the last hope of Greece" and the bondage of the members of the Achaean League.

The relations between the members of the League, whether it had general laws or not, depended upon the authority of the constituent cities and the degree of strength and practically unequal basis of the union.

The culture of the city states was high, and was so brilliant that each independent state could hardly enter into a union on equal terms without sacrificing its pride, prestige and its own peculiar political issues. Naturally political democracy was confined to meetings in the market-place of the free citizens, who used their slaves as machines for production and served the public in no other capacity than as mere consumers. To them the Achaean League was only a piece of political mechanism to prevent external invasion and diplomatic impropriety.

Aristotle, in his *Politics*, touches on a hundred institutions in his remarkable survey, but though there had been instances of union before the time of Aristotle, he never discusses the form of federal government, which had been of the loose kind, and the "federal revival" began many years after his death, when the Achaean League was constituted on a new basis.

At the time of Aristotle there was a variety of city states scattered around the Athenian democracy. He criticised, analysed and compared the numerous political institutions from his ethical standpoint and furnished and contributed the *Politics* to the growth of political philosophy on the basis of "political justice."

From his definition of the state he denounced an alliance of any sort, because "a state exists for the sake of a good life," but not "for the sake of alliance or maintenance of injustice," and an alliance is a mere society if intercourse with one another is of the same kind after as before the union.[1] And he said further that "there are no magistracies common to the contracting parties who will enforce their engagements, different states have each their own magistracies; nor does one state take care that the citizens of the other are such as they ought to be, nor see that those who come under the terms of the treaty do no wrong or wickedness at all but that only they do no injustice to one another,"[2] and he added that "the community becomes a mere alliance which differs only in place from alliances of which the members live apart, and law is only a convention,"—"a surety to one another of justice," as the sophist Lycophron says, and "has no real power to make the citizen good and just."[3]

On this argument the state exists for the sake of a good life on the basis of relative equality and freedom and justice.

This relative justice and relative freedom should be based upon the virtue of good government and adapted to the varying functions of good citizens. The great mind of Aristotle could not acknowledge federalism as a good governmental organisation, since its principles were animated by compromise.

Polybius described the Achaean League, and although he recognised the unitary laws, weights and measures, coinage, supreme administration, councils and judges, which made a union much closer than a mere treaty or alliance—in fact created a union which, if enclosed within town walls, would be a single state, even then he did not realise that a new state distinct from the individual states had been created, i.e. the relation of the member states to the collective state.[4]

And Strabo, a Greek geographer and historian, also described only cursorily and superficially the Achaean and Lykian Leagues, which he called *systema*; after him we hear nothing for centuries about the union of states.[5]

Although neither from "enlightened" monarchy, which Plato emphasised, nor from the "mediating middle class," to which Aristotle adhered, did the actual experience in the Grecian states tend to uphold the Achaean League; nevertheless a bridge was built by which thought passed from the narrow unit of the city to the wide cosmopolitanism on which Stoicism was based.

[1] Aristotle: *Politics*, trans. by Benjamen Jowett, 1923, pp. 118–119.
[2] Ibid., p. 118.   [3] Ibid., p. 118.
[4] Polybius: *Historiæ*, ed. Bekker, II, p. 37. S. Brie: *Der Bundestaat*, 1874, p. 10. G. J. Ebers: *Die Lehre vom Staatenbunde*, 1910, p. 4.
[5] Strabo: *Geography*, VIII, 6, Secs. 18, 25; IX, 3, Sec. 7; XIV, 3, Sec. 3.

Modern federalism has gained little from the legacy of Greek politics except a vague experience of confederation, and it is experience which is the real root of political philosophy.

The Roman Empire dominated Europe under the auspices of the Roman Emperors, and developed the brilliant unitary sovereign empire until the growth of barbarian power put an end to its shadowy supremacy.

The Roman Empire derived its political philosophy from Stoic cosmopolitanism and its moral virtue from the Christian Fathers. Its political frame was formulated partly by the fundamental ideas of Athenian democracy. Nevertheless, on the one hand the Roman law had infallible supremacy in the secular sphere, while on the other hand Christianity was a general guardian of virtue in the spiritual sphere. Several cities or towns independently made unions for the purpose of political relations, in order to preserve their independence, but still throughout the Empire there was a single sovereign law, which subjugated all the members.

Though the people of Rome had been in favour of ruling men by kindness rather than by fear, and conquered foreign nations by faith and friendship rather than by hard bondage, yet, as Grotius said, "it is true that it often happens that he who is superior in the league be much more powerful than the rest, and he by degrees usurps a sovereignty over them especially if the league be perpetual."

In these periods, the legists in order to distinguish between empires and kingdoms which were composed within the state, applied to this latter the term *universitas*. But the hard fact was that there were within the Empire kingdoms and cities which had actual independence—i.e. the rule of the Emperor was little more than nominal. All the jurists clung to the idea that the *universitates* were only groups which constituted each a single legal unit, but not a "state."

Only a few pre-eminent thinkers, such as Engelbert von Volkersdorf and Dante, ascribed to the Emperor the realisation of general prosperity or the fostering of the higher interests of the state, and to the individual states the realisation of the prosperity of the individual nations and care for this particular interest, and thus approximated to the idea of the federal state.[1]

---

[1] *Engelberti abbatis Admontensis Liber de Ortu, Progressu et Fine imperii Romani* (in the Maxima bibliotheca veterum patrum, tomus XXV, Lugduni, 1577), Cap. 15 argum. tertium and cap. 17. Dante: *De Monarchia*, ed. Alessandro, Torri, 1844, Lib. I, cap. 16.

Bartolus, a Roman jurist, laid down that the essential tendency of the state was sovereignty, and divided all unions into two forms:—(a) *Universitates*, subject to no superior; (b) *Universitates*, recognising a superior. The former was restricted to the state conception and the latter represented the union, but he made no distinction between *civitas*, *regnum* and *imperium*, the differences between which were, from the standpoint of the human organisation, merely quantitative.[1]

This was the first step towards making clear the conception of federation.

But for a long time the traditional doctrine prevailed. Leagues of states were discussed on the same basis as colleges of doctors, students, etc. They were discussed as if they were bodies corporate without any special political nature or characteristic.

In the Holy Roman Empire the term *universitas* (subject to no superior) was enlarged to include all *universitates*, which had no superior except the Emperor—and by this they were recognised as having something of sovereignty; but still no clear distinction was drawn between corporations whose status was based on private law and those based on public law.

The downfall of the Roman Empire was followed by the anarchical stage of feudal Europe. Nevertheless, the mediaeval political system implanted a germ of federalism in the community by its employment of co-ordinated authority. The impulse towards constitutional methods was almost certainly inaugurated by the conciliar movement which sought to reduce papal domination to constitutional authority.

But I am quite in agreement with Gierke that no federalism had been explicitly manifested until the conception of sovereign states came into existence.[2] Just as in the ecclesiastical so in the international community, in relation to the unions of states the conception of sovereignty was first expressed by the theory which excluded every possibility of one state being over the others.

Ever since the federative structure was constructed, attention was drawn by the political and legal thinkers to the choice between the adoption of federal relations between a number of fully sovereign states and that of a corporate unitary state (*ein gegliederter Einheitsstaat*).

Accordingly the modern national state is based on sovereign authority, and is a ferment to produce a right idea of federalism.

[1] Otto Gierke: *Das deutsche Genossenschaftsrecht*, 1881, III, pp. 355–356. *Johannes Althusius*, 1880, pp. 231–232.   [2] Ibid., *Johannes Althusius*, pp. 235–237.

It is therefore not surprising that the first advocate of the federal idea on a theoretical basis was Jean Bodin, who was the founder of the modern theory of sovereignty.

Bodin in 1577 emphasised the co-operative character of federalism, and since there was no compatibility between this and the conception of sovereignty, he was convinced that the unions must be based on treaty and divided them into *foedera aequa* and *foedera iniqua*.[1]

His idea of unequal federation was that in which "the one acknowledgeth the other to be superior in the treatie of alliance; which is in two sorts, that is to wit, when the one acknowledgeth the other to be his superiour for honour, and yet is not in his protection: or else the one receiueth the other into protection, and both the one and the other is bound to pay a certaine pention or to give certaine succours, or owe neither pention nor succours"; that is to say, the members of the federation were absorbed into a single common sovereignty. Yet obviously this is nothing but a unitary state, constituted either by annexation or conquest.

Equal federation meant federation of powers marked by a diversity of form of government, strength, riches, etc., this being not more than a mere association of friends.

By the term, *aequum foedus* he meant that "the one is in nothing superiour unto the other in the treatie; and that the one hath nothing above the other for their prerogative of honour, albeit that the one must do or give more or lesse than the other for the aid that the one oweth unto the other."

Under this heading he criticised the position of the canton in the Swiss Confederation and the various Grecian and Roman leagues and referred to the "Estate of the Empire of Germans, which we will in due place show to bee no monarchie, but a pure Aristocratie, composed of the princes of the Empire, of the seuen electors and the imperiall cities."[2] In his doctrine such a social confederation cannot be called a state but is a mere confederation. It was a mere loose union of several sovereign states which did not recognise anything more vital than the purpose of defence and attack. He assumed that the cantons in Switzerland were not in any sense a nation or a state at all.

It was impossible to recognise or to reconcile the corporative and constitutional union of the states with his conception of sovereignty.

In the overwhelming domination of Bodinian absolutism, a

---

[1] Jean Bodin (*Bodinus De Republica*, Lib. I, cap. 7): *The Six Books of Commonweale*, trans. by Richard Knolles, 1606, p. 73.   [2] Ibid., pp. 75–84.

writer who went further into the question of federal union than any other thinkers or jurists and set up the popular sovereignty against the dominant influence of the Bodinian absolute conception of sovereignty, was Johannes Althusius. His famous *Politica* was published in 1603, and in it he tried to explain the federal principle on the basis of the doctrine of the people's sovereignty.

Althusius divided confederations into two kinds, the *confederatio plena* (complete confederation) on the one hand, and the *confederatio non plena* (incomplete confederation) on the other.[1]

To him *confederatio plena* meant that all the component bodies were dissolved into a single state in which was vested one sovereign authority, whilst the *confederatio non plena* was that the confederated states maintained their full sovereignty and pledged themselves to mutual assistance for their common good.

There were innumerable examples of such unions in the mediaeval Italian cities, each of which was governed by a single authority in accordance with the common pact between the members of its union.

The complete confederation as such was based upon a sovereign state, in which no federal spirit whatsoever was embodied.

Incomplete confederation was a union of states for some particular purpose, and was nothing more than an association of friendly powers.

There were three types of federation in this category:—

i. The first system of federation was a mere alliance between states or provinces or towns, of such a kind as the league between Venice and Florence, or England and France to resist papal dominance.

ii. The second was a personal union, such as the union between Denmark and Holstein.

iii. The last was a confederation such as the Swiss Confederacy, in which the component cantons sent their representatives to the confederation and they met together to discuss and settle matters by their delegated authority. The problems with which they dealt were referred back to the citizens of each canton and decided by referendum. This idea of the ratification of legislation was due to Swiss political expediency.

Althusius, in his third edition of the *Politica*, 1614, made an immense advance in the federal idea.[2] He defined the complete confederation as follows: "Plena consociatio et confederatio est,

[1] Johan. Althusii, U.J.D.: *Politica, methodicé digesta atque exemplis sacris et profanis illustrata*, 1603, Chap. VII.   [2] Otto Gierke: *Johannes Althusius*, pp. 14–15.

quâ alienum regnum, ejusque regnicolae, vel provincia, aut consociatio universalis quaevis alia, communicatis legibus fundamentalibus regni, et juribus majestatis, in plenum integrumque jus et communionem regni adsumuntur, cooptantur, et quasi in unum idemque corpus conjunguntur et coalescunt, tanquam unius ejusdemque corporis membra."[1]

As to the incomplete federations he said: "Non-plena confederatio est, qua diversae provinciae vel regna, salvo singulis suo majestatis jure, quoad auxilia mutua contra hostes ferenda, vel quoad fidem praestandam et pacem inter se et amicitiam colendam, vel quoad communes amicos, vel hostes communi sumptu habendos, ultro citroq; solemniter icto federe, seu pacto inito, ad tempus certum, quod melius vel incertum, se obligant."[2] As to these, Althusius pointed out that it is necessary to take great care lest any agreements entered into by one of the parties should be of such a nature as to affect adversely the others.

As to the competence of the confederation Althusius wrote: "Ideoque hic ponderanda sunt 1. potentia confederandi socii; 2. fides et constantia confederandi socii ex anteactis; 3. similitudo morum; 4. aequa et honesta conditio inter confederatos, an ex federe nihil, aut parum utilitatis, ad conferedatum veniat."[3]

The obligations and pacts of the confederates were, he said, laid down in definite laws and conditions duly recorded and confirmed by the oaths of the parties to them. These "laws" concern mainly three matters: "1. de defensione mutua contra vim et injuriam; 2. de concordia inter confederatos fovenda et conservanda; 3. de administratione communium jurium sociorum confederatorum."[4]

The first of these classes of laws or pacts dealt with the mutual defence of the members against external or internal attack, with the obligation to give aid quickly, and to act as loyal allies in peace and war. The second class provided for the amicable settlement of disputes between the members of the confederation by conciliation or even arbitration, and for mutual obligations not to make war on each other or to assist any confederated state to attack another, not to levy taxes against one another, and not to harbour fugitive criminals, and to facilitate commercial intercourse, etc. And the third class of laws provided for contributions to common expenditure in war, the equitable distribution of territorial gains or monetary indemnities, and so on.[5]

---

[1] Johan. Althusii, U.J.D.: *Politica methodicé digesta atque exemplis sacris et profanis illustrata*, 5th ed., 1654, Chap. XVII, Sec. 27.   [2] Ibid., Sec. 30.
[3] Ibid., Sec. 31.   [4] Ibid., Sec. 33.   [5] Ibid., Secs. 34–40.

As to the relationship between the states and the confederation, though the joint assemblies had the right to decide general affairs, even by a majority vote, yet the states should remain fully sovereign. But he did not assume it as *Republica Corpus*, but as that which maintained its own territory and its supreme rights, "tantum communicans cum sociis, quantum interipsos est conventum."

At the same time, in his definition of the constitution of the United Provinces of Netherland, he used the expressions "Concilia universalis consociationis," and especially "Comitia sociorum confederationum." He said, "superest, ut nunc etiam quaedam dicamus de conventibus, conciliis et comitiis confederatorum sociorum, qui singuli separata majestatis jura habent et usurpant, atque ita diversas Respublicas et politias constituunt. Jus igitur convocandi confederatos socios, et conventus publici indicendi ex communi sociorum consensu constituitur, et plerumque est ambulatorium, à principe, vel primo socio confederato hebdomadatim progrediens usq; ad ultimum, ut à confederatis sociis Belgicis fieri solet: vel uni ex sociis communi consensu conceditur."[1]

Thus he made no clear demarcation between the union and the league.

The greatest merit of Althusius, and one for which Otto Gierke, the champion of the *Genossenschaftstheorie* in the nineteenth century, was indebted to him, is his theory of the corporation. Althusius formulated the federal idea on the basis of both actuality and his religious and political doctrines, and laid down its system and principles.

The main weakness of his theory was that he firstly accepted the conception of social contract as a principle and built it into his structure, thereby dissolving all public law into private law.

He asserted that there is a natural law structure of society in which families, vocational associations, communes and provinces all exist as necessary and organic members intermediate between the individuals and the state and in which the wider union is consolidated from the corporative unities of the narrower unions and thereby obtains its members. These narrower unions as real and organic communities create by themselves a distinct common life and a legal sphere of their own, and at the same time give up to the larger union so much as it needs in order to fulfil its specific purposes. Finally the state was generically similar to its

[1] Johan. Althusii, U.J.D.: *Politica methodicé digesta atque exemplis sacris et profanis illustrata*, 5th ed., 1654, Chap. XXXIII, Sec. 122.

member unions, and was differentiated from them only by its exclusive sovereignty which, as the highest earthly legal authority, has a fulness of new and special attributes and functions, but encounters an insuperable obstacle in the "own rights" of the narrower unions, and if it encroaches on them will break down before the revival of the members' sovereignty resulting from the violation of the pact of union.

Althusius' corporation theory affected the development of doctrine in two different directions—those of the conception of the consolidated state on the one hand, and of the conception of confederation on the other.

Hoenonius, as the follower of Althusius, made a clear distinction between the *respublica simplex* which consisted of a single town, and the *respublica composita* formed of a number of towns or developed into a *regnum* or *imperium* by transference of the federal idea. And Otto Casmannus in 1603 also distinguished between the *composita respublica* and the *civitates confederatae*.[1]

In amplifying this formula, he understood by a "consolidated" state any state which consisted of several states, cities and districts joined together under the same government, or brought together in a single political organisation, so that a kingdom was the corresponding union of several states or duchies under the government of a king, and an empire was several kingdoms under the rule of an emperor. So, according to him, confederated states come into existence as soon as neighbouring states join together for protection against common enemies, or for interests of trade and communication, or for other reasons make a compact about particular matters involving mutual trust upon a purely voluntary basis.

Christoph Besold, however, limited the idea of the *civitas composita* to the case in which a number of *gentes* with different *leges* are bound together in a single *corpus politicum* with a single *imperium*—a case quite different from that of the state made up of communes and corporations or from alliances and personal unions. He adduced as the main example of the *civitas composita* the Germanic Empire, the state form of which he expressly stated to be that of a "state made up of states," in which the *majestas* belonged exclusively to the whole, but the members had the nature of subordinate and relative states.[2]

---

[1] Gierke: *Johannes Althusius*, p. 245.
[2] Christoph Besold: *Diss. de jure territorium*, Chap. IV, Secs. 2–3; *Diss. praecogn. philos. compl.*, Chap. VIII, Secs. 1, 3–4 (cited by Gierke: *Johannes Althusius*, p. 245).

His theory of *Staatenstaat* developed into the conception of Ludolph Hugo, whose system was far more scientific and who developed the idea of a division of power, based on general principles, between the sovereign super-state and the states in the federation. Hugo's work, *De statu regionum Germaniae*, published in 1661, was an outstanding contribution to the German federal idea.

At the same time the other direction of federal development in the seventeenth century produced great men such as Grotius and Pufendorf.

Hugo Grotius, the founder of international law, made an advance on the natural right theory by his idea of the league, and formulated the theory of unions of state on an historical survey in his work *De Jure Belli et Pacis* in 1625.

He placed the conception of *unio* nearer to the *systema civitatum foederatarum*, and admitted the idea of equal and unequal leagues.[1]

In the political system, Grotius remarked that a federal society which was composed of a number of provinces or states had as its main purpose the continuation of the union. But with the independent security of sovereignty provinces or states made a federation for the permanent purpose of the common good. But in his historical survey of the league between Carthage and Rome he asserted that although this conditional surrender of the former to the latter by the league "is not so much the lessening the sovereign jurisdiction, as the perfect transferring of it to another," yet actually they might be admitted to a league not upon equal terms, but under the dominion of Rome.[2] The Provinces of the Netherlands combined to form the Dutch Republic and the Swiss cantons to establish the Swiss Confederation. Sovereign authority still remained in the hands of the provinces and cantons. But though nominally and legally the general authority was not transferred from sovereign states to the federal council, yet in actual practice the latter was allowed to exercise that authority. This united society was called a federated nation.

In the history of political science the conception of a federative nation originated with the introduction of the international law of Grotius.

Following on this remarkable contribution, Pufendorf developed the federal ideas on the firm basis of political theory in his book called *De Jure Naturae et Gentium*, published in 1672.

[1] Hugo Grotius: *De Jure Belli et Pacis*, 1702, II, Chap. XV, Secs. 5–6; I, Sec. 7.
[2] Ibid., Sec. 7.

His philosophy was based upon the ideas of Hobbes and Grotius. Though he condemned the theory of absolute sovereignty, yet he accepted Hobbes' general philosophical scheme and Grotius' limited ethical conception of sovereignty. Hobbes' main idea was that of absolute sovereignty, not to be sub-divided by any power.

Pufendorf, writing under the pseudonym of Severinus de Monzambano (1667), criticised the nature of the German Empire, which appeared to him as "irregulare aliquod corpus et monstro simile," and he placed it between the limited monarchy and the system of federated states. In his later works, *De republica irregulari* in 1671 and *De systematibus civitum* in 1677, he developed the theory of federalism, that is of a state containing states within itself, and consequently a personal union and the mere confederation appeared to him as the normal form of union of states.[1]

He regarded the German Empire as a transitory form between the system of the state and the unitary state. This was explained by the particular assumption of "irregularity" as a corrupt (*verderblich*) constitutional error. Therefore he characterised the German Empire "as a monstrous structure remediable only by the formation of a system of a regular state."[2]

On this assumption he divided states into the following types: (i) the regular state; (ii) the irregular state.

The "regular" state was a single sovereign state and the "irregular" state was an aggregate body politic of independent states or provinces bound together for the permanent carrying out of common aims and purposes. Such a federation was formed on the basis of administrative expediency by the collective body of powers which were transferred from sacred independent sovereignty to the collective state, which was an association for a common and permanent aim. He defined such a state as being formed "when several states are by some special bond so closely united that they seem to compose one body and yet retain each of their sovereign commands in their respective dominions." This he called the "systems of states."[3]

He declared that the "system of state" existed when several sovereign states united permanently, with a full guarantee of their sovereignty, and united by contract, or rule of alliance,

---

[1] S. von Pufendorf (*Severinus de Monzambano*): *De statu imperii Germanici*, Chap. VI, Sec. 9; *Diss. de Systematibus civitatum; De Republica Irregulari; De Jure Naturae et Gentium*, Book VII, Chap. V, Secs. 12–21.
[2] Otto Gierke: *Johannes Althusius*, p. 247.
[3] S. von Pufendorf: *De Jure Naturae et Gentium*, Book VII, Chap. V, Sec. 16.

for continuous common action for specific purpose. War, peace, foreign intercourse and alliance vested in the federal authority set up for the common purpose, and to whose support the states contributed by taxes or subsidies. Such powers as negotiation of traffic subsidies for particular cases in any single state, the appointment of magistrates, the enacting of laws, powers of life or death over their respective subjects, and ecclesiastical authority should be entirely left to the discretion of each sovereign state.

The federal state was faced with the difficulty of reconciling the independent sovereignty of each member state with the promotion of the common interests of all the states under its rule.

In the first place there must be a definitely fixed place and time of assembly for the exercise of federal functions.

To Pufendorf the federal Assembly, however permanent it might be, had difficulty in carrying out its own functions owing to the hindrance which its members caused by selecting each time representatives from the mandatory states for specific purposes.

In the second place there must be unanimity of voting in the Assembly. No majority, however large, could pass measures involving action by all the states on common lines. The members must have equality of voting rights, for it must frequently occasion great injustice if in a confederative system the plurality of votes were to bind the whole body.

In these circumstances, if the system could not operate in such a way, the union would return to the "law of nature."

Other contemporary and seventeenth-century thinkers hardly went beyond Hugo's and Pufendorf's ideas of federalism. Up to the time of the American federalists, the federative union was nothing more than a union either temporary or permanent of independent authorities for special common purposes in the face of foreign powers. Such a union is commonly termed a confederation.

The federal idea in the modern sense is one not merely of a co-partnership of the state and local units, but also involves a co-operative unity of members of each component body directly related to the federal government, and of the citizens of the community as a whole. Direct contact with the citizens of each state for the common aims has been an essential part of the idea of federalism in all political speculation since 1787.

§ 2

Before we enter into the discussion of the federalist idea we must endeavour to understand the underlying doctrine of political philosophy on which federalism is based.

The political ideas of the seventeenth century, in which Machiavellianism predominated as the gospel of *The Prince* since 1532, shifted from the continent to England and were replaced by the publication of *Leviathan* in 1651.

The ideas of "social contract" and "law of nature" were embodied in political doctrine by Hobbes, who set up the supremacy of sovereign power created by contract and laid down that all the rights of man were to be handed over to the sovereign head.

John Locke, on the other hand, established the principle of consent and destroyed the theory of divine right, emphasising that by "social contract" the people should form their own government, in order to preserve "life, liberty and property." The legal limitation of governmental power produced the justification of resistance against authority.

Natural right, democracy and resistance under the idea of the social contract brought about the sacred principle of the later democratic majority rule. His doctrines, such as representation, the rights of man, consent, and the forms of parliamentary representative government, were the basic doctrines of political philosophy in the development of federal speculation.

On the other hand, Locke contributed the utilitarian conception to political philosophy. Whatever line of analysis be adopted no philosophical theory can take the place of utilitarianism in the federal idea.

In this respect, David Hume was the first and foremost writer to adhere to the theory of utility throughout his works. Usefulness is the adaptation of means to the end of morality, both in spiritual and practical problems.

His philosophy is based upon his unique scepticism, in which experience is the principal guide. Sentiment rather than metaphysical reason is the source of human morals. He set up a philosophy founded on empiricism vis-à-vis *a priorism*.

He denied the idea of the social contract and condemned the existing authority, because nearly all government had originated in "usurpation or conquest." He advocated democratic political organisations and freedom and liberty. And his remarkable conception of utility no doubt greatly influence the essential nature of federalism.

These three figures (Hobbes, Locke and Hume) gave nothing to federalism, but contributed the fundamental philosophical basis to the federal idea along with those whose work and influence I shall proceed to describe.

In the development of federal ideas Montesquieu must not be omitted even though he had little to say about the relations between states.

His main contribution to political philosophy was twofold; firstly, the theory of relativity in which "all knowledge is knowledge of relations," and secondly, the historical interpretation of politics.

Based on his philosophy of utility, the historical survey of various forms of government, in the relation between surroundings and morals, set out his general laws of politics, and arrived at administrative expedients such as the "separation of powers."

He emphasised that "laws," in their most general signification, are necessary relations arising from the nature of things;[1] further, law in general is "human reason inasmuch as it governs all the inhabitants of the earth"[2] in relation to the climate of each country, to the quality of its soil, to the degree of liberty which its constitution will bear, to religions and customs, etc. These relations he should examine, since all these together constituted what he calls the "*Esprit des Lois.*"

Montesquieu criticises federal unions for not having made any fundamental progress since the time of Grotius. His argument is that the federal form of the state is very important in regard to security, and mutual defence, especially for small republics.

It is a convention that contrives a kind of constitution that "has all the internal advantage of a republican, together with the external force of a monarchical government"—what he calls "a Confederate Republic."[3] "This form of government," he said, "is a convention by which several petty states agree to become members of a larger one which they intend to establish; it is a kind of assemblage of societies that constitutes a new one, capable of increasing by means of further association, till they arrive at such a degree of power as to be able to provide for the security of the whole body." Each confederate preserves its sovereignty, but transfers a part of its functions to the federal government for the "security of the whole body."

Montesquieu penetrated to the very root of the nature of federalism when he said that the republic of this confederation, "able to withstand an external force, may support itself without

[1] C. de Montesquieu: *De L'Esprit des Loix*, 1748, Book I, Chap. I.
[2] Ibid., Chap. III.   [3] Ibid., Book IX, Chap. I.

any internal corruption," and "this form of this society prevents all manner of inconveniences."

With regard to the relation of authorities between the confederacy and confederated states, the ideal balance of power should be that which would be required "if a popular insurrection should happen in one of the confederated states, the others are able to quell it," or "if abuses should creep into one part, they are reformed by those that remain sound." Only by means of the association of petty republics could their internal happiness and external strength be maintained.[1] And he suggests two essentials of federalism; firstly, that a confederate government ought to be composed of states of the same "nature," especially of the republican kind,[2] and secondly, that in preference to equal representation it is important that representation be proportional to the power and extent of the various confederate states.[3]

He refers to the distinction between Holland and Switzerland and Germany, and the comparison between the Lycian Republic and the United Netherlands.

These ideas are an important focus of the federal functions, but Montesquieu imbued the later federal thinkers with his views—i.e. relativity and expediency, rather than with those of *a priori* federal ideology.

The particularity of political and civil laws in each state and the "separation of powers" affect the later federal and decentralised ideas, especially among the American federalists. It is clear that the *Esprit des Lois* inspired the federalists, who were the founders of modern federalism.

Rousseau started from the natural freedom of man in the Golden Age in his *Discours sur l'inégalité*, and ended with "general will" in his *Contrat Social*.

In his metaphysical conception he convinced his adherents that by social contract the state must depend upon sovereignty based on the "general will," i.e. will of a whole, not will of all. No sovereignty was justifiable without the sanction of the "general will." He attacked representative government, and emphasised the significance of the individual. He advocated democracy in a small state, since the legislative assembly could come into direct contact with the whole people; and he drew a line between sovereignty as such and the government as a mere executive.

His metaphysical speculation sought to find a harmonious autonomy, and it was manifest that the theory of federation, so

---

[1] C. de Montesquieu: *De L'Esprit des Loix*, 1748, Book IX, Chap. I.
[2] Ibid., Chap. II.   [3] Ibid., Chap. III.

far from being a mere offshoot, sprang from the very root of Rousseau's political ideal.

Rousseau wrote at some length on the federal principle, but unfortunately the document was destroyed in one of the early months of the French Revolution when the friend to whom he had given it took fright. Nevertheless, the federal ideal finds expression here and there in his various writings, such as, the *Institutions Politiques* and the *Contrat Social*, and in phrases in *Émile* and *Le Gouvernement de Pologne*.

He laid down definitely that "it is useless to bring up abuses that belong to great states against one who desires to see only small ones; but how can small states be given the strength to resist great ones, as formerly the Greek towns resisted the great King, and more recently Holland and Switzerland have resisted the House of Austria? If we make such a union, we should not expect to avoid its natural disadvantages."[1]

And he adds in *Émile* that "we shall examine finally the kind of remedy that men have sought against these evils in leagues and federations, which, leaving each state master in his own home, arm it against all unjust aggression from without. We shall inquire what are the means of establishing a good form of federal association, what can give it permanence, and how far we can extend the rights of the federation without trenching on those of sovereignty."[2]

Advising the three separate parts of Poland to form a union, he insists on "perfecting the form of the *Diétines* (County Councils) and enlarging the authority of the respective Palatinats, while carefully drawing the line of the boundaries of the states, and not destroying legislation by, and subordination to, the Republic."[3]

To Rousseau federalism, from one point of view, was not "new" and "modern"[4] but was the dream arising from his essential principle—which he applied to enlarge and perfect the system of federal government—which was "to reunite the advantages of the great states and those of the small ones."[5]

It is uncertain how far his federal ideas had advanced, but judging from his main conception, which made him the apostle of the small state, where every citizen could take a direct share in politics, it is hardly possible to regard him as a modern federal

---

[1] J. J. Rousseau: *Du Contrat Social*, 1762, Chap. XIII, pp. 281–305.
[2] Ibid., *Émile*, Book V. MS. Geneva 205, Vol. II in Vaughan: *The Political Writings of Rousseau*, Vol. II, p. 158.
[3] Ibid.: *Le Gouvernement de Pologne*, Chap. V.
[4] Ibid.: *Lettres de la Montagne*.   [5] Ibid.: *Le Gouvernement de Pologne*, Chap. V.

thinker; rather, he was a believer in the confederation of the United States of America between 1781 and 1787.

The only system under which his doctrine could be fully applied would be "one of federated self-governing communes, small enough to allow each member an active share in the legislation of the communes."[1]

The author of the *Social Contract* thought little of kingdoms and favoured the small states which would never be swollen into empires. Rousseau laid down the fundamental basis of an international league in his famous essay *Projet de Paix Perpétuelle*, which was written by him on the manuscript of the Abbé de Saint-Pierre.[2] In order to preserve peace in Europe, it was necessary to get rid of the dangerous rivalries among the European states; and he urged that this could be done "only by a confederative form of government which, uniting nations by bonds similar to those which unite individuals, submits them all equally to the authority of the laws."[3]

Looking at the historical confederations of the past, he argued that these institutions were far from the perfection which they might have attained, "because the best schemes never work out exactly as they were supposed, and because, in politics as in morals, the growth of our knowledge reveals only the vast extent of our woe."

He declared that "it would be a great mistake to hope for this state of lawlessness ever to change in the natural course of things and without artificial aid."[4] If the equal distribution of force should be maintained as the result of the existing Europe, he without doubt insisted on deducing "a conclusion of importance to the project for establishing a general league; for to form a solid and durable confederation, all its members must be placed in such a mutual state of dependence that not one of them alone may be in a position to resist all of the others and that minor associations which would have the power to injure the general body may meet with sufficient hindrances to prevent their formation, without which the confederation would be vain, and each would be really independent under an apparent subjection." He went further. If these obstacles were such as he described above, that "all powers are entirely free to form leagues amongst themselves

---

[1] T. H. Green: *Works, Philosophical*, 1906, Vol. II, p. 398.
[2] J. J. Roussseau: *Lettre à M. de Bastide*, December 5, 1760.
[3] Ibid.: "Extrait du Projet de Paix Perpétuelle de M. l'Abbé de Saint-Pierre," in Vaughan: *The Political Writings of Rousseau*, 1915, Vol. I, p. 365.
[4] Ibid., p. 370.

and to make offensive alliance, it can be surmised what they will become when there is a *great armed league* always ready to prevent those who undertake to destroy or resist it."[1]

The means of attaining this great purpose—to bring about a real confederation, a true political body, out of the free and voluntary fellowships which united the European states, was to "increase its advantages" and to "force all parties to co-operate for the common good."[2]

In this respect he insisted that a federal rather than a confederal basis be given to this international league, though he projected a European federation which would be far closer than a "loose and general bond of humanity." "It is," he said, "necessary that the confederation should be so general that no considerable power would refuse to join it; that it should have a judicial tribunal with power to establish laws and regulations binding on all its members; that it should have an enforcing and coercive power to constrain each state to submit to common counsels, whether for action or for abstention."[3]

Accordingly, five articles were necessary:—

By the first, the contracting sovereigns shall establish amongst themselves a perpetual and irrevocable alliance, and name plenipotentiaries to hold in some fixed place a permanent Diet or Congress, where differences between the contracting parties would be regulated and settled by way of arbitration or judicial decisions.

By the second, there shall be specified the number of sovereigns whose plenipotentiaries are to have a voice in the assembly, those who are to be invited to agree to the treaty, the order, time and manner in which the presidency shall pass from one to the other for equal terms, and, finally, the relative quotas of contributions towards the common expenses and the manner of raising them.

By the third, the confederation shall guarantee to its members the possession and government of all the states each of them controls at the moment, as well as the succession, elective or hereditary, according to whichever is established by the fundamental laws of each country; and in order to put an end once and for all to the disputes which are constantly reviving, it shall be agreed to take present possession and the latest treaties as the basis of the mutual rights of the contracting Powers, at the same time renouncing for ever and reciprocally all anterior pretension, with

---

[1] J. J. Rousseau: "Extrait du Projet de Paix Perpétuelle de M. l'Abbé de Saint-Pierre," in Vaughan: *The Political Writings of Rousseau*, 1915, Vol. I, p. 373.
[2] Ibid., p. 374. [3] Ibid., pp. 374–375.

the exception of future contested successions and other rights which may fall due, and which shall all be decided by the ruling of the Diet, no member being permitted under any pretext whatsoever to take the law into his own hands, or take up arms against his fellow-members.

By the fourth, the cases shall be specified in which any ally guilty of infringing the Treaty is to be put under the ban of Europe and proclaimed a common enemy—that is to say, if he refuse to carry out the decisions of the great Alliance, if he make preparations for war, if he negotiate treaties contrary to the terms of the confederation, and if he take up arms to resist it or to attack any one of the allies.

Lastly, by the fifth article, the plenipotentiaries of the European federal body shall always have the power, on the instructions of their courts, to frame in the Diet by a majority of votes, provisionally (and by a three-quarter majority five years afterwards, finally), the regulations which they shall judge to be important in order to secure all possible advantages to the European Republic and each one of its members; but it shall never be possible to change any of these five fundamental articles except with the unanimous consent of all the members of the confederation.[1]

These conditions which Rousseau set up for the European federal body corporate indicated majority rule and the recognition of the federal administrative and judicial authority over the member states.

Kant also appealed for the "federation of free states." From his philosophical basis of "providence"[2] he derived an ideal "cosmo-political constitution" among the nations which assumed the form of federation regulated by law, according to the "right of nations as concerted in common."

He condemned international trade competition and the existing world credits, and favoured the abolition of standing armies and the use of poisonous weapons, and advocated the promotion of international morality and confidence.

One of his interesting proposals in respect of the world federation was that "in order to promote perpetual peace" the civil constitution in every state should be "republican."

---

[1] J. J. Rousseau: "Extrait du Projet de Paix Perpétuelle de M. l'Abbé de Saint-Pierre," in Vaughan: *The Political Writings of Rousseau*, 1915, Vol. I, pp. 375–376.
[2] I. Kant: *Principle of Politics*, III, p. 74. Providence is the life force of nature which embodies harmony of force "rationally and in order." It is to Providence we must look for the relation of the end of humanity in the whole of the species, as furnishing the means for the attainment of the final destination of man, through the free exercise of his powers so far as they go.

To Kant, the republican constitution was a constitution which was formulated firstly "according to the principle of 'liberty' of the members of society as men"; secondly, "according to the principle of the 'dependence' of all its members on a single common legislature as subjects"; and, thirdly, "according to the law of the 'equality' of its members as citizens."

Republican government was the "only one" which sprang from the idea of the original contract[1] upon which "all rightful legislation of a people" was based, and the principle of republicanism embodied his conception of public right[2] originally and essentially as the basis of "the civil constitution in all its forms."

His metaphysical assertions as to these political metaphors arose out of his infallible theory of "practical reason." To him democracy was not always compatible with republicanism.

Whatever may be said as to his fundamental idea, this suggestion is worth taking into account in any consideration of federalism, and particularly in observing the federal development of the German constitution.

[1] The fundamental law, thus indicated (liberty, equality and self-dependency in the civil state), which can only arise out of the universal united will of the people, is what is called the "original contract."

[2] "Law of right is represented as a reciprocal compulsion necessarily in accordance with the freedom of every one under the principle of a universal freedom. Public right is the sum of the external law which makes such a complete agreement of freedom in society possible."

CHAPTER II

DEVELOPMENT OF THE IDEAS OF MODERN FEDERALISM IN THE UNITED STATES OF AMERICA

Modern federalism has been evolved since the failure, due to inefficient administration, of the confederation of the thirteen states of North America during the period 1776–1787.

The political ideas previously prevalent among the leaders of American independence were chiefly the consequence of the idea of "natural right," the theory of consent and right of self-government and of resistance against coercion developed by Sydney and Locke, and the administrative expediency of the "separation of powers" advocated by Montesquieu. Harrington was not alone in his advocacy of the political ideas set forth in his *Oceana*[1], wherein government should be based on "law," not on "man"; in 1696 Sydney also formulated his democratic principle of government and theory of resistance to unjust law. Sydney condemned in every particular the theory of the divine right of kings which Sir Robert Filmer advocated in *Patriarcha*, and particularly denounced the latter's fallacious arguments, since "'Tis an eternal truth that a weak and wicked prince can never have a wise council or receive any benefit by one that is imposed upon him."[2]

Sydney believed that since the time of Adam, liberty was the natural right of human beings. He assumed that in the breasts of all men God has implanted the principle of liberty; a liberty, however, which "is not licentiousness of doing what is pleasant to mankind against the command of God" but one which is simply "an exemption from all human laws, to which the people have not given their assent." For the rights of a people proceed only from the laws of natural liberty, that ever lived "before the name of Christ was ever known in the world." He also indicated that men are therefore perfectly justified in making use of the reason that God has given them to exercise laws that control their actions which usurp sway over them; if otherwise, he said, man is "looked upon as a little different from beasts."[3]

Liberty produced virtue, order and solidity, which are the essential basis of popular government.

[1] Harrington wrote *Oceana* in 1656.
[2] Algernon Sydney: *Discourses concerning Government*, 1751, Chap. I, Sec. 3.
[3] Ibid., Chap. I, Sec. 2.

In civil society, he said, "men cannot continue in the perpetual and entire fruition of the liberty that God hath given him—the liberty of one is thwarted by that of another." The ground of all just government should be "general consent."

The only lawful basis of government is the consent of the ruled, and, he said, "by common consent joining in one body, and exercising such a power over every single person as seemed beneficial to the whole," such a man is a "perfect" democrat and is free.

Whatever government is formed on the basis of liberty, "the difference between the best government and the worst doth wholly depend upon a right or wrong exercise of that power."[1]

Administration is so important that the choosing of a magistrate is just as vital as the making of laws. Those who administer power must possess ability in management, in doing justice and in procuring the welfare of the people, but they must not presume on a name or dignity. From his liberal interpretation of the Scriptures he was convinced that natural rights are from God and nature, not from God.

Popular or mixed government is a better form of government for the welfare of the people as a whole than absolute monarchy. Sydney, therefore, favoured elected magistracy, and thought that contract between magistrates and the people was the most expedient for the preservation of liberty.[2]

With vivid historical illustrations and precise logic he presented conclusions deduced from sound experimental premises.

No law is just and valid unless it is based on the common good of the people as a whole, and also on general consent.

Liberty is the highest virtue by which the happiness of men can be attained. No unjust law is entitled to force anyone to obey. Disobedience to an unjust law is a natural right of mankind.

Thus during the later years of the seventeenth century Algernon Sydney vigorously appealed to the justice of popular government and theory of consent and right of resistance, and soon after the Revolution of 1688 John Locke published (1690) his famous *Second Treatise of Civil Government*, and then throughout a hundred years and more the liberal movement in every country was inspired by Locke's ideas of government.

In order to make clear the basic theory of the federalists, I shall describe briefly the ideas of the early American colonists prior to the doctrine of Sydney and Locke.

The early colonies set up a strong ecclesiastical and political

[1] Algernon Sydney: *Discourses concerning Government*, 1751, Chap. I, Sec. 10.
[2] Ibid., Chap. II, Secs. 1, 2, 3, 4, 5, 6, 21.

regime, which was reminiscent of Geneva under John Calvin's overwhelming personality. Puritan and Quaker covenants were the guiding principles of colonial life. The ordinance of the ministers was predominant, and puritanism was the basis of judgment in both ecclesiastical and political life.

The Puritans set up a political organisation derived from their own interpretation of the Scriptures, and the life of New England in the eighteenth century was theocratic in character and entirely under the Sabbatarian laws.

The conflicting views with regard to the relation of the powers of church and state were represented by Roger Williams and John Cotton.[1]

Williams' view of separation between church and state indicated that the state is entirely secular in character, whilst John Cotton —though he agreed with Williams that the church, although not "essence of the state . . . pertains to the integrity of the city" —said that "religion is the best good to the city, and therefore laws about religion are truly called civil laws."[2]

But the theocratic supremacy in the American colonies could not be destroyed until the revolutionary sentiment replaced the church covenant.

Democracy, as then understood, was "the meanest and worst of all forms of government"[3] and could not be found in colonial life, except in local self-government[4] and the establishment of the "body politic" on the basis of contract.[5]

The tendency towards political democracy was a characteristic of the Englishman, but not of the Puritan, and was due to the legacy of democratic ideas handed down from the seventeenth-century English political thinkers, such as Milton, Harrington, John Locke and Algernon Sydney.

[1] Roger Williams wrote *The Bloody Tenet of Persecution for the Cause of Consciousness* (1644), indicating that the state is distinct from and should exist without the church. He said: "the church is like unto a corporation, society or company of East India or Turkey merchants or companies in London." The essence of church and state is a different entity, because religion may radically change, whilst the government of cities and states remains unchanged. Even though John Cotton agrees that the church is a separate society distinct from the state, yet he held that the growth and welfare of the state depends on the purity of the church, and therefore the church pertains to the integrity of cities.
[2] John Cotton: *Works*, 1647. *The Bloody Tenet Washed and Made White*, Chap. LXVII.
[3] Letter of John Cotton to Lord Saye and Sele, 1636.
[4] Body of Liberties in Massachusettes Bay (1641). Fundamental Order of Connecticut, 1639.   [5] *Mayflower* Covenant in 1620.

Thomas Hooker, a famous Connecticut divine, set out democratic ideas in his work *A Survey of the Summe of Church Discipline* in 1648. The idea of contract was clearly manifested in his writings; he said: "In the building, if the parts be neither mortised nor brased, as there will be little beauty, so there can be no strength. It is so in setting up the frames of societies among men, when their minds and hearts are not mortised by mutual consent of subjection one to another, there is no expectation of any successful proceeding with the advantage to the public."[1] The "sinews of society" are the mutual subjection wherein explicit contract is based on consent, and binds every part into a common whole.

The immediate revelation of God's spirit to be each individual soul's "inner light" brought about a little more democracy in the Quaker society of Pennsylvania.

Anti-ceremonialism, denunciation of sacraments, denial of need for a special priesthood, condemnation of church tithes, and the non-necessity of oaths—all these were the essence of the puritanism of the New England colonies.

The followers of William Penn in Pennsylvania were more tolerant in their form of government. Their aims of government were to "support power in reverence with the people and to secure the people from the abuse of power." Government is free for the people, and "the laws rule, but the people are a party to those laws." The people in Quaker communities were granted religious freedom, and no religious limitations, either in the community or in governmental offices, were imposed.

In the year 1787 two states only out of the thirteen, being more democratic, set up a unicameral instead of a bicameral assembly; these were Pennsylvania and Georgia.

The love of democracy had already been manifested in the early life of the colonists. They had been freed from English coercive power, and voluntarily enforced a strict theological order in their daily life, wherein the germ of the ideal of self-government gradually developed into political expediency.

The arbitrary oppression of George III and his ministers fomented revolutionary sentiments in the minds of the colonies. It was the Stamp Act (1765) and the Townsend Act (1767) which accelerated the colonial antagonism to the Royal prerogative.

Successive failures in British colonial policy culminated in the issue of the Boston Port Bill in 1774 and the "Committees of Correspondence," which were constituted for united resistance

[1] Thomas Hooker: *A Survey of the Summe of Church Discipline*, 1648, p. 188.

against the usurpation of the mother country, and led up to the first Continental Congress of 1774. The crisis of the relations between them and the mother country helped to strengthen the bonds between the colonies and brought complete union in the federation of 1774. And in May 1775 the Continental Congress made a declaration of resistance against the British Government.

The eloquent orations of Edmund Burke and Chatham, which emphasised a liberal policy towards America, and popular appeals in England for the freedom of these colonies, were unavailing.

The ideas of the American revolutionary leaders shifted from those of the English seventeenth-century radicals to those of Thomas Paine. In the year 1776 Jefferson, Adams and the leaders of the colonies drafted and issued the Declaration of Independence.

The political theories which were gaining ground in America were revealed in the Declaration, and were manifested successively in the formation of the constitutions of the thirteen states.

In the development of the revolutionary ideas in America, John Adams in 1774 said, "the fealty and allegiance of America is undoubtedly due to the person of King George III, whom God long preserve and prosper."[1]

The leaders of the colonies insisted that by the charters of colonies, and the contracts therein, the colonists were bound to obedience to the king but not to Parliament.

However fallacious the early revolutionary literature might be, the existing conception—namely, "taxation without representation is tyranny"—reached its climax when Thomas Paine wrote *Common Sense*, addressed to the people of America. Sydney's inscription in the album of the University of Copenhagen, which read as follows: "This hand, an enemy to tyrants, seeks with the sword peace and contentment under a free government," was fully justified by the revolutionary leaders in America.

In 1776 the underlying political theory in America was largely identical with that of the seventeenth century (1688) in England. The belief in the state of nature, the conception of natural right, the idea of consent and government on the basis of contract produced the Declaration of Independence and the assertion of the inalienable and absolute validity of individual "inherent" rights.

Government is merely a "common umpire" within the ambit of the compact.

The legal limitation of governmental action resulted in the proportional strength of the legislative parliament and the

[1] John Adams: *Works*, IV, p. 146.

justification of the right of resistance against arbitrary power in order to preserve "life, liberty and property."[1] At this time, John Adams strongly insisted that the rights were founded on "the frame of nature, rooted in the constitution of the intellectual and moral world," derived from "the great legislator of the universe."

Hamilton, in his youth, asserted that the sacred rights of mankind "are written as with a sunbeam in the whole volume of human nature, by the hand of the divinity itself, and can never be erased or obscured by mortal power."

The fundamental axioms in the Declaration of Independence were that "All men are created equal, that they are endowed by their Creator with certain inalienable rights, that among these are life, liberty and the pursuit of happiness."[2]

In order to secure these rights "governments are instituted among men, deriving their just powers from the consent of the governed."[3]

The Declaration of Independence asserted that "whenever any form of government becomes destructive of these ends, it is the right of the people to alter or to abolish it and to institute new government."[4]

In order to preserve enjoyment of life and liberty, with the means of acquiring and possessing property and pursuing and obtaining happiness and safety, the right of freedom of speech and meeting, equality of men before the law, religious toleration and the abolition of the standing army were accepted as fundamental principles.

Of all the liberal thinkers of the French Renaissance, the man who chiefly inspired the American fathers was Montesquieu, who set up elaborate schemes of administrative principles called the "separation of powers" in *L'Esprit des Loix*, published in 1748.

"Political liberty," he said, "is to be found only in moderate government," and "it is there only when there is no abuse of power," but "constant experience shows us that every man invested with power is apt to abuse it."[5]

He formulated the tripartite division of powers because "to

[1] John Adams: *Works*, IV, p. 139.—"The preservation of life, liberty and property is the essential means of formation of government by social contract, advocated by John Locke in the *Second Treatise on Government*."
[2] The Declaration of Independence of U.S.A., July 4, 1776.
[3] Ibid.
[4] Ibid.
[5] Montesquieu: *The Spirit of Laws*, 1878, Eng. trans., Book XI, Chap. IV.

prevent this abuse it is necessary from the very nature of things that power should be a check to power."[1]

Therefore adequate mechanism for this power was due to this principle by which, he said, "a government may be so constituted that no man shall be compelled to do things to which the law does not oblige him, nor forced to abstain from things which the law permits."[2]

With this criterion the idea of "separation of powers" was framed; the powers of executive, legislature and judicature must be independent and act each as a check upon the others.

No liberty exists when "legislative and executive" powers are united in the same person, or in the same body of magistrates," and no liberty can be obtained "if the judiciary power be not separated from the legislative and executive."[3] Tyranny is the result when these three powers are united in the "same man" or the "same body."

Montesquieu's technique greatly influenced the Fathers of America in framing their constitution in 1787.

Their successful revolt against the tyrannical usurpation of the British Government and their hatred of the aristocracy naturally caused an over-estimation of the intrinsic value of the "separation of powers."

In agreement with the Virginian democratic ideas, Jefferson and his friends asserted that the legislative, executive and judicial power should be separate and distinct.[4]

The driving forces in revolutionary thought, such as the theory of natural right or the separation of powers, provided the foundation of the confederation, the "perpetual" union of the thirteen states in 1781.

In this confederation each component state "retains its sovereignty, freedom, independence, and every power, jurisdiction and right."[5] These thirteen states "enter into a firm league of friendship with each other for their common defence, the security of their liberties and their mutual general welfare."

In order to "secure and perpetuate mutual friendship and intercourse" between the people of the thirteen states they formulated a mere league and alliance for common defence, i.e. it was a *Staatenbund* and not a *Bundesstaat*.

The delegated authority in the congress, such as the right of

---

[1] Montesquieu: *The Spirit of Laws*, 1878, Eng. trans., Book XI, Chap. IV.
[2] Ibid. [3] Ibid., Book XI, Chap. VI.
[4] Ibid.
[5] Articles of Confederation (1781-1787), Art. 2.

recall, short terms of delegation and no eligibility to Congress for anyone who held government office, could not become effective legislation without the conferment of the power to enforce it.

All foreign relations, declarations of war and peace, the supreme command of the army and navy, judiciary and arbitration, regulation of coinage, standards of weights and measures, post office, etc., and other powers, such as arbitration of disputes between the component states, commercial treaties, and the levying of duties and customs, were vested in the Congress or Committee of States at the time of recess of Congress; but the strong feeling of sovereignty of each state, the prejudice against the national Government, and expenditure on the affairs of Congress according to the value of land, resulted in the impossibility of an adequate functioning of this confederation.

After the peace of 1783 the United States of America entered on a new era and the formation of the existing constitution.

The economic stagnation, financial, industrial and commercial, and the administrative inefficiency of the confederation produced the elaborate schemes of political speculation of the federalists.

CHAPTER III

IDEAS OF THE FEDERALISTS

§ 1

Hamilton told the people that, whatever logical and philosophical theories might be formulated, the basis of union must be the highest utility of the union to their political prosperity, and that the proposed constitution would afford additional security to the preservation of the republican species of government, to liberty and to property.[1]

The culmination of the federal experiments, in political history, was not only due to theoretical justification, but chiefly to the urgent needs of the union in face of threats, both political and economic, from neighbours. The federalists also emphatically urged the necessity for union in order to prevent the catastrophe of political and economic peace under the ineffective bond of the confederation of 1781, and called for united action in the face of the existing internal and external emergencies.

Against the danger of foreign arms and influence, as well as that of domestic trouble, the preservation of peace and tranquillity entirely depended on a "cordial union under an efficient national government."[2]

The eighty-five articles of the federalists were not only masterpieces of federal theory, but were also valuable contributions to political science, because political science not only requires the theoretical justification of right and wrong in the body politic, but ought also to study actual principles of administration which are no less important than the former in the field of politics.

From this point of view the federalists asserted that their federal speculation was chiefly based on the experimental examination of political organisation, executive, legislative and judicial, and presented the historical and theoretical justification for the new constitution of 1787. "Experience is the oracle of truth" and "utility of union on the principle of federal compromise" were the main maxims of Hamilton, and formed the general assumptions of the Conventions of Philadelphia in 1787.

First of all the efficiency of the federal government would promote the ability of the administrative services. "When once

[1] *The Federalist*, I (Hamilton). [2] Ibid., III (Jay).

an effective national government is established the best men in the country will not only consent to serve, but will generally be appointed to manage it."[1]

Men of talent and wisdom, who were required in the offices of national government, would give their proper and suitable services without interfering with the efficient administration of local affairs.

Secondly, designed or accidental actions affording just causes of war are less to be apprehended under one general government than under several smaller ones, and one good national government affords far greater security against unlawful violence than does anything else.

Jay condemned any form of confederation, either that of 1781 or that of two or three separate confederations, because of the lack of success resulting from intrigues of foreign diplomacy which continually played off one state against another.

He assumed that the absence of uniformity, whatever elaborate constitutional code might be formed, conduced to a relative inequality of strength which is prejudicial to the union. Both human wisdom and historical experience have already in numerous instances vindicated the justness of his theory. Differences of economic interests and social environment produce distrust which creates distrust, and "by nothing is goodwill and kind conduct more speedily changed than by insidious jealousies and uncandid imputations."[2]

Thirdly, like Hobbes, Hamilton asserted that "love of power" and "desire of pre-eminence" are terms contradictory to the desire of equality and safety and the human provisions of uniformity; unless there is the formation of union for common ends and prevention of secret jealousy, faction in the states of the union must inevitably occur.

Hamilton pointed out that "experience, the least fallible guide of human opinion," negatived the idea that commercial republics were less induced to war than monarchies, and he quoted the dictum of the Abbé de Mably that "neighbouring nations are naturally enemies of each other, unless their common weakness forces them to league in a confederative republic, and their constitution prevents the differences that neighbourhood occasions, extinguishing that secret jealousy which disposes all states to aggrandise themselves at the expense of their neighbours."[3]

Not only the diversity of commercial interests provokes the

[1] *The Federalist*, III (Jay).   [2] Ibid., V (Jay).   [3] Ibid., VI (Hamilton).

underlying motives of jealousy and hatred between neighbours, but, moreover, the large vacant lands in the West of America would be the cause of faction between the states unless they were preserved as the common property of the union. The "justice of participating in territory acquired or secured by the joint efforts of the confederacy" and "the habit of intercourse on the basis of equal privileges" would give a keener edge to discontent among the thirteen states. In addition to this problem the public debts of the union would be a further cause of disturbance among them. The diversity of political and economic conditions and the possibility of laws in violation of private contracts would threaten destruction to the loose ties of 1781.

Hamilton solemnly condemned the action of some of the state legislatures as to contractual rights, with the spirit of retaliation to which it gave rise, and the danger that "a war, not of parchment, but of the sword, would chastise such atrocious breaches of moral obligation and social justice."[1] He added that "*Divide et Impera* must be the motto of every nation that either hates or fears us."[2]

The strengthening of the executive arm of the government against both external and internal danger was an absolute necessity.

It was inevitably necessary for this defence that the standing army should be controlled by the federal command, not by state authority, partly because the absence of standing armies in the states brought about the impossibility of the use of force in the case of conflicts, and partly because "the industrious habits of the people" of his day, absorbed in the pursuit of gain and the various developments of science, had produced an entire revolution in the system of war, and established the need of constant discipline in the army.

From this realistic standpoint Hamilton and Madison regarded their opponents as ideologists and their ideas as "airy phantoms," just as Bentham thought that *Naturrecht* was "nonsense upon stilts."

Hamilton's federalism gave rise to a new political speculation, that of the *Bundesstaat*, in the history of political ideas.

The community which he had in mind rested upon the broad and solid foundation of human utility as revealed by the highest wisdom and experience.

Hamilton conceived that politics are a science, in the develop-

[1] *The Federalist*, VII (Hamilton).   [2] Ibid.

ment of which the truth of various political theories and the efficacy of administrative principles have been criticised and analysed in the world laboratory since the dawn of history.

His ideal of federalism is a little more than Montesquieu's "Confederate Republic," a kind of constitution that has all the internal advantages of a republican, together with the external force of a monarchical, government.[1]

The first essential characteristic of the confederacy, as contrasted with the consolidation of states, had been declared to be "the restriction of its authority to the members in their collective capacities, without reaching to the individuals of whom they are composed." Hamilton admitted that this had been generally the case, but asserted that there had been extensive exceptions, and that the prevalence of the principle had been the cause of "incurable disorder and imbecility" in government.[2]

He defined a confederate republic as "an assemblage of societies," or "an association of two or more states into one state." The extent, modifications and object of federal authority are mere matters of discretion. At the same time the separate state constitutions exist for local purposes with parts of the sovereign authority, under the general authority of the union; this is in the rational sense of the term conformable with the idea of federal government.

In order to understand Hamilton's federal principles I will now examine the underlying political ideas on which they are based.

Hamilton, holding *The Wealth of Nations* in his hands as soon after its appearance as a boat could cross the sea,[3] landed on the virgin soil of America from his native place, the West Indies, a little before the beginning of the Revolution. Before and during the war with Great Britain he was a young and enthusiastic agent of revolutionary theories, and he advocated the natural right of the equality of man and the sacred right of property.

Being a politician of the eighteenth century, as Edmund Burke was, he turned from being an apostle of Locke to one of Hobbes, during the ten years 1776–1786.

Like Hobbes, Hamilton thought that "men are ambitious, vindictive and rapacious," the "love of power and the desire of predominance" being as imperative as the desire for equality and safety.

---

[1] Montesquieu: *The Spirit of Laws*, Vol. I, Book IX.
[2] *The Federalist*, IX (Hamilton).   [3] C. G. Bowers: *Jefferson and Hamilton*.

Therefore, criticising Montesquieu's model of the excellent confederate republic of Lycia, where there was a common council with votes proportional to the size of the members, he reached a conclusion that these distinctions insisted upon "are the novel refinement of an erroneous theory."[1]

At the same time Madison asserted that the diversity of faculties in the human being was the latent cause of social faction. As long as "reason" and "self-love" co-exist man's opinions and passions "will be a reciprocal influence on each other; the former will be objects to which the latter will attach themselves."

The diversity in the faculties of men produced the original right of property, and these innumerable differences in human nature are not less "an insuperable obstacle to a uniformity of interests."[2]

The protection of these faculties is the first object of government.[3]

From this assertion the economic interpretation of the constitution of the United States of America has been derived. He emphasised his view that "from the protection of different and unequal faculties of acquiring property, the possession of different degrees and kinds of property immediately results; and from the influence of these on the sentiments and views of the respective proprietors ensues a division of the society into different interests and parties."[4] The shrewdness of his mind foresaw the diversity of political sentiments and views resulting from the different interests, and that the "most common and durable source of faction" is the various and unequal distribution of property.

Even though, in the formation of his constitution, Madison drew advantage from the interests of financiers, and from the commercial and large landed interests, nevertheless he clearly explained that "the regulation of these various and interfering interests forms the principal task of modern legislation, and involves the spirit of party and faction in the necessary and ordinary operations of the government."[5]

The only remedy for the effect of this faction in hindering united action is not to remove the cause so as to take away liberty as the essential source of human life, but to control the effects so as to promote impartial justice by keeping equilibrium between the different interests under an adequate constitution.

---

[1] *The Federalist*, IX (Hamilton).   [2] Ibid., X (Madison).
[3] Ibid.   [4] Ibid.   [5] Ibid.

Madison, in agreement with Hamilton, who was a man of a century later than Hobbes, really recognised the essential source of democratic politics from his experience of self-governing colonial life. The shift from absolute sovereignty, guided by Hobbes' *Leviathan*, to conservative democracy, based on the aristocratic rules of Burke's Whiggism, was the chronological development of English Toryism. So, too, Hamilton was co-ordinate with Edmund Burke in his political ideas and beliefs, both in his utilitarian conception and in his realistic and empirical attitude of mind. "Experience is the oracle of truth, and where its responses are unequivocal they ought to be conclusive and sacred."

Madison foresaw the interests, private and public, that would conflict with justice and social good under purely democratic or mere majority rule, and he concluded that "the causes of faction cannot be removed, and that relief is only to be sought in the means of controlling its effects."[1]

He therefore condemned his opponents who adhered to the idea of pure democracy, saying that "theoretic politicians, who have patronised this species of government, have erroneously supposed that by reducing mankind to a perfect equality in their political rights they would, at the same time, be perfectly equalised and assimilated in their possessions, their opinions and their passions."[2] To a democracy he preferred a republic, which differed from the former in the delegation of government to an elected body of citizens and the greater area and number of citizens to which it could extend.

Any civil society is "nerveless" unless it is based on power. Hamilton was convinced that among the primary truths, on which all subsequent reasoning must be based, are those maxims "in ethics and politics that there cannot be an effect without a cause that the means ought to be proportioned to the end; that every power ought to be commensurate with its object; that there ought to be no limitation of a power destined to effect a purpose which is itself incapable of limitation."[3]

From these political ideas Hamilton and his fellow-federalists drew the elaborate picture of the "federal state," which was the first outline in the history of federal literature.

More advanced than the European precedents of federal ideas, Hamilton said, "we must extend the laws of the federal government to the individual citizens of America."[4]

[1] *The Federalist*, X (Madison). [2] Ibid.
[3] Ibid., XXXI (Hamilton). [4] Ibid., XXIII (Hamilton).

The maxim that "the means ought to be proportionate to the end" resulted in his assertion that "the persons from whose agency the attainment of any end is expected ought to possess the means by which it is to be attained." Hamilton thought that "all observations founded on the danger of usurpation ought to be referred to the composition and structure of government, not to the nature or extent of its powers."[1] Therefore he emphasised that the aim of government is that "it ought to contain in itself every power requisite to the full accomplishment of the objects committed to its care and to the complete execution of the trusts for which it is responsible, free from every other control but a regard to the public good and to the sense of the people."

The duties of the federal government were to establish national defence of public peace against foreign or domestic violence, and at the same time to set up a national fiscal system to secure the responsible and effective administration of the federal government.

He said, "money is, with propriety, considered as the vital principle of the body politic, as that which sustains its life and motion, and enables it to perform its most essential functions."[2]

As far as the resources of the national wealth permit, complete power to secure a regular and adequate revenue may be regarded as "an indispensable ingredient in every constitution."

The federalists proposed that a power of taxation, subject to constitutional limitation, should be vested in the national federal government. They condemned the quota system and land value assessments, a mere *ignis fatuus* of finance, because of the diversity of natural resources and economic and social conditions in various localities.

Hamilton expressed his fundamental idea of national finance, "as a position warranted by the history of mankind, that in the usual progress of things the necessities of a nation, in every stage of its existence, will be found at least equal to its resources."[3]

He held that "the federal government must of necessity be invested with an unqualified power of taxation in the ordinary modes," and whilst he favoured the exclusive right of the union to levy import duties he argued that it must not be limited to this form of taxation, and that the power of imposing other duties must be "concurrent and co-equal in the united states and the individual states."[4]

The security against an unequal distribution of the financial

[1] *The Federalist*, XXXI (Hamilton).   [2] Ibid., XXX (Hamilton).
[3] Ibid.   [4] Ibid., XXXI–XXXII (Hamilton).

burden of the community is the control of the House of Representatives, wherein an adequate representation of interests is equally proportioned among merchants, learned and professional classes and land-holders, and, secondly, the choice of the best men who have an extensive knowledge of administration and a "thorough knowledge of the principle of political economy," and who know that "the most productive system of finance will always be the least burdensome." In these circumstances the power of taxation in the federal government should be vested in the federal legislature, and its administration must be directly carried out by the federal executive.

The need of efficiency of federal government, both legislative and executive, had the result of vesting in it national defence, regulation of commerce and unified policy in foreign diplomacy and finance, and of bringing about an adequate distribution of power between the federal authority and the state ones, and between the tripartite divisions of governmental powers. According to Hamilton all this serves to demonstrate the utility of the union.

To Madison the compromise between the vital principle of liberty and the energy and stability of government is due to the genius of republican liberty and federal wisdom.

Madison explained the American federal practice to which his posterity and the world would be indebted for "the example of numerous innovations displayed on the American theatre, in favour of private rights and public happiness."[1]

Not only Hamilton but also Madison attached very great importance to the promotion of the happiness of the individuals in America and, at the same time, of the general good of the nation as a whole and of the component states as well.

Madison stated the relation between the idea of democracy and of republicanism as follows: "As the natural limit of democracy is that distance from the central point which will just permit the most remote citizens to assemble as often as their public functions demand, and will include no greater number than can join in those functions; so the natural limit of a republic is that distance from the centre which will barely allow the representatives to meet as often as may be necessary for the administration of public affairs."[2]

The fabric of union of the thirteen states, the adoption of which was a novelty in the political world, was the accomplishment of a "revolution which has no parallel in the annals of human society."[3]

[1] *The Federalist*, XIV (Madison). [2] Ibid. [3] Ibid.

§ 2

What was the real character of the government which the federalists desired to form?

In the proposed constitution, the Act of the Constitution with the assent and ratification of the people and of the states is not a national but a federal one.

With regard to the ordinary powers of government the House of Representatives derives its power from the people of America; so far the government is "national" not "federal." The Senate derives its power from the states "as political and co-equal societies." In this case, so far the government is federal not national, but at the same time the executive power is derived from "a very compound source."

The authority to amend the constitution in its greatest power "departs from the national and advances towards the federal character, and loses again the federal and partakes of national character" in that it requires a majority of the people of the union and the sanction of the federated states.

Madison said, "the proposed constitution is, therefore, in strictness neither a national nor a federal constitution, but a composition of both."[1]

From this notion of government the distribution of powers between the federal and state governments and the tripartite division of governmental powers were formulated.

The significance of the federalist principle and its difference from the preceding federalism is shown in the following categories.

First of all, the essential source of modern federalism is a federal state, not a federation of states. The power on which federal government is based is the sanction and ratification by the people of the country and the extent to which its operation and the execution of its powers reach the individual citizens of America directly.

Whether the source of power is the compound sanction of the people or of the component states, the power of the federal administration is to be carried out under its own discretion in the ambit of the rights vested in the federation by the constitution.

Secondly, by the nature of the republican form of government, the predominance of the legislative assembly is an inevitable "usurpation" upon the other governmental powers. The

[1] *The Federalist*, XXXIX (Madison).

federalists thought that the danger of usurpation is due to the structure of government and not to the nature or extent of its power.

In the form of federation, the state governments, from their original constitutions, are endowed with complete sovereignty. The sacrifice of the established power of the state for the welfare of the whole nation naturally aroused furious antagonism and hatred, and the strength of the federal government led the members of the union to the "state of absolute scepticism and irresolution."

But the genius of the new nation of America struggled against all obstacles, and set up the "federal state" with due preservation of the constitutional equilibrium between the general and the state governments.

In this compound sovereign authority the federalists believed that the mirror of political liberty reflected the truth of the adequate separation of powers in the new constitution. When "the pulse of liberty was at its highest pitch," absolute independence and non-interference between the main governmental powers seemed to these Fathers the inalienable and absolute need of every constitution.

But the federalists, whose political ideas were based on experimental utilitarian conceptions rather than on theoretical dicta, required "further examination of Montesquieu's separation of power," which seemed to them "an invaluable precept in that science of politics."

Madison justified, to some extent, his opponent's view of the infallible validity of this political maxim, saying that "no political truth is certainly of greater intrinsic value, or is stamped with the authority of more enlightened patrons of liberty, than that on which the objection is founded."[1]

The principle on which this political criticism was based took as a standard the British constitution, which "was to Montesquieu what Homer has been to the didactic writers on epic poetry."[2]

The great French author's point of view as to the essential evil of the consolidation of powers was that "where the *whole* power of one department is exercised by the same hands which possess the *whole* power of another department, the fundamental principles of a free constitution are subverted."[3] It is essential to the preservation of liberty that "each department should have a will of its own," and in this due foundation of separate

[1] *The Federalist*, XLVII (Madison). [2] Ibid. [3] Ibid.

distinct functions of governmental power "it should have as little agency as possible in the appointment of members of the others."[1]

Nevertheless, in practical constitutional working experience has shown that "unless these departments be so far connected and blended as to give each a constitutional control over the others, the degree of separation which the maxim requires, as essential to a free government, can never in practice be duly maintained."[2]

This connection, in the presidential power concerned with appointments and foreign negotiations, by the power of Senate consultation, was an inevitable necessity in administration.

Legislative supremacy was "elective despotism," for which the federalists proposed a remedy.

Even Jefferson insisted on his view that in the legislative assembly, executive and judicial powers had "accordingly, in many instances, decided rights which should have been left to judicial settlement, and the direction of the executive, during the whole time of their session, is becoming habitual and familiar."[3]

In Pennsylvania the Council of Censors was appointed to inspect and survey the adequate working of the separation of powers.

The federalist remedy for legislative despotism "is to divide the legislature into different branches, and to render them, by different modes of election and different principles of action, as little connected with each other as the nature of their common functions and their common dependence on the society will admit."[4]

The federalists asserted that a mere demarcation on parchment of the constitutional limits of the several departments was not a sufficient guard against those encroachments which lead to a tyrannical concentration of governmental powers in the same hands, and also occasional appeals to the people would be neither a proper nor effective provision for that purpose because the passions and not the reason of the public would sit in judgment.

The federalists conceived the formation of a government which was to be administered by men over men; the great difficulty lay in this, "first, you must enable the government to control the governed, and in the next place oblige it to control itself."[5]

Though dependence on the people is the primary control on

[1] *The Federalist*, LI (Hamilton or Madison).   [2] Ibid., XLVIII (Madison).
[3] Ibid.   [4] Ibid., LI (Hamilton or Madison).   [5] Ibid.

government, "experience has taught mankind the necessity of auxiliary precautions."[1]

They asserted that "this policy of supplying, by opposite and rival interests, the defect of better motives, might be traced through the whole system of human affairs, private as well as public." It was shown especially in all the subordinate distributions of powers, "where the constant aim is to divide and arrange the several offices in such a manner as that each may be a check on the other."[2]

In the compound republic of America all the power surrendered by the people "is first divided between two distinct governments, and then the portion allotted to each subdivided among distinct and separate departments. Hence a double security arises to the rights of the people. The different governments will control each other, at the same time that each will be controlled by itself."[3]

Against the evil of sinister rule, both hereditary and majority despotism, compound republican federalism is the best security. The federalists held that "justice is the end of government" and of civil society, and that in a wide territory like that of the United States, with a great variety of interests, parties and sects, a coalition of a majority on principles other than those of justice and the general good was less likely than in a small state. They laid down the principle that the larger the society the more capable will it be of self-government, and, "happily for the republican cause, the practicable sphere may be carried to a very great extent by a judicious modification and mixture of the federal principle."[4]

Thirdly, the form of government in every state of the union ought to be republican, in the same manner as Kant suggested for the "Federation of States."

The purpose must be "to guarantee to every state in the union a republican form of government," and "in a confederacy founded on republican principles and composed of republican members the superintending government ought clearly to possess authority to defend the system against aristocratic or monarchical innovations."

"Where else could the remedy be deposited than where it is deposited by the constitution?"[5]

The uniformity of political institutions in republican form is the real force making for the uniformity of the members of

[1] *The Federalist*, LI (Hamilton or Madison). [2] Ibid.
[3] Ibid. [4] Ibid. [5] Ibid., XLIII (Madison).

the union, much more than the mere union of their representatives.

Fourthly, the three-fourths majority sanction for federal decisions, in the case of constitutional amendments and the ratification of conventions, is a new characteristic of federalism.[1] Unanimity had been the fundamental condition in the old confederation.

Having destroyed the tradition of the old league the enlightened genius of a new nation set up the principle of the federal nation, i.e. *Bundesstaat*.

Madison stated that the great principle of self-preservation and the transcendent law and happiness of society are "the objects at which all political institutions aim, and to which all such institutions must be sacrificed."[2]

The "principle of reciprocity, which is the fundamental thesis of the confederation, seems to require that its obligations on the other states should be reduced to the same standard."

No compact between independent sovereigns based on legislative authority is recognised as more than a mere league.

Since the slightest friction among members owing to differences of opinion is liable to cause the dissolution of the federal pact, the delicate problem of alteration in the idea of complete equality in confederation has to be solved. The validity of the constitution must be based on the highest utility of the greatest number of mankind.

Even though the constitution and all laws formed by the federal legislatures of the united state should be the supreme laws of the land, and the interpretation of these laws by the Supreme Court of Justice must prevail over that of other Courts, yet the constitutional equilibrium between the general and the state governments grants and justifies the complete authority of state sovereignty.

Constitutional federalism under American democracy was to be federal in character, republican in method, but not entirely confederate or allied in nature.

Fifthly, Hamilton was convinced that "it may be laid down as a general rule that this confidence in, and obedience to, a government will commonly be proportioned to the goodness and badness of its administration."[3]

The positive justification of the constitution involved the power to make all laws necessary and proper for carrying out executive

[1] *The Federalist*, XLIII (Madison).   [2] Ibid.   [3] Ibid., XXVII (Hamilton).

and all other powers in the government of the United States in every department.

In order to preserve efficient administration, federalists set up devices to establish energy and stability in government, to promote efficacy and equity in law and justice, and to maintain the adequate combination and blending of the tripartite governmental powers.

"The energy in executive," Hamilton said, "is a leading characteristic in the definition of good government." It is the "genius of republican government" and the true foundation for the enlightenment of government and the preservation of liberty and peace. The more the idea of modern federalism is put into practice, the more significant the republican method becomes.

The ingredients which constitute energy in the executive are unity, duration, adequate provision for its support, and competent powers.

In order that there may be a barrier against the fear of "unveiled mysteries" of a "future seraglio," the executive must have, first, "a due dependence on the people, and, secondly, a due responsibility."[1]

Hamilton asserted that the unity of the executive in the single responsibility of the President of the United States was "one of the best of the distinguishing features of the constitution," as saving it from the experiences of the administrative vices of the plurality of executive responsibility.

Prior to 1787 the value and nature of the executive in a democratic system had never been so thoroughly discussed. The danger of encroachment on the liberty of the people by a strong executive was to be checked by the right choice of the President both in method and principle, and an adequate limitation of executive power either by the constitution or by the machine of government, but not by the nature of the power itself.

Hamilton said that it was "desirable that the sense of the people should operate in the choice of the person to whom so important a trust was to be confined."[2]

It was due to that love of aristocracy and of intellectual pre-eminence which characterised him that he drew up the "convention" method of electing the Chief Magistrate of the United States under the pretext of the danger of "opportunity of tumult and disorder," which would inevitably result from a method of direct election. The reason he adduced for the election

[1] *The Federalist*, LXX (Hamilton).   [2] Ibid., LXVIII (Hamilton).

of the President by convention was that such an important position required the highest possible perfection of choice after a due "deliberation and judicious combination of all reasons and inducements."[1]

The President so elected was empowered to be the head of the people for a period of four years, with a certain complement of power laid down in the constitution of the United States of America.

As the President of the United States was "the elective periodical servant of the people," his powers were limited to such things as the power of appointment of officials and judges of the Supreme Courts of Justice and other Courts, the conduct of foreign negotiations with "the advice and consent of the Senate," power over the military and naval forces of the nation as a mere director or Commander-in-Chief, a qualified control over acts of the legislative bodies (power of veto in certain instances), the grant of pardon for offences except in the case of impeachment, and the right to adjourn Parliament for a limited time.

The judicial power, as well as the executive, has a duty as the faithful guardian of the constitution, and as a barrier to encroachment and oppression by the representative body.

The security of a steady impartial administration of the law is a citadel of public justice against the danger of legislative and executive preponderance.

The appointment of judges by the President with the advice and consent of the Senate is a proper method of choice to such posts, as they require special legal knowledge. The tenure of the office must be "during good behaviour."[2] "The standard of good behaviour for the continuance in office of judicial magistracy is certainly one of the most valuable of the modern improvements in the practice of government."

The sword of the community was held by the executive and the purse of society was possessed by the legislature, but no direction either of the strength or the wealth of society depends on judicial power.

The business of the judge is not to have "force" or "will," but "merely judgment." Therefore a standard of good behaviour and permanent salaries and remuneration are essential to the stability of the judiciary.[3]

The precautions taken to secure a sense of responsibility are

---

[1] *The Federalist*, LXVIII (Hamilton).   [2] Ibid., LXXVIII (Hamilton).
[3] Ibid., LXXVIII–LXXIX (Hamilton).

that the judges are "liable to be impeached for malconduct by the House of Representatives and tried by the Senate; and, if convicted, may be dismissed from office, and disqualified for holding any other."[1]

The federal judicature extends "(i) to all those cases which arise out of the laws of the United States, passed in pursuance of their just and constitutional powers of legislation; (ii) to all those which concern the execution of the provisions expressly contained in the articles of union; (iii) to all those to which the United States are a party; (iv) to all those which involve the peace of the confederacy, whether they relate to the intercourse between the United States and foreign nations, or that between the states themselves; (v) to all those which originate on the high seas, and are of admiralty or maritime jurisdiction; (vi) and lastly, to all those in which the state tribunals cannot be supposed to be impartial and unbiassed."[2]

The constitutional survey of the legal validity of enactments is a standing restriction on the federal and state legislatures, and there must also be "a direct negative on the state laws," or preferably "an authority in the federal courts to overrule such laws as might be in contravention of the articles of union."

Judicial supremacy over constitutional functions is the characteristic of the federalists, whose ideal was a "government of laws, not of men."

In the governmental powers the legislative authority is the foundation of the constitution on the one hand, and performs intermediate functions of administration on the other.

The House of Representatives was formed by the representatives of the population elected for a certain period of years.

It is a maxim that "the continuance of the government may become more democratic, but the soul that animates it will be more oligarchic," and the principle is to secure "a sufficient number for the purpose of safety, of local information and of diffusive sympathy with the whole society."[3] The federalists assumed that one representative for every thirty thousand inhabitants would make the House of Representatives a safe and competent guardian of the interests which will be confided to it.

At the same time the Senate was appointed by the state legislatures, each member holding high qualifications and retaining office for six years.

---

[1] *The Federalist*, LXXIX (Hamilton). [2] Ibid., LXXX (Hamilton).
[3] Ibid., LVIII (Hamilton or Madison).

Equality of representation in the Senate is the "result of the compromise between the opposite pretensions of the large and small states," and also the product of the "compound republic" which was founded on "a mixture of proportional and equal representation."

It is a principle that "the equal vote allowed to each state is at once a constitutional recognition of the portion of the sovereignty remaining in the individual state and an instrument for preserving that residuary sovereignty"; and also it must prove an impediment against improper acts of legislation.[1]

The President, with the advice and consent of the Senate, has certain executive powers. The constitutional mechanism which provides the presidency with the advice and consent of the Senate on certain matters gives the latter executive power, and the Senate itself has judicial authority, i.e. in regard to impeachment and trial; therefore the Senate holds the position of an intermediate body of governmental powers. The Senate is a collective and federal trustee for the proper interests of the component states.

Finally, the distribution of powers between the federal and state governments was an essential part of the federal principle, and the degree and extent of the power of federal authority under modern federalism were derived from this constitutional equilibrium of governments, and ought to be commensurate with its purpose of securing effective administration.

The principle of distribution of powers, to which the federalists adhered, should be directed to the highest utility of mankind by the best exercise of human wisdom and experience; firstly, whether such a power be necessary and tending to the public good, and, secondly, in the case of an affirmative answer to that question, how to guard effectively against a perversion of power to the public detriment.

Justice is the end of civil society, but the reverence for laws and government inculcated by the voice of enlightened reason, even by Aristotle, "would not find superfluous advantage" to have "the passion and prejudices of the community on its side."

Federalists understood that "in every political institution a power to advance the public good involves a discretion which may be misapplied and abused."[2]

In order to form a correct judgment on this problem, Madison

[1] *The Federalist*, LXII (Hamilton or Madison).   [2] Ibid., XLI (Madison).

divided the powers of the union into six categories relating to the following different objects:

(I) Security against foreign danger.
(II) Regulation of intercourse with foreign nations.
(III) Maintenance of harmony and proper intercourse among the states.
(IV) Certain miscellaneous objects of general utility.
(V) Restraint of the states from certain injurious acts.
(VI) Provision for giving due efficacy to all these powers.[1]

In the first place common defence, security of liberty and the general welfare are the primitive objects of civil society and the avowed essential objects of federation.

The powers in this first category involve those of the "declaration of war and granting letters of marque; of providing armies and fleets; of regulating and calling forth the militia; of levying and borrowing money."

These powers, vested in the government of the union, must be effectively confined to the federal executive.

The second category consists in the powers which "regulate the intercourse with foreign nations, to wit: to make treaties; to send and receive ambassadors, other public ministers and consuls; to define and punish piracies and felonies committed on the high seas, and offences against the law of nations; to regulate foreign commerce, including a power to prohibit after the year 1808 the importation of slaves, and to lay an intermediate duty of ten dollars per head as a discouragement to such importations."[2]

This class of power is of importance for efficient administration. The regulation and the carrying out of these powers must properly be accorded to the federal administration.

The third class of powers comprises those which provide for harmony and proper intercourse between states and contain "the restraints imposed on the authority of the states and certain powers of the judicial department."[3]

The powers under this classification are "to regulate commerce among the several states and Indian tribes; to coin money, regulate the value thereof and of foreign coin; to provide for punishment of counterfeiting current coin and securities of the United States; to fix the standard of weights and measures; to establish a uniform rule of naturalisation and uniform laws of

[1] *The Federalist*, XLI (Madison). [2] Ibid., XLII (Madison). [3] Ibid.

bankruptcy; to prescribe the manner in which the public acts, records and judicial proceedings of each state shall be proved, and the effect they shall have in other states; and to establish post offices and post roads."[1]

The federal experiments of his day had not reached maturity in regard to such matters as the laws of divorce and labour and educational legislation for which federal control has proved to be essential.

The rules as to federal control must be changed in accordance with the development of society.

The placing of the administration of justice under the federal control is requisite for the solution of judicial relations of states with others and with foreign jurisdictions.

The fourth class of powers is of a miscellaneous character, but some of the powers included in it are extremely important in federal politics:—

(A) A power to promote the progress of science and useful arts by securing, for a limit of time, to "authors and inventors the exclusive right to their respective writings and discoveries," must coincide with public good and individual right and be under the control of the federal government.

(B) The power to exercise exclusive legislation, in all cases whatever, over such district (not exceeding ten miles square) as may, by cession of particular states and the acceptance of the Congress, become the seat of government, and to exercise the same authority over places, such as forts, magazines, arsenals, dockyards and other needful buildings.

(C) Power "to declare the punishment of treason—but no attainder of treason shall work corruption of blood, or forfeiture except during the life of the person attainted"—is vested in the federal authority in order to punish treason committed against the United States, but it is necessary to restrain the federal government "in punishing it from exceeding the consequence of guilt beyond the person of its author."[2]

(D) The power to admit new states into the union, by which no new state shall be formed or created within the jurisdiction of any other of the states, nor any state be formed by the junction of states or parts of states "without the consent of the legislature of the states concerned and the Congress," is not only to promote order in the union, but also to prevent discord in federal administration.

(E) Power to dispose of and make all needful rules and

[1] *The Federalist*, XLII (Madison). [2] Ibid.

regulations respecting the territory and other property belonging to the United States is necessary in order to avoid the friction of jealousy and ambition of the states, especially with regard to Western territory.

(F) Power to "guarantee to every state in a union a republican form of government, to protect each of them against invasion and, on application of the legislature and of the executive, against domestic violence" is of very great importance.

In order to preserve the virtue of the federal free constitution, the maintenance of the existing republican governments is a substantial guarantee of federal cordiality, and, moreover, the more alike the governments the greater the interests and rights to be co-ordinated.

In democratic federalism conflicts between states, whether a majority or a minority of the union, may require "other umpires" outside of the two disputing parties.

Madison asserted that "it is a sufficient recommendation of the federal constitution that it diminishes the risk of a calamity for which no possible constitution can provide a cure."[1]

(G) The power "to consider all debts contracted, and engagements entered into, before the option of this constitution as being no less valid against the United States under this constitution than under the confederation" is a mere declaratory proposition which brings about the improvement of the national credit, within and without.

(H) The power to provide for amendments, to be ratified by three-fourths of the states, with two excepted matters only—namely, the equality of suffrage in the senate and certain provisions restricting temporarily the powers of Congress, provides a reasonable amount of flexibility.

And the provision that the ratification of the Convention by nine states "shall be sufficient for the establishment of this constitution between the states ratifying the same" is one of the most striking novelties in the American federation.

For the safety and happiness of the whole of the members of the union the aim of the federal pact must be preserved, and it must be incumbent on the majority of the members to avoid the unnecessary dissolution of a federal state. The validity of the federal compact should be, morally and legally, dependent on moderate and prudent relationship, and on the mutual expectation of justice in the union.[2]

[1] *The Federalist*, XLIII (Madison).   [2] Ibid.

The fifth class of provisions in the federal authority consists of the following restrictions on the powers of the constituent states:—

Firstly, no state shall enter into any treaty, alliance, or confederation; grant letters of marque or reprisal; coin money or emit bills of credit; make anything but gold and silver a legal tender in payment of debts; pass any bill of attainder, any *ex-post facto* law, or law impairing the obligation of contracts; or grant any title of nobility.

Secondly, no state without the consent of the congress can lay any imposts or duties on imports or exports except what are necessary for the execution of inspection laws, and the net produce of all duties on imports laid by any state shall be for the use of the treasury of the United States. Also "no state shall without the consent of Congress lay any duty on tonnage, keep troops or ships of war in time of peace, enter into any agreement or compact with another state or with a foreign power, or engage in war unless actually invaded or in such imminent danger as will not admit of delay."[1]

The last class of powers which the federalists assigned to the federal authority is the provision on which the efficacy of the federal government is to be based. "To make all laws which shall be necessary and proper for carrying into execution the foregoing powers, and all other power vested by this constitution in the government of the United States in any department or office thereof" is the substantial power of government to carry on effective administration.

The extent of executive or judicial power, when it supersedes the legislature or other departments, depends not upon the degree or extent of power itself, but on the composition or structure of government. There must be scope for "construction and inference" within necessary and proper limits.

The constitution and the law of the federal government in the consolidated republic is the supreme power as the law of the land. "The constitution and the laws of the United States are all treaties made, or which shall be made, under the authority of the United States, and shall be the supreme laws of the land and the judge of every state shall be bound thereby, anything in the constitution or laws of any state to the contrary notwithstanding."

Such a power as this may infringe the independence of state sovereign authority, for the federal power in the federal state,

[1] *The Federalist*, XLIV (Madison).

in the sphere allotted by the constitution, must be absolute and supreme.

The question of sovereignty in the federal power is also due to the compound nature of legislative authority, but sovereignty, in the function of federal authority so far as the constitution extends, rests with the federal government.

It is the fundamental principle of government that the authority of a whole society should not be subordinate to that of a part.

The oath and affirmation to support the constitution binding upon the Senate and the officials both of the United States and every state, or some other provisions for giving efficiency to the federal authority, either in the executive or judicial departments, are characteristic of modern federalism.

Thus by the genius of the federalists there was built up the elaborate architecture of the "federal state," constructed with federal material and republican technique.

Unlike "the reveries of those political doctors whose sagacity disdains the admonitions of experimental instruction,"[1] modern federalism was formulated by an eminent group of political scientists whose ideas were those of the utilitarian conception based on empirical philosophy.

The "federal state," which was federal in character and republican in method, secured the greatest possible equilibrium between political expediency and the psychological and philosophical schools of thought of the later eighteenth century.

Hamilton justified his utilitarian philosophy in the following quotation from David Hume: "To balance a large state or society, whether monarchical or republican, on general laws, is a work of so great difficulty, that no human genius, however comprehensive, is able, by the mere dint of reason and reflection, to effect it. The judgment of many must unite in the work; experience must guide their labour; time must bring it to perfection, and the feeling of inconveniences must correct the mistakes which they inevitably fall into in their first trials and experiments."[2]

---

[1] *The Federalist*, XXVIII (Hamilton).
[2] D. Hume: *Essays*. "The Rise and Progress of Arts and Sciences," *The Federalist*, LXXXVI (Hamilton).

CHAPTER IV

THE FEDERALISM OF JEFFERSON

A series of pamphlets published contemporaneously with the rise of the federalists embodied the arguments for and against the views set out in their Essays.

Some of the pamphleteers, such as Elbridge Gerry, Alexander C. Hanson, Edward Randolph, Richard Henry Lee and George Mason, attacked the federalist doctrine from the point of view of the danger of over-consolidation of the federal state and consequent suppression of the individual state initiative.[1]

Nevertheless, there appeared no effective counterblast to the federalists until Jefferson's advocacy of the "Federo-Republican State" became generally diffused and approved.

Jefferson, being one of the most eminent champions of the American fathers, drafted the Declaration of Rights and wrote the famous articles on the constitution called *Notes on Virginia*. He was a prominent opponent of Hamilton's proposed constitution. Since to Jefferson love of liberty and zeal for free government were fundamental ideas, Hamilton's desire for energy and stability of government provoked his strong indignation against the new constitution of 1787.

The friction between Hamilton and Jefferson was chiefly due to the different nature of their minds and fundamental philosophies, rather than to a different idea of the federal mechanism. They both admired republicanism, but each of them tried to set up his own distinct criterion of republican democracy.

Jefferson believed that "man was created for social intercourse; but social intercourse cannot be maintained without a sense of justice; then man must have been created with a sense of justice,"[2] whilst Hamilton thought that "man is ambitious, vindictive, and rapacious." From the psychological point of view Jefferson was a follower of Locke, as modified by Rousseau, and Hamilton of Hobbes. Jefferson was grieved to see that his friend M. Dupont also "adopted the principles of Hobbes and the humiliation of human nature."

He said, "The sense of justice and injustice is not derived from our natural organisation, but founded on conventional duty."

[1] P. L. Ford: *Pamphlets on the Constitution*, 1787–1788, 1888.
[2] Thomas Jefferson: *Writings*, ed. by Paul L. Ford, Vol. X. To Francis W. Gilmer, June 7, 1816, p. 32.

It was Jefferson who gave a precise definition to the term "republican government": he said, "purely and simply, it means a government by its citizens in mass acting directly and personally according to rules established by the majority; and every government is more or less republican, in proportion as it has in its composition more or less of this ingredient of direct action of citizens."[1]

Being an eighteenth-century liberalist, like Montesquieu and Rousseau, he asserted that "such a government is evidently restrained within narrow limits of space and population." Nevertheless, democracy in large states could take its part in Parliament by the method of representation by consent, instead of by an assembly of people in the market place.

But the pure republic ought to be formed by representatives who are chosen either *pro hac vice* or for such a short term as should render secure "the duty of expressing the will of the constituents."[2]

The nearest approach to the pure republic is the closest connection of government with the hearts of people, but republicanism may also be found in "forms of government where the executive, judiciary, and legislative functions and the different branches of the latter are chosen by the people more or less directly for longer terms of years or for life or made hereditary; or where there are mixtures of authorities, some dependent on, and others independent of the people."[3]

He laid down the axiom that "the further the departure from direct and constant control by citizens, the less has the government of the ingredient of republicanism," and he rebuked Hamilton's republicanism that was to him an amalgamation between republicans and federalists "of name only, not of principle."[4]

Jefferson expressed his opposition to Hamilton in the following letter: "All indeed call themselves by the name of republicans, because that of federalist was extinguished in the battle of New Orleans. But the truth is that finding that monarchy is a desperate wish in this country, they rally to the point which they think next best, a consolidated government. Their aim is now therefore to break down the rights reserved by the constitution to the states as a bulwark against that consolidation, the fear of which produced the whole of the opposition to the constitution at its birth. Hence

---

[1] Thomas Jefferson: *Writings*, ed. by Paul L. Ford, Vol. X. To John Taylor, May 28, 1816, pp. 29–30.
[2] Ibid., p. 30.   [3] Ibid., p. 29.
[4] Ibid., To William Johnson, October 27, 1882, p. 225.

the new republicans in Congress preaching the doctrines of the old federalists and the new nicknames of Ultras and Radicals."[1]

Further than this Jefferson condemned Burke's Toryism and praised Priestley's and Paine's radicalism. He said, "Mr. Paine's answer to Burke will be a refreshing shower to their Tory minds."[2]

From his republican point of view, he condemned the new constitution as giving effect to a principle of "consolidation," and its effect would be to melt down the thirteen states into one general government. He defended the liberties of the people by insisting that the declaration of their natural rights was essential in order to restrain the unchecked license of government.

The renunciation of the power of keeping a standing army, the absence of security for the liberty of the press or for freedom of commerce against monopolies, the abolition of trial by jury in civil cases, the proposition of supremacy of the law of the federal legislature over those of the states, the abandonment of rotation of office, and the re-eligibility of the President were Jefferson's main objections to the new constitution.

Jefferson's chief resentment was against those who supported the overweening power of the executive and judiciary and held that once the constitution was formed the people had no right of resistance save in the extremest cases.

If the constitution be "a matter of compromise," a "capitulation of conflicting interests and opinions," as Jefferson asserted, a constitutional guarantee of fundamental rights must be necessary for the security of liberty, in so far as the present political organisations are concerned.

The Jeffersonian democracy is no less vital in federal organisations than in a unitary one. Because, even though I put aside the philosophical assertion of right and duty, whether duty reflects rights or vice-versa, no citizen in an existing civil society can be himself at his best without the necessary rights.[3]

If the foregoing stipulation be accepted, since constitutional law is the supreme law of the land, the legal guarantee of the "natural "rights of the people by the constitution is one of the greatest importance, especially in the federal state.

[1] Thomas Jefferson: *Writings*, ed. by Paul L. Ford, Vol. X. To William Johnson, October 27, 1882, pp. 225–226.
[2] Ibid., Vol. V. To Benjamin Vaughan, May 11, 1791, p. 334.
[3] The rights to which I refer are the Natural Rights in the modern sense, that is to say, the meaning of "Natural" is not considered as in the eighteenth century's "Naturrecht," but as indicating essential and necessary rights such as those to live, to work, to have freedom of speech, etc.

Even though in modern federalism a part of the state sovereignty is handed over to the federal government by the common consent of the component states, the "natural" rights of the people cannot be legally guarded without a bill of rights in the constitution.

The federal mechanism prevented the realisation of principles for the welfare of humanity, such as the prohibition of child labour, which cannot be abolished in the United States, and also the establishment of methods of election designed to protect the equality of franchise.

It seems to me that Jefferson's claim to this right is justified by experience.

The second objection, in regard to the re-eligibility of the President and the stability of executive and the abolition of rotation of office, was derived from his extreme love of liberty and hatred of arbitrary authority which was based on the prevailing political theory of his day, but not the result of any conscious political expediency.

He emphasised the necessity of union, saying that "harmony" between the legislative and executive branches and between all and the general government "are so many steps towards securing that union of action and effort in all its parts, without which no nation can be happy or safe."[1]

He rejected the power of veto of the President and said that "the negative proposed to be given men on all the acts of the several legislatures is now for the first time suggested to my mind. *Prima facie*, I do not like it, it fails in the essential character that the hole and the patch should be commensurate."[2]

Nevertheless, however democratic Jefferson may have been, he could hardly go farther than the contemporary liberal thinkers, such as the utilitarian radicals in England, and the Renaissance thinkers in France.

Jefferson recognised the merit of "natural aristocracy" as "the most precious gift of nature, for the instruction, the trusts and government of society," and he thought it best to put the *pseudo-aristoi* into the governmental organisation.[3]

Thirdly, his life-long struggle against judicial control over the legislature was demonstrated in several articles into which we cannot enter further at the moment.

If judicial decision is "the last resort" of governmental power,

---

[1] Thomas Jefferson: *Writings*, ed. by Paul L. Ford, Vol. IX. To James Sullivan, June 19, 1807, pp. 75–76.
[2] Ibid.   [3] Ibid., To John Adams, October 28, 1813, p. 425.

as the federalists asserted, Jefferson thought that such a constitution is a "complete *felo de se*."[1] Even though the power of impeachment was possessed by the legislative authority, still the constitution, on this hypothesis, would be "a mere thing of wax in the hands of the judiciary."

Jefferson considered that it is "an axiom of eternal truth in politics that whatever power in any government is independent, is absolute also; in theory only, at first, while the spirit of the people is up, but in practice as fast as that relaxes."[2]

Therefore he claimed that "they are inherently independent of all but moral law," and that "independence can be trusted nowhere but with the people in mass."

Against the federalists' doctrine of inter-connections between the tripartite powers, he expressed his own conviction in the statement that "each of the three departments has equally the right to decide for itself what is its duty under the Constitution, without any regard to what the others may have decided for themselves under a similar question."[3]

His firm conviction that the three departments must be "co-equal and co-sovereign" within themselves led to the conclusion that a remedy for the unconstitutionality of the executive and legislative functionaries is dependent upon the establishment of the responsibility of the people in their elective capacity.

His final survey of these problems revealed that what people need was not only elaborate machinery to control inevitable evils, but "to inform their discretion by education."

The "two hooks," on which his republicanism was hanging, were his characteristic political ideas, public education on the one hand and decentralised local government on the other.[4]

The public contest between Jefferson and Hamilton on the stage of the early federal theatre in America was of incalculable value in the political history of the bourgeois democracy, but was not a conflict between profoundly different political theories, and was nothing but the dispute between large capitalistic interests and those of the petty bourgeois and agricultural interests, which produced later the two lines of politics in America, the Republican party on the one hand, and the Democratic on the other. Charles Beard has asserted that "it may be truly said that the constitution

---

[1] Thomas Jefferson: *Writings*, ed. by Paul L. Ford, Vol. X. To Judge Spencer Roane, September 6, 1819, p. 141.
[2] Ibid., p. 141. [3] Ibid., p. 142.
[4] Ibid., Vol. IX. To Joseph C. Cabell, January 31, 1814, p. 453.

was a product of the struggle between capitalistic and agrarian interests."[1]

Jefferson said that "it is the only thing which can yield us a little present protection against the dominion of a faction, while circumstances are maturing for bringing and keeping the government in real unison with the spirit of their constituents."

Therefore Jefferson's idea of federalism in the strict sense did not differ much from that of the federalists in nature, but only in method.

Jefferson's belief that the relationship between the general and state governments generally supposed the latter subordinated to the former, was clearly manifested by his remark that "this is not the case, they are co-ordinate departments of one single and integral whole."[2]

He said that "to the state government are reserved all legislation and administration in affairs which concern their own citizens only, and to the federal government is given whatever concerns foreigners or citizens of other states; these functions alone being made federal. The one is domestic, the other the foreign branch of the same government, neither having control over the other, but within its own department."

The claims to the same power put forward by departments was an exception for which Jefferson provided a "common umpire." Jefferson's democratic nature reached the following conclusion: "In cases of little importance or urgency, the prudence of both parties will keep them aloof from the questionable ground; but if neither can be avoided nor compromised, a convention of states must be called, to ascribe the doubtful power to that department which they may think best."[3]

He thought that the significance of the constitution lay in the *Lex Legum*.[4]

Not only from the standpoint of the composition of the government, but also from that of the security of public liberty, Jefferson thought that the "preference of a plural over a singular executive" would lessen the dangers of the simple executive, and he asserted that "the true barrier of our liberty in this country is our own state governments."[5]

Suggesting a safeguard against this possible usurpation, he said: "Seventeen distinct states, amalgamated into one as to their

---

[1] Charles Beard: *Economic Origins of Jeffersonian Democracy*, p. 3.
[2] Thomas Jefferson: *Works*, ed. by Washington, Vol. VII. To Major John Cartwright, January 5, 1824, p. 358.   [3] Ibid., p. 358.
[4] Ibid., p. 359.   [5] Ibid. To M. Destutt Tracy, January 26, 1811, pp. 567, 570.

foreign concerns, but single and independent as to their internal administration, regularly organised with legislature and governor resting on the choice of the people, and enlightened by a free press, can never be so fascinated by the arts of one man as to submit voluntarily to his usurpation."[1]

In this definition of the federal state the differentiation of state and general prerogative was precisely illustrated by his statement that of those powers transferred by the constitution to the general government "the general executive is certainly pre-ordinate—e.g. in questions respecting the militia," therefore "the government must be subject to receive orders from the War Department as any other subordinate office would."

In this assertion Jefferson emphasised that:—"The way to have good and safe government is not to trust it all to one, but to divide it among the many, distributing to everyone exactly the functions he is competent to." He asserted that "the wit of man cannot devise a more solid basis for a free, durable and well-administered republic."

Jefferson's ideal security of liberty and democracy was an elaborate system of decentralisation from the national to the state governments and down to county and ward. The ward was a unit of local government six miles square[2] and would become a small republic within itself within a county which "is estimated at an average of twenty-four miles square."

He said that "the article, however, nearest my heart is the division of county into wards; these will be pure and elementary as republics, the sum of which taken together compose the state, and will make of the whole a true democracy as to the business of the wards which is that of nearest and daily concern."

The powers which each ward ought to possess, are as follows:—

1. An elementary school.
2. A company of militia with its officers.
3. A Justice of the Peace and constable.
4. Care of its own poor.
5. Its own roads.
6. Its own police.
7. One or more jurors elected to attend the Courts of Justice.
8. Votes given at their "Folk House" for all functionaries reserved to their election.

[1] Thomas Jefferson: *Works*, ed. by Washington, Vol. IX. To M. Destutt Tracy, January 26, 1811, p. 570.
[2] Ibid., Vol. VII. To Major J. Cartwright, June 5, 1824, p. 357.

Thus each ward was a "small republic within itself."[1] The affairs of the larger sections, of the county and of the state and of the union were to be delegated to agents elected by themselves.

Thus the wards must be "of such a size as that every citizen can attend when called on, and act in person."[2]

The government of the wards is to be organised for all things relating to themselves exclusively.

The county administration is to be carried out by officers and judges elected and chosen by every ward within the county.

Jefferson said that "by making every citizen an acting member of the government and in the offices nearest and most interesting to him" these decentralised systems of government "will attach him by his strongest feelings to the independence of his country, and its republican constitution."[3]

The justices thus chosen by every ward "would constitute the county court, would do its judiciary business, direct roads and bridges, levy county and poor rates and administer all the matters of common interest to the whole county."

The citizen in a free government should thus make the government into a composite whole which can be described as:—
"(i) the general federal republic for all concerns, foreign and federal; (ii) that of the state for what relates to its own citizens exclusively; (iii) the county republics for the duties and concerns of the county; (iv) the ward republics, for the small and numerous interesting concerns of the neighbours; and in government as well as in every other business of life it is by division and subdivision of duties alone that all matters, great and small, can be managed to perfection."[4]

Such a system of government as he described was his ideal federation and he believed that it was the wisest invention that had ever been devised by the wisdom of mankind "for the perfect exercise of self-government and for its preservation."

His ideal was that "the whole is cemented by giving to every citizen personally a part in administration of public affairs."

Thus, all the power was distributed by dividing and subdividing these republics from the great national governing one down through all its subordinations until it ends in the administration of every man's affairs by himself; "by placing under everyone what his own eye may superintend, that all will be done for the best."

[1] Thomas Jefferson: *Works*, ed. by Washington Vol. VII. To Major J. Cartwright, p. 358.   [2] *Writings*, ed. by Paul L. Ford, Vol. X. To Samuel Kercheval, July 12, 1816, p. 40.   [3] Ibid., p. 41.   [4] Ibid.

In this decentralised federal state the organisations from the elementary republics of the wards up to that of the union set up a "certain grade of authorities on their own basis of law," allotting to each its "delegated share of power," and "constituting truly the system of fundamental balances and checks for the government."[1]

The share in the direction of the ward or some of the higher divisions and the participation in governmental affairs on the basis of a free republic anticipated the relationship between grades of political institutions as "federal co-ordination"—that is to say, these divisions were not various branches of an integral unitary government, but each with its own independent law was to form a federal state.

Jefferson's democracy was based on the doctrine of John Locke on the one hand and on the ideas of the later eighteenth century radicals, such as Godwin and Paine, on the other. At the same time his fundamental idea, manifested throughout his official and literary writings, was really based on the utilitarian conception and led to the claim that his philosophy was of English origin.

In his generous mind, no matter what views others held, Jefferson could not grasp any idea but his anxiety for liberty, and his desire for a free government was so strong that his continued struggle against Hamilton's aristocracy sometimes led him to extremes far removed from his own convictions.

Nevertheless, his logical and liberal mind kept his friends and himself in constant efforts for the establishment of the republican federal state.

His views as to the revision of the constitution were a reflection of his radicalism.

Jefferson said, "the earth belongs to the living, not to the dead, the will and the power of man expires with his life by the natural law." In each generation a nation is bound by the will of the majority, but none can "bind the succeeding generations, more than the inhabitants of another country."

Therefore, he emphasised his views that as the generations of men may be considered as bodies and corporations, "so each generation has the usufruct of the earth during the period of continuance," but "when it ceases to exist, the usufruct passes on to the successive generations" free, unencumbered, and for ever.

From Buffon's table of mortality, Jefferson calculated that as every eighteen years and eight months one half of the inhabitants

[1] Thomas Jefferson: *Works*, ed. by Washington, Vol. VI. To Joseph Cabell, February 2, 1816, pp. 543–544.

would be dead, the right of majority rule would terminate in nearly nineteen years.[1] The law of nature commands beings to alter or adjust themselves to the majority will in their generation. Laws and contracts would be obliterated by this natural transformation.

He said, "this corporeal globe and everything upon it belongs to its present corporeal inhabitants during their generation."[2] In these conditions, the right to direct what concerns themselves and to declare the law by the discretion of the majority is completely justified. This majority has a right to depute representatives to a convention and to make and alter the constitution to "what they think will be the best for themselves."

In his later years, in 1816, he proposed certain amendments of the constitution, embodying his political tendencies. These were:—

1. General suffrage.
2. Equal representation in the legislature.
3. An executive chosen by the people.
4. Judges elective or movable.
5. Justices, jurors and sheriffs elective.
6. Ward divisions.
7. Periodical amendment of the constitution.[3]

His fundamental proposal was for a republican federal constitution wherein each component state might make distribution of its powers between the general, state, county and ward republics, and set up such decentralised system of administration, within or without each government, dividing and subdividing the duties, as it might deem fit.

The federal idea to which Jefferson adhered was pure federalism, in which each government in the country has its own sovereign right to carry out its own duties at its own discretion. The perfect working of the administrative machine to produce unity is based on the harmonious wills of all citizens combining to form one whole.

His first principle of republicanism is that "the *lex majoris partis*" is the fundamental law of every society of individuals of equal rights; and obedience to the will of society enounced by the majority of a single vote, as sacred as if unanimous, is the first of all lessons of importance.

[1] Thomas Jefferson: *Writings*, ed. by Paul L. Ford, Vol. V. To James Madison, September 6, 1789, pp. 118–119.
[2] Ibid., Vol. X. To Samuel Kercheval, July 12, 1816 p. 44. [3] Ibid., p. 41.

With these political ideals Jefferson proposed rigorously to "maintain the line of power marked by the constitution between two co-ordinate governments, each sovereign and independent in its own department, the states as to everything relating to themselves and their state, the general government as to everything relating to things or persons out of a particular state."[1] Within the constitutional line of demarcation each state has its own exclusive power and this justified the right of secession. He thought that certain states owing to local and occasional discontents might "attempt to secede from the union." It is probable that this local discontent can spread to sound parts of so extensive a union. Such a majority grievance might result either in secession of the states from the union or in redressing it by laws peacefully and constitutionally.

He condemned the idea that "if on the temporary superiority of the one party, the other is to resort to a scission of the union, no federal government can exist."[2]

The safeguard against the calamity of a secession was a little patience, and "we shall see the reign of witches pass over." Even though Jefferson justified the sovereign exercise of state powers, yet he proposed, just as Bentham preferred order to liberty, that resistance at home must be by the way of patience till "luck turns and restores the opportunity of winning back the true principle of government."

The fundamental security for the liberty of the people is the power of the state. Democracy is based on direct participation of citizens in the administration of government. The decentralisation of government from the federal government to the wards exercising their own independent powers is the wisest device of governmental technique ever formulated by the political experience of mankind for the preservation of self-government. He rejected the strong arm of the executive and the supreme authority of the judicature.

The best general key to the solution of the question as to which of the powers may be exercised by the several governments is the fact that "every foreign and federal power is given to the federal government, and to the state every purely domestic."

The one instance of control vested in the federal over the state authority, which is purely domestic, is that of metallic monetary tender. The federal government is in truth "our foreign govern-

[1] Thomas Jefferson: *Writings*, ed. by Paul L. Ford, Vol. X. To Samuel H. Smith, August 2, 1823, p. 263.
[2] Ibid., Vol. VII. To John Taylor, June 1, 1788, p. 264.

ment, which alone is taken from the sovereignty of the separate states."

Therefore, in the federal state, the state naturally is the entire root from which the Jeffersonian democracy of self-government has grown.

The federal state to which Jefferson referred, is federal in nature and decentralised democracy in method. His ideal is the "federo-republican" state.

He asserted that the real line of demarcation between the powers of general and state government can hardly be drawn precisely except under the most urgent necessity. At the same time the common claim of society is self-government in each generation. The amendment of the constitution is of vital importance for the preservation of physical liberty and the maintenance of moral emancipation.

He emphasised the view that the federal constitution must be based on the greatest utility of mankind in each generation and in each place. The majority will of all citizens, which is derived from the decentralised system of self-government, is as inviolable as unanimous will.

His love of liberty extended not only to democratic constitutional status as guardian of a nation, but also to the self-constituted influence of voluntary society.[1]

The standards of social welfare were not indeed merely based on the functionaries of government, but also on the sincerely conscientious reason and experience of voluntary associations— i.e. conscious solidarity of the opinions of citizens.

His federalism is based not only on the utilitarian conception, but also on the democratic theory of his day.

He himself said, "I am an epicurean" and at the same time "a sympathiser with the unitarian movement."

Even though he condemned religious dogma, which he described as "priest poison," he said, "Epictetus and Epicurus give laws for governing ourselves, Jesus a supplement of duties and charities we owe to others."[2]

His assertion of the moral principle by which the government is to be animated was based on the philosophy of Locke on the one hand, and that of Montesquieu on the other. "Liberty, truth, probity and honour" are the four "cardinal principles of society."

[1] Thomas Jefferson: *Writings*, ed. by Paul L. Ford, Vol. X. To Jedediah Morse, March 6, 1822, p. 205.
[2] Ibid., To William Short, October 31, 1819, pp. 143-144.

He said that "morality, compassion, generosity are innate elements of the human constitution."

His "natural right" theory, on which he insisted throughout his life, was to secure the recognition of individual rights, such as the right of independence of force, the right to property founded on natural wants, and the right to liberty. No one has a right to obstruct another, and justice is the fundamental law of society.

Jefferson predicted of the democracy of America that "everyone owns property," and Americans will continue to be virtuous and retain their democratic form of government as long as they remain an agricultural people.[1]

Jeffersonian democracy did not require any modification of the property system,[2] but rather encouraged and favoured the perfect development of *laissez-faire* economics against the capitalist monopoly on the grounds of his principle of natural right.

The philosophy on which Jefferson's ideas were based derived from the utilitarian conception on the one hand, and from "natural right" on the other.

His utilitarianism was dependent upon reason and wisdom rather than mere expediency. His experimental criterion for the evolution of good and evil was the highest utility of mankind on the ethical basis of justice.

His ideal "federo-republican" state was a definite model of federalism in modern political science, as William James' ideal of being distributive, and the practical application of his theory in the United States of America was manifested in the real validity of federalism of this kind, and reached its culmination when John Calhoun asserted the absolute justification of state sovereignty in his work *A Disquisition on the Constitution and Government of the United States*, published in 1854.

From this survey of Jefferson's doctrines and that of Hamilton's theories in the preceding chapter it will be seen that federalism in the modern field of politics was evolved from the highest wisdom of two great political thinkers, Hamilton on the one hand and Jefferson on the other. Regarded from the standpoint of political theory, each of the theories of these great men possessed particular merit; the theories of the latter were chiefly derived from ethical sources, those of the former were largely founded on expediency.

Each decried the ideas of the other from his own point of view; Jefferson rebuked Hamilton as the promulgator of the rankest

[1] Thomas Jefferson: *Writings*, ed. by Paul L. Ford, Vol. IV. To James Madison, December 20, 1787, pp. 479–480.
[2] Charles Beard: *The Economic Origins of Jeffersonian Democracy*.

doctrine of the old federalists which embodied the "government of wolves over sheep," whilst Hamilton considered Jefferson's ideas as "airy phantoms." The conflict between the two resulted in the triumph of Jefferson, his election to the presidency and exuberant presidential address, and the amendments he made to the federal constitution. His theory produced the political system of federalism, and at the same time Hamilton's idea took form as the administrative organ in federal functioning.

"The choicest talents and the noblest hearts which had ever appeared in the world" were incarnated in this contest of federalism in Hamilton and Jefferson and others, such as John Adams, Madison, Jay, Marshal and Morris, who brought about the great social revolution which was to consolidate the thirteen states into the one great nation of the United States of America.

Modern federalism set up its principles in the constitution of the United States of America, which has been the most permanent political institution ever devised by the highest wisdom and experience of mankind.

Even though the federal conceptions both of Jefferson and Hamilton have been subject to severe and detailed criticism by many later thinkers, yet it cannot be denied that modern federalism is still imbued with their spirit to the present day.

CHAPTER V

THE FEDERAL IDEAS OF DE TOCQUEVILLE

The victory of Jackson in the presidential election in 1828 was a landmark in the political history of the United States. It embodied a material change in economic and social conditions and revealed a marked political transformation from the ideas of the intellectual aristocrats, such as the federalists and Jefferson, to those of the frontier democrats in the West and South, such as Andrew Jackson, from 1829 to 1837.

Eleven new states had joined the American federal government since the promulgation of the federal constitution by the thirteen states in 1787.

Jacksonian democracy was manifested by his first exercise of the presidential power of veto on the one hand and by administrative changes on the other. His belief in the equal co-ordination of the tripartite governmental power brought about the elevation of the executive and the degradation of the legislative power, because he was convinced that the new democratic regime was a triumph for the executive, representing the people, over the congressional "aristocracy."

At the same time the principle of rotation in office, abandonment of religious and property tests for office-holding, the abolition of property qualification for the franchise and the separation of the state and church were the realisation of Jefferson's idea.

After the Revolution the first remarkable manifestation of political literature in respect of American politics was the publication of De Tocqueville's *Democracy in America* in 1835.[1]

Alexis de Tocqueville was one of the most brilliant and able French political thinkers of the early nineteenth century. His political ideas, illustrated in his work *Democracy in America*, became so popular as to acquire the laudation of M. Royer Collard: "Since Montesquieu there has been nothing like it." No matter what criticism may be applied to him as a French liberal thinker, his earnest search for legitimate equality led him to study and investigate the new democratic country on the other shore of the Atlantic and say that "among the novel objects that attracted my attention during my stay in the United States,

[1] The ideas of the American federal thinkers during the intervening period will be discussed in Chapter VI.

nothing struck me more forcibly than the general equality of conditions."[1]

The main thesis of his great work was the criticism of republican democracy, which was the desirable and inevitable course of human progress; but he believed that even though the "principle of sovereignty of the people, which is to be found, more or less, at the bottom of almost all human institutions, generally remains concealed from view," the country in the world where the doctrine of the sovereignty of the people could be fairly appreciated and is practically put into a concrete form is assuredly America.[2]

He said that "at the period of their first emigrations the parish system, that fruitful germ of free institutions, was deeply rooted in the habits of the English, and with it the doctrine of the sovereignty of the people had been introduced into the bosom of the monarchy of the House of Tudor."[3]

The principle of popular sovereignty and the love of equality and liberty had been nurtured in the townships and municipalities. He emphasised the view that "a nation may establish a system of free government, but without the spirit of municipal institutions it cannot have the spirit of liberty."[4]

The formation of the great federal union in America proved that "nothing but a general combination can protect their liberty" and preserve equality in society against the aggression of power. He asserted that democracy could be applicable to an Anglo-American country, but in old European countries, such as France, the American form of democracy, socially, politically and economically, was impossible to adopt.

Tocqueville thought that the main contributions to the maintenance of the democratic republic in the United States of America fell into the following three categories:—

1. That "federal form of government which the Americans have adopted, and enables the union to combine the power of a great empire with the security of a small state."

2. "Those municipal institutions which limit the despotism of the majority, and at the same time impart a taste for freedom and a knowledge of the art of being free to the people."

3. "The constitution of judicial power." The judicial power is exercised in such a manner by the Courts of Justice as to repress the excesses of democracy and check and direct the impulses of the majority without stopping its activity.[5]

---

[1] Alexis de Tocqueville: *Democracy in America*, trans. by Henry Reeve, 1889, Vol. I, p. 1.   [2] Ibid., p. 52.
[3] Ibid., p. 25.   [4] Ibid., p. 57.   [5] Ibid., p. 303.

He believed that following on the dissolution of the confederation of 1781 the federal constitution was a novel product of the "choicest talents and the noblest hearts, after the long and mature deliberation" in the National Convention whose proposals "offered to the acceptance of people the body of general laws which still rules the union."[1]

The union was formulated to "absorb the individual importance of each in the general importance of all" and consolidate the thirteen states into one nation, and to preserve the particular interest of each state within its own sphere of self-government.

As the union divided the sovereignty of the people between two different governments, the federal government on the one hand and the state governments on the other, so the former, represented by the union, should endeavour to form a compact body to "provide for the general exigencies of the people," and the latter should govern by themselves in all matters concerned with internal prosperity and touching the daily life of the nation. Therefore the claims and obligations of the federal government could be formidable with the "express purpose of meeting the general exigencies" of a nation, whilst those of the state were "so complicated and various" that it was hardly possible to define precisely its share of authority, since unforeseen contingencies were bound to arise. All authority which was not included amongst federal rights was declared "to constitute a part of the privileges of the several governments of the states."

In this connection Tocqueville asserted that the "government of the states remained the rule, and that of the confederation became the exception."[2]

The two governments being completely independent and separate, the one should fulfil ordinary duties and respond "to the daily and indefinite calls of a community" and the other was to be responsible within a certain limit of laws and only exercise "an exceptional authority over the general interests of the country."[3]

In the ambit of the federal constitution the federal government retained the absolute exercise of a portion of sovereignty in the nature of centralisation of government, such as foreign and general powers and unlimited authority of levying taxes in order to fulfil its engagements. In the balance of power the larger portion of sovereign authority was still reserved to the constituent states.

[1] Alexis de Tocqueville: *Democracy in America*, trans. by Henry Reeve, 1889, Vol. I, p. 109.   [2] Ibid., p. 110.   [3] Ibid., p. 55.

He said, therefore, that the United States formed not only "a republic but a confederation."

Tocqueville thought that even though the United States federal constitution was apparently more centralised than that of France or Spain in certain respects, the ultimate result of absolute sovereignty of the crown was no less than that of the popular sovereignty, as the former would infringe on the rights of the people and take "by force whatever the constitution of the country denied."

Like his contemporaries, Tocqueville asserted that the "gradations of popular morality and enlightenment" could more generally be found in a small state than in a great empire, and "small nations have ever been the cradle of political liberty."[1]

In the small nations the direct contact between citizens and the affairs of the state usually prevented the violation of the rights of the people, and freedom was "in truth the natural state of small communities."[2] But "the history of the world," he said, "affords no instance of a great nation retaining the form of republican government for a long series of years."[3]

The relationship between physical strength and moral and intellectual power had hitherto produced inconsistencies, because the advantages of superior physical force in a large state were cancelled by the relative lack of moral power which could more easily penetrate the whole of a smaller state and contribute to its internal prosperity.

Tocqueville believed that the "federal system was created with the intention of combining the different advantages which result from the greater and lesser extent of nations."[4] The danger of centralisation was that it arrogated to itself too detailed a control over daily administration to allow of the maintenance of liberty. The remedy for this was to grant each constituent state a large measure of administrative and political power. The result of this federal practice might, however, tend to inefficiency unless regulated by the strong arm of the federal government which should control the legislation affecting general problems.

This advantage of federalism was coincident with the special ability of Anglo-American political conditions and the spirit of amelioration which was constantly alive in the American republic and produced the elaborate working of the functions of divided sovereignty.

---

[1] Alexis de Tocqueville: *Democracy in America*, trans. by Henry Reeve, 1889, Vol. I, pp. 158–159.
[2] Ibid., p. 158.   [3] Ibid., p. 159.   [4] Ibid., p. 161.

This was due to the fact that the law and the custom of American republican government "were engendered in the townships and in the provincial legislatures."

Tocqueville insisted that in the American federal system "the public spirit of the union is, so to speak, nothing more than an abstract of the patriotic zeal of the provinces. Every citizen of the United States transfuses his attachment to his little republic into the common store of American patriotism."[1]

Political passion and the natural endowments of America smoothed away those obstacles to the federal system which had been stumbling-blocks in Europe.

He admired federal America in that the union was "as happy and as free as a small people and as glorious and as strong as a great nation."[2] Nothing checked the spirit of enterprise in the United States of America.

Thus federalism, to Tocqueville, was the product of political wisdom and experience and based upon a compromise of the advantages of small states and of a great empire. It was the finest political expedient ever devised by political talents and liberal hearts, through which liberty and equality were well balanced against authority.

From this conception federalism was the highest invention in the science of politics and the only road to democratic republicanism in the large state.

In the federal organisation the legislative authority, which was the source of the sovereignty of the people, was manifested by a "spirit of conciliation" which resulted in two chambers, the House of Representatives on the one hand, and the Senate on the other, owing to the acceptance of two different principles. The aim of the federal constitution was not to destroy the independence of the state, but to restrain it within certain limits.

Since these two systems were theoretically irreconcilable, the diversity of interests thus created produced natural obstacles to their application in any political structure; for instance, the minority of state interests paralysed the majority will of the people. Nevertheless, through such an illogical and irrational combination of the two parts of the legislative function the federal compromise in America avoided friction in the American legislative body, chiefly because all the states were "young and contiguous, and their customs, their ideas and their exigencies are not dissimilar," and, moreover, the habitual use of constraint in enforcing the

[1] Alexis de Tocqueville: *Democracy in America*, trans. by Henry Reeve, 1889, Vol. I, p. 162. [2] Ibid., p. 163.

decision of the majority moulded the state influence into the mechanism of the federal government.

Differing not only in methods of election, but also in functions, the House of Representatives was purely legislative, its only share in judicial powers being "in the impeachment of public officers," whereas the Senate co-operated in the work of legislation and exercised the judicial function and at the same time acted as the executive council of the nation. Tocqueville believed that the executive power had a very important influence on the destinies of nations.

The President was an elective magistrate. However independent he might be, the senatorial council had the unequal authority of the legislative, and the executive had made the latter subordinate and dependent. This dependence of the executive power was one of the defects inherent in the republican constitution. And presidential responsibility and sole representation were as limited and particular as "the sovereignty of the union in whose name it acts."

The novel invention of the veto power of the President was, "in fact, a sort of appeal to the people."[1]

One of the federal characteristics was that "everything can be provided for by the laws," and all "political institutions can prove a substitute for common sense and public morality."[2]

The President was absolutely an outsider in respect of the formation of laws, but he was the executor of the laws and agent of sovereign power. Tocqueville said, "The dangers of the elective system increase in the exact ratio of the influence exercised by executive power in the affairs of the state."

The energy and stability of the executive in the face of capricious and dangerous demands by the majority were desirable and urgent, but by an inadequate duration of tenure and mode of election the federalists' policy of re-eligibility rendered "the corrupt influence of elective governments still more extensive and pernicious," and made the President an "easy tool in the hands of the majority."[3]

Tocqueville, being a magistrate, considered the judicial institutions as the most important governmental power and said that in an Anglo-American community the judicial institution "occupies a prominent place among what are properly called political institutions."[4]

In republics the government held generally two means of resistance against the encroachment of the people: "the physical

[1] Alexis de Tocqueville: *Democracy in America*, trans. by Henry Reeve, 1889, Vol. I, p. 118.
[2] Ibid., p. 119.   [3] Ibid., pp. 134–135.   [4] Ibid., 136.

force which is at their disposal, and the moral force which they derive from the decision of the Courts of Justice."[1]

He was convinced that "the great end of justice is to substitute the notion of right for that of violence and to place a legal barrier between the power of government and the use of physical force."[2]

He believed that "federal government stands in greater need of the support of judicial institutions than any other."[3] The reason why he emphatically expounded this view was that federal organisation was naturally weak and incompetent because based on the union of several independent states; for the *de facto* working of the sovereignty of the union was far weaker than the *de jure* constitution.[4]

He insisted that as the new federalism was based on the principle of "one people in relation to federal government," the union required the entire national judiciary to be centred in one tribunal, such as the Supreme Court of the United States, in order to enforce the obedience of citizens to the national laws, and to "repel the attacks which might be directed against them."

He added that the object of the federal tribunal was to prevent the several Courts of the states from deciding matters which affected the national interests and to form a uniform body of jurisprudence by "the interpretation of the laws" of the constitution; that is to say, "the Supreme Court of the United States was therefore invested with the right of determining all questions of jurisprudence."[5]

Although the judicial power of the federal Courts appeared to be preponderant over the state sovereignty, the precise limit of the federal supremacy laid down in the constitution and the *de facto* weakness of the federal government caused the jurisprudence of the tribunal of the union to extend and narrow its sphere exactly "in the same ratio as the sovereignty of the union augments and decreases."[6]

Tocqueville asserted that "the privileges of the Courts of Justice are extended with the increasing liberties of the people."[7]

In this respect the judicial power of the Supreme Court was concerned with all cases arising from laws, treaties and admini-

---

[1] Alexis de Tocqueville: *Democracy in America*, trans. by Henry Reeve, 1889, Vol. I, p. 137.   [2] Ibid.   [3] Ibid.
[4] Tocqueville thought that in federalism the independence of the component states naturally resulted in that they entertained no real intention of obeying the central government, and very readily ceded the right of command to the federal authority and very prudently reserved non-compliance to themselves.
[5] Alexis de Tocqueville: *Democracy in America*, trans. by Henry Reeve, 1889, Vol. I, p. 140.   [6] Ibid., p. 144.   [7] Ibid., p. 148.

THE FEDERAL IDEAS OF DE TOCQUEVILLE

strative ordinances made either by executive power or by legislative authorities, and all cases of special or ordinary jurisdiction which dealt with the general needs of the nation.

Although the constitution was based entirely on legal mechanism, yet the notion of federal sovereignty was of a political nature.

Nevertheless, he believed that without the co-operation of judicial power the constitution would be "a dead letter."[1]

However great the power which the judges of the federal Supreme Courts possessed, it was "clothed in the authority of public opinion,"[2] and it was merely the guidance of people in popular enactment of laws they formed. He was convinced that the federal judges, as a matter of fact, "must not only be good citizens and men possessed of that information and integrity which are indispensable to the magistrate, but they must be statesmen."[3] The real need of an effective federal organisation was to consolidate judicial power independently and extensively, so as to promote the liberty of people against any infringement of democracy.

At the same time Tocqueville, like the federalists, was of the opinion that the "federal constitution is superior to all the constitutions of the states."[4]

In federalism the sovereign prerogative *de jure* was divided between the federal and state governments, but *de facto* the state sovereignty usually nullified the national activity of the federation. Tocqueville insisted that even though politically federal government was exceptional, the federal constitution theoretically was superior to those of the states.

He asserted that the chief cause of the superiority of the federal constitution was the character of the legislators who had drawn it up with their past experience.

The danger of democracy, resulting from "the abuse of freedom" introduced by Americans into the confederation, caused the Americans of 1787, animated by a sincere love of liberty, to propose certain restrictions. The stability of the two chambers, the strong armed force vested in the executive, and the independence and supremacy of judicial power imposed restraints on the evils of excessive democracy—namely, "the complete subjection of the legislative body to the caprices of the electoral body and the concentration of all the powers of government in the legislative authority."

[1] Alexis de Tocqueville: *Democracy in America*, trans. by Henry Reeve, 1889, Vol. I, p. 149.
[2] Ibid., p. 149.　　　　　[3] Ibid.　　　　　[4] Ibid.

The growth of these evils had been checked by the policy of the state, but the restraint and supervision of federal control over the state excesses of freedom were still urgently needed. The federal constitution was drawn up in such a manner as to restrain, by the highest exercise of wisdom and experience, the encroachments of the states.

Tocqueville pointed out the distinction between "confederations" before and after 1789, viz. the confederation and federal state.

He assumed that the powers which were vested in the confederate government were nearly identical with the privileges of the federal government.[1] The federal governments, such as the Swiss Confederation, the Germanic Empire, and the Republic of the United Provinces, were remarkable for their weakness and inefficiency and were doomed to perish, but the union of America in its new phase of federalism was bound to prosper owing to its "vigorous and enterprising spirit."

In the year 1789 federalism faced a novel theory which must be considered a great invention in modern political science and a practical application of democracy in the liberal political doctrines which had been adduced more than a century ago. This was the "federo-republican" state.

The federal theory of 1789 was to form a federal government, on the agreed principle of the constitution in virtue of the majority consent, between the several states, for the purpose of united action for common and foreign interests and in order that the federal government "should not only dictate the laws" but "execute its own enactments."[2] Therefore, he said that in both the confederate and federal state "the right is the same but the exercise of the right is different."[3]

In confederation the administration of federal government depended upon the authority of the separate component states, and however extensive the sovereign power possessed by the federal government, yet the failure to exercise these rights and powers was due to "the plea of inability" which was put forward, and so a state of anarchy arose in consequence of the conflict of interests between the confederates and the union.

Tocqueville stated that in the new federal state "the subjects of the union are not states but private citizens." The federal government ruled not over the "communities," but directly over individuals, and its force was not borrowed, but "self-derived"; it exercised its administration by its own civil and

---

[1] Alexis de Tocqueville: *Democracy in America*, trans. by Henry Reeve, 1889, Vol. I, p. 154.   [2] Ibid., p. 155.   [3] Ibid.

military officers, and performed judicial duties in its own courts of justice.

The real defect of the confederation had been inadequacy of normal power, whereas the federal state had "the power of enforcing all it was empowered to demand."

Tocqueville assumed that modern federalism had been formulated by the human understanding which "more easily invents new things than new words,"[1] that is to say, it depended upon the most exact equilibrium between human wisdom and passion in political science.

Tocqueville pointed out the weakness of the federal system and said that federalism was "like those exquisite productions of human industry which ensure wealth and renown to their inventors, but which are profitless in any other hands."[2]

He stressed the fact that the fundamental evil of the federal system was the "very complex nature of the means" it employed. The two divisions of sovereignty caused legal friction, and federal organisation had to be based on a "theory which is necessarily complicated, and which demands the daily exercise of a considerable share of discretion on the part of those it governs."[3]

He said, "The union is an ideal nation which only exists in the mind and whose limits and extent can only be discerned by the understanding."[4] The technique and structure of federal government were "artificial and conventional," and its function and practice were adaptable only to those who had been accustomed to self-government, or in whose state a "science of politics has not descended to the humblest classes of society."[5]

Considering the love of "one's native country which is instinctive in human hearts," vis-à-vis the intellectual ties of association for common ends, the principle of divided sovereignty in federalism revealed its weakness and defects in theory and practice; but the sovereignty of union was abstract and "factitious" and that of the state was natural, not exceptional.

Numerous federal experiences in the political history of the world had resulted in dissolution and anarchy. Only the modern federal theory of the United States, owing to their social and geographical advantages and their political abilities, resulted in a permanent institution of political science, in which the relative perfection of its laws compensated for the defects of its nature.

Tocqueville asserted that federalism was a true political

---

[1] Alexis de Tocqueville: *Democracy in America*, trans. by Henry Reeve, 1889, Vol. I, p. 156. [2] Ibid., p. 166.
[3] Ibid., p. 165. [4] Ibid., p. 165. [5] Ibid.

system and "one of the combinations most favourable to the prosperity and freedom of men." He said that ever since the formation of the new federation "the term federal government is no longer applicable to a state of things which must be styled an incomplete national government."[1]

Tocqueville's analysis of federalism was on so scientific a basis that he was regarded as the founder of the federal theory which prevailed for a long time in Germany. He accomplished "the transference into German scientific knowledge of the characteristic difference between the two forms of union which were set up by the American Fathers."[2]

[1] Alexis de Tocqueville: *Democracy in America*, trans. by Henry Reeve, 1889, Vol. I, p. 157.
[2] Ebers: *Die Lehre vom Staatenbunde*, p. 101.

CHAPTER VI

DEVELOPMENT OF FEDERAL IDEAS IN THE UNITED STATES OF AMERICA FROM KENT TO CALHOUN AND WEBSTER

§ 1

The federal ideas of America had by the time Tocqueville wrote developed into a theory which stood midway between the federalists' doctrine and that of Jefferson.

The fundamental idea of the former strongly favoured the theory of consolidation and that of the latter the theory of state rights.

Chief Justice Marshall, Kent and Story more or less adhered to the federalists' conception of federalism, and the tendency of consolidation resulted in the progress of federal supremacy with regard to the execution of the federal principle and especially that of the judiciary.

The supremacy of the Supreme Court of Justice as the final authority in legal and political decrees, of which the power was defined in the Judiciary Act (25th Section), was endorsed by successive stipulations, such as the Acts of May 19, 1828, and of March 3, 1833. Nevertheless, since Jefferson put forward "the Federo-Republican State" in opposition to the Federal Constitution of 1787, the Jeffersonian federalism, both legally and politically, had encouraged Jacksonian democracy and the theory of nullification,[1] and reached its climax when John Calhoun boldly advocated the supremacy of state rights in *A Discourse on the Constitution and Government of the United States* in 1854.

Before examining the ideas of Calhoun I shall describe several leading federal thinkers of these two parties.

Chief Justice Marshall gave a celebrated decision in justification of the prevailing theory of the federalists. In the case

[1] *Doctrine of Nullification.*—"That the Doctrine of Nullification may be clearly understood it must be taken as laid down in the Report of a special Committee of the House of Representatives of South Carolina in 1828.

"In this Document it is asserted that a single state has a constitutional right to arrest the execution of a law of the United States within its limits, that the arrest is to be presumed right and valid, and is to remain in force till three-quarters of the states in a Convention shall otherwise decide" (James Madison: *Works*, Vol. IX, p. 573).

of Virginia *v.* Cohen, regarding the supremacy of state rights, he said, "If such be the constitution, it is the duty of the Court to bow with respectful submission to its provisions; if such be not the constitution, it is equally the duty of this Court to say so, and to perform that task which the American people have assigned to the Judicial Department."

James Kent, a Professor of Law at Columbia College, defined the law of the nation in his work *Commentaries on American Law* in 1826, and assumed that "the government of the United States was erected by the free voice and joint will of the people of America, for their common defence and general welfare."[1]

Historically he asserted that the great value of a federal union had sunk deep into the minds of the Americans.[2] Of necessity the union developed from the confederation to the federal state in which "the final destiny of republican government was staked on the experiment which was then to be made to reform the system of our national compact."

He was convinced that the achievement of the convention "was laying the foundations of the fabric of the national polity, where alone they ought to be laid, on the broad consent of the people."[3]

Joseph Story, a judge of the Supreme Court of Justice, put forward his federal ideas in his *Commentaries on the Constitution of the United States* in 1833. By legal argument he expounded the theory of divided sovereignty, and denied that the Federal Constitution of 1787 was a compact, asserting that it was a law accepted by the people.

He held that "the term sovereign or sovereignty is used in different senses"—its larger sense on the one hand and the limited sense on the other.[4]

Sovereignty in the former sense meant "supreme, absolute, uncontrollable power, the *jus summi imperii*, the absolute right to govern,"[5] but sovereignty in the latter sense is a term used to designate "such political powers as in the actual organisation of the particular state or nation are to be exclusively exercised by certain public functionaries, without the control of any superior authority."[6]

Being a follower of Blackstone, who said "sovereignty and legislature are, indeed, convertible terms, and one cannot sub-

---

[1] James Kent: *Commentaries on American Law*, ed. by John N. Gould, 1896, Vol. I, Part II, p. 203. [2] Ibid., p. 203. [3] Ibid., p. 219.
[4] J. Story: *Commentaries on the Constitution of the United States*, 1891, Sec. 207.
[5] Ibid., Sec. 207. [6] Ibid.

sist without the other," Story said, "in every limited government the power of legislation is, or at least may be, limited at the will of the nation, and therefore the legislature is not in an absolute sense sovereign."[1]

In this application the term sovereignty could be used in a more limited sense "in which it expressed merely the positive or actual organisation of legislative, executive and judicial powers" than when it was morally personified in the "appellation of state" as Mr. Justice Wilson advocated. Therefore Story asserted that "the state has power to do this or that; the state has passed a law, or prohibited an act, meaning no more than that the proper functionaries, organised for that purpose, have power to do the act, or have passed the law, or prohibited the particular action."[2] Therefore the sovereignty of a state, "considered in reference to its association as a body politic, may be absolute and uncontrollable in all respects, except of the limitation which it chooses to impose upon itself."

He said, "the sovereignty of government organised within the state may be of a very limited nature"; "it may be unlimited to some; it may be restrained as to others."[3]

From this assertion sovereignty in the limited sense is divided and in the larger sense is absolute.

He was convinced, with regard to federal sovereignty, that "strictly speaking, in our republican forms of government, the absolute sovereignty of the nation is in the people of the nation; and the residuary sovereignty of each state, not granted to any of its public functionaries, is in the people of the state."[4]

At the same time he asserted the federal constitution to be not only a federal, social, original, voluntary and written compact, but also a compact "by which the several states and the people thereof respectively have bound themselves to each other and to federal government," and by which "the federal government is bound to the several states and to every citizen of the United States."[5]

On this constitutional basis Story asserted that the fundamental maxim of the federal constitution of the United States was based on the doctrine of *inter leges silent arma*, not on that of *inter arma silent leges*.[6] He assumed that in the free state people ordain and establish "in their sovereign capacity." They "meet and declare what shall be the fundamental law for the

[1] J. Story: *Commentaries on the Constitution of the United States*, 1891, Sec. 207.
[2] Ibid., Sec. 208.   [3] Ibid.   [4] Ibid.
[5] Ibid., Secs. 317–318.   [6] Ibid., Sec. 334.

government of themselves and their posterity"; and the constitution was considered "as fundamental law, and not as a mere contract of government during the good pleasure of all the persons who were originally bound by it or assented to it."[1]

Since the constitution of the United States had laid down that its laws and treaties, etc., shall be "the supreme law of the land," the people of the United States, not the separate people of a particular state with the people of the other states, ordained and established "a constitution, not a confederation."[2]

He considered "as a political heresy" the opposed view of the constitution which upheld the doctrine of compact, viz. that any state had a right to withdraw from the union at pleasure and repeal its operation.

Historically, politically and legally the federation of 1787 in the United States was "the consolidation of the union," and ordained and established by the people of the United States "in their collective capacity."[3]

Story set up the supremacy of political jurisprudence as the final interpreter, which "is a final and common arbiter provided by the constitution itself, to whose decisions all others are subordinate; and that arbiter is the supreme judicial authority of the courts of the union."[4]

Story thus justified the federalists' ideas from a legal standpoint.

Madison also, in his later years, presented a view of the federal state as a new model of governmental organisation, with no similitude or analogies to other existing systems of government. It was a mixture of both consolidated and confederated government and was based on the concurrent operations of "divided sovereignty."[5]

He stood on "the ground of compromise" between the theory of state rights and that of consolidation, saying, "let, then, the advocates of the state rights acknowledge this rule of measuring the federal share of sovereign power under the constitutional compact, and let it be conceded, on the other hand, that the states are not deprived by it of that corporate existence and political unity which would in the event of a dissolution, voluntary or violent, of the constitution replace them in the condition of separate communities, that being the condition in which they entered into the compact."[6]

Justifying the theory of compromise and that of compact,

[1] J. Story: *Commentaries on the Constitution of the United States*, 1891, Sec. 338.
[2] Ibid., Sec. 352.   [3] Ibid., Sec. 363.   [4] Ibid., Sec. 375.
[5] Madison: *Works*, ed. by G. Hunt, Vol. IX, pp. 384-394.   [6] Ibid., p. 570.

his inconsistency, which was apparent here and there regarding federalism, did not merely proceed from the sophistry of his mind, but resulted from the actual existence of the federal state of America, the definition of which, as he said, should be "derived from the content of the constitution and the facts of the case."[1]

From the nature of the contract Madison argued "it is the nature and essential of a compact that it is equally obligatory on the parties to it, and of course that no one of them can be liberated therefrom without the consent of the others, or such a violation or abuse of it by others as will amount to a dissolution of the compact."

He explained a division of sovereignty which "is in fact illustrated by the exchange of sovereign rights often involved in treaties between independent nations, and still more in the several confederacies which have existed, and particularly in that which preceded the present constitution of the United States."[2]

Since the constitutional compact of the United States had divided the supreme power of government between the United States by special guarantee and the several states by general reservation, a political act of this competent authority was "an act of the majority of the people in each state in their highest sovereign capacity, equivalent to an unanimous act of the people composing the state in that capacity."

He strongly emphasised the view that "without admitting the divisibility of sovereignty," that is the idea of sovereignty as divided between the union and the members composing the union, and even accepting the view as to the unity and indivisibility of the moral being created by the social contract, no existence of the compound system of government in the federal state could be justified in theory as well as in practice.[3] He believed that the acceptance of this assumption was the only method of justifying the view of the federation, even that of the moral personification of the union—and this sovereignty of both the union and the states was equal, and each was a moral person created by the "social compact."

Assuming the divisibility of sovereignty as the essential character of federalism, he denied the theory of nullification because "the main pillar of nullification is the assumption that sovereignty is a unit, at once indivisible and inalienable."[4]

Moreover, from the nature of the constitutional compact, the

[1] Madison: *Works*, ed. by G. Hunt, Vol. IX, pp. 385-475.
[2] Ibid., pp. 571-572. [3] Ibid., p. 572. [4] Ibid., p. 599.

people of the several states must be sovereign as they are a united people. This was the true character of the political system of the United States "sustained by an appeal to the law and the testimony of the fundamental charter."[1]

From the survey of the political system of the federal state he rejected the nullifying doctrine as being that of "polemic adversaries," for the reason that "nullifiers in stating their doctrine omit their particular form which is to be carried into execution."[2]

He denied Jefferson's appeal to the right to summon a convention at the pleasure of a single state, as it would lead to "a calamitous interregnum" during its deliberation, and "no man's creed was more opposed to such an opposition inversion of the Republican order of things."[3]

Although the doctrine of nullification of South Carolina needs in the last resort the sanction of one-third of the component states, which is derived "not from a single, but a concurrent interposition," yet no "unconstitutionality" could be recognised or nullification permitted by the federal states if the decision in question was one arising under the term "common defence and general welfare."

With this assumption "the centripetal or centrifugal tendency" of authority in the federal states is a problem which experience must decide, and "depends not upon the mode of grant, but the extent and effect of powers granted."

Madison asserted that the final appeal "must be to the authority of the whole, not to the parts separately and independently."[4]

The "concurrent interposition" in such a case was a resort to ultra-constitutional interpositions. As he assumed that the judicial supremacy of the constitution was the vital principle of the union, he was convinced that the constitution and laws of the United States should be "the supreme law of the land, anything in the constitution and laws of any of the states to the contrary notwithstanding."[5]

§ 2

An opponent of Kent, Story and others was St. George Tucker, a Virginian jurist, who in his *Commentaries on Blackstone* in 1803

[1] Madison: *Works*, ed. by G. Hunt, Vol. IX, p. 600.   [2] Ibid., p. 471.
[3] Ibid., p. 472.   [4] Ibid., p. 607.   [5] Ibid.

proclaimed that the states were united in a confederacy, but still retained their independence and sovereignty.

Even though the common government of the United States was formed, yet there still existed the natural right of which "no force or compact can deprive the people of any State, whenever they see the necessity and possess the power to do it."[1]

Tucker considered the federal constitution partly as a social and partly as a federal compact; he said, "although the federal government can, in no possible view, be considered as a party to a compact made anterior to its existence, yet as the creature of the compact it must be bound by it to its creators, the several states of the union and citizens thereof."[2]

At the same time he accepted the division of sovereignty between the states and federal governments.

On this assumption he drew up a scheme of the state rights which the state retained, i.e. rights of withdrawal from the union and of revolutionary resistance and secession.

William Rawle, in 1825, put forward his interpretation of federation in a work entitled *A View of the Constitution of the United States of America*. He remarked that "the states are no longer to be known to each other as merely states," since they formed the intention to create a new political society to establish a new government.[3] Nevertheless, the people of the states united with each other without alteration of their sovereignties and without destruction of their previous organisations.

He believed that all powers necessary for the attainment of the general objects for which the states separately or confederated had been found incompetent were the necessary outcome of the national needs of America, and the powers reserved to the states were "not necessary for the attainment of those objects."

He continued that even though "two governments of concurrent rights and powers cannot exist in one society," yet the principle and the composition of the federal state present "the novel and supreme spectacle in political history."[4]

Rawle discussed the phases of the political system of the American federal state as differing from the previous federal organisation, saying that "the state is as much a member of

[1] H. St. George Tucker: *Commentaries on Blackstone*, 1803, pp. 187.
[2] Tucker nevertheless thinks that a state may at will withdraw from confederation.
[3] W. Rawle: *A View of the Constitution of the United States of America*, 1825, p. 25.
[4] Ibid., p. 26.

the union and forms as much a part of the greater society as the people themselves, yet the state does not enter into the union upon the federal principle"—that is to say, has not merely a confederated character. He assumed that whatever controversial views might have existed with regard to supremacy of powers as between the union and the state, the true nature of the constitution was to be "applied in all cases of impartial and correct exposition" deducing from its entire text and being consistent with the unity and harmony of the whole.[1]

His idea of federalism was based upon that of the federalists.

He added that the main source of the union was "the association of the people of the republic."[2] Each state was pledged to preserve the republican form of government by compact and had consequent responsibility to the rest beyond the mere compact, and each was guaranteed and authorised by the federal government to employ and enforce the "paternal" authority of the union. Nevertheless, he asserted that no intervention as such could be justifiable, "if the people of a state should determine to retire from the union."

It depended upon the state itself whether to retain or abolish the principle of representation, "because it must depend on itself whether it will continue a member of the union."[3]

He said, "this right must be considered an ingredient in the original composition of the general government," and added that it was "competent for a state to make a compact with its citizens, but reciprocal obligations of protection and allegiance might cease in certain events;" and it was further observed that "allegiance would necessarily cease on the dissolution of the society to which it was due."[4]

In agreement with Montesquieu, he thought the characteristic feature of federalism depended on "the principle on which alone the union is rendered valuable, and which alone can continue it"—the preservation of the republican form. Even though the federal organisation of the United States permitted the use of the organised force of the union, by the engagement to protect each state government from domestic and foreign violence, yet the majority of the people of a state could reserve the right to relinquish the republican form of government, and consequently cease to be a member of the union.[5]

He assumed that however desirable the interposition of the union in the particular concerns of a state, the right of self-

[1] W. Rawle: *A View of the Constitution of the United States of America*, 1825, p. 28.
[2] Ibid., p. 288.   [3] Ibid., p. 289.   [4] Ibid., p. 290.   [5] Ibid., p. 291.

government of the states ought to be firmly preserved against infringement by the union at its pleasure. And he urged that the excellent system of the United States federation provided "the utmost care to avoid encroachments on the internal powers of the different states, whenever the general good did not imperiously require it."[1]

He preferred judicial interposition to intervention by armed force. The high tribunal provided for the reduction of the combatants to an equal level as suitors, without destroying the dignity of sovereign power of the states, for "in this case the political estimation of neither state could receive any degradation." The decision of the disputes would only be regulated by "the purest principles of justice."[2]

Rawle asserted that the right of secession entirely "depended on the will of people of each state," because only the people possessed the right to alter their constitution.

On this assumption he argued that "the constitution of the United States is to a certain extent incorporated into the constitutions of the several states by the act of the people."[3]

He stood, like other federal thinkers, midway between the extremists—the nationalists on the one side and the particularists on the other.

§ 3

Calhoun's theory of state right was so systematically expressed that it is considered one of the ablest political treatises written in the first half of the nineteenth century, after those of the federalists.

Calhoun, a politician of South Carolina, formulated his political ideas on the basis of the Aristotelean conceptions on the one hand, and of Hobbesian psychology on the other. Assuming as an incontestable fact that man is so instituted as to be a social being, he asserted, as a generally proved phenomenon, not merely of human nature but of all animal existence, that "his direct or individual affections are stronger than his sympathetic or social feelings."[4]

Even though the social feeling may be combined with intel-

[1] W. Rawle: *A View of the Constitution of the United States of America*, 1825, p. 292.
[2] Ibid., p. 293. [3] Ibid., p. 295.
[4] Calhoun: *Works*, ed. by R. K. Cralle, 1854, Vol. I, *A Disquisition on Government*, pp. 1–3.

lectual and moral culture to limit individual abuses, yet the controlling power over these evils, "wherever vested, or by whomsoever exercised, is *government*."[1]

He continued, "Man is so constituted that government is necessary to the existence of society, and society to his existence and the perfection of his faculties," and he added, "it follows, also, that government has its origin in this twofold constitution of his nature; the sympathetic or social feelings constituting the remote—and the individual or direct, the proximate cause."[2]

The appropriate function allotted to human beings by the infinite wisdom of the Creator was the "social and political state." The preservation and perfection of our race and of our society were necessary for the existence and well-being of mankind.

So far as the government was administered "by men in whom, like others, the individual are stronger than the social feelings," the power vested in government to prevent injustice and oppression on the part of others was essential for the welfare of the community. He rejected the assumptions of *Naturrecht* philosophy, saying that the state of nature was an "unwarrantable" hypothesis, and he totally repudiated the theory of social contract, since the political state was the outcome of the needs of human beings. As Burke said, "government is a contrivance of human wisdom to provide for human wants."

The instrument which prevented the abuse of the government was what Calhoun termed "constitution."

He said, "having its origin in the same principle of our nature, constitution stands to government as government stands to society; and, as the end for which society is ordained would be defeated without government, so that for which government is ordained would, in a great measure, be defeated without constitution."[3] The striking difference between constitution and government was due to the fact that the latter was dependent upon necessity and the former upon volition—one of the most efficient tasks imposed on man was to form a constitution worthy of the name.

Calhoun asserted that "constitution is the contrivance of man, while government is of Divine ordination."

One of his greatest political problems was the organisation of constitution—in other words, what structure of constitution may

[1] Calhoun: *Works*, Vol. I. *A Disquisition on Government*, p. 4.
[2] Ibid.
[3] Ibid., p. 8.

resist and prevent government from oppressing the subjects of the sovereignty.

On this assumption he emphasised the view that "power can only be resisted by power—and tendency by tendency."[1]

From this criterion government which was based solely on numerical majority, even though it was dependent upon the idea of democracy, was absolute government, just as monarchical and aristocratic governments were apt to be absolute, uncontrolled and irresponsible bodies of concentrated powers, which paid no heed to "the sense of community." For the attainment of constitutional government the responsibility of the rulers to the ruled through the right of suffrage was the indispensable and primary principle. Unless this right was "properly guarded and the people sufficiently enlightened to understand their own rights and the interests of the community and duly to appreciate the motive and conduct of those appointed to make and execute the laws," it would be "a great and dangerous mistake" and an "erroneous opinion" of forming constitutional government.[2]

Nevertheless, the organisation of the entire sense of community ought to be based on interests as well as on numbers, because the diversity of interests and the conflicts between different portions of the community were so deeply seated that it would result in action of government to favour the interest of one section of the community. The consent of each interest and of every citizen through "its majority and appropriate organ"—in consequence the united sense of all—was what he called "concurrent or constitutional majority,"[3] just as John Stuart Mill proposed the "plural vote."

The government which depended on the "concurrent voice" of every citizen and his interest was constitutional government—that is to say, government based on right of suffrage on the one hand, and the appropriate organ whose power was to be constituted by the mutual negative among its various conflicting interests on the other. This negative power, such as veto, interposition, nullification, check or balance of power, was the power of preventing or arresting the action of government—which by its own interior structure, or, in one word, its organism—should be so formed as to be able to resist any tendency to abuse its power. Such organisation as would furnish the means of resistance on the part of the ruled to the oppression and abuse of

[1] Calhoun: *Works*, Vol. I. *A Disquisition on Government*, p. 12.
[2] Ibid., p. 13.   [3] Ibid., pp. 15–35.

power of the ruler was "the first and indispensable step towards a constitutional government."[1]

Calhoun asserted that in the form of constitutional government "it is indeed negative power which makes the constitution, and the positive which makes the government."[2] He was convinced that the principle of constitutional government was based on "compromise," and that of absolute government on "force."[3]

The protection and perfection of society was the fundamental aim of government, to guard against injustice, violence and anarchy within, and attack without, and for the betterment of society and for the utmost development of human faculties, intellectual and moral, through liberty and security. The cardinal co-ordination of governmental organisation with the requisite proportion of liberty and security—physical and moral force—sprang from the theory of compromise, and from the same source progress and civilisation would be engendered. The government of concurrent majority was Calhoun's ideal political organisation in which "individual feelings are from its organism enlisted on the side of social, and made to unite with them in promoting the interests of the whole, as the best way of promoting the separate interests of each."[4]

Calhoun added that "to enlist the individual on the side of the social feelings to promote the good of the whole is the greatest possible achievement of the science of the government," while to effect numeral majority, "to enlist the social on the side of the individual, to promote the interest of parties at the expense of the good of the whole, is the greatest blunder which ignorance can possibly commit."

Calhoun asserted that unless every conflict was to be adjusted by a compromise without appeal to force, the foundation of a constitutional government could hardly be realised.

From this assumption Calhoun considered federalism as a novel and refined political system, for the structure of which "we are far more indebted to the superintending Providence that so disposed events as to lead, as if by an invisible hand, to its formation than those who erected it."[5] And this was based on compromise but not on force, and so he asserted that "war, however just and necessary, gave a strong impulse adverse to federal and favourable to the national line of policy."[6]

In federal organisation the several governments which com-

[1] Calhoun: *Works*, Vol. I, *A Disquisition on Government*, pp. 15–35.
[2] Ibid., p. 35.   [3] Ibid., p. 37.   [4] Ibid., pp. 69–70. Cf. p. 38.
[5] Calhoun: *Works*, Vol. I, *A Discourse on the Constitution and Government of the United States*, p. 199.   [6] Ibid., p. 361.

posed the union preceded the federal government "which was created by their agency." The former had a separate political entity, each possessing its own written constitution and acting separately and having a sovereign character, whilst the latter maintained federal government in the same character, but "jointly instead of separately."[1]

The entire powers of government, legislative, executive and judicial, were divided into two kinds, one of a general character delegated to the federal government, and the other comprising all powers "not delegated, being reserved to the several states in their separate character."[2]

In its appropriate sphere each had to perform all functions of government, but "neither is perfect without the other." The entire and perfect government was formed by the two co-ordinated and combined.

Calhoun was convinced that modern federalism, which proceeded from the model of the United States government, must be federal as well as democratic, and "federal, on the one hand, in contradistinction to national, and, on the other hand, to a confederacy."[3] The fundamental principle of democracy was no doubt the great cardinal maxim, "that people are the source of power," and at the same time the federal government of the United States was a federal organisation but not national. From the convention of 1787 and on historical assumptions he asserted that "United States" was "the baptismal name" of these component states—received at their birth.[4] Therefore the government of Washington was the "federal government of these states or the general government of the union." Like previous thinkers he emphasised the view that under the constitution and government the political relations between the states were substantially of a confederated character, as they "are declared to be free, independent and sovereign states,"[5] expressly, instead of a mere unity of the American nation.

Although the government must necessarily partake of the character of the constitution "as it is but its agent to carry its power into effect," yet, politically and historically, the whole structure of the United States "was in strict accord with the federal character of the constitution, but wholly repugnant to the idea of its being national."[6]

Then Calhoun asserted that since the allegiance of every

[1] Calhoun: *Works*, Vol. I, *A Discourse on the Constitution and Government*, p. 111.
[2] Ibid., p. 112.   [3] Ibid., p. 113.   [4] Ibid., p. 116.
[5] Ibid., p. 116.   [6] Ibid., p. 126.

citizen was due to the source of sovereignty it was constitutionally and historically dependent upon the people of the United States.

Calhoun answered categorically the questions of by whom, for whom, for what and over whom the constitution "was ordained and established."

He assumed that, as the preamble of the constitution said, "We, the people of the United States, in order to form a more perfect union—do ordain and establish this constitution for the United States," and "the United States" meant the several states of the union, so the people of the United States were no doubt those of the several states of the union, and the constitution was federal and these states were "united as independent and sovereign communities."[1]

The fundamental nature of the union had to rest, without material change, on the same basis of confederated character—"that federal and confederated states meant substantially the same thing."

Calhoun insisted that the change which took place in the federal state constitution of 1787 was "not in the foundation, but in the superstructure of the system."[2]

Politically and geographically the framing of the federal constitution was delegated by the states, and the ratification of the convention by the nine states out of the thirteen created the federal government; but when it was ratified by the people of the states respectively, it was binding on each only in consequence of being ratified by it; until then it was a mere plan of constitution without any binding force.

What was the character of the federal government and its constitution? Calhoun answered the question as to whether the constitution of 1787 did or did not divest the several states of their character of separate, independent and sovereign communities, and merge them all into one great community called the American Nation.

By and for the people of the several states it was ordained and established; and the purpose of ordaining and establishing it was to perfect their union to establish justice and to ensure defence and liberty at home and abroad. As the constitution ordained and established by the "joint and united authority of the states ratifying its effect among them, extended between them," not over them, so the binding powers, as a compact, were appropriately applied.

[1] Calhoun: *Works*, Vol. I, *A Discourse on the Constitution and Government*, p. 129.
[2] Ibid., p. 117.

Calhoun asserted that "these states, in ratifying the constitution, did not lose the confederated character which they possessed when they ratified it, as well as in all the preceding stages of their existence; but, on the contrary, still retained it to the full."[1]

From the federal character of ratification and amendment of the constitution and of the federal governmental functionaries, he was emphatically convinced that "the people of the several states still retain that supreme ultimate power, called sovereignty —the power by which they ordained and established the constitution, and which can rightfully create, modify, amend or abolish it at their pleasure."[2]

As he entirely rejected the "theory of nationality of the government" which "is in fact founded on fiction," so he assumed that "the powers in the constitution called granted powers are, in fact, delegated powers—powers granted in trust—and not absolutely transferred."[3]

The tenth amending Article, that "the powers not delegated to the United States by the constitution, nor prohibited by it to the states, are reserved to the states respectively, or to the people," indicated expressly and precisely the source of sovereign right.

This reservation of powers to the states and the people was what he called "reserved power" vis-à-vis "delegated power" in federal government.

He was convinced that the highest sovereign power "was included among the two spheres of powers," and "this with others not delegated are those which are reserved to the people of the several states respectively."[4]

On this assumption he objected entirely to the prevailing theory of divided sovereignty. Like the later German federal thinkers, he said decisively that "sovereignty is an entire thing;—to divide is—to destroy it."[5] As the theory of compromise maintained that sovereignty in America rests on the people, so Calhoun believed that although he assumed the fundamental source of democracy, yet sovereignty was never transferred to the government but to the people and remained, without transference to the people as a nation, to the people of the several states.

Therefore, the powers delegated to the federal government of the United States were delegated in the confederated character, and the distinction between confederation and federal state with regard to distribution of powers and governmental functionaries

---

[1] Calhoun: *Works*, Vol. I, *A Discourse on the Constitution and Government*, p. 131.
[2] Ibid.   [3] Ibid., p. 143.   [4] Ibid., p. 144.   [5] Ibid., p. 146.

indicated that the federal constitution could not vest delegated power in the Congress alone, but also "in all the other departments of the government, whilst the articles of confederation could with propriety vest them in Congress."[1]

From his federal conception Calhoun emphatically objected to the federalists' opinion, as it cast a mist over the system, and he especially attacked the national notion of federal government.

He asserted that the whole—including the federal as well as the separate state governments—"taken together, form a federal community; a community composed of states united by a political compact—and not a nation composed of individuals united by what is called a social compact."[2]

Calhoun derived the distinction between the confederation and federal state from his "state right theory."

Assuming that the difference between them was based not on the foundation, but on the structure of the system, he asserted that the federal state held the delegated powers to the extent of having a confederacy for its basis, and differed from it "inasmuch as the powers delegated to it are carried into execution by a government, not by a mere congress of delegates as is the case in a confederacy."[3]

He added that "federal government, though based on a confederacy, is, to the extent of power delegated, as much a government as a national government itself," and is a more effective organisation than an assembly of diplomatists in a confederation.

The system of the federal state substituted "a government in lieu of such a body," as the latter was better adapted to a confederated kind of government.

The distinction between the two kinds of government was based not on the restriction or limitation of powers but on essential views as to the structure of the system.

The confederation was constituted by a "solemn league or compact, entered into for the purpose specified," and constructed in such a manner as to become "a union in consequence of being ordained and established between the people of the several states, by themselves and for themselves, in their character of sovereign and independent communities."[4]

From the same source of sovereignty, and the same power of ordaining and establishing the authorities by consent or

[1] Calhoun: *Works*, Vol. I, *A Discourse on the Constitution and Government*, p. 149.
[2] Ibid., p. 162.   [3] Ibid., p. 163.   [4] Ibid., pp. 165–166.

mutual understanding by the people of the several states, the federal and state governments stood in "the relation of equal and co-ordinate constitutions and governments."

To Calhoun, like other federal thinkers, the striking quality of the federal state was the manner of execution of delegated powers which acted directly on individuals without appealing to the agency of state governments.

This is the essential distinction between a federal government and a confederacy which involves "substituting a government in the place of the congress of the confederacy."

But he indicated that it now remained to be shown that the government was a republic—"a republic or (if the expression be preferred) a constitutional democracy in contradistinction to an absolute democracy." According to his views the government was regarded "as the trustee or agent to carry its power into execution and is composed of two elements"; on the one hand "the states regarded in their corporate character," and on the other "their representative population—estimated in what is called federal number."[1]

Moreover, he adhered to his view that the three departments, the legislative, the executive and the judiciary, were co-operate in function and federal in nature.

The legislature consisted of two chambers, the Senate and the House of Representatives, the natures of which were entirely based on concurrent and not simply numerical majority.

Though executive power was vested in the President of the United States, yet his election, and that of the Vice-President, depended on the concurrent voice, and although the exercise of judicial power also rested with the Supreme Court of Justice, the appointment of Judges also depended on a concurrent majority. The states, regarded in their corporate capacity, played an important part in the concurrent exercise of government. Therefore, in the federalism of the United States the government and the constitution rested on "the principle of concurrent majority" and formed a republic—"a constitutional democracy, in contradistinction to an absolute democracy."[2]

Therefore, he asserted that "the government of the United States is a democratic federal republic."[3]

The division of the powers of government between the several states and the United States was the main problem of any

[1] Calhoun: *Works*, Vol. I, *A Discourse on the Constitution and Government*, pp. 173–174.   [2] Ibid., p. 185.   [3] Ibid., p. 187.

system of government in federation—that is, the divisions of powers of governments "into such as are delegated, specifically, to the common and joint government of all the states, and the reservation of all others to the states respectively."[1]

In each sphere of its organisation and functions, each government, federal and state, maintained perfect and supreme powers, but it required "the two united to constitute one entire government."[2] For the purpose of the common good of all the states, external and internal, the joint federal government was formed, and as Calhoun did not adhere to the *Naturrecht* theory he thought that without the causes of the need of union—such as foreign relations on the one hand, and preservation of mutual peace and safety within on the other—the bond of the federal fabric was never strong enough to establish a "joint supplementary" government.

The organisation of government as such was expressly and tacitly based on the division and distribution of powers between the two co-ordinate governments—the power to be delegated, and the residue of powers to be reserved.

Assuming that it was one of the main purposes of federalism that the knowledge of the local interests and domestic institutions of the states respectively should be much more acute, and the responsibility of each to their respective people much more perfect through the state governments, the interference of the federal government in their interior and local concerns was obviously to jeopardise the ends of the federal constitution, which were "to establish justice, ensure domestic tranquillity, and secure the blessings of liberty." [3]

Calhoun laid it down that the principles of the federal constitution of the United States consisted, "in the first place, in the enumeration and specification of powers delegated to the United States, and the express reservation to the states of all powers not delegated; in the next, in imposing such limitations on both governments and on the states themselves, in their separate character, as were thought best calculated to prevent the abuse of power, or the disturbance of the equilibrium between the two co-ordinate governments; and finally in prescribing that the members of the Congress and of the legislatures and all executive and judicial officers of the United States and of the several states shall be bound by oath or affirmation to support the constitution of the United States."[4]

[1] Calhoun: *Works*, Vol. I, *A Discourse on the Constitution and Government*, p.197.
[2] Ibid.   [3] Ibid., p. 215.   [4] Ibid., p. 226.

The "federal" and "republican" principle in the co-ordinate distribution and preservation of the equilibrium of the powers depended on the relative force of powers delegated and reserved, without encroaching on or absorbing one another. If the balance of powers were to be disturbed, federalism would end in consolidation on the one hand or in dissolution on the other.[1] Contrary to the federalists, Calhoun feared the tendency towards an overpowering federal government and encroachment on the states' liberty, and he said the real struggle had been to control the government of the United States.[2]

He assumed that "the result has shown that, instead of depending on the relative force of the delegated and reserved powers, the latter in all contests have been brought in aid of the former, by the states on the side of the party in possession and control of the government of the United States—and by the states on the side of the party in the opposition in their efforts to expel those in possession and to take their place."[3]

Therefore, the real authority, instead of being limited to the delegated powers alone, must habitually include also that of the states and of their population, ranked on the federal side. This united strength naturally bestowed greater powers on the federal government than on the states in opposition.

From this practical point of view he laid down the political axiom that "there can be no constitution without division of power and no liberty without a constitution," and added a kindred axiom that "there can be no division of power without a self-protecting power in each of the parts into which it may be divided; or in a superior power to protect each against the other," and concluded that "without a division of power there can be no organism; and without power of self-protection or a superior power to restrict each to its appropriate sphere the stronger will absorb the weaker, and concentrate all power in itself."[4]

On this political hypothesis he deplored the party system and believed that it spoiled the confederated character of the legislative organs, and he accused the extreme enthusiasm of presidential elections of nullifying the federal nature of the executive function, and he very strongly objected to the supremacy of the Supreme Court of Justice over state rights and liberties. He said: "law must be proper as well as necessary, in order to bring it within its competency," but it was "not

[1] Calhoun: *Works*, Vol. I, *A Discourse on the Constitution and Government*, p. 227.
[2] Ibid., p. 229.   [3] Ibid.   [4] Ibid., p. 237.

to injure others" and it ought to rest "on the fundamental principles of morals."[1]

The equality of jurisprudence in co-equal government was important in order not to deprive a state of right to its sovereignty.

The remedy for this "spoiled" system was to give to each of the states a concurrent voice in making and administering the laws and a veto in action. His fundamental idea of a concurrent majority was the preliminary to nullification.

He asserted that the mutual negative on the parts of the two co-ordinate governments where they did not agree as to the extent of their respective powers was the main aid to federalism in guarding against consolidation on the one hand and in preventing disunion and conflict between them on the other. He emphatically confirmed the view that sovereignty in federal America was vested in the people of the several states, not in the government, and the power of the federal government was due to mutual agreement between the peoples of the several states without any restriction in the exercise of their sacred and absolute power.

Therefore the states stood to the federal government in the relation of parties to the "constitutional compact," and the binding force between them merely depended on the nature of the compact, but not on the sense of the constitution of a single government; i.e. the power vested neither in nor over them.

"Rights must be exercised with prudence and propriety," and "the highest moral obligation" to the "constitutional compact" proceeds from harmony and unanimity resulting from the conviction that no one section or interest could overthrow another.

The whole resources of the union, moral and physical, depended upon the concurrent confidence of the federal constitution and governments, and their free and unanimous exercise in theory as well as in practice. He clearly formulated his federal axiom of the state right theory, which was based on the original sovereign power of the several states as parties to the "constitutional compact."

The negative power of the states produced the theory of nullification, and the physical resistance to federal oppression of state right brought about the theory of secession.

He rejected totally the prevailing theory of compromise and of divided sovereignty and set up the state right theory. This

[1] Calhoun: *Works*, Vol. I, *A Discourse on the Constitution and Government*, p. 254.

appeal to the right of the states gave the people of the southern section of the American union the firm conviction of their right to secession when the problem of slavery reached its climax in 1861.

§ 4

Webster denounced the state right theory, to which Calhoun adhered, saying that "he has no foothold on which to stand while he might display the powers of his acknowledged talents," as a strong man struggling in a morass and sinking deeper and deeper "into the bottomless depths of this Serbonian bog."[1]

Webster's main theory of the fundamental constitution was based on that of a fundamental law, not on a "constitutional compact."

He defined the constitution as "certainly not a league, compact or confederacy, but a fundamental law; that fundamental regulation which determines the manner in which the public authority is to be executed is what forms the constitution of a state."[2]

He asserted that there was no compatibility between compact and constitution, because "the constitution of the United States was received as a whole and for the whole country." "Not as a Massachusetts man, nor as a Northern man, but as an American, and a member of the senate of the United States . . . I speak to-day for the preservation of the union."[3] Webster said: "On entering into the union the people of each state gave up a part of their own power to make laws for themselves, in consideration that, as to common objects, they should have a part in making laws for other states; in other words, the people of all the states agreed to create a common government, to be conducted by common counsels."[4] On this assumption the people of the United States adopt, ratify, ordain and establish the constitution or form of government and do not merely accede to it.

He continued that although the constitution is founded on consent, "the fruit of the agreement exists, but the agreement itself is merged in its own accomplishment"; in other words, the result of this agreement is "not a compact, but a law."[5]

[1] Webster: *Works*, III, 1853.—*The Constitution not a Compact between Sovereign States.*" (A speech delivered in the Senate of the United States on February 16, 1833, in replying to Mr. Calhoun's speech on the Bill "further to provide for the collection of Duties on Imports") (pp. 449–450).
[2] Ibid., pp. 465–466.   [3] Ibid., V, 1853, pp. 325–326.
[4] Webster: *Works*, III, 1853, p. 462.   [5] Ibid., p. 468.

At the same time, with regard to the nature of sovereignty, he attacked Calhoun's view of indivisible and inalienable sovereign power, as he believed that "the sovereignty of government is an idea belonging to the other side of the Atlantic," and is "of feudal origin."

The government of the United States was limited and all power rested with the people.

He asserted "that the states in many respects are sovereign nobody doubts, that they are sovereign in all respects nobody contends," because "the true idea of the constitution of the United States and also of the constitution of every state in the union is that powers are conferred on the legislature, not by general, vague description, but by enumeration."[1] Then the people "alone are sovereign; they elect what governments they please, and confer on them such powers as they please."[2] Sovereignty in the European sense had no validity at all, being essentially different from the political system of the United States.

The maintenance of the constitution is "not a matter of resting in state discretion or state pleasure," as his opponents contended, but it does depend on "the plighted public faith," and lays "its hand on individual conscience and individual duty" and individual obligation.[3]

The constitution and the federal government of the United States "create direct relations between the government and individuals"; the power of the government extends to every citizen of the United States in the sphere of powers granted by the constitution, whilst government is pledged to high and solemn duties to protect the rights and interests of the people of the country.

As all these relationships are based on "the connection as dear and as sacred as can bind individuals to any government on earth," so the federal government is not a mere agency—"power of attorney"—but a proper government, directly affecting individuals, granting to them protection on the one hand and demanding from them obedience on the other.

The confederation promised, engaged and plighted the faith of each component state, whilst the federal state proceeded from the individual conscience and depended upon individual duty.

Finally, the individuals, the people of all the states, united themselves under one general government for certain definite

[1] Webster: *Works* V, 1853, p. 389.
[2] Ibid., III, 1853, p. 469.
[3] Ibid., p. 471.

common objects, and to the extent of this union restricted the separate authority of the states.

Webster asserted that the people of the United States were "one people," and the power of direct legislation and execution of administration and law over the people were characteristic features of the federal state.

He emphasised the view of the federalists, that "the fabric of American empire ought to rest on the solid basis of the consent of the people," and endorsed the consent of people, called by Europeans the "social compact."[1]

Although he assumed that the people of the United States form the American nation, the people of the federal state "live under two governments" and owe obedience to both the federal and state governments; and at the same time each government protects and guarantees their rights and interests within the separate sphere of its particular powers or duties.

To Webster the demarcation of the spheres of activity between two governments was so distinctive that there was no such dispute between "a government *de facto* and a government *de jure*," as had been seen in the disputes of the "rival" houses of parliament in England.

The union is considered as "perpetual and immortal," and is "the association of the people under a constitution of government, uniting their power, joining together their highest interests, cementing their present enjoyments, and blending in one indivisible mass all their hopes for the future."[2]

From this nationalist theory of union he deduced that the theory of nullification was entirely unconstitutional.

Since the constitution was not formed by a mere accession of the people of the states, and not derived from a compact which was formed by the states as parties, but was ordained and established by the people of the American nation, the word "accession" or "secession" was totally wrong in any sense of constitutional interpretation.

The liberty which American people desired was not "political liberty in any general undefined character, but our own well-understood and long-enjoyed American liberty."

From this conception that the people of America formulated the constitution for their common benefit, happiness and prosperity, he assumed that "to reject an established government, to break up a political constitution, is revolution."[3]

Even though the doctrine of nullification or secession did not

[1] Webster: *Works*, III, 1853, p. 477. [2] Ibid., p. 478. [3] Ibid., p. 456.

embody the revolutionary attitude, yet state right as such was termed, in Calhoun's conclusion, "revolutionary rights."

By the medium of nullification the absolute duty of congress to pass and to maintain laws would be impaired, and the obligations of the constitution would be disregarded. The constitutional rights and duties could hardly be fulfilled if this intervention was permissible. They belonged to the people of the United States, not to the peoples of the particular states.

The state right theory seemed to Webster "the wildest illusion and the most extravagant folly."

He said that "secession, since it must bring these consequences with it, is revolutionary, and nullification equally revolutionary,"[1] because "to begin with nullification, with the avowed intent, nevertheless, not to proceed to secession, dismemberment and general revolution, is as if one were to take the plunge of Niagara and cry out that he would stop half-way down."[2]

He denounced Calhoun's idea of absolute majority and concurrent majority as a mere dogma. The construction of federal government had wisely provided for concurrent majority in legislature, the Congress represented the people on the one hand and the senate represented the state interest on the other, and so, too, in the executive and judicial departments. The theory of nullification, on the other hand, resulted in minority government, which is contrary to popular government. It is interference with the common interest of the whole for the sake of the interest of the few. He believed that whoever argues against the principle of popular government "argues the impracticability of all free government."

If the constitution of the United States be a government proper enforcing the "supreme laws of the land," the interposition of a state to enforce her own construction, and to resist, as to herself, that law which binds the other states, is a violation of the constitution. Nullification, in disobeying the supreme laws of the land and consequently in breaking the union into fragments, is "as revolutionary as secession."

The nullifying state "would not belong to a government, while it rejected its authority. It would not repel the burden, and continue to enjoy the benefits." "It would not undertake to reconcile obedience to public authority with an asserted right of command over that same authority."[3]

He strongly condemned the nullifying principle of South

---

[1] Webster: *Works*, III, 1853, p. 459. [2] Ibid., p. 461.
[3] Ibid., pp. 490–491.

Carolina, which approved "the forcible seizure of goods, before duties are paid or secured, by the power of state, civil and military."

The direct application of physical and military force to resist the laws of the union was an entire violation of the free constitution of the United States.

The unconstitutionality of the claim to the rights of nullification and secession was proved by the motives of the claim.

What is the motive of law? Webster answered that "it is a settled principle, acknowledged in all legislative halls, recognised before all tribunals, sanctioned by the general sense and understanding of mankind, that there can be no inquiry into the motives of those who pass laws for the purpose of determining on their validity."

And he added that "if the law be within the fair meaning of the words, in the grant of power, its authority must be admitted until it is repealed."[1]

Even though a power of discrimination may be assumed in the exercise of legislation and government within the granted powers, the ultimate confidence of people in the constitution was the justification of constitutionality.

The remedy for the usurpation of the federal government over state rights was the judicial review of federal legislation and administration. It was the duty of government to suppress revolutionary attacks on the supreme law of the constitution.

With a national impulse Webster laid the new foundation of the nationalist theory of the union in his controversy with the particularist doctrine of Calhoun.

The nationalist doctrine developed into a concrete and scientific argument wherein the latent force of the national spirit was distinctly manifested after the Civil War, and the nature of federal America tended to follow the nationalist school and to create a new phase of federal ideas in the last quarter of the nineteenth century.

[1] Webster: *Works*, III, 1853, p. 496.

CHAPTER VII

DEVELOPMENT OF FEDERAL IDEAS, 1866–1900

§ 1

The history of American federal politics in the middle period of the nineteenth century repeated the conflict between the Southern planting interests and the Northern industrial and financial magnates, and caused the federalists to draw a distinction between the federal principle, based on the theory of limited state rights, on the one hand and the nationalist theory on the other.

In order to maintain peace, statesmen had to find a way of reconciling these two conflicting interests.

Jeffersonian democracy and Jacksonian democracy were gradually making Southern influence supreme in the federal government at Washington.

The overwhelming victories of the democratic administration at the two successive presidential elections of 1852 and 1856 were caused by the judicial guarantee of the "Missouri Compromise," in the famous Dred Scott case, decided by Chief Justice Taney in 1857.

The tariff for revenue only, the pro-slavery programme of the democratic government, and finally President Buchanan's veto of the Homestead Bill swept away the Hamiltonian programme of the Whigs and the abolitionists' appeal for the overthrow of slavery in America.

The whole political condition of America under the dominance of the planters was gradually changed by a series of storms which cleared away the Hamilton-Webster programme and replaced it by the predominance of the economic and social schemes of the Southern interests, and so brought about a slow consolidation of forces on the side of the republican party.

In the struggle of these two groups the problem of slavery came to be considered as one of political expediency rather than a matter of humanity and justice, except by small groups such as the Garrison socialist groups or a few abolitionists.

The political transformation was marked by the victory of Lincoln in the presidential election of 1860. It was answered by the Democratic Convention in Charleston, where the "Divine Blessings were invoked" on the new issue by a unanimous vote, and South Carolina declared her independence.

The bombardment of Fort Sumter led the eleven Southern states, confronted by twenty-three states in the federal union, to elect Jefferson Davis of Mississippi as a provisional president in February 1861. They drafted a permanent constitution at the Congress of Montgomery, and decided on Richmond as the capital of the confederacy in November of the same year.

The fierce conflict caused each of the belligerent states to maintain a stringent military and autocratic administration for four years.

The natural advantages, economic and political, possessed by Lincoln's Northern states for the conduct of the war overrode the pro-slavery Southern states in the name of justice and humanity, for the abolition of slavery and the equality of every citizen in the American union.

The federal theory during this conflict permeated the hitherto prevalent state right theory of Calhoun, and developed into a new nationalist theory, expressed in Lincoln's dogma that "No state could lawfully withdraw from the union," and that secession was consequently either insurrectionary or revolutionary, according to circumstances.

The verdict of 1864 was the triumph of Webster's federalism, based upon constitutional law, over Calhoun's "compact" doctrine based upon the theory of confederation.

All theologians started with the same Bible as their guiding light, but evolved very different dogmas from it. In the same way, each federal theorist, starting from the letter of the federal constitution, evolved his own particular theory of federalism, thus rendering the problem almost impossible of solution.

The outbreak of the Civil War seemed at first to exemplify Calhoun's state right theory, and to show the weakness of the orthodox nationalist doctrine of the union.

The nationalist theory of federalism, legally based on constitutional law, was challenged by South Carolina's declaration of secession. We might regard the state right and the nationalist theories as based upon the social contract theory, the latter being derived from Locke's theory of limited competence, and the former being deduced from Hobbes's theory of the necessity of a strong central authority.

A valid defence of the nationalist doctrine required the establishment of a new theoretical basis, in justification of Lincoln's federal policy.

At the same time the history of political ideas was marked by a great advance not only in theory but in the field of practical experiment.

Bentham and Hegel repudiated the ideas of social contract on the one hand and of the eighteenth century's "natural right" on the other hand, and built up their own philosophical theory which was the starting-point of the nineteenth-century thought; utilitarianism became popular in England, and the metaphysical theory flourished in Germany.

The democratic regime in England began with the Reform Act of 1832, and the enlightened bureaucracy of Frederick the Great gave birth to the German Confederacy of 1815.

The *Political Ethics* of Francis Lieber,[1] published in 1839, was the inspiration of a new school which restated the nationalist theory of federalism, and in order to make this new theory of federalism clear I will describe briefly Lieber's attitude to political science.

He started his philosophy from the prevailing rationalism of his day, which laid down that "man is a rational animal," who is capable of controlling emotions and impulses and at the same time is responsible for his actions.

He said, "man is endowed with intellect, and the faculty of reflection," and also that "man is endowed with sympathy and fellow-feelings"—a fact which is "of the greatest importance in everything at all concerned with man's social state," and causes him to acknowledge himself as a citizen of the state.

Criticising Locke's empiricism he held that the idea and consciousness of right and wrong—"ought" or "ought not"—are derived from the original and innate power of "the subtlest intellect and the most vigorous mind," independently of experience or revelation.

Justifying Kant's attitude towards the "categoric imperative" he asserted that "man does not live long, even in the rudest stages of society, without feeling approval or disapproval at certain actions independently of their judiciousness or expediency.

---

[1] Dr. Lieber was a German scholar who went to America and was appointed Professor of History and Political Economy in South Carolina College, after a long vagabond life in Europe. He left his country in 1820 at the time of the Greek revolution because of his indignation at the armed injustice of the Prussian Government. In later years he resigned his South Carolina post, accepted the Professorship of the same subjects in Columbia College, and was elected to the Chair of Political Science of the Law School in New York. He died in the seventy-third year of his age. An enthusiastic belief in nationalism and a love of liberty and equality were the dominant characteristics of his nature, and appeared throughout his writings.

These actions are gradually made the subject of reflection, the character of this approval or disapproval is meditated upon, and finally man arrives at certain ethic results clearly represented to his mind."[1]

He asserted that man's whole ethical nature was naturally founded upon his individuality and sociality, which were "the two poles round which his whole life revolves." Being in nowise a follower of Rousseau, Lieber's ethical principle was by no means dominated by any metaphysical hypothesis.

The difficulty of applying the ever-same truth to ever-changing reality cannot be solved merely by the adoption of fundamental criteria, but by experience; because, as he said, "in many cases doing right means nothing more than selecting that which experience has shown to be best."[2]

Experience is requisite with regard to the habits, practice and exercise which are requisite for the application of ethical principles to politics. Without ethics experience degenerates into mere expediency. From these principles he deduced his "political ethics," which dealt with political relations in all matters from municipal to international.

Political ethics are, to Lieber, a fundamental guide wherein man is led to ends of the highest importance, physical, intellectual and moral, as man is endowed with both individuality and sociality.

In his philosophy, however different their conceptions of natural law on the basis of the state of nature might be, he, like Spinoza, asserted the science of natural law to be necessary to the axiom that "I exist as a human being, therefore I have a right to exist as a human being."[3]

On this assumption natural law is the quest for the rights of man, derived from his nature, both physical and moral; in other words, "it is the law" or "body of rights" which human beings have deduced from the essential nature of man.

Man's individuality is the consequence of the fundamental nature of mankind, and of his very existence; and the recognition of the essential rights of man, what Lieber called "primordial rights," follows inevitably.

Man's sociality was manifested first in the family, in which social affection led him to become instinctively gregarious and developed the idea of association, and in which also a natural division of labour, for the maintenance of the family life, developed barter, exchange and trade with others.

---

[1] Francis Lieber: *Manual of Political Ethics*, 1839, p. 46.
[2] Ibid., p. 55.   [3] Ibid., p. 46.

Combining individuality—involving the development of the right of property, which was an indispensable condition of human civilisation—and the sociality of the family—which was the first "focus of patriotism"—the state thus evolved because of the natural necessities of human beings.

Men must live in a greater union where they could establish relations and develop ideas which they could not do sufficiently in the family.

He assumed that "a union of a different character is required —it is called the state."[1]

The fundamental idea of the state, more than that of the family, which was merely the intercourse of the members, was "justice, right which exists between man and man."

Among the various relations of human society the state was a society founded upon the relation of right, but he assumed that "a man is a moral individual, yet bound to live in society."

To fulfil his destiny man was by inescapable necessity compelled to live in the state, which Lieber designated a "jural society."[2]

Lieber's conception of the state was not of an institution based on social contract, but of one evolved from human necessity and nature, in that it is the jural and moral society "which has to protect the free action of everyone, as its first basis; and as all the other enumerated relations imply actions, each of these relations becomes likewise a relation of rights either claiming to be enforced or to be protected against infringement."

The object and essence of the state was not only to protect individual security, but also social security, and to guarantee human individuality which could not be absorbed by any power; so these were the primordial rights on the one hand and also stood incalculably above individuals on the other, as the state was the society of societies, which it was the duty of members collectively to form for the essential necessities of human existence.[3]

---

[1] Francis Lieber: *Manual of Political Ethics*, 1839, p. 151.   [2] Ibid., p. 160.
[3] Ibid., p. 171.

"We have arrived, then, at the following important truths:

"(1) The state exists of necessity, and is the natural state of man.

"(2) The state is a jural society.

"(3) The state is a society of moral beings.

"(4) The state does not absorb individuality, but exists for the better obtaining of the true ends of each individual, and of society collectively.

"(5) The state, being a human society, jurally considered and organised, is the society of societies; a bond for weal and woe.

"(6) The state does not make right, but is founded upon it.

"(7) The state is aboriginal with man; it is no voluntary association; no

From this standpoint his ethical theory of the state repudiated the natural right theory, for he treats firstly of the duties of man, and only secondly of his rights derived from his duties.[1]

Accordingly he set up man's primordial rights as almost a necessity, on the axiom that "by my existence I prove my imprescriptible right to my existence as a man, physical, intellectual and moral."[2]

Therefore the state ought to protect and secure his rights for the fulfilment of his individuality, and at the same time to interfere with individual liberty for the benefit of the society as a whole, but as little as possible, according to the requirements of progressive civilisation, because Lieber believed that "no policy can be sounder than to leave as much to private exertion as the public weal, comfort and morality allow."[3]

For this mission of the state it must be given a certain power to carry out its objects. The idea of sovereignty came to be examined and tested by this unique criterion.

From his axiom that man cannot live without a jural society he deduced the "necessary existence of the state and that the right and power, which necessarily and naturally flows from it, is sovereignty"; in other words, it is based on an absolute necessity of man's living with man in a relationship subject to law and with a power to enforce rules for the protection of individuals and the well-being of the human community.[4]

Therefore, since sovereignty ought to be based upon society, he asserted that "the sovereignty of society manifested itself by public opinion, by the formulation of law and by power."

"Public opinion is the aggregate opinion of members of the state, as it has been formed by practical life; it is the common sense of the community, including public knowledge, and necessarily influenced by the taste and genius of the community."[5]

Without this sense of public opinion the law is "a mere husk." Law ought to be the expression of the public will—not only the law which is laid down by the legislatures, but also judge-made law ought to be based upon the sense of the community.

In the functioning of sovereignty the power of society, which

contrivance of art, or invention of suffering; no company of shareholders; no machine, no work of contract by individuals who lived previously out of it; no necessary evil, no ill of humanity which will be cured in time and by civilisation; no accidental thing, no institution above and separate from society; no instrument for one or a few; the state is a form and faculty of mankind to lead the species toward perfection—it is the glory of man."

[1] Francis Lieber: *Manual of Political Ethics*, 1839, p. 62 (pp. 214–215).
[2] Ibid., p. 189.   [3] Ibid., p. 186.   [4] Ibid., pp. 229–234.   [5] Ibid., p. 239.

Lieber called "the self-sufficient plenitude of sovereignty," overrules any other powers.

Set up in order to exercise this power of the state, government is only an institution which derives its power from society. Whatever various forms of government there may be, the best government is that which is best administered, in that there are "the greatest number of laws and institutions essential to that state founded, developed or secured, with which the nation works heart and hand for just and great ends."

But the main weakness of his theory as starting the federal idea on its ultimate development into the pluralistic state was his erroneous conception of organism.

His ideal state was "hamarchy," a polity that had an organism, an organic life "in which a thousand distinct parts have their independent action, yet are by the general organism united into one whole, into one living system."[1] In a unique historical survey he attacked "autarchy," which "acts by power and force." He believed that federalism could only survive if it constituted a polity of "hamarchy," and asserted that "the various united states, with their counties, judiciaries, state legislatures and congress, and their thousand semi-official meetings, form a 'hamarchy'; some of the states, without the American union, would have little of a hamacratic character; the federal government, without the state legislatures and sovereignties, would probably soon lose its hamacratic character."[2]

His ethical principles were antagonistic to the abuse of power, and greatly favoured liberty and self-government. He favoured the division of power and judicial supremacy and independence. His ideal form of government would be an organic government, founded on the principle of justice, which federated every grade of local and social institutions within the state into an organic whole—what he meant by "hamarchy." However different the modern idea of the state might be, when formulated in terms of psychology and philosophy in political science, his doctrine of the ethical basis of the state struck the first blow at the orthodox theories of federalism, which gave it a legal and contractual character, and was the first inspiration of the new conception of American federalism.

J. C. Bluntschli said that "he [Lieber] is a liberal both as a man and as a scholar," and "belongs to the first representatives"

---

[1] Francis Lieber: *Manual of Political Ethics*, 1839, p. 383.—His idea of organism is based on Bluntschli's Theory of Organism, which is entirely independent of the organic idea of *Genossenschaft* Theory. [2] Ibid., p. 385.

of the union of the philosophical and historical methods in jurisprudence and political science.[1]

Lieber also criticised federalism in his numerous lectures and writings, at about the climax of American federal history both in practice and theory.[2] Applying his historical method he showed the nationalist aspect of the federal government of the United States.

He emphatically asserted that the characteristics of the modern state were due to the fact that nationalism was the main source of its activity, and that the aim of the state was the formation of a national state in which the nation had an entity closer and more powerful than a mere aggregate of people.

The Cis-Caucasian races, whose spirit of self-government and love of liberty were manifested in ancient Greece and in modern England, took part in a great migration of nations after the period of maritime discovery.

The great period of colonial policy produced one of the most remarkable facts in that the history of the American states, particularly that of the United States, had commenced. North America was settled by English dissenters, who came from a country "national for many centuries," in which "the principle and habit of self-government existed," and where, moreover, "the representative system, and the representative system with two houses, had developed itself in contradiction to the continental system of three estates, or in recent times the unicameral system of what may be called the French democracy."

He said that the early settlers in North America "were imbued with the idea of self-evolving and independent common law, uncouth in many respects, but instinct with protection of individual rights and personal freedom."[3]

When the *Mayflower* touched the American coast, the first volume of Hugo Grotius' immortal work, *The Law of War and Peace*, foretold the development of federalism. At the same time Milton's *Areopagitica* elevated the spirit of the liberal colonists and those who fled from England to enjoy liberty of conscience,

[1] Bluntschli's address on Lieber's *Service to Political Science and International Law*.

[2] His contribution to federalism appeared first in his lecture on *The Rise of our Constitution and its National Features*; secondly, in *What is our Constitution—a League, Pact, or Government?*; thirdly, in *An Address of Secession and Amendments of Constitution*; and lastly in his other writings, chiefly in *Liberty and Self-Government*.

[3] Francis Lieber: *Miscellaneous Writings*, 1880, Vol. II, *The Rise of our Constitution and its National Features*, p. 36.

settling in North America under the various forms of colonial government, such as the Proprietary, Charter and Crown Colony.

The "republican nerve" of the Anglo-Saxon apparatus of government and institutions embodying that *jus divinum* of civilisation, which Chief Justice Marshall long afterwards expounded, was implanted in the various colonies from Massachusetts down to South Carolina.

The same political concepts, the same traditions, the same language, the same historical associations, and the same physical and spiritual aspirations, however different their forms of government might be, inspired and animated "the manly consciousness of partaking in the great system of Anglican liberty."

At the same time, though the colonists in the early times retained the spirit of loyalty towards the mother country, the "sub-national consciousness" was manifested on various occasions.

Defence against the Indians and protection against the encroachment of the Dutch led to the "United Colonies" of New England in 1643. As early as 1638 Connecticut and New Haven proposed the union which was completed only five years later; the completed confederacy lasted say about forty years and consisted of the colonies of Massachusetts, New Plymouth, Connecticut and New Haven. At the close of the seventeenth century there was a comprehensive scheme for a union of all the colonies; Lieber mentioned that in 1697, more than half a century after the New England confederacy, a plan was drawn up by William Penn to form a general grouping of all the American colonies of Great Britain for "their better understanding and the public tranquillity and safety."

Finally, these national features in American history were manifested distinctly in the Albany plan of union, which was drafted by Benjamin Franklin in 1754.

The Albany plan of union was the first important outline of the American federal union, for the "mutual defence and security" of certain colonies from Massachusetts to South Carolina. Lieber remarked that "this sounds national and is what the Greeks would have called Pan-American."

By this proposal "one general government may be formed in America, including all the said colonies, within and under which each colony may retain its present constitution."

This general government was to be administered by a "President General," who was to be appointed and supported by the Crown, and a "Grand Council," chosen by the representatives of the people of the several colonies meeting in their respective assemblies.

The rights and duties of the "Grand Council" were to extend to legislation, the levying of contributions to a general treasury, the appointment of civil and military commissions under "this general constitution," and the control of the actions of the executive. These were explicit symbols of "one general government and of the nation."

The second event in the direction of the formation of a national character of the United States was the "Declaration of Rights" by congress at New York in 1765, when the indignant opposition of the Americans against the mother country was roused by the Stamp Act of that year.

The revolutionary movement was clearly manifested in every respect and in every event.

As soon as the American leaders recognised the necessity of secession or independence (*Abfall*) there was a "national spontaneity, which characterised their actions and continued to characterise them to the end."[1]

The national conscience was roused and the feeling of the country sprang from no other source than the general consciousness of what is called national sovereignty.[2] Lieber remarked that "the highest of all authorities—the self-sufficient universal consciousness—lifted up that authority yielded to it." And "the people, who had struggled against separation, fell into the formation of a new nation, greatly aided in this by geographic separation from the mother country and geographic union within, and continued and farther developed their precious and inherited self-government."[3]

On September 5, 1774, the delegates of the colonies and provinces in America of Great Britain met and held a congress at Philadelphia, at Carpenter Hall. It was swayed by a unanimous determination to create an American nation and to maintain and preserve American liberty.

The congress chose Washington to be the General and Commander-in-Chief of the "United Provinces of North America," to combat the enemy of the country and to defend America's inherent and inalienable right.

The Declaration of Independence of July 4, 1776, was an irrevocable declaration of American nationalism.

However slow the growth of the American union may have been, Lieber emphasised that it was organic integration, not

---

[1] Francis Lieber: *Miscellaneous Writings*, 1880, Vol. II, *The Rise of our Constitution and its National Features*, p. 48.
[2] Ibid., pp. 46–75. [3] Ibid., p. 48.

disintegration, which was "the prescribed law and end of all life —physical as well as psychologic, individual as well as social."[1]

He analysed the Declaration of Independence psychologically as being "modest and manly in a touching degree—a decent respect to the opinion of mankind," and politically as being "thoroughly national" and "for one people."[2]

He asserted that this Declaration was not only to be considered in its potential national character, but as imbued with the light of political philosophy, and as a quasi-Bill of Rights.

The formation of the confederation, a perpetual union between the states in 1777, and the more permanent union established by the constitution of the United States in 1787 were the outcome of American national sentiment and the desire for the noblest preservation of that justice, humanity and liberty which were inherent in Anglo-American freedom and self-government.

From this historical standpoint Lieber examined the federal state of America and discussed whether it was based on the idea of a league, of a compact or of a government.

His investigation led him to believe that the pabulum, on which the minds of Northern statesmen were nourished, was Algernon Sydney's *Discourse Concerning Government*, and that the minds of the Southern statesmen were impressed and moulded probably by Montesquieu's *Spirit of the Laws*.

Nevertheless, the theory of contract, according to which all government was originally based on an agreement, had been of dominant importance in the political ideas of the seventeenth and eighteenth centuries, and in those days the Jeffersonian demand for the continuance of democracy and liberty was derived from the theory of an initial contract.

Lieber condemned that idea; though plausible at the first glance, "yet it is erroneous and unphilosophical throughout."

He asserted that no historical instance of a body politic based on such a contract had ever been adduced. He said, "Hobbes in his *Leviathan* derives an atrocious despotism from contract, and Locke in his *Essay on Government* derives the constitutional polity from it."

His *Jus*, law and government, was the result of natural and necessary evolution, as the family was the first society. The question whether the constitution of the United States was founded on a mere contract or whether it was an organic system was not only important from the historical or scientific point of view, but was

---

[1] Francis Lieber: *Miscellaneous Writings*, 1880, Vol. II, *The Rise of our Constitution and its Natural Features*, p. 68.   [2] Ibid., p. 70.

also significant "as a problem of political life and of social existence, of public conscience, of right and truth in the highest spheres of human action and of our civilisation."[1]

In the solution of this problem we ought to consider what was the fundamental character of the document called the "Constitution of the United States," and to inquire on what basis it was founded, examining for this purpose not merely its phraseology, but also its internal history and its original contents and provisions.

He emphasised the view that the national life of the whole community was dependent on a single term of the constitution, according to Cicero *constituere rempublicam*.[2]

His attack on the particularist theory of state rights was based not merely on the legal justification of the nationalist doctrine, but on the logical and philosophical principle of the modern state, aided by his unique historical method.

He said that "fallacy has its rules—to seize upon one point—one term, to narrow down the meaning even of this one point, and then keenly to syllogise from that single starting-point, irrespective of all other modifying and tributary truths or considerations."[3] To him the search after truth ought to be impartial and indifferent—"it may be symbolised by the soaring eagle rising to the regions of light."

First of all Lieber discussed whether the constitution of the United States was a contract or government, with reference to the view of a certain Senator Webster from Louisiana who said, "a contract broken at one end is broken all over."

Was it really true that the constitution of the United States was based on Webster's theory of a contract, and was broken by a single action of secession by one component state?

For the sake of argument he inquired what sort of contract it was. The particularistic publicists adhered to the government which was founded either on an original pact or a political pact, and at the same time they argued that the government contract was one in perpetuity. Therefore they justified society as continuous and did not recognise the contracting members as a *fuoruscito*.

Not only was this argument logically feasible, but also the idea

---

[1] Francis Lieber: *Miscellaneous Writings*, 1880, Vol. II, First Lecture, *What is our Constitution?* p. 89.
[2] Ibid., p. 90.—Cicero mentioned *Constituere rempublicam*, which means "organising the common weal, putting it in order and connecting all the parts in mutual organic dependence upon one another." [3] Ibid., p. 90.

of common contract did not leave one party the right to depart from it without the consent of the other parties.

If the thirteen original states of the United States with their own sovereignty were leagued together by the constitution, there was no justification for President Jefferson acknowledging that "neither he nor anyone had the constitutional power of purchasing foreign territory," or in asking "the English Parliament for acts of indemnity for having broken the law."

Then Lieber condemned the theory of "lawful secession," which was founded upon the idea of "reserved rights of the states."

In the formation of the union the federal state admitted the component members to become full participants in the union and left them the same full self-government as was enjoyed by the already existing states.

No idea of contract was valid unless it recognised mutual obligations for some common purpose, and the element of reserved right left the opportunity of mutual injury.

In these conditions no state could ever evolve, and no supreme law of the land could exist, and no government could function; there would be that anarchical state to which nullification and secession logically led.

Lieber thought that the essential character, genesis and substance of the modern state were not based upon the Athenian city-state, nor upon the medieval federal system, nor upon a political league, but upon a national polity.

The highest type and the fullest development of modern states was "the organic union of national and local self-government: not, however, national centralism or a national unity without local vitality."[1]

From the historical records of "United America" it was clear that the North Americans came generally from the Netherlands and from England—"manly, venturous, clad in the armour of self-government and belonging to a race with institutional instincts."[2]

The national current of the United States of America, ever since the Albany Plan of union, developed and culminated in the formation of a national government under the constitution of 1787. Besides this historical justification of the American nation the argument regarding federal sovereignty was Lieber's unique exposition of a new conception of federalism.

According to the Articles of Confederation of 1777 the union

[1] Francis Lieber: *Miscellaneous Writings*, 1880, Vol. II, First Lecture, *What is our Constitution?* pp. 96–97.   [2] Ibid., Second Lecture, p. 99.

was perpetual, but at the same time was formed by the several states, each of which "retains its sovereignty, etc." No word of sovereignty appeared in any constitution or other document except the Articles of Confederation.

What was sovereignty? Edward Coke, a great jurist in England, had declared in the Commons that English law did not know the word "sovereign."

Although an undesirable development of the idea of sovereignty, the modern sense of sovereignty means not only the highest overruling power within the state, but also, in the metaphysical sense, the original self-sufficient source of authority and powers, from which all other authority was derived. To Lieber, as I have already said, sovereignty was based upon a necessity of the human community—that is to say, not upon man, but upon the moral worth of public opinion—in other words, "the soul of the people."

From this criterion he deduced that in relation to foreign states no government other than that of the United States has ever been sovereign, and also that the feeling of union—of mutual dependence—underlay the whole system from the beginning, as history proved that the colonies exercised a very high degree of self-government, but never absolute autonomy, from the moment of independence.

The colonies never acted as fully independent sovereigns, except as United America. In these circumstances he assumed that "if the distinction between *de jure* and *de facto*, or between practical, or rather factal, and theoretical character, is inapplicable to anything, it is to sovereignty."[1]

He was convinced that the framing and adoption of the constitution of 1787 was the establishment of a fundamental law of the land as "it ought to be understood by everyone who aspires to a dignified consciousness of his rights and duties as an American citizen and to become a guardian of American citizenship, without a minute knowledge of our history and a truthful study of the debates which led to the framing and adoption of the constitution."

The total absence of the word "sovereignty" and the existence of the three words, "Union," "Constitution" and "People," in the preamble to the fundamental law clearly indicated the government of the whole nation and testified to its entirety and unity.

He said that "the mere *modus* of adopting the constitution proves nothing."

Hundreds of records of debates in this time and other historic

[1] Francis Lieber: *Miscellaneous Writings*, 1880, Vol. II, Second Lecture, p. 110.

evidence demonstrated that there was most urgent need to establish a national government; Madison considered that America would almost be lost if a constitution were not established.

The provision in the constitution of 1787 with regard to treason against the United States provided for the allegiance of every citizen to the federal government, not merely to the states; as Lieber remarked, "allegiance is the faith and loyalty due to the sovereign—in our case the nation or country."

Even though he fully accepted the contention of Bluntschli that under the Helvetic constitution the Swiss publicists spoke of the sovereignty of Switzerland and the cantonal sovereignty of each canton, meaning thereby "its self-government, with an entire organisation of government," yet he assumed that the constitution depended on the national government, equipped "with most of the usual attributes of sovereignty."[1]

Owing to the wide legislative and executive powers of the federal government the two houses had a complete national character,[2] and the President was "the standard-bearer, the *gonfalonier* of the union."

The constitution of the United States broadly declared and decreed that "all laws made in pursuance of the same shall be the supreme law of the land."

The constitution was a national law, with all attributes essential to a law which could enforce obedience, and was a fundamental national law proceeding from a national conscious will and necessity, and establishing a complete national government— "an organisation of national life."

Condemning the state right theory as logically absurd and morally wicked, he was convinced that the constitution of the American federal government was dependent upon a "general government, nationally uniting a number of states with the framework of local governments," which "is that very thing which America has contributed as her share to the political history of our race."[3]

---

[1] Francis Lieber: *Miscellaneous Writings*, 1880, Vol. II, Second Lecture, p. 113.
[2] Ibid., p. 114.—"The constitution gives to the House of Representatives a complete national character, by founding the representation on the population, and making the representatives vote individually. It gives even this representative and national character to the Senate, inasmuch as the Senators also vote individually, and not by states, although each state by sending two Senators, irrespective of its population or wealth, is so far represented as state. No one in Congress has a deputative character, in the mediaeval sense, or is there as attorney, depending upon previously given instructions, as the ambassadors of the German princes in the German Diet." [3] Ibid., p. 117.

Starting from this general assumption Lieber inquired what secession was. The validity of the right of nullification or secession depended mainly on the answer to the question whether or not the constitution regarded the states as the possessors of the final sovereignty.

To Lieber, sovereign right was possessed neither by the union nor by the states, but belonged to the crystallised public opinion of the nation. Was secession revolutionary? Was it treason against "the supreme law of the land"? His answer was explicitly and wisely that the constitution of federal America did not grant any right of secession at all. But the provision that every power not granted by the federal instrument was reserved to the state authority would result in the supposition that the constitution itself contained, and tacitly acknowledged, the right of secession, that is the principle of self-destruction, so far as the seceding states were concerned.

It was the case in such contemporary constitutions as the first democratic constitution of France, which recognised "that if the government acts against the law, every citizen had the duty to take up arms against it."

This was American democracy tempered by extreme particularism and excessive love of liberty and natural right. As Lieber expressed it, "this was, indeed, declaring Jacobinical democracy tempered by revolution, as a writer had called Turkey a despotism tempered by regicide."[1]

The imagination and ability of the framers of the constitution of 1787, far-seeing and thoroughly schooled by experience as they were, yet failed by some "oversight" to make any provision for one important matter, namely the possibility of secession.

However guilty of neglect on this point they might be, Lieber assumed that "those that so carefully drew up our constitution cannot be blamed for not having thought of this extravagance, because it had never been dreamt of in any confederacy, ancient, mediaeval or modern."

If there were not such a provision in any federal constitution, and if we could not deduce any guiding principle from the idea of sovereignty, the solution of this problem could be found only by reference to the common law of mankind.

From the ancient Achaean League down to the Swiss Confederacy, the Germanic federation or the United States of the

[1] Francis Lieber: *Miscellaneous Writings*, 1880, Vol. II, *An Address on Secession*, p. 130.

Netherlands, a much weaker union, such a right of secession or nullification had never been contemplated.

Moreover, the framers of the constitution implicitly ignored the right of secession when the firmer union of the federal state was constructed by "the better understanding of politics, and a nobler consciousness of the mission as a nation" of great America.

Then secession involved revolution. Revolution for what? He answered, "To remedy certain evils."

He reached the conclusion that this problem was to be solved by the discovery of ways of remedying certain evils. Did we favour revolution or peaceful (lawful) remedies?

He pointed out that "right" and "wrong," or "truth" and "justice," meant nothing in the case of revolutions, and if there were no probability of success from the outset, unsuccessful revolutions were not only "misfortunes" but became "stigmas."

He strongly recommended provision for systematic and lawful reforms in order to prevent violent outbreaks.

The record of the debates in the congress and the convention showed that the framers of the constitution were men like ourselves and considered the constitution as being far from infallible.

"As long as life lasts, so long there is change." As the law of civilisation is not stationary, so the condition of life changes sometimes for the better and sometimes for the worse. Nevertheless he said that "cessation of organic change is death." Law must change in the course of time. If the law were made by men, the everlasting change of generations could hardly force the positive law of human society on anyone either by virtue of the sovereign will or by an inalienable and absolute law of right. He asserted that "reality is sovereign and will allow no master," and added that "both solid conservatism and arrogant aggression lead to ruin."[1]

Law and constitution remained simply a means (though an indispensable and necessary means), in the same way as the state and government were simply a means of promoting and securing the highest objects of human life. And the objects of human life must not be sacrificed to the means.

From this test of constitutional validity he deduced that the amendment of the constitution was of the greatest importance for the welfare of the political community. He condemned the extreme constructionists as upholders of a hyper-constitutional

---

[1] Francis Lieber: *Miscellaneous Writings*, 1880, Vol. II, *Amendment of the Constitution*, p. 142.—His conservatism consisted in an unalterable adherence to the principle of continuance in the absence of the need for change.

hypothesis, because "the axiom of mechanics, that nothing is stronger than its weakest point, may not wholly apply to laws and constitutions; and the lapse of so long a period, with its wear and tear, has revealed feeble points and flaws in the cast of our fundamental law which demand close attention and timely repair, lest the injury become irreparable."[1]

He endeavoured to prove the truth of union and nationality by his historical survey, and maintained the view that the constitution had established a representative government over the whole, and, like Hamilton, he emphasised that the efficient government of a great nation must be of the natural type, imbued with the highest spirit of federal self-government.

Therefore, if the state right theory were admitted in the federal state, the dual allegiance would result in divided sovereignty on the one hand, and "damnable" perplexity between two exclusive sovereign theories and political reality on the other.

This double allegiance would be a "fearful see-saw for a conscientious citizen."

He demanded the proposed amendments dealing with "the necessity of the integrity of our country, allegiance, the treasonable character of elevating so-called state sovereignty above the national government, the extinction of the Dred Scott principle, and the total abolition of slavery." The proposed amendment for the abolition of slavery ought to provide for the representation of the ex-slaves in the national assembly as free persons. Though all citizens had equal rights, he concluded that the representatives should be male citizens of a certain age "having qualifications requisite for electing members of the most numerous branch of the respective state legislatures on the basis of each census."

The prohibition of slave-trading of any kind should be explicitly laid down in the constitution, and the free inhabitants without any exception of colour, race or origin should be entitled to the privileges of citizens, both in the courts and elsewhere.

He proposed the amendment of the constitution which the Northern statesmen equally desired. But however earnestly and strongly he emphasised the need for the amendment as essential to human happiness he failed to deal with the problem of the constitutional process of amendment. He tacitly acknowledged the existing method of amendment in which the practical measures of the alteration ran counter to the belief in the organic changes of life.

[1] Francis Lieber: *Miscellaneous Writings*, 1880, Vol. II, *Amendment of the Constitution*, p. 144.

His federalism was far removed from previous federal doctrines and was based on the idea of organism. The main thesis of modern federalism—the federal state—had been dependent either on the recognition of divided sovereignty or on single sovereignty.

Even Hamilton and Webster could hardly deny the reserved rights of the states. The difference between the particularist doctrine and the nationalist theory of federalism was as to whether the constitution of the federal state was based upon the sovereignty of the states or upon that of the union.

Madison's agreement with the theory of divided sovereignty was derived from the idea that sovereignty was based on the people in the states, but not upon the governments of the states. The implicit recognition of the "people's" sovereignty brought about the controversy between Calhoun and Webster as to whether "people" meant the people as the whole or in the several states.

The argument on the letter of the constitution was never-ending, but Lieber's conception of a nation which differed from the people showed the way to an apparent solution of those problems which especially excited the national temper in the Civil War.

At the same time Lieber was convinced that sovereignty was based on the universal opinion of the national and public conscience. Applying this criterion of sovereignty the main question of the previous federal theories—whether the sovereign authority rested in the state or in the federal government—was not the central argument, and the sovereignty of federal America did not flow from the fountain of the sovereign power of people, but from the common reservoir of the national universal will and consciousness.

Supposing that the sovereign authority of the federal state rested upon the national will of the people, the theoretical ground of federalism in politics would undergo a material change, and tend to be based upon the idea of "organism" with its living functions.

His federalism in the modern state would not merely be a mechanical political system, but a relationship of federal functions between the general and state governments with a complete sense of self-government and liberty. From his own axiom of the nature of the modern state, republican federalism was the highest form of political organisation on the basis of organic sense, and the noblest decentralised institution expressive of self-government.

In Lieber's view the characteristic of American liberty should permeate "representative republicanism and the principle of confederation or federation." He explained that "federalism is taken, of course, of its philosophical and not in its party sense."[1]

According to Lieber the establishment of a federal republic is justified not merely by political expediency, but as being the embodiment of the highest possible philosophical good.

In this assumption the relationship between federal and state governments was dependent, not upon a mere correlation of sovereign bodies, but upon the political entity of the organic units of a collective whole—in that it was federal in character and decentralised in method. It was the foreshadowing of a new conception of federalism, and of the development of the federal idea.

The question as to how far his idea of federalism influenced the later American thinkers and whether or not it affected the development of federal ideas after 1865 involves a further investigation of the federal principle.

§ 2

The triumph of the Washington government in 1864 ended the bloodshed of the revolutionary battlefields in favour of the Lincoln party.

The thirteenth, fourteenth and fifteenth amendments of the constitution secured a firm foothold in republican politics.

Just at the time of the beginning of the Civil War, the western frontiers were the main focus of capitalistic and speculative enterprise.

After the construction of roads and canals for the development of commerce and trade, railway construction became the dominant form of enterprise.

As soon as the federal government decided to develop the western territory various subsidies were granted by congress for that purpose, and especially for railway construction. Owing to these subsidies granted by the Lincoln government the dream of trans-continental railway construction was realised on May 10, 1869, when the two advancing hosts of construction from east and west met at Promontory point, near Ogden, and the Union Pacific line was established.

Following this construction several railways were made, and after the boom and depression of the railway enterprises James J.

[1] Francis Lieber: *Civil Liberty and Self-Government*, ed. by T. D. Woolsey, 1880, p. 258, note 1.

Hill succeeded in establishing the continental railways on a large scale.

Trans-continental telegraph services were inaugurated in 1861 to facilitate trade between the east and west. The Homestead Act, passed in Congress in 1862, greatly stimulated the new migration for the development of the western regions, and also the new entry of foreign emigrants from the Far East and Scandinavia began.

At the same time the rapid increase of population in these newly settled districts began to be realised by the ambitious adventurers who wished to invade the fertile lands in the Indian territories.

The aggressive republican federal government accepted their demand to send an army to expel the Red Indians from their own free lands.

The overwhelming ambition of business enterprise in the west was the adumbration of an imperialistic policy on the part of the American government.

Industrial development in the east and middle north and the rapid expansion to the west and south required labour on the one hand and capital on the other. The need for labour produced the problem of immigration and the demand for capital required systematic banking and financial provision. Inter-state trade and commerce gave an incentive to the rapid establishment of transport and communication.

The Civil War brought about the destruction of the old economic basis of the slave-owning aristocracy, and led to the establishment of the new capitalistic large-scale business enterprises.

The common economic interests of the states became closer and closer, and the economic interdependence of the southern agrarian states and northern industrial and financial states and the middle western agricultural and mining regions brought about an increasing consciousness of the unity of the American nation.

The economic adventures and enterprises along the western frontiers and the unity of purpose in the wars with the Southern confederacy and the Red Indians stirred and encouraged the growth of full national consciousness, as England attained to national existence in the great adventurous days of Queen Elizabeth, and Prussia in the time of Frederick the Great.

These material changes in the economic and social life of the United States in the sixties and seventies of the nineteenth century largely affected the political system in federal America in fact as well as in theory. The main force in American thought from 1864 onwards tended to be realistic, and the political aim was nothing but the practical and theoretical realisation of the national unity. The key to open the national gate was the acknowledgment that the supreme power—sovereignty—rested on the basis of the nation. Consequently the idea of political systems naturally changed from the mere theoretical political philosophy which had hitherto prevailed into one judicially formulated, or which sought to base itself on an ethical or metaphysical conception of the state. Therefore, under the sway of nationalism the main political ideas tended to assume either a juristic or an idealistic character rather than a mere political one.

But Anglo-American thought could not move entirely from empiricism to full acceptance of metaphysical mysticism. Nevertheless, the urgent demand of the American thinkers after the Civil War is simply for the supremacy of the sovereignty of the union, to which Austinian absolutism serves to give an English origin.

In these circumstances the foreign political ideas which mainly influenced the people of 1864 were not *Naturrecht* or *Contrat Social*, but German transcendentalism on the one hand, and the English utilitarian conceptions, such as those of Austin, on the other.

The real contribution of Francis Lieber to political science affected no doubt not merely the political system of federal government, but also the whole science of politics on the ethical basis.

Being neither a Hegelian nor entirely a Benthamite, his purpose in formulating his political maxims was to philosophise the idea of self-government, giving it an ethical justification, and to apply it to political systems and functions.

At that time, in opposition to Lieber's *Political Ethics* and the Germanic idea of the state, the utilitarian theory of jurisprudence, especially that of John Austin, influenced American thinkers more than any other doctrine.

Austin's analytical juristic school repudiated the social contract theory, and advanced its own theory of government. Austin criticised and analysed every political institution from the standpoint of reality and formulated his definitions and classification of the various systems and institutions by the empirical method. Government, to him, had to grow, and grew, through "the perception of the utility of political government, or the preference of the bulk of the community of any government to anarchy."

His classification of federations was twofold, designated,

respectively, "composite states" and "systems of confederated states," following, in this, writers on positive international law.

He defined a composite state as follows: "The several united societies are one independent society, or are severally subject to one sovereign body: which, through its minister the general government, and through its members and ministers the several united governments, is habitually and generally obeyed in each of the united societies, and also in the larger society arising from the union of all." The system of confederated states was that "the several compacted societies are not one society, and not subject to a common sovereign: or each of the several societies is an independent political society, and each of their several governments is properly sovereign or supreme."[1]

From his assertion of sovereignty, which was derived from fact, not from law or right, and incapable of legal limitation, the several united governments of a composite state, "as forming one aggregate body," or they and its general government, "as forming a similar body," were "jointly sovereign in each of the united societies, and also in the larger society arising from the union of all."

In the composite state, where the common and general government ought to be federal, not supreme, each of the several governments, parties to the federal compact, is in that character "a limb of a sovereign body."

Consequently, even though several governments were subject to the sovereign body of which they were constituent members, they were not, as such, purely in a state of subjection, and at the same time the common and general government was not sovereign or supreme.

From his analytical survey of federal states he drew the conclusion that if the political powers of the common or general government were merely delegated to it and created by the several united governments, "it is not a constituent member of the sovereign body, but is merely its subject minister."

Therefore Austin set up his unique justification of national sovereignty in a composite state by saying that "the sovereignty of each of the united societies, and also of the larger society arising from the union of all, resides in the united government as forming one aggregate body"; i.e. as signifying their joint pleasure or the joint pleasure of a majority of their number agreeably to the modes or forms determined by the federal compact.

[1] John Austin: *Lectures on Jurisprudence*, ed. by Robert Campbell, 1873, Vol. I, p. 269.

On this basis the political powers of the federal government were conferred and determined and enforced, and at the same time it was competent to abridge the powers of its constituent members. To the sovereignty of that aggregate body the several state governments, although not at all subordinate, were in a state of subjection.

Even though the power to interpret laws and issue commands, within the sphere determined by the federal compact, were conferred upon the tribunals of the general or several governments, the final power of every court as such was derived from that sovereign power of the aggregate body.

Austin maintained that the supreme government of the United States of America came within the foregoing description of a composite government and said that "the sovereignty of each of the states and also of the larger states arising from the federal union, resides in the state's government as forming one aggregate body; meaning by a state's government, not its ordinary legislature, but the body of its citizens which appoint its ordinary legislature, and which, the union apart, is properly sovereign therein"; in other words, it resides "in several individuals" or "those several oligarchies as forming a collective whole."[1]

Contrasted with this composite state the system of confederated states was a mere alliance with permanent duration and there was no allied government which was subject to the sovereign body except a loose and impotent assembly of ambassadors of the competent sovereign societies, as in the German Confederation or Swiss Confederacy.

Partly inspired by the national crisis of the Civil War, and partly influenced by new political conceptions, chiefly those of Lieber, Hegel and German jurists and John Austin, the American political thinkers of the last part of the nineteenth century were schooled either in transcendental philosophy or in the utilitarian doctrine.

O. A. Brownson, in his work *The American Republic*, put forward in 1866 a view of the American political organisation which was derived from Austin, but also influenced by de Maistre's catholic philosophy.

He, unlike the others, but like Jameson, assumed that the constitution of the United States was twofold, written and unwritten; the latter was due to the natural growth of the American community, what he called "Providence," and the

[1] John Austin: *Lectures on Jurisprudence*, ed. by Robert Campbell, 1873, Vol. I, p. 268.

former to the positive expression of the latter. Not unlike his contemporaries, his main argument was not federal organisation, but the theory of the constitution. Naturally, sovereignty was the essential thesis of his work. In opposition to the orthodox popular sovereignty, which had no ground of reason, sovereignty in his mind was vested in the states united but not in the states severally.

He held that while "the sovereignty is in, and must be in, the states it is in the states united and not in the states severally."[1] The states in the federal United States "are all sovereign states united, but disunited are not states at all." As life is "in the body but not in the members," so sovereignty rested in the union but not in the states individually. The Americans were the people of the United States collectively or as a society, not people individually. Therefore he asserted that no theory of the constitution could ever exist, but only the fact of the constitution —a simple historical fact which "precedes the law and constitutes the law-making power."

From his observation of United States history he concluded that the state and the union were born together and grew up together, whilst instinct rather than deliberate wisdom expressed itself in the United States in both "constitutional unity and constitutional multiplicity."

Sovereignty in his nature was coincident with domain and the domain was in the United States. Provided that sovereignty was inseparable from the states—the United States of America—the wills of the people, unless there are no states, "have no laws, have no force, bind nobody and justify no act."

This doctrine of federalism was chiefly directed to two problems, the mode of the formation of the United States and the division of powers of government between the states in their united capacity and their individual capacity.

In the mode of the federal constitution the powers of the United States "are indeed grants and trusts," not from a mere conventional assembly of the people, but "from God through the law of nature, and are grants and trusts or powers always conceded to every nation or sovereign people."[2]

In his view sovereignty was based on "unwritten constitution born with and inherent in people"—providence. Applying this theocratic criterion he condemned Madison's popular sovereignty, because Madison and his followers' philosophy and political theory "may sometimes affect the phraseology they adopt, but form no rule for interpreting their works," and at the same time

[1] O. A. Brownson: *The American Republic*, 1866, p. 224. [2] Ibid., p. 233.

he rebuked the state right theorists because they advocated and insisted on "reserved" power derived exclusively from their own dogmas. That was utterly incompatible with the notion of a national state whose members had sovereign authority. Either states ceased to be sovereign in the federal state or they retained their sovereignty by agreement whether in alliance or confederation.

He said that "the powers reserved to the states severally are reserved by order of the United States, and powers so reserved are reserved to the people of the United States." Sovereignty to him resided in the states united as its domain, and in the people of the United States as its constituent element; he condemned state sovereignty as "squatter sovereignty."

He was convinced that "sovereignty, in the republican order, is in organic people or the states"—that is to say, organic American people do not exist as a consolidated people or state, they exist only as organised into "distinct but inseparable states"; in other words, "each state is a living member of the one body and derives its life from its union with the body, so that the American state is one body with many members."[1]

Therefore the differences between Madison's views and his own turned upon the determination of the source of sovereignty; the former believed that sovereignty was derived from people who had formed a convention, whereby they became an organised community, and the latter insisted on the existence of the real living solidarity of the community as the work of providence prior to the convention.

In order to live and act, sovereignty must maintain "an organ" through which people express their will. This organ, according to Brownson, in the American system was "Convention."[2]

On this assumption federalism in the United States was dependent not only upon the federal organisation of the body politic, but also upon the federal function of exercising the supreme powers to be applied.

The distribution of powers was an essential characteristic of the American Republic. Strictly speaking, as the source of sovereignty is one and indivisible, so government is one though its powers are divided and exercised by two sets of agents and ministers. Therefore the division of powers of government was the origin of the providential fact of American polity and formed the federal constitution, unwritten and written by the people themselves.

He asserted that this division of the powers of government

[1] O. A. Brownson: *The American Republic*, 1866, pp. 245–246.   [2] Ibid., p. 247.

"is particular to the United States and is the effective safeguard against both feudal disintegration and Roman centralism."

On this assumption he condemned the theory of secession as a doctrine of state "suicide," and at the same time he equally condemned the reaction against secession and disintegration, because it would strengthen the tendency to centralism which could "succeed no better than disintegration."

This centrifugal and centripetal play of political forces would be brought to an equilibrium by public opinion, by which the government was directed "on its constitutional path."[1]

This feature of the federal system of America was not due to an antagonism of classes, estates or interests, and also was in no sense a system of checks and balances.

The division of power between general and particular governments—federal and state—and into three departments was derived from administrative expediency which drew a line between two separate interests—"the general relations and interests and the relations and interests of the people of the United States." In this federal system, the federal government in the general relations and interests took charge of public authority and rights, and the state governments in particular were concerned with protection of private rights and personal freedom.

The powers of each government were equally sovereign and both federal and state governments were co-ordinate, standing on the same level and derived from the same source of sovereign authority. The only subjection of each co-ordinate government in the federal republic was to the immediate sovereign body, e.g. the convention.

Theoretically and practically the actual facts proved that the demarcation of power on the basis of these relations and interests was unreal and the co-existence of both governments was a complete real government in "its plenitude and integrity."

Brownson concluded that the American method of the division of power "demands no such antagonism, no neutralising of one social force by another, but avails itself of all the forces of society, organises them dialectically, not antagonistically, and thus protects with equal efficiency both public authority and private rights."[2]

On this argument he believed that the return of the seceded states to the union was a matter of restoration, but not of creation, because the Civil War was a "territorial war," and even though the states revolted against the union and secured territorial

[1] O. A. Brownson: *The American Republic*, 1866, p. 252. [2] Ibid., pp. 270–271.

integrity, yet all the power of a sovereign rests in the United States and the people of the seceded states remained people of the United States. He believed that the solidarity of the race was that requirement of human life which had founded society, and the territorial division "formed merely particular societies, states or nations."

His federalism in the large sense was divided into several territorial regions but maintained the solidarity of the race; the nation was based on international law, and the federal state or confederation on the nation, which subdivided into states, counties and municipalities.

Territorial democracy was to him an essential fact in the federal organisation in the face of humanitarian democracy and socialistic centralisation. Although his federal doctrine was vague, both on the basis of experimental facts and on metaphysical grounds, yet when he emphasised that the divine essence was the main source of the division of the powers of government in America his doctrine of federalism became theocratic in nature, and was of no value in the scientific study of political systems.

Besides Brownson, Joel Tiffany in 1867 formulated a theory of the sovereignty of the nation. The people of the United States, in the conduct of the national federal government, acted "in virtue of their powers as men, and as members of an organised government or society," and occupied "a place above political constitutions which were derived from them."

He concluded that "the inevitable consequence of establishing a national government extending its jurisdiction that it might execute the national authority throughout the nation was the necessary subordination of the state governments to such an authority."[1]

John N. Pomeroy, a professor of political science in the University of New York, held the same view of sovereign power, namely, that it "consists in the collective will and in the faculty of wielding and disposing those forces which obey that will."[2]

He conceived that sovereignty was indivisible in its nature and appertained "to the totality of members of the body politic—to the entire people."

He sought to base his assertion that the federal constitution is an organic law on the attributes of sovereignty of "a political unity."

He regarded the whole civil polity as resting upon two grand

[1] Joel Tiffany: *A Treatise on Government and Constitutional Law*, 1867, p. 312.
[2] John N. Pomeroy: *An Introduction to the Constitutional Law*, 1868, p. 5.

ideas, that of self-government on the one hand and that of centralisation on the other; the former was a habit descended from the civil politics of the Anglo-Saxon and Germanic races, and the latter was a legacy from Rome. The first was the safeguard of liberty and the second the source of power.[1]

These two elements were essential to the well-being of the nation. The American political system, in a federal organisation, like that of Lieber, was destined to be based on the idea of self-government in which "we have an ascending scale of towns, counties, states, nation."[2]

He, like French federalists, assumed that federalism by its very nature possessed the function of administration which could preserve an impartial balance of liberty and authority.

Empirically-minded Americans could not ignore Austin's analytic legal doctrine. John C. Hurd put forward his views in the *Law of Freedom and Bondage* in 1851 and criticised political arguments from the theoretical point of view in *The Theory of our National Existence* in 1881. He emphasised that there had previously been a tendency to assume that "the existence of political facts is not determined by the observing intellect employing the bodily senses, but by knowledge of certain principles of morals."[3]

Political facts were the result, not of theory, but of events; there must be someone who formulates certain rights and laws which need general acceptance before they become effective or who skilfully acts as if they are so accepted.

Hurd's political ideas were entirely based upon empiricism, and the search for truth leading to a legitimate conclusion was no more than an inquiry as to the actual facts, by analysis and inductive methods.

He said that "a fact is known by the observing intellect aided by bodily senses, as existing, whether in the judgment of the moral sense it ought to exist or not."[4]

The controversy at the time of the revolution of 1861 was not as to the *a priori* validity of obligation to the law, or as to the rules of right and wrong, but as to the political obligation arising from a set of facts. The reasoning *a posteriori* was the induction from fact which for convenience we will call theory or principle.

Political creations, such as supreme power in the state, must

---

[1] John N. Pomeroy: *An Introduction to the Constitutional Law*, 1868, pp. 100–102.
[2] Ibid., p. 102.
[3] John C. Hurd: *The Theory of our National Existence*, 1881, Preface, p. vi.
[4] Ibid., Preface, p. ix.

be examined in the light of the political facts which determined people in a certain territory to live together, and not by abstract doctrines as to rights of human existence. However imperfect Hurd's doctrine might be, his empirical attitude towards the federal system started a new school of federal theory. This was a new liberal doctrine of federalism, but it was very little more advanced than that of Austin.

Hurd held that sovereignty was a power exercised by one individual or a body of individuals over others who were conscious of it being so exercised. Therefore such a power did not rest upon any theoretical ground of general will or any pretence of general consent or public opinion, but upon the actual will of the majority of the holders of such authority, i.e. the majority of the electorates established by the constitution.

Hurd asserted that sovereignty could not be an attribute of law: "because by the nature of things law must proceed from sovereignty." It was not based by its nature on law at all, but on fact; as he said, "to give a constitution: that is to recognise a sovereign."

His assertion of sovereignty from the standpoint of the "analytical jurist" furnished a test of the legal basis of federalism.

As Austin thought that the judicial power was the final authority of arbitration, so Hurd believed that the actions of the executive and legislative should under a written constitution be ultimately subject to judicial inquiry, indicating the final determination of the nature, extent and legal effect of political power within the territory.

He was convinced that "on the ground of the determination of political relations, beyond the scope of the judiciary, these opinions are not here [in America] presented as authority but as on the same plane as testimony, with others from some other sources."

Accordingly, he regretted that there had been no theory of the constitution "accepted by any member of the court since 1861 and certainly not by a majority."

Opinions of the court came to light. Chief Justice Chase's views of the "perpetuity and indissolubility of union," although vague in nature, indicated that the states now stood under "the loss of distinct and individual existence or of the right of self-government."

The new tendency of the national union brought about a marked era of constitutional development in which "the states are not only bound to regulate themselves by its provisions, but the constitution compels them to be what they are—to exist—

to be a state." Historically each of the states in the union was completely and individually sovereign, and each agreed to the adoption of the constitution, with the voluntary cession of certain portions of those sovereignties for the formation of the federation.

The history of the federal government, since 1787, had shown the progress of the national power which, in fact though not in law, transformed itself from an international personality into "a newly born political person, to whom the name of the United States, or, less formally, the union was applicable."[1]

In reality a portion of sovereign power was held by the union or the United States in the same manner and sense as the sum of sovereignty was possessed by an independent nation, "not by law but as fact," whilst the remainder of sovereign power not ceded to the union was held by the several states in the same manner and sense as if they were independent countries. Even though the views of the Madison-Webster school might have previously prevailed, the fact that the 10th Amendment of the United States' Constitution assured reserved rights, had shown that these were not held by the states, or by the people of the states, "as severally sovereign but as joint sovereign only."

Hurd argued that the states would not as such possess these reserved powers unless they held the power as being delegated to them by the federal government, and added that "it was because they were united states, and only as they were such, that they held either class or power."

From this it followed that the state in the union possesses "sovereignty as a unit." Therefore Hurd asserted that sovereignty in the American Republic was not popular sovereignty, but that of so many millions of human beings.

Hurd described the political system in America, organised by the people of the states, as "democratic oligarchy."[2]

He believed that "the political people of the several states in union instituted the general government, under the constitution as law, to be the means for exercising their sovereignty over the people considered as a mass of inhabitants without reference to the state boundaries."[3]

From his assumption that sovereignty was based on the consent of the majority will of the holders of sovereign power, the test as to the actual seat of supreme power was one of fact, not of law.

Consequently, condemning the theoretical doctrine of state rights as "consigned to the limbo of political vanity," Hurd,

[1] John C. Hurd: *The Theory of our National Existence*, 1881, p. 102.
[2] Ibid., p. 140.
[3] Ibid., p. 141.

like Austin, insisted that the fundamental fact to be recognised was how many organised political people of the several states in the union were holders of the supreme power; for them the government of the United States was an instrument "as truly as the governments of each state are instruments for the organised political people of the states."

The actual location of sovereignty in the federal states was not based upon a purely "intrinsic connection between political doctrine or ethical problem of right or wrong and domestic institutions, but a question of fact of whether the supreme power was held by this or that group of organised political people within the federal boundary."

On this assumption he opposed that doctrine of the sovereignty of the federal union which based it on public opinion, to which Lieber and his followers adhered.

It was hardly acceptable as a political fact that, in the theoretically perfect democracy, "public opinion and that of the governing body must be one and the same thing."

In the form of representative government which was dependent for its existence on the majority will of the electors, he assumed that public opinion, when adverse to the government, would represent the demands of the majority of people in contradiction to the majority demands of the electorate.

Hurd therefore held that the main problem of federalism was that of reconciling two vital factors—the national existence on the one hand and the location of sovereignty on the other.

Firstly, as to the supreme power in the union of the states, voluntarily remaining united by organised political people of the several component states—i.e. the supremacy of the national government—he asserted that the question of loyalty to the sovereign must be "one which more than any other has divided men in their political, social and even domestic relations."

Secondly, the distribution of sovereignty was not only among political authorities—that is, among nations—but was more obviously among the subordinate organisations, such as the states and their provinces, cities, towns, communes, families.

The federal state on the basis of national sovereignty was the legal representative of the joint will of the majority of the political people of the several constituent states, and differed from the international personality of the confederation.

Though Hurd and his followers laid stress on the actual facts, rather than on the strict law or right, yet in their final judgment they arrived at the same conclusion as those other exponents, like Jameson or Burgess, who adhered to Lieber's view of federal supremacy.

§ 3

Differing from Austin's theory of sovereignty of the determinate human superiority, Jameson derived from the Germanic doctrine of sovereignty the conclusion that "sovereignty resides in the society or body politic; in the corporate unit resulting from the organisation of many into one."[1] Sovereignty, being indivisible and inalienable, acted as the agent or representative of the sovereign and constituted the civil government directly by the organic movements of political society itself, without any legal agents, as the manifestations of "public opinion."

In his mind the constitution, therefore, was twofold; there was the written constitution, which sprang up from the unwritten constitution, which sprang from the organic life of a political community.[2]

From this idea that sovereignty ultimately resided in the people of the United States, his historical survey of facts and principles naturally led him to the vexed question of American nationality.

As a political society constituted a nation, so an influence on its authority was exercised by the "locus of sovereignty."

Considering the state right theory, of which he said that Jefferson was a founder and Calhoun an apostle and expositor, as a mere heretical dogma, federalism was to him a political expedient arising from the political circumstances of 1787.

Writing in the *Political Science Quarterly* during 1890 he laid great emphasis on the conception of "national sovereignty." So that his notion of federalism was not more advanced than that of Lieber, and was influenced by the reaction of sentiment brought about by the War of Secession.[3]

Nevertheless he recognised that the state authority was interwoven with the machinery for the exercise of the fundamental rights of sovereignty, as for example the organic force of the constitution exemplified in the convention of the constitutional amendment.[4]

He concluded that as the development of the constitution had shown that the people of the United States, not simply as a

---

[1] J. A. Jameson: *Constitutional Convention*, 1876, Sec. 21.   [2] Ibid., Secs. 75–77.
[3] *National Sovereignty*, in *Political Science Quarterly*, Vol. V, June 1890.
[4] J. A. Jameson: *Constitutional Convention*, Sec. 57.

political unit, but as disseminated among the states, had a sanction of the highest authority. Whatever authority therefore a state convention might possess, "it will be used to signify the possession by such people of quasi-sovereign rights in subordination to the real sovereign, the American nation."[1]

In 1877 Theodore D. Woolsey, a disciple of Lieber, analysed the federated system of states on the basis of a juristic classification. There were several forms of union. Firstly, the league of two or more states for mutual defence, permanent or temporary, with special duties was formed by agreement, by the free will of each. This constituted an international union. The other forms of union were what the Germans called *Staatenbund* and *Bundesstaat*.[2]

In the federal union each member of the federation must be wholly independent in the exercise of those powers which concerned itself alone, but each and all must be subject to the common power of the federal government, which was concerned with the whole body of men collectively.

The settlement of these two bases of federal union was the fundamental problem of government. Woolsey assumed that "this central power or government of the federal union must, in the nature of the case, be the result of an agreement of parts with one another; but, when founded, it no longer depends on the desire of any one member to continue in the union."[3]

He thought that the main problem was whether or not the relation of such a federal government to the member states was different from the relationship between the state and the municipality. He assumed that the latter had no sense of independence, whereas the states in the union had more competence and independence in so far as their own powers were concerned. Distinguishing between *Staatenbund* and *Bundesstaat*, he laid down that the former word denoted "a league or confederation of states," while the latter meant "a state formed by means of a league or confederation."[4]

The main test of this distinction was the inquiry "whether the political body in question has the essential qualities of a state or not."

He pointed out that the rights of the *Bundesstaat*, or of a state resulting from confederation, might vary from the one extreme of parts so consolidated that they had ceased to be parts to the opposite extreme of a loose union.

[1] J. A. Jameson: *Constitutional Convention*, Sec. 62.
[2] T. Woolsey: *Political Science or The State*, Vol. II, 1886, pp. 167–169.
[3] Ibid., p. 167.   [4] Ibid. p. 169.

Also the *Staatenbund* as a league might approach very nearly in fact to a state constituted by confederation or to an alliance for a number of purposes; and sometimes might be mistaken for a mixed government.

Federal government, which constituted a state over states, was an artificial construction devised by human wisdom, "more complicated than any other kind of government," and presented particular difficulty because of the co-existence of states and of a paramount state.

He assumed that in the *Bundesstaat*—that is, a state formed out of states—"there is not one sovereignty more but there are many sovereignties less, and the supremacy is lodged in the federal union," as the constitution and the law of the United States should be "the supreme law of the land." The federal government maintained its own executive organ to carry out its own law, and interpreted and executed its own laws by its own judges.

The power to punish treason against the union was given to the federal authority. The success of the federal union was due to the fact that there existed common feeling and a common language, common law, common religion, common institutions and common notions of liberty, and especially approximately uniform systems of government among the members of the federal union.

The federal union was to Woolsey one of the most difficult and complicated forms of government, unless it possessed the above-mentioned qualities. He remarked that in the United States the constitution of 1787 created a state formed by a league, and not a mere confederacy of states, "without merging the existence of the members into that which they created."

In this respect Burgess more precisely and scientifically explained the federal organisation.

In his articles in the first volume of the *Political Science Quarterly* in 1886, Burgess definitely laid down that "sovereignty resided alone in the people of the whole nation, and a state could be legally bound in organic changes against its will."

The consequences of his notion of sovereignty were so far-reaching that he asserted the functions of the commonwealth to be mainly "jural and police functions."[1]

This jural and police relation of the federal organ to the state governments was limited to making the citizenship national, decreeing the equality of civil rights, and imposing upon the

[1] Burgess: *American Commonwealth*, in *Political Science Quarterly*, 1886, Vol. I, p. 22.

local organs "the duty of maintaining republicanism," and restricting the whole of their authority by the national law and its judicature.

The remaining rules of confederation, such as equal representation in the Senate or the rule as to amendment of the constitution as to federal functions, were "the relics of the usurpation of 1781."

Disagreeing with John Hurd and other previous thinkers, he adhered wholly to the German metaphysical theory of the state, saying that "the commonwealth really exists only in its governmental organisation, whilst a nation has a physical and ethnical existence as well as a governmental."[1]

Federal history had already established the principle that the sphere of the commonwealth government is "judicial administration more than executive administration."[2]

Not only did these tendencies manifest the decline of the state authority, but also the more recent inclination to organise constitutionally the municipalities of the commonwealth accelerated the downfall of the state rights and the state had ceased to be, in many respects, "the natural local government."

This showed itself in "the gradual dissolution of the commonwealth through the consolidation of the municipalities" and through the necessary centralisation of the national authority.

But he conceived that the history of the United States had multiplied the formation of communities from the time of colonisation down to the advance of the western frontier. The state government at the time was by nature a real local government. But since the network of communications had been established all over the continent, no one had really considered, from either the geographical or ethnological standpoint, the existence of several commonwealths side by side. Still he could not ignore the real basis of the American system, "the commonwealths and the nation"; the former are the pivots of real local self-government.

The cardinal maxim which Burgess proposed was the adjustment of these two forces in federal America. He thought that the commonwealth areas were too large for local government, and too small for general government. Whether America became a platonic state or a federal state depended on future development, but he believed that the commonwealth or state would occupy a less important place in the political system, the nation would attain a much higher place and the municipality would secure a much more distinct and independent sphere.

[1] Burgess: *American Commonwealth*, in *Political Science Quarterly*, 1886, p. 25. [2] Ibid., p. 32

He prophesied that the future cardinal principle of federalism would be that of "the nation, sole and exclusive sovereign, distributing the power and functions of government between central organs, commonwealth and municipality, defining, guaranteeing and defending the fundamental principle of the civil right—in accordance with the dictates of the nation's political and juristic policy."

Being a disciple of Bluntschli he maintained the latter's doctrine that the origin of political society was geographical and ethnological unity. From this assumption he deduced that federalism was "the more natural arrangement and the one more easy of attainment" when the populations of several states vary in their ethnical character and possess about equal political capacity.[1] Nevertheless, as he had a definite conception of the state, which was also that of Bluntschli, so the state is a "particular portion of mankind viewed as an organised unit."[2] The state ought to be "all-comprehensive," "exclusive," "permanent" and "sovereign." Starting from this general conception of the state as an unlimited sovereign unitary body, he emphasised the facts that the distinction between the state and government was of great importance, and that the government is not the sovereign organisation of the state.

As with Lieber and Woolsey, his theory of the historical genesis of the state was one of evolution, condemning the theory of the social contract as an unhistorical statement of origin, and admitting only harmony with social contract theory in respect of the later transitory stage of the developed state.

Common language and common customs, common psychology, common interests and a state consciousness were the essence of the modern national state, which was the highest product of recent political development.

As regards the forms of the state, he accepted generally the classification adopted by Bluntschli.

Bluntschli had examined several forms of the state, and finally divided them into "states having colonies or vassal provinces, states in personal union, confederated and federal unions."

The first of these were not states, but local governments with a measure of self-governing autonomy, and the second was only a governmental division. The third, confederation, was not a state entity, because it had no sovereignty in the union, which "is only government."

[1] John W. Burgess: *Political Science and Comparative Constitutional Law*, 1890, pp. 40–41.   [2] Ibid., p. 50.

Finally, with regard to the federal state Burgess was convinced that "this is no component state, there is no such thing as a federal state." He added that "what is really meant by the phrase is a dual system of government under a common sovereignty."[1]

He asserted that the so-called federal state was to be distinguished by the political facts that several states might consolidate to form a single state with a federal and dual system of government, or a single state might be constructed on the above system of administration with a vast scope of independent governmental activity within the sphere assigned by the supreme constitution. Therefore Burgess was inclined to deny any principle of federalism in the state form at all.

Nevertheless, he endeavoured to criticise the American constitution from the actual facts of history, and at the same time he acknowledged the state as the holder of a legal share of constitutional functions.

Though he did not pretend to hold a pragmatic conception, and admitted the German conception of the state, yet he derived his conception of the American system from the real facts and evidences of history, holding the dogmatic conception of the "indestructibility of the union" to be an unwarranted abstraction. But in fact his attitude towards federalism had a far more philosophical and legal basis than these propositions. His weakness on the political side was due to the fact that he was influenced more by the German idea of *Staatslehre* than by the pragmatic study of political facts.

His historical interpretation of politics was nothing more than an attempt to find a justification in facts for the legal theory of the legitimacy of the national system.

Though he was a student of German political ideas, he could not ignore the importance of the self-governing community. The only service which the American transcendental school of politics rendered was the foreseeing of the tendency of federalism, which was midway in the transition from the loose union of states to a unitary state, administratively decentralised.

§ 4

The federal idea, for nearly two decades after the close of the War of Secession up to 1888, was nothing but the theoretical

[1] John W. Burgess: *Political Science and Comparative Constitutional Law*, 1890, Part I, Book II, Chap. III, p. 79.

justification of Lincoln's dictum that "measures otherwise unconstitutional might become lawful by becoming indispensable to the preservation of the constitution through the preservation of the nation."[1]

Both John Hurd and Burgess, each from his own point of view, established the notion that sovereignty was based on the nation as a whole, not on people or states severally.

Empirically and metaphysically sovereign authority in the state was supreme, indivisible and inalienable.

As Calhoun had rejected the compromise theory of federalism because he upheld the state right theory, so they objected to the doctrine of divided sovereignty and accepted that of single and unlimited sovereignty, with the total repudiation of the theory of contract.

The theory of "organism" or of "historical evolution" had taken the place of theories of "natural right" and of "social contract."

Though an early defender of the union, like Daniel Webster, propounded the nationalist theory, he did not wholly deny the Hobbesian idea of the social contract as an indication of the way in which the union was formed.

But the nationalist theory of the seventies and the eighties of the nineteenth century was based on an entirely different conception of law and philosophy.

The conceptions of "organism" and "social evolution" were used as philosophical explanations of political society. The growth of *Staatslehre* in Germany established itself strongly from Waitz to Seydel and later from Laband to Jellinek, whose influence on America was very great.

The new nationalist theories, from Brownson to Burgess, proclaimed that sovereignty was based not upon the states, but upon the people of the United States, the nation. But none of them could repudiate the states as integral parts of federal America. Brownson and John Hurd proclaimed that the political sovereign people of the United States consisted of those of the "states united."

Even Woolsey acknowledged that the federal union of America was the state constituted by the confederation without absorbing the member states into the union.

Nevertheless, the instinctive force of social evolution so developed itself as to show that the states had no self-subsisting authority, either sovereign or semi-sovereign, but were merely organs of

[1] Lincoln: *Works*, 1894, Vol. II, p. 508.

government of the nation; the supreme sovereignty resides in the nation, not in the casual collection of people.

Therefore, the ideas of Lieber and of John Austin were the guiding principles of federal theory in America at this period, and not much advance could be made.

The outlook of political thinkers in those days had changed immensely and a new conception of organism was stimulated by Darwinian biology, and rationalistic empiricism was given a great impetus by the growth of the study of psychology. A landmark of modern philosophy was the publication of William James' *Principles of Psychology* in 1890.

At the same time the Hegelian metaphysical conception made great progress in the English-speaking countries after its introduction by T. H. Green, and was hastened by the growth of idealist revival, such as the Neo-Kantian and the Neo-Hegelian schools on the continent.

The science of physics brought about the publication of Giddings' *Dynamic Sociology* in America, and the study of psychology produced a new phase of empirical philosophy in James' pragmatism.

But before our own day the greatest contribution to the federal idea was made by James Bryce.

CHAPTER VIII

BRYCE'S THEORY OF FEDERALISM

Since the federalists and De Tocqueville there had been no such explicit and luminous exposition of American federalism as that contained in the three volumes of *The American Commonwealth* of James Bryce, published in 1888.

Nearly two decades after the War of Secession, federal solidarity had been asserted by various publicists or political thinkers and there had been established a common belief in the "indestructibility of the union."

Bryce had at his disposal a far larger amount of material than De Tocqueville was able to employ in his *Democracy in America* (published in 1835), and used it to advantage in his minute investigation of the federal system over a period of a century.

The convention of 1787 influenced American politics for nearly thirty years under the great leadership of Washington, Hamilton, Jefferson and Madison.

The tenure of the White House for the next thirty years, until the outbreak of the Civil War, was either by robust frontier politicians such as Andrew Jackson, or by honest servants of party politics.

Finally, the bombardment of Fort Sumter determined the trend of American politics towards consolidation and a belief in the necessity of the union for the common benefit of the American body politic. The victory of the North in 1864 inaugurated a new phase of federal America based on national patriotism.

Both the followers of Lieber, such as Jameson and Burgess, and those of John Hurd equally condemned the state right theory, and formulated their ideas on the basis of national sovereignty.

The hundred years' experiment of federal administration, and the rapid growth of communications throughout the vast continent, gave rise to the spirit of national solidarity and a belief in a common national existence, inspired not only by the prevalent tendency of nationalism all over the world, but also by the recognition of the need for common political action in respect of common economic and social matters.

The industrial revolution turned the United States from a rural democratic republic into a half-rural and half-urban democratic state. The Benthamite democracy which was the ideal of the fathers faced the alternative of a new democracy. Monopoly, trusts and other forms of combination in business and industrial enterprises naturally created the bourgeoisie on the one hand and the proletariat on the other. The working class was the new social force in America created by the rapid progress of plutocracy. Socialism, communism, internationalism and the humanitarian movement vis-à-vis militarism, nationalism and imperialism came into being in the last thirty years of the nineteenth century.

Bryce had been led to study these three great events in American political history by the immense development of democracy in his own England both in politics and in economics. Gladstonian liberalism and the Tory democracy of Disraeli had already established the main outlines of the present constitution of Great Britain under the principle of parliamentary representative government to which J. S. Mill adhered.

France had already passed the miserable era of political unrest after the first revolution of 1789 and established the Third Republic in 1870, and Bismarckian dictatorship had followed the formation of the German Empire. The loose confederation of Switzerland was transformed in 1848 into the new Swiss federal state, on the model of the American constitution. Italy had attained its unity by the diplomacy of Cavour and the bravery of Garibaldi. Japan had rapidly risen from a mediaeval state to a modern monarchical constitutional country. Thus the world of 1888 had witnessed the establishment of modern nationalism.

In America the pride of liberty and equality in economics as well as in politics had freely developed a great nation. The enormous natural resources and vast unoccupied lands produced and resulted in the successful enterprises of *laissez-faire* economics and a diversified development of civilisation during the rapid expansion of the country, and common language, common habits and common traditions of Anglo-American descent successfully established *laissez-faire* politics, with a national pride in increasing the stars and stripes of the flag.

Bryce wrote the *American Commonwealth* after his third visit to America and after a full and detailed investigation of both personal and official information. It is not too much to say that it was the first time that federalism in America had been thoroughly criticised and analysed. And it can be said with truth that his observations and criticisms on this subject did not arise from the standpoint of federal classification favoured by the

German legal mind, but from the point of view of objective fact. The materials which he utilised were not limited within the narrow compass of legal interpretation, but he had abundant historical materials of such a wide extent that his survey of American politics ranged from national federal government to American social institutions. A real picture of American democracy in 1888 was presented by his careful pen, just as the book of De Tocqueville had been the mirror of federal democracy for his European followers.

Bryce described the American republic as a federal state differing from a confederation, such as the German confederation from 1815 to 1866 or the permanent union of the United States from 1781 to 1787, or from the decentralised state of England or the Government of France before the political consolidation under Cardinal Richelieu.

The federal state of the American republic was itself "a commonwealth as well as a union of commonwealths."

As to all other federal thinkers, so to him the difference between the federal state and the confederation depended on the extent of federal government, either by direct control over every citizen of the constituent states or by the permanent governmental organ of the federal government, with its power of enforcing its will and of restraining the component states within their own allotted spheres.

The power of the federal government was not a delegated power of the component sovereign states, but the direct authorised representative power of the people of the states. The elaborate organ of the federal republic of 1789 was the union, which gave the independent self-governing smaller communities full play for their authority within their limited sphere, and gave the large national federal government free exercise of the powers granted by the constitution and a claim to the subordination of the smaller states within the attributes of powers which the sovereign people of the states were allowed to possess.

In his historical survey he held that the federal constitution of 1787 was "not a new thing," but was based on the government before 1787. This was constituted by the reconciliation of two outstanding interests, on the one hand admitting a deep-rooted local desire for self-government within the wide-spreading community, and on the other hand establishing efficient administration, within and without, on the ground of national work and national unity.

What James Bryce conceived as the underlying influences

on the political theory of the statesmen of 1787 were, firstly, the experience of the English constitution, which was theoretically developed at that time according to the prevalent legal conceptions by Mr. Justice Blackstone, and, secondly, the effect on their political philosophy of the treatise *L'Esprit des Lois* of Montesquieu.

They were not so much influenced by Harrington, Locke and Sydney at that time as they were in the revolutionary period, and also not so much by Burke or Rousseau as were the people of the European continent.

Bryce asserted that: "No general principle of politics laid such a hold on the constitution-makers and statesmen of America as the dogma that the separation of these three functions"—the legislative, the executive and the judicial—"is essential to freedom."[1]

The main guidance of their fathers was by the empirical idea of political philosophy which David Hume laid down in his utilitarian theory.

Bryce scrutinised the origin of the federal state not from the *a priori* theory of federation, but from the practical necessity of American politics, and the hereditary political legacy of free institutions.

He credited the framers of the federal constitution "with a double portion of the wisdom which prefers experience to *a priori* theory, and the sagacity which selects the best materials from the mass placed before it, aptly combining them to form a new structure."[2]

The immediate impulse to the formation of a perpetual union in 1781 came from the fact that the fear of foreign interference, the sense of weakness both at sea and on land against the "military monarchies of Europe," weighed on the minds of the fathers and "made them anxious to secure at all hazards a national government capable of raising an army and navy and of speaking with authority on behalf of the new republic."

The federal system was chiefly derived from the experience of American colonial and state governments, which had been tested by administration under the English prerogative or by the necessity for united action during eight years of the revolutionary period.

They were trained in these traditions, but also in the precedents and practice of the so-called English constitution, often vague and always flexible, but nevertheless a working compromise. And they had learned also how far central power might employ

[1] Bryce: *The American Commonwealth*, 1888, Vol. I, p. 36.   [2] Ibid., pp. 43-44.

direct action and to what extent local initiative could be responsible by itself.

The main guarantee of the smooth functioning of federalism was found in the fact that America had a "principle of the English common law whose importance deserves special mention," the principle of the English common law that an act by any official person or law-making body in excess of his or its legal competence is simply void.

Bryce tested the federal system thoroughly by pointing out that its main problem turned on two points; namely—how far the powers of the component states should be recognised "as independent and separate factors" in the constitution of a national government, and what kinds and amounts of those powers should be withdrawn from the states and be vested in the federal government.

The verdict of the Civil War in 1864 settled this problem in America, and by 1888 general agreement had been reached on the following principles:—

Firstly, "every state on entering the union renounced its sovereignty and was for ever subordinated to the federal authority as defined by the constitution."

Secondly, "the functions of the state as factors of the national government are satisfactory," i.e. sufficient to secure the strength and the dignity of these communities.

Lastly, the demarcation of powers between the national and state governments, determined by the constitution, "is convenient and needs no fundamental alteration."

His survey of federalism, after the general assertion of the "indestructibility of the union" as a nation, recognised a national government as a solid and permanent authority created by the rigid constitution on the one hand and self-governing local government with power of initiative on the other.

The main problem in federalism was the distribution of powers between the federal and state governments. Bryce said that this delimitation "is effected in two ways, positively by conferring certain powers on the national government, negatively by imposing certain restrictions on the states."[1]

Even lawyers thought that the restriction of powers of the national government was unnecessary and "inartistic," since *ex hypothesi* it could not exercise powers not expressly granted. However, the practical exercise of powers was so complicated that "it is not the mere existence of the national power," but its

---
[1] Bryce: *The American Commonwealth*, 1888, Vol. I, p. 417.

exercise, which is "incompatible with the exercise of the same power by the state."

Therefore Bryce classified the powers of government in the following five categories :—

(1) Powers vested in the national government alone.
(2) Powers vested in the states alone.
(3) Powers exercisable by either the national government or the states.
(4) Powers forbidden to the national government.
(5) Powers forbidden to the state governments.[1]

It was unnecessary to inquire into the first two classes of powers because they were distinctly enumerated in the federal constitution.

But the question of authority for the exercise of powers either by the national or state government, such as bankruptcy or electoral laws, must be determined neither by the Congress nor by the President nor by the state government, but by the authentic interpretation of the constitution by the federal or state courts.

Bryce mentioned that the constitution failed to indicate whether the national or state governments should determine such powers as those of establishing a particular form of religion; of endowing a particular form of religion or educational or charitable establishments connected therewith; or of extending the electoral franchise, and so forth.

These omissions from the constitutional determination of powers were chiefly due to the fact that the Convention of 1787 had no wish to secure uniformity between the states in government or institutions, and cared little about protecting the citizens against abuses of state power. It sought chiefly to secure the national government against encroachments on the part of the states, and to obviate disputes.

In the federal system the power vested in the states was "original and inherent" power which belonged to the union and might be understood as *"primâ facie* unlimited." And the powers granted to the national government were theoretically "delegated power," determined and created by the constitution of the union. As Bryce presupposed that the supreme sovereignty rested in the people of the states, so to him "the union is an artificial creation" whose government could have nothing but

[1] Bryce: *The American Commonwealth*, 1888, Vol. I, p. 418.

what the people have conferred on it by the constitution, and whose powers were positively granted.

However, like others, he asserted that the characteristic of the federal state was the direct and immediate authority of the federal government within a prescribed sphere. In this system the federal authority could be exercised by the federal officials, selected and appointed by the federal chief, the President.

Inasmuch as the direct control of federal authority from the White House at Washington extended all over the local areas, "there is no local self-government in federal matters."[1]

As the federal government was "the creation of its own inhabitants," so they framed their political organ with "the least contact and the least danger of collision."

He said that "their aim was to keep the two mechanisms as distinct and independent of each other as was compatible with the still higher need of subordinating, for the national purpose, the state to the central government."

This delicate working of the federal machine was the characteristic of the *Bundesstaat* as distinct from the *Staatenbund*.

He emphasised a further consequence of the federal principle, namely, "that the national government has but little to do with the states as states."

The tie between them proceeded from the relationship with their citizens who "are also its citizens," rather than with them as ruling commonwealths.

Whether the federal constitution maintained the two separate governments or co-ordinated the functions of both, the national government required from the state the election of representatives, presidential elections, the provision of militia and the maintenance of republican forms; and at the same time the national government was not allowed to ask for any contributions, or to issue any administrative orders to the states, or to require the states to submit their laws to it and veto such as it disapproved.

Even though the sphere of activity in each assigned function was limited by the supreme rules of the constitution, a remarkable omission from the federal constitution was the absence of any concurrent power granted to the federal government so that its authority might be used to coerce "a recalcitrant or rebellious state," and of any limitation on the right of nullification or of secession.

On this problem Bryce laid down that "there is no abstract or theoretic declaration regarding the nature of the federation

[1] Bryce: *The American Commonwealth*, 1888, Vol. I, p. 425.

and its government; nothing as to the ultimate supremacy of the central authority outside the particular sphere allotted to it, nothing as to the so-called sovereign rights of the states."[1]

He ascribed this omission to the practical genius of the statesmen of 1787, to whom experience in politics was more valuable than any "abstract inquiry and metaphysical dialetics." They conceived that the human mind is not to be restrained by mere abstract theories, but after a century's experience of federalism it had become necessary to subscribe to the doctrine of the "indestructible union of indestructible states."

The "inextricable" difficulty put before the American lawyers and publicists up till 1861 was solved by incalculable sacrifices of lives and money. It began to be admitted that "the union is not a mere compact between the commonwealths, dissoluble at pleasure, but an instrument of perpetual efficiency emanating from the whole people and alterable by them only in the manner which its own terms prescribe—"indestructible union of indestructible states."[2]

The recognition of the "indestructibility" of the union entitled the union to exercise force for its preservation. The question whether the American nation would turn federal into unitary government or not depended on how far public opinion as a whole would favour this tendency.

The characteristic feature and special interest of the American federal state was the fact that two governments with separate and independent activities existed on the same ground.

Being itself the creature of the constitution the federal system in the delicate working of its mechanism required less friction and more harmony, otherwise there was no means of correcting the defects of this machinery except by each government.

Hence the cardinal necessity of preventing collision or friction, which Bryce thought to be secured by the concurrent application of certain devices.

The first of these was the restriction of the working functions of the federal government "to the irreducible minimum of functions absolutely needed for the national welfare"; and the second was the giving to that government, in so far as those functions extended, "a direct and immediate relation to the citizens in order to render the federal authority able to act, not through the state organs, but by its own federal executives."

These two were fundamental principles of federalism, established by the sound political wisdom and experience of the

[1] Bryce: *The American Commonwealth*, 1888, Vol. I, p. 428.   [2] Ibid., p. 430.

later eighteenth century. This was the orthodox federal theory as to the relationship of the two governmental mechanisms whose principles were applied in all other countries to frame federal and quasi-federal constitutions in the following nineteenth century, such as the Swiss Constitution of 1848 and the Canadian and Australian federal governments.

The application of these principles to federal functions was sought by Bryce under two heads—firstly, the relation of the national government to the states as corporate bodies, and secondly, its relation to the states as individuals, i.e. the citizens of the union. The corporate relationships between the national and state governments he divided into three.[1]

First of all the states served to help the formation of the national government by choosing presidential electors, by choosing senators, and fixing the franchise which qualifies citizens to vote for the members of the House of Representatives, without any restriction except in respect to the fifteenth amendment, that persons could not be deprived of the right of suffrage "on account of race, colour or previous condition of servitude."[2]

Secondly, owing to the formation of the constitution the states gave up certain powers which they would otherwise enjoy. Any question of the transgression of the federal constitution either by the federal or by a state power could only be solved by the decision of the Courts of Law, firstly of the State Court and finally of the Supreme Court of Justice.[3]

Thirdly, the President as national executive and Congress as national legislature had the right of interfering with the governments of the states in certain matters.

If the constitution had granted to Congress the power to legislate on certain special matters or had forbidden the states to do so, the state statutes, even though previously valid, became invalid owing to the federal statute which was constitutionally superior to the former—for example, a unification of bankruptcy law.

Bryce said "the field of this so-called concurrent legislation is large, for congress has not yet exercised all the powers vested in it of superseding state action."[4] Such restraint was due to the presumption in favour of the states. Even though the federal legislature possessed *primâ facie* the right of prohibiting state legislation, "the appropriate legislation" could hardly be enforced, because opinion arising from habit and tradition might conflict

---
[1] Bryce: *The American Commonwealth*, 1888, Vol. I, p. 433.
[2] Ibid., p. 434.   [3] Ibid., p. 435.   [4] Ibid., p. 436.

with the legitimate authority—for example, in the case of prohibition of electoral discrimination based on race or colour.

The President as the national executive had the right and duty of giving effect to the legislation of Congress, and of exercising the discretionary power bestowed on him by the constitution of enforcing the maintenance of republican forms in every component state, and of sending federal troops to suppress transgressions of the constitution.

Nevertheless, the power to interfere in state action was confined to the preservation of peace and order in federal affairs; the punishment of crime was entirely a matter for the discretionary authority of the states.

The legitimate authority, which the federal authority could exercise, was limited to three cases. Offences against federal statutes, resistance offered to the enforcement of federal authority, attacks on property of the federal government and disturbances thereof were suppressed and punished by the federal authority. But since there was no common federal criminal code, the judgments of the federal courts pronounced in civil cases were left to the execution of the officers of those courts. Other cases of disorder and offences were entirely left to the states, who "are, however, entitled in one class to summon the power of the union to their aid."

With regard to the individual relations between the national and state governments, federalism had the remarkable feature that the people of the union were at the same time those of the states, and owed "allegiance to both powers." In the federal organisation the right of the state to the obedience of the citizens was larger and wider, and applied to every order of a competent state, whereas the national government could legislate and command only within a certain limited sphere.

Not only the legislature and the executive, but also the judicial power, were strictly confined to their respective spheres. The main test of the allegiance of citizens to each authority was to "ascertain whether the federal law is constitutional." The federal authority, either executive or judicial, was exercised by the whole machinery of the union, with its own federal officials under the command of the President and its own federal judges under the supervision of the Chief Justice of the Supreme Court, "just as the nerves act over the human body."

In the enforcement of the authority of the national government the federal official was empowered "to summon all good citizens to assist him" when he was opposed by physical force, and also if necessary to call upon the President to aid him by sending federal troops.

The delicacy of the federal functions was due to the principle of the common law by which "all citizens are bound to assist the ministers of the laws, but the deficiency of federalism revealed in this function is that it is true in one country as in the other that what is everybody's business is nobody's business."

Resistance to the federal authority was rarer in the more ordered and civilised states than in the less civilised states. But the resistance by citizens to the orders and laws of the federal government should be less difficult to deal with than that by the duly constituted authority of the state.

The problem of the right of nullification and secession, from the Kentucky and Virginia resolution down to the upheaval of the Civil War of 1861, has been definitely solved by that war.

The doctrine of federal supremacy in the union must be deemed to be that "no state has a right to declare an act of the federal government invalid," and "no state has a right to secede from the union."[1] The final decision as to the constitutionality of acts of Congress and the actions of the national executive is the majority decision of the nine judges of the Supreme Court of Justice. An unconstitutional act of the state legislature is *ipso jure* void, so citizens who disobey the federal authority are punishable by the federal power, not by the state sheriff.

The main objection to this doctrine is the absence of any provision in the constitution in regard thereto. But Bryce's answer to this was that "such a provision would have been superfluous, because a state cannot legally act against the constitution," and "all that is needed is the power, unquestionably contained in the constitution [Article III, Sec. 3], to subdue and punish individuals guilty of treason against the union."[2]

The sphere of activity of the national government was kept to a minimum and left to the state the largest activity possible. Therefore in the federal system there was to be no interference with the state activities outside that provided for by the constitution, which kept steadily in view as the wisest policy local government for local affairs and general government for general affairs only. As Bryce accepted *laissez-aller* as a necessary principle of federalism, so he recognised that "reason and experience" were important in determining its real functions. He was convinced that "no doctrine more completely pervades the American

---

[1] Bryce: *The American Commonwealth*, 1888, Vol. I, p. 447.
[2] Ibid., pp. 448–449.

people, the instructed as well as the uninstructed."[1] Philosophically the efficacy of federalism could be tested by comparison with the ruling of natural or divine order.

To Bryce federalism was the method of *laissez-aller* in politics and the theory of *laissez-faire* in economics. The defects of these methods were naturally elaborated as well as their merits. Examining the question of how far the federal system and its organisation affected political ideas, Bryce classified its demerits as compared with unified government as follows:

1. Weakness in the conduct of foreign affairs.
2. Weakness in home government, i.e. deficient authority over the component states and the individual citizens.
3. Liability to dissolution by the secession or rebellion of the states.
4. Liability to divisions into groups and factions by the formation of separate combinations of the component states.
5. Want of uniformity among the states in legislation and administration.
6. Trouble, expense and delay due to the complexity of a double system of legislation and administration.

The first two were inevitable and undeniable weaknesses of federation, but as regards the third the claim of right of secession had already been rejected. The victory to the union in the Civil War had established the doctrine of the legal indestructibility of the union.

The fourth and fifth defects were necessary evils of federation, but at the same time consequential on the merit of decentralisation. The last defect was due to the organisation of the federal state, and was deemed to be an inevitable defect.

Bryce formulated the merits of the federal system as follows:

Firstly, federalism provided "the means of uniting commonwealths into one nation under one national government without extinguishing their separate administrations, legislatures and local patriotisms."[2] Federalism alone could furnish a unique system of co-ordination of the centripetal and centrifugal forces which sprang out of "the local position, the history, the sentiments and the economic needs of those among whom the problem arises." As Bryce said: "That which is good for one people or political body is not necessarily good for another. Federalism is

[1] Bryce: *The American Commonwealth*, 1888, Vol. I, p. 452.   [2] Ibid., p. 464.

an equally legitimate resource, whether it is adopted for the sake of tightening or for the sake of loosening a pre-existing bond."

Secondly, federalism supplied "the best means of developing a new and vast country."[1]

The newly developed areas required special laws and orders differing from those of the long-established parts of the country, and he also mentioned that "the spirit of self-reliance among those who build up these new communities is stimulated and respected."

Thirdly, the federal system had the peculiar merit that it prevented the rise of a despotic central government, absorbing other powers and menacing the private liberties of the citizens.[2]

Lastly, federalism itself was furnished with an incalculable source of self-government experience in the local governments.

These local self-governments maintained the interest of people in their local political affairs and gave the opportunity of educating the citizens in their daily round of civic duties, and enabled them to understand the value of the public services which served the highest political aim of promoting harmony between individual liberty and collective prosperity.

Not only this, but the spirit of self-government could secure "the good administration of local affairs by giving the inhabitants of each locality due means of overseeing the conduct of their business."

These benefits of local self-government were not confined only to the federal system, but existed also in unified countries, but what this self-governing system especially evoked was due to the fact that "the more power is given to the units which compose the nation, be they large or small, and the less to the nation as a whole and to its central authority, so much the fuller will be the liberties and so much greater the energy of the individuals who compose the people."[3]

This was the axiom of self-government which Bryce found in "American democracy," and it was a principle of federal advantage—of centralisation and localisation of power—established as a matter of historical experience and general expediency.

The further merit of federalism was that it enabled people to try experiments in legislation and administration within a certain area of the country under the state power without risk to the whole state; such an experimental administration could not be tried in a large centralised country.

---

[1] Bryce: *The American Commonwealth*, 1888, Vol. I, p. 465.
[2] Ibid., p. 466. [3] Ibid., p. 467.

Federalism had the further advantage that, if it diminished the collective force of a nation, it diminished also the risk to which its size and the diversities of its parts expose it. Not only political, but also social and economic, maladministration could stop at the state frontier without spreading over the country and becoming an evil prevalent throughout the nation.

The final advantage was that it relieved the national legislature of a large burden of legislation and enabled it to legislate deliberately and efficiently as the national council of the whole country.

These merits of federalism were deduced from the American experiments in which Europeans "are startled by the audacity with which Americans applied the doctrine of *laissez-faire*: Americans declare that their method is not only the most consistent but in the end the most curative."

Better control of taxation, better oversight of public works, better political education of the people, better experiment in legislation and administration were the counterpoises to the dangers of the limitations of the central government which are "the quality of federalism's defects."

Bryce asserted that the main problem "which all federalised nations have to solve is how to secure an efficient central government and preserve national unity while allowing free scope for the diversities, and free place to the authorities, of the members of the federation."[1] He added that "the characteristic merit of the American Constitution lies in the method by which it has solved this problem." The direct authority of the federal government over all citizens and the wide scope of the day-to-day political powers of the states' governments maintained that equilibrium of the centripetal and centrifugal forces which was necessary to preserve the love of local independence and self-government, to encourage the sense of community, and to develop a strong national pride out of the free and conscientious devotion of the whole society.

The strength of American federalism lay not only in the nature of its political machinery, but also in the temper and circumstances of the people, especially in the legal habits impressed on the mind of the nation.

The elaborate fabric of the union was preserved not only by the suitability of the federal device, but also by legitimate patriotism and self-reliance.

He ascribed the growing tendency towards a strong national

[1] Bryce: *The American Commonwealth*, 1888, Vol. I, p. 472.

government chiefly "to sentimental forces that were weak a century ago, and to a development of internal communications which was then undreamt of." Like De Tocqueville, he concluded that "the devices which we admire in the constitution might prove unworkable among a people less patriotic and self-reliant, less law-loving and law-abiding than are the English of America."[1]

His survey of American federalism did not add much to De Tocqueville's general observations, but the main basis of Bryce's judgment on federalism was his thorough study of American political life in the eighties of the last century, and the examination of the value of territorial federalism from the standpoint of English democracy. His impartial criticism of the merits and demerits of federalism was not only a noteworthy contribution to the federal system, but was also of great service in resolving the problem of self-government between central and local government.

[1] Bryce: *The American Commonwealth*, 1888, Vol. I, p. 474.

CHAPTER IX

DEVELOPMENT OF AMERICAN FEDERAL IDEAS FROM THE BEGINNING OF THE TWENTIETH CENTURY TO THE PRESENT DAY

§ 1

Since federalism after the Civil War had revealed itself in the general acceptance of the superiority of the union, the vital problem of federalism played a less important part in American political discussion. The general acknowledgment of the "indestructibility of the union" removed the theories of nullification and of secession from the field of debate. The dominant political theory of social contract, on which the early federal idea was based, was entirely replaced by the evolutionary theory, which was based on the interpretation of history. The idea of dual sovereignty and the theory of compromise, which had been the main subject of argument, was totally destroyed and was replaced by a new nationalist theory of the union, derived from either the abstract theory of organism or the legal doctrine of sovereignty, which were both founded on *a priori* and empirical philosophies. As there had been no outstanding theoretical defenders of the state right theory since John Calhoun, so there were no advocates of the union more distinguished than Francis Lieber and John Hurd.

But the federal system was the main characteristic of the American Constitution and not only sprang from the theoretical justification of 1787, but was in the main the natural outcome of political circumstances and of social and economic forces. Therefore, as long as the constitution of 1787 remained the supreme law of the land in America, no discussion of political doctrines could ignore the nature and function of federalism.

Nevertheless, the conditions of America in 1890 presented an economic and social state entirely different from that of 1787. At the same time the new outlook of the science of politics had resulted from the long experiences of the modern state. Popular government in the form of American federalism had a century's experience, and the novelty of federal functions in 1787 now furnished an old-established example which various other countries had already copied.

In Germany the compromise theory of federalism had been introduced by Waitz in consequence of the elaborate picture of American democracy painted by De Tocqueville, but the forcible contribution of Calhoun's state right theory greatly influenced the German federal theory advocated by Seydel; and Gerber's and Haenel's *Herrschaft* theory laid the foundation of juristic personality to the federal state idea.

The elaborate idea of *Kompetenz-Kompetenz* was set up by that school of jurists and became the prevailing theoretical justification of separation of powers under the notion of the absolute indivisible conception of sovereignty. Their theories had already been criticised by Laband, who set up the idea of "non-sovereign state" and theory of "own right."

The theory of "own right" was presented in the elaborately developed argument of Jellinek. The new phase of German doctrine started by Gierke's *Genossenschaft* theory was introduced. Brie set up an elaborate basis of the doctrine of the "all-sidedness" of the state.

Whatever legal character the German doctrine might have had, the theoretical justification of the actual federation undoubtedly influenced the American legal and political thinkers.

Not only the federal conception in Germany, but also German political philosophy, was affected by some American political thinkers, such as Woolsey and Burgess, whose doctrines were more extreme and transcendental than those of the later famous German political thinkers, such as Jellinek and Brie.

Along with these German influences the school of utilitarian politics gradually developed, not only in the sphere of politics but also in federal discussion.

John Hurd's idea of federalism did not differ from that of John Austin, but nevertheless this school of thought could not be overridden by German schools in American politics. At the same time the study of administration became an important necessity in modern government, whose business increased in volume and complexity year by year. The great landmark of political science was the publication of Walter Bagehot's *English Constitution* in 1867.

A graphic picture of English politics was drawn by him, and a background of reality, strangely contrasting with the propositions of John Stuart Mill's *Representative Government*, was clearly depicted.

Since the Civil War the defenders of the union were nearly all advocates of the supremacy of the union, starting from the point of view of the national sovereignty and from the absolute doctrine of John Austin.

The 14th Amendment of the constitution gave great authority to the federal government by establishing equal rights for the whole people, with entire disregard of colour and race and, by implication, asserting the solidarity of the nation.

The problem of 1887 was not the problem of 1787. The democracy of 1887 had less economic equality than in 1787, but more political equality. America had already developed into a nation. The west frontier had extended to the Pacific coast in 1890, and the great rapidity of industrial development, from mining and railways to textile and manufacturing industries, made great changes in the national life of America.

The units of political life in rural politics in 1787 had gradually changed into units of urban politics in 1887. The United States were not only an agricultural country, but also a great industrial and commercial nation.

City politics and municipal undertakings were the natural outcome of urbanism. The enormous increase in the population was absorbed by the rapid growth and expansion of the country and the development of industry and commerce. The problem of socialism introduced by liberal politicians was contested by the old doctrine of conservatism. The victory of competition resulted in the establishment of great capitalist combinations and trusts.

Industrialism naturally brought about extreme economic inequality instead of that economic liberty at which the American fathers aimed in 1787; and the political democracy of the eighteenth century had changed to industrial democracy by 1887.

The political development of President Roosevelt in the first four years of his Presidency indicated the very pronounced advance of American imperialism and the growth of capitalist enterprise.

The organisation of commerce, facilitated by transport and communication, extended its scope and activity not only in inter-state relations, but also in international relations.

In these circumstances political theory was affected not only by the general change in political ideas, but also by the actual needs of social progress.

The Darwinian theory of the survival of the fittest was generally acknowledged as the competitive doctrine of economics.

Accordingly, Lord Hugh Cecil's *Conservatism* was the gospel of American statesmen and leading trade magnates in those days.

Ever since the Civil War had brought about the general understanding of the union and set up the idea of an American nation, industrialism had naturally influenced the political ideas of the day, and the financial or business magnates did not desire a really strong government, but neither did they want one that was too corrupt or too weak to be able to be used as their agent when required. Therefore, the federal problem was not at this time of great importance for contemporary politicians and business men.

Their demand was not for the protection of their interests against attack either from the working class or from the government. The complete *laissez-faire* doctrine prevailed in economics, but the *laissez-aller* was repudiated in politics by state intervention in the life of the individual.

It is not too much to say that the main issue in the politics of the last twenty years of the nineteenth century and at the beginning of the twentieth century was not the federal problem as a whole, but the problem of dealing with economic liberty conceived as *laissez-faire* in the federal sphere under the new regime of social and industrial organisation.

The great issue in the building up of industrial democracy in the fully developed capitalistic state was the creation of liberal democracy on the basis of socialistic propositions, which were the main force in American politics even though the violent doctrines of communism and anarchism were propounded in vain in those days.

The most prominent statesmen of the time, Roosevelt and Wilson, always adhered to liberal democracy against a strong conservative movement.

Not only this industrial development, but also material social changes resulted from the enormous increase of immigration after the Civil War. The variety of racial types ranged from Nordic to Latin, and from Negro to Chinese, and produced the problem of American "fundamentalism" for Anglo-Americans.

The menace to the American community was the prevailing alien influence, and the maintenance of alien customs and traditions presented a new problem of political life.

After 1914, and especially in recent years, public attention has been brought to bear on these issues.

However apparently remote these questions may be from federalism, their solution can proceed only from a pluralistic idea, and not from the monistic illusion of unitarism, and should depend for its character and method upon the federal idea.

The problem of federalism, therefore, is not merely a subsidiary problem of American political machinery; it has become a basic problem of American life.

Federalism became a more important principle in the distribution of governmental powers, in order to adjust political functions to the newly established industrial scheme. Accordingly, federalism was of paramount significance, with regard to determining the functions of the federal government under the constitution and also in affecting the administrative action of governments whose powers were granted and limited by the constitution.

Therefore, the federal problem after 1887 was not the problem of the sovereignty of the union of the component states, but was the allocation of those powers in order to carry on the state successfully as an American nation.

Consequently, the problem now concerns not only political theory, but the principles of public administration.

In view of this line of development, the great need in American politics was undoubtedly for a fresh study of public administration in the federal union, and this was of equal importance and necessity in the municipalities, the states and the national government in their respective spheres.

Therefore, we can divide the federal ideas after 1880 to the present day into a new political and administrative federal doctrine, and the judicial interpretation of federalism.

The legal justification of federalism was not altogether foreign to contemporary political ideas, and the two always coincided with each other in their general view of politics.

However independent and superior the judicial tribunal might be, according to the spirit of the federal constitution, the appointment of the judges by the President with the sanction of the Senate reflected the historical development, in that the judicial interpretation of federalism wavered between the nationalistic doctrine on the one hand and the state right theory on the other, in so far as the judgments were coincident with the general opinion of the time.

Since the appointment of Chief Justice Taney in 1835, judicial bias in favour of the Southern democrats, accompanied with the 10th Amendment as to the reserved rights of the states, had culminated in the decision in the Dred Scott case, and in the Merryman case in 1861. The downfall of Taney's influence was indicated by the concurrent transfer of political powers from the Southern slave-holding interests to the Northern industrial and financial interests.

The three vacant seats in the Supreme Court of the United

States gave an opportunity to the Lincoln party to change the judicial attitude towards the constitution, and after the appointment of the three new judges in 1862 the famous Prize cases decisively justified Lincoln's governmental blockade and the armed suppression of rebellion.

The appointment of Chief Justice Chase on December 6, 1864, gave a stronger turn of legal opinion towards the federal idea, in conjunction with successive amendments of the constitution, especially the 13th, 14th and 15th Amendments, and the numerous acts and regulations of the Congress against social injustice.

The first admission of a negro lawyer, John S. Rock, of Massachusetts, to practise before the bar of the court, six weeks after Chief Justice Chase came into office in 1865, was judicial recognition of the 14th Amendment.

A sincere nationalist and patriot, Chief Justice Chase, in his first six years gave the decisions of the Court a nationalistic trend, sustaining the powers of the federal government to the fullest extent. In the Bank Tax cases in 1865 the long struggling National Bank system was judicially accepted as constitutional.

The series of decisions on the constitution, especially the settlement of disputes regarding the validity of the statutes of the Southern confederated states, was in accord with the nationalist doctrine of federalism.

The Supreme Court, after the death of Lincoln, faced a new antagonism on the part of the radical republicans in the famous Milligan case in 1866, and the legal question of the validity of the Reconstruction law in 1867.

In the first case, "the laws are no longer silenced by clash of arms" was asserted in opposition to the executive authority and supported the current popular desire to uphold civil liberty and congressional supremacy against military government in the South.

In the second, the great reconstruction law was endorsed by the legal tender case, in which it was indicated that economic interests were likely to be a dominant consideration in judicial decisions.

But no decisions of the Supreme Court, however impartial and indifferent they might be between the extreme claims of the two contesting political interests, could have been generalised without the concurrence of the dominant opinion of the time.

The extreme nationalist doctrine engendered by the war was mitigated by successive decisions of the Supreme Court of Justice after the Milligan case.

The new democracy, to check the economic usurpation of the large capitalist monopolies, put forward a series of social enactments, such as the Sherman Anti-Trust law of 1890 and Clayton law in 1914, and in case after case the judgments of the Supreme Court were in favour of the democratic liberalism of Roosevelt and Wilson.

In the judicial decisions the general tendency of federalism coincided completely with the nationalist doctrine. In the legal interpretation of federalism from the Civil War up to the present no judicial sanction of the federal supremacy was more precisely and explicitly expressed than by Chief Justice Chase's decision in the case of Texas *versus* White. He laid down that "the union of the states never was a purely artificial and arbitrary relation ... It received definite form and character and sanction by the Articles of Confederation. By these the union was solemnly declared to be 'perpetual.' And where these articles were found to be inadequate to the exigencies of the country, the constitution was ordained 'to form a more perfect union.' It is difficult to convey the idea of indissoluble unity more clearly than by these words. What can be indissoluble if a perpetual union, made more perfect, is not? But the perpetuity and indissolubility of the union by no means implies the loss of distinct and individual existence, or of the right of self-government by the states. ... It may be not unreasonably said that the preservation of the states and the maintenance of their governments are as much within the design and care of the constitution as the preservation of the union and the maintenance of the national government."

"The constitution, in all its provisions, looks to an indestructible union composed of indestructible states. When, therefore, Texas became one of the United States she entered into an indissoluble relation. ... There was no place for reconsideration or revocation except through revolution or through consent of the states. Considered, therefore, as a transaction under the constitution, the ordinance of secession adopted by the Convention, and ratified by a majority of the citizens of Texas, was absolutely null and utterly without operation in law. The obligations of the state as a member of the union, and of every citizen of the state as a citizen of the United States, remained perfect and unimpaired."

The doctrine of the "indestructible union of indestructible states" was the outstanding judicial decision of federal America asserted by the Supreme Court of Justice, to which all the rest of the numerous decisions were merely supplemental. The political federal doctrines were judicially justified by the series of decisions of the Supreme Court from time to time, but *de facto* federalism in America superseded *de jure* federalism in practice.

§ 2

Now we will return to the political ideas of federalism after 1887.

A graphic picture of American politics was presented in the *Congressional Government* of Woodrow Wilson, published in 1885.

To show the living reality of American politics as contrasted with the paper description was Wilson's real aim in trying to give a complete critical account of the federal constitutional government of the United States. He asserted that "the noble charter of fundamental law given us by the convention of 1787 is still our constitution; but it is now our form of government rather in name than in reality, the form of the constitution being one of nicely adjusted, ideal balances, whilst the actual form of our present government is simply a scheme of congressional supremacy."[1]

Apart from the balance of tripartite governmental powers, he believed that nothing was so quintessential as the balance between national and state governments. In the course of the history of federal encroachments upon the states as well as state encroachments upon federal powers, the federal authority was "in most cases the only, and in all cases the final, judge."

He concluded that "in short, one of the privileges which the states have resigned into the hands of federal government is the all-inclusive privilege of determining what they themselves can do."

On the doctrinal side of the federal system the powers reserved to the states and state prerogatives were much emphasised, whereas the effect of the federal court system was that in actual fact the sense of federal power as a power of powers, and of federal authority as it were over the very habits of society, was carried into every community of the land either through governmental federal officers or by federal officers in direct contact with the people.

The vivid sense of subordination to the powers at Washington resulted not only from the victory of the union party, but from the actual federal predominance in administration in the course of the development of internal improvements.

He said that "it was imperatively necessary; the union of the

[1] Woodrow Wilson: *Congressional Government*, p. 6.

form and of law had become a union of sentiment, and was destined to be a union of institutions."[1]

Hamilton's ideal of national unity and community had been already fostered by the development of intercommunication. Whatever amount of state independence remained in the blood of the federal body politic, the maturity and the growth of that body had already built up a strong conception of federal supremacy for the benefit and advantage of every citizen of the nation as a whole.

In describing the judicial recognition of federal supremacy, he asserted in *The State* that the national government in the United States "is the organic frame of the states."[2]

He recognised that the federal constitution of 1787 was, as a result of the weakness of the confederation, absolutely necessary in order to create a better union for the maintenance of peace and goodwill within and without.

In the course of the struggle for supremacy between the federal and state governments, the Civil War brought about a change of the most profound character in the federal state.

The full acknowledgment of the vital importance of federal life, as a national life, brought about a new understanding of the relationship between national and state governments which were not "dual governments" but a "double government" upon which the present integration of its state and federal parts depended. Wilson said, "the government with us has ceased to be plural and has become singular, the government of the United States."

The balance of power between the state and the federal governments was not only adjusted under the public law and operated effectually and harmoniously in the sphere of allotted powers but also fitted into "each other with perfect harmony of co-operation, wherever their jurisdictions cross or are parallel, acting as parts of one and the same frame of government, with an uncontested subordination of functions and an undoubted common aim."[3]

As he did not criticise from a doctrinaire standpoint, but from a survey of actual political conditions, he asserted that the relationship between the federal and state governments was derived not from the administrative divisions, as we have seen that between central and local government to be, but from "the constituent members of the union, co-ordinate with the union in their powers, in no sense subject to it in their appropriate spheres."[4]

[1] Woodrow Wilson: *Congressional Government*, p. 32.
[2] Ibid., *The State*, p. 297.   [3] Ibid.   [4] Ibid., p. 298.

The principle of self-government, or self-direction, in the federal constitution in each appropriate sphere was the characteristic feature of federalism in America.

Wilson held that the member states of the federal union as such possessed the rights of a state "even though self-determination, with respect to their law as a whole, has been lost by the member states." No matter what power of their own they had, they could not determine it or extend it without appeal to the federal authority; yet the members of the union were "still states," because their powers were "original and inherent, not derivative; because these political rights are not also legal duties; and because they can apply to their commands the full imperative sanction of law."[1]

In the juristic interpretation, he asserted that "their sphere is limited by the presiding and sovereign powers of a state superordinated to them, the extent of whose authority is determined under constitutional forms and guarantees by itself."[2]

In this assumption federalism was a unique political structure whose form of *Bundesstaat* differed from the unitary decentralised state to which his contemporaries Burgess or Willoughby endeavoured to assign it. He recognised fully that the federal constitutional system of the United States was based not upon theory but upon fact. As the fact of constitutional government was based upon organised opinion and a common consciousness of the interests of the community, so after the colonial period of Great Britain federalism, expressed in and developed from the constitution of 1787, had created a strong sense of community of interest, which resulted in unity among themselves and the formation of a national character.

Wilson observed that it was no political accident that the state had survived the union of 1787. The common aim of the leading politicians in 1787 in formulating the federal constitution was to secure a strong and consolidated central government for the national welfare in face of the jealousy of local interests.

In the twentieth century the predominance of economic over political and social life was so marked that Wilson could hardly escape from the economic interpretation of federal organisation, as he recognised the vital social economic differences existing between the states.

The great synthesis of the long-delayed problems of the federal state made by the Civil War was accompanied by economic

[1] Woodrow Wilson: *An Old Master and Other Essays*, pp. 94, 95.
[2] Ibid.

and social development, and created that vital unity of American politics—that federal supremacy—from which Wilson called a nation into being.

The change of federal conception, he believed, was not due to political, but mainly to psychological, differentiation, i.e. "the spirit of our action rather than of its method."[1]

Therefore the principle, upon which the federal state had been based, did not require any reconstruction for the making of the new America, but only the detailed and legitimate alteration of the constitutional understandings as to the sphere of national government.

As he recognised the difference of economic interests between the different sections and the continuous growth of territories along the western frontier up to 1890, so he pointed out that the federal system in America was a great contribution towards the adjustment of local circumstances and the national diversity between regions and regions and even states and states.

The vitality of variety on the one hand and the unity of sentiments on the other were the basis of the American political system. Therefore he conceived that the United States "is a country not merely constitutionally governed, but also self-governed."[2]

Self-government was a charter of federalism, but at the same time was not merely a form of institution but also a form of character. Is the idea of self-government really a constituent part of federalism? If so, federalism can only survive in a community where the sense of self-government can be attained.

Though most of Wilson's writings dealt with the constitutional functions of the modern state, he did not discuss any form of federalism in particular. Did his omission of any criticism of federalism weaken his views?

The reason why such a great American statesman and political scientist did not argue the problem of federalism, was not because he neglected its importance, but because it had generally been settled by the federal experiences of the last hundred years.

The criticism of the political mechanism of federation had already been exhausted by previous publicists and jurists; but the vital problem of federalism in our day is not merely its mechanical system or the seat of the sovereign power, but the technique of federal administration in adapting and readjusting

[1] Woodrow Wilson: *Constitutional Government in the United States*, p. 50.
[2] Ibid., p. 51.

the principle of federalism to the new structure of the fully developed and highly complicated community.

The expansion of the western frontier of the United States ended in 1890 and then their ambition turned to imperial development, in the South and on the Pacific.

The pulse of the nation was counted by the Washington government through the well-arranged nerve system of federal officialdom.

The recognition of the evolution of a great American nation was established among the people of the several states, and the vital point of federal disunion was one quite distinct from the question of sovereignty.

Wilson, however, realised the importance of the relationship between the national and state governments, which was a cardinal question of the American constitution.

He regarded this relationship between the powers granted to Congress and those reserved to the state governments as the vital problem in view of the economic and political development of the United States. Approached not as a theoretical question of federal distribution of powers, but as a practical question, the principle to be adopted must be based on the actual circumstances of national life; in other words, the determination of whether a particular matter should be included in the federal or state powers must be reached by an adequate analysis of the life of the nation. The principle to be applied in the distribution of powers in the federal system was, therefore, that of the search for impartial truth in order to ensure adequate division between two co-ordinate governments, in the ceaseless current of human activities. This was the spirit by which the founders of the government were inspired.

The tests for the determination of the scope and character of distributed powers in the federal system were not so simple as to be formulated in general terms; but the guidance and direction of practical politics were to be decided not solely by the political considerations with which the Fathers of 1787 were chiefly concerned, but also by the conditions of national life resulting from economic evolution, this being more important in our eyes than any political theory or lawyers' discrimination of functions.

In formulating a right constitutional understanding, based on practical facts, the vital importance of the federal scheme required the most carefully deliberate wisdom and experience.

Supposing that the unified regulation of political or economic conditions was harmful in such vast territories and among such various peoples as existed in the United States, this unsatisfactory position was not due to the fact of the distribution of powers in the federal system, but to a failure in the adequate functioning of state government. The provision of efficient and sensible federal organisation was not a mere question of the mechanism of distribution of power but depended upon the solution of a deeper political problem.

The recent repudiation of representative government in the states, and the false conception of democracy involved in the initiative and referendum, showed the real basis of constitutional government.

Returning to representative government and self-government in the states, the political and economic growth of the country should be directed not only by formal amendment of the constitution but also and chiefly by the instrumentality of the judicial interpretation of the courts, whose decisions might mean the adaptation of the constitution to changes in material conditions.

As Wilson preferred conservative progress to radical and revolutionary change, he recommended that this progressive modification and transference between federal and state governments should take into account the actual and substantial development of interests, and of that national consciousness which required the amendment of powers.

Even though he recognised that the trend of economic forces was in favour of the transference of power from the states to the federal government, no paternal action, at the judgment and choice of the central authority, could bring about vital changes in habits and methods unless sustained by local opinion and aims or local convenience. Wilson was convinced that local interests and conveniences with their harmonious co-operation would constitute a nation, capable of vital action and control, either by the reform of state government or by an adequate transfer of the power of social control from the state to federal governments.

He concluded that "the object of our federal system is to bring the understandings of constitutional government home to the people of every part of the nation, to make them part of their consciousness as they go about their daily tasks."[1]

[1] Woodrow Wilson: *Constitutional Government in the United States*, p. 197.

§ 3

The shift of political theory from the Newtonian theory of the universe to the Darwinian theory of evolution brought about an absolute repudiation of the federal principle, as based upon the theory of social contract; and instead of the dynamic mechanism of political instruments the living reality of political functions, in relation to evolutional development, and co-ordinated with other social and economic material facts, became of vital importance.

The sociological survey of politics, either in metaphysical or empirical political philosophy, replaced obsolete political metaphors.

Federalism in this way was tested and analysed not merely by political principles but by the administrative efficiency with which the most complicated schemes of governments were put into concrete application.

Wilson's first contribution to the *Study of Administration*, in the second volume of the *Political Science Quarterly*, was the first adumbration of the importance of the study of administration.

He emphasised that in the science of administration there must come first, instead of the "closest doctrine," the comparative study of political organisations throughout the world, as he said that "the cosmopolitan what-to-do must always be commanded by American how-to-do-it." He was convinced that the duty of America is "to supply the best possible life to a federal organisation, to systems within systems; to make town, city, county, state and federal government live with a like strength and equally assured healthfulness, keeping each unquestionably its own master and yet making all interdependent and co-operative, combining independence with mutual helpfulness."[1]

He was convinced that the federal state was a national state with an interdependent relationship of political organs, federal and state, in which, without the states losing their character, the federal self-government was superordinated to states' self-government.

Federalism in that sense, apart from the arguments as to the legal conception of sovereignty, is more or less the outstanding modern conception up to the present time.

Lowell, on the contrary, attacked Austin's conception of

[1] Woodrow Wilson: "Study of Administration," in *Political Science Quarterly*, June 1887.

sovereignty which was the dominant legal conception among English-speaking people, taking the place of Bentham's final test of democratic supremacy of legislation.[1]

John Hurd's followers had set up Austin's conception of unlimited sovereignty which had a predominant influence in the determination of the sovereignty of the union. Though Lowell recognised that this doctrine "was of real importance," was not a mere matter of intellectual speculation and was based upon the fundamental notions of the existing political system, yet he condemned the conception that every nation must have "one and only one sovereign and every sovereign together with its subjects must constitute a nation."

If this conception was justifiable, it naturally brought about the acceptance of either the extreme nationalist theory, or of the state right theory, in federal discussions. He argued that there was a possibility of the existence of two sovereign authorities within the same territory, issuing commands to the same people touching different matters.[2]

The attributes of sovereignty within a prescribed territory were distributed among several communities, the same people having independent competence in each case; that is, the dual sovereignty of the federal system.

Therefore, as the notion of national sovereignty was to be based upon a mere hypothesis, so it was in fact conceivable that the limit of sovereign power might be fixed by means of a kind of declaration which enabled members of the society to distinguish between those commands and others and by which the competence of the sovereign was defined in each limited respect and limited sphere.

He was the only man during the last quarter of the century whose arguments as to sovereignty reverted to the federal ideas of Madison.

Contrary to Wilson and Lowell, Willoughby first advocated in America the juristic analysis of the character of the union, and applied the elaborate classification of German *Staatslehre*.

As he called himself a follower of T. H. Green, his fundamental theory of political philosophy could be described as a "theory of proportion," designated by Hobhouse as the "theory of harmony." Consequently, he tried to base his characteristic study of law and politics on the English idealistic conception, but borrowing the methods of German *Staatslehre*, and adapting

[1] Lawrence Lowell: "The Limits of Sovereignty," in the *Harvard Law Review*, 1888–1889, Vol. II.   [2] Ibid.

the means of the English analytical jurisprudence. Therefore he adopted the scientific method of federal classification, copying that of Jellinek, and at the same time being a defender of John Austin, on the juristic side, and an advocate also of T. H. Green's political ideas. His discussion of the union did not have so much influence as that of his contemporaries, though it differed from them only in his application of the juristic methods of scientific classification.

He classified the forms of union into "unorganised unions," and "organised unions," following the example of Jellinek.[1]

As regards the former class, Willoughby,[2] in opposition to Jellinek's opinion, argued that such a loose form of union as an alliance or the relationship between the United States and some Indian tribes was a close relation of sovereign states which were morally and legally bound by international treaties. Such a contractual relationship as an alliance could hardly be designated as a union of a legal character; it was a mere treaty relationship.

In the latter class—"organised unions"—Jellinek included the following categories:

(1) The International Administrative Union.
(2) The Real Union and Personal Union.
(3) The Confederacy (*Staatenbund*).
(4) The Federal State (*Bundesstaat*).[3]

Of these the two last categories—*Staatenbund* and *Bundesstaat*—provided the essential framework for true unions.

Although many various definitions of these two unions had been put forward by various publicists and jurists at different times, Willoughby assumed that it was still necessary to have a proper analysis of the problem of a purely juristic kind.

This attitude, however, is entirely a German characteristic. Although Willoughby employed these scientific juristic methods to analyse the nature of the distinct forms of the unions, these *a priori criteria* could hardly be applied to the American federal state. What Willoughby wanted to put into definite premises was that, firstly, "sovereignty signifies the legal competence of the state to determine its own legal right and duty as well as that of all persons natural and artificial": secondly, sovereignty, thus denoting the legal omnipotent will of the states, is indivisible and

---

[1] For this see Vol. I, Part III, Chap. III, pp. 477–487, 487–524.
[2] W. W. Willoughby: *The Nature of the State*, p. 234; *The Fundamental Concepts of Public Law*, p. 184.   [3] Cf. Vol. I, Part III, Chap. III, pp. 487–524.

inalienable: thirdly, two or more states each possessing this sovereignty and legal omnipotence cannot enter into relations with one another which are of a strictly legal character: and, lastly, therefore, a sovereign state cannot be created through a joint action of two or more previously existing sovereign states.[1]

According to this criterion, sovereignty could not be produced by a treaty relationship and, at the same time, no states could be called sovereign states when they had joined with one another to form a union. Therefore, with regard to a state with legal personality there can be no question as to whether it possessed absolute sovereign power or not.

Willoughby, therefore, made a distinction between *Staatenbund* and *Bundesstaat*, that in the former "these federated units are severally sovereign, in which case the central body is wholly without this attribute," and in the latter a "so-called central federal body possesses the sovereignty in which case the federated units are wholly without sovereignty."[2]

In these circumstances, the members of the union retaining full sovereignty and legal independence and there being, strictly speaking, no central state organization, the central government was nothing more than the common and complex organ uniting several sovereign states and established and maintained for carrying out certain purposes in accordance with the authority delegated by each state. In this treaty relationship, therefore, the right of nullification or secession might be justified, and would be the final test of the confederation.

In this category were included historical unions such as the old German unions from 1815 to 1866, the Swiss confederation under the pact of 1815 and the American confederation from 1781 to 1787.

The federal state, on the other hand, involved the existence of a true central sovereign state, composed of constituent members whose legal rights were not themselves sovereign.

Therefore from a juristic point of view the central government of the federal state was to be conceived as the organ of a true centralised state, not as a common organ within which the members—the states of the union—had certain independent authority. In other words the central authority of the federal state exercised its own will through its own power without any interference from the states.

[1] W. W. Willoughby: *The Fundamental Concepts of Public Law*, pp. 191–192; *The Nature of the State*, pp. 240–242.
[2] Ibid., *The Fundamental Concepts of Public Law*, p. 192.

Whatever the historical facts might be as to the formation of the union by the common desire and by the joint co-operation of the states, Willoughby assumed that to the federal state there must be conceded the possession of national sovereignty.

He tried to distinguish between the federal state and the confederacy by means of a juristic interpretation based on facts.

He denied the validity of that principle of distinction which was based on the amount of the power actually vested in the central government and in the individual states, and of that distinction between the two types which consisted in the fact that the federal state could enforce its own laws directly upon the individual subjects or citizens, whilst the confederacy could enforce its decisions only through the state governments. He also condemned the distinction which was based on the absence of any requirement as to the unanimous consent of the states to any amendment of the constitution of the union, and the distinction between federal and confederated states by means of enumerated or unenumerated powers.

These distinctions were utterly contradictory to the historical facts of federal organization.

The real test he deemed to be "the power or lack of power of the individual state to determine the extent of its own obligations under the articles of union, and, in the last resort, if its view be not acquiesced in by the general government, to withdraw from the union."[1]

In other words the extent to which "the federal tribunal's decrees are enforceable by the executive" was the decisive test of the distinction of the *Bundesstaat* and the *Staatenbund*.

The right of nullification, therefore, was the central test in the distinction between the confederation and the federal state; in the former the right was positive and in the latter negative.

Willoughby believed that the outstanding types of federal union in our day were those of the United States on the one hand, and the German Empire on the other. But their forms of federation differed entirely in this respect, that the United States were legislatively decentralised and governmentally centralised; whilst the German Empire was legislatively rather more centralised and executively much more decentralised.

In the United States the supremacy of the federal authority, especially the competence of executive and judicial departments, was firmly established by the outcome of the Civil War in 1864.

[1] W. W. Willoughby: *The Fundamental Concepts of Public Law*, p. 202.

The weak German federal system, which was executively decentralised, had been replaced largely by the effective superiority of Prussia.

In the federal state federal citizenship was recognised; the existence of federal territory and dependencies, either "incorporated" or "unincorporated," was acknowledged; equality between the states was not an essential part of the federal organisation. The residual power was admitted to reside in the national government, and federal supervision over states and the federal coercion of the member states and the necessary powers for the maintenance of federal union were constitutionally and judicially recognised as being vested in the federal government in the course of federal history.

Willoughby's exposition of the advantages and disadvantages of the federal system was no more of a novelty than that of Bryce.

He emphatically argued that "the special advantage of the federal form consists in the fact that it permits the satisfaction in fuller form than is possible under any ordinary system of local government, of the desire that may be felt by the citizens of the individual states to preserve their rights of self-government, while at the same time yielding obedience, as to certain matters, to a common political authority."[1]

With this criterion of federalism, as I have explained above, Willoughby tried to analyse American federation, neither admitting the state right theory nor the nationalist theory.

From his fundamental criterion of the conception of the state, on the one hand, and from consideration of historical controversy on the other, he reached the conclusion that the originality of the United States was that it was "a confederacy of sovereign states united only by a treaty or compact," but "it nevertheless is a fair juristic reference from the events that occurred soon after the union was established that the confederate conception of the union was no longer in consonance with the facts, and that the opposing nationalistic conception had been impliedly accepted by the American people when they acquiesced in the powers which the national government had asserted and exercised."[2]

He was convinced that the establishment of national sovereignty had been manifested even before 1860, but the fundamental recognition of national sovereignty evolved from the long historical experience and was finally tested by the secession of the Southern states, judicially and constitutionally, and federal supremacy

[1] W. W. Willoughby: *The Fundamental Concepts of Public Law*, p. 221.
[2] Ibid., p. 252.

over the states was established either through the 14th Amendment of the Constitution, or the successive decisions of the Supreme Court in the so-called Debs case.[1]

His view of United States history was that of an organic evolution of national sentiment and feelings, whereby what he called the federal state could be realised after a long struggle between the state right and nationalist theories.

§ 4

It is quite essential in the discussion of the federal state that we consider the problem of "non-sovereign political bodies." The meaning given by Willoughby to "non-sovereign bodies" was an invention of German terminology.

The excessive use of terminology in German *Staatslehre*, however useful for classification, was the cause of confusion in the formation of political ideas based on juristic metaphor but not on political actuality.

The main purpose of German jurists in their treatment of the federal state was to set up a conception of the state applicable to a member of the federal state, confederation or other type of union. In other words, how far did the members of the federal union retain their sovereignty in the forming and working of the federal state.

The question whether the members of a confederacy retained their status as states is not touched by Willoughby's idea of *Staatenbund*; the main question is how far the members of the federal state retain their status as states.

Brie and Rosin laid down that the fundamental characteristic of a state, whether sovereign or non-sovereign, is "its aims or ends." As Rosin drew a line between the sovereign and non-sovereign state according as its aims are national or local, so Brie assumed the distinction to lie in the universal character of the former vis-à-vis the particular character of the latter.

Brie's conception made "all-sidedness" the test of statehood, and by this the members of the federal state, even though they partially lost their sovereignty, retained statehood, because he asserted that the so-called "non-sovereign state" retained the essential character of "all-sidedness."

The most remarkable defender of the statehood of the member states in German federal history was Laband, in whose later

[1] W. W. Willoughby: *The Fundamental Concepts of Public Law*, p. 250.

works "own right" or "own right of domination" meant omnipotence of power, an original legal superiority of the dominating power over the dominated persons—that is, power to coerce or command the governed through its own will and force.

Laband regarded the member states of the *Bundesstaat* as still retaining their statehood, and being more than mere administrative divisions, because their "own right" continued. Jellinek, for reasons which were more political, took the same view, but differed from Laband in the meaning which he gave to "own right"—he regarded as the chief characteristic of such right the fact that its holder "is legally not answerable for its exercise."[1] The possession of this decisive power is shown by the existence of independent organs for its enforcement.

Willoughby, however different his principles and methods, stood on the same footing as to the juristic conception of state sovereignty as Laband and Jellinek. Nevertheless, as Austin's one and indivisible conception of sovereignty was Willoughby's main thesis, so the latter fell into the same pit of dogmatism as Burgess, who regarded the federal state not as a separate entity, but merely as one particular type of the unitary state.

The *Kompetenz-Kompetenz* was not a political metaphor at all, as the legal competence of the members of the composite state was derived from the federal constitution.

According to Jellinek, and even to Wilson's distinction of state rights between "original" and "derivative," the distinction between the non-sovereign state and mere administrative agency depended on how far the legal competence retains its own right to exercise power within its own sphere.

Willoughby's argument was that unless the doctrine of divided sovereignty was tenable, the idea of a political entity exercising its own original political power was inacceptable, but Jellinek and Laband had their conception of sovereignty as being indivisible and inalienable.

The actual facts of the federal state had already given the federal government the supreme authority to intervene and give commands to the states within spheres assigned to it legally and constitutionally.

Jellinek himself recognised "the sovereignty of superior state as contrasted with the non-sovereign state," as being shown in the following ways:

"First, in the negative control by it of the activities of the latter; second, in the power of the sovereign state to use the

[1] W. W. Willoughby: *The Fundamental Concepts of Public Law*, p. 260.

non-sovereign state for its own ends, be it as the direct object of its will or as a relatively independent member of a federal union; thirdly, the sovereign state had at all times the right to take to itself, in a constitutional manner, the highest rights belonging to the non-sovereign state."

If sovereignty were one and indivisible, it was not correct to say that certain subordinate or non-sovereign political bodies could express independent wills of their own on any matter whatever.

If the term "state" was to be regarded simply as a "technical one," then the wills of the non-sovereign states or administrative agencies, as they were termed, were dependent upon the will of the sovereign state in each case. Then the whole issue in the search for the scientific precision desired by the analytical jurists, but not necessary for practical purposes, turned on the scope of the discretionary action granted by the constitution or law. Therefore the discussion of the theoretical and juristic difference between the forms of the member state of the federal state and of the autonomous administrative local area of the unitary state, or, in other words, between the non-sovereign state and the administrative agency, reached the negative conclusion that both were local agents possessing their own powers derived and emanating from the national or sovereign state. But as a matter of practical fact, the distinction between them was marked firstly by a difference of instruments, secondly by a difference of quality, and finally by a difference in the amount of discretionary powers.

However incompatible it might be with the juristic interpretation, the historical fact was that the states, before the formation of the union, were independent states and were, therefore, the creators of the union, and at the same time the powers of the supervision and coercion allowed to the states by the central government were less limited than those of any local self-government.

The complete framework of government in the federated states of the *Bundesstaat* practically marked them as being fully organised bodies politic. The possession of their own law-making power, the possession of their own executive under their competence and of their own judges in their own courts, within the limits of their own constitution, gave them an authority far more independent and self-determining than that possessed by any autonomous local government.

Therefore he concluded that "in the federal state a true central state is created, the several units are legally and constitutionally united, and sovereignty—the power of ultimately determining its own legal competence—resides in the federal body"; and "in the confederacy on the other hand the individual states retain their character as states, and their relations to each other are of an international or treaty character."[1] Now Willoughby converted the idea of the federal state into the form of a decentralised pluralistic state. Willoughby's federalism is that of Georg Jellinek, which has no relation to actual American federalism. Therefore it seems to me that his criticism of federalism is merely the application of the German federal theory of 1880 to American politics.

Merriam also described the nature of the American federation by saying that divided sovereignty was firmly accepted at the time of the formation of the union through the doctrine of social contract dominant in 1787. The question of the location of sovereignty, whether it was vested in the people as a whole or in the several states, gave rise to the contest which culminated in the struggles between Calhoun's state right theory and Webster's nationalist theory, and led to the Civil War.

But since the war had settled the "vexed question of secession" and political ideas were transferred from the theory of contract to the doctrine of evolution, the final test of the political system was not the letter of the constitution but the organic and evolutionary nature of the body politic.

The idea of the nation was precipitated by the organic theory and the notion of sovereignty, as juristically interpreted, determined that the nation was supreme, that sovereignty was one and indivisible, and that the sovereignty of the federal authority was indisputable. He asserted that "the state has in fact in many cases become a less important unit, economically, politically, and socially than the city, and, on the whole, the tendency of this time is overwhelmingly national, both in fact and in theory."[2]

Now federalism to Willoughby and Merriam was not an absolute necessity, to be designated as such, since the United States has been called "an indestructible union composed of indestructible states." The essential problem of federalism was not as to the framework of the body politic, but as to the nerve function of its system.

Therefore, however different might be Willoughby's methods and principles, the ideal state can now be considered to be administratively decentralised, legislatively centralised, and judicially predominant, in federal form.

[1] W. W. Willoughby: *The Nature of the State*, p. 254.
[2] C. E. Merriam: *American Political Theories*, p. 304.

Dunning, Willoughby, H. J. Ford, Merriam and others advocated nearly the same doctrine from their own different political standpoints. The scientific study of politics, especially the comparative study of various governments, on both sides of the ocean, contributed greatly to the new developments of political science.

§ 5

Though the German influence of *Staatslehre* prevailed among the political thinkers or jurists in the last quarter of the century, the American underlying principle of empirical philosophy was more enlightened and systematised by the introduction of pragmatism, in method and principle, into both political ideas and legal conceptions. Woolsey's and Burgess' contributions to German metaphysical study of politics affected the development of the federal idea less than the pragmatic study of politics and of administration.

The most fundamental contribution to the theory of federalism during the last fifty years was that of William James' great system of pragmatism. The empirical philosophy, which had developed during the last part of the nineteenth century, from Bentham's quantitative theories to John Stuart Mill's qualitative principle, was brought back to the founder of empirical philosophy, to David Hume, and polished and finished by the pragmatic conception of philosophy.

Apart from German metaphysical influence in America, pragmatism became the spring of political ideas in politics and administration, and even in legal theories. The study of federalism, therefore, started on a new phase, from the basis of pragmatic theory rather than that of the eighteenth century philosophy of social contract.

Roscoe Pound criticised and analysed sociological jurisprudence in the spirit of pragmatism, John Dewey set up a new mode of ethics and logic on the pragmatic philosophy, Goodnow in public administration, Merriam in political science, Croly and Lippman in political and social inquiries from the same angle, and Charles Beard's economic interpretation of politics were the natural outcome of American politics. Under these new conditions Beard's thorough study of federal functions on the basis of economic materials exemplified in America the pragmatic study of the political and economic federal state.

Beard assumed that the principle of the federal system was

generally based on the doctrine of limited government.[1] By the federal constitution, the sphere of individual liberty and right and the rules of laws, in legislation, administration and judicature, were limited by the powers allotted to the national and state governments.

He asserted that though the doctrine of delegation was theoretically justifiable and affirmed by the 10th Amendment, which legalised the reserved rights of the state prerogative, still, in reality, the supremacy of federal authority, as the supreme law of the land, was strongly established by the Supreme Court as a constitutional principle. Regarding individual liberty, freedom of speech and press and even of religion, the general attitude to these problems utterly shifted from the notion of Bentham's liberty to that of J. S. Mill; that is from Jeffersonian democracy to Lincoln's suspension of Habeas Corpus and Wilson's Espionage Act of 1917.

The federal authority had the right to interfere with individual liberty, but the right of property, except property in man, such as slavery or involuntary servitude, was still left to the powers of the state governments.

Beard conceived that the federal system, despite its complexity, was operated successfully by the American genius of co-operation and by the highly developed legal habit, whereby the judiciary secured the supreme and final authority over the other co-ordinate governmental powers.

The federal constitution ensured the inter-state relationships of the citizens of each state, and in this relationship of the states the federal judiciary was empowered to determine finally their legal rights and control the conduct of business and industry.

The standard of citizenship and suffrage was also generalised by the federal authority.

The main driving force of the new federalism was not only the general change in political and legal theories, but the great need for federal control over the complexity of administration and the rapid progress of industry and commerce.

The epoch-making 14th Amendment secured judicial control over all activities of the states in regard to the fundamental questions of persons and property. Not only this, but federal control of economic activities had also been established.

The federal control over railways, the control of industrial corporations, federal labour legislation, control of immigration, post office services and miscellaneous legislations, such as the

[1] Charles Beard: *American Government and Politics*, p. 105.

Pure Food and Drug Act of 1906 and National Bill of Lading and Warehouses Act of 1916, and such moral legislation as the Lottery Act of 1895 and Prohibition in 1920 were outstanding features of federal progress.

In the progress of federal co-ordination with the state governments, no better testimony to the federal supremacy could be found than the federal subsidies to the states, such as those of the Weeks Act of 1911 and of the Health and Hygiene and Industrial Rehabilitation Act of 1920.

It is quite true, as Beard points out, that if the rigid interpretation of the constitution were adopted by the strict constitutionalists, no federal administrative services such as the General Lands Offices or the Bureaus of Mines and Education could be maintained.

Now the problem of federalism is concerned not only with the political structure of independent states possessing the highest freedom within the appropriate powers distributed between federal and state governments, but also with the political distribution of administrative functions.

It is plausible that, as Beard assumed, "by a skilful adjustment of relations between the supervising federal authorities and the executing state and local authorities, national standards and local initiative may be combined."[1]

However, the school of public administration has not yet postulated the fundamental principles of federalism, but has given great impetus to the study of the matter of technique, that is, how the federal principle can be so applied as to bring about the greatest administrative efficiency.

The opportunism of Goodnow put forward a principle of administration, based on the ideal of centralisation of administration with decentralisation in legislation, on the basis of responsibility for political action.

The founder of the study of public administration in America unfortunately overestimated administrative efficiency and underestimated the federal importance of decentralised administration.

However, we are convinced that general guidance and direction in legislation and administration must be centralised in the general government, but that a large scope of freedom and initiative must be decentralised to local governments in a state having a federal character.

Such extensive self-government as the new chartered cities in

[1] Charles Beard: *American Government and Politics*, p. 450.

Missouri obtained in 1875 was incompatible with Goodnow's ideal.[1]

But no initiative can preserve and inspire merely decentralised legislation under a centralised administration such as the French or Prussian system. It is possible only where the English traditions prevail.

Nevertheless, the recent study of administration had illuminated federal principle by showing the possibility of an adequate decentralised system under the final control of a central authority. It is not too much to say that federalism in America has tended to lose its orthodox principles and to formulate a pluralistic state of federal character.

In this development of the federal idea, Laski's challenge to the orthodox conception of sovereignty was a landmark in the history of political ideas, as well as in that of the federal principle, substituting pluralism for monism, relativity for absolutism.

As we have seen the historical drama of the struggle between Hamiltonian and Jeffersonian democracies being played on the federal stage in America, so in 1925 we see the same drama of the contest between federal centralisation and federal republicanism being re-acted by Thompson and Judson on the same stage but on a far more elaborate scale.[2]

The great maxim of a new federalism is William James's view that "the pluralistic world is more like a federal republic than like an empire or a kingdom."

No political thinkers nor jurists among our contemporaries have fully explained William James's suggestion.

Federalism in its new conception was not the result of the discovery of any new form of organisation, but of the further development of federal functions both in politics and economics, which facilitated the application of the pluralistic ideas to the practical functions of the state in a federal form. Laski expounded the new conception of federalism in his *Grammar of Politics* more explicitly and clearly than any other thinker.

Now the history of federal ideas in America was the history of the federal state. The verdict of territorial federalism has shown the inevitableness of the transition of the American federal state to a highly decentralised state with a federal character.

The federal mechanism now becomes a skeleton of federalism, and federal function in the state organ comes to be the central point of federal discussion.

[1] F. J. Goodnow: *Politics and Administration*.
[2] Walter Thompson: *Federal Centralisation*, 1923. H. P. Judson: *Our Federal Republic*, 1925.

The state in the pluralistic sense gives rise to a new conception of federalism as a political system, and decentralization as a new federal function in administration.

Now federalism as a piece of political machinery is no more valid than a highly decentralised state, but it has revealed its validity as a political idea in the philosophical sense, to be applied not only in political organisation but in economic and other forms of organisation as well.

PART II

THE HISTORY OF BRITISH FEDERAL IDEAS

CHAPTER I

DEVELOPMENT OF BRITISH FEDERAL IDEAS FROM THE SEVENTEENTH CENTURY UP TO THE PRESENT DAY

§ 1

Whether or not the idea of modern federalism has its origin in Great Britain is the first and most interesting inquiry that must be made with regard to England.

In order to make this problem clear we must first of all investigate the fundamental source of the federal idea. The federal experience in political organisation had sprung neither from doctrinaire ideals nor from metaphysical speculation, but from the actual exigencies of political experiment.

Ever since the first appearance of the Achaean League in Greece the spirit of federalism had gradually crystallised into a political formula, and had already been tacitly recognised as a political organism when the immortal work of Althusius, *Politica*, was put before the public in the year 1603.

The modern federal idea was actually formulated by the rise of the United Provinces of the Netherlands, and theoretically by the publications of a group of publicists, such as Althusius, Hugo Grotius and Pufendorf, and it was firmly established in 1787 by the creation of the federal state in America, and revealed in the collected papers of *Publius* written by eminent American federalists. But every historical union, without exception, even the formation of the North American federation in 1787, had arisen owing to the necessity for external defence and general internal utility. It being granted that the idea of federalism was based upon experience and necessity, and sprang from the experiments of statesmen or politicians, can we really find and trace the main source of the federal idea?

The multiplicity of the Grecian city states and the anarchical states of mediaeval Europe produced the Grecian leagues on the one hand and the confederated leagues on the other. The success and failure of these confederations, up to the North American federal state in 1787, were really proved and justified by the historical test that these numerous confederations were entirely based on legal relationships of international character.

A proof of this was that nearly all publicists who criticised federalism to some extent considered confederation to be a state formation based on international law. But the final verdict as to the historical confederation had not been laid down by any previous thinkers until the Federalists in America published a series of papers in justification of the federal constitutional state of 1787.

Every theoretical justification of federation, from its adumbration up to modern federalism, proceeded from and was based upon the actual necessity and the facts which had caused federation to be adopted as a political expedient by statesmen and men of affairs.

However, no federalism could succeed unless the people had a certain sentiment or political inclination towards association. These qualities which were inherent in a people could have been displayed by a free people, by citizens enjoying self-government and by men of legal mind. The question of whether or not these qualities can be attained by all races is an interesting problem which I will discuss in the future, but as a matter of fact the attainment of this unique characteristic is, so far as the past generations are concerned, confined to the Nordic races, which Francis Lieber called the Cis-Caucasian races.

In this argument we cannot fail to realise that the political organisation of Great Britain has taken the form of a self-governing community from the time of the early settlers. Laws were formed for their own purposes by the people themselves, and their habits and customs were determined by the maxims of the art of ruling derived from their own wisdom and experience. The association in a small community was a homogeneous unit of free men, from which early England grew up.

The birth of Great Britain was the union of the Crowns of England and Scotland in 1603, after the enlightenment resulting from the intellectual and liberal administration under the regime of Queen Elizabeth. The union of the two kingdoms of England and Scotland by the Act of Parliament in 1706–1707 was a striking event in the history of Great Britain, in that the idea of devolution was discussed.[1] The United Kingdom formed by the union of England and Scotland was the genesis of the great and complex British Empire of to-day.

The modern constitution of Great Britain emerged from the great declaration of Magna Charta in 1215, and developed into parliamentary democracy.

[1] *State of the Controversy betwixt United and Separate Parliaments*. Pamphlet printed in the year 1706.

The growth of parliamentarism and the numerous services of the local parishes manifested England as the most tolerant country in the world except the Netherlands in the seventeenth and eighteenth centuries.

It was not surprising that Montesquieu in his utilitarian politics took for his ideal the English constitution, as the greatest example of self-government and liberty in his day. Even though Rousseau denounced the British representative government, his metaphysical assertion of the ideal state in his *Social Contract* could hardly have been materialised unless the federal idea had formed part of his political system.

The ideas of self-government and of liberty in politics and economics, however much they might vary in the progress of civilisation, were a fundamental principle of the democratic body politic in the past, and are so in the present and must be so in the future.

Federalism was, of course, a particular kind of political mechanism adapted to particular conditions of states, such as a vast country like the United States or a small group of countries in a certain area such as Switzerland and Germany. But federalism is either a system of united corporate associations or a corporative entity of various different communities acting unitedly in respect chiefly of matters of international importance and general internal welfare.

This co-operation in action and the united will of the component states and peoples thereof produce the highest possible harmony between individual liberty and social sentiments, and between the sense of self-government on the one hand and that of obligation to the whole society on the other.

The idea of federalism, based upon the harmony of the ideas of individuality and collectivity and upon the utility of co-ordination, requires for its realisation a highly decentralised system of self-government on the one hand and a unified and central organisation for general purposes on the other.

Experience in local self-government and the training given by parliamentary institutions, enlightened by the tolerant teaching of Protestantism and the growth of political philosophy, determined the essential features of federalism as developed by the people of Great Britain.

The intellectuals of England at the time of the discovery of Greek philosophy favoured Aristotelian experimentalism rather than Platonic idealism, which was shown through the contributions of John of Salisbury and Thomas Aquinas in the thirteenth century. Maitland asserted that "in no department of philosophy, except perhaps that of deductive logic, has the influence of Aristotle been so long and so strongly felt as in that of politics. No history of the British constitution would be complete which did not point out how much its growth has been affected by ideas derived from Aristotle."[1]

Philosophy in the seventeenth century emerged from the influence of Thomas Aquinas and produced a new trend of thought, through the medium of Bacon, the empirical philosophy of Hobbes and Locke on the one hand and English intuitionism on the other.

David Hume founded the utilitarian empirical philosophy from which the Benthamite *laissez-aller* policy in politics and Adam Smith's *laissez-faire* policy in economics were evolved. In English politics the deep-rooted underlying philosophy ascertained and justified the federal idea and its application to actual political mechanism and reality.

But though British political ideas and institutions were the cradle of modern federalism, yet Great Britain was formed by the union of the Scottish and English Crowns, and there were very few political thinkers at that time who contributed any ideas to the development of federalism.

The reason for this failure was the fact that a small island like Great Britain did not really require any system of federation except that of well-organised local self-government which was efficient in nature and in practice.

The real necessity of federalism was only recognised by the people after the development of the elaborate imperial relationships of the British Empire, or when the burden upon parliament had brought the need of devolution.

In these circumstances the study of federalism in England tended naturally to be critical or analytical of the actual forms of federalism which existed mostly in America or on the continent. But the federal relationship between the motherland and her widely scattered colonies became an actual political problem in England and produced an extensive literature, and also the vast dominions, such as Canada and Australia, with their own self-government (responsible government), were naturally faced with the problem of federalism in their own domains.

It will be convenient, therefore, to divide my discussion into two parts, and to deal with the general federal idea on the one

[1] Frederick William Maitland: *Collected Papers*, ed. by H. A. L. Fisher, 1911, Vol. I, p. 5.

side and with the progress of British federal practice on the other.

The former was limited to a small number of thinkers who examined it generally, and mostly analysed and investigated it from the negative presupposition of its practice in political reality; and the latter was confined to special thinkers who dealt with the particular problems of colonial relations and of devolution.

No political thinker up to the end of the eighteenth century —that is until the formation of the North American federation of 1787—had dealt with the federal state in any treatise.

John Locke, in his *Second Treatise of Civil Government* in 1690, used the word "federative" in speaking of the powers which were universal and common to all members of the state, as individuals possessed these powers before they contracted to form the state; and in his assignment of the distribution of powers he assumed that these "federative" powers also existed in the relationship between all states and their members.[1]

This federative power was a common power operating through the medium of "one body" of the Commonwealth, exercising "the powers of war and peace, leagues and alliances, and all the transactions with all persons and communities without the Commonwealth."

These powers, which Locke called "federative" as distinct from "executive," were the common powers which the confederation had generally enjoyed under its delegated authority.

In the eighteenth century David Hume, one of the greatest philosophers that England ever produced, proposed his "ideal of a perfect commonwealth," and visualised it as being such as "the Commonwealth of the United Provinces, formerly one of the wisest and most renowned governments in the world."

His *Oceana*, concerning an aristocratic representative republic, stood for a state with equal representation, freely and annually elected, of the towns and counties—the provinces being democratic and autonomous within limits, and with a general government entrusted with the conduct of affairs common to all the provinces. He asserted that even though there might be a frequency of disturbance occasioned by the jealousy and envy of particular interests, yet the government of the federation might "become more expeditious and secret in their resolutions than was possible for the States-General." As he assumed that "a small commonwealth is the happiest govern-

[1] J. Locke: *The Second Treatise of Civil Government*, 1694, Book II, Chap. XII.

ment in the world within itself," he was convinced that the federal system in the state organism was probably the best one for the security and stability of a free government.[1]

Until Bentham wrote *The Constitutional Code* in 1823 no political thinker had entered upon the criticism of federalism.

To Hume as to other thinkers of his day federalism was a political system directed towards liberty and freedom, by the equilibrium of force and liberty. Still, he left this balance to his sceptical conclusion, i.e. of "something" which he could not tell.

§ 2

I will first briefly describe the federal practice in the British Empire. Though both the inter-colonial and the imperial federal movement or devolution were outside federalism in the strict sense, yet the federal ideal has always been the motive force of political development within and without the United Kingdom.

After the period of maritime discovery and the opening of the new route to the East and America, the New World was the source of the wealth of the European nations. The balance of trade was regarded as the determining factor in national prosperity. The colonies of the New World were subjected to the trade monopoly of the mother country, and this was the origin of a new and exclusive system of mercantilism.

The wealth of nations rested upon the possession of colonies in the New World and the maintenance of the strength of great naval forces for the protection of the empires, Spain, Portugal, England and Holland were the great colonizing powers of that day, and competition in expansion resulted in successive wars between them. This rivalry in colonial development was the cause of most of the diplomatic intrigues and political unrest in Europe, and resulted in the formation of the great British Empire in the eighteenth century after the Treaty of Utrecht.

It was not until the middle of the eighteenth century that nations began to consider the nature and importance of the relationship between the mother countries and their colonies.

Colonies existed for the benefit of the mother country through the trade monopoly, which compensated for the heavy expenses incurred for the maintenance of the colonies. The Roman idea of colonisation predominated over the Greek conception.

[1] David Hume: *Political Discourses*, 1752, *Idea of a Perfect Commonwealth*, Chap. XII.

The Navigation Ordinance of 1651 in England established the *raison d'être* of colonies under the mercantile system of monopoly. The growth of colonisation in the fifties and sixties of the eighteenth century in England led to the constant struggles between the aggressive policy of George III, for the sake of existing monopolistic interests, and the growing resentment among the leaders and the rank and file of the thirteen American colonies.

The Stamp Act, 1765, led to the formation of the Continental Congress on the other side of the Atlantic, and at the same time inspired the liberal thinkers on this side of the ocean to advocate separate autonomy on the one hand or the formation of union on the other.[1]

Though Hume left the colonial problem untouched in his *Political Discourses*, yet his pessimism as to the probability of Imperial Union revealed itself in his objection to the adoption of federalism because of the vast distances and the difficulty of communication between the colonies and the mother country.

Nevertheless, the idea of federal union as applicable to the British Empire was first put forward implicitly by Governor Powell, who said in 1765 that the leading problem of the great Empire "of whom Great Britain should be the commercial and political centre is the precise duty of government at this crisis."

Adam Smith was the first man who explicitly asserted the federal union between Great Britain and the North American Colonies in his great work, *The Wealth of Nations*, in 1776.

As the founder of free trade he analysed and criticised the evils of the exclusive monopoly trades and the effect of the

---

[1] Discussion of the American Colonies in 1776, when Adam Smith published *The Wealth of Nations*, was the fashion of that time. David Hume wrote the following letter to Adam Smith in February 1776:

"Dear Smith,—I am as lazy a correspondent as you, yet my anxiety about you makes me write. By all accounts your book has been printed long ago: yet it has never been so much as advertised. What is the reason? If you wait till the fate of America be decided, you may wait long. . . . The Duke of Buccleuch tells me that you are very zealous in American affairs. My notion is that the matter is not so important as is commonly imagined. If I be mistaken, I shall probably correct my error when I see you, or read you. Our navigation and general commerce may suffer more than our manufactures. Should London fall as much in its size as I have done, it will be the better. It is nothing but a hulk of bad and unclean humours. Yours," etc.

"It is not, perhaps, uncharitable to suppose that the following eulogium would have been more warm, had the person it was addressed to not been one of 'the barbarians who inhabit the banks of the Thames' " (J. H. Burton: *Life and Correspondence of David Hume*, 1846, Vol. II, pp. 483-484).

mercantile system in theory and in practice. He asserted that no attempts to prevent the disruption of the relationship between the mother country and the colonies would be effective without the formation of a "general confederacy." His free and tolerant colonial policy sapped the old one at its roots.

He assumed that "in order to render any province advantageous to the Empire to which it belongs it ought to afford, in time of peace, a revenue to the public sufficient not only for defraying the whole expense of its own peace establishment, but for contributing its proportion to the support of the general government of the Empire." And he added that "every province necessarily contributes, more or less, to increase the expense of that general government. . . . The extraordinary revenue too, which every province affords to the public in time of war, ought, from parity of reason, to bear the same proportion to the extraordinary revenue of the whole empire which its ordinary revenue does in time of peace."[1] This was the maxim of colonial policy from which he deduced the principle of the Imperial Union, and derived his theoretical justification of confederated representation in the parliament of Great Britain.

Now Adam Smith, like his contemporaries, assumed the maxim of taxation that no taxation could be imposed without the consent of the taxpayer, and pointed out that the crux of this problem was whether colonial taxation for the general revenue of the empire could be levied by the colonial assembly or by the parliament of Great Britain. Although the King in Parliament was legally sovereign and could levy taxes in the colonies at his own pleasure, the colonial assemblies had refused to levy any taxes, partly as a result of "unavoidable ignorance of administration, concerning the relative importance of the different members of those different assemblies" and other offences and blunders in the monopolised evils, and partly because of the unsatisfactory system of management and the improper function of representation in the general affairs of the hitherto unknown great empire.

Whatever natural disparity might exist between the affairs of particular interests of local organisations and those of the general government of the empire, the parliament of Great Britain in operating the scheme of taxation by requisition should be guided by equality of rights between the constituents of the mother country and those of the colonies, in other words, by the principle of equal rights and duties towards all the citizens

[1] Adam Smith: *The Wealth of Nations*, 1776, Vol. II, Book IV, p. 225.

with entire disregard of the difference between the motherland and the colonies.

Now, on this assumption political experience has already shown that no parliament or assembly could determine the proportional amount of taxes for all the affairs of the empire without having a power of "inspection and superintendency" over all the matters of the whole empire. If the colonial assembly was organised "in the way that suited best the circumstances of the provinces," the parliament of Great Britain, which was charged with supervision of the general affairs of the whole empire, was better equipped to determine the proportion of the contributions to general government from all the parts of the empire, according to the "relative degree of wealth and importance," to the general defence and support of the whole. But he thought that there was no probability that the parliamentary requisition would be unreasonable even though there was no colonial representation in the British parliament, and explained that "the parliament of England had not upon any occasion shown the smallest disposition to overburden those parts of the Empire which are not represented in parliament."[1]

Nevertheless, the necessity of representation in the British parliament was a matter of psychology due to a belief in free government and to the sentiment of the leaders of politics. Without representation no one could feel sure of the preservation and defence of his existence, especially those of property, and the duration and stability of every form of a democratic government. It was a "desire" and "ambition" of the high-spirited leaders of the natural aristocracy.

Adam Smith, a man of the eighteenth century, faced the political system with the prescription of intellectual supremacy and its virtue, and believed that the free play of initiative of individuals or associations would bring about harmonious cooperation for the achievement of legitimate aims.

[1] Adam Smith: *The Wealth of Nations*, 1776, Vol. II, Book IV, p. 228.—The reason he believed this was his assumption that the British colonies differed from those of Rome.

"The whole burden of the debt contracted on account of the war would in this manner fall, as it always has done hitherto, upon Great Britain; upon a part of the Empire, and not upon the whole Empire. Great Britain is, perhaps, since the world began, the only state which, as it has extended its empire, has only increased its expense without once augmenting its resources. Other states have generally disburdened themselves, upon their subject and subordinate provinces, of the most considerable part of the expense of defending the empire."

Therefore the only way to prevent the resort to arms by the leaders of America in defence of their own right of existence was to satisfy the demand for civil rights by the grant of a share in the determination of the policy of the general government—that is, by the formation of "the general confederacy" of the British Empire.

He proposed that "if to each colony, which should detach itself from the general confederacy, Great Britain should allow such a number of representatives as suited the proportion of what it contributed to the public revenue of the empire, in consequence of its being subjected to the same taxes and in compensation admitted to the same freedom of trade with its fellow-subjects at home; the number of its representatives to be augmented as the proportion of its contribution might afterwards augment."[1] This method was derived from "the wheel of the great state lottery of British politics." The distance between the different constituents of the empire could be virtually abolished, and the diversity of their feelings and customs harmonised, by the idea of representation, which was unknown to the ancient world.

Therefore union was a possible, and was indeed the only possible, solution of the problem of empire. The fact that the citizens were of the same race and spoke the same language meant that there would be no difficulty in harmonising this "general confederacy," which had no parallel with the failure of the Roman republic. He asserted that, though the "Roman constitution was necessarily ruined by the union of Rome with the allied states of Italy, there was not the least probability that the British constitution would be hurt by the union of Great Britain with her colonies," and he was convinced that the constitution, on the contrary, would be completed by it and seemed to be imperfect without it, and "the assembly which deliberates and decides concerning the affairs of every part of the empire, in order to be properly informed, ought certainly to have representatives from every part of it."[2]

Representation in the British parliament in proportion to the produce of American taxation should minimise the fear of overturning the balance of the constitution on the British side and facilitate the working of the constitution by bringing about a better equilibrium of forces between the monarchical and democratic parts of authority. And at the same time on the American

---

[1] Adam Smith: *The Wealth of Nations*, 1776, Vol. II, Book IV, p. 231.
[2] Ibid., p. 234.

side this system of representation would sweep aside the fear of oppression resulting from the distance from the seat of government, and give satisfaction by the constant increase of the number of members of parliament owing to the rapid progress of American wealth, population and improvement.

Edmund Burke, on the contrary, maintained the impossibility of a federal union of this great empire. Nevertheless neither Lord Morley nor any other thinker could deny that Burke's axiom, on which his political philosophy was based, was one of the greatest enunciations of statecraft ever made in England.

His ideas were due to the application of two distinct methods, the historical method on the one hand and philosophical reasoning on the other. He recognised that the struggle in method and principle was derived from "expediency" and judicial right, in other words "the natural operation of things" and "the metaphysical distinction."

His early speeches and writings especially produced "effective eloquence," which embodied more reason and judgment than the mere declamation and passion of his later works. His utilitarian exposition of political justice was one of the federal maxims by which the relative validity of federal and local mechanism and their functions was ascertained. "To show the thing you contend to be reason, show it to be common sense, and show it to be the means of attaining some useful end" was Burke's rule of judgment which was the key to wise policy: "Nobody shall persuade me when a whole people are concerned that acts of lenity are not means of conciliation."

He set up the doctrine of "no taxation without representation" as the liberal principle of British politics, saying that "I don't examine whether the giving away a man's money be a power excepted and reserved out of the general trust of government . . . the question with me is not whether you have a right to render your people miserable, but whether it is not your interest to make them happy. It is not what a lawyer tells me I may do, but what humanity, reason and justice tell me I ought to do. I am not determining a point of law: I am restoring tranquillity, and the general character and situation of a people must determine what sort of government is fitted for them." He hated even "the very sound" of metaphysical a priorism, and at the same time the "true touchstone of all theories which regarded man and the affairs of men ought to be derived not from a mere expediency, but from the highest and noblest reasons and wisdom of their experience."[1] His appeals against the American policy of the government of George III founded modern liberalism, and had fuller reason and judgment and more lucidity than his later attitude towards the French Revolution, which combined strong conservatism and declamation.[2]

It cannot be denied that his utilitarian conception of politics, however different its method and principle, yet contributed something to the development of federal ideas. The ideal of English politics was embodied in Burke's speeches and writings, which deserved Morley's admiration that "public life was the actual field in which to test and work out, and use with good effect, the moral ideas which were Burke's most sincere and genuine interests. And he was able to bring these moral ideas into such effective use because he was so entirely unfettered by the narrowing spirit of formula."[3] His test of the justification of American taxation was determined by his attitude of mind, which was that "the spirit of practicability, of moderation and mutual convenience, will never call on geometrical exactness as the arbitration of an amicable settlement; consult and follow your experience."[4] This was the touchstone of relative validity in human affairs and mankind, from which the real idea of federation was evolved. The wisdom and legitimacy of statesmanship were sometimes twisted and distorted by the overwhelming influence of environment at the time of the highest pitch of passion and excitement. Even Burke started with liberalism and ended with conservatism, as a result of the

[1] John Morley: *Edmund Burke, A Historical Study*, 1867.—"The idea of a right as a mysterious and reverend abstraction to be worshipped in a state of naked divorce from expediency and convenience was one that his political judgment found preposterous and unendurable. He hated the arbitrary and despotic savour which clung about the English assumptions over the colonies. And the repulsion was heightened when he found that these assumptions were justified, not by some permanent advantage which their victory would procure for the mother country or for the colonies, or which would repay the cost of gaining such a victory, not by the assertion and demonstration of some positive duty, but by the futile and meaningless doctrine that we had a right to do something or other, if we liked" (p. 146). "The defenders of expediency as the criterion of morals are commonly charged by their opponents with holding a doctrine that lowers the moral capabilities and that would ruin society if it were unfortunately to gain general acceptance" (p. 150).

[2] John Morley: *Edmund Burke*, 1923.—"In the pieces on the American war, on the contrary, Burke was conscious that he could trust nothing to the sympathy or the prepossessions of his readers, and this put him upon an unwonted persuasiveness" (p. 118).

[3] Ibid., p. 303.

[4] Edmund Burke: *Works*, Vol. II, 1815, *On American Taxation*, p. 431.

cataclysm witnessed during his lifetime. Statesmanship has tended towards practical application rather than to the formulation of abstract principles and speculations.

However vague and inexact the empirical criterion and principle may have been, the maxim on which the federal idea was based depended on this rather than on the metaphysical criterion of right and wrong. Can we totally deny that the great federalists, Hamilton, Madison and Calhoun were schooled by Burke? Do we assert that the English colonial federalists, Lord Durham, John MacDonald and Sir Henry Parkes, did not stand on the same footing as Burke? Even Bismarck, however different his political views may have been, could not have formed the federal empire of Germany without sharing Burke's greatness.

Though Burke's utilitarian philosophy could not have the entire credit for the federal maxim, yet his political morals were a great contribution towards the development of federal practice, because federalism was derived from the recognition of necessity in politics and economics.

Nevertheless the political ideas of his age did not allow him to assert the practical possibility of federalism. His attitude towards the colonies, especially to America, was entirely in favour of their self-government and the abandonment of imperial coercion, as evidenced by his declaration, "Leave America if she has taxable matter in her to tax herself."

He assumed a kind of union: "My idea, without considering whether we yield as a matter of right, or grant as matter of favour, is to admit the people of our colonies into an interest in the constitution, and by recording that admission in the journals of parliament, to give them as strong an assurance as the nature of things will admit that we mean for ever to adhere to that solemn declaration of systematic indulgence."

But he opposed the federal union of the British Empire, with American members in the British House of Parliament, because of the impracticability arising from the distance of "6,000 miles in two voyages."

He said "it costs him [Lord Grenville] nothing to fight with nature and to conquer the order of Providence, which manifestly opposes itself to the possibility of such a parliament."

His objection to imperial union was mainly due to the impossibility of parliamentary practice rather than to any political opposition to it.

He emphasised that "to clear up my [Burke's] idea on this subject—a revenue from America transmitted hither—do not delude yourselves—you can never receive it—no, not a shilling. We have experienced that from remote countries it is not to be expected." Burke's conception of colonial relationship was dependent upon his opinion that "for that service, for all services whether of revenue, trade or empire, my trust is in her interest in the British constitution." He was convinced that the "hold of the colonies is in the close affection which grows from common names, from kindred blood, from similar privileges and equal protection," and he added—"Let colonies always keep the idea of their civil rights associated with your government,—they will cling and grapple to you, and no force under Heaven will be of power to tear them from their allegiance."

He believed that such ties, though "light as air," were "so strong as links of iron"; and he emphasised that "the last hopes of preserving the spirit of the English constitution, or of reuniting the dissipated members of the English race upon a common plan of tranquillity and liberty, does entirely depend on their firm and lasting union."[1]

On this assumption Burke's argument was not completely antagonistic to the imperial relationship in a loose bond, but was so to the complete union, to which Adam Smith did not think there was an "insurmountable hindrance" in practice.

These conflicting opinions as to colonial relations were put forward in the seventies of the eighteenth century by two great men, Adam Smith and Edmund Burke, whose sagacity and prudence foretold the coming controversies of two schools, the Imperial Federalists on the one hand and the Separationists on the other.

Whether or not federalism could be applied to the vast spreading field of the empire as such and to the racial diversity of inhabitants within it, is a question of the validity not only of territorial federalism, but also of the probability and possibility of international federalism. For this reason—the question of the possible scope of federalism—I will trace briefly the trend of ideas of the British Imperial Federalists and their opponents, who were called "Little Englanders."

Now Burke's eloquence and Adam Smith's sagacity were incapable of terminating the struggle for American Independence in 1783, and the colonial problem of the colony was left to work itself out until the famous Canadian report of Lord Durham in 1838, not only because of the bitter experience in North America, but also because of the continual unrest in Europe from the French Revolution in 1789 to the appearance of the Holy

[1] Edmund Burke: *Works*, Vol. III, *Letter to the Sheriffs of Bristol*, p. 202.

Alliance in 1815. The world was striving for the establishment of tranquillity and peace against the social unrest and militant and autocratic aggression in Europe.

Moreover, the independence of North America and the formation of a democratic government in the United States provoked sympathy towards the emancipation of the colonies.

During this period, not only philosophical radicals, like William Godwin and Thomas Paine, but also Bentham and his followers, decisively expressed the view that the colonial system was "hurtful to Europeans only because it is hurtful to the colonies."[1] They thought that the colonies did not compensate by any trade benefit for the governmental expenses of possessing them, and moreover induced war on a large scale which entailed additional expense, "by which the ruling few always profit at the cost of the subject many."[2] Bentham advised the French National Convention in 1793 as follows: "I will tell you a great and important, though too much neglected truth—Trade is the child of capital: In proportion to the quantity of capital a country has at its disposal will in every country be the quantity of its trade. . . . Is not the monopoly against the colonies clogged with a counter monopoly? . . . Hear a paradox—it is a true one. Give up your colonies. . . . They are yours: keep them, they are ours. . . . Give up your colonies because you have no right to govern them, because they had rather not be governed by you, because it is against their interest to be governed by you, because you get nothing by governing them, because you cannot keep them, because the expense of trying to keep them would be ruinous, because your constitution would suffer by your keeping them, because your principles forbid you keeping them, and because you would do good to all the world by parting with them."[3]

§ 3

After the Congress of Vienna produced the first foreshadowing of international leagues—the Holy Alliance—the modern states made immense internal progress, in the field of economics, passing through an industrial revolution and in the field of politics reforming governmental systems on democratic and representative lines.

The shadow of the mercantile system, despite American

---

[1] Bentham: *Works*, ed. by Bowring, 1843, Vol. III, *Manual of Political Economy*, p. 56.   [2] James Mill: *Article on Colonies*, p. 33.
[3] Bentham: *Works*, Vol. IV, *Emancipate your Colonies*, pp. 409, 419.

Independence, still caused the statesmen in England to hesitate in reforming the irresponsible system of colonial representative government. The Canadian rebellion under the vain Papineau in 1837 led through Lord Durham's appointment as High Commissioner to the Canadian Reform of 1838.

His report was really a landmark in the history of the colony and the first foreshadowing of the Canadian federation. Lord Durham, a philosophical radical, described the existing vice of colonial government by saying that "the natural state of government in all these colonies is that of collision between the executive and the representative body," the struggle of which "has aggravated the animosities of race, and the animosities of race have rendered the political difference irreconcilable."[1]

The entire separation of the legislative and executive power —irresponsible government—was a natural error and a complete nullification of representative government, such as we know by experience was the real cause of the English Revolution of 1688 and the French Revolution of 1830.

He proposed the first constructive reform of responsible government that had the wisdom of adopting the true principle of representative government and facilitating the management of public affairs "by entrusting it to the persons who have the confidence of the representative body."

The responsibility of the colonial administration based on the confidence of the representative legislature, and the nominal authority of the sovereignty of the British Crown represented by the governors, produced good government and harmony in the relationships between the colonies and the mother country.

With responsible government in the North American colonies the federal principle was the only panacea for the settlement of discontents and the promotion of harmony and co-operation with the mother country.

The permanence of the bonds between the Canadian provinces and the motherland, and the possibility of upholding the noble spirit of Anglo-Saxon national pride, were attainable only by means of a federal union of the separate self-governing provinces of British North America. He was convinced that, basing true responsible government on the capacity and integrity of the provinces, the true principle of the limitation of powers in a constitutional balance "was that apportionment of it in many different depositaries which has been adapted in all the most free and stable states of the Union."

[1] *Lord Durham's Report*, 1838.

The entrusting of the conduct of local matters to the legislative authority of the union of Canadian provinces, and a perfect subordination to the control of the mother country as to the constitution and form of government, regulation of foreign relations and of trade with the mother country, the other British colonies and foreign nations, and the disposal of the public land, were in this colonial organisation balanced by the security of the colonies against foreign aggression under the protection of the military and civil power of the home government.

In this respect Durham's ulterior scheme did not approach to imperial federation, but was based upon the strong links of the perpetual bond formed by the endurable and firm "sentiment of the national pride," which the colonists "are accustomed to view as marks of nationality which distinguishes them from their republican neighbours."

Durham's characteristic of national loyalty, however vague and ambiguous, was the only possible tie between the rising colonial nationality and the mother country.

To him federalism was applicable only to the inter-colonial system of government.

In his argument he emphasised one of the important questions of federalism, that is whether or not the conflicts arising from diversity of race within a territory could be solved by the political mechanism of federation—whether it offered the possibility of a settlement of the conflicts between the French inhabitants and the government in Lower Canada. Even though he was strongly inclined to the project of a federal union, especially influenced as he was by the advice of Roebuck on his first arrival in Canada, yet his actual investigation of the Lower Provinces led him to object to the federal solution on the grounds of racial antagonism. Reunion was a necessary preliminary to the constitutional synthesis. He proclaimed that "I was fully aware that it might be objected that a federal union would, in many cases, produce a weak and rather cumbrous government; that colonial federation must have, in fact, little legitimate authority or business, the greater part of the ordinary functions of a federation falling within the scope of the imperial legislature and executive."[1] Time and the honest co-operation

---

[1] *Lord Durham's Report*, 1838.—"If the population of Upper Canada be rightly estimated at 400,000, the English inhabitants of Lower Canada at 150,000, and the French at 450,000, the union of the two Provinces would not only give a clear English majority, but one which would be increased every year by the influence of English emigration."

of the various parties would be required to aid the action of the federal constitution; but time was not allowed owing to the violence of the hostility in Lower Canada, and co-operation could "not be expected from a legislature, of which the majority shall represent its French inhabitants."[1]

The introduction of federalism in a territory occupied by diverse races was likely to prove successful in course of time, provided that the gradual and harmonious co-operation of these peoples allowed free play to its application; without this any federal compromise would inevitably result in disintegration.

In these circumstances the only possible remedy was a complete legislative union, such as the union of England and Scotland, so as to compel the obedience of any refractory population to the popular legislature.

In spite of the federal union of Lower Canada, Durham proposed a general federal union for all the North American Provinces.

He believed that the more the mother country granted freedom and liberty to the colonies, the closer and more harmonious would be the co-operation of the colonies with the mother country by the establishment of good and responsible governments in the union for common purposes. No fear whatever of separation could arise from the application of the great maxim that "the first duty is to secure the well-being of our colonial countrymen," and it was "the hidden decree of wisdom by which the world is ruled" that the practical relief from undue interference, which would be the result of such a change, would strengthen the present bond of feelings and interests; and that the connection would only become more durable and advantageous by having more of equality, of freedom and of local independence.[2]

His federal maxim was entirely based on this liberal principle of democracy, through which small unimportant provinces developed into states and the spirits of the inhabitants were upheld by the united consciousness arising from a common federal government, which was to solidify and absorb the North American colonies into one more powerful nationality.

---

[1] *Lord Durham's Report*, 1838.—He explained that the main inducement to federation, the necessity of conciliating the pretension of independent states to the maintenance of their own sovereignty, could not exist in the case of colonial dependencies liable to be moulded according to the pleasure of the supreme authority at home.   [2] Ibid.

This comprehensive system of responsible government in an effective union offered the fullest scope for human activity and legitimate ambition.

Like Adam Smith, Durham emphasised that the primary task of a wise government was to provide for this inherent endowment of human morals, to pacify "the turbulent ambitions" and to employ "in worthy and noble occupations the talents which now are only exerted to foment disorder."[1]

Inspired by legitimate and noble ambitions and by the natural morality of free and civilised society, and by the solidarity of national feelings arising from common usages, laws and customs and common beliefs, union for common defence against foreign enemies is the natural bond that holds together the greater communities of the world.

Not only the need of defence, but also internal needs furnished and strengthened reasons for union. The postal services, common fiscal regulations, a common custom-house service and the common regulation of duties levied on all commerce, a common monetary and banking system and a common currency should greatly gain "both in economy and efficiency by being placed under the common management." The local and provincial institutions and establishments would be gradually changed and the administration of justice necessarily developed, and finally the future legislatures would provide for complete reconstruction on the uniform and permanent footing of union, and a "general appellate tribunal for all the North American colonies should be established for the upholding of justice and peace."

Durham unfortunately changed his original idea of union into that of legislative union because of the insoluble problem presented by national antagonisms in Lower Canada. But his sincere recommendation of the principle of colonial responsible government, and his underlying patriotic imperialism, brought about an attempt on his part to devise a distribution of powers based on a broad distinction between imperial and colonial affairs. The distribution of power as such, however different it might be from the strict sense of federalism, was the fundamental idea of federal organisation, as was also the formation of a general legislative union and a general executive answerable to and possessing the confidence of the people, and the self-governing responsible governments in a union were, at least, the germ of the future federal union of Canada.

[1] *Lord Durham's Report*, 1838.

Moreover, the firm assertion of the need for a decentralised system of colonial government, in which he emphasised that the establishment of a good system of municipal institutions throughout these provinces was a "matter of vital importance,"[1] preshadowed a sound basis of future federalism.

It cannot be denied that Durham originated the idea of federalism in Canada, and first propounded the idea that the principle of responsible government should be applied to colonial politics.

Lord Sydenham and successive conservative administrators of the viceregal government made no material changes in Canadian policy, and it was not until the second outbreak of unrest in 1849 that any essential reform took place.[2]

The reunion of Lower and Upper Canada under the unreformed executive government of the Governor lasted a decade after the Durham Report, whilst the colonial policy of Lord Russell was based on conventional fallacies.

The last memories of Metcalf's ostentatious administration faded before the enlightened rule of Lord Elgin, whose viceroyship turned the dark prospect of political storm into a bright and hopeful clearness such as Canada had never before experienced.

The great statesmanship of Earl Grey, who was Colonial

---

[1] *Lord Durham's Report*, 1838.—He said: "A general legislature which manages the private business of every parish, in addition to the common business of the country, wields a power which no single body, however popular in its constitution, ought to have; a power which must be destructive of any constitutional balance."

[2] W. P. M. Kennedy: *The Constitution of Canada*, 1922, p. 198.—"Meanwhile the Act for the reunion of the Canadas had passed the imperial parliament and Thomson had been raised to the peerage in recognition of his services. He must henceforth appear in the history as Baron Sydenham of Sydenham and Toronto. It is hardly necessary to analyse the Act in detail. The two provinces were to be formed, by proclamation, into one province of Canada within fifteen months after the passing of the Act. The general scheme of government was little changed. There was erected one legislative council, members of which held office for life on good behaviour, and one house of assembly, the members of which were to consist of an equal number from each old province and must possess property worth at least £500. Provision was made for altering 'the apportionment of the number of representatives.' The speaker of the council was to be nominated by the governor, and of the assembly to be elected by its members. The status of the Church of England, of the Roman Catholic Church, of waste lands, and of religious toleration was clearly defined. Arrangements were made for a consolidated fund out of which the expenses of the judiciary, government, and pensions might be paid."

Secretary,[1] and Elgin's liberal-minded principles of administration laid the foundation-stone of responsible government in Canada, as well as in colonial administration generally. Elgin sent for La Fontaine and Baldwin, the opposition leaders, to form a cabinet which was the first real cabinet in Canada.

The establishment of responsible government and the new phase of the position of the Governor-General in Canadian affairs raised the whole level of Canadian politics. Lord Elgin's consistent and dignified assertion of his political principles turned the rebels of 1849 to "loyal rioters", and gave every possibility for the development of that constitutional responsible government which he strenuously advocated.

The hitherto insoluble problem of the British and French-Canadian conflict was solved by impartiality and the giving of equality of political opportunity to the two races.

Elgin's liberal-conservatism cemented the formation of the federal union of Canada, especially when the power of the cabinet under Elgin's governorship passed into the hands of J. A. MacDonald and Taché, and when the growing consciousness of self-governing capacity prevailed not only in the two Canadas, but also all over the British North American colonies. New Brunswick received responsible government in 1848, Prince Edward Island in 1851 and so on.

The triumph of Earl Grey's principle of the constitutional responsibility of the majority party in the legislative assembly in Canada overthrew the old imperialist doctrine of Her Majesty's sovereign control over the provinces without any reference to the opinions of the colonists.

Now this new phase of colonial policy, except in the "native" colonies, opened up an entirely new problem for the British Empire, that of the relation between the self-governing dominions and the mother country.

The successive failures of cabinet governments in Canada and the other provinces, and the increasing inconvenience of inter-colonial relations, and especially the desire for the construction of inter-colonial railways, turned the minds of the leaders of the Canadas from the idea of legislative union to the federal solution.

Moreover, the spread of rumours as to Palmerston and Russell's

[1] W. P. M. Kennedy: *The Constitution of Canada*, 1922, p. 251.—"His statesman-like faith is all the more remarkable for two reasons. He was willing to trust the untrained, untamed, uncouth colonials to work out their own future. He found a *via media* between the *non-possumus* of the Tory and *laissez-faire* of the Whig in a conception of empire which is largely that of to-day."

arrogant and warlike attitude towards the United States federal government no doubt gave a strong impetus to the formation of the union by the realisation of the need for defence, just as every federal movement has received an incentive from fear of foreign attack, and there was also the recognition of the weakness of the separate governmental organisations of the various peoples.

So there came the formulation of the idea of the federation of the British North American provinces in the epoch-making Quebec Resolutions of October 10, 1864. These resolutions indicated that "the best interests and present and future prosperity of British North America will be promoted by a federal union under the Crown of Great Britain," and that the "system of government best adapted under existing circumstances to protect the diversified interests of the several provinces and secure efficiency, harmony and permanency in the working of the union" would be a general government charged with matters of common interest to the whole country and a local government for each of the provinces charged with the control of local matters in their respective sections.[1]

Federalism in Canada, in the strict sense, was not a federal state at all, because the sovereignty of the United Kingdom of Great Britain and Ireland was the legal basis of the Canadian federal Act. However independent and responsible the Canadian federal government might be, the final authority should be vested in the King in Parliament at Westminster. Even though Canada was not a federal state in the legal sense of possessing international personality, but rather a decentralised state in respect of her position in the British Empire, yet she has proved to be one of the great countries where political experiments have been tried, and where real working practice of federalism has been experienced.

The ideas of federalism adopted in Canada were not at all new, but were more or less modelled on and copied from those of the United States. The practical statesmen both in the colonies and the mother country were very critical of the federal idea and its value, as seen in the United States, until the formation of the Canadian federation.

There were three reasons why the federal ideas of the British dominions differed from that of the United States. Firstly, the

[1] The Two Canadas, the provinces of Nova Scotia, New Brunswick, Prince Edward Island, and also, on equitable terms, Newfoundland, North-West Territory, British Columbia and Vancouver, were to belong to the proposed union.

territorial federalism in the United States had already shown the direction of the federal functions and administrations. Secondly, though the federal government in Canada and elsewhere in the British Empire was the responsible government, yet it was no sovereign body in the legal sense; that is to say, federalism was limited to federal functions and was not based on the possession of sovereignty in the distribution of powers, but only on demarcation of governmental powers under the sovereign power of the United Kingdom. And thirdly, the internal necessity of co-operation between the provinces and past experience of the neighbouring federal state had taught them the advantages of unified action under a general government, especially in railway development and in the customs and postal services, etc.

Federalism in Canada was an embodiment of the *Bundesstaat*, in which no sovereignty was vested.

Therefore the federal union of Canada was not concerned with the question as to whether sovereignty was vested in the federal government or the provincial ones. The question of *ultra vires* the distribution of sovereignty in the British Dominions depended on the relationship between the King in parliament in London and the federal government of the Dominion of Canada in Ottawa, but not on the relationship between the federal government and the provincial ones, i.e. it was one of subordination, not of co-ordination. The basis of the federal system in Canada, in so far as federalism was concerned, was confined to the federal functions of the United States constitution of 1787. But, in so far as the Canadian federation was a part of the British Empire, and inasmuch as the framers of the Act for the union of Canada endeavoured to avoid the weaknesses shown by the federal experience of the United States, Canadian federalism had characteristics which were in a measure unique.

The enumeration of the distribution of powers between the general parliament and the local legislative bodies adopted by the conference of delegates which drew up the Quebec Resolutions was more or less similar to that of other federal states. But MacDonald's ideas as to the formation of a strong central government were the result of the bitter experience of the United States in 1861, which strengthened the resolve to save Canadian federation from the fatal weakness of federalism.

In order to avoid this, MacDonald and his colleagues framed the provisional federal constitution in which the federal and provincial powers were enumerated but the undefined residuum of powers, what the Americans called reserved rights, were possessed by the federal government, and moreover, "the federal government was given power to appoint and dismiss for due cause the provincial Lieutenant-Governors and disallow the provincial Acts."[1]

MacDonald, in his speech in 1865, declared that to discuss state rights in the federation was to begin at the wrong end of the federal argument. "Here we have adopted a different system. We have strengthened the general government. We have given the general legislature all the great subjects of legislation. We have conferred on them, not only specifically and in detail, all the powers which are incident to sovereignty, but we have expressly declared that all subjects of general interest not distinctly and exclusively conferred upon the local governments and local legislatures shall be conferred upon the general government and legislature. We have thus avoided that great source of weakness which has been the cause of the disruption of the United States."[2]

Of course the rights of sovereignty were preserved, and the requirement of the consent of the Crown to any measure either of the general parliament or of the local legislatures, and the rights of veto which this involved were reserved to the Governor-General as an agent of the Crown.[3]

Following the monarchical constitution of Great Britain the executive in the Canadian union was legally Her Majesty's government under the practical authority of the premier of the Canadian federal government.[4]

This was the second respect in which the Canadian general constitution differed from that of the United States. The executive in the federal government was dependent on the majority party in the House of Parliament, and so Canada escaped the evil of independent executive government.

A further difference from the United States federation was that the legislature, not only the House of Commons, but also the legislative council (the senate), was based on population. Moreover, MacDonald and Taché—but not the Liberal Brown—were in favour of the nomination and life membership of the members of the legislative council instead of election for a limited term.

---

[1] W. P. M. Kennedy: *The Constitution of Canada*, 1922, p. 303. A. B. Keith: *British Colonial Policy*, 1918, Vol. I, p. 254.
[2] A. P. Newton: *Federal and Unified Constitution*, 1923, p. 190.
[3] A. B. Keith: *British Colonial Policy*, 1918, Vol. I, p. 258.   [4] Ibid., p. 246.

This mode of appointment of the second chamber, however strongly MacDonald and his colleagues argued that it promoted the efficiency of federal government, could not escape from the criticism that it tended towards centralisation.

Not only this, but the prevailing principle of equal representation in the federal legislature through the medium of the second chamber was utterly betrayed by the scheme of making east Canada the "pivotal province" for representation, in that the representation in the general legislature of the federation should not be necessarily on the basis of equal equilibrium of the component states, but in that of the unequal balance of representation according to the real quality of the component parts. MacDonald and Taché and even Brown tended to this principle of representation in the second chamber in proportion to the population from excessive fear of the evil of sectionalism and of the future possibility of local conflicts, such as they had seen result in the bloodshed of the Civil War amongst their neighbours.

But the problem of equal representation in the general legislature was of great importance in the federal argument, which I will examine in a later chapter.

This principle by which the "pivotal province" was the determinant of representation in the federal government caused there to be 24 legislative councillors for the three divisions of east Canada, and 65 members for Lower Canada in the House of Commons.[1]

The differences between the liberal-conservatism of MacDonald, and the liberal-radicalism of Brown, and the sectionalism of the smaller provinces of Maritime Provinces, Prince Edward Island, New Brunswick and others, with the desire of the newly developed Western Provinces for entry into the union, delayed the final formation of the North American union. Apart from objections on a few minor points, the imperial government was in favour of the establishment of the Canadian union.

The support of the imperial government, especially the guarantee of a loan for the construction of inter-colonial railways, the economic negotiations with the United States[2] and the fear of Fenian invasion, together with the great efforts of MacDonald, Brown and Galt, hastened the agreement for

[1] A. B. Keith: *British Colonial Policy*, 1918, Vol. I, p. 248.
[2] It was the case of the Reciprocity Treaty concluded by Lord Elgin with the United States Government in 1854. Its expiration in 1866 was followed by many efforts on the part of Canada to secure its renewal.

the formation of the union, which was reached at a meeting of Canadian delegates, led by MacDonald, and delegates from Nova Scotia and New Brunswick at the Westminster Palace Hotel in London on December 4, 1866—a year after the Quebec Resolutions were introduced to the Canadian parliament in MacDonald's epoch-making speech.

This conference passed sixty-nine resolutions, which were based on the Quebec Resolutions, and forwarded them to the Colonial Secretary.

On February 19, 1867, the Earl of Carnarvon, Secretary of State for the Colonies, introduced the British North America Bill in the House of Lords and explained the characteristic features of the colonial federation. The Bill provided for a Canadian union, not merely of the existing "common centre of the confederation, such as the provinces of Upper Canada, of Nova Scotia and New Brunswick," but also, in the future, of Newfoundland, Prince Edward Island and all the Western territories of a Canada extending from the Atlantic to the Pacific.

He explained the nature of the federal government, which was twofold: a "central parliament" and "local legislatures." The central parliament comprised two chambers, the "upper chamber" to be styled the "Senate," and the lower chamber to be termed, according to English tradition, the "House of Commons."

The duties of the senate in the federal union were not only to resist "the sudden gusts of popular feeling" and to moderate and harmonise public sentiment, but also to be made "a fundamental principle of the measure of the several contracting parties," the object of which "is to provide for a permanent representation and protection of sectional interests." The membership of the upper chamber should be based on the principle of life nomination by the Governor-General and unequal representation of the local provinces (taking as standard Lower Canada where 1,100,000 inhabitants are represented by 65 members); and of the House of Commons on the principle of population. This equal representation in the senate, and proportional numbers of members of the House of Commons, would remove the previous dissatisfaction of Upper and Lower Canada, and of the small and large provinces as to the terms of their entry into the union. The complete self-government of the local provinces without interference from the central authority was the basis of the federal constitution, and naturally the distribution of powers between them was the most important matter in the federal organisation.

Lord Carnarvon declared that "the real object which we have in view is to give the central government those high functions and almost sovereign powers by which general principles and uniformity of legislation may be secured in those questions which are of common import to all the provinces; and, at the same time, to retain for each province so ample a measure of municipal liberty and self-government as will allow and indeed compel them to exercise these local powers which they exercise with great advantage to the community."[1]

He explained the divisions of powers into four groups:

(a) those subjects of legislation which are attributed to the central parliament exclusively;
(b) those which belong to the provincial legislature exclusively;
(c) those which are the subject of concurrent legislation;
(d) a particular question which is dealt with exceptionally.

It was noticeable that in the first classification the enactment of criminal laws was vested in the central power and its administration in the local authority, which was far better than the system of the United States. And as cases of concurrent power he instanced immigration, agriculture and public works, explaining that even though the two first would in most cases be matters only of local interest, yet it would be possible that "they may have under the changing circumstances of a young country a more general bearing, and therefore the discretionary power of interference is wisely reserved to the central power." Moreover, in public works, although some public enterprises must be left to the municipal or local authority, yet public works such as railways, telegraphs or canals clearly must come under the central control. It was also an interesting contrast with the United States federation that education was not entirely left to the free action of the local authorities. In spite of religious prejudices the "central parliament of the confederation" had discretionary right to interfere in the educational administration.[2] He emphasised that whatever powers the Act might enumerate, the residue of legislative power must be vested in the general parliament of the Dominion of Canada.

[1] Speech introducing the British North America Bill, February 19, 1867. *Hansard's Parliamentary Debates*, 3rd Series, Vol. 185 (1867), Cols. 557–576b.
[2] British North America Act, March 29, 1867, Sec. 93.

The experience of the American federation tended to show the absolute necessity of not restricting the "generality" of the powers of the central authority, and of not enumerating them, but of extending those powers to the making of all laws requisite for "the peace, order, good government" of the confederation.[1] The Canadian federation, in its first document, embodied the doctrine of indestructibility of union which in the United States federation had been evolved only from its ninety years' federal history.

Lord Carnarvon laid emphasis on the fact that the failure of the legislative union, which Lord Durham had indicated, was the inevitable result not only of racial differences between the provinces of Upper and Lower Canada, but also of the ill-imposed subjection of the Maritime Provinces to the general union, saying that "it is in their case impossible, even if it were desirable, by a stroke of the pen, to bring about a complete assimilation of their institutions to those of their neighbours."[2]

The federal union offered the only solution, from the political standpoint, of these problems. He pointed out also that the embodiment of the monarchical principle in the Canadian union was "a challenge" to republican America, and asked the comprehensive question as to "how these provinces, when united, can be one whit more or one whit less of a kingdom than when separate."[3] The idea of the federal union of Canada was only a means to the solution of all the problems which presented themselves in Canada, a solution desirable not only on grounds of political expediency, but also because it would benefit the intellectual and moral aspirations of the Canadian nation.

One of the most fascinating problems, the development of harmonious co-operation out of national diversity, was shown to be solved by the formation of Canadian federal union, which indicated the need and demand for interests superior to and more important than racial antagonisms. The federation, therefore, was the only solution of this complex problem.

At the same time it was a test of federalism which showed that its main value was not in the system, but in the function; for the Canadian federation was not a federal state in strict

---

[1] The Earl of Carnarvon's Speech introducing the British North America Bill, February 19, 1867. *Hansard's Parliamentary Debates*, 3rd Series, Vol. 185 (1867), Cols. 557-576b.   [2] Ibid.   [3] Ibid.

legal form, but yet the object of federalism was apparently attained.

As MacDonald indicated in his speech, the whole scheme of confederation as propounded by the conference, as agreed to and sanctioned by the Canadian government, and as presented for the consideration of the people and the legislature, "bears upon its face the marks of compromise."

Federalism should be based upon the theory of compromise, that is, upon "a spirit of conciliation" of the interests of component parts of the whole, for their "best interest and present and future prosperity."

§ 4

The seventies of the nineteenth century formed the epoch-making period of federal history, not only in England but also all over the world. The enactment of the British North America Act in the House of Commons in 1868, and the publication of Freeman's *History of Federal Government* in 1863, marked the dawn of imperial federalism.

The constant advance of the colonial governments towards responsible government, and the appearance of European rivals in colonisation, in trade and in diplomacy, inspired the enthusiastic spirit of the Union Jack both in the colonies and in the mother country.

In the face of the imperial federalists a champion of the disintegrationists, Goldwin Smith, fiercely attacked the imperial federalists from the economic standpoint. But the leaders of the several English-speaking colonies, such as Godley and Sir Julius Vogel in New Zealand, and Joseph Howe in Nova Scotia, maintained the integrity and the permanent bond of the British Empire, as the standard of the true metal whose stamp was effaced in proportion to the extent to which weakness may be discovered in "the instinct of natural pride" or in the "love of empire."

"The home of our fathers"—that is, "the cradle of our race" —was the main source of imperial federalism. The Honourable Joseph Howe insisted on the unified *Organisation of Empire* in 1866, maintaining that in face of the separationists' attack, the grant of responsible government and the reform of the imperial parliament to allow the colonists to secure equal opportunity in the legislature of the empire on the "compromised basis of representation" were essential for colonial unity.¹

Along with the concurrent colonial development the autonomy of the colonies consolidated new communities by means of a gradual breaking away from the influence of the mother country, and in each the ruling class in politics and economics became predominant over the rest of the community. Like the old democratic community of the early nineteenth century the small group of ruling aristocracy dominated the self-governing dominions—this kind of government was termed "Benthamite democracy." Still the belief in intellectual superiority was the chief barrier against liberty and characterised the Victorian democracy under the rule of aristocracy.

Though colonial responsible government was mostly based on popular democracy, politics centred round the agents of the Crown and particular groups of statesmen and the large interests. Nearly all imperial federalists, both in the colonies or in the mother country, except a few theorists, were statesmen or business men who were connected with colonial trade or industry, and their advocacy of federalism was more or less the result of their own practical experience of administration, or of their own interests, and not of theoretical aspirations.

The movement in favour of imperial federalism was not confined to a considerable number of literary contributions; it developed also into an effective propaganda and the formation of various societies.

The first incentive to imperial federation was Edward Jenkins' article on *Imperial Federalism* which appeared in the *Contemporary Review* in January 1871. He pointed out the possibility of forming an imperial parliament, and indicated the lines of demarcation between imperial and provincial matters with which each government should deal.²

Before this, Goldwin Smith's series of letters, published in the *Daily News* in 1862–1863, pointed to the disintegration of the colonies and had an impressive effect on contemporary liberals. John Morley's admiration caused him to speak of them as that "masterpiece of brilliant style and finished dialectic" in which

---

¹ Hon. Joseph Howe: *The Organisation of Empire*, 1866.—Representation in the Imperial Parliament should be based on a decennial census of the following: the number of people; the value of real and personal property; the amount of exports and imports; the tonnage owned; new ships built; the number of fishermen and marines employed (p. 22).

² Edward Jenkins: *"Imperial Federalism,"* in *Contemporary Review*, January 1871.

that "negation of a policy was advocated more than twenty years ago."

Goldwin Smith opposed imperial federation partly because of belief in free-trade economics, and partly because on grounds of public finance he objected to futile expenditure in keeping up the navy and army in order to maintain the colonies.

Also Sir Robert Rogers, the permanent head of the Colonial Office who for eleven years had the guidance of several of its political chiefs, favoured Goldwin Smith's view as to disintegration and held that the colonies were preparing for "being cast adrift or for self-reliance."

In opposition to this trend of opinion and a liberalism dominated by the Cobden-Bright *laissez-faire* policy, which would have culminated in the disintegration of the Empire, the Tory democracy of Disraeli took the place of the police-services state and laid the foundations of the new state administration.

The reform of the home government and aspirations towards the unity of the empire became the two main and coincident lines of Tory policy. The problem of the relationships between the local and the national government was one and only one aspect of a twofold problem of political expediency—how to secure the permanent unity of the colonies with the mother country, and at the same time to promote the intercolonial federal movement. The solution of this problem of imperial unity was to be found either in a "federal council" or in an "imperial federation."[1]

In 1869 the Social Science Congress at Bristol and the historical Cannon Street meetings "presented no practical plan of organisation such as is required to turn to account that noble sentiment as a means of giving us the strength, security and cohesion of a united nationality."[2]

At the conference on colonial questions on July 20, 1871, at the Westminster Hotel, de Labillière read a paper on *Imperial and Colonial Federalism*, in which he advocated the direct choice of members of the imperial parliament by the people, not by the provincial governments of the different parts of the empire, and insisted that the number of this legislative body should be large enough to choose and form the federal cabinet from it.

Jenkins in 1871, criticising the policy of Goldwin Smith as "a policy of mammon," asserted that a federal imperial system

[1] F. P. de Labillière: *Federal Britain*, 1894, pp. 12–13.
[2] Sir F. E. Young: *Imperial Federation of Great Britain and Her Colonies*, 1867, "Letter from a Constant Reader," p. 68.

would keep the expense of defence "at a minimum," and "imperial influence judicially exercised would assimilate the commercial policy of the province to that of Great Britain."[1] Also at the Social Congress at Devonport in October 1872, Jenkins and de Labillière read papers advocating federation.

Disraeli's famous announcement in favour of imperial federalism was made at the Crystal Palace on June 24, 1872, when he said: "I cannot conceive how our distant colonies can have their affairs administered except by self-government. But self-government, in my opinion, when it was conceived, ought to have been conceded as part of a great policy of imperial consolidation. It ought, further, to have been accompanied by the institution of some representative council in the metropolis which would have brought the colonies into constant and continuous relations with home government.... In my opinion, no minister in this country will do his duty who neglects any opportunity of reconstructing, as much as possible, our colonial empire, and of responding to those distinct sympathies which may become the source of incalculable strength and happiness to this land."

C. W. Eddy's paper on *Permanent Unity of the Empire*, which was read after his death, was a remarkable plea for federal unity on the basis of a federal council.

The attitude of the contemporary statesmen and colonists towards imperial federalism stimulated and inspired the formation of the "Royal Colonial Institute" founded in 1868. The Duke of Manchester gave special support to this institute, and also S. W. Silver, a great sympathiser with the federal movement, lent the help of his colonial paper to the advocates of the imperial federalism. The contributions in the columns of *Colonies* in 1873–1876[2] were the first beginnings of the practical discussion of imperial federalism, just as we have seen that American federalism was first put before the American public in the famous series of articles in the *Federalist*, which was the first foreshadowing of the modern federalism.

In this series of letters the main arguments had regard to two schemes for the imperial unity of the British Empire. Sir Frederick Young argued for the establishment of imperial federation among the Anglo-Saxon British colonies, excluding India and native colonies, whereas a writer calling himself "Colonus"

---

[1] Edward Jenkins: *The Colonies and Imperial Unity*, delivered at the Conference on the colonial question at Westminster Palace Hotel in 1871 (p. 26).

[2] Sir F. E. Young: *Imperial Federation of Great Britain and her Colonies*, Appendix.

proposed the establishment of federal councils as the first step towards federal unity. These series of letters were not concrete recommendations, as were those of the American federalists, but a general appeal to sentiment for the establishment of imperial unity.

One of the contributors, calling himself "An Imperialist," manifested most clearly the mental attitude of the imperialists when he said that "the delighted people have seen the glorious truth shining in the blaze of recognition by the whole world that England, after all, is as strong and, above all, as high-spirited as ever, their hearts have been stirred within them that they are, what the noble history of their fathers revealed at every time, Englishmen. . . . So the federation movement is advancing in the colonies, Canada achieved a great dominion not long since, whilst conflicts of interest and feeling, which the solution of arduous problems created, furnished a grand political education to all its members. They learned the necessity and excellence of the most characteristic of English virtues—compromise."[1]

Imperial federation could be formed simply because of the imperial sentiment born of the noble history of "Englishmen." Federalism could never be adopted successfully except by a mediaeval people under a Grand Duke before the Reformation; a people possessing liberty and self-government could hardly form a federal union until the necessity and demand for federal unity had really arisen.

That excellent and characteristic English virtue—compromise—was, of course, useful in the establishment of federalism, but would have been of no value had there not been the need and demand for federal unity. About the year 1883–1884, S. W. Kelsey advocated a scheme of federation in the *British Colonial World* and in *The Journal of Commerce*.

He pleaded for imperial federation as essential for colonial defence against foreign aggression, and because of the economic need for an imperial *Zollverein*.

The only way to tie the "Gordian Knot" of the British Empire was to form a federation with an adequate representative system. He remarked that "to meet the circumstances of the time we must be prepared for a great constitutional change, the leading features of which should be a great extension of local self-government, and a real representation of the empire, both home and colonial."

[1] Sir F. E. Young: *Imperial Federation of Great Britain and her Colonies*, pp. 53–55.

For this purpose he proposed the abolition of the existing Houses of Lords and Commons and the creation of a new legislative body which should possess similar privileges and authority, but be smaller in number and represent a group of various corporate bodies throughout the United Kingdom and the colonies.

Observing the inefficiency of the existing parliament under the burden of increasing legislation, the scheme of his imperial senate must be considered as providing not merely for colonial representation for imperial legislation, but also for the application of the principle of devolution to the United Kingdom.

He divided England into eight grand municipalities with an average population of three million.

The centres of these municipalities should be London, York, Manchester, Exeter, Winchester, Oxford, Cambridge and Lincoln. Ireland should be divided into four provinces with, as centres, in Munster—Cork; in Ulster—Belfast; in Connaught—Galway, and in Leinster—Dublin. In Scotland two divisions, Aberdeen and Edinburgh, would be deemed to be sufficient, and Wales could be one municipality with its capital at Cardiff. Each of these municipalities was to be entitled, in respect of administration, to complete self-government. Each municipality should have its Lord Mayor, Archbishop, Chief Justice, Military Commandant and Municipal Council of Aldermen. Each of these councils should be independent and supreme in its own area, with appeal from it only in matters of imperial interest.

The imperial senate, which was to be the central legislative body for the British Empire, was to be partly composed of officials and partly elected from the municipal councils. The basis of representation of each part of the imperial unit was to be one member of the imperial senate for each 250,000 of population. In this scheme Kelsey calculated that there would be 146 members from the United Kingdom and 54 members from the colonies. In addition to that, official members from the grand municipalities of the British Isles might be 32 in number. And also he proposed "colonial" representation; 18 or 20 seats must be given for the native races of the empire.

This scheme seemed very sound, but there were great obstacles in the way of its realisation. The problem of the representation of the native races in the imperial federation was a very difficult one. Kelsey recognised that the native populations of India and Africa would require special treatment, but that was no reason why their claim to representation should be disregarded.

W. E. Forster's appeal for "imperial federation" was based on the powerful impetus which would be given to the principle of the empire's unity by the fact that "each member of the federation would find in the common nationality at least as much scope for its aspirations, as much demand for the patriotism and self-reliance of its citizens, as it would if trying to obtain a distinct nationality for itself."

He urged that the idea of the eventual independence of the colonies, "i.e. disunion," must be replaced by that of the formation of an association of the self-reliant colonies on equal terms "to transform our colonial empire into a federation of peaceful, industrious and law-abiding commonwealths."[1]

The imperial federal movement gradually consolidated itself by the formation of the "Imperial Federation League" on November 18, 1884. This league was composed of eminent statesmen and politicians both in England and the colonies, including the Marquis of Normanby, Earl of Rosebery, Mr. Mowat (Premier of Ontario), Sir John MacDonald (the Premier of Canada), Sir William Fox, W. E. Forster, Sir Frederick Young and de Labillière.

The league had many branches in Canada and Australia and circulated a large quantity of literature, had meetings and public lectures and issued a monthly journal, *Imperial Federation*. Also men of business organised "The United Empire Trade League" for the harmonising, as much as possible, of "tariffs and commercial systems" and the promotion of trade facilities, such as "cheapening and improving imperial postage." There was also the powerful aid of other kindred organisations, such as the "United Services Institution" and the "London Chamber of Commerce." The effective movement towards "Britannic federalism" was launched by the meeting of the first colonial conference in 1887 in London, to which all the self-governing colonies sent delegates.

At this time a number of pamphlets and books were published by various enthusiastic imperialists on the subject of imperial federation, and they generally supported the idea of a "supreme parliament" for the unity of the empire either from militaristic or from imperialistic points of view.[2]

A pamphlet published by "Centurion" proposed a federal system for the empire as "potential federation," not as an

[1] F. P. de Labillière: *Federal Britain*, 1894, p. 27. Rt. Hon. W. E. Forster's address on "Our Colonial Empire," delivered at Edinburgh, November 5, 1875.
[2] C. C. Cunningham: *A Scheme for Imperial Federation*, 1895.

"imperial" one. It suggested that the system of the empire should be based upon such an assembly as "an assemblage of the leading cabinet ministers of the empire," which was to be designated the "Supreme Council of the Empire."

The assembly must be representative of the colonies, responsible for their government and a "secret and deliberate body" without the "hegemony" of the government of the mother country.[1]

N. D. Davis suggested a short plan of imperial federation, proposing intercolonial federation on the guiding principle of a single chamber dealing with the general affairs of each group of colonies. The unity of the empire was to be based on groups of federated colonies, confederated with parent states.

The imperial legislature should be one chamber consisting of two hundred and be called a "Council of Representatives," and the imperial executive should be chosen as responsible to the House. He proposed that the "decisions" of the "Councils of Representatives" should be binding upon all subordinate legislatures, this being an application of the Canadian federal principle.

He further suggested that the supreme power of the "Council of Representatives" should extend to the following groups of subjects: firstly, defence of the empire; secondly, protection of the trade of the empire against foreign governments; thirdly, emigration; fourthly, such other matters as imperial communications by steamships and telegraph services, uniform currency, including the question of the decimal system and bimetallism, naturalisation, patents, copyrights, uniform commercial, penal and civil codes, uniformity in respect of quarantine, uniform system of weights and measures, and a single system of land transfer for the empire.

All these pamphleteers, even though they expressed vague and indefinite views, mostly proposed devolution on the one hand and imperial or "potential" federation on the other.[2]

However indefinite the nature of the Colonial Conference might be, an enthusiastic exponent of "imperial federalism" conceived that "the conference itself was undoubtedly a federal assembly, though of a very elementary description."[3]

Though this Imperial Federation League did not last after 1893, it did an enormous amount of work in promoting imperial unity.

[1] *An Essay on Practical Federation*, by "Centurion," 1887.
[2] N. D. Davis: *A Short Plan of Imperial Federation*, 1887.
[3] F. P. de Labillière: *Federal Britain*, p. 33.

At this time one of the most excellent literary works on imperial federalism was de Labillière's *Federal Britain*, published in 1894. At the time the champions of the anti-imperial federalism were Goldwin Smith and John Morley, whose exposition was unquestionably a powerful blow to the federalists. John Morley's liberal mind[1] naturally favoured "Little Englandism," and criticised the imperialistic attitude of the federalists, and especially the ideal set forth in Seeley's *Expansion of England*, a book which had a great influence.

Morley criticised and analysed imperial federation from his standpoint of Burkian liberalism both in economics and politics. As he favoured the disintegrationist ideas of Goldwin Smith, his incurable scepticism as to imperial federation extended not only to the preconceptions from which the imperial federalists started, but also to their detailed schemes. He insisted that any political organisation must be examined in relation to the practical life, the material pursuits, the solid interests, and the separate frontiers and frontier policies of the colonies.

Seeley laid down his political unification of the empire as a remedy for pauperism in Great Britain, and as providing for the military defence of the empire. Morley replied that, looking at the actual directions taken by British emigration, a mere emotion of patriotic sentiment could hardly change the current of emigration without "the calculation of prudence," saying that "no true patriot can honestly wish that it should be otherwise, for patriotism is regard for the well-being of the people of a country as well as affection for its flag."[2] As regards imperial defence, accepting Sir Henry Parkes' opinion that the familiar plan for solving colonial relations by the representation of the colonies in the imperial parliament "would be abortive from the first and end in creating new jealousies and discontents," and agreeing with Forbes' expert view as to the impossibility of defence of the vast area of the empire, he was convinced that "this vague craving for closer bonds, this crying for a union on the part of some of our colonists, is in truth a sign of restless malaise, which means if it were probed to the bottom, not a desire for a union at all, but a sense of fitness for independence."[3] Morley asserted that the colonial interests in trade and finance

[1] He wrote in his *Recollections* that he was a strong adherent of Liberalism, "the last remnant of the Manchester School: Harcourt and Morley from conviction strong; Mr. Gladstone in a lesser degree."—John, Viscount Morley: *Recollections*, 1917, Vol. II, p. 78.
[2] John Morley: "*Expansion of England*," in *Macmillan's Magazine*, February 1884, p. 247.   [3] Ibid., p. 249.

were coincident with one another, and that one of the most certain results of that foreign policy in Europe, "which is so dear to the imperialist or bombastic school," would be to bring about that "disintegration of the empire which the same school regards as the crown of national disaster."

Condemning the formation of an imperial *Zollverein*, he declared his conviction that the food-supply of Great Britain was dependent not merely upon the colonial supplies, but to an increasing degree upon foreign countries. The protectionist appeal for a preferential tariff, which would compel the colonies to impose a system of customs duties—as part of the federal constitution, whatever the changes in their own opinions or conditions might be,—might be simply the "destruction of self-government." Morley's ideal of *laissez-faire* in which "free trade is of extreme importance but freedom is more important still," agreed with that of Cobden and Bright. He agreed with Cobden that imperial federation would be a mistake, not because of the distance between the mother country and the colonies, but because of the liability to imperial taxation and debt. With the increasing population, growing social complexity and industrial and commercial development the vital interests of Great Britain required that attention should be concentrated on domestic legislation, and that her capital should be reserved for her own purposes.

Sympathising with Forster's views, he assumed that the federal council would be without doubt deliberate and executive, but would be aiming at an artificial concentration. He was convinced that the federal union, in its own nature, must be "a bond of political and national interests, and not of sentiment merely, though the sentiment may serve by way of decoration," and that imperial federalism from its very nature denied to its members the right of secession, even though the members stood on an equal footing as to rights and powers.

Finally, Morley emphatically insisted on Mill's view as to the impossibility of forming a federal condition when "countries are separated by half the globe," and although they had sufficiently similar interests, "could not have a sufficient habit of taking council together"; and he asserted that no federal machinery was capable of being established unless there were solidarity of needs and interests. He suggested that "the problems of government arise from clashing interests, and in that clash the one touch of nature that makes the whole world kin is the resolution not willingly to make sacrifice without objects which are thought to be worth them."

Therefore imperial federalism, whatever form it might take, was an artificial concentration, the abolition of the principles of self-government and love of liberty and freedom and responsibility of government; and the more free play were granted in the empire, the closer and the greater unity would be realised.

As Turgot compared the colonies "to fruit which hangs on the tree till it is ripe," the closer union of the British Empire would absolutely fail.

Morley's criticism of federalism was the greatest blow to its adherents because federalism of any kind must be based not upon mere sentiment, but also on practical mutual benefits and common interest between the members.

Nevertheless, Labillière endeavoured to defend his own federal polity and attacked the idea of disintegration as a mere "will o' the wisp."[1] He formulated the essential principles of imperial federalism at the Colonial and Indian Exhibition, which was held under the auspices of the Royal Colonial Institute in 1886.

He declared emphatically that the vital force of imperial federation was chiefly derived from the sentiment of unity, which embodied a practical principle which "will realise itself by this country and the colonies succeeding in producing such an effective federal government as will meet their joint (our British fellow-subjects') requirements, and be in harmony with their views and institutions—a government which will safeguard all their common interests without interfering with their provincial affairs." As William Fox insisted that "national character is coloured quite as much by sentiment as by laws and constitutions," so Labillière was convinced that "sentiment is one of the great mainsprings of human action, it makes and maintains nations, but not without organisation . . . a nation is but a mob without organisation."[2]

On this assumption the federal machinery was but an organisation of government wherein the separate parts of the British Empire acquired a united system of government with the connecting ocean highways between them, for the protection and security of their "common interests."

Labillière proposed four applications of the essential principle of imperial federation.

Firstly, he laid it down as a fundamental maxim of imperial federation on the basis of equity that "any system of imperial

---

[1] F. P. de Labillière: *Federal Britain*, 1894, p. 214.
[2] William Fox: *Letter to Colonies*, December 7, 1872. F. P. de Labillière: *Federal Britain*, 1894, p. 190.

federation should combine on an equitable basis the resources of the empire for the maintenance of common interests and adequately provide for the organised defence of common rights."

Secondly, on the principle of "the equitable basis," he asserted that for the adequate expression of common interests in the imperial government there must be equitable representation in a parliament of the empire. The imperial parliament, at the present day, should consist of representatives from Canada, Australia, South Africa and the West Indies. He excluded India because of the non-existence of an elected Indian legislature and her particular ideas, oriental history and tradition; and proposed that "India, governed as a dependency by an imperial federal parliament and executive, would be in as good a position as she is at present under the control of the existing imperial parliament." But he expected that India would be one of the federal powers in the future. He thought that it was unpractical and unwise that the "equitable basis" of representation should be fixed with mathematical accuracy, taking into account the natural factors such as population, wealth and territory, and that the federal distribution of representation must be adjusted "so as to satisfy the fair claim of all people of the empire." He said that "it might be so in the case of Mauritius and Malta, Natal and one or two of the West India Islands if they could not be satisfactorily included in groups." At the same time he recognised that, as in the existing federal systems, the franchise system must be left to the unfettered discretion of the provinces.[1]

Thirdly, on the equitable basis of representation, he believed that "there could be no practical or sentimental grievance in a parliament, in which the whole empire was fairly represented, directly imposing taxes throughout all its dominions."[2] On the British political principle of "no taxation without representation," the federal constitution, which would be formed by the equally proportioned delegations from all parts of the empire, might even specify certain sources of revenue to be, either wholly or partially, reserved for taxation by the parliament of the empire. Labillière's ideal of imperial federation was based on the type of the *Bundesstaat* instead of that of *Staatenbund*.[3]

[1] F. P. de Labillière: *Federal Britain*, 1894, p. 193.   [2] Ibid.
[3] Ibid., p. 194.—"Suppose, for example, tobacco, wines and spirits were thus set apart, they alone would yield a very large Imperial revenue. An income-tax, not to exceed 3d. in the pound, would also bring in considerable sums from all quarters of the Empire. It can easily be seen that if it were desirable to

Fourthly, it was an essential principle of federalism that "the self-governing colonies should retain complete control of all their provincial affairs."

The discretionary power to regulate their fiscal systems and determine their various economic policies, allowed to the governments of the dominions and colonies, was the federal compromise between the centrifugal and centripetal forces of federal and provincial governments. The principles of free trade and of protection varied in different parts of the federal empire. However desirable the unification of fiscal and trade systems might be, the federation offered more valuable advantages than the removal of existing trade restrictions in the diversity of the circumstances in the old and new territories of the empire.

In order to ensure efficient organisation, federalism in the British Empire should be based on the most elaborate system of the "federal states" which had been experienced in other countries.

There must be a complete legislative parliament and executive ministry on the basis of the federal state on the one hand, and a complete system of provincial self-government on the other. Labillière favoured the principle of a responsible executive characteristic of the British constitution rather than that of an independent executive as in the United States federation.

The ministry of the imperial federal government must rest on the confidence of the imperial parliament. As to the imperial parliament he had a little doubt as to whether an imperial upper house was necessary or not. He thought that this was a matter of practical convenience rather than of theory.

Therefore the second chamber in the imperial parliament was not altogether of importance because "the control of land systems and regulation of private property would be vested in the provincial parliaments."

At the same time the imperial lower house was to have sufficient members to be able to form a ministry. By this formation of an imperial parliament the existing burden of the House of Commons would be relieved by a desirable division of labours which would divert imperial matters to the imperial parliament, and leave the House of Commons free to devote itself to the British Isles. It would be a great help to the over-burdened

limit the taxing powers of the Federal Parliament, ample margin could be given it to enable it to raise, even from a very few items, sufficient revenue for purposes of peace or war."

existing House of Commons when the devolution movement in the British parliament was realised.

Labillière's ideal of imperial federalism was entirely based on the "federal state," not on the "confederated state." And however vague and provisional his propositions might be, the federalism to which he adhered derived from the principles of the British constitution and the parliamentary executive, and was superior to the preceding United States federation. And at the same time, whatever principle might be applied as an equitable basis to all parts of the federal empire from Great Britain to the West Indies, the question of sovereignty, in so far as the noble sovereignty of the King was recognised, was entirely removed from the main discussion as to a federal compromise. Therefore the main problem of federation was much more easily solved than in the United States.

Labillière also tried to demarcate the distribution of powers in his ideal imperial federation. He divided them into the following three groups:—

1. Questions which are obviously of imperial or common concern.
2. Those which are obviously provincial.
3. Those which may be left to the control either of the imperial government or the provincial government.

In the first class—imperial concerns—the imperial parliament was entitled to legislate, and the imperial executive was empowered to deal with the following matters:—

1. Imperial defence against external foes was the first important question of common concern. The establishment of land and sea forces all over the empire was entirely in the control of the imperial power.

2. Joint revenue and expenditure for joint defence and common matters were vested in the imperial parliament with the right to levy taxes; and he said, "It is only necessary here to remark that a complete imperial government should have direct power to levy taxes, and not merely to impose subsidies upon the various provincial governments of the empire."

3. With a joint system of defence it was a natural consequence that all those who help to maintain it should have a voice in conducting foreign relations. It was absolutely necessary that all treaties and negotiations with foreign nations should be conducted through an imperial foreign minister responsible to the

imperial parliament in which every portion of the empire should have a fair share of representation.

4. The extensions of the empire should naturally be controlled by the imperial government, because of its responsibility to administer all colonies, and especially India.

5. The federal empire required the control of India because serious difficulties might arise in conducting foreign relations with other nations if India were left to the control of the United Kingdom. Also, if the federal system of the empire should be established, the federal empire bore a great responsibility and obligation to India, and also would be fully sensible of the prestige rising from its possession. Methods of Indian representation in the federal parliament should be carefully considered.

6. In the federal empire naturalisation must be regulated by the imperial authority.

In the second class—powers of the provincial governments—he indicated that the following questions should be entirely under the control of the provincial governments, without any interference by the imperial federal authority: (1) church establishment; (2) education; (3) land laws; (4) taxation and tariffs; (5) internal defence; (6) Irish Home Rule; (7) inter-federation; (8) alterations of provincial constitutions; (9) native races.

Included among these, the power of altering provincial constitutions, was a conditional power; the constitutions could not be changed by the provincial parliament in particulars affecting the interests other than their own "without the amending Acts being reserved for the sanction of the imperial government."

This should be the only case of imperial supervision of the provincial powers, but *de facto* there had never been interference in the history of the self-governing dominions.

The third class of matters were those left to the concurrent powers of the imperial or provincial governments.

The following "concurrent powers" were mostly better and more conveniently regulated by the federal parliament of the whole empire than by the several provincial parliaments, with the different traditions and customs of their territories: (1) law of marriage; (2) wills; (3) coinage, copyright and patent laws; (4) domicile; (5) railways, streams and telegraphs.

Even though the construction of means of communications for the opening up of the provincial territories might be primarily under the control of the provincial government, yet the main lines of communication between the separate parts of the empire, even the intercolonial ones, such as the Canadian Pacific Railway, would be more conveniently regulated by the imperial government than by the provincial government.

(6) Emigration. The problem of over-population of the United Kingdom could be easily solved by the federalists because the imperial federation would bring about a notion of "one nation," not a particular nationality, Canadian or Australian. "One of the truest policies for building up the empire would be to put its waste people upon its waste lands."

(7) A final Court of Appeal should be the legal security of liberty for the people of the empire, there being a right to appeal from the inferior courts of the colonies to the Judicial Committee of the Privy Council, in which the highest ability and greatest judicial intellects of the great empire were gathered.

He insisted that with imperial federation it would certainly be necessary that, at least in all cases affecting imperial rights, there should be an appeal to the highest division of the imperial courts in the metropolis of the empire, even if branches of that court were established in the colonies.

(8) Reciprocity in commercial relationships between each part of the empire was an avenue to reach an imperial policy. As we have seen that the main controversy as to forms of federation arose from the diversity of the political and economic conditions of the various parts, so imperial reciprocity was one of the chief obstacles to imperial federation; for even the intercolonial federation of Australia could not be attained owing to local antipathy between free trade New South Wales and protectionist Victoria. However, through the idea of reciprocity and enlightenment as to imperial unity, the people of the great empire would be "disposed to regard their interests as identical and to promote the most unrestricted trade among themselves."[1]

In this distribution of power Labillière preferred the federal organisation of the directly elected parliament to a confederation of the federated dominions with delegates from their parliaments.

A real feeling of central government would be the product of a directly representative parliament for the federation.

Adopting the principle of direct popular election, even though the franchise and electoral divisions would be left to the provincial or inter-federal constitutions, the imperial federal constitution should fix the number of members to be chosen by each dominion or province, and the federal parliament should contain at least two hundred members with not less than three years' tenure.

[1] F. P. de Labillière: *Federal Britain*, 1894, p. 116.

And the question of the second chamber was naturally of more importance in a federation than in a confederation. Labillière in his early writings described the senate of the empire as the "most brilliant legislative assembly," consisting of "picked men from the hereditary peerage of England and from the aristocracy of intellect and statesmanship of the whole empire."

But the essential purpose for which the imperial upper house existed, the protection of private property, such as capital and land, was to be entirely under the control of the provincial parliaments, and not under that of the imperial parliament.

In these circumstances he was rather inclined to favour a parliament of one chamber, saying that "the Britannic constitution could dispense with a second more easily than could that of any other federal union."[1] And he proposed that the framing of the imperial federal constitution should be carried out through the medium of a preliminary conference or convention.

Along with the evolution of intercolonial federation, progress towards an imperial federal constitution resulted from the successive efforts of groups of imperial federalists, and finally the Imperial Federation League determined to draft a broad scheme for an imperial federal constitution at the suggestion of Lord Salisbury in 1891. The league set up a committee of eleven to frame a federal scheme, and after more than a year's deliberations it published a report, laying down the essential principles of federation. The league sent a deputation to the Prime Minister and urged the government to assemble a Colonial Conference to make the great attempt. The sympathy of even the great leader of the liberal party, Gladstone, towards imperial federalism manifested the general progress of opinion among the eminent persons of all parties in 1893, when he said that "the maintenance of the unity of the empire, and the consolidation of that union, is the reason that the Imperial Federal League had reached the limit of its effective action"; and Gladstone's remark that "the imperial initiative would be the proper mode of setting to work" indicated that "the Imperial government was always open to entertain the question of organised union and partnership of the empire."

From that time onwards the imperial federation movement advanced in the colonies rather than in Great Britain. The Imperial Federation League of Australia was formed in order to maintain the unity of the British dominions and to strengthen

[1] F. P. de Labillière: *Federal Britain*, 1894, p. 67.

it in the future by some form of federation. A series of pamphlets was published by this league down to 1911.[1]

Nevertheless, though the ideal of imperial federation as the keystone of imperial unity was the "finest pile of brick and stone" of a grand imaginary political edifice, it remained a phantom, not a reality.

§ 5

The formation of the Colonial Conference in 1887 practically closed the door to ideal federation, but it opened a new phase, that of the grand council with a simple confederated character.

After the Indian Council was formed many imperialists proposed an "Imperial Council," advocated the "council system" of a joint committee of representatives—what some people called Agents-General—which was parallel to the India Council, whilst others proposed separate ministries for the colonies with several under-secretaries representing the colonies.

This idea of a council gradually developed into the meeting of the Colonial Conference in 1887.

The representation of the colonies at the Colonial Conference was the product of nineteenth century democratic politics, which constituted "a clearly defined development of a regular body of opinion connected by a network of cross-references."

Viscount Haldane published a pamphlet on *Federal Constitutions within the Empire* in 1900, which put forward a new idea of an imperial federal movement. He assumed that the constitution of the empire was derivative "after having arrived at a joint conviction of its justice and utility." Just as "the sovereign has ceased to govern and now only reigns" as the outcome of a slow process, so the powers of the self-governing dominions had evolved from the very fashion of the general government at home, ever since Sir George Brown, a man of real ability, sent a despatch in 1860 as Governor of Queensland. Through various judicial decisions,[2] the Governor, even though he was a sovereign agent, was liable to be sued for an illegal action and he was empowered under the Colonial Office Regulations of 1892 to obtain "the advice of the Imperial Law officers through the Secretary of States."

Out of the multitude of precedents regarding the relationship

[1] *Pamphlets of the Imperial Federal League of Australia* (Dominions Office Library).
[2] The Cases of Hill *v.* Bigge (3 Moore P.C. 465); Cameron *v.* Kyte (3 Knapp 332); Musgrave *v.* Pulido (5 Ap. Cas. 102).

between parliament and the self-governing dominion governments "the acts which constitute them are but the skeletons which the practice of governors, ministers, parliaments and judges have to endow with flesh and blood before the dry bones can live."[1] As he assumed that the substance of the imperial relationships was unwritten and evolved from the principle of responsible government, so he endorsed the decisions of Lord Mansfield that constitutional restrictions had "other than legal sanction and has become much more definitely recognised, as the theory of colonial government has developed during the last quarter of a century."

As the Canadian federal constitution evolved from the storehouse of tradition, and the Australian federal commonwealth was formulated on a scheme framed not at Whitehall but by the deliberations of Australian statesmen, responsible government was granted to the dominions free from interference from Downing Street "so far as purely dominion affairs were concerned."

Therefore Lord Haldane was convinced that the bonds of the empire are the bonds, "not of any law written or unwritten, but of a common heritage of history, of interest, and of blood." On this assumption it was of great importance for the unity of the empire to preserve the absolute right of autonomy, and to maintain the existing institution with "a spirit which is imperial in the nobest sense" and at the same time it was essential that the Houses of Parliament still remained "in theory and law supreme."

In his view, however ideal imperial federation might be, the rigidness and inelasticity of a federal constitution would weaken the essential basis of the empire, and he, like Dicey, thought that it would have to be attained "by other means than federation in the legal sense."

In these circumstances the federal movement in the British Empire led to the second achievement, the inter-federation of Australia.

The demand for and grant of the establishment of colonial responsible government were not confined to the North American provinces in the forties of the last century, but prevailed all over the English-speaking colonies.

The report of the Committee of the Privy Council for Trade and Plantations in 1844 proposed the grant of self-governing constitutions to the Southern Australian colonies, mentioning that "the colonies of South Australia and Van Diemen's Land being on the other hand at once willing and able to provide by local resources for the public expenditure of each, or at least for

[1] Lord Haldane: *Federal Constitutions within the Empire*, 1900.

so much of that expenditure as is incurred with a view to colonial and local objects, the time has in our judgment arrived when parliament may properly be recommended to institute in each of these colonies a legislature, in which the representatives of the people at large shall enjoy and exercise their constitutional authority."[1]

Therefore, proposing the division of New South Wales into two independent colonies, New South Wales in the northern division of old New South Wales, with its capital at Sydney, and Victoria in the south, with capital at Melbourne, the committee recommended the creation in each of a legislature with responsible government under the exercise of Her Majesty's prerogative, in which the "representatives of the people should exercise their constitutional authority and influence." The committee's report urged not only responsible government, but also proposed a general assembly of these constitutional colonies, New South Wales, Victoria, South Australia and Van Diemen's Land, owing to the need for an adequate and uniform fiscal system in order to carry on the administration, whilst "the complete control over the colonial expenditure ought to be given to the respective legislatures."

The question of revenue, which was chiefly derived from duties, gave the main impetus to the proposal for a general assembly and provided the future motive for the federation of the Australian Commonwealths.

This recommendation embodied, no doubt, certain common subjects under the rule of the Governor-General, and was the first foreshadowing of the later movement of federalism. The general assembly was to consist of the Governor-General and the House of Delegates, to be composed of not less then twenty and not more than thirty elected by district constituencies each having a population of 15,000. It was to deal with the common problems, ranging from the "imposition of duties" to "proceedings of the Supreme Court."

In the same way the New Zealand House of Representatives asked for responsible government in 1854. Earl Grey's reply was that "Her Majesty's government have no objection whatever to offer to the establishment of the system known as responsible government in New Zealand."

From the time Earl Grey gave responsible government to the colonies of Australia in 1850, incessant efforts towards the forma-

[1] *Report of Committee for Trade and Plantations of the Privy Council on proposed Australian Constitution.* A. B. Keith: *British Colonial Policy,* 1918, Vol. I, p. 198.

tion of Intercolonial federation had been continuously fomented by eminent men in various colonies, but none of these efforts received much support. The six colonies of Australia started their own careers as separate states and developed their own specific interests and policies. The prospects of federation were far from promising realisation, the obstacle to united action being the diversity of interests—principally in the matter of tariffs.

In 1855 a tariff agreement provided a compromise scheme of import duties between New South Wales and Victoria, which was terminated in 1873. The fiscal conference of 1863 also suggested inter-colonial free trade, which made no progress, and especially this movement of colonial unity was hindered by the Imperial Acts of preferential duties. In 1873 the Australian Colonies Duties Act was repealed.

In 1870 Charles Gavan Duffy's Royal Commission in Victoria was formed for the purpose of considering the best means of accomplishing a federal union of the Australian colonies. The incentive came from the formation of the Canadian federation in 1867 and the new and threatening aspect of foreign affairs.

The commission recommended the grant of the power of contracting obligations with foreign states; "the want of this power alone distinguishes their position from that of states undoubtedly sovereign." The report said that "if the Queen were authorised by the imperial parliament to concede to the greater colonies the right to make treaties, it is contended that they would fulfil the conditions constituting a sovereign state in as full and perfect a manner as any of the smaller states cited by jurists to illustrate this rule of limited responsibility; and the notable concession to the interests and duties of humanity made in our own day by the great powers with respect to privateers and merchant shipping renders it probable that they would not on any adequate ground refuse to recognise such a state as falling under the rule . . . it must not be forgotten that this is a subject in which the interests of the mother country and the colonies are identical."[1]

Though Duffy's scheme for the neutrality of Australia in the foreign affairs of the empire was a foreshadowing of the later development of colonial relations, at the time it appeared to mean nothing less than separation or independence.

The first consignment of criminals in 1864 to be sent to New Caledonia by the French government, and the invasion and interference of German and American interests in the Samoan

[1] *Parliamentary Papers*. Victoria, 1870, 2nd Session, Vol. II, p. 247.

group in 1875, gave a fresh incentive to the settlement of the conflicts caused by the jealousies between the colonies.

When the intercolonial conference discussed various subjects and also the tariff problem, Sir Henry Parkes produced a Draft Bill before the conference in 1881, but the proposal fell through again. As Joseph Chamberlain recalled, when he introduced the Bill establishing the Commonwealth of Australia in the House of Commons, Sir Henry Parkes was one of the great figures in British federal history, just as great as MacDonald in Canada.

The movement towards federal government culminated in the Convention of the Colonies of Australia in 1883, which was a revival of Sir Henry Parkes' scheme and the idea of Sir Samuel Griffith.

It accepted the creation of "a federal Australian Council," the purpose of which was to deal with the following common problems: (1) the marine defence of Australia beyond territorial limits; (2) matters affecting the relations of Australia with Islands of the Pacific; (3) the prevention of the influx of criminals; (4) the regulation of quarantine; (5) such other matters of general Australian interests as may be referred to it by Her Majesty or by any of the Australian legislatures.

This convention admitted that "the time has not yet arrived when a complete federal union of Australian colonies can be attained, but, considering that there are many matters of general interest with respect to which united action would be advantageous, adopts the accompanying Draft Bill for the constitution of a Federal Council."

In 1884 all the colonies, except New South Wales and New Zealand, adopted this Bill, and in August, 1885 sent the "Federal Council of Australia Act" for the royal assent.

The federal council was strictly not a federal representation, but what Sir Henry Parkes called "a unique body," delegated and nominated, not elected.

A second stimulus to the federation of Australia was a result of the Colonial Conference of 1887.

The Australian contribution of the sum of £126,000 per annum and the periodical inspection of Australian forces turned colonial minds towards federation.

Sir Henry Parkes' constant effort was to awaken public opinion to the great national service which federation could render. The main difficulty which he encountered was in his own state, New South Wales. At last he assumed that the time was ripe for the consolidation of the federal Australian Commonwealth and his invitation to the meeting of the representatives of the colonies was accepted at Melbourne on February 6, 1890 by seven colonies.

A unanimous resolution was passed accepting Sir Henry Parkes' proposal for "the union of these colonies under one legislative and executive government on principles just to the several colonies." A national Australian Convention was empowered to consider and report upon a scheme for a federal constitution, and the Conference resolved that to the Convention should be "delegated not more than seven members from the self-governing colonies and four from each of the crown colonies."

The National Australian Convention met at Sydney on March 2, 1891, and designed the framework of a federal constitution,[1] which was based in outline on the federal constitution of the United States rather than on the model of the federal Dominion of Canada followed by Sir Henry Parkes' scheme.

Though the draft was formulated, and several colonial parliaments approved it, the failure of Sir Henry Parkes' bargain in New South Wales made the immediate adoption of federation utterly hopeless. Then Sir George Dibbs, the new minister of New South Wales, failed in his attempt at the unification of Victoria and his colony, and his government faced a financial crisis. In the course of time public opinion was converted to Sir Henry Parkes' views and the intercolonial federation movement became popular from 1893: the Australian Natives' Association had supported the cause from its formation in 1884. In January 1895, a conference of Australian Premiers was held at Hobart, and resolved on the holding of a convention, formed of ten representatives of each colony, directly chosen by the electors, for the framing of a federal constitution. In 1897 the convention election took place and the first meeting was held on March 22, 1897, at Adelaide. The constitution adopted was based on the general principles of the federal constitution of 1891.

But the main discussions in the succeeding sessions of the convention turned on the conflicts of power, especially the financial power of the senate, between the large and small states, on rights in rivers, and on railway rates.

Finally, in 1898, the famous "Braddon Clause"[2] provided the solution of the federal problem of Australia, and there was a favourable referendum in each colony but still there was only a small majority for the Bill in New South Wales and federation

[1] W. H. Moore: *Commonwealth of Australia*, 1910, pp. 42–43.
[2] Commonwealth of Australia Constitution Act [63 & 64 Vict.], Chap. XII, Sec. 87.

without New South Wales was not a matter of practical politics. But then some amendments of the draft constitution were proposed by New South Wales and were accepted at the Conference of Premiers in Melbourne in January 29, 1899, at which all the six colonies were represented. These amendments related to matters of rather minor importance,[1] but a referendum on this new draft constitution proved favourable in each of the colonies and the recommendations of the Convention were sent to the home government for royal sanction.

On May 14, 1900, the Australian Federation Bill was introduced in the House of Commons in a speech by Joseph Chamberlain.

Now federalism in the Commonwealth of Australia was evolved from the same conditions as in the United States. The same language, the same customs, the same laws and the same traditions, and common descent from the peoples of the British Isles had resulted in more or less identical forms of self-government and similar social conditions in the various colonies. But the responsible governments of the colonies, all going their own separate ways, had gradually created a diversity of interests and produced in the course of time unexpectedly high barriers between them.

At the same time the situation of the great continent in the Pacific, far away from the conflicts of European powers, meant the absence of any strong impetus to the unification of defence policy, so that the declaration of "the Monroe doctrine of Australia" provided the same sense of security as in the United States.

Therefore no solution of the problem of federal unity could be found except in a mutual understanding between the vested interests of the self-governing colonies.

In these circumstances the task of establishing federation in Australia was far more complicated and difficult than in Canada, because the latter was faced with the continuous risk of aggression by a neighbouring power. From this general point of view the form of federalism adopted was naturally that of the United States, rather than that of the special case of Canada.

Australian federalism revealed itself as the federal state, on the model of the United States, with an entire disregard of sovereignty. In his introductory remarks on the Australian Commonwealth Constitution Bill, presented to the House of Commons on May 14, 1900, Joseph Chamberlain emphasised his opinion that "it is true to say, that on the whole this new constitution, although it

[1] W. H. Moore: *Commonwealth of Australia*, 1910, pp. 50-51.

is in important respects unlike any other constitution at present existing, still in the main, and more than any other, follows the constitution of the United States of America."

Chamberlain contrasted the federal establishment of a new Commonwealth with that of the Dominion of Canada, in that the latter was settled in conference between the Canadian delegates and Her Majesty's government, while the former was framed by the people of Australia through their representatives, who "have worked alone without inviting or desiring any assistance from outside."

The separate states in Australia, having enjoyed self-government for a much longer period than had the provinces of Canada, had naturally attained the conviction of having a "complete independent self-governing existence"; moreover the Australian states were in a more independent position geographically and less threatened from foreign countries than the Canadian provinces which always faced the menace of the growing power of the United States.

Moreover, Chamberlain pointed out that the people of Canada had before them an object lesson of the "danger of exaggerating state rights" in a federal constitution, which had resulted in the Civil War in the United States, whilst the people of Australia had been remote from, and not influenced by, that example.

Therefore Canadian federation "was substantially to amalgamate the provinces into one dominion, whilst the constitution of Australia created a federation, for distinctly definite and limited objects, of a number of independent states, and state rights have throughout been jealously preserved."[1] The reserved rights in the Canadian federation—that is, every power which was not expressly given to the provinces—were vested in the central federal government, whereas the federal government in the Australian federation was only empowered to possess "powers over matters which are expressly stated and defined in the constitution."[2]

The senate in Canada was comprised of the representatives of the provinces substantially in proportion to the population, whilst the senate in Australia consisted of six members from each of the member states on an equal basis, even though both of the lower houses were similarly framed on the representative basis of population.

[1] Joseph Chamberlain's introduction of the Australian Commonwealth Bill in the House of Commons, May 10, 1900. Keith: *British Colonial Policy*, Vol. I, p. 347.   [2] Ibid.

The senate in the Australian federation was more advanced than that of the United States in the way in which it was formed, in that the senate was not chosen by the state legislatures or by separate constituencies in each state, but by the same constituency in each state, which the French call *Scrutin de liste*. The object of the senate was not to be an intermediary between the legislative and executive functions, but to be a check on the first chamber on the one hand, and a safeguard of state interests on the other.

The federation which was being formed after a hundred years' experience was put forward as the final decision, but state right had been strongly protected by the referendum which left that decision to the majority of votes in a majority of the states.

In the distribution of powers thirty-nine distinct matters were vested in the new federal parliament.

The federation of 1900 enormously increased the range of enumerated powers in comparison with that of the United States. They extended from the tariff to marriage, divorce, old age pensions, and insurance, and included, as Chamberlain specially pointed out, matters which affected interests outside Australia: firstly, the fisheries; secondly, copyright; thirdly, legislation dealing with the people of any race not being natives of any of the states (I think that contemplated legislation in regard to Asiatics); fourthly, "external affairs,"—a phrase of great breadth and vagueness which, unless interpreted and controlled by some other provision, might easily give rise to serious difficulties; and, fifthly, the relations with the islands of the Pacific, which also involved, of course, many questions in which foreign nations were concerned.[1]

The problem of sovereignty, even though the federation of the dominion was free from legal controversy regarding the location of sovereignty in the federal state, still remained as *ultra vires* between the federal government and the imperial government in the mother country.

Chamberlain's speech as to self-government was emphatic: "We recognise fully the unwisdom—I had almost said impossibility—of pressing views on great self-governing communities to which they are absolutely opposed. However great we might think the mistake they are making, and however great we might think the injury to the empire, still we should have to set against

[1] Joseph Chamberlain's introduction of the Australian Commonwealth Bill in the House of Commons, May 10, 1900. Keith: *British Colonial Policy*, Vol. I, p. 350.

that the danger of interfering with those rights which they regard as their undoubted palladium."[1]

Nevertheless, he believed that the problem of relationships between federal government and the independent governments should be determined by a tribunal in which all parties have confidence.

The main problem in this respect was that there must be an adequate relationship between the Supreme Court of the Federation and the Judicial Committee of the Privy Council. Chamberlain insisted that, if the position of the imperial parliament was that of trustee for the empire, then, although the policy of reconstruction may be a different matter, "the right of reconstruction" undoubtedly depended upon the imperial government in so far as sovereignty rested in the Crown. Therefore, it was of the highest importance to set up "such a permanent constitution of the Judicial Committee as would make it certain that on every occasion when a colonial case was involved there was a colonial judge with full knowledge of local conditions well qualified to advise his colleagues."

On this assumption he emphasised that "what we propose, pending further consideration which must be given to any greater scheme, is to appoint for seven years a representative from each of these colonies and India, to be members of the Privy Council, who shall also act during that period as Lords of Appeal, and upon whom will be conferred life peerages, so that they may continue to sit in the House of Lords, although they will not act as judges after the term of their service has expired."[2]

But the question of *ultra vires* in judicial appeals to the imperial government was a matter not only for federal discussion, but also one affecting the relationship between the central and local governments.

The federalism of Australia was an entirely typical model of the modern federal state. But the experience of a hundred and twelve years did not suggest any reform in the federal mechanism, and no novelty could be found in the Australian federation except the increasing power of the federal government, which was not so federally decentralised as that of the United States, and not so federally concentrated as that of Canada.

The central federal power in the Australian Constitution went

---

[1] Joseph Chamberlain's introduction of the Australian Commonwealth Bill in the House of Commons, May 10, 1900. Keith: *British Colonial Policy*, Vol. I, p. 370.   [2] Ibid., p. 380.

into greater detail and dealt with more matter than that of the United States. The state rights in the Australian federation were less, and more power was given to the Commonwealth; and the Commonwealth parliament was enabled to legislate for a state, upon the state's request, a thing which lay quite outside the function of congress. In the judiciary a complete system of federal courts was not yet established, and consequently the state courts were allowed to perform the duties of a federal judiciary. In Australia the "Federal High Court" was the Court of Appeal from the state courts, but in the United States each state Supreme Court was the final Court of Appeal for the state.

In Australia there was no such limit on the legislative power to deal with individual rights, as we have seen in the "Bill of Rights" in other federal constitutions.

Australian federal government was responsible and cabinet government, whilst the United States government was an independent executive.

The senate depended upon the election by the people, not by the state legislatures; it had no power of amending, but only of suggesting amendments to, money bills, and there was the possibility that "new states may have a smaller representation in the senate than original states."

The head of the executive was not elected by the people, as in the United States, but was nominated by the Crown.

No veto of the executive existed *de jure* in the sense of the United States constitution, but the veto was exercisable by the Governor-General, who, as an agent of the Crown, was invested with the sovereignty of the Crown.

The Canadian federal constitution prescribed the constitutions of the several provinces which were subject to federal veto, whilst the Australian constitution took the state constitutions as existing and made no change in them "except as the federation controls or supersedes them."

The Canadian federal constitution determined that all the reserved powers were to be vested in the provinces, whilst the Australian left all powers to the states except in so far as they were expressly given to the federal power.

As to the executive, the Canadian federal authority had power to appoint the Lieutenant-Governors, whilst the Australian constitution provided that the appointment of the state governors should be left to the home government.

With regard to the veto, the dominion government of Canada possessed the authority to be exercised through the Governor-

General, but in Australia the federal government had no right whatever to interfere with the state statutes.

In respect of the judiciary, Canada had no special federal courts other than the Supreme Court of the dominion, whilst Australia had two distinct sets of courts, federal and state, and lacked the power to establish federal courts other than the High Court, and simply invested the state court with federal agency.

The senate in Canada was nominated, but that of Australia was elective.

It was of great importance that Canada had no power to amend the constitution except through the King in the United Kingdom parliament, but Australia provided a method whereby the Commonwealth might amend the constitution by legislative enactment with royal sanction. In this respect Australian federalism was far more advanced and democratic than that of Canada.

§ 6

Although the two great dominions, Australia and Canada, were constructed through the mechanism of federalism and governed large territories by federal technique, the large colonies in South Africa failed to frame a federal constitution at the time when Sir G. Grey's scheme of a political federation was not approved by the home government, on the ground that federalism was premature where no responsible government had been experienced up to 1858? Moreover, Lord Carnarvon's proposal for federation in 1875 fell flat owing to Froude's disastrous conduct of his mission, and also because of the conflict of interests of the colonies, especially the ambitions of the Cape as regards the ownership of the diamond mines in Griqualand West. The problem of the consolidation of South African colonies was so difficult that it was not until after the Boer War that the ideal of union came within the field of practical politics and was strengthened by the success of federalism in the two other dominions.

The grant of responsible government to the Transvaal in 1906 and to the Orange River colony in 1907 led to the establishment of a joint South African Constabulary for both of these.

The voluntary union of the four colonies and Rhodesia, under the High Commissioner for South Africa, renewed the Custom Union in 1906.

The establishment of responsible government was naturally followed by the movement towards federal consolidation. Successive events, such as the recognition of the federal High Court of South Africa as a Court of Appeal, to some extent in the place of the Privy Council, and the Colonial Conference of 1907, resulted in the Conference of 1908. The labours of the delegates appointed for the formation of the constitution developed into the reverse of federalism, and resulted in the framing of the Act of Union, with a highly decentralised unitary government. This new form of government was due partly to adherence to the North America Act and in part was the fruit of full consultation with the imperial government concerning means of removing the federal difficulties.

The intercolonial federal movement in the British Empire came to an end for a while after the consolidation of the South African Union was formed.

Now Baron Felix von Oppenheimer, an Austrian, prophesied as to the imperial unity of empire that "the federal council and similar institutions do not satisfy the colonies. An imperial parliament in which the representatives of the self-governing colonies would have votes is a remote possibility and one scarcely to be realised. The only real means of bringing the colonies and the mother country closer together is the recognition and mutual promotion of their essential economic interests."[1] The demand for imperial federation received a final verdict when the first Imperial Conference met in 1911. Asquith, then Prime Minister, asserted that "we cannot, with the traditions and the history of the British Empire behind us, either from the point of view of the United Kingdom or from the point of view of our self-governing dominions, assent for a moment to proposals which are so fatal to the very fundamental conditions on which our empire has been built up and carried on. Therefore, with the highest possible respect, as we all have, for the skill and ability with which Sir Joseph Ward has presented his case, and a great deal of sympathy with many of the objects he has in view, I think we must agree that on its merits this proposal is not a practical one, and that, even if it were so, even if it could be shown to be so, the fact that it not only does not receive the unanimous consent of all the representatives of the dominions, but is repudiated by them all except Sir Joseph Ward himself, is for the purposes of this conference a fatal and, indeed, an insuperable objection to its adoption."[2]

Along with imperial federation, the movement for devolution in

[1] Baron F. von Oppenheimer: *British Imperialism*, 1905, pp. 86–87.
[2] Mr. Asquith's speech regarding Imperial Federation at the first Imperial Conference, 1911. Keith: *British Colonial Policy*, Vol. II, p. 303.

Great Britain gradually gained ground, the argument being that as the House of Commons had reached the maximum capacity for legislation, "England herself had been compelled to submit to a curtailment of her demands."[1]

T. A. Spalding, in 1896, insisted on the principle of devolution and argued that federalism was the only way to fulfil the permanent mission of parliament, in face of its ever-increasing burdens in the attempt to fulfil its legislative function on the one hand and on the other the function of controlling the administration and of ventilating grievance by means of debate.[2] He contended that the problem presented by the over-burdening of the House of Commons must cause and promote a movement towards federal devolution.

In the decade 1850–1860, despite the vital importance of foreign and colonial matters, these took up only 19·5 per cent. of the total debates, even when the Crimean War and Indian Mutiny were raging. The paralysis of parliament within and without crippled the efficient discharge of its mission, both in the internal problems of the three kingdoms, England, Scotland, and Ireland, and in foreign and colonial problems.

In 1850 the burdens of domestic legislation brought about a tacit recognition of federalism in debate in the House of Commons, where, in "state" questions which were not of interest to members of the other two states, a new convention was established by an understanding that disinterested members did not attend these debates.

He emphasised that "the Scottish night" was the first sign of federal institutions in the House of Commons.

In his argument as to whether the definition of federation was applicable to the development of devolution, Spalding, starting from Dicey's conception of federalism, under which a rigid and written constitution was the first essential for a supreme law over the non-sovereign bodies of federal and state governments, endeavoured to find the federal conception in the evolution of a federal function within the unitary state.

The primary objection to his federalism was that it was an organism in which the central government with sovereign power did not guarantee the state rights, and moreover the power of constitutional revision was not beyond the control of the national government. But he expounded his view that the solution of urgent political problems was of more importance than "a mere question of nomenclatures," and he defended himself by the

[1] T. A. Spalding: *Federation and Empire*, 1896, p. 64.   [2] Ibid., pp. 77–80.

utilitarian creed that "so the thing be understood I am indifferent as to the name."[1] He concluded the description of evolutionary federalism by approving the making of the House of Lords into the final Court of Appeal; just as in the House of Commons matters relating to any particular division of the United Kingdom were entrusted to the members from that division, so in the same way, quite properly, it was the legal members in the upper house who constituted this final court, thus emphasising the progression of evolutionary federalism.

He asserted that "it is dangerous to attempt to lay down any hard-and-fast rules as to the inevitable consequences of a federal system of government, and it might be possible that, under certain conditions, a form of government having all the advantages of federation might gradually be evolved without developing either a written constitution or a constituent assembly outside and controlling the federal assembly."[2]

On the assumption of devolutional federalism he proposed that "any federal system which would be adapted to the peculiar needs of the United Kingdom would consist of an imperial parliament composed, as at present, of two chambers and the crown, and three state assemblies which would consist of one popular elected chamber." He thought that the creation of a state "second chamber would be either anomalous or superfluous," because the second chamber of the imperial parliament would fulfil that function as a central body in legislation and a final Court of Appeal.[3]

This movement towards devolution was finally concluded by the formation of the Conference on Devolution in 1920. The report put forward a practical way of putting devolution into operation, but did not consider whether the principle of devolution was desirable or not. The majority report, proposed by the Speaker, and the minority report, signed by Murray Macdonald and his supporters, both set up three areas, England, Scotland and Wales (including Monmouthshire), for the establishment of provincial legislatures. The majority report recommended that the local subordinate legislature should consist of two chambers, but the minority report proposed that each of the areas "shall have a directly elected chamber." Regarding the second chamber,

[1] John Locke: *Of Civil Government*, 1694, Chap. XII.
[2] T. A. Spalding: *Federation and Empire*, 1896, p. 248.
[3] Ibid., pp. 304–305.—The "three state assemblies" meant the three different legislative assemblies of England, Scotland and Ireland. The federal nature is due to the fact that there is a distribution of powers between the Imperial Parliament and the three state assemblies and a limitation of functions.

Macdonald favoured the proposal of Lord Bryce's Conference on the Reform of the Second Chamber, and recommended that "peers shall not be disqualified for election to the popular elected chambers." Both recommended that the "inherent and supreme rights and powers of the parliament of the United Kingdom must remain absolutely unimpaired," but also proposed that absolute rights of the subordinate legislature should be granted by the method of special enumeration. This distribution of powers was of the utmost importance in federal devolution.

The right to determine the question of *ultra vires* was vested in the Secretary of State, with the final decision left to the Judicial Committee of the Privy Council, who "shall decide upon its validity or otherwise."

The practical value of this distribution of legislative powers between the United Kingdom and the local subordinate legislatures ought to be estimated not only by the advantage of freedom from the overburden of legislation, but also by considerations of efficient and adequate administration, and the possible confusion arising from diversity of legislation in three areas. This latter consideration had already manifested the demerits of existing federal states, the tendency of which had then been to centralise legislation for joint and general purposes.

The question of a remedy for the condition resulting from the overwhelming increase of local legislation in the national parliament is the main problem for reformers. The solution may be found in some new system of parliamentary procedure based on the application of the federal idea.

At the same time Mr. and Mrs. Sydney Webb's proposal of a pluralistic scheme of two parliaments in the British constitution was a characteristic federal feature of their ideal Socialistic Commonwealth, and aimed at the co-ordination of the industrial and political functions of parliament.

For their Socialistic Commonwealth the Webbs proposed two parliaments—one entrusted with the national administration of the industries and services by and through which the community lives, and the other charged with strictly political matters. It was a distinction between *Wirtschaft, gestion*, "housekeeping," on the one hand, and *Verwaltung, autorité régalienne*, police power, on the other.

The two national parliaments were to be "co-equal and independent, and neither of them first nor last."[1] The co-operative

[1] Sidney and Beatrice Webb: *A Constitution for the Socialist Commonwealth of Great Britain*, 1920, p. 111.

commonwealth of the Webbs' ideal state was based on the co-ordinate and equal independent powers and functions of the two national assemblies in the federal co-independence.[1]

G. D. H. Cole's *Guild Socialism* propounded the pluralistic idea of a federated state in which the Industrial Congress of Guilds took the highest place, but all the functions of industrial and social departments were to be co-ordinated; joint consultation between them was to be the means of arriving at the final decision in any conflict.

The difference between the Webbs' ideal state and Cole's

[1] *Addendum.*

Mrs. Webb's article on "A Reform Bill for 1932" in the *Political Quarterly* for January 1931 is of striking importance as setting out a definite scheme of reform of the democratic parliamentary state. In view of the growing inefficiency of the existing legislative and administrative machinery, resulting from the overburdening of the executive and the congestion of parliament, few can deny the need for a comprehensive change.

Accepting the existing basis of the British constitution, namely that the supreme authority rests formally "with King, Lords and Commons in Parliament assembled"—which under the Parliament Act of 1911 means with the Cabinet and the House of Commons, and rejecting the schemes of devolution recommended by the Conference on Devolution in 1920 and by Murray Macdonald's ideal suggestion, Mrs. Webb proposes a more limited and explicit type of devolution; "a devolution not of subjects at all but of specific statutes or groups of statutes."

Territorial devolution is regarded as out of date, and unsuitable to a small and densely populated area like Great Britain. What is proposed is the establishment of a National Assembly (or, if Scotland pressed for a separate organisation of its own, two such assemblies), and the devolution upon that body of a large body of business at present dealt with by the Cabinet and Parliament. The National Assembly would not, like the London County Council or the Manchester Municipal Corporation, be wholly without legislative powers: it would have the powers of amending and extending statutes which have been increasingly given in recent years to Government Departments—the complaints as to these powers would not arise if they were exercised by an elected body or committees of it. And the powers of the National Assembly would always be subject to the ultimate control of Parliament. The powers proposed to be transferred to the National Assembly are, broadly speaking, those which relate to purely domestic matters—health, education, labour (including factory administration), agriculture, mining, transport, power, and so on—the broad test being whether the subjects are national or local and political or economic. The scheme is, therefore, one of functional federalism on a national and not on a district basis: as regards the distribution of powers between federal organs, it does not show any advance upon orthodox federalism.

If it be accepted that federation on a territorial basis is "out of date" for Great Britain, it follows that functionalism will be the central problem of the future development of the idea of federalism. Mrs. Webb's scheme is undoubtedly a valuable indication of the line on which the British constitution might well advance to a new form of federalism.

guild state was that the former was based on the consumer's state, whilst the latter was based on the producer's supremacy in the state.

But both the Webbs' and Cole's pluralism placed their political ideas on the basis of that "theory of harmony" which Hobhouse proposed from the ethical value. Their appeal to functional democracy in the working of the state led them to look for the solution of political discord in the power exercised by the "invisible hand."

But the pluralistic aim could be attained even under the present parliamentary system, provided that it could be sufficiently reformed to admit of functional representation.

The pluralistic conception of the state manifested itself in respect of parliamentary efficiency by the establishment of the committee system, which enabled the treatment of various social and economic problems to be co-ordinated by parliament. Laski and Finer recommended the committee system, instead of the "German Economic Council."

Laski observed of devolution "nor does the experience of America indicate that the mere multiplication of legislatures is a sovereign remedy; on the contrary, its real lesson is rather the startling rapidity with which we limit the number of members genuinely gifted with legislative insight."[1]

The theory of "a joint congress of supreme bodies representing each of the main functions in society" was faced with the problem of the administrative difficulty arising from the existence of co-ordinate bodies. Laski assumed that "territorial unity shall not destroy functional independence and individual freedom."

In Cole's and the Webbs' proposals there was no power of final decision, but any dispute between two parties or states had to be settled by the joint decision of the disputants. But Laski, although an ardent upholder of pluralism in politics, yet assumed that "the state is made responsible by informing its co-ordinating power with notions of justice"[2]—that is, the state ought to possess the power of universal reference as far as every group in the state has a right to share in any decision.

[1] H. J. Laski: review of *Devolution in Great Britain*, by Wan-Hsuan Chiao, *Economica*, No. 19, March 1927, p. 107.
[2] Ibid., *Grammar of Politics*, 1925, p. 140.—"A state is made responsible by informing its co-ordinating power with notions of justice. It is made to play its due part in the communal synthesis by making it directly accessible to the interests which compose that synthesis. It then becomes a one which partakes of the nature of a many because the many enter into it and transform it." Cf. Part II, Chap. II, pp. 318–319.

Therefore the state was not at all to coerce the various functions of men, because the justification of groups in the state community was that they offered the only means of attaining a co-operative creation in which man could be realised at his best. But the state should be umpire as to final administration. "For the purpose of convenience the administration of the general rules of community is probably better managed by a simple than by a complex institution, granted the necessary safeguards." On this argument Laski assumed the parliamentary state with a federal character to be the best.

In the criticism of the increasing discontent with the idea of the "Economic Council," Finer proposed the substitution of the committee system for the existing parliament, instead of the special formation of an economic council.[1]

Imperially and internally the federal movement in the constitution of Great Britain did not give effect to the orthodox principle of federalism, but revealed itself as the committee system, with the Imperial Conference on the one hand and the recommendation of a new form of committee system for parliament and decentralised administration, with a centralised generalisation of the legislature, on the other.

In the evolutional development of the British constitution, both internal and imperial, the federalism of 1864 in the United States exercised a predominant influence on imperial federalism on the one hand, and on the idea of devolution on the other, during the latter half of the last century and down to the present day. The verdict on the former was given at the Imperial Conference of 1911 by the setting up of the system of the grand council of the Imperial Conference, and the dominions of the British Empire were recognised on their entry into the League of Nations in 1919 as independent members. And the Speaker's recommendation in the Conference on Devolution in 1920 was the final expression of sympathy with the devolution movement.[2]

Not only the distance which separates the dominions from the mother country, the diversity of interests and the consolidation of their own interests and nationalities, but also the absence of that necessity and demand which are essential to federation were antagonistic to the establishment of complete imperial federation. Labillière's and Kelsey's ideal was ended by the half-way device

[1] H. Finer: *Representative Government and a Parliament of Industry*, 1923, pp. 210–230.
[2] *Conference on Devolution*. Letter from Mr. Speaker to the Prime Minister. Published by H.M. Stationery Office, 1920 (reprint 1924), London.

of the committee system of the empire, taking various forms of conference, such as the Economic Conference, and the Imperial Defence Conference, and other committees relating to health and educational matters, which were a slight bond of the scattered empire, derived from the common sentiment of the Anglo-Saxon race, and the economic connections between colonial interests and the City of London.

In 1917 J. A. Murray Macdonald wrote a pamphlet arguing of imperial federation that the only safe and assured means of constitutional union among British people is the accustomed and familiar means of a parliament with an executive responsible to it.[1] He proposed the creation of an imperial parliament with 300 members from the constituencies of the whole empire in the House of Commons and representatives in the House of Lords from all parts of the empire.

Nevertheless, the general understanding of imperial unity, except in the case of a few of its advocates, has not gone beyond imperial co-operation.

Dicey gave as his verdict that imperial federation "is at the bottom a delusion, and a delusion perilous not only to England but to the whole British Empire"; the characteristics of federalism were not reconcilable with the actual unity of the whole empire under "the formation of a federal or any other brand-new constitution."

The needs of the empire were, firstly, defence and the expenditure thereon, and, secondly, constant consultation between England and the dominions in co-related matters. The Imperial Conference was therefore a step in the right direction and the best mode of inter-communication between the mother country and the dominions.

He concluded that "my full belief is that an imperial constitution, based on good will and fairness, may within a few years come into real existence, before most Englishmen have realised that the essential foundations of imperial unity have already been firmly laid. . . . The ground of my assurance is that the constitution of the empire may, like the constitution of England, be found to rest far less on parliamentary statutes than on the growth of gradual and often unnoted customs."[2]

The ideal of the "Little Englander" was the foreshadowing of the actual developments which have taken place in the British dominions; but while these dominions are practically self-

[1] J. A. Murray Macdonald: *Notes on the Constitutional Reconstruction of the Empire*, 1917.   [2] A. V. Dicey: *Law of the Constitution*, 1924, introduction, lxxxvi.

governing, and also quasi-independent, yet in the strictly legal sense of the term their status as sovereign powers is still doubtful even though internationally they appear as such.

Now the history of federation in Great Britain showed an unintentional and unconscious leaning to the ultimate aims of federalism—the decentralised state in the pluralistic sense.

However much the enthusiastic and earnest advocacy of the imperial federalists had influenced public opinion, and however logically and scientifically the devolutionists had urged the necessity for some form of devolution, no practical result had followed, either in domestic or imperial affairs, except in so far as essential necessity had led to the adoption of some special forms—either the loose form of councils of a confederated character or that of committees in the House of Commons.

Now we may inquire into the nature of federalism in the light of the history of the British federal movement.

Federalism was based on "utility"—that is, on the existence of a demand. The essential character of federalism was the equal position of co-ordinate powers and the existence of similar political institutions among the component parts of the federal body. And the members of the federal union, whether sovereign or non-sovereign states, should have more or less "original state" character, in other words, be states based on responsible government.

The idea of sovereignty has been and is established in our time as a common belief whose mystic force is the greatest obstacle to the development of federalism. Natural hindrances, such as distance, difference in climate, domestic and social habits, language and so forth, are the second obstacle to federal development. Firstly, it is of vital importance to notice that the failure of imperial federation is due to the fact that the actual necessity for imperial federation had not yet reached the point where the formation of the "federal state" was practicable. And, secondly, some of the natural obstacles had increased the improbability of its realisation. And, moreover, the absolute notion of sovereignty, as being vested in the King in Parliament at Westminster, was always an obstacle to the establishment of an equitable basis for membership of the British Isles and the self-governing dominions and colonies.

But apart from these legal criticisms and independent of sovereignty, as J. S. Mill observed, the British Empire has developed into a kind of confederation in the loosest form.

The Imperial Conference was constituted under the terms of the resolution of the Colonial Conference of 1907, and is a permanent conference of delegates of His Majesty's governments in the United Kingdom and in his self-governing dominions beyond the seas for the promotion of the common interests of the empire; it is to be held every four years.

The Prime Minister of the United Kingdom is ex-officio President, and the Prime Ministers of the self-governing dominions are also ex-officio members of the conference. The Secretary of State for the Dominions is also to be an ex-officio member of the conference and to take the chair in the absence of the President: other United Kingdom and dominion ministers may attend. Each government possesses only one vote in the conference. As the executive organ, a permanent secretarial staff under the direction of the Secretary of State for the Colonies is set up for the conducting of the business of the conference. Since the Imperial War Conference of 1917, India has been admitted to full representation at the conference, and since the grant of self-government to Ireland in 1922 the Irish Free State has naturally become a permanent member of the Imperial Conference.

Besides the Imperial Conference there are also specific conferences and committees, such as the Imperial Education Conference, the Imperial Economic Conference, the Committee of Imperial Defence, and the Foreign Affairs Committee as means of imperial co-operation. Under the secretariat there are numbers of bureaux and committees which are standing and executive bodies not entitled to enforce their decisions; there is the "Judicial Committee of the Privy Council" as the final Court of Appeal, and there are hundreds of voluntary unions which together create a unique example of a quasi-confederated union.

Though *de jure* the self-governing dominions are non-sovereign bodies, yet His Majesty's government in Great Britain has never ventured upon a coercive policy in the exercise of a sovereign will against the majority will of the dominions; and these are even legally quasi-sovereign states possessed of international personality, since the self-governing dominions of the British Empire are independent members of the League of Nations. Except in this last case, *de facto* the British Empire is based on the confederative form of federalism. Nevertheless, in the German sense of federalism, its ordinary definition, the British Empire is in no sense a federated state, but a unitary sovereign state with enormous colonies and dominions all over the world.

Therefore I conclude from the actual history of British federalism that in our time Great Britain has failed in, and proved unsuitable to, federation, imperial and domestic, but has travelled on the right road towards the natural end of federalism—that is, towards the decentralised state in the pluralistic sense, internally, and towards disintegration imperially. I believe that the recent revival of colonial patriotism and the strengthening of imperial unity is a temporary phenomenon.

If the essential federal bond between the mother country and the several dominions and colonies is to be based on the actual needs and demands of both sides and evolved from the interests of both under the existing regime, the necessity and the desire for federation will gradually decline; but so long as the natural co-operation of the Anglo-Saxon race and the fortunate co-ordination of economic interests are not broken by some great upheaval on both sides, the great empire will continue to stand as an elaborate political structure, the like of which has never been and never will be seen again in the history of mankind.

Even though the fundamental virtues of federalism—the principles of self-government and of responsible government based on the theory of compromise—are deep-rooted in the minds of Englishmen, practical needs and desires have not availed to create a federal structure in Great Britain. The British federal movement has taught us that no unitary state, however important its decentralisation may be, can form a federal state, and also that federalism itself is an intermediate political system between the loose *Bund* and a decentralised state with a federal character.

In 1930 federalism came before the English and Indian public as a fresh subject when the Round Table Conference set up the federal structure sub-committee under the chairmanship of Lord Sankey. No one expects that such a vast country as India can be governed satisfactorily on a dominion status without consideration of the federal idea. The existing conditions of India, which are the consequence of divergences in her social and state structure —the differences between the Indian states and British India and those of religion and race—demand solution by means of the federal device. Though no other solution of these problems can be nearly so effective as the federalist one, yet historical federal experience has already taught us that the application of orthodox federalism cannot bring about a really satisfactory solution unless the basis of federal India is reconstructed.

Nevertheless, the federal structure can of itself mitigate the disadvantages arising from the differences in political, economic and social conditions during the transition period to the ideal federal state. In this respect the sub-committee made recommendations as to the distribution of authority between the Indian states and British India, and their relation to the federal authority, and at the same time proposed a bicameral legislature and a federal authority, though not of a wholly satisfactory kind.[1] Wholesale differences may exist as to the basis of the state structure between the German Empire of 1871 and federal India, but a certain similarity between them can be found in the relations of the federal state to British India as well as in those of the Indian federal government to them both, except that there would be no possibility of federal hegemony in a federal India.

In these circumstances, federal India, even in the sphere of orthodox federalism, would still be far less advanced than federal Canada or federal Australia. The only omission in federal India, likewise in Australia and Canada, is the elimination of the hypothesis of legal sovereignty in its formation, except the question of *ultra vires* of the distribution of power between the British sovereign and the federal government as well as between the federal state and its component parts.

With dominion status the final settlement of federal disputes is vested in the Privy Council. In this respect, as in other federal dominions, Indian federalism is confined to the problem of the distribution of power in respect of federal functions. So far as concerns in our time the conception of sovereignty within the federal organisation, the centralised tendency of federalism might overcome state right theories like those of John Calhoun and Max Seydel. But in federal India the problem would still remain as to the structure of the future Indian states and their relation to federal government and British Indian provinces, and as to minorities.[2]

The minority question, which turns mainly on the relations of Moslems and Hindus, cannot be solved by any territorial federal mechanism except the establishment of a new federal idea of functionalism and the enlightenment of the Indian peoples so as to overcome their traditional social complexities. For the sake of India, no matter how theoretically inadequate the projected structure of federal India may be, the thorough study of the German Empire, as well as of other federal states of republican

---

[1] *Indian Round Table Conference*, London (published by H.M. Stationery Office). Cmd. 3772, 1931, pp. 8–9, 14–27.   [2] Ibid., pp. 45–49.

form, is necessary to avoid as much as possible the evils which they experienced and to secure as far as may be the advantages which they have secured, and to show the ways in which the difficulties which the future federal India must face may be overcome by a process of gradual reform which will cope with them as they arise.

CHAPTER II

MODERN FEDERAL IDEAS IN GREAT BRITAIN

§ 1

From this actual history of federal discussions in Great Britain I will return to the theoretical discussions of federalism, and examine the extent to which they have influenced the development of federal theory, why the British federal movement has failed, and why it will ultimately develop to that form of federalism which the United States and other federal states are now facing—namely, the change from federation into the decentralised unitary state.

First of all, I shall briefly summarise the most important discussions of federalism by the chief British political thinkers since about the year 1800.

Bentham noticed nearly all the problems of democratic government, the aims of which, he incessantly insisted, should be based on the principle of "the greatest happiness of the greatest number," but not on the "self-preference principle." His survey of every function of government, ranging from the appointment of minor local judges to the ends of government, resulted in his thorough statement of a "Constitutional Code," in which his ideal state, based on the greatest happiness principle, was fully set out.

Federalism, in his eyes, was an alternative form of government in which the "federative government is the only one whose circumstances admit of the formation of the present code." His Constitutional Code, "though penned on the supposition that government is to be of the simple kind, is not the less adapted to the purpose in view, if the only form employable is the federative."[1]

It was his fundamental thesis that federalism is that form of democratic government of the republican kind of which the main purpose is to give the greatest appropriate powers to the sub-legislatures. He made a ratiocinative and instructive analysis of federative government, and of its advantages and disadvantages.

His political attitude, however, was that the simple form of government was preferable to the complex one. Therefore the federation could only survive as a "matter of necessity" or a "fit object of government" in the form of government.

Starting with this general assumption, he examined the federal

[1] J. Bentham: *Works, Constitutional Code*, ed. John Bowring, 1843, Vol. IX, p. 644.

constitution by a twofold method, the "analytic" and the "synthetic."

According to the analytical method, he assumed the federal constitution to be that of "a number of sub-legislatures," and he conceived them, "one or more, or all of them as to this or that point, or any number of points, supreme: not subordinate with relation to the legislature."[1] At the same time, by the synthetic method, he conceived it as "a number of republics, each independent: in each of them the authority of the legislature is supreme, but agreeing to stand as to certain specified points, one or more, subordinate to a central legislature, the members of which shall be deputed from the several thus confederated states."[2]

In these two definitions, what Bentham designated as the federative government was a highly organised confederation or the federal state of Madison's ideal.

He compared federative government with the simple one and enumerated the several disadvantages.

In the federal system there were difficulties which could be divided into two classes: those which "regard the substance of the arrangements," and those which "regard the form."

He sub-divided those regarding the substance into "the personal and real"—that is, "men and money worth." The difficulty of arrangements as to men was far easier of solution than that of money, because the main question was "whether the men contributed by each state shall be kept distinct or mixed indiscriminately in the central army." As to money's worth, he put forward two difficulties; one was "how to settle quotas between state and state," and the other, "how to secure the actual furnishing" of the quotas.

He thought that the quotas should be settled on the statistical basis of the wealth of the states, actually and relatively to population.

[1] J. Bentham: *Works, Constitutional Code*, ed. John Bowring, 1843, Vol. IX, p. 644. —In the first section, Art. I: "In every District is a sub-legislature." "By sub-legislature understand a political body, exercising, under the authority of the Legislature, either as to the whole, or as to a part of its logical field of service, functions of the same nature as those of the Legislature."

"Sec. II: By each sub-Legislature, under the authority of the Legislature, are exercised, within its local field of service, the several functions following:—

"(1) Its Ministerial function; (2) Its Institution-rearing function; (3) Its Money-supplying function; (4) Its Expenditure-watching function; (5) Its Transfer-compelling function; (6) Its Information-elicitative function; (7) Its Publicity-securing function." It was a highly organised self-governing local autonomy under the authority of the national government (pp. 640–644).

[2] Ibid., p. 644.

As to the method of securing it, the most simple was taxation fixed by the legislature, but there were difficulties as to its administration and collection.

He criticised and compared the single taxation and double taxation systems, each of which had its own merits and defects; the former was the method of the confederacy and the latter that of the federal state.[1]

However ambiguous his federative government might be, that is, as to whether it was a confederation or a federal state, his criticism of federalism was concerned with the federal state as it existed in the United States, which stood mid-way between the ideals of Madison and Calhoun.

He was opposed to the double system of government, firstly on the ground of expense, in that "of two branches of the additional establishment, namely, administration and judiciary, the maximum of the addition will be re-duplicated in both cases," and secondly, because of the danger of disagreement, ill will and consequent rupture of the association of states. The main problem arose from the existence of the *imperium in imperio* in the federative government, and the risk of the violation of the rights of one party or its oppression by the others, and the repugnancy which would inevitably result from the double allegiance of the people.

From this standpoint of internal administrative expediency, his verdict undoubtedly favoured the simple system rather than the complicated one, but the validity of this determination depended chiefly upon an administrative method of carrying out its purpose.

In regard to form—by reason of the diversity of interpretation

---

[1] J. Bentham: *Works, Constitutional Code*, ed. John Bowring, 1843, Vol. IX.—"Each state, to its own taxes imposed for its own peculiar purpose, adds others, imposed on the same sources, or say contribution-yielding subject-matters of taxation, or on other and additional ones. In both cases it collects the money by its own collectors; and from the aggregate fund thus composed, periodically conveys the quota agreed on, or such lesser share as it chooses to part with, for the use of the whole confederacy to the central spot. Call this the Single-taxation system. Each state under such restrictions and conditions as are agreed on, gives permission and authority to the Central Government to impose, as its own choice, taxes to the stipulated amount on the citizens of the several Confederated States.

"In this case follow, as a necessary consequence in each State, two separate Department Official Establishments: to wit, a branch of the Administrative and a branch or the whole of a Judiciary Establishment: the one, for the collection of the correspondent part of the revenue, in uncontested cases; the other for the collection of it, in contested cases. Call this the Double-taxation system" (p. 645).

—however sincere and impartial, his verdict was due to the difficulty of finding, in any part of the field, locutions sufficiently well adapted for the purposes of demarcation between the authority of the central government and that of the confederated states.

In order to attain a complete solution of this problem, the fullest possible knowledge of "the art and science of logic" was an absolute necessity.

There must be a thorough investigation of actual facts, from which the actual distribution of these two powers could be derived.

The various evils of the federal system were increased with the magnitude of the aggregate territory. He asserted that "the distance and consequent length of time would cause tardiness and infrequency of communication" between the seats of the central government, administration and judiciary, and the seats of the local government.

These vices were more obviously and significantly exemplified in the judiciary than in the administrative department. However much these evils might be minimised by the application of registration or the publication system, especially his ideal "Pannomion," the rapid dispatch of government business was naturally hampered.

In the adjustment of territorial limits as between the states, it was highly important to settle questions as to the use of water, either of the river or of the sea—such as fishing, irrigation and navigation.

None of these questions, such as water or trades, could be solved without judicial arbitration or conciliation. But Bentham thought that the probability of continuing in a state of amity was not to be increased "by coalescence into a confederated state" under judicial authority, but the question could be peacefully adjusted by a judicature composed of agents from each state.

In the federal system the publicity of judicial discussions or appeals to the tribunal of public opinion could hardly check mischievous action among the states, such as any plan of conquest or oppression by one of another; the only check was superior military power.

Bentham's discredit of the federal system was minimised in "the case of the Anglo-American states." He said that "to establish an effective and permanent union of this kind, nothing more is necessary than to take for the model, and for subject-matter of exact imitation, the system exemplified in the case of the Anglo-American states."

The essential difference of this confederacy from others depended upon the fact that in the United States there existed the "eminent altitude in which the public mind was seated, in respect of political and legislative intelligence, at the time of the establishment of the confederacy," whilst in the others, such as those which had been subjected to Spanish tyranny and Portuguese misrule, the public mind was in a very low state as compared with the former.

From the historical failure of the Athenian type of alliance and the loose confederacy, he conceived that the remedy was a more extensive union; e.g. "the greater the power in the hands of the central government, and thence of the several individual functionaries sharing in it."

Bentham's instruction to the federative government was nothing more than that of Hamilton's appeal to the Convention of 1787.

He totally rejected the confederated system of state because of his opinions as to federal deficiencies.[1] He counted the advantages of a simple government as being not less "undeniable." Firstly, corruption might be far easier in the federal system than in the simple one; secondly, the danger of conflict between the central and local government was everlasting and never settled; and thirdly, the equal power, the same degree of civilisation and the same republican form of government produced weakness in federal government and strengthened the local government.

He admitted that the main advantage of the federal system was that in a given space there were "a number, more or less considerable, of political debating assemblies, instead of no more than one—the additional and all-pervading strength thus given to the public mind in every part of the country, each particular government operating as a check upon the central government, as well as upon every other."[2]

[1] J. Bentham: *Works, Constitutional Code*, ed. John Bowring, 1843, Vol. IX.—"Sec. III. Art. I. Exceptions excepted, in no instance will a Federal Constitution, or say a confederated form of government, be employed in preference to the simple, or say, unconfederated. Reasons:

"1. Complicatedness of the Federal form.

"2. Thence difficulty of the several operations of creation and preservation in relation to it.

"3. Difficulty of effecting an agreement as to the purport of the arrangements to be established.

"4. Difficulty of framing apt expressions for the designation of those same arrangements.

"5. Danger of jealousies, from supposed partiality as to this or that particular state.

"6. Danger of disagreement and eventual hostility on the part of the states, a confederacy of which is formed, or in contemplation to be formed" (p. 646).

[2] Ibid., p. 647.

This decentralised legislature was so important in a democratic government that he recognised that the fall of the French republic was mainly due to its absence.

Bentham asserted that this necessity of decentralised legislature in the federal system might be met by the powers and duties of his ideal "sub-legislatures," through which the majority of the defects of federative government could be eliminated and its aim might be fulfilled.

However great the difference between the various political mechanisms of the federative governments, the "one soul" in the final determination ought to be essential in any political technique. He was convinced that "in the federative form there cannot but be as many souls as distinct governments, and amongst them there may any day be jarring ones."[1]

His final judgment of federalism was that it depended upon the nature of the actual political circumstances, which must be tested by his utilitarian calculus.

Suggestive as his analysis was, this argument was critical rather than constructive, but it was a fair criticism of the federal state which existed in his day.

§ 2

John Austin, a great jurist and the founder of the analytical school of jurisprudence, discussed federalism in his lectures on *The Province of Jurisprudence* in 1832. As I have already explained fully in a previous chapter (Part I, Chap. VII, § 2), his real contribution to the theory of federalism was his exposition of the new type of federalism which sprang up in the United States after the Civil War of 1861.

At the time of the failure of the orthodox federalism, no influence was stronger than that of Austin's conception of sovereignty upon the minds of the framers of the new federal doctrine in the United States. John Hurd and his followers, in the face of Germanic legal transcendentalism, put forward the sovereignty of the union based on the utilitarian conception of law. As Austin criticised the federal union it is worth while quoting his general conception of a composite (federal) state and a system of confederated states. He said "a composite state and a system of confederated states are broadly distinguished by the following essential difference. In the case of a composite state, the several united societies are

[1] J. Bentham: *Works, Constitutional Code*, ed. John Bowring, 1843, Vol. IX, p. 647.

one independent society, or are severally subject to one sovereign body, which, through its minister, the general government, and through its members and ministers, the several united governments, is habitually and generally obeyed in each of the united societies, and also in the larger society arising from the union of all. In the case of a system of confederated states, the several compacted societies are not one society, and are not subject to a common sovereign: or (changing the phrase) each of the several societies is an independent political society, and each of their several governments is properly sovereign or supreme. Though the aggregate of the several governments was the framer of the federal compact, and may subsequently pass resolutions concerning the entire confederacy, neither the terms of that compact, nor such subsequent resolutions, are inforced in any of the societies by the authority of that aggregate body. To each of the confederated governments, those terms and resolutions are merely articles of agreement which it spontaneously adopts: and they owe their legal effect, in its own political society, to laws and other commands which it makes or fashions upon them, and which, of its own authority, it addresses to its own subjects. In short, a system of confederated states is not essentially different from a number of independent governments connected by an ordinary alliance. And where independent governments are connected by an ordinary alliance, none of the allied governments is subject to the allied governments considered as an aggregate body: though each of the allied governments adopts the terms of the alliance, and commonly enforces those terms by laws and commands of its own, in its own independent community. Indeed, a system of confederated states and a number of independent governments connected by an ordinary alliance cannot be distinguished precisely through general or abstract expressions. So long as we abide in general expressions, we can only affirm generally and vaguely that the compact of the former is intended to be temporary: and that the ends or purposes which are embraced by the compact are commonly more numerous, and are commonly more complicated than those which the alliance contemplates."[1]

In Austin's idea of federalism the question of sovereignty had more influence than any other consideration, because his federal notion as to its fundamental thesis was not quite novel in actual contents.

Other English authorities on international law, such as Twiss

[1] John Austin: *Lectures on Jurisprudence*, 1873, Vol. I, p. 269.

and Phillimore, more or less, had a similar conception of federalism as it was propounded in North American literature. And the federation was assumed to be an international personality, confirming a national existence.

§ 3

John Stuart Mill, the most eminent political thinker in England in the nineteenth century, criticised the federal system in his *Representative Government* in 1861, when the Civil War in America was opened by the declaration of secession by the eleven southern states.

The greatest happiness principle was for Mill dependent not upon Bentham's quantitative validity, but upon qualitative justification. His utilitarian rationalism brought about his conception of the state as the best where government was organised under such a representative constitution that the merits of political institutions—such as order and progress—were well-balanced in the form and functioning of that government.

To Mill, the ideal government was "an organisation of some part of the good qualities existing in the individual members of the community, for the conduct of its collective affairs," so that individual and public interests and the virtue and intelligence and morals of its wisest members were kept directly and constantly in contact with the business of the government which was to be best fitted to promote the interests and qualities of any given society.[1]

Nevertheless, whatever moving force the best governmental machinery might derive from the good qualities of people, his socialistic inclination brought about the recognition of the good

[1] J. S. Mill: *Representative Government*, 1861.—"What we have said of the arrangements for the detailed administration of the government, is still more evidently true of its general constitution.

"All government which aims at being good, is an organisation of some part of the good qualities existing in the individual members of the community, for the conduct of its collective affairs. A representative constitution is a means of being the general standard of intelligence and honesty existing in the community, and the individual intellect and virtue of its wisest members, more directly to bear upon the government, and investing them with greater influence in it, than they would have under any other mode of organisation; though under any, such influence as they do have is the source of all good that there is in the government, and the hindrance of every evil that there is not.

"The greater amount of these good qualities which the institutions of a country succeed in organising, and the better the mode of organisation, the better will be the government" (pp. 32–33).

quality of governmental mechanism which "makes them instrumental to the right purposes."

His love of democracy and liberty led him to regard as the ideal government a representative government such that the supreme power in the last resort—that is, the sovereignty—should "rest in the entire aggregate of the whole community," where every citizen ought not only to possess a voice in the performance of the ultimate sovereignty, but also was occasionally called to take an actual part in government by the personal discharge of some public function, local or general. The desire for participation in the exercise of sovereignty as well as in its execution was an ultimate aim of the good government.

With this presupposition he criticised the federal system as one of the necessary functions of government. Political necessity among some portions of mankind required the federal union as advantageous for their mutual defence within and without and for other foreign relations.

He did not attempt any classification or theory of the union, like German publicists, but analysed objectively federal representative government as one system of machinery and functioning of the body politic. The actual federal systems he had in mind were no doubt those of the United States after 1787 and Switzerland after 1847.

Mill observed that even the British Empire in relation to the dominions and the mother country was "the slightest kind of federal union."[1] The free colonies had full powers over their own affairs and were less restrained by the mother country, except in foreign affairs, than the member states of the United States. But the power of veto, however rarely it might be exercised, was reserved to the King in Parliament at Westminster; and the inequality of rights in respect of foreign affairs manifested that it was not a federation in the strict sense.

First of all he asserted that, in order to operate the federal machine successfully, certain political conditions were essential.

It was necessary for the maintenance of an efficient federal bond to have a sufficient amount of mutual sympathy among the population, not only a united feeling in respect of a common enemy, but also a common sympathy arising from community of race, language and especially religion, and above all the same political institutions which should aim essentially at creating a common feeling as to the identity of the political interests to be served.

[1] J. S. Mill: *Representative Government*, 1861, p. 316.

It also required the stability of federal government, because, if otherwise, the confidence in the federal authority would decline, and the sacrifice of the liberty of the separate states for the sake of the federal tie would be disappointed, and their cognisance of the reserved rights would hasten the sectional breach and the destruction of the bond.

A last condition, less important than the others, was that there should not be a very marked inequality of strength between the contracting states. However inevitable inequality of natural resources might be, still it was absolutely essential that there should not be any one state stronger and more powerful than the rest combined, or any two whose power might be irresistible by the rest.[1]

Like other publicists, he tried to divide the modes of organising a federal union into two.

Firstly, the federal authorities could be delegated by the governments solely and their acts could be an "obligation only on the governments as such," what we called confederacy—for example, the German confederacy and the Swiss Government before 1847.

Secondly, the federal government could hold "the powers of enacting laws and issuing orders which were binding directly on individual citizens" within appropriate limits placed on the federal government by the constitution, such as the American union of 1787.

He reduced the confederation to a "mere alliance which was subject to all contingencies which render alliances precarious." In these circumstances no mandates of the federal government, if the local majority disagreed, would ever be executed, and no settlement, if the recalcitrant states should resist incessantly against the federal issue, was probable without the use of physical force. Mill expressed the opinion that the most "instructive" treatise on the federal discussion, therefore, was the collective papers of the American "Federalists," where the weaknesses and defects of the method of confederations were exposed and there was presented the more perfect mode of federation—what we call the "federal state."

An effectual confederation of two or more kingly governments under a single king appeared to be a mode of union, but intrinsically was far nearer a unitary state under the single will of the crown.

[1] In the case of the German Bund, Austria and Prussia nullified formation for a long time until Prussia became predominant over Austria in 1867.

On his argument, the only mode of federation which held the probability of efficient discharge of federal governmental functions was the "federal state," not the confederation which was a mere alliance, and not the real union which was federated under the command of a single crown.

It was in the nature of the federal state that the double obligation of the citizens towards the authorities of the states and of the federation produced a double obedience, which necessitated undoubtedly a clear constitutional demarcation of their authorities on the one hand, and made it of the utmost urgency to establish an impartial "Umpire" for the decision of disputes between them or their functionaries on the other.

The federal state, therefore, set up and empowered a supreme court of justice as the highest and final federal tribunal, which preserved supreme power over governments both federal and state, and had the right of deciding the constitutionality of all laws made by them.[1]

The main pillar of the federal state was the highest confidence in, and the fullest reliance on, the supreme court of justice for federal functions.

The passive character of the judicial umpire as to the unconstitutionality of law did not matter very much in the early experience of America, and the confidence placed in the judicial tribunal was not sufficient, and its authority was weakened, ever since Chief Justice Taney's judgment on slavery made it lawful within the territories of the "Missouri Compromise."

The way to reach ideal federation was to promote the stability of federal institutions in which confidence would be maintained, and the proper discharge of their duties secured by the legal supremacy of a court vested with the final judgment as to constitutionality.

The key of the federal state, distinguishing it from the international relationship, was that war and diplomacy were precluded by the federal union. The judicial arbitration in the federal union was the means by which the supreme court of justice "dispensed the international law," that is, it was the foreshadowing of a real international tribunal of arbitration.

With regard to the distribution of powers in the federal union, Mill implicitly expressed a view as to the main controversy of federalism in his day. In this problem no speculative political thinker since the Federalists, except John Calhoun, in "a posthumous work of great ability," had vindicated "the general

[1] J. S. Mill: *Representative Government*, 1861, p. 303.

principle of limiting the tyranny of the majority and protecting minorities by admitting them to a substantial participation in political power." He thought that with regard to general subjects, except foreign affairs, the real question turned upon the extent people in general desired and were willing to give up their local freedom and surrender to the federal tie in order to enjoy the greater happiness and benefit of being one nation.

In the fifties of the last century, the federal problem, in Calhoun's reply to Webster, came to a climax, which was incapable of solution without either the formation of an entirely new conception or the use of physical force to compel the surrender of one doctrine to the other.

Mill did not put forward any suggestions as to federal solidarity, but his remedy was an evolutionary solution, drawn from the actual experience of a federal people.

He emphasised the necessity of the bicameral system of federal legislature, a representative house based on population, on the one hand, and the senate, with equal representation of every state, on the other.

The senate system which he advocated was the expression of his ideal plural representation and the securing of the authority of intellect in politics, and also was to guard against the evils of centralisation by giving equal representation to the component states.

These statutory methods produced the practice of co-operation, in which the weak, by unity, can meet on equal terms with the stronger, and the value of the federal organisation cannot be minimised by any attempt at aggressive policy, either by the use of arms or even by the prestige of the superior powers. No organisation other than the federal one produced more real peace and good will with voluntary conscientious co-operation.

In Mill's argument as to whether a country, when it was determined to unite, should form a complete unitary state or federal union, the main thesis was that the test is a political one. He thought that territorial magnitude was one of the considerations which must be taken into account in determining whether a single central government was capable of governing or supervising numerous matters throughout vast areas, because there might be a limit to the administrative capacity even of a good government. This limit of administrative capacity prevented an effective rule from a remotely distant seat of government, even through an instructed agent of the central authority—except in the case of savages who were unable to govern by themselves. Therefore, the federal system was the natural product of the political conditions of a large country but not of a country the size of Italy. Another consideration was the extent of the desire of the citizens in the various provinces for different legislatures, different ministries and administrative bodies. Nevertheless, as a matter of fact, differences of legal systems and traditions were not altogether essential in the federal state, and, on the other hand, even in the unitary state, the co-existence of different legal systems and traditions was possible under a highly decentralised system, such as the Union of England and Scotland.

If the people of the several states did not insist on maintaining permanently different legal systems or separate ministries or law-making bodies or fundamental institutions, it was practicable to reconcile minor differences in order to preserve unity of government.

What was necessary was to give to the local authority a large sphere of initiative and activity in the sense of liberty and self-government. He asserted that "identity of central government is compatible with many different degrees of centralisation, not only administrative, but even legislative."[1]

It was essential that people should have the desire and the capacity for forming a closer union in the sense of high decentralisation rather than a mere federal one, if their local peculiarities and diversities and details of administration were to be preserved.

A real desire of this kind was safeguarded by the guarantee of the constitution to maintain the federal principle on the one hand, and centralised efficiency on the other.

Federalism, to Mill, was not only dependent upon political organisation, but also upon political needs in every system of government.

The qualitative validity of the utility of desire of the given inhabitant in the given territory is the key to political organisation. Therefore, federalism was in essence the general desire for co-operation between the peoples of the individual states of the union, whereby harmony between them was ensured, and was consequently of great importance in upholding the legal supremacy of the union as a whole.

Mill tried to test the real value of federalism not by the federal system, but by the federal functions, in that he justified federal ideas as essential and important in any political organisation.

[1] J. S. Mill: *Representative Government*, 1861, p. 312.

§ 4

A little later, in 1863, Edward A. Freeman, an historian, put before the English public *The History of Federal Government in Greece and Italy*, which was the first and most exhaustive survey of the federal idea and of the history of federal government, beginning with the Amphiktyonic Council in Greece and going down to the Lombard League in Italy.

His general view of federalism was characterised by the British conception, with a background of historical federations from the Achaean federal constitution to the formation of the Southern American confederation in 1863.

Freeman generalised federalism as being a system of which the essential principle was derived from "compromise between two opposite political systems," in other words, "its different forms occupy the whole middle space between two widely distant extremes," and some of these intermediate forms shade off imperceptibly into the extremes on either side.

He laid down a definition of federal government not from the legal or philosophical standpoint, but from an historical point of view, and asserted that "the name of federal government may, in this wider sense, be applied to any union of component members, where the degree of unity between the members surpasses that of mere alliance, however intimate, and where the degree of independence possessed by each member surpasses anything which can fairly come under the head of merely municipal freedom."[1]

Like other thinkers, he was convinced that the full ideal of federalism could only have a possibility of realisation in "the most finished and the most artificial production of political ingenuity," because, as he was a follower of De Tocqueville's federal ideas, he emphasised that "it is hardly possible that federal government can attain its perfect form except in a highly refined age and among a people whose political education has already stretched over many generations."[2]

To constitute a perfect federal government, there were two requisites:—firstly, each member of the federal government must be absolutely independent in the internal matters which only concern that member, and secondly, all must be subordinate to a common power in matters which concern the whole body of members collectively.

[1] Freeman: *History of Federal Government in Greece and Italy*, p. 2.   [2] Ibid.

The appropriate powers in each case are not a matter of privilege or concession from any higher power, but a matter of absolute right by virtue of inherent powers as independent commonwealths on the one hand and of the sovereignty of the union on the other. Sovereignty within each sphere of activity—of private and internal affairs on the one side, and common and international matters on the other—is co-independent and non-interferent and vested in each appropriate government. Therefore, he assumed that "a federal union, in short, will form one state in relation to other powers, but many states as regards its internal administration."

With this idea of federal government, he, like the American federalists, asserted the principle of divided sovereignty, saying that "this complete division of sovereignty we may look upon as essential to the absolute perfection of the federal ideal."[1]

And he defined the true and perfect federal commonwealth as "a collection of states" in which it is equally unlawful for the central power to interfere with the purely internal legislation of the several members on the one hand, and for the state powers to intervene in the common legislation and enter into diplomatic relations on the other. No real federation could exist unless these two divided sovereignties were permitted to co-exist within their respective spheres; otherwise such a union might be either municipal independence or a mere "confederacy."

Then Freeman, like many other thinkers, classified federal governments into two groups.

The first consists of unions where the federal power represents only the governments of the several members, and their "immediate actions" are confined to those governments; these are "confederacies or systems of confederated states."

The other kind of union, where the federal power can act not only on the several governments, but also directly on every citizen of the states, and in which the federal government is co-ordinate with the state governments, each being sovereign in its own sphere, is a "composite state" or "supreme federal government."[2]

In the former the administrative duties are vested in the state governments, so that the federal government in the strict sense can hardly be called "a government"; whilst in the latter case the full functions of government in respect of administration are vested in the federal government with its own civil service, which can act directly upon every citizen of the component states,

[1] Freeman: *History of Federal Government in Greece and Italy*, p. 3.   [2] Ibid., p. 9.

without any reference to their governments, within the matters enumerated by the federal constitution.

"External unity" and "internal plurality" were to Freeman essential characteristics of federal commonwealths, but from the historical facts he deduced that the "composite state" is the natural tendency of federal development.[1]

The true and perfect form of federalism in his time was presented by the "federal states" or what he called "composite states"—to which he, being an historian, did not apply any legal test of divided sovereignty. However, from the assertion that in the federal state "sovereignty is, in fact, divided," and from the equality of co-ordinate authority to which each government could claim allegiance within its own sphere, his compromise theory of federalism emerged and was justified.

Emphasising his doctrine that federalism is a compromise, he pointed out that it is not a form of government to be contrasted with that of monarchy, aristocracy or democracy, but is rather a cross-classification with them: "a federal commonwealth may be either aristocratic or democratic or some of its members may be aristocratic and others democratic," and "though federal states have commonly been republican, there is nothing theoretically absurd in the idea of a federal monarchy."[2]

Federalism, therefore, was to Freeman a mechanism of compromise between two extreme political demands under any of these classes of governments; that is, it was an intermediate political system to solve the problem of "whether several small states shall remain perfectly independent or shall be consolidated into a single great state."

The federal tie, to Freeman, was the creation of harmony between the advantages of union to the several states and a certain advantage in maintaining their independence.

From these general propositions, Freeman concluded that federalism is a compromise between a large state and a small state, and federal government is a middle course between the systems of the large state and the small state. This was not a new suggestion; other federalists, especially De Tocqueville, had put forward the same idea.

To Freeman federalism had the merits of both the large and the small state, and at the same time, being a compromise, it was liable to have some of the demerits inherent in all compromises.

[1] Freeman: *History of Federal Government in Greece and Italy*, pp. 10–11.
[2] Ibid., pp. 12–13.

In a small state the development of all the faculties of individual citizens is raised to a pitch far superior to that of the average citizens of a large state, and the highest and noblest feelings and emotions of human nature produce great patriotism on the one hand, and the fullest scope for human genius of every kind on the other; but such small states had so far generally been short-lived, owing to the constant temptation which they offered to war-like states and the excessive violence of internal political rivalries.[1]

On the other side, in the large state the representative system of constitutional government, whatever the form of state organisation, had grown up by force of circumstances, and even when Freeman wrote, in 1863, was universally accepted as a political right, though the extent of that right varied.

Through the medium of the representative system, the system of local government was derivative, but modern federalism was creative.[2] The systems of concentration and of local freedom were counteracted and balanced either by the weight of the municipality or by that of federalism.

Though the English towns and counties and self-governing dominions possessed a large amount of internal power, no less in extent than that of the Swiss canton or the American state, these extensive rights were "a creation of common or statute law, and the varieties of local law and custom existed purely on sufferance."

The function of the large state is to secure peace within and without, far better than a small state can, that bitterness of party strife which is a frequent characteristic of small states being diminished, and international peace being promoted by the lessened risk of war, as the interests of the nation are recognised and regulated by "the public law of nations."

This common security of peace and order in a large state, with a representative system, offsets the possibility of a lower level of political education among the citizens and might avail to maintain the high standard of political intelligence often found in a small state and exemplified especially in the city commonwealth.[3]

Ignorance, carelessness and corruption among the electors are the inherent vices of representative government on a large scale; and though corruption might be insignificant in existing political conditions, still it is, Freeman thought, an inevitable

---
[1] Freeman: *History of Federal Government in Greece and Italy*, pp. 29–42.
[2] Ibid., pp. 56–60.   [3] Ibid., p. 40.

vice in the consolidated large state—much more so than in the decentralised or federal state.

So the city commonwealth, the type of the small state, "sacrificed everything else to the full development of the individual citizens," and "the great modern kingdom" which is the type of the large state "sacrifices everything else to the peace, order and general well-being of an extensive territory."[1]

The system intermediate between the two is the "federal republic"; it is a "compromise," with the merit of combining the two systems.

Freeman was convinced that "a federal government does not secure peace and equal rights to its whole territory so perfectly as a modern constitutional kingdom. It does not develop the political life of every single citizen so perfectly as an ancient city-commonwealth. But it secures a far higher amount of general peace than the system of independent cities; it gives its average citizens a higher political education than is within the reach of the average subjects of extensive monarchies."[2]

The federal form is "a more delicate and artificial structure" than any other form of government, and therefore, in Freeman's view, can only be attained in "a late growth of a very high state of political culture."

In this argument he put forward as the characteristic of federalism that it is essentially the creature of circumstance.[3] The circumstances, which Freeman thought of, were particular and exceptional. No city-commonwealth, such as Athens in her prosperity, could stoop to a federal union with other cities, and no great state like the United Kingdom could restore quasi-federal rights to Scotland and Ireland.[4] From this historical fact he deduced, as an important maxim of federalism, that it should arise by the formation of "a closer tie between elements which were before distinct, not by the division of members which have been hitherto more closely united."[5]

From his discussion of federalism, following the lines of De Tocqueville, Freeman drew the general deduction that a federal constitution must be assumed to be republican, whilst the constitution of a large consolidated state would be monarchical. Monarchical federalism is, indeed, theoretically possible, and in the feudal system the relationship between lords and vassals or between sovereigns and princes, based upon the principle of

---

[1] Freeman: *History of Federal Government in Greece and Italy*, p. 68.
[2] Ibid., p. 69.   [3] Ibid., p. 70.   [4] But it has done so.
[5] Freeman: *History of Federal Government in Greece and Italy*, p. 70.

contract, approximated to monarchical federalism, though it fell short of federalism in the true sense, for "to produce anything like true federalism all national affairs should be ordered in a National Assembly, an institution which in feudal France was never attempted and to which the Imperial Diet of Germany presented only a very feeble approach."[1] A nearer approach to true federalism was to be found in the case of the union of two or more kingdoms under one king, like the Austrian Empire and the union of Sweden and Norway. But "on the whole the general tendency of history is to show that, though a monarchic federation is by no means theoretically impossible, yet a republican federation is far more likely to exist as a permanent and flourishing system."

He pursued his inquiry to show that the nature of federalism differed according to the different size of the member states.

Greek federalism with its member cities and the Swiss federation with its member cantons constituted one type of federalism, whereas states of the size of the American or German federation naturally presented quite different types. So federalism with small member states had chiefly the merits and demerits of the small commonwealth, and federalism with large member states showed the advantages and disadvantages of large monarchies and republics. But broadly it combined the merits of the two systems to a considerable extent, though it also had some of the demerits inherent in "compromise."

In a federal government the peace and order and the perfection of the political education of every citizen could theoretically be secured just as well as peace and order in a large state and the political education of people in a small state. But the fact that sovereignty is legally divided between the federal and state governments can weaken the federal power in conflicts between member states on the one hand, and in international disputes on the other. Even in the closest union, "the mere threat of nullification or secession by the several states may weaken the action of the federal power in a way which their constitutional opposition in the federal assembly could not do." On the other hand, political education in the federal state is far greater than in the large kingdoms, but practically less than in city commonwealths. The amount and development of that education in the federal state differ according to "the size of the member states."[2] An understanding of public affairs and the influence of every

[1] Freeman: *History of Federal Government in Greece and Italy*, p. 75.
[2] Ibid., p. 81.

citizen can be attained only through self-government. Federalism, by its very nature, is favourable to self-government, in that it results in a far greater amount of political intelligence and a far higher political good sense and rational confidence on the part of every citizen than does the consolidated republic.

Federalism is essentially "the system of union and of that strength which follows upon union"—that is to say, the federal basis is dependent on the agreement of the members to the political nature of their union. Therefore Freeman emphasised that "it requires a sufficient degree of community in origin or feeling or interest to allow the several members to work together up to a certain point," and also "it requires that there should not be that perfect degree of community, or rather identity, which allows the several members to be fused together for all purposes."[1] Therefore federalism is inappropriate when there is no community at all, or when community has developed into identity—that is, it stands on the intermediate point between two systems, "capable either of being despised as a compromise or of being extolled as the golden mean."

The alleged weakness of federalism is that it is "artificial." In a sense this is a "truism," but the essential fact of federalism which assures its permanence is that it is based "not on sentiment, but on the reason of its citizens."

Freeman grasped the right idea of the tie of federalism—that it is based on the reason of the members and on demands and circumstances which required a particular kind of union; on this point his federal ideas were superior to those of any of the English imperial federalists. This essential fact of federalism brought about his conclusion that the federal union is essentially a compromise, and may be as permanent as any other.[2]

Finally, he examined the rights and wrongs of secession. The idea of secession could be most plainly justified on the ground of expediency. Rebellion was sometimes necessary, just as Jefferson believed that revolution was justifiable in order to secure the alteration of government to meet social changes.

But as a federal union is essentially a perpetual union, it cannot make provision for its own dissolution. Freeman observed that "the federal power is entitled to full obedience within its own sphere, and the refusal of that obedience, whether by states or by individuals, is essentially an act of rebellion."

Nevertheless, a federation, even though legally perpetual, is

[1] Freeman: *History of Federal Government in Greece and Italy*, p. 84.
[2] Ibid., p. 88.

"something which is in its own nature essentially voluntary," so that *ipso facto* there is "a sort of inconsistency in retaining members against their will."[1]

There is another reason: no state will think of secession as long as it has an interest to remain in the union, because federalism is mainly derived from the desire and reason of human association.

Freeman asserted that "an American state can secede if it pleases; but no Swiss canton will ever desert the protection of its brethren because it knows that secession, instead of meaning increased independence, would mean only immediate annexation by the nearest despot."[2]

Freeman concluded of Switzerland that "the federal system, in short, has here, out of the most discordant ethnological, political and religious elements, raised up an artificial nation, full of as true and heroic national feeling as ever animated any people of the most unmixed blood."[3]

He suggested in comparative politics that in the federal state the bi-cameral system was "absolutely necessary." This was still the accepted principle.

Freeman's federalism was based on the conception of compromise between the highest merits of the large state and the small state respectively. His justification of divided sovereignty and his theory of compromise were not novel, but there is force in his argument that federalism rests on reason and not on sentiment, and that it is the result of the pressure of circumstances. It is quite true that federalism has been derived from the co-operate union of self-governing independent states or provinces and not from the introduction of a decentralised system into a unified consolidated state. The compromise between the powers of centralism and local freedom was of greater importance in federalism than in the smaller states.

Freeman's contribution to the study of federalism was, no doubt, of great significance as the presentation of ancient federal history, but his general discussion of federalism had more influence on that study than on the English federal movement itself.

§ 5

James Bryce's contribution to federalism was that orthodox principle of federalism which I have already discussed in a previous chapter. He presented the division of powers as the

[1] Freeman: *History of Federal Government in Greece and Italy*, p. 91.
[2] Ibid., p. 93.   [3] Ibid.

problem of "centrifugal and centripetal forces," and he remarked that the United States and Switzerland, in comparison with unitary states living under rigid constitutions, such as France, Denmark, etc., suggested the observation that "the service which rigid constitutions may render in strengthening the centripetal tendency can best be rendered where a federation is to be constructed."[1]

The centrifugal force of state rights and the centripetal force of the federal constitution were well-balanced in the working of federalism.

With his orthodox federal ideas he maintained that "the perfection of the federal system may be tested by the degree of thoroughness with which the federal principle is worked out in its application not only to the legislative, but also to the executive and judicial branches of government."[2]

As a matter of theory he asserted that federalism was the intermediate organ between the centripetal and centrifugal forces of the state, and was a natural harmony of these forces; "for nothing is more difficult than to observe exactly, and the ripest fruit of historical study is that detachment of mind, created by the habit of scientific thinking, which prevents observation from being coloured by prejudice or passion."[3]

Now if we assume the harmonious balance of natural forces to be the highest development of the human mind, then federalism should be derived and a federal technique evolved from the scientific examination of experience.

Then in political science the value of federalism was dependent not only on its structure, but on the ideas through which its mechanism and function were worked out. However, Bryce did not touch any philosophical matter, but merely studied and criticised thoroughly federal constitutions and organisations in the light of his political studies.

Two great contemporaries of Bryce also dealt with federalism. These were A. V. Dicey, who discussed it in the *Law of the Constitution* in 1885, and Henry Sidgwick, in his *Elements of Politics* in 1881.[4]

Henry Sidgwick was an English thinker whose *Elements of Politics* had an outstanding reputation. He considered federalism as a political device for dividing functions between the central and the local governments, in contrast with the division into

[1] James Bryce: *Studies in History and Jurisprudence*, 1901, Vol. I, pp. 252–253.
[2] Ibid., p. 445. [3] Ibid., p. 262.
[4] The following discussion is based on the later editions of these two works.

areas for the purpose of local administration. This division of functions might result from the fact that the states, or parts of the states, which had either been formally independent or had enjoyed a large amount of practical autonomy, were united—voluntarily or compulsorily—into one political community, in which "the portions thus combined are likely to desire to retain important differences in laws and customs." The sentiment of nationality would oppose complete absorption either because of differences of history, race, or religion or because of physical circumstances, and the distance of territories in the case of a world-wide colonial empire.

Sidgwick designated as a "composite state" the state formed by parts which were to a large extent politically separate, and he distinguished "dependencies" from the "federality" in this kind of composite state.

He asserted that if with an approximate equalisation of political status "there is a general desire to maintain the political separateness of the parts as well as their union in the larger whole, an obvious method of satisfying this desire is to introduce a stable constitutional division of function between the government of the whole and the governments of the parts, securing to the latter a substantial amount of legislative independence." He therefore reached the general idea of the federal state "as a whole made up of parts politically co-ordinate and constitutionally separate."[1]

He distinguished the federal state from the highly developed unitary state with large autonomy of local government on the one hand and from a league or confederation of independent states on the other.

If the balance and combination of unity of the "whole aggregate" with "separateness of parts" constituted "federality," he regarded the following three things as essential to the federal state.

In the first place, the federal state, differing from other forms of the state, must maintain the autonomy of its parts, and this implied the definite division of functions between the federal and state governments guaranteed by the constitution. It was a principle of federality that "the federal parts are to be independent as regards internal matters, while they have common government for external matters." The usual and most expedient line of division was: Firstly, matters external to the parts but not to the whole, which are often of the most vital significance to the modern state—he asserted that "hardly any point is likely

[1] Henry Sidgwick: *The Elements of Politics*, 1919, p. 532.

to be more vital for the cohesion and stability of a federal state than to secure free trade among the federated part-states"—were included in the sphere of the common government.

Secondly, matters which had to be regarded as strictly domestic to each part, but were of serious common interest to the whole, such as currency, patents, copyright, bankruptcy, etc., were included in the sphere of the common government.

Lastly, the management of all foreign relations and the control of the military forces necessary to deal with the external attack and internal unrest were naturally confided to the federal authority.

But at the same time the powers of the part governments depend not only on a definite enumeration of powers in the constitution, but are left undefined in so far as constitutionally they fall within the reserved rights of the part-states.[1]

In the next place, in the very nature of the federal state the separate political existence of the part-states, as the members of the whole state, should be represented in the structure of the common government.

This structure of the federal government distinguished the federal state from the confederation.

In the federal government, "as the part-states, if independent, would be formally equal in international rights, their partially retained independence may be represented by giving to all equal shares in the election of some important part of the common government, so that normally any decision of the body or individual so elected will represent the decision of a majority of the part-states."[2]

But if the part-states were very unequal in size and rejected the constitutional rights of a majority of citizens, the structure of government required another system of federacy—that is, a confederacy in which "a representative body may be constituted as part of the common government, in which representatives of each part-state vote not individually but collectively, according to the decision of a majority of their number; the aggregate voting power of each set of representatives being proportioned to the size of the part-state that they represent."[3]

In the third place, how far and by what means stability could be maintained in the balance of governmental powers between the whole and the part governments was the main problem of federalism and also the chief distinction between it and the unitary state.

[1] Henry Sidgwick: *The Elements of Politics*, 1919, pp. 533–534.
[2] Ibid., pp. 534–535.   [3] Ibid., p. 535.

In the unitary state this division of powers depended entirely upon "the will of the central legislation," whilst in the federal state, as its characteristic, the central legislation possessed no such unlimited power, but the division was entirely fixed by the federal constitution which the central as well as the local government must obey. Therefore the immutability of the constitution was of the essential nature of federalism. Sidgwick himself, like other thinkers, condemned this immutability, as such an idea was "indefensible from a utilitarian point of view."

He said, "we realise too fully the inevitable changes of social needs and conditions, and the limitations of human foresight, to approve of establishing constitutions that cannot be altered without illegality."[1]

But he assumed that "the principle of federalism, strictly taken, requires that the consent of any part-state should be given to any change in the constitutional division of powers between the whole and the parts; on the view that the powers allotted to the part-states belong to them independently, in their own right, and being not conferred by any authority external to the state, cannot legitimately be withdrawn by any such authority."[2]

By these three outstanding features of federalism he distinguished more definitely the federal state from other forms of union.

The loosest type of the union was to be designated as a "mere alliance for a limited time which does not result in the formation of any important common organ of government."

But the confederation, being a permanent union of states uniting for permanent common action in important matters, established a "common organ having power to make decisions of importance" with regard to common purposes, of which the most obvious were "security and strength in foreign relations." In order to secure this permanently the union ought to have a common council as well as common command of military force in case of war. If this permanent organ of common government had been organised, then the union was beyond a mere alliance and ranked as a confederation.

In order to secure the strength of the union, and to preserve internal peace and prevent the otherwise inevitable disputes among the confederates, the union ought to establish a judicial authority, and, finally, in order to ensure the continued stability of the union it ought to possess an authority to determine the contribution from the confederated states to the general fund.

[1] Henry Sidgwick: *The Elements of Politics*, 1919, p. 536.
[2] Ibid., pp. 536–537.

Now these requirements of common organs to strengthen the union and to secure the efficient and complete discharge of governmental tasks, transformed the union from a confederation to a federal state.

The answer to the question whether we could notify "any definite point of transition at which unity predominates over plurality" would indicate the demarcation between the confederation and the federal state.

As long as the united states or part-states "retained the right of withdrawing from the union at will," however great the "revocable" power granted to the common authority, Sidgwick thought that this stage of union was still that of confederation.

"Irrevocability" was not sufficient for this distinction, but when the federal community was completed and controlled by "a single common government" in all foreign relations and in all important matters relating to the common welfare, it was conceived as a single state with international personality, however great the extent of independence in internal matters which might be allowed to the part-states.

The distinct line of demarcation was that, in order to attain a stable and adequate realisation of federalism, the federal government should enter nominally into "important direct relations with the citizens of the several part-states, instead of merely acting on them through the governing organs of part-states."

Then federal legislation framed laws which bound directly all citizens; the federal judiciary decided the application of the laws, and in the last resort interpreted the laws and the constitution; and the federal executive enforced laws and collected taxes directly from the individual citizens of the whole state.

Sidgwick believed that these governmental functions in federal governments were not only essential to the conception of the federal state, but were the basis of the federal moral obligation.

He laid emphasis on the distinction between the federal state and confederation by reference to the fundamental question of allegiance of citizens to the authority. He asserted that "the distinction between the two cases seems to me very profound from the point of view of an individual member of the community; since in the latter case the individual citizen will have a habit of undivided allegiance to the government of his part-state—with which, therefore, he will naturally side if any dispute should arise between central and local organs; whereas, in the former case, it will be his recognised and habitual civic duty to obey either government within its own sphere."[1]

To him "the habit of divided allegiance" was the fundamental and essential characteristic of the federal state.[2]

From the philosophical point of view Sidgwick's definition of the federal state in contrast to the confederation was quite legitimate. In so far as he based federalism on the division of the functions of power between the central and local authorities, allegiance—the obligations of citizens to authority—was of great importance to the political organism.

As to the ultimate consequence of this division of allegiance the constitution of the federal state was to lay the important foundation, as the "supreme law of the land," and to direct the common guidance of all governmental and individual matters in the federal states. Therefore, the divided and limited functions of the federal government and the supreme position of the judicial functionary became the legitimate results of the "federality," and "the more stability is given to the constitution by making the process of changing it difficult, the greater becomes the importance of this judicial function of interpreting its clauses."

In order to ensure the perfect performance of federal functions the Supreme Court of Justice was properly formed, but it was a delicate problem to secure its due functioning "without at the same time giving the Supreme Court too predominant a power."[3]

So far as the federal state maintained the security guaranteed by the constitution, the federal sentiment would be in favour of keeping the constitution stable and permanent "by requiring the assent of a large majority of part-states" to any change.[4]

For the federal state to be in a satisfactory condition the part-states ought to be "either numerous or not very unequal in size." If they were few and unequal in size the federal state would turn into a unitary state by absorbing the weaker part-states into "dependencies," because equal representation in the senate of the federal government was difficult to attain when there was a preponderance of a large part-state. Therefore it was far better that the part-states in the federal state should be "few," for "the fewer they are the smaller is the inequality that would be the danger."

In this regard the history of federation in North America and the European continent—in the United Netherlands and Switzerland and Germany—had manifested the weaknesses

[1] Henry Sidgwick: *The Elements of Politics*, 1919, p. 539.
[2] Ibid.   [3] Ibid., p. 540.   [4] Ibid., p. 541.

and disadvantages of federalism and had already shown the gradual growth of federal authority to the extent that the nation realised "the maximum liberty compatible with order" and the necessity of efficiency of administration in its relations with the central authority.

Sidgwick concluded that "it may be observed that federalism arising from historical causes is likely to be in many cases a transitional stage through which a composite society passes on its way to a completer union: since, as time goes on, and mutual intercourse grows, the narrower patriotic sentiments that were originally a bar to full political union tend to diminish, while the inconvenience of a diversity of laws is more keenly felt, especially in a continuous territory."[1]

At the same time he was convinced that even though the confederation naturally developed into the federal state, "still the development of modern democratic thought and sentiment, so far as it favours liberty and self-government, tends in favour of federality." The great extent of autonomy in the self-governing colonies caused his assertion that under the well-developed self-governing dominion "the principle of federation is *primâ facie* applicable."[2]

Even though he did not thoroughly agree with imperial federation in view of the hindrances arising from the physical and natural diversity between the mother country and the colonies, yet he recognised highly decentralised local government as a stage in the progress of political liberty and favoured the establishment of well-organised self-government.

On this assumption Sidgwick was convinced that federalism was a transitory stage in development from the mere composite state to the unitary state in the existing form of federal organism. The function of federalism, its essential nature and purpose, was the ultimate aim of every modern democratic country.

Therefore, Sidgwick's outstanding contribution to federal ideas was that the functions of federalism are fundamental to its nature and that these functions are the ultimate aim not only of the federal state as it now exists, but also of the democratic unitary state in so far as it is decentralised by the division between central and local government.

His notion of federalism, especially his last argument, is in my judgment quite acceptable and plausible.

A. V. Dicey, a great British legal philosopher, who gave a new impetus to the study of the British constitution and developed

[1] Henry Sidgwick: *The Elements of Politics*, 1919, p. 544.   [2] Ibid., p. 548.

new ideas about it, especially with regard to parliamentary sovereignty and *droit administratif*, indicated federalism as an important form of political organisation in his famous work, *The Law of the Constitution*, published in 1885.

Both statesmen and political thinkers in England in 1884, even J. S. Mill, Bagehot and Maine, generally included the nature of federalism in a comparative study of constitutions in order to justify the English representative government as the best form of body politic.

Dicey noted that the essence of federalism was the distribution of limited power among bodies, "executive and legislative and judiciary, each co-ordinate and independent of each other."

The underlying basis of the federal state must be groups of states or provinces so closely connected "by locality, by history, by race, or the like, as to be capable of bearing in the eyes of their inhabitants an impress of common nationality," and was generally "the slowly-matured fruit" from which the states had been "bound together by close alliance or by subjection to a common sovereign."

In the second place, the first essential to the formation of the federal state was "the existence of a very particular state of sentiment" among the people of the component states—that is, "they must desire union and must not desire unity." This notion of "the combination of union and separation," the sentiment for which naturally emerged from the sense of common interest and common national feeling on the one hand and the strong loyalty and allegiance to the locality on the other, was the foundation of federalism.

To Dicey the reconciliation of these inconsistent elements was the aim of federalism, which was "to give effect as far as possible to both sentiments."

Federalism, therefore, was "a political contrivance" by which the reconciliation of the two political forces could be attained; that is, it was an attempt to conciliate the national unity and power with the maintenance of "state rights." This was the essential character of federalism.

Starting with this conception Dicey argued that the real source of federalism was a combination of the notions embodied in the preamble to the federal constitution of the United States of 1787 and those of its 10th Amendment.[1]

[1] A. V. Dicey: *Law of the Constitution*, 1924, p. 139.—"The preamble to the Constitution of the United States recites that 'We, the people of the United States, in order to form a more perfect union, establish justice, ensure domestic

Dicey's federal ideas were far more adequately manifested by his principle of reconciling the distribution of powers and forces between "national unity" and "state rights," than were those of Freeman by the principle of "compromise," and the possible harmony of the merits of large and small states. Dicey observed and criticised federalism by examining its functions, whereas Freeman analysed it as a piece of mechanism. But different as were their lines of argument—one was the historian's and the other the lawyer's—federalism was to them both, the conciliating or compromising mean between the two extremes. But I believe that in so far as the importance of political federalism has been transferred from mechanism to function, the notion of federalism has more validity in respect of function than in respect of mechanism.

Federalism in the future should be based on the fundamental notion of *droit administratif*, which is of more importance than that of any political system.

In that sense even Dicey could not penetrate to the real source of the federal idea, but criticised and analysed it on the basis of legal validity.

From his conception of federalism Dicey deduced the three leading characteristics of completely developed federalism: firstly, the supremacy of the constitution; secondly, the distribution of powers among bodies with limited and co-ordinate authority; and lastly, the authority of the courts acting as the interpreter of the constitution.

As to the nature of the federal state he asserted that the federal constitution was founded on a "complicated contract" and the basis of this agreement by the component states was dependent upon "the article of treaty, or in other words of the constitution."[1] Therefore the federal constitution must necessarily be a "written" constitution or what Dicey called a "rigid or inexpansive constitution."[2]

Upon this assumption his federal ideas were derived from the "compact" theory of federalism.

As regards the supremacy of the constitution, in the face of "the absolute legislative sovereignty or despotism of the King in tranquillity, provide for the common defence, promote the general welfare, and secure the blessings of liberty to ourselves and our posterity, do ordain and establish this Constitution for the United States of America.' The Tenth Amendment enacts that 'the powers not delegated to the United States by the Constitution nor prohibited by it to the States are reserved to the States respectively or to the people.'"

[1] A. V. Dicey: *Law of the Constitution*, 1924, p. 142.   [2] Ibid.

Parliament" in the British constitution, the federal constitution was declared to be "the supreme law of the land," and the federal state derived its existence from the constitution just as "a corporation derives its existence from the grant by which it is created" —"the Act of Parliament," and the immutability of the constitution, quite outside and beyond the ordinary legislative bodies, was the main object of federal institutions.[1]

In the case of the founding of the American constitution in 1787 the federal aim was to prevent the encroachment of state right upon the security of the United States. It was of primary importance to maintain this. Dicey argued that the supremacy of the constitution and its immutability were compatible with and appropriate to this idea of federalism; namely, "the maintenance of the respective spheres of the national and the state government": otherwise there was "no guarantee" of state rights against the power of the federal government and the authority of the federal power in face of the state sovereignty was "illusory."

Therefore, as the Congress and other legislative bodies were mere subordinate law-making bodies, any law which had gone beyond the limits of the constitution was invalid and unconstitutional.

On this supposition *ultra vires* and "unconstitutionality," even though the comparison was an apparent absurdity, were not different from one another; that is, Congress and the Great Eastern Railway Company under the constitution on the one hand, and under the Corporation's Act of Parliament on the other, "are in truth each of them nothing more than subordinate law-making bodies."[2]

Regarding the distribution of powers, the federal distribution of power was rigidly prescribed by the constitution, which delegated special and closely defined powers to the executive and legislature and to the judiciary of the union. Dicey remarked that "the principle of definition and limitation of powers harmonises so well with the federal spirit that it is generally carried much farther than is dictated by the mere logic of the constitution."[3]

However inflexible the constitutional division of powers might be, there was no possibility of harmony in the operation of these powers without a satisfactory relationship between the federal and state governments. Therefore it was of importance that the

[1] A. V. Dicey: *Law of the Constitution*, 1924, p. 144.
[2] Ibid., p. 147.　　　　　　　　　　　　　　　　[3] Ibid., p. 148.

state constitutions throughout the union should be "formed upon the federal model." But the tendency of federalism is "to limit on every side the action of government and to split up the strength of the state" among the co-ordinate and independent authorities, and, so Dicey concluded that "federalism means the distribution of the force of the state among a number of co-ordinate bodies each originating in and controlled by the constitution."[1]

This being the nature of federalism the necessity of putting the principle into effect led legitimately to the creation of the Supreme Court of the federal state, which formed the final body charged with the juristic interpretation of "the supreme law of the land," without any favour either to federal authority or to state rights. The due maintenance of justice through the supreme tribunal was the characteristic feature of political jurisprudence. In federalism Dicey asserted that this political jurisprudence was really a "true merit," that the wisdom of the federalists who created the union applied with extraordinary skill the notions which they had inherited from the English law to the novel circumstances of the new republic.

Apart from the English juristic conception, and far from the French conventional idea of constitutionality, the essential characteristics of federalism—the supremacy of the constitution, distribution of powers, and especially the authority of the judiciary as the supreme power of the constitution—were manifested "in every true federal state."[2]

Dicey showed by analysis that federalism was weak in nature because of the check and balance in the distribution of powers. In respect of inefficiency of administration and weakness in the conduct of foreign relations the federal state contrasted unfavourably with the unitary state. But the recent tendency of federalism, which was no doubt due to the desire to strengthen the federal authorities at the expense of state independence, diminished the inherent weakness of the federal state. At the same time, the federal system appeared as possessing a merit "which does not commend itself to modern democrats, and no more curious instance can be found of the inconsistent currents of popular opinion which may at the same time pervade a nation or a generation than the coincidence in England of a vague admiration for federalism alongside with a far more decided feeling against the doctrine of so-called *laissez-faire*."[3]

Federalism, therefore, tended "to produce conservatism,"

[1] A. V. Dicey: *Law of the Constitution*, 1924, p. 153.
[2] Ibid., pp. 160–161.
[3] Ibid., p. 169.

and the effect of the federal system, with its rigid and supreme constitution, was to maintain the *status quo* in politics and be incompatible with schemes for "wide social innovation."

This definition is partly acceptable in respect of the American federal constitution owing to the difficulties of amendment, but it naturally invites criticism when regarded as being essential to the nature of federalism.[1]

Dicey, like all other thinkers, observed the danger of the judicial supremacy. He assumed that no one can doubt that when set to determine matters of policy and statesmanship most honest judges "will necessarily be swayed by political feeling and by reasons of state," that "the moment that this bias becomes obvious a court loses its moral authority," and the "irresistible temptation to appoint magistrates who agreed with the views of executive" was the inevitable consequence of the control of the courts over the action of government.

But the reverence for law and the legal spirit was in reality the cause of the success of federalism. He concluded that "federalism substitutes litigation for legislation, and none but a law-fearing people will be inclined to regard the decision of a suit as equivalent to the enactment of a law."[2]

To Dicey the development of the legal spirit among the people, in the sense of constitutionalism, was the highest merit of federalism.

In the introduction to later editions of this work he elaborates the federal principle not merely in the legal sense, but on the basis of political doctrine.

Whatever delusions or illusions about federalism English thinkers may have held, the federal mode of thought is now a natural trend of political ideas, evolved from the democratic body politic. The security of the nation and the stability of the general government emerged from the homogeneous co-operation of a diversity of local particularities.

Not monistic absolutism but pluralistic liberty is the real motive force of the democratic institutions of to-day.

Describing "federalism" as a "natural constitution for a body of states which desire union and do not desire unity," an essential condition for the success of the federal government, whether a confederation or a federal state or even real union, was the "physical contiguity" of the states which entered into the union.

That meant, as he stated, that an approximate equality in

[1] Cf. Part II, Chap. II, pp. 321–322.
[2] A. V. Dicey: *Law of the Constitution*, 1924, p. 175.

the wealth, population and historical background of the member states was favourable to the creation of the federal complex. He asserted that the underlying idea of federalism was that "each of the separate states should have approximately equal political rights and should thereby be able to maintain the limited independence."[1]

The equal representation of the member states in the federal legislature, whether or not, as Walter Bagehot argued, it was adverse to political justice,[2] was yet essential to the federal mechanism, in the sense of the orthodox federalism; if otherwise, the danger of a dominant part was imposed formally and threatened the maintenance of federal equality.

The great contribution made by Dicey to federalism in the modern state was his decisive pronouncement that "federalism, when successful, had generally been a stage towards unitary government; in other words, federalism tends to pass into nationalism."[3]

This was proved by the history of federalism in the United States, the German Empire and Switzerland. From his examination of the nature of federalism he postulated the ultimate destiny of the federal state.

First of all, he assumed—like all other publicists—that the federal constitution was a weaker form of government than a unitary one. In the technique of federalism, the division of power was the basis of federal institutions—a division not only between the federal and state governments, but between the functionaries of each. This distribution of powers was the essential characteristic of federation, but the constant effort of federal statesmanship was to compare the claims of one particular state with the federal state as a whole, and to hold the balance between too great federal solidarity on the one hand and excessive particularism on the other.

In the second place, for the harmonious working of this division of powers between the federal and state governments, the significant necessity was the "predominance of legalism," or in other words, "a general willingness to yield to the authority of the law courts."[4]

He emphasised that, to impartial critics, "nothing was more praiseworthy than the reverence paid by the whole of American

[1] A. V. Dicey: *Law of the Constitution*, 1924, p. lxxv.
[2] Walter Bagehot: *The English Constitution*, 1922, p. 98.
[3] A. V. Dicey: *Law of the Constitution*, 1924, Introduction, p. lxxvi.
[4] Ibid., p. lxxviii.

opinion to the Supreme Court of the United States," even at the time of violent political controversy. Impartiality of judgment, and the practice of constitutional righteousness as to the federal distribution of power, was a practical matter as to which Dicey had entirely negative conclusions owing to the difficulty of suppressing the influence of party politics.

Lastly, he emphasised that "federalism creates divided allegiance."[1] He said that this is the most serious and the most inevitable of the weaknesses attached to the form of government under which "loyalty to a citizen's native state may conflict with his loyalty to the whole federated nation."

The history of the *Sonderbund* in the Swiss federation and the secession in the United States had shown the impossibility of divided loyalty.

As to the special weakness of federalism, Dicey asserted that "in any estimate of the strength and the weakness of federal government it is absolutely necessary not to confound, though the confusion is a very common one, federalism with nationalism."[2] It was quite true that a truly federal government means "the denial of national independence to the member states of the federation," and "no single state in the American union is a separate nation." The experiment of federalism in Canada and Switzerland was a union of states for common needs and not the sacrifice of independent separate existence for the sake of national prosperity, whereas an entity such as the union of England and Scotland was founded on a certain federal sentiment of willingness and confidence to bring about a national unity. But it is quite true, as Dicey said, that "the aspiration and the effort towards actual national independence is at least as inconsistent with the conditions of federal as with the conditions of a unitary government."[3]

He emphatically concluded: "Nor does historical experience countenance the idea that federalism, which may certainly be a step towards closer national unity, can be used as a method for gradually bringing political unity to an end."[4] His assertion that federalism was a transitional stage in the development of the body politic is a sound and judicious observation.

Two great English political thinkers, Dicey on the one hand and Sidgwick on the other, thus put forward their understanding of federalism as a "transitional state" through which "a composite

[1] A. V. Dicey: *Law of the Constitution*, 1924, Introduction, p. lxxviii.
[2] Ibid., p. lxxix.   [3] Ibid., p. lxxx.   [4] Ibid.

society passes on its way to a complete union," and out of which a political unity was brought into being.

To sum up as to English federal ideas. Freeman treated federalism as the compromise between two extreme bodies politic, between a large and small state, from the historian's point of view. Dicey analysed federalism as an intermediate political organ for the division of the state functions between general and particular powers, from the standpoint of legal philosophy. Mill and Sidgwick treated federalism as a piece of political technique, securing the division of functions between local and central governments, from their standpoint of political philosophy.

However different their methods, federalism was to them all an intermediate political system and a compromise as to the technical division of political functions. The theory of compromise was the outstanding principle of federalism contributed by English thinkers.

On the whole, the discussion of federalism by nearly all English thinkers was in general more critical and analytical than doctrinaire, and it did not start with the dogmatic hypotheses on which arguments as to federalism had frequently been based.

§ 6

In these circumstances even in the United States the contribution to American federal ideas by European thinkers, such as De Tocqueville, Bryce, Austin and Dicey, was far greater than that of the numerous American thinkers during the last century, except the American federalists and Jefferson and Calhoun. Nevertheless, ever since the problem of sovereignty in the federal state of the United States had *de facto* been solved by the verdict of the Civil War and guaranteed under the decisive interpretation of the constitutional sovereignty by Chief Justice Chase of the Supreme Court of Justice, the federal idea made immense progress in theory and in practice, and was impartially criticised and scientifically analysed by various thinkers.

The greatest contribution to the federal idea in Great Britain is, without doubt, the rise of the pluralist theory of the state, into which I will not go in detail here.

At the same time, by the aid of the Germanic conception of the *Staatslehre* and the movement for the promotion of the new philosophy of "pragmatism," the federal idea was given great scope throughout the whole field of human activity.

By the unique *Genossenschaftstheorie*, Otto Gierke gave a new impetus to the federal idea from his philosophical basis of "organism," and Maitland—the greatest legal philosopher of England—recognised the value of the *Genossenschaftstheorie*, and asserted that "there seems to be a genus of which the State and Corporation are species. They seem to be permanent organised groups of men; they seem to be group units; we seem to attribute acts and intents, rights and wrongs to these groups, to these units."[1]

Neither the English pluralist nor the French could take up the *Genossenschaftstheorie* at once as his criterion. Maitland, as a typical English jurist, could not write of Gierke's theory without referring to the English historical theory of "Trust." He, breaking away from the famous dictum of Pollock that "the greatest artificial person, political speaking, is the state," asserted that if there is to be group formation, the problem of personality cannot be evaded, "at any rate if we are a logical people."

Every English pluralist quotes Gierke's dictum that "our German Fellowship is no fiction, no symbol, no piece of the state's machinery, no collective name for individuals, but a living organism and a real person, with body and members and a will of its own. Itself can will, itself can act; it wills and acts by the men who are its organs as a man wills and acts by brain, mouth and hand. It is not a fictitious person; it is a *Gesammtperson*, and its will is a *Gesammtwille*; and it is a group-person, and its will is a group-will."[2]

But in agreement with the French expression of "civil personality" or of "congregations" Maitland reached the conception of group personality, and gave to it the following definition: "(i) If the law allows men to form permanently organised groups, those groups will be for common opinion right-and-duty-bearing units; and if the law-giver will not openly treat them as such, he will misrepresent, or, as the French say, he will 'denature' the facts: in other words, he will make a mess and call it law. (ii) Group-personality is no purely legal phenomenon. The law-giver may say that it does not exist, where, as a matter of moral sentiment, it does exist. When that happens he incurs the penalty ordained for those who ignorantly or wilfully say the thing that is not. If he wishes to smash a group, let him smash it, send the policemen, raid the rooms, impound the minute-book, fine, imprison; but if he is going to tolerate the group, he must recognise its personality, for otherwise he will be dealing wild

[1] F. W. Maitland: *Political Theories of the Middle Ages* (by Gierke), 1922, Translator's Introduction, p. ix.   [2] Ibid., p. xxvi.

blows which may fall on those who stand outside the group as well as those who stand within it. (iii) For the morality of common sense the group is person, is right-and-duty-bearing unit. Let the moral philosopher explain this, let him explain it as illusion, let him explain it away; but he ought not to leave it unexplained, nor, I think, will he be able to say that it is an illusion which is losing power, for, on the contrary, it seems to me to be persistently and progressively triumphing over certain philosophical and theological prejudices."[1]

Maitland assumed that whether the association is incorporated or unincorporated is not a matter of much practical importance. He pointed out that legally Gneist was mistaken in describing the English county system of his time as self-government, since it "was due in a large measure (so it seems to me) to the work of the Trust," but he observed that "much had been done behind the hedge of trustees in the way of constructing *Körper* (bodies) which to the eye of the plain man look extremely like *Korporationen*, and no one was prepared to set definite limits to this process."

Maitland pointed out that this reacted upon the English system of local government. Action and reaction between *Vereine* and *Communalverbände* were the easier in England, because there was no formal severance of public from private law,[2] such as existed in the German legal system. So he put the state as a group on the same footing as the county or borough or the Stock Exchange.

Maitland mentioned the distinction between the borough and the country in that the former is a corporation and the latter is not, though the country council is, but said: "I am sure that it does not correspond to any vital principle."

Thus he considered the cases of Lincoln's Inn, or Lloyd's, or the Stock Exchange, or the Jockey Club, or the church or a trade union, as a group which had a perfect group personality and group will, though these were behind the wall of trustee and concealed from the direct scrutiny of legal theories. That is "something that contract cannot explain"—i.e. the "personality of the organised group," which, he said, "was, on the whole, pretty well recognised in practice." He asserted that since an *Anstalt* or *Genossenschaft* has "to live in a wicked world . . . this sensitive being must have a hard exterior shell which is provided by the 'trust' of English law." He did not need to be told "that we are dealing in fiction, even if it be added that we needs must feign,

[1] F. W. Maitland: *Collected Papers*, 1911, Vol. III, pp. 314–315.
[2] Ibid., p. 398.

and the thought will occur to us that a fiction that we needs must feign is somehow or other very like the simple truth." But as long as the something of this sort of group personality depends on one single fact, and inasmuch as the English idea of trust is extremely elastic and all manner of groups can flourish within the hedge of trusteeship, Gierke's task of recovering and revivifying "the organic idea and giving to it a scientific form" is, according to Maitland, to admit morally something in a group personality which in the strict legal sense is not accepted.

His conception of group personality is fully explained by Laski's sentence: "Clearly there is compulsion in our personalising . . . we do it because we feel in those things the red blood of a living personality. . . . Here are no mere abstractions of an overexuberant imagination. The need is so apparent as to make plain the reality beneath." Maitland laid the foundation of real personality, which has gone some way in England "to ascribe to the state or to, more vaguely, the community, not only *a* real will, but even *the* real will," and formed the pluralistic thought that "not only will our philosophic *Staatslehre* be merging itself into a wider doctrine, but we shall already be deep in the *Genossenschaftstheorie*."

As Maitland suggested, "what is true of religious bodies is hardly less true of many other *Vereine*"; the work of John Neville Figgis, *The Church in the Modern State*, published in 1913, was the first literature of political pluralism. The guild socialists, A. J. Penty and S. G. Hobson, placed the state on the same line as the "National Guild." G. D. H. Cole, a prominent economic and political thinker of to-day, expounded his guild socialist state based on the pure pluralistic conception, as William James aimed at pluralism being distributive. Cole attaches as little value to the state as to a pair of shoes for the satisfaction of human desire. The Webbs' theory of the pluralist state is not exactly similar to that of Cole, but insists on the state as the highest consumer's community on the basis of pluralist function.

Ernest Barker's famous essay, *The Discredited State*, was the presentation of the typical English pluralist principle. It started by accepting "as perhaps not untrue" the saying that "the state has generally been discredited in England." Applauding Maitland's group theory and Figgis' federal idea of the state, with the inherent right of association, he clearly found the way for the ideal group of personality to escape the cramping limits of a "charter of delegation such as must go to the creation of a *persona ficta*." "We may eliminate personality and will—

transcendent personality and transcendent will—from associations; we may be content to speak of associations as schemes in which real and individual persons and wills are related to one another by means of a common and organising idea."[1]

He condemned the Austinian notion of sovereignty. The reality which that notion seeks to contain is, he said, "the associating and organising idea of law and order." Externally it has some value; "internally, it leads to a false unification and simplification of the rich complexity of the facts. It substitutes unitarism for federalism, a 'corner' in lieu of competition." Such a view might seem to be anarchism; Barker regarded it as being "polyarchism." The problem which that presents—the problem of unstable equilibrium—would, he thought, "be settled by the needs of mere ordered life." Law and order is the necessary force, as the state is partly an organ of freedom and partly a vehicle of force. The demand for a return to law and order may revive and prevail, but will be in no way threatening to the state, though it may be a great menace to other societies and ideas. "The idea of law and order, when it is roused, is one of the cruellest things in history," as shown in the suppression of the Paris Commune in 1871.[2] The discredit of the state is a sign that the state has done, and is doing, its work well. It will come into credit again as soon as it is seen to be doing its work badly. "In our social life we are swarming hither and thither after associating ideas, not only of law and order, but of religion, nation, class. If it comes to a pinch, we shall forget that we are anything but citizens. Through our mouths the state, which is nothing but ourselves organised in an ordered life, will then say to itself, 'It is necessary to live.'" The state which Barker believes to be worthy to live is the decentralised state federally organised with a variety of ideas and schemes.

Tawney's ideal of the revival of the mediaeval community is that of a functional state in the place of our modern acquisitive society.

Modern pluralism cannot be independent of functionalism. The greatest authority on this pluralistic state theory in our time is Harold J. Laski. He has elaborated the "pluralistic conception of the state," based on Maitland's legal philosophy, and confirmed the federal idea as essential to the state function from his ethical basis of "pragmatic utilitarianism." Gierke valued the federal idea relatively more than the notion of the whole, as the whole was comprised of numerous atoms, and

[1] Ernest Barker: "*The Discredited State*," in the *Political Quarterly*, February 1915, p. 113.   [2] Ibid., p. 121.

said, "what man is, he owes to association of man with man"; while Laski gave the federal idea more weight than the notion of individual value in the compound whole.

Laski, more than anyone else in Great Britain, has shown the abuse of the state dominion under the conception of sovereignty, just as in the last century Hugo Preuss condemned the conception of sovereignty which is an erroneous foundation for the formation of a properly constituted theory of state. As Laski is a pluralist and a socialist, who stands side by side with the Marxists, his opposition to the absolute notion of sovereignty is mainly due to his firm belief that the new movement for conquest of self-government "finds its main impulse in the attempt to disperse the sovereign power, because it is realised that where administrative organisation is made responsive to the actual association of men, there is a greater chance not merely of efficiency but freedom also."[1] He analysed the conception of sovereignty from his pragmatic point of view, which even Preuss had never dreamt of. Considering, on the one hand, such failures in the assertion of theoretical sovereignty as the non-success of attempts of the British government to override the opposition of colonial legislatures, the non-success of the Privy Council as a supreme authority on matters of church doctrine, and, on the other hand, the success attending the issue by the church of a new doctrinal order, or the declaration of a strike by a trade union, Laski holds that "sovereignty is, in its exercise, an act of will" whether to do or refrain from doing, behind which "there is such power as to make the expectation of obedience reasonable." And he added: "Now it does not seem valuable to urge that a certain group, the state, can theoretically secure obedience to all its acts, because we know that practically to be absurd."

So a trade union, ordering a strike, is "exercising a power that differs only in degree, not in kind, from that of the state." Completely analysed, sovereignty is not very formidable: "it is the obvious accompaniment of personality and the main characteristic of personality is the power to will." He defined sovereign power by a remarkable phrase, in saying that "sometimes wills, whether individual or corporate, conflict, and only submission or trial of strength can decide which is superior."[2]

Taking for granted this maxim, though Kelsen ascribed the same character to sovereignty on the basis of his altogether

[1] H. J. Laski: *The Foundations of Sovereignty*, "The Pluralistic State," p. 243.
[2] Ibid., *Studies in the Problem of Sovereignty*, 1917, Appendix A, "A Note on Sovereignty and Federalism," p. 270.

opposite hypothesis of the "norm," the federal controversy which has been raging between federalists and particularists in Germany, as well as in the United States, may result in quite a simple compromise.[1] Laski does not ignore, as Gierke and Preuss did, that the modern state is the sovereign state, i.e. "every state in the modern world is a territorial community in the name of which some agent or agents exercise sovereignty."[2]

He holds that the legal expression of sovereignty, although unquestionably logical, has no value in political philosophy; and assumes the rise of the sovereign state to be historically "an incident in its evolution, the utility of which has now reached its apogee." But as a theory of political organisation he thinks that there must be in every social order some single centre of ultimate reference, some power that is able to resolve disputes by saying a last word that will be obeyed. In the realm of political science, what is important in the nature of power is "the end it seeks to serve and the way in which it serves that end."[3] That is what he calls sovereign power to universal reference. That is the chief point at issue as to the pluralistic state between his theory and G. D. H. Cole's ideal of establishing democratic justice on the basis of functional equality. That is, Laski's state is based on Gierke's expression of unity in plurality. In the modern complicated community he admits that the state is, in some form or other, an inevitable organisation, as will be apparent to anyone who examines the human nature that we encounter in daily life, but he emphatically refuses to admit its inevitability as having a moral pre-eminence of any kind. The only possible inevitableness the state can possess is the "national minimum," to which all members, individuals or groups, within and without, will subscribe with full knowledge of what their consent entails. Therefore, in agreement with Ihering, he asserted that "after all the state is not itself an end but merely the means to an end, which is realised only in the enrichment of human lives," and he added that "its power and the allegiance it can win depend always upon what it achieves for that enrichment."[4]

Laski's main approach to this conclusion is the problem of allegiance, i.e. how far or whether you and I should obey one group or other group, with full satisfaction of freedom for the

---

[1] H. J. Laski: *Grammar of Politics*, p. 53.—"It has been pointed out that the discovery of sovereignty in a federal state is, practically, an impossible adventure; but that difficulty is not confined to the federal state."
[2] Ibid.; "*Law and the State*," in *Economica*, November 1929.
[3] Ibid., *Grammar of Politics*, pp. 44–45.
[4] Ibid., p. 88.

fulfilment of our desires. This is his basic principle of the pluralistic theory of the state, which admits the group personality on the one hand and the recognition of natural rights inherent to persons and groups against authority on the other.

Criticising the English legal assertion of fictitious personality, Laski entirely agreed with Maitland that "it is clear enough that unless we treat the personality of our group persons as real, and apply the fact of that reality throughout the whole realm of law, what we call justice will in truth be no more than a chaotic and illogical muddle."[1] He added that though English lawyers are reputed to dislike abstractions, and such excursions as this into legal metaphysics may appear to them dangerous, yet "life is a series of precipices, and we have to act upon the assumptions we make."

Like Maitland, he asserted that "the distinction between incorporate and voluntary association must be abolished," and that the "trust must be made to reveal the life that grows beneath" its "fictitious protectiveness." He stands, therefore, firmly by the side of William James's predicate of the "pluralistic world."

Admitting the state of polyarchism, he said, "sovereign your state no longer is, if the groups within itself are self-governing. Everywhere we find groups within the state which challenge its supremacy. We find the state, in James's phrase, to be distributive and not collective."[2]

Therefore, since men belong to one group and at the same time to others, a "competition for allegiance is continuously possible." His essential task, "to find how to divide my allegiance between the different groups to which I belong," is really the highest pluralist approach to the ground of obligation, in which the highest possible satisfaction of the desires of the persons in each group, including the state, can consciously be attained by the full chance of "continuous initiative" of every member and of access, spiritually and materially, to the final decision of every group by means of consent. This is the democracy of pragmatic utilitarianism. In this respect the ultimate aim of the state is to find out how to bring the satisfaction of the desire of individuals, as well as of groups, into complete harmony with the desire of the state as a whole. Laski clearly indicated in *The Grammar of Politics* that "the group is real in the same sense as the state is real. It has, that is to say, the interest to promote, the function to serve . . . the group is real, I suggest, as a relation or a process.

[1] H. J. Laski: *The Foundations of Sovereignty*, "The Personality of Associations," p. 168.   [2] Ibid., p. 169.

It is a binding together of its individual parts to certain modes of behaviour deemed by them likely to promote the interests with which they are concerned. In that sense it possesses personality. It results in integrated behaviour. It enables its members to find channels of satisfied activity which otherwise would be absent. It has life only through that behaviour."[1]

Therefore no allegiance is permanent, in that the interests of members in the group have for them a marginal utility which exists in "the perspective of knowledge that loyalty may be transferred elsewhere." In this respect Laski's demand for co-operation is "federal and not imperial in character," and "the centre of significance is no longer the search for unity, but rather what that unity makes," i.e. "a creative adjustment." The political inference from this is that "the structure of social organisation must be federal if it is to be adequate. Its pattern involves, not myself and the state, my groups and the state, but all these and their interrelationships."

With the response to the demands of the state there grows up between it and the individual a process which alters both response and demand. But for the state to validate its demand for an alteration of the relation of the individual to the various groups to which he belongs, it must show "that its demands represent a general reciprocal increase of good—a good which is a co-operative creation," and elicit "a response which enables me to experiment with the growing realisation of my best self." Therefore his main point is that "since society is essentially federal in nature, the body which seeks to impose the necessary unities must be so built that the diversities have a place therein."

Since "society is federal, authority must be federal."[2] To give effect to this aim means joint research to find the "common place" in which each group feels that his purpose attains a just realisation. But that means a division both of decision and administration and functions, and on the other hand an attempt at creative co-ordination by erecting an "authority which co-ordinates a system of guarantees or limitations." That system must needs be intricate; its framework is a "system of rights postulated as natural because experience has shown them to be the necessary condition of a good life." As Duguit put *solidarité sociale* as the substitute for the Bodinian notion of sovereign supremacy, so Laski urges natural rights as the foundation of state action in this modern world. The ethical importance of his political pluralism consists in the full justification of the conscious

[1] H. J. Laski: *Grammar of Politics*, p. 256. [2] Ibid., p. 271.

allegiance to authority in its efforts to maintain the security of the functional and local units controlled by the state. Laski in this respect think that no matter what definition of the state may be adopted, the essential criterion is to give the individual the right to pass, whether by himself or in concert with others, judgment upon its validity by examining its substance, by which only and through which the state action stands "on a moral parity with the acts of any other association."

According to Laski, that is, freedom of speech and of association, a living wage, adequate education, proper self-government, suitable employment, and the power to combine for social efforts "are all of them integral to citizenship" and "are natural rights in the sense that without them the purpose of the state cannot be fulfilled." They are "inherent in the eminent worth of human personality." He held them to be "outside the power of the state to traverse," and upheld in them the ethical supremacy as a limit upon "the sovereignty of the state." For the attainment of these rights, industrial democracy is no less important in the modern state. "Unless there is approximate equality of property as between its different members their rights will in the mass be merely relative to the property they possess. The chief social motive must therefore be service." In order to avoid this fundamental error, of rights being merely relative to property, liberty, which means the exercise of initiative by each man in the attempt to secure the fulfilment of his best self, must be combined with equality. Laski's ideal is a "society in which men are given an equal opportunity of self-realisation"—that is, "a society in which there is justice." With this aim in view, the only possible state to which man owes allegiance is the state in which he discovers moral adequacy. For this the pluralistic state "protects the wholeness of men, over and above those parts which express themselves through groups more specific in character." As he bases the state and its sovereignty on the plural reality, the theory of the federal state is easier for Laski than for any other thinker to reconcile with the division of sovereignty. Dicey's assumption of federalism which "attempts to reconcile the apparently inconsistent claims of national sovereignty and state sovereignty" is to him only thinly veiled "sarcasm," since sovereignty is bound to degenerate into a mere "power to will."

Since, according to Laski, federal government has no final arbiter, the legislature of the United States or of Canada is on the same level as an English railway company—that is to say, a non-sovereign law-making body. Though theoretically existent, in actual practice parliamentary sovereignty is absurd since, for example, it has a legal superiority over colonial legislatures which in practice it cannot realise. The American Revolution was on the English side "an experiment in applied Austinianism, and it is surely obvious that a sovereignty so abstract is practically without utility." Since, after all, the sovereign authority is *de facto* a power of one group to be superior to the other, in the variety of the group life, as in the federal organism, the wide distribution of sovereign authority is admissible in the federal constitution. And Laski doubts whether it is true that federalism is conservative, and expresses the opinion that in respect of any federal constitution there is to-day a "growing impatience with its rigid encasement, the ever insistent demand that the form shall be made equally elastic with the spirit."[1]

On the whole, the English political pluralism, which Laski has now more scientifically formulated, is typically more English in character than Gierke's *Genossenschaftstheorie*.

The chief contribution of his works is the overthrow of the traditional belief in the monistic theory of the state and the preparing the way for the pragmatic approach to the nature of the state. The state should not be a unitary whole on an *a priori* synthesis, but a voluntary territorial community federal in character and distributive in technique. Relativity is the highest test of the social structure. The national state is not the final unit above or below. The decentralised pluralist state on the basis of true democracy is ethically and materially the highest form of state, for which the upholding of natural rights is the fundamental system, and the best means to that end is the creation of a state organisation federal in character and especially federative in authority. I will conclude this statement of Laski's ideal by saying that the tendency of all social systems, whether political or economic, and social organisations towards a pluralistic structure is a real force of progress.

The contributions of American and English thinkers towards the development of federalism have laid the fundamental basis of the federal idea in theory and in practice. This substantial *Grundbegriff* of federalism emerged from long experience and practice, and it has gained in importance as a federal idea more than as a mere political scheme. Federal functions have come to be more essential than its mechanism, both in the worn-out unitary sovereign state and in the existing inefficient federal states.

[1] H. J. Laski: *Studies in The Problem of Sovereignty*, Appendix A, "A Note on Sovereignty and Federalism," p. 275.

In this sense Anglo-American federalism has been far more elaborate and has contributed by its ideas and schemes more to progress than has continental federalism, but at the same time continental federalism is much more inclined to the legal interpretation and the legal form of federalism than the Anglo-American—this is especially the case with the German jurists' contribution of the *Staatslehre*. The contribution of the French thinkers towards federal ideas is novel and suggestive, but rather of a general than of a detailed nature. No realisation of the new federalism can be attained unless these two forms of thought—the Anglo-American and the continental federalism—harmonise and form a synthesis of the best that is contained in both sets of ideas.

PART III
THE HISTORY OF GERMAN FEDERAL IDEAS

CHAPTER I

DEVELOPMENT OF FEDERAL IDEAS FROM HUGO AND PUFENDORF TO GEORG WAITZ

§ 1

The foundation of the Achaean League of the Grecian City States, 281 B.C., constituted the origin of federalism on the continent of Europe. A cursory survey of the theory of federalism at the height of the Greek Renaissance was undertaken by a few thinkers, such as Polybius and Strabo, who conceived it as a mere expedient for a union of states against foreign aggression.

Every aspect of Grecian life was so deeply influenced by city-state politics that even Aristotle's experimental political studies had not touched on any federal form of government.

The transformation of the political system of Athens into that of Rome was shown by a slight resemblance between city states and the early Roman states and municipalities before the triumphant formation of the Roman Empire.

Roman democracy, which was followed centuries later by the unified supremacy of Justinian legalism, went only so far as to create a decentralised political scheme, but did not form any federal system at all. After Caesarism replaced the democratic rule of the *Comitia*, the idea of federalism remained in abeyance until the downfall of the gigantic edifice of the Roman Empire.

Mediaeval Europe was governed by feudal politics until the great social revolution of the Reformation, out of which the modern state emerged.

The historian Gibbon assumed that feudalism was in its origin a kind of federalism. His assertion had no accurate foundation in the sense of modern federalism, but the anarchy of mediaeval Europe was without doubt the main impetus to the establishment of federated unions, such as the Swiss Confederacy of 1291 and the Italian City and Hanseatic Leagues. Feudalism certainly had for its basis the idea of contract just as federalism was based on the *Vertrag-theorie*, but in the feudal organisation of society there was scarcely any foreshadowing of federalism.

The basis of feudal society was not wholly statehood but estate, and the law on which the feudal theory was founded was far nearer the *Landrecht* based on public law. From the juristic point of view no idea of the *Bundesstaat* could spring out of the feudal status.[1] The subordination of the vassal to the lord, and of the lord to the king, was entirely in contradiction with the co-ordinate relations between the members of a federation. And the contract between the vassals and the lords and the lords and the king was characterised far more by a moral than by a legal obligation, whereas the best form of federalism was a union of states in which the members of the federation could be republican. From this last consideration it is clear that feudalism by its very nature was the antithesis of federalism.

Federalism, therefore, was revived in its form and nature when the notion of the modern state destroyed the idea of feudalism and the dynastic ideal replaced the feudal practice. But in the feudal political system federation was possible only in the form of a league or an alliance of princes or dukes for aggression towards neighbouring powers. One or two princes predominated over the others not only in the federal pact, but also in the final responsibility for federal policy and administration, as even in the case of the United Provinces of the Netherlands. At the same time the ideas of constitutionalism and limited monarchy, such as those of Marsiglio, were instrumental in ridding the minds of would-be reformers of the superstitious beliefs of the Holy Roman Empire.

But these feudal-natured confederations and numerous leagues in mediaeval Europe had in some way or other terminated by the time of the formation of the national confederated state of the United Provinces of the Netherlands in 1579.

Though the Union of the Netherlands was characterised by a confederated republican nature, the supremacy of the *Statthalter*, William of Orange, was one of the legacies of the mediaeval *Staatenverbindung*, and at the same time a transitional stage in the development towards modern federalism. Federalism on the continent of Europe up to the formation of the Swiss federal state in 1848, and the German federal state in 1919, was, strictly speaking, by no means the ideal form of the federal state as compared with that of the United States of America.

Except for a few Roman jurists, no federal ideas were put forward by anyone until the publication of Bodin's *Six Livres de la République* in 1577. Althusius' *Politica* in 1603 was the first landmark in the history of federal ideas.

Althusius sought to define confederation as a statehood differ-

[1] Siegfried Brie: *Der Bundesstaat*, 1874, p. 13.

ent from a unitary sovereign state, by designating the former a *Confederatio non plena* and the latter a *Confederatio plena*.[1]

He then divided the *Confederatio non plena* into three forms of union: the mere alliance, the personal union and the confederation. His theory of corporation laid down, as Gierke pointed out, the basic foundation of the German federal idea.

His political speculations with regard to federalism paved the way for two kinds of federation, one of which approximated to a federal state and the other to the state consolidated from states. The federal idea in the former was much more clearly and precisely expounded by Hugo Grotius, the father of international law, in his *De Jure Belli et Pacis* in 1625, and elaborated by Pufendorf in his work *De Jure Naturae et Gentium*.[2]

These two jurists claimed for confederation an international legal personality, but unlike Althusius they could hardly dissociate the confederated nature of federalism from the absolute recognition of the sovereignty of the component states on the one hand and the enumerated restriction of federal practice on the other. Althusius' theory of corporation in the consolidated state, mentioned above in relation to the federal idea, was more closely followed by Ludolph Hugo than by the other jurists of his time.

Federal ideas made no material progress until the speculations of the American federalists in 1787. And even though the epoch-making contribution of the creation of the federal state by the United States Constitution of 1787 gave an example to continental federal development, no federal state appeared until the revision of the Swiss Constitution in 1847 and the formation of the federated German Empire in 1871.

Feudal-coloured federalism continued to shed its dim light upon the continental federal idea, and there was no striking literature regarding the federal state until the remarkable contribution of De Tocqueville in 1836. The idea of modern federalism was transfused into the continental federalism by the medium of his *Democracy in America*, and gave a new impetus to the federal principle in the German confederacy and the Swiss confederation. Georg Waitz, a German political historian, introduced modern federalism into the worn-out, half-destroyed confederacy in his work *Das Wesen des Bundesstaats*, in 1853.

Therefore the history of federal ideas on the continent is naturally the history of German federal principles, except as

[1] Cf. Part I, Chap. I, pp. 27–30.   [2] Ibid., pp. 31–32.

regards the instructive suggestion of economic federalism first propounded by Proudhon in France in his *Principe Fédératif* of 1863.

§ 2

The mediaeval Germanic principalities and feudal states had been grouped together and formed the Holy Roman Empire under the Hapsburg dynasty. The elaborate phantom of the Holy Roman Empire upheld this gigantic and sacred edifice until the great social revolution of the Reformation in the early sixteenth century.

Feudal groups and leagues under the sacred power of the Emperor, as Freeman expressed it, can hardly be designated "confederations" in the modern sense of the word. The Imperial Diet furnished the highest legislative body; the *Reichskammergericht* constituted the Supreme Court of Justice and the office of the emperor chosen by the electors, together with his own *Reichsrat*, was the executive organ. But as later events showed, the loyalty of the electors towards the emperor was shattered by the unparalleled phenomenon of the Reformation.

Luther's appeal "To the Christian Nobility of the German Nation" in 1520 was the first adumbration of the rising of Germanic political unity. The bankruptcy of the ecclesiastical supremacy of the Roman papacy started in Germany, and resulted in the anarchy of the peasant revolt of 1525, and in the tumult of the Reformation and Counter-Reformation, not only in theological strife, but also in the physical conflicts of blood and iron. The Thirty Years War changed the great empire, once based on the sacred dignity and revered name of the Holy Roman Empire, into a crippled and decrepit body politic. The Peace of Westphalia established the principles of religious emancipation from the spiritual supremacy of the Vatican.

Under the shadow of the now impotent Holy Roman Empire the substance of imperial authority was practically in the hands not of the emperor, but of the *Reichsrat*, which was composed of the representatives of the estates and entrusted with the control of the imperial treasury.

Even though theoretically the emperor possessed sovereign power in the Diet and *Reichskammergericht*, his impotence in administration caused the rise of dynastic powers, such as those of Prussia and Bavaria, destined to overthrow the feudal lords and produce an entire change in the Germanic social structure.

The only alternatives to the Holy Roman Empire were to transform the empire into a federal system of government, or to base the empire on the political hegemony of the Hapsburg dynasty, independent of the conventional pretensions of spiritual supremacy.

Except for the rise of the Prussian dynasty, the dim halo of the emperor kept for him an historical authority over the Germanic people until the Napoleonic aggressions at the very end of the eighteenth century.

During the greater part of the seventeenth and the eighteenth centuries federal ideas were generally neglected, except in Pufendorf's, Hugo's and Pütter's contributions, but the successive contributions of the administrative principle in Germany, such as the school of *Kammeralists*, and the doctrine of Stewardship of Frederick the Great, caused immense progress in German political ideas, replacing the doctrine of Absolutism.

During this epoch the political principle of how to rule was so widespread as to exclude the possibility of any progress in the principle of organisation in which both ruler and ruled could participate.

The great mistake of the emperor who received the Napoleonic challenge in 1796 resulted in the entire disruption of German unity, when Prussia remained neutral and Bavaria intrigued to repudiate the imperial allies. The Peace of Lunéville in 1803 resulted not only in the loss of territory to the empire, but also in the formation of the notorious *Reichsdeputations-Haupt Ausschuss* which overturned the foundations of the feudal Germanic states under the hegemony of the dynastic kings.

The whole, or virtually the whole, of the spiritual principalities in the empire, together with all but six of the fifty-one free imperial cities, were swept away and were consolidated under the Hapsburg or Hohenzollern hegemonies or the Bavarian kingdom or in the Grand Duchies of Baden and of Nassau.

The Napoleonic ambition of a Pan-European empire gave rise to the *Rheinbund*, which united sixteen German states in 1806, and of which the kings of Bavaria and Württemberg, as well as the Grand Duke of Baden, were members.

Meanwhile, under the spiritual influence of Lutheran liberalism, Prussia had begun its existence under the Elector of Brandenburg, and was established as a kingdom in 1701. By his successful administration, based on the doctrine of Stewardship, Frederick the Great (1740–1786) made the Prussian kingdom one of the most powerful states in Germany.

It was he who originated the *Fürstenbund*, that first adumbration of the Germanic federal union, but which had not the faintest prospect of success so long as Prussia and its allies declined to contemplate any organic change in the moribund diet of the empire.

The benevolent despotism of the Prussian monarchy had by 1800 created one of the strongest militaristic states and one of the *Kultur* states of the Holy Roman Empire. Although Napoleonic aggression inflicted an almost fatal blow on Prussia in 1806, yet this very defeat produced the real Germanic national spirit already brought into being by the constant appeal of the patriotic literature of Fichte, Schiller and others.

The bloodshed on Prussian fields and humiliating defeats by the Napoleonic army not only transformed Fichte's individualism into Rousseauan absolutism, but also produced an intellectual and romantic element in every aspect of Prussian life, and firmly established German nationalism both in Prussia and in all German states.

Not only the romantic appeals of literature, but also unparalleled contributions of political philosophy emerged from this struggle and started the German trend of thought which led to the formation of the German Empire in 1871.

In the development of political theory the idea of social contract and *Naturrecht* of the eighteenth century had ended in its great historical embodiment of 1789 and shifted from the notions of Althusius, Locke and Rousseau to the historical metaphysical school of thought on the one hand and the Benthamite utilitarian school on the other. The German school of thought repudiated the latter and accepted the former.

Political philosophy in Germany was revived and animated in the later eighteenth century by the immortal contributions of Kant, the only philosophy of outstanding value since the time of Althusius and Spinoza. He investigated Hume's empiricism and scepticism, and set up his own philosophy of the categorical imperative on the basis of "pure reason."

His doctrine was that the highest virtue of human beings was freedom of will, the manifestation of which was the greatest human aim, i.e. the rational conscious purpose subject to the universal laws of nature.

Reason in creatures was the innate faculty "of which it is characteristic to extend the laws and purposes involved in the use of all powers." Kant went far beyond Hume's empirical assertion of the derivative reason on a psychological basis, by arguing that man possessed an animate rational sense.

Deducing from "something" which Hume left as sceptical, individual freedom of will was rationalised subjectively by pure reason, as it was to be universal and eternal, common and absolute. The individual free will in a nature of variety was purified and strengthened by the rational reason and transmitted to a synthetic universe which was compatible with the universal law of nature.

Kant himself, in his long deliberate meditation in his study at Königsberg, deduced and formulated the universal law of nature which he designated as a categorical imperative and doctrinised *Practical Reason* as the basis of politics. As he, like T. H. Green later, assumed that human beings leaned towards the general principle of self-love or individual happiness, objectivity must be superior to subjectivity or empiricism—in other words, principle had to overrule practice.

On this postulate objective necessity must be based on *a priori* grounds.

On this assumption of *Practical Reason* the greatest liberty could only be realised by the perfectly just civil constitution, which was the highest necessity of human beings. As the philosophical entity of the civil union was devoid of men's "unsociableness" under the constitution, so every state in the relation with another "may rely for its safety and its rights, not on its own powers or its own judgment of right, but only on this great international federation, on its combined powers, and on the decisions of common will according to law." From his ideal federation of a free state his synthetic notions of the constitution of the federated state could be idealised. But the federation, to which Kant adhered, was derived from "Providence," and not from utility or necessity. To him federalism was based naturally on the *a priorism* of interstate morality, but not on the empirical outcome of the solidarity of desires and necessity of human association.

Although Kant rationalised human activities into his categorical imperative, yet he made allowance for the empirical nature of human association and regarded federalism as the highest manifestation of ideal human association.

Nevertheless, his ethical basis of the state and the federation of free states set up a synthetic whole of morals and *Politik*. Fichte, on the other hand, had like Rousseau, passed on the same road from individualism to the general will; but as he drew a distinction between morals as ideal and politics as expediency, he never approached the problem of federation as the final expedient for German survival.

Hegel founded the indefeasible basis of German idealism on the purely ethical ground that the state was "the realised, ethical idea or ethical spirit" that was the reflection of the general will which furnished the universal synthesis of real will and was based on rational freedom of self-consciousness. He deemed the state to be a completed reality which is an ethical whole and the actualisation of freedom, and therefore the state was an "organism" based on "political constitution."

Since the state was "not a private person, but itself a completely independent totality," the relation between the states, according to him, ought to be intrinsically right, and in mundane affairs that which is intrinsically right ought to have power. But there is no power to decide what is intrinsically right and to give effect to this decision. The absolute power on earth which is the spirit substantively realised and directly real is sovereign independence.

There is to Hegel no judge over the state, at most only a referee or mediator; and even the mediatorial function is only an accidental thing, being due to particular wills. Kant's idea of eternal peace by means of an alliance of the states was by no means compatible with his ideal that "the substantive weal of the state is its weal as a particular state in its definite interests and conditions, its particular external circumstances and its particular treaty obligations."

As long as the spirit of the nation is an existing individual having in particularity its objective actuality and self-consciousness, "the destinies and deeds of states in their connection with one another are the visible dialectic of the nature of the spirit." His idealistic conclusion reached the highest stage that "out of this dialectic the universal spirit, the spirit of the world, the unlimited spirit, produces itself"; and he concluded that "in the state self-consciousness finds the organic development of its real substantive knowing and will, in religion it finds in the form of ideal essence the feeling and the vision of this truth, and in science it finds the free conceived knowledge of this truth, seeing it to be one and the same in all its mutually completing manifestations, namely, the state, nature and the ideal world."

His idealistic deduction was simply the absorption of all the ingredients of social functions and associations into a divine-natured state, and left no room for self-government and objective particularity, and naturally never produced federalism in his metaphysics.

Now in the beginning of the nineteenth century every branch of German social science saw its ideals through the medium of Hegelian transcendentalism.

With this trend of political ideas the German Confederation of 1815, under the supreme authority of the Hapsburg dynasty, was the first appearance of federation in Germany.

The transference from the *Naturrecht-Theorie* to Historic-Metaphysics produced a new aspect of jurisprudence, Roman law, for example, receiving a new great attention, especially historically. Savigny founded historical jurisprudence, which was applied mainly to Roman law, and tested juristic philosophy by that of history. Besides the notion of historical interpretation, even Savigny required a logical foundation and strengthened his historical statements by metaphysical argument.[1]

No matter to which school of legal thought one belongs, it must be conceded that the only complete method of establishing the principle of jurisprudence is the combination of the historical and logical; this has been manifested in every phase of legal history. Classical Roman law had its origin in Stoic philosophy and later Roman law in Christianity, and even early American legal history could hardly be understood without taking Puritanism into account.

Stahl's religious interpretation of jurisprudence did not differ much from the law of nature or Kant's or Hegel's metaphysical ethics. This ethical jurisprudence on an historical basis was formulated by Kant's metaphysical *Anfangsgründe der Rechtlehre*. Kant's formula of justice was the idea of right, and every legal rule, doctrine and institution must be in some way or other the complete and perfect realisation of his ideal "right," which comprehends the whole of the conditions under which the voluntary actions of any one person can be harmonised in reality with the voluntary actions of every other person, according to a universal law of freedom.[2]

The reconciliation between individual self-assertion and supervision by authority, i.e. government and liberty, was Kant's ideal dictum of "right."

If we thought that the highest aim of law was a compromise between the need of stability and that of change, then the

[1] R. Pound: *Interpretations of Legal History*, 1923, pp. 17–18.
[2] Kant: *Philosophy of Law*, trans. by Hastie, 1887, p. 45.

formula of "right" laid down by Kant was the necessary postulate for the everyday administration of justice unless it was not based on a system.

Thus federalism could theoretically be analysed by Kant's ideal dictum of right. But as Roscoe Pound remarks, "the historical critique to which legal rules and doctrines and institutions were subjected in the last century comes directly from these metaphysicians who thought they understood law—from Kant and Hegel."[1]

By Kant ethical jurisprudence was formulated, and by Hegel, along with the historical school, political jurisprudence was founded which developed into positivism.[2]

Hegel's right and law clarified the conception of legal history in which the development of the spirit of legal philosophy was "the march of freedom in civil relations."

Hegel's ideal of "freedom as an idea" was the highest manifestation of law, and the realisation of the idea that "existence generalised is existence of free will" was the synthetic co-existence of the political idea with the legal idea as unfolded in juristic rules and doctrines and institutions.

The philosophical solution of jurisprudence was based on philosophical, political metaphysics as realised in civil relations.

This conception of Hegel's legal idea suggested the historical interpretation in the terms of particular races and nations, and gave jurists an idealistic sociological interpretation.

The conception of jurisprudence based on Hegelian principles was the main current of thought underlying philosophy in the nineteenth century, until the advent of Comte's positive philosophy.

The positivists developed their juristic doctrine out of the material of the historical school and their juristic conception out of the Hegelian doctrine.

This mechanical sociology in jurisprudence shifted in the latter part of the nineteenth century to biological jurisprudence, under the influence of the rise of biological science and Darwinian sociology. In the eighties the rise of psychology exerted a profound influence on the idea of law, and the Darwinian notion of organic evolution gave place to Gierke's *Genossenschaftstheorie*. The rise of Stammler, the "Neo-Kantian," and of Kohler, the "Neo-Hegelian," both opposed to the prevailing psychology and pragmatic jurisprudence, created the two divergent schools of legal thought now existent.

[1] R. Pound: *Interpretations of Legal History*, p. 32.   [2] Ibid., p. 47.

In the course of the development of legal conceptions and political ideas modern German federalism actually took shape owing to the dissolution of the Holy Roman Empire and the formation of the German Confederation of 1815 under the Hapsburg hegemony.

The Confederation of 1815 was a mere *Staatenbund* of the kings, princes, dukes and a few free principalities, and the Diet of Frankfurt was a mere gathering of ambassadors from the member states, and had somewhat less authority than the congress of the Permanent Union of the United States of 1781.

The Revolution of 1848 in France dealt the first blow to Germanic autocracy and bureaucracy, and gave the liberals an opportunity of revolting against the authorities. The Frankfurt liberals were successful in forming the *Vorparlament* of Frankfurt —May 18, 1848—an unparalleled event in the history of Germany.

The delegates of this assembly, one for every fifty thousand inhabitants, were elected by manhood suffrage and represented all the peoples in the Germanic conferation.

The 586 members, who, however, included none of the ruling princes, met in the *Paulus-Kirche* at Frankfurt, and the meeting was a landmark in German federal history just as the Convention of 1787 in the Independence Hall in Philadelphia formed one in the United States.

The main object of the Frankfurt parliament was to revise the Act of Confederation of 1815 and to convert a loose confederation into a liberal, constitutional, monarchical federal state.

The new theory of federalism demanded by the political ideas of 1848 went far beyond the classical conceptions of Pufendorf.

The Frankfurt liberals aimed at the same ideals as Hamilton and Madison had succeeded in establishing in the federal state of America in 1787. The difference between the Convention of 1787 and the Frankfurt parliament was not that of the formation of the assembly, but was due to the conditions of member states, the American states being based on a republican constitution, and the German on a variety of state forms none of which had any legal constitution.

Therefore one of the main characteristics of a federal state, a uniformity of state governments, was one that the German federal movement lacked, ranging as the governments did from the feudal system and the free principalities to kingdoms which lasted till the formation of the present federal constitution of 1919.

The political ideas of 1848 demanded a definite conception

of federalism—the creation of a monarchical federal state—criticised the classical federalism of Pufendorf, and formed a new theory.

Germany's transcendental trend of thought had already demarcated the sphere of social sciences and limited the scope of political science to that of *Staatslehre*.

Looking back at Kant and Hegel, the distinction between politics and public law had already been drawn and developed by Karl Marx and Stein, but their sharp demarcation of political ideas and jurisprudence was mitigated and modified by the introduction of the new *Allgemeine Staatslehre*, in which the two branches of *Politik* and *Staatsrecht* began to be indistinguishable and to be more or less two aspects of the theory in which the conceptions of the origin, aim and form of the state were discussed.

This *Allgemeine Staatslehre* was generally dealt with by the jurists and criticised and analysed the various phases of the state and its functions from the juristic rather than from the sociological or philosophical standpoint.

All the exponents of *Staatslehre*, from Bluntschli and Jellinek to Brie and Rehm, each in a somewhat different manner, based their theories of federalism on their *a priori* principles of jurisprudence.

With the exception of Gierke's *Genossenschaft* theory the jurisprudence on which their final doctrine was mostly based was positivism, developed from Hegelian historical to political jurisprudence, and formulated the theory of the state on the basis of their own juristic conception. To these jurists federalism was a mere system of states, and the object of their *Lehre von den Staatenverbindungen* was to fit every kind of union into a particular category of states either according to its general functions or to its mode of federal formation.

The close relation of the federal principle to the Germanic federation was shown in the works on *Deutsches Staatsrecht*, which were mostly here juristic interpretations of the existing constitutions of the German Empire, quite independent of the underlying political idea of federalism.

But even though the history of federal ideas in Germany had an entirely different aspect from that of Anglo-American federalism, yet the development and change of the notion were more or less coincident with the actual transformation of federal theories.

In 1848 German jurists awakened to the need for a new theory of federalism in order to justify and encourage the Frankfurt decision as to the formation of a federal state, and to meet the increasing discontent with the imperfect functioning of the federation.

The federal experience of the United States of America had already served as an example for more than fifty years, and the epoch-making contribution of De Tocqueville gave the first and most powerful impetus to European federal ideas.

The federalism expounded by Tocqueville was evolved from the American federal system as it was in 1833, when the theories of compact and of divided sovereignty were universally accepted under the designation or theory of "compromise." He assumed that federal government was "exceptional" and state government normal, and the co-ordinate existence and harmonious working of the division of sovereignty between the federal and the state governments were the highest form of democratic technique in political organisation.

According to Tocqueville's theory federalism was the harmonious political mechanism used in determining the merits of large and small states; in other words, it reconciled authority with liberty.

Agreeing with Madison's compromise theory Tocqueville weighed federalism in the scales of political ideas and functions rather than in the balance of legal sovereignty.

His literary charm and philosophical insight into American federalism gave an immense blow to the continental metaphysical and legalistic theories, but except Waitz, and, in a sense, Gierke, German federal exponents could hardly rid themselves of the deep-rooted fallacy of the indivisible and inalienable notion of sovereignty. Until Hugo Preuss proposed a new conception of federalism nearly all federal exposition in Germany or elsewhere on the continent of Europe was confined to the abstract legal justification of federalism on the hypothesis and dogmatic idea of sovereignty.

Therefore the problem of sovereignty, with regard to its origin and its location in the federation, and the classification of federal unions into legally rigid formulas were the main points of discussion among German federalists.

This juristic character of federalism was no doubt of great importance in the history of federal ideas. Federalism itself is an artificial political mechanism, and its technique is to be operated according to the legal nature of the federal constitution which in some way or other is derived from the contract of the federated states; in other words, the solidarity of consent of the federated members of the union. The German federal argument in this respect has been a leading influence in the development of federal principles, and contributed to the transformation of the federal idea from the theory of compromise to the federal goal of the pluralistic decentralised state.

§ 3

The first man in Germany to introduce in a scientific form the conception of one state formed by a combination of the states was Ludolph Hugo in his work, *Dissertatio de Statu regionum Germaniae*, published in 1661.[1] His opening sentence reads as follows: "It is clear that our empire is guided by a twofold government, for the empire as a collectivity forms a common state-entity, and the separate territories of which it is composed have their own princes, or judges, their own courts of justice and diets, and moreover a separate state individuality which is subordinate to the higher state."[2] He pointed out that his own task was to indicate the cause and nature of this difference, and then briefly to show what lay within the province of the supreme imperial government as compared with the provinces of the single governments.

He started from the difficulty of exercising efficient and unitary rule over a great empire which had followed the normal course of German historical development since the foundation of the great Frankish Empire. For the solution of this difficulty in the life of the state it was necessary to divide the whole into a certain number of territories, and to give to the ruler of each state a "universal" authority.[3]

With regard to the ruling authorities of each territory the German territorial authorities alone could be considered as independent and therefore regarded as possessing "state authority," even though they were subordinate to the whole state.

On the other hand, comparing the German *Bund* with certain confederations such as the Achaean, Netherland and Swiss, the

---

[1] Brie: *Der Bundesstaat*, 1874, p. 17. Otto Gierke: *Johannes Althusius*, p. 246. Hugo Preuss: *Gemeinde, Staat, Reich*, pp. 12–14. Ludolphi Hugonis: *De Statu Regionum Germaniae*, 1689.
[2] Ludolphi Hugonis: *De Statu Regionum Germaniae, Propositi Explicatio*, Sec. 1.
[3] Ibid., Chap. II, Secs. 1–3.

German states were subject to a higher state authority, whereas in the others the member states were not in a position of actual subordination.

Hugo, however, admitted that subordination to a higher power was incompatible with the Aristotelian definition of the state, and accordingly doubt could be thrown on the designation of the German territories as states. He then modified certain of his statements, but concluded that the German territories might at least be considered as analogous to states, in spite of the fact that the powers of the empire over its territories were closely akin to sovereignty.

In support of this view he maintained that there was a division of sovereign rights between the supreme state and the member states.

The main point was that the empire had to safeguard the common welfare of the empire and the individual states their own territorial welfare.

This principle was modified by the sound principle which laid down that to each power should be assigned the task it could accomplish better than others.

In opposition to the prevailing theory, Hugo did not consider state power to be "absolute" and "inalienable." He did not seem to consider closely whether and how far such a division could be reconciled with the "universal nature" of state authority. With regard to justice the territorial authorities were allowed to make their own laws so long as they were compatible with the imperial constitution, but the imperial court of law could intervene to rectify errors of territorial law and prevent a miscarriage of justice.

The harmony between the whole and the parts and of the parts with one another was maintained by the fact that the constitutions of the individual principalities, because of a similar nationality and their formation by the imperial ministry, and also owing to deliberate imitation, were copies of the imperial constitution, although not an exact one since they differed in many respects.[1]

Hugo's exposition of the German Empire, although not accurate and scientific in the modern sense of federalism, contained the first reference to a division of the *Staatsgewalt* and a new conception of federal authority over that of the state. Although the German Empire of his day did not exactly correspond to his theoretical plan, it was nevertheless really the first

[1] Ludolphi Hugonis: *De Statu Regionum Germaniae*, Chap. IV.

manifestation of the theory of *Staatenbund* as contrasted with the orthodox theory of confederation.[1]

His theory of federalism set out the confederated nature of the German Empire, and did not follow closely the generally accepted *Staatenbund* theory of his time.

Hugo's treatise received immense applause from learned circles, and his new theory not only obtained acceptance, but also gave an impetus to the development of the idea of "federalism," and especially that of the "federal state" in Germany.

Samuel Pufendorf put forward and developed federal ideas based on the fundamental political creeds of Grotius and Hobbes. In agreement with Bodin and Hobbes, Pufendorf was convinced that the absolute unity of state power, as well as the complete independence of the highest will in each state, followed logically from the essential nature of the state. On this assumption he not only rejected the theory of mixed states, but also that of a state containing many states in itself. Nevertheless, Pufendorf was convinced that a number of states, belonging to the same nationality, might need closer union, without, however, giving up their individuality as states.

But in order to obtain this he recognised only two methods; one being an association in respect of the person of the ruler, and the other a permanent treaty-based association for the exercise of certain supreme rights, but yet maintaining the complete sovereignty of the single states. Since he was a firm believer in sovereignty he regarded decisions by majority vote of the confederated states with regard to common affairs, not only as a transition to a unitary state, but, in any event, as a deviation from the real nature of a state system. Therefore he considered it abnormal that "any member of the state system should possess by virtue of its priority any power over the other members."[2]

But applying this principle to the actual German Empire he pointed out that the lack of the federal pact and the existence of a head of the union could allow it to be characterised as a system of union states, whereas the sovereign position of the princes in their own territories and their common decisions in regard to general affairs did come nearer to this system, and that the practical significance of an association of states was far behind that of a regular state.[3]

---

[1] Ludolphi Hugonis: *De Statu Regionum Germaniae*, Chap. II, Sec. 8.
[2] Brie: *Der Bundesstaat*, p. 23. Otto Gierke: *Johannes Althusius*, pp. 250–254.
[3] Cf. Part I, Chap. I, pp. 32–33.

In so far as he correctly indicated the actual political situation of the German Empire and the prevailing tendency towards the development of federalism he was no doubt the first exponent of federalism in the scientific sense, and by his remarkable and precise statement he had relegated into obscurity for a long time the prevailing theory of a state formed by combination of other states, the weakness of which was undoubtedly shown in Hugo's exposition.

This theory of the state formed by a combination of other states, which had for a long time been neglected by the German jurists, began gradually to be revived in the latter part of the eighteenth century.

Johann Stephan Pütter, in an entire agreement with Hugo's theory, more explicitly than J. J. Moser,[1] set out not only the Aristotelean rigidity of the state form, but also made a clear statement of "a higher division of the state body" by his rational systematic method, and he is the first man who designated definitely the German Empire as "the state consolidated from states." More precisely in his later work, *Beyträge zum Teutschen Staats und Fürstenrechte*, in 1777 (which did not altogether agree with Hugo's theory) Pütter put forward the view that the state was not only an organisation as a large state, but might arise from the union of several states into a greater whole. He argued that many different states could be blended into a unified state, but that it was also possible for them to be united for common protection against foreign powers and for certain other purposes, while still maintaining their equality and independence.

He emphasised the importance of the fact that the hitherto independent states should be joined and united into a union, in which "all states should uphold their own governments with their supreme rights in their internal constitutions, but have a still higher common power over them."[2] He observed that the usual process with regard to the formation of the consolidated state was the combination of the separate states; but the reverse process could and actually did take place in the German Empire —that empire which earlier was in every respect only one state and was gradually divided into several separate states which, however, as time went on, came to be united into a unitary state under a common supreme ruler.

[1] J. J. Moser: *Von Teutschland und dessen Staatsverfassung*, 1766.
[2] Pütter: *Von der Regierungsform des teutschen Reichs*, Secs. 9–14, 18.—One of his works was translated into English under the name of *An Historical Development of the Present Political Constitution of the German Empire*, in 1790.

From his observation of the actual situation in his time Pütter was led to ascribe to the individual states "as a rule and on the whole, government possessed of all the supreme rights," whereas he did recognise that the general authority of imperial legislation tended to eliminate the supremacy of the individual states and interfere in internal relationships. As he considered the emperor to be the possessor of the highest powers, so he designated the participation of the estates of the empire in the imperial government a *Mitregierungsrecht*.[1]

When Pütter drew an important distinction between the constitution of the empire and the constitution of all other limited monarchies, he pointed out that in Germany the estates of the empire were not private owners or elected representatives of certain communities, but true royal envoys of their own member states.

From this Pütter concluded that in decisions affecting the governments of separate states political weight must be laid more on the estates of the realm than on the emperor himself, and the German imperial constitution was more or less similar to the so-called "system of federated states."

Also, the most distinguished members of Pütter's school of thought, such as Häberlin and Leist, laid down unaltered in their handbooks on German public law Pütter's view of the constitution of the German Empire as a state compounded of several states.

This was almost universally adopted by the publicists of the last decade of the empire.[2]

Nevertheless, however widely their idea of the federated state had spread, the general theory of federalism did not develop during the whole of the eighteenth century beyond the point to which Pufendorf had brought it. And in spite of Pütter's strongly expressed and generally accepted views as to the system of the federated state, the *Staatenbund* still remained the nucleus of the federal idea in Germany.

Even later and greater political thinkers in Europe, such as

---

[1] Pütter: *Von der Regierungsform des teutschen Reichs*, "Beyträge," III, Secs. 6, 7.
[2] Häberlin: *Handbuch des teutschen Staatsrechts*, 1797, I, pp. 150–153, 259–260. Leist: *Lehrbuch des teutschen Staatsrechts*, 1803, Secs. 15–17, 20, 57. Schmalz: *Handbuch des teutschen Staatsrechts*, 1805, Secs. 30–32. Von Roth: *Staatsrecht deutscher Reichslande*, 1788, Secs. 4, 23–25. J. C. Majer: *Teutsche Staatskonstitution*, 1800, Sec. 12. N. T. Gönner: *Deutsches Staatsrecht*, 1805, Secs. 2, 87.—The German land "is considered as a state body which is constituted not by the confederation, but by a union under a common higher state authority, namely, as a state."

Montesquieu in his *République Fédérative*, Wolff in his *Civitas Maxima* or Kant in his *Föderalismus der Freyer Staaten* or *Völkerbunde*, failed to throw any new light on or even to develop or clarify the federal-state theory as Pütter conceived it.[1]

The German federal idea had never developed during the time when the Holy Roman Empire maintained the gigantic and unstable edifice founded on the different and independent elements of the states, and particularist tendencies retarded the unified co-operation of the German nation.

The French Revolution of 1789 led the German monarchies and princes to react against the liberal movement in German politics, but on the other hand the later Napoleonic despotism destroyed the old political structure, on the ruins of which a new federal system was soon to be erected.

The destruction of the feudal system and the formation of the *Rheinbund*, along with the rise of Germanic nationalism, brought about a new phase of German federal history which, however, was destined to be only a transient one.

The study of the *Rheinbund* now became the focus of the speculations of the publicists. Since the *Rheinbund* under the protection of Napoleon could not be regarded as a state, but only as a confederation, comparison was necessary to determine and establish the resemblances and differences between the two supreme authorities in an organised union of states in order to reach the conception of the composite state.

In order to formulate these conceptions, German jurists sought to build up a clear and comprehensive terminology, and to consider the necessary relationships between the various systems of federated states.

One of the most distinguished publicists at the time of the *Rheinbund* was K. S. Zachariä, a German jurist of Saxony, whose individual characteristics were mirrored in his works: *Geist der neuesten deutschen Reichsverfassung*, 1804; *Das Staatsrecht der rheinischen Bundesstaaten und das rheinische Bundesrecht*, 1810; and *Vierzig Bücher vom Staat*, 1839.

The political changes following on the Peace of Lunéville in 1804 required a clear knowledge of the German Empire, and Zachariä, in opposition to the prevailing theory, asserted that the so-called German Empire was not a "national state," but a "national union, i.e. confederation."

He based this assertion far more on actual political experience

[1] Otto Gierke: *Johannes Althusius*, pp. 246-247.—Even Spinoza in his expression of Aristocracy stood nearer to the federal state conception.

than on theoretical argument, and founded the legal distinction between the two kinds of unions of states on the actual events and requirements of state life.[1]

He assumed that the essential requirements of a state were an absolute and unlimited "will" and an amount of physical power sufficient to enable it to withstand any internal resistance, whereas as a matter of fact in a union of sovereign states each one retained its own power of decision in regard to right and wrong. Neither the majority vote nor the decisive authority of the German imperial diet was sufficient to make it a supreme power, since its authority could be rendered invalid by the appeal of any one of the component estates, and the executive power of the estates of the empire could therefore not be enforced. Differing from the views of Pütter and his school, Zachariä concluded that for legal reasons the federal empire could not be in any case regarded as "a national state." From this standpoint the fall of the Holy Roman Empire and the formation of the *Rheinbund* were not to be considered as marking a complete change, but as the natural evolution of the system of unions, as "a mere association of sovereign states" without the valid authority of the *Bund*.

In his résumé of the *Jus Publicum Civitatum* of the *Rheinbund*, published in 1807, he laid down as the essential characteristic of a *Staatenbund* the possibility of its dissolution by agreement of the individual states—this power of dissolution being an integral part of each state entity.[2] As real examples of consolidated states formed by states, he cited the North American federal state and the Swiss confederation.

K. S. Zachariä's views regarding state aims and state power in the federal state were discussed in detail by G. H. von Berg in his work *Abhandlungen zur Erläuterung der rheinischen Bundesacte* in 1808. Berg disputed the view of the *Rheinbund* as a state by reference to its limited sphere, and also the admitted sovereign authority of the individual members of the union.

He asserted that the *Rheinbund* had for its object protection against external enemies and internal unrest, yet this union, differing from the German Empire, lacked the general purpose of the state which could not be attained without "a universal supreme state authority." His exposition of the relationship of

---

[1] Brie: *Der Bundesstaat*, p. 35. K. S. Zachariä: "Geist der neuesten deutschen Reichsverfassung," in Waltmann's *Zeitschrift für Geschichte und Politik*, Jahrg. 1804, pp. 34–64.
[2] K. S. Zachariä: *Jus Publicum Civitatum quae foederi Rhenano*, 1807, Sec. 60.

the state purpose to the state authority was his standard in ascertaining whether a union should be placed in the category of the *Staatenbund* or in that of the *Staatenverbindung*.

Therefore, Berg conceived that in the German Empire the authority of the single states might be dependent on limited state power, whereas the federal assembly in a *Staatenbund* was "a political authority (*Behörde*) for the maintenance of peace among the different sovereign states of which the *Bund* was composed."[1] On this assumption the *Rheinbund* was not a *Bundesstaat*, but a mere *Staatenbund*—an association for external and internal peace, "an idea arising from the acceptance of an imperial constitution."

W. J. Behr, in his work *Systematische Darstellung des Rheinischen Bundes*, 1808, discussed the difference between a *Völkerstaat* and a *Staatenbund*.[2]

Like other thinkers, Behr asserted that the real nature of the *Staatenbund* consisted in the association of several independent states for the common attainment of legal security at home and abroad, whereas the national state was a union of states, which was subject to a common higher power and a single ruler; he defined the head of the national state as a human being elected and chosen. He pointed out that the highest power in the *Völkerstaat* was to be a real state authority, which must possess legislative, judicial and executive powers in which the "subordination of nations federated under the constitution" under the "common supreme authority" must extend to every branch of the federal and state authorities, whereas in the *Staatenbund* individual states had a self-imposed limitation only in their external affairs.

Behr developed his principles in more detail by contrast between the *Rheinbund* and the German Empire in which he maintained that, in contrast with the *Völkerbund* as a mere association of sovereign states, the *Völkerstaat* in its activities had a share in the inner life of the members of the union, and also made secure the co-existence of the individuals who constituted the nation.

He further assumed that the laws of the empire "settled not only the legal relationship of the territories to one another, but also the legal relationship of the territorial rulers to their people, and even those of the members to one another, and

[1] Berg: *Abhandlungen zur Erläuterung der rheinischen Bundesacte*, 1808, pp. 1–10.
[2] W. J. Behr: *Systematische Darstellung des Rheinischen Bundes*, 1808, III, Secs. 12–15, pp. 55–64.

pledged them all equally as direct or indirect subjects of the empire.[1]

With regard to the subordination of the heads of the individual states to a higher state authority, he drew the conclusion that these must be merely organs (or officials) of the national state authority, and "may not decide or undertake anything by their own general determination, but only on the determination of the national state authority."

He took this impossible relationship as an argument against the national state and in favour of confederation: he conceived that "the constant strife between the head and the members and the entire neglect of the real purpose of the union" was an inherent evil of the national state, whereas in the *Staatenbund* the supreme power in the member states was entirely concentrated on the state purposes, and at the same time the self-imposed limitations in regard to external affairs were not oppressive, and therefore such a union was a guarantee of permanency and strength.

The national state authority thus possessed competence to determine the main distinction between the *Völkerstaat* and the *Staatenbund*.

Behr designated the elective Emperor in the German Empire as a "completely adequate" head of a federal state, and recognised the veto of the emperor. He set up as indispensable for the federal assembly in every form of federation the equal voting right of all members and the unconditional validity of the majority vote.[2]

The formation of the *Rheinbund* was the first adumbration of the federal state organisation in both the theory and practice of the federal idea in Germany.

From Hugo, who assumed the German Empire to be a kind of federation, down to Behr, who considered it to be a federal state, the expositions of all federal thinkers were based either on their own hypotheses or on their own views as to the actual conditions in the German Empire.

The *Rheinbund*, even though not a proper and complete form of federal union, gave great stimulus to the federal idea in Germany, but it was not until the Congress of Vienna in

---

[1] Behr: *Das teutsche Reich und der rheinische Bund*, in Winkopp's *Zeitschrift*, Band 7, p. 113.—His articles published in Winkopp's *Zeitschrift*, Band 6, pp. 418–447; Band 7, pp. 99–138, 361–408; Band 8, pp. 3–63.

[2] Behr: *Das teutsche Reich und der rheinische Bund*, in Winkopp's *Zeitschrift*, Band 7, pp. 363–370.

1815 that modern federalism in that country was really inaugurated.

No literature of that time had formulated any clear and scientific conception of a federal state, or even assumed that the confederation was to be considered as a *Bundesstaat* or evolved the idea of a "federal state" out of the political life of Germany.

Both statesmen and publicists in Germany were indifferent at that time to the conception of a federal state, and not only did the dualism of Austria and Prussia in the German confederation hinder the transition to the German federal state, but also the hitherto prevailing idea of the independence of the individual German states prevented this new development from going beyond the diplomatic conventions of the Congress of Vienna which produced the German confederation.

Even though the restoration of the imperial supremacy was resented by the spokesmen of the small states, no idea of a federal state had as yet been propagated, except that in imitation of the Holy Roman Empire they needed a common head for their union and some amendment in the old form of the empire.

In the opening address of the diet, an Austrian member, Buol-Schauenstein, declared that "Germany is only a confederation and not a federal state"—that is, "the equality of the German princes and free cities united in the German union."

Klüber, in his epoch-making exposition of the origin and law of the German *Bund*, said that the German union was a *Staatenbund*, not a *Bundesstaat*, while Freiherr von Gagern would not admit that Germany was only a *Staatenbund* and claimed for it the equality of a federal state.[1]

On the other hand, a great historian, Heeren, took the view that the German *Bund* was constituted as "a political unity," and as a consolidated power in its relation with foreign countries, and therefore went beyond a mere alliance.[2]

A noted philosopher, Fries, went back to an earlier point of view and demanded "a real supreme government of the union," and especially legislation over the internal affairs of the individual

---

[1] J. L. Klüber: *Uebersicht der Diplomatischen Verhandlungen des Wiener Congresses*, 1816, pp. 122–127. J. L. Klüber: *Oeffentliches Recht des teutschen Bundes und der Bundesstaaten*, 1817, Section 103. Heinrich von Gagern: *Das Leben des Generals Friedrich von Gagern*, Erster Band, p. 387.

[2] A. L. Heeren: *Der deutsche Bund in seinen Verhältnissen zu dem Europäischen Staatensystem* (Historische Werke, Abhandlung V), Göttingen, 1816, p. 21.

states which he, like Gagern, considered to be the most essential characteristic of a federal state.[1]

F. W. Tittmann argued against Behr and Klüber that the object of the federal authority in the federal state need not be a person, but in both kinds of state unions the higher collective will could be formed just as well by the majority will of all the members: but he limited the scope of the federal authority by considering "the internal relationships of the individual state to be quite outside the conception of the whole union."[2]

In his *Darstellung der Verfassung des Deutschen Bundes*, 1818, Tittmann first divided unions of states into those which have and those which have not a federal authority. Such authority may be either coercive (i.e. armed with the power necessary to enforce its decisions) or non-coercive—in the former case the enforcement of the obligations of the members is a right inherent in the higher authority set up by the pact of union; in the latter case the enforcement can only be by war, a means which any one of the parties to an international law agreement can adopt. Tittmann next pointed out that it was customary to divide unions of states into federal states and confederations, though the meanings to be given to the terms were not always very explicit. He himself explained the term federal state (*Bundesstaat*) as connoting that the federal state is a state, and is to the individual states of the union what the state is to its citizens. "In so far as every subordination of the collective legal relationships of the members under a union has in itself the character of a state, every union of states with federal authority is to be called a federal state." But the federal authority differs from state authority, for (as stated above) it can exist without having coercive power, whereas the idea of such power is inseparable from that of state authority. Tittmann held therefore that the term "federal state" could properly be applied only to those unions of states in which the federal authority had coercive power.[3] A union in which the federal authority was not so equipped was to him a mere confederation. Tittmann pointed out, however, that a union of states cannot be in so strong a position in respect of the legal relations of its members as the state in respect of the legal relations of its citizens: the analogy between the federal power and state power is one of direction, not of extent. For the

[1] J. F. Fries: *Vom deutschen Bund und deutscher Staatsverfassung*, 1816, pp. 162, 165, 167, 168.
[2] Friedrich W. Tittmann: *Darstellung der Verfassung des Deutschen Bundes*, 1818, pp. 15, 16.   [3] Ibid., pp. 5–6.

strength is in each case made up of the strengths of the members, but whereas in the state the strength of the individual citizen is small, and he is not capable of resistance to the state power, the strength of the individual member of a union of states may be very great. So in his view of the union of states the federal state may take on the character of a confederation or vice versa: and consequently the distinction is by no means clear-cut. As an example he said that the German *Reich* of his time should unquestionably be a federal state, but actually more closely resembled a mere confederation.[1]

Discussing next the question of sovereignty, he defined it as being to the government (*Regierung*) of a state what freedom is to the individual. Just as the independence of inner life is essential to the freedom of the individual, so independence of external control in domestic affairs is essential to the sovereignty of the state. "Every exercise of power over the internal affairs of a state is a limitation of its sovereignty."[2] If the subordination to federal authority of legal relationships in the internal affairs of the members is included in the conception of the federal state, then the federal state is incompatible with the sovereignty of the members. But he himself believed that "the inner relations of the individual state lie outside the conception of all unions of states." In such unions the only limitation which comes into consideration is that of the external relations of the members. So the federal state is only an international law relationship (it is a *Staatenstaat*), not a constitutional law relationship. But he admitted that there are stages of independence; and the characters of the state and the federal state tend to approximate.[3]

Tittmann observed that there was no agreement, definitely expressed in current terminology, as to whether sovereignty could be attributed only to those states which possessed independence in their external affairs, though recent diplomatic language tended to attribute it to states which did not possess such independence (e.g. the members of the *Deutsche Bund*). And this he held to be correct. The freedom of the individual does not mean independence in legal relations of the power of the state; and in the same way a state can rightly be called sovereign, although in the determination of its international law relations it recognises a higher power[4]—at any rate, a federal authority. "If the individual or the state has given up independence only in so far as seems necessary for the setting up of a

[1] Friedrich W. Tittmann: *Darstellung der Verfassung des Deutschen Bundes*, 1818, p. 8.   [2] Ibid., p. 15.   [3] Ibid., p. 17.   [4] Ibid., p. 19.

higher whole, of which he or it is a member, so that in a higher circle of social life the reasonableness of the relation is brought about by a definite form, there is no need to drop the terms "freedom and independence."[1] Tittmann, therefore, held that the general opinion was right in holding that the states of the *Deutsche Bund* in his time were "sovereign," and that the princes in the former German Empire were only "half-sovereign."[2]

As to the *Deutsche Bund* he laid down the propositions that (1) the member states were sovereign; (2) the German states formed in it a *"Bund, confédération, lien fédératif,"* an international law relationship, a union of states, not a union state; (3) that union was a relation between equals, but (4) there was a fundamental inequality owing to the inequality of voting power in the *Bundestag*; (5) the activity of the *Bund* was not merely a treaty arrangement, but federal authority, since as a rule decision was by majority vote.[3] It was not definitely settled how far the *Bund* had the power to enforce its decisions on its members: and consequently if (as he held) the existence of a coercive supreme authority determines whether a union of states is a federal state or not, it remained at the time he wrote (1818) undecided whether the *Deutsche Bund* was a federal state or a confederation.[4]

After thus analysing the actual *Deutsche Bund* of 1815, Tittmann favoured its federal state character, not for merely abstract reasons, but because of natural needs. And he quoted a speech of the Austrian representative at the *Bundestag*: "Time and human civilisation know no absolute limit; and so we will hold the structure of the *Deutsche Bund* as sacred, but never as finished and complete."[5]

After the German confederation was formed, the history of the federal idea in Germany was a transition from the idea of a confederation to that of a federal state, just as we have seen the change in the American federal development after 1781.

§ 4

The development of the German federal idea was not marked until the revision of the Swiss constitution in 1847 and the revolutions of 1848, which gave a great incentive to the formation

---

[1] Friedrich W. Tittmann: *Darstellung der Verfassung des Deutschen Bundes*, 1818, pp. 19–20.   [2] Ibid., p. 20.
[3] Ibid., pp. 21–25.   [4] Ibid., p. 31.   [5] Ibid., pp. 39–40.

of the German *Bundesstaat*, both in theory and in practice. The conviction of supreme sovereignty belonging to the individual states in the *Bundesstaat* prevented liberal thinkers from accepting internal interference with the member states save in very exceptional cases. The old theory of the *Bundesstaat* as a whole remained unaltered so long as the subordination of the individual states under a higher state power, and the competence of the *Bund* in relation to internal general affairs were considered as the characteristic distinction between the *Staatenbund* and the *Bundesstaat*.

The unity of the German nation required uniformity of public law, whilst the independent existence of the individual states in the *Bund* was considered of the utmost importance.

Therefore the erection of the federal state was the signal not only for the rise of liberalism, but also for the alleviation of the existing evils of inefficient administration due to the dualism of the German *Staatenbund*.

In the progress of this movement all the jurists and statesmen naturally tried to set up a theoretical and legal justification of the federal state.

Though previous thinkers had recognised that the federal power dealt with the general affairs of the nation, they failed to conceive the necessarily direct relationship of the power of the federal state with the citizens of the individual states, and consequently the representative organ of the federal government was not one composed of citizens elected from all the peoples, but merely an assembly made up of representatives of each state.

Out of the several influences such as that of Schurig's *Fürstenbund*,[1] the old conception of the union together with the constitutional hereditary monarchy, the establishment of the emperor and the rise of the North American federal state, a new idea of a *Bundesstaat* was evolved from the practical demands for national unity by famous liberal exponents such as Friedrich von Gagern, Paul Pfizer and Carl Welcker.

Friedrich von Gagern, deriving a system of federal organisation from his firm conviction of nationalism, remarked that "the natural desire to build up a power as a great nation in order to cast the whole weight of the nation into the balance in all political questions is again a claim for the unity and federation whose most appropriate and powerful form is the federal state."[2]

[1] Schurig: *Darstellung des Fürstenbundes*, 1787.
[2] Heinrich von Gagern: *Das Leben des Generals Friedrich von Gagern*, Erster Band, 1856, p. 387.

Rejecting the hitherto prevailing idea of a "supreme head" of the union, Gagern formulated a complete definition of the federal state, saying that "the federal state is the union of several states which subordinate themselves to the common state authority for the attainment of state purposes without the rulers of the individual states relinquishing all their supreme rights."[1]

He went on to say that the individual states should be deprived of their supreme rights in regard to those internal affairs which could be better carried out by the co-operation and collective power of the federal state—that is to say, that the sovereign power of the separate states in the government of their territory should be limited, but only in so far as the constitution of the federal state should determine.

With regard to federal affairs legislation should be in the hands of the individual states only in respect of certain matters, without prejudice to the whole, and the officials of the states should all be appointed to the service of the highest state powers.[2]

Gagern assumed that in the federal state the government of each individual state was "an intermediate stage between the commune and the highest state power, which in the most effective manner and with more freedom and independence took the place of the highest administrative authorities which great states set up for their provinces."[3]

With regard to the problem of the co-existence of the powers of the empire and of the individual states, he asserted that "unity as an idea is not removed, although the exercise of the international and external supreme rights can be separated, and the internal highest right in relation to the territories can exist even though the power of the states is subordinated to the authority of the empire—otherwise half-sovereign states were entirely inconceivable."[4]

The legal impossibility of combining the subordination of the individual state power to the higher authority with the ideal unity of state power was his main difficulty in setting up the conception of the federal state based on the harmony and coexistence of the two powers.

He thought that the hereditary monarchy with a representative constitution was an ideal form of the state, combining

---

[1] Heinrich von Gagern: *Das Leben des Generals Friedrich von Gagern*, Erster Band, 1856, p. 372.   [2] Ibid., p. 377.
[3] Ibid., p. 377.—Gagern's account of the services of the individual state government to the federal administration is the main difference between German and American federations up to 1870.   [4] Ibid., p. 383.

the order and solidity of monarchy with the freedom and activity of the republic, and asserted that the *Bundesstaat* was the highest possible form in which the principles set out above could be most easily realised.

In his ideal hereditary, monarchical, federated *Bundesstaat* he included the consideration of equal opportunity and of balance between the power of the empire and the individual states; therefore he asserted that there should be a chamber in the federal empire representative of the half-sovereign princes on the one hand and another chamber representative of the people of the individual states on the other.

Ardent nationalist as he was, Gagern's ideal for his country was a federal state with constitutional assemblies both for the whole and for each member state.

P. A. Pfizer, who differed in certain respects from Gagern, placed his ideal in a future republican federal system, in a new formation of Germany by the initiative and under the protection of Prussia, with the separation of the Austrian provinces.

He favoured the continuation of the German individual states and their princes, and their representation in general affairs through the Prussian Government, and also the representation of the German people, consisting of delegates from the states.[1]

In 1835 Pfizer discussed the historical-political development of the union of states in his work *Ueber die Entwicklung des öffentlichen Rechts in Deutschland durch die Verfassung des Bundes*, and emphasised that unity and freedom in the Germany of the future were of great importance to the new national formation.[2]

In order to reach this goal he thought that the *Staatenbund* was not a suitable form of union, because of the supreme and equal powers of members of the union, and the fact that secession by any member state must be permissible.[3] Nevertheless, the *Bundesstaat*, on the other hand, was not only empowered to restrict the internal legal relations of the member states "through its constitution and legal order," but also legally to extend its federal authority not merely "to the individual states or their governments, but to the citizens of all the individual states."[4]

An extension of the federal authority over all matters affecting national welfare and its direct connection with everything concerning the citizens of the states was Pfizer's conception of

---

[1] P. A. Pfizer: *Briefwechsel zweier Deutschen*, 1831, in which he conceived that Prussian protection would be necessary from the military point of view.
[2] P. A. Pfizer: *Ueber die Entwicklung öffdes entlichen Rechts*, 1835, p. 40.
[3] Ibid., pp. 44–45. [4] Ibid., p. 45.

the *Bundesstaat*, which emphasised its difference from the *Staatenbund*.

Besides internal peace and protection from foreign foes, Pfizer desired for his country "national union and freedom."[1]

Though he recognised the Madisonian conception of the federal state with regard to the federal authority, yet he, like other thinkers of his day, asserted that the federal state was theoretically to be organised on the basis of the legal equality of the individual states. Nevertheless he realised practically that the inequality of powers in the German *Bund* between the powerful and weaker princes and of the size of the territories and number of population between the individual states, and the need for unity absolutely required that Prussia should be entrusted with complete authority, while, on the other hand, the legislative power in the federal diet was to be exercised in common with a national assembly.[2]

His ideal for the *Bundesstaat* was that it should represent the unity of the German nation as well as the unity of the princes, and that as the organ of freedom it should moderate the power of the princes so as to place the coping-stone of the German federal state on the edifice of German unity and freedom.

Of great importance in the study of the nature and law of the union of states, especially of the federal state, was Carl Welcker's contribution *Ueber Bundesverfassung und Bundesreform, über Bildung und Gränzen der Bundesgewalt* in 1834, to which he was incited by the struggle for reform of the Swiss confederation.

A little later Welcker clearly expounded his views regarding the conditions and needs of Germany in his work, written in co-operation with von Rotteck, the *Staats-Lexikon* in 1836, and a further exposition of the federal idea in Germany was his work *Wichtige Urkunden für den Rechtszustand der deutschen Nation*, 1844, published under the supervision of J. L. Klüber. For an understanding of the origin and development of the union of states, Welcker claimed that a thorough and scientific knowledge of political as well as natural science was essential.[3]

Although certain great thinkers, such as Aristotle and Montesquieu, sought to make such knowledge the basis of their systems of states, yet later thinkers failed to recognise the different nature of political unions in confining themselves merely

---

[1] P. A. Pfizer: *Ueber die Entwicklung des öffentlichen Rechts*, 1835, pp. 46–47.
[2] Ibid., pp. 100,102–103.
[3] Carl Welcker: *Bund* in *Das Staats Lexikon*, ed. by Carl von Rotteck and C. Welcker, 1843, Vol. II, pp. 709–710.

to logical development on purely philosophical principles: "every basic division in every sphere of knowledge must be derived from the fundamental principles of science, having regard to the different kinds of subjects under discussion."[1]

Starting with this assumption, he claimed that legally the most essential differences in the *Bundesvereine* were due to essential differences in the basic law or to the different purposes and conditions of the unions. Therefore he asserted that the "*Bund* itself was in its most essential characteristic a union." His argument started from an empirical method of investigation of the actual conditions of various forms of the union, and set up a juristic criterion to classify them into a system of his own.

He took into account all existing forms of the union, from a mere alliance to a federal state, and classified them into the following legal categories:

(i) "Private and public personality or constitutional law."
(ii) "Actual and pure supreme law."
(iii) "Obligatory or administrative law."[2]

The *Bundesstaat* was a union of states based on public law in which the participators were united in "a sovereign community or a common moral personality and subordinate to the collective will as members," and thus came under the first category.[3]

The *Staatenbund*, which was a union of several sovereign states maintaining their external sovereign rights in common or as "joint property," was based on international law and the law of property, and must be placed in the second category.[4]

Finally, a mere union of states or an alliance was a kind of union either based on international law or on the law of contract, which united and pledged several sovereign states by an obligatory treaty.[5]

Welcker tried to derive the theory of the federal state from the existing North American federation, which differed in certain respects from the Swiss and German unions.

The essential duty of the federal state, under such a legal relationship, was to remain firm and unwavering and maintain harmony in its administration and politics. By its very nature he was convinced, like the American federalists, that the fun-

[1] Carl Welcker: *Bund* in *Das Staats Lexikon*, ed. by Carl von Rotteck and C. Welcker, 1843, Vol. II, p. 710. [2] Ibid., p. 711.
[3] Ibid., Welcker: *Urkunden für Rechtszustand der deutschen Nation*, 1844, p. 36.
[4] Carl Welcker: *Bund* in *Das Staats Lexikon*, ed. by Carl von Rotteck and C. Welcker, 1843, Vol. II, p. 711. [5] Ibid.

damental legal character of the federal state—that is, the public law and personal or constitutional union of states—consisted in the fact that "several quasi-sovereign states and governments united into a real moral personality or *universitas*," and into a "common higher constitution of the state," and were "subordinated" to the higher federal state. He assumed that the purpose for which several different states subordinated themselves to a higher "common state" without giving up their entire independence and sovereignty could "rationally be entirely no other than identical with the aim of the state or that of the nation itself."[1]

For the carrying out of the federal law, not only for external, but for moral and national higher aims and the laws of the land, and as an ethical personal unity of the different states, the federal state was established as "an internal and external union of all members of the federation in a real and at the same time a sovereign community."[2]

This community set up "the universal and absolute legal validity of the majority vote in common affairs and a common will," as the supreme authority for the carrying out of federal government, a real obedience and duty as subjects of all the federal governments, and "not only a general but a personal limitation of their sovereignty."[3]

As the laws and obligations of the federal powers were founded on an "inexhaustible substance" (*unerschöpflicher Inbegriff*), the legal position as to the freedom and independence of the member states was debatable.

Nevertheless, Welcker asserted that the federal state unite into a nation and must be based on direct relationship with all citizens, and added "the citizens are united by the general national law of life." The federal rights and duties should be exercised directly upon the citizens of all the different states, and in so far as these had legal freedom and their free co-operation and their right to vote was dependent "on all internal association relations," they must also be recognised as being in direct relations with the federal state and its government; otherwise simultaneously with the legal freedom all real internal unity of life and strength would be lost to the *Bund*."[4]

Regarding the functions of the federal state, he was a close

---

[1] Carl Welcker: *Bund* in *Das Staats Lexikon*, ed. by Carl von Rotteck and C. Welcker, 1843, Vol. II, p. 714. Welcker: *Urkunden für Rechtszustand der deutschen Nation*, p. 37.   [2] Ibid., p. 714, Welcker, *Urkunden für Rechtszustand der deutschen Nation*, pp. 37–38.   [3] Ibid., p. 715   [4] Ibid., p. 717.

adherent of the American federalists in emphasising that the federal organisation should consist of three government authorities, co-ordinate and harmonious in their own independent spheres.

The principal object of this method of representation was that particular interests and general national unity and freedom should harmoniously co-exist and be included in the main purpose of the federal state.

In order to carry out the common affairs of the federal state, there must be three well-organised functions of federal government as "an organ for the maintenance of the unity and order of the union both for the executive power and representation of the unity especially in regard to foreign powers."[1] He, however, like the American federalists, favoured "a natural possible unity" for which no better organ could be devised than authority more or less monarchical, "the head of the union."[2]

At the same time a "naturally more democratic organ," namely, the participation or representation of the citizens in the federal assembly, was of the utmost importance for the maintenance of the "general constitutional and national freedom of the citizens, and for the development of the internal life and freedom of the whole nation, and also to represent the right of all the citizens to participate in forming the federal decision."[3]

Finally, on account of the nature of the federal state, an organ for the maintenance and representation of the independence and the particular interests of the individual states and their government was also necessary—that is to say, "a kind of upper house composed of equal representatives of every different government" —this was a senate of an aristocratic character.[4]

With regard to the judiciary, even though Welcker recognised the constitutional law of the federal states, he failed to emphasise the highest and final authority of its supreme court of justice.

He concluded from the nature of the federal state, from its common fundamental law, purpose and organisation, and its need of healthy existence, that the individual states must harmonise in the essential principles of their constitutions, and the

[1] Carl Welcker: *Urkunden für Rechtszustand der deutschen Nation*, pp. 40, 41.
[2] Ibid., p. 40. Welcker: *Bund* in *Das Staats Lexikon*, ed. by Carl von Rotteck and C. Welcker, 1843, Vol. II, p. 719.
[3] Carl Welcker: *Urkunden für Rechtszustand der deutschen Nation*, p. 41.
[4] Ibid., pp. 41–42. Welcker: *Bund* in *Das Staats Lexikon*, ed. by Carl von Rotteck and C. Welcker, 1843, Vol. II, p. 720.

permanency of these constitutions must be guaranteed by the *Bund*.

While his exposition approximated closely to the American federal state of his day, yet he did not make use of his legal theory in solving the main problem, namely, the allocation of sovereignty in the federal state. Though he recognised the possibility of the division of sovereign authority between the states and the federal government, yet he did not indicate agreement or disagreement with the theory of divided sovereignty. He laid emphasis on the federal state as an harmonious combination of freedom and initiative with unity and order, and thought that it needed the highest political culture, and was the most difficult to form of all political creations. At the same time he observed that the legal basic characteristic of the *Staatenbund* was the self-imposed limitation of sovereign rights; it was no sovereign community, but an association of independent states with equal treaty rights and obligations. A confederation could not be designated as a national union, and consequently the citizens of the union had no direct participation in the affairs of the union, but only through the governments, viz. there was no representation of the people as individuals.

His view of the distinction between the federal state and the confederation, although legally not clear, was the first comprehensive discussion of the problem in Germany.

Von Gagern, Pfizer and especially Welcker attempted to establish a federal doctrine by the same method of commentary as was used by Kent and Story in commenting upon the American constitution about the same time.

The French Revolution of 1848, by the liberal wave of feeling it sent across Europe, and the revision of the Swiss constitution stimulated new federal proposals in Germany, e.g. those for the reform of the German constitution which were made in the Frankfurt parliament in 1848.

Although the revision of the Swiss constitution brought about the transformation from a confederation to a federal state, yet the leading idea in this movement was not more significant than, or showed any advance upon, Welcker's proposals. Nevertheless, that revision was an undoubted epoch in the history of European federal ideas, as it led to the formation of a real constitution and a more complete federal state.

In 1831 a politician, Kasimir Pfyffer, had sought to promote the material interests of the Swiss confederation by its transformation into a federal state. He desired to guarantee the rights of the people vis-à-vis the government by the formation of a central organ composed of freely voting delegates of cantons, and advocated a more unitary form of the executive.[1] The revision committee appointed by the *Tagsatzung* (the Swiss federal assembly) decreed equal representation of the cantons as alone consistent with the federal principle.

At the same time, from both political and scientific considerations, Troxler asserted that in the federal state the "national" and "cantonal" elements, mutually conditioning and binding one another, were indissolubly united, and consequently in addition to the existing representatives of the governments of the cantons he desired national representatives to be elected according to population, and that these two chambers should take decisions without depending on special instructions.[2]

The principles to which these federal thinkers adhered were derived from the North American constitution.

Ludwig Snell, in his work *Handbuch des Schweizerischen Staatsrechts*, 1839, amplified the characteristic distinction between *Bundesstaat* and *Staatenbund*. He set out as the essential difference the fact that the confederation was based on "the treaty of the member states: a permanent and international principle of pact," whereas the federal state was based "on the decision of the majority of all the citizens," and thus "on the constitution which formed the member states into a nation."[3]

He pointed out that a second distinction with regard to the sphere of central authority was that the federal state not only aimed at protection from foreign foes as did the confederation, but also at establishment of law and maintenance of internal order. In the confederation the external purposes of the state were the main object of the union, by which "the need of the central power should be limited," whilst in the federal state the scope of the state extended not only to external, but also to part of the "internal state objects." With the progress of law and the advance of culture the federal state enlarged the sphere of the central authority.

Snell was entirely in favour of Welcker's conception of the federal constitution, and advocated the reform of the Swiss *Bund*. Even Stettler, a constitutionalist of Bern, agreed with

---

[1] Kasimir Pfyffer: *Zuruf an den eidgenössischen Vorort Luzern bei Uebernahme der Leitung der Bundes Angelangenheiten*, 1831.
[2] Troxler's Essay on *Worauf muss die Bundesverfassung begründet werden?* 1833.
[3] Ludwig Snell: *Handbuch des Schweizerischen Staatsrechts*, 1839, Vorwort, pp. xxi–xxii.

Snell's exposition of the federal state in his work *Das Bundesstaatsrecht der Schweizerischen Eidgenossenschaft* in 1847.

Nevertheless, the Swiss publicists were neither willing nor capable of developing or improving Welcker's federal idea.

The revision of the Swiss constitution took place almost unnoticed amidst the European unrest, whereas in the German movement the essential factors towards the recognition of the federal state were the consciousness of the lack of cohesion in the existing constitution and the strong feeling for the old empire.[1]

The prevailing view of that time, embodied in the works of such publicists as Pfizer and Carl Welcker, was that the transformation of the German confederation into a federal state was of the highest importance for the formation of the future German nation.

The diversity of opinion regarding the precise nature of the reform of the imperial constitution was due to the difference between practical politics and theoretical aspirations. The practical requirement of reform in actual politics naturally brought about a certain modification and adjustment of the theory.

In 1847 the publication of the programme of the *Deutsche Zeitung* and, soon after the February revolution, the famous Bassermann proposal [2] put forward the plan by which the German confederation would be transformed into a federal empire, but did not advance much beyond Welcker's principles.

The downfall of the Metternich cabinet in Austria and the strike in Berlin gave new activity to the federal ideal, and resulted in the declaration of the King of Prussia that "Germany will transfer from the *Staatenbund* to the *Bundesstaat*."[3]

The consultations and decisions of the *Bundestag* (composed of seventeen persons with full authority) for the revision of the federal constitution on a real and national basis were a landmark in the history of the federal idea in Germany.

The national assembly recognised the existence of the

---

[1] Prof. Rüttimann: *Das nordamerikanische Bundesstaatsrecht verglichen mit den politischen Einrichtungen der Schweiz*, Vol. I, 1867, pp. 25–50. J. Blümer: *Handbuch des Schweizerischen Bundesstaatsrechtes*, Vol. I, pp. 127–140.

[2] Klüpfel: *Die deutschen Einheitsbestrebungen in ihrem geschichtlichen Zusammenhang*, pp. 459–460. Roth und Merck: *Quellensammlung zum deutschen öffentlichen Recht seit 1848*, 1850, Vol. I, pp. 30–58.

[3] Roth und Merck: *Quellensammlung zum deutschen öffentlichen Recht seit 1848*, 1850, Vol. I, pp. 145–148. H. A. Zachariä: *Deutsches Staats- und Bundesrecht*, 3. Aufl., Bd. I, p. 202.

individual states and their dynasties on the one hand, and proposed a constitution based on national unity on the other.

The establishment of a supreme law by the imperial constitution would lead the empire to the federal state—but, in fact, to a "Prussian-German federal state."[1]

The discussion on federal practice for and against the new resolution of the Frankfurt national assembly not only had no practical result owing to the refusal of the King of Prussia to accept the position of emperor of the newly reformed federation, but also did not apparently influence the minds of the people as a whole.

The main difficulty which the Frankfurt parliament faced was not diversity of opinion on the essential problem of federalism, but the division of opinion as to the form of the state—that is, whether monarchy was to be overthrown or not. And when Prussia decided against liberalism the Frankfurt project failed.

Nevertheless, the theoretical discussion of the federal idea opened the road to the examination of the main problem as to whether or not the central authority could carry out its administration and its direct fiscal activities through its own independent organisation, and finally led to an analysis of differences as to origin, organisation and competence from the standpoint of the general difference between the conception of federal state and that of the empire.

§ 5

Until Waitz laid down the theoretical basis of federalism in Germany, Bluntschli, Dönnigen, H. A. Zachariä and Stahl and Radowitz were outstanding figures in the shaping of a new federal theory.

J. C. Bluntschli, a great Swiss jurist and an outstanding authority on constitutional law, paved the road for the development of the federal idea from Welcker's federal theory to Waitz's new conception of federalism in his work *Geschichte des schweizerischen Bundesrechtes* in 1849.

Analysing all the details of the Swiss constitution he arrived at the conclusion that no state could be formed like Switzerland without the principle of federalism, and the main characteristic of the Swiss federation was "the union of the independent and republican" states.[2]

[1] Brie: *Der Bundesstaat*, pp. 79–80.
[2] Bluntschli: *Die Geschichte des schweizerischen Bundesrechtes*, 1849, Vol. I, p. 552.

While the prevailing conception of the "federal state" in Germany was that on the one hand the central authority must be based on competence, and that on the other the participation of the individual state in the federal decision was an essential principle, Bluntschli put forward the concrete notion of a federalism which differed from the empire.

First of all he tried to differentiate an alliance from the *Staatenbund*. To him an alliance was a mere union for foreign affairs, which possessed a "passing by" purpose and a limited duration, whilst a confederation was a permanent organisation, and in so far as the duration was not restricted it was eternal. And supposing that the former would also be permanent, yet the alliance was not based upon "a common authority of the state whole in relation to foreign countries," and lacked "internal connection" in the organisation of the union and institutions.

Nevertheless, the confederation was constituted not merely "as a plurality of the state" vis-à-vis foreign powers, but also as "a common body of state" and created "its internal common organ," that is to say, it possessed statehood in international law.

His main contribution to federal ideas was the distinction between *Staatenbund* and *Bundesstaat* and *Reich*.

Firstly, he like other thinkers laid down the distinct demarcation between the *Staatenbund* and the *Bundesstaat*. He thought that the antithesis between them was based upon the "more or less" extent of the power of the central authority, and upon the "more or less" extent of the independence of the individual states in the union.

The conception of a distinction between the "more and less" powers of the central government of the federation brought about differences in grade, but not in kind, of the state form. But he assumed that this distinction could be considered "in fact as the different kinds of the state form in itself," out of which "the difference between these more and less in the origin and strength of the central power exists again within the different confederations and several federal states."[1] For example, the Swiss confederacy, since its formation up to 1848, was organised as a *Staatenbund*, but the power of the federal authority before 1798 was far less than at the time of the "mediatising constitution."

However, Bluntschli assumed that the "real distinction" between the confederation and the federal state was to be found in the different organisation of each.

He asserted that in the *Staatenbund* the individual states were

[1] Bluntschli: *Die Geschichte des schweizerischen Bundesrechtes*, 1849, Vol. I, p. 553.

united in forming a state-entity. Nevertheless, this "was not in itself organised as a central state, differing from the individual states, but the federal authority was either entrusted to the individual states or composed of the heads of the individual states." On the contrary, in the federal state the entity did not merely consist of "organised individual states," but was also a "completely organised central state."[1]

With regard to external relations there was no difference between them, and the confederation might appear externally as "an indivisible unity." The powers of the individual states, such as the right to determine war and peace and the right to conclude treaties with foreign powers, might be very much limited or even withheld. Nevertheless, in the *Bundesstaat* the relationship of the collective state and its parts to foreign countries was usually placed in the "hands of the central authority," because the "constitution" of the federal state was more favourable to the extension of power of the central authority than in the case of a confederation.[2]

Regarding the internal relationships, the distinction between them was apparent, though "the existence of the federated individual states" was common to both kinds of state form, and in both cases the individual states were not "mere parts (provinces) of the collective state," but themselves state-entities each equipped with its own legislature and its own government.

Therefore he asserted that "the organism of the union and the central authority" were quite different.[3]

In the legislature he assumed that in the federal state the legislative body was to be without any restraint within the sphere of the common interests—that is to say, could be designated as "a national or federal parliament"; while in the confederation it was an assembly of the union composed of the delegates of the individual states.

Consequently, the law of the federal state depended on the "free decisions of the legislative bodies," whilst that of the confederation was derived from common decisions and orders which were ruled by the instructions, and had the full authority, of the confederated states—that is, from treaty-based decisions.

The institution of the national head of the union was far more organised in the federal state than in the confederation.

The federal state was constituted by a unitary federal government in which "the full authority of the government was con-

[1] Bluntschli: *Die Geschichte des schweizerischen Bundesrechtes*, 1849, Vol. I, p. 554.
[2] Ibid.
[3] Ibid., p. 555.

centrated to regulate with the ministry the different expression and relationships of the state life," but the confederation on the contrary maintained an organ, subordinated to the federal assembly, only for some special activities, such as military office, inspectors' or chancellors' office, etc.

Nevertheless, Bluntschli asserted that the powers of the union could not entirely be limited by a single principle, and that in all forms of union of states there was the spirit of collectivity on the one hand and that of the single state on the other. The constitution, therefore, was a manifestation of the "comparison and conclusion of these two spirits," and the argument as to federal mechanism turned for him on their comparative importance.[1] He assumed that the federal state favoured the "national spirit," which was manifested by the existence of the *Bund*, whilst the confederation was under the dominance of particular organs in which it led "the national interests and consciousness" to the federal form, and carried on through the "channel" of the common decisions of the national assembly of the delegates of individual states.

On this assumption he tested every form of federated state by the criterion of the degree of power.

To him the lowest form of confederation was a *Bund* in which the federal organs had a mere cantonal character, and the highest form was one "in which the federal organisation possessed a federal character." It was "federal in so far as it was neither exclusively cantonal nor on the contrary purely national, i.e. it was organised without regard to the individual states, but based upon the union of the individual states into the federal body politic."[2]

In this category the federal state "opened to the national principle a definite scope on the side of the federal principle."[3]

Consequently, he assumed that the "federal confederation" was a "subordinate form of the state," because it did not give free play to the whole-state idea.

But this form of federal union was intrinsically the "most consistent and perfect manifestation of the federal idea." He emphatically asserted that "federalism is nothing other than the federal form for the federal spirit."[4]

On the contrary the federal state could be considered the formation of the states; therefore he concluded that it was not "a pure federal form," but "a mixed and transitory form

[1] Bluntschli: *Die Geschichte des schweizerischen Bundesrechtes*, 1849, Vol. I, p. 556.
[2] Ibid., p. 556.   [3] Ibid., p. 556.   [4] Ibid., p. 557.

from the union to the national state," and also not a unitary state.[1]

He laid down the conception, epoch-making in German federal history, that the *Bundesstaat* was impossible to compare with the empire. The empire was an organisation of a state which was "derived not entirely from individual states, but from the collectivity," and it was not organised by the union of the individual states, but the unity of the whole was the foundation of the empire, every branch of which was a mere formal division, as in the old German Empire or the new Austrian Empire.[2]

Bluntschli's federal conceptions gave a new direction to the federal idea in Germany, but his classification of the federal form was mainly based upon a comparison of power and of the federal organ.

How far and how much sense of power was embodied in the federal organ was the essential criterion for the demarcation between *Bundesstaat* and *Staatenbund*.

Federalism to him was the co-existence of the spirit of the whole and that of the particularity—that is, the national principle on the one hand and particularism on the other. In other words, the national sense in the form of the federal principle was the characteristic of the *Bundesstaat*, which was entirely different from the unitary state on the purely nationalistic basis.

According to him the federal state appeared as a transitory—mixed—form between *Staatenbund* and *Staatenreich*.

Though his criticism was imperfect in the legal sense as being without reference to the source of power in the *Bund*, yet it was a remarkable contribution to the federal idea that the *Bundesstaat* was the highest form of federalism, and a "mixed" and "transitory" form from the union to the unitary state, and the *Reich* was in no sense a contradiction of the federal idea.

Heinrich A. Zachariä in *Deutsches Staats- und Bundesrecht* in 1841 set out, like Blunschli, a clear statement of federalism with regard to the characteristics of those days, and he also considered the *Staatenstaat* or the federal state as the intermediate form of the state in its course of development from the confederation to the unitary state.[3]

On the whole his contribution to federalism showed no progress of any kind, but J. Stahl's exposition of the federal state was an advocacy of the establishment of a central efficient power,

[1] Bluntschli: *Die Geschichte des schweizerischen Bundesrechtes*, 1849, Vol. I, p. 557.
[2] Ibid., pp. 557–558.
[3] Heinrich A. Zachariä: *Deutsches Staats- und Bundesrecht*, 1865, Vol. I, p. 100.

whereas a number of brochures, especially those of Dönniges, were based on the principle of assigning more power to the individual states than to the central authority.

An outstanding figure was Radowitz, whose essential maxim was chiefly derived from the fundamental notion of the *Dreikönigsverfassung*. He emphasised the need of the federal state that the central power should itself be able to carry out its own laws based on the constitution, and not do this through the individual state.[1]

This postulating of the decisive distinction between central and state authorities was of the highest importance in upholding the *Bundesstaat* in the development of *Unions-Politik*. The direct control by the central power of its own administration without any intermediate organ of the individual states certainly had great influence on the new creation of federalism in Germany.

Nevertheless, practically and theoretically no material progress had been made until Waitz proposed his federalism on a Hamiltonian basis as elaborated in the great work of de Tocqueville in 1833.

[1] J. von Radowitz: *Reden und Betrachtungen*, 1852, p. 116.

CHAPTER II

DEVELOPMENT OF FEDERAL IDEAS FROM GEORG WAITZ TO MAX SEYDEL

§ 1

In 1862 a great historian, Georg Waitz, published the *Grundzüge der Politik*, which was a landmark in the development of federal ideas in Germany. His attitude towards politics was more philosophical than juristic, and he started from the assumption that the state is "an institution for carrying out the moral duty of mankind, in so far as this institution is manifested in the collective life of nations."[1]

Having denied the mechanical formation of the state, either through "human contract" or through "the authority of one or a number of individuals," he emphasised his view of the origin of the state, that it "rests on the higher moral conditions of mankind—not as a physical, but as an ethical organism," and on historical evolution.[2]

As the state was an association of permanent duration it was "a divine institution like the family and the church," and therefore the conception of the state on this moral basis was "closely connected with the conception of the nation."

As the land and the people were the main factors in the state the formation of the nation did not altogether resemble the formation of the state.[3] But the community, which as a state itself rested upon other grounds, was seldom constituted as a national state. So he assumed that "the national state is a completion of the national life, as it is the highest function of the state."

With this idealistic conception of the state he asserted that "the state as organism embraces in its code the law of its existence,

---

[1] Georg Waitz: *Grundzüge der Politik*, 1862, p. 5. Cf. his early work, *Das Wesen des Bundesstaates in der Kieler Allgemeinen Monatsschrift*, 1853, pp. 494–530, in which he advocated the same federal idea as Radowitz.
[2] Ibid., p. 5.—"If we are convinced that there has been progress in the development of humanity on the whole, we must also admit that there has been progress in the formation of the state. The historian may believe in progress that is not always periodical, but actually extending although not constantly and uniformly in the more highly civilised races, when we compare the people of the present day with those of the past."
[3] Georg Waitz: *Grundzüge der Politik*, 1862, p. 7.

derived not from outside but inherent in itself."[1] According to the inherent power of the state itself, the code of the state was "the law," which is an outcome of the national life.

From this assumption he deduced that "the state may be called the legal state in so far as it has become conscious of its code of law and has its existence within the sphere of that law," and as the state stood as an "organism" so the state was itself a "purpose."

Starting from this principle he asserted that the power of the state rested "upon the code itself," and the authority "on the sphere of the state."

For this reason the state authority was "the unity of authority or power existing in the state" and was given independently with the state.

Following from the principle that the state rested on the nation, the state authority stood on and proceeded from the nation.[2]

He assumed that the other expression of state power was sovereignty, which was independent and supreme and without which a real state could not exist.

What he called "popular sovereignty" (*Volksouveränität*) had no foundation in a correct conception of the state. He assumed that the sovereignty, which rested with the ruler, determined "in itself nothing as to the relation of the ruler to the state authority."

The ruler normally ought to unite a whole-state authority, out of which the two divisions of the code of law were to be demarcated, namely, the determination of the code—legislation—on the one hand, and the execution of the code—government and judicature—on the other.

This division of the state authority could not take place "in such a way that one power stands on one organ of the state and the other power on other organs," which would split the state within itself. If what belonged to the state authority were handed over to the members of the state, the state would be dissolved. Nevertheless, he assumed that all power could not be exercised by a single organ.

Therefore Waitz concluded that "the condition in which the code of state is determined, its sphere well defined, obedience and freedom united, is that which corresponds in its nature to an ethical organism." But he added that owing to the imperfection of human affairs "the real state can never be more than an approximation to this ideal."[3]

[1] Georg Waitz: *Grundzüge der Politik*, 1862, p. 9.   [2] Ibid., p. 18.   [3] Ibid., p. 20.

This attitude to the state authority showed that Waitz admitted the sovereignty of the people, as Madison approved "people's sovereignty," and at the same time justified the general notion of "divided sovereignty."

With these general political ideas he criticised and analysed the union of states as a form of the state.

He classified states into two kinds: firstly according to power, and secondly according to organisation—whether it was a single or collective form.

As to the nature of power he, like other thinkers, considered it to be divided into republican, theocratic and monarchical, and as regards organisation he determined four forms—the unitary state, the collective state, the federal state and the confederation.

For him the unitary state existed "so long as the state authority has one central point within the state, whether it is limited by the formation of special authorities or has incorporated in itself other state bodies which yet remain independent."[1]

Therefore, the feudal state comes within the conception of the unitary state.

Secondly, in classifying the various state formations he distinguished collective states from others.

The two main forms of state in this category were:

(1) The real union, in which the state was united, such as a consolidation.

(2) "The personal union, in which various state bodies really only have a ruler in common, but where there frequently exists also a community of certain state relationships" such as belong to the collective state. In regard to this category he thought that when the feudal state ceased to be a unitary state, as we had seen in the German Empire in its later development, it could be spoken of only as a collective state.[2]

Thirdly, he said that the federal state was "that kind of state formation in which a part of state duty and state life is common and another belongs to the individual parts and independent states," and depended upon a twofold organisation of the people in the state, "partly in collective and partly in independent parts."[3]

Finally, in the case of the confederation, he held that the essential thing was that the states were joined together as such and united for common direction of certain definite affairs.

[1] Georg Waitz: *Grundzüge der Politik*, 1862, p. 42.
[2] Ibid., p. 43.
[3] Ibid., pp. 43–45.

As the confederation was not a mere league or alliance, so there must be essential duties of state life for which the union was made, and consequently it must be of a permanent character.[1]

The federal discussion, however, was mainly confined to the categories of *Bundesstaat* and *Staatenbund*.

Waitz held that it was quite unnecessary to deal with the need for the establishment in his time of a federal authority for the future of Germany, for this had already clearly been manifested by various previous thinkers.

Justifying the formation of a strong national authority as a German political expedient of his day, he concentrated his argument on the attempt to set up a new and clear conception of the federal state.

Criticising the case for the federal state set out by Dönniges, who formulated this general demand better than any other exponent, Waitz founded his federal conceptions on the federalism of Tocqueville, whose comprehensive exposition of the North American constitution had taught him most. Though Welcker had cleared away the clouds of the prevailing conception of the federal state, still he had failed to set out clearly the nature of the *Bundesstaat*.

Even when a great jurisprudent like Bluntschli had expounded the nature of the federal state, he had, nevertheless, just like Zachariä and Pözl, left many parts untouched.

First of all, Waitz set out a clear statement of the idea of the federal state, differing from the comprehensive notion of the nature of the confederation.[2]

The confederation was, according to his definition, "A union of different states for the common fulfilment of the task of the state life." Being different from a mere union of the states, the *Staatenbund* presupposed "a real association of the political interests and the state activity."

What he called a union was itself an individual state acting as an independent political body and forming by its union a new state body politic which appeared as an independent whole. But the union should be based on treaty or agreement and its character must be dependent upon international law.

The scope of common affairs in the confederation was so varied that they could be narrowly limited or widely extended according to circumstances, but every state in the confederation should have a share in the determination of common affairs.

Waitz's fundamental assertion was that an essential condition

[1] Georg Waitz: *Grundzüge der Politik*, 1862, pp. 45–46. [2] Ibid., pp. 153–155.

of confederation was the need for the unanimity of all the member states in the common decisions of the confederation and that it depended "on their will"—that is, the individual states through treaty of an international character formed a political body of the several member states for common affairs, and each state maintained the inalienable right of independent sovereignty. But the application of the majority principle, except in regard to alteration of the federal pact, was not altogether incompatible with the nature of the confederation.

But at the same time the history of confederation showed that the individual states, such as the Swiss cantons and the German states, were not made into unions merely by the treaties of 1815, but these treaties were actually only a more exact formula for "the older and inalienable law of interdependence" (*Zusammengehörigkeit*).[1]

If the resistance of individual states would hamper the whole activity of the union, then the main principle of the real community of essential state interests in the confederation could not be permanently maintained, in so far as the majority principle failed to carry out the object of all states and to prevent the dissolution of the union.[2]

Nevertheless, the form of the common direction, or government, was not "of effective significance."[3]

The central organ of the confederation was to be representative "of the states but not of the nation"—that is, it was to be an assembly of the delegates of the individual states for the common purposes.

From the inefficient functioning of historical confederations Waitz concluded that the confederation "is a malformed and insufficient organisation of state life," and served only "as a transitory stage to other formations of the state."[4]

This later assertion was amply justified by the historical evidence which we have seen in the development of federal practice as well as theory.

Waitz recognised the confederation as a rising state body of an independent whole, considering it as a little more than "moral personality," as an international personality. But his notion of confederation did not extend to regarding it as that corporation of which the later thinkers dreamed.

Though he regarded the confederation as a form of the state, in that it was based on the essential state interests of a permanent

[1] Georg Waitz: *Grundzüge der Politik*, 1862, p. 157.
[2] Ibid.   [3] Ibid.   [4] Ibid., p. 159.

body politic, he totally rejected the idea that in the *Staatenbund* there could be any superior authority or any subordination of power between the member states themselves and the confederated power, and he emphatically objected to the existence of sovereignty over sovereignty, and accepted the sovereignty of the individual state as the sovereign supremacy.[1]

From this conception of the *Staatenbund* he deduced that the *Bundesstaat* differed from the confederation and also from the old German Empire.

Criticising Stahl's notion of the German Empire as a federal state, and also the Prussian scheme of the "Vienna Congress" in which the princes joined with the emperor in common rule for common affairs, he held that these notions were entirely contradictory to the nature of the federal state, partly because of the "subordination of the member states under the higher imperial authority, and partly because of the complete independence of the state life that was a *Staatenreich*—where, as little in Empire as in the confederation, the nation possessed a direct control over the united state authority.

Waitz defined the federal state as being a state, "as its name indicates."[2]

He asserted that as the state, from the scientific standpoint, appeared not as an accidental union of individuals, which was brought about through agreement or through power, but as the organisation of the people to carry out the higher tasks of life, so the federal state was the same form of the state "where a part of all the common tasks of the state life is to be fulfilled in common by the whole nation and the other part to be carried out separately by the individual races and divisions of the people."[3]

Following Tocqueville's conception,[4] the individual state and the federal state were "necessary complements of one another." It was essential that the people "should be in an equal relation to the individual state and federal state" for the determined parts of the state activity, each of which was based on "the national foundation."

Waitz drew attention to the fact that there was no distinction of rights between the confederation and the federal state as to

---

[1] Georg Waitz: *Grundzüge der Politik*, 1862, p. 161.
[2] Ibid., p. 162. [3] Ibid., p. 163.
[4] A. de Tocqueville: *Da la Démocratie en Amérique*, 1840.—"Une forme de société dans laquelle plusieurs peuples se fondent réellement en un seul quant à certains intérêts communs, et restent séparés et seulement confédérés pour tous les autres."

the amount of power entrusted to the federal authority in respect of foreign affairs. Nevertheless, he emphasised that in the federal state determined parts of the state life were entirely left to the federal government on the one hand and to the individual member states on the other.

Therefore, he asserted that "every division is really a state in itself."[1] In the confederation there was no "collectivity"; in the state empire there were no "members"; but the federal state must embody "both"—there the collective state and the individual states co-existed.

From his doctrine as to the state power he deduced that the essential thing for every state was that the state was "independent, excluding every authority foreign to itself."

As the municipalities of the empire were not states, because they had not supreme power over themselves, so the confederation was never considered as a state, because, however wide and strong the competence of the federal authority, the confederated power was always dependent upon the delegation or power of attorney of the individual states, and there was no independent law for itself.

But in the federal state the collective state and the individual state had each a smaller sphere than the unitary state, "but within that sphere the right of the two former is no less than that of the latter."[2]

Therefore, rejecting Stahl's view of a federal state, in which sovereignty did not rest with the individual state, but with the central authority, he asserted that the federal state must be based on the conception that sovereignty rested "not with one or the other but with both the collective state (central power) and individual state (state power)," each of which was independent in its own sphere.

Justifying the notion of de Tocqueville, who declared regarding the United State that "it is true that the union of 1789 has only a limited sovereignty; but as within its sphere it has formed only one and the same people, within its sphere it is sovereign," Waitz asserted that the "federal state is founded on the real obedience or allegiance of all governments of the federation, and also on an actual—not only real but personal—limitation of their sovereignty," that is, "the restriction of the sphere, but not of the content, of the sovereignty and the division of state power in which one is just as good as the other."[3]

This idea of divided sovereignty clearly distinguished the

[1] Georg Waitz: *Grundzüge der Politik*, 1862, p. 164.   [2] Ibid., p. 166.   [3] Ibid.

federal state from other unions and "not the ambit of the collectivity, but the kind of authority exercised by it determined the distinction."

Self-governing independence in each sphere of activity of state life appeared as a unitary state in organisation and in function. In this real federal state the internal impulse led the people to this form of state. Accordingly, Waitz recognised that "the theory of politics, from whatever general principles it seems to have arisen, is nevertheless only the proof of the law which is the foundation of the living products of national life."[1]

Then Waitz considered the nature of federal power under which the people as a whole stood in respect of the common share of state life in direct relation with the federal state. The *Bundesgewalt* within its sphere "must be based on the same general conditions and tasks of state life for the nation as a whole," as the unitary state was for the whole ambit of state activity.

Naturally, he examined the problem of the mode of exercise of federal power. Criticising the old German constitution he asserted that "the state which merely has to make laws and issue general regulations, but must place their exercise in the hands of others, loses itself in abstract ideas without value and significance or wastes the power which it has in the attempt to maintain its authority."[2] And at the same time, when the individual state was ruled or administered by the law which was handed over to the other, it was "deprived" of its detailed administration, and therefore of a state characteristic.

Therefore, he emphasised that the direct power of enforcement of law both by the central authority and by the individual states within their respective spheres was of the utmost importance in the federal state.

There was no centralisation in the customary sense, which was established in quite a different manner.

With regard to the centralisation there existed the *centralisation administrative* against the *centralisation gouvernementale*; the former was the French centralisation and the latter was the American centralisation, that was federal centralisation.

This notion of federal centralisation was the main political issue in regard to the federal state, on which all federal thinkers and jurists have chiefly concentrated in their efforts to formulate their respective principles.

Especially the legalist federal doctrines in Germany endeavoured to establish a clear conception of this problem.

[1] Georg Waitz: *Grundzüge der Politik*, 1862, p. 168.   [2] Ibid., p. 169.

In the history of the German federal ideas Waitz made a great advance on Welcker's view of the federal state, in which, though Welcker considered it as a union in direct relation with the people, yet he did not go on to advocate the direct administration of the federal state and based his principle on a fundamental misconception of the *Dreikönigsverfassung* in the Frankfurt constitution.

Radowitz was the first in Germany to lay down the real conception of the federal state—that "central power" constitutionally should be independent and act by itself, and not through the individual state—yet he failed to demand the thoroughgoing power of administration, such as legislation and supervision.[1]

Waitz, following Tocqueville's federal idea, for the first time in Germany set up the view that the federal government should not only dictate the law, but also enforce its own enactments, and that the subjects of the union were not the states, but the private citizens.

The main issue which Waitz expounded was the "self-independence" of the federal state power.

This "self-independence" manifested itself in the "organ," which in the federal state as in any other state must be threefold—executive government, legislative assembly of the people and judicature. And he asserted that "it is not different powers of the state which they represent, but the state as an organisation to exercise its independent power through its separate organs which have maintained their own independence of one another, whilst the state life can be carried on only through their common activities."[2]

He inquired further on what basis the federal state should be independent of the individual states.

After considering the organs of the federal government in the Greek federations and in the Italian and Germanic unions in the Middle Ages he held that the government of the federal state must be based on the new conception of the North American federal state.

But he also drew the conclusion that neither the "directory" federal government elected by the common assembly, on the Swiss principle, nor even a monarchical federal state, was altogether incompatible with the true nature of the federal state.[3] The main principle in the federal state was a "direct connection of the nation with the federal (collective) state and its organi-

[1] Georg Waitz: *Grundzüge der Politik*, 1862, p. 171.
[2] Ibid., p. 173.   [3] Ibid., p. 175.

sations"—this he called "the national element of the federal state." The direct participation of the people in every organ of the federal state was in accordance with the general political principle.

Consequently, he thought that it was not "inconceivable" that the absolute monarchical state system could exist in the federal state, because "neither in the individual states nor in the collective state would the nation actively share, so that both governments could exist separately."

But he assumed that no permanency could be imagined for such a constitution, and also conflict would be unavoidable in such a dual system of authoritarian rulers.

Nevertheless he vindicated the federal dual representation, saying that "not for the sake of twofold rule, but in order to make more completely possible the full display of its life and activity, will a nation give up the single system of the unitary state for the divided one of the federal state."[1]

To him the federal state always considered as of the first importance "a more active consciousness of the nation and its duties and a more active participation in its general affairs," and this could be accomplished only when the people took a real share in the life of the state.

In this argument, unlike Tocqueville, he waived the consideration of whether or not the federal state would only be possible on a republican basis.

Far more than the unitary state did the federal state require the establishment of a national assembly to work in full cooperation with the legislature and by the establishment of state management of finance to exercise due influence on the rest of the conduct of the state.

This representation should not and could not be that of "the individual states or representative bodies of the individual states," but "the nation, which had direct relationship to the collective state as to the individual state, should be represented here in the existing organisations."[2]

In his objection to the representation of the individual states in an electoral assembly because of the mixture of different objects, which was politically wrong, he asserted that the nature of the federal state did not permit of the inclusion of the individul state as "a member" or a "subdivision of the state body."[3]

As in the state assembly each individual member should not always regard the particular interests of special districts, but must

[1] Georg Waitz: *Grundzüge der Politik*, 1862, p. 176. [2] Ibid., p. 177. [3] Ibid.

act for the whole, so the representative in the greater assembly of the collective state should never deal with the concerns of the state to which he belonged, but with the common affairs of the federal state as a whole.

Accordingly, eligibility should be uniform throughout the whole federal state, whereas the election itself must take place in districts within the limit of the individual states.

In this respect he thought that the Swiss constitution and the proposed German constitution were more logical than the North American union, whose system was a "general" election, but with the state determination of the electoral franchise.

Nevertheless, he did not lay down any definite principle as to the electoral law, since it seemed to him that the different circumstances and changes in respect of the individual states made the formulation of any general rule impracticable. Representation in the federal state must be based on the nation as a whole, yet the actual procedure to attain that representation must naturally depend on political expediency, according to the nature of the relations of the whole state with the individual states.[1]

In general, the constitution of the federal state provided for a House of Representatives of the people on the one hand and a House of the States, called "Council" or "Senate," on the other.[2]

This system of two chambers was not only advantageous in itself, but also enabled the individual states to represent their interests—a matter of "the utmost importance in the organisation of the federal state."

From the complete division of the two spheres of state activities between the individual states and the collective state, no participation in the matters arising from the particular needs of the individual states should be included in the general functions of the collective state.

However debatable this system might be, the federal nature of the divided competence brought about a compromise by establishing a federal council to share in the federal decisions of the legislature as well as in its executive functions.

This need of "compromise" resulted in the formation of a *Staatenhaus*—the American senate.

Waitz—like others of his contemporaries—assumed that although the establishment of the senate in the American union was originally due to political expediency, yet effective care was also

[1] Georg Waitz: *Grundzüge der Politik*, 1862, p. 179. [2] Ibid.

taken in the formation of a House of Representatives, the necessity for which the political wisdom of American legislators fully recognised.

On this basis of expediency the Swiss federal constitution followed more or less the same principles as the American, but the inequality and differing sizes and the monarchical systems of the German states necessitated modifications of those principles. Besides its legislative function the United States senate possessed executive functions, in respect of the sanctioning of treaties and the appointment of federal officials and judges. It depended "on many relationships to the republican state system as a whole, together with the individual states," giving the latter a motive for participation in the legislative body and for sending delegates to the *Staatenhaus*, even though they could not appear as the representatives of the state government.

Whether or not the same method could be applied in a monarchical federal state such as Germany was a matter for consideration.

He doubted if one could avoid considering "as unnatural" this dual functioning in respect of what was essentially the same need, and thought that the only effect of that duality would be to make any free action on the part of the state far more difficult.[1]

Nevertheless, he assumed that it was not altogether "objectionable" if the common affairs did not develop to the competence of the general assembly, that they should be submitted to a council with representation of the individual states and particularly of their governments.

Such an arrangement could not interfere with the independence of the federal government and its competence to act within its sphere with full strength and responsibility.

He asserted that the institution of the federal council (*Bundesrath*) should be of such a kind that its activity should not only be restricted to certain definite purposes, and the preparation of a scheme of laws, but should also "not be decisive, but only a sort of advisory voice."[2]

The main task of the federal council was not only to restrain the federal authority to its sphere, but also to secure harmonious co-operation between the national unity and the multiplicity and variety of interests on which the individual states were based—that is, the compound purpose of unity and diversity of interests in the federal state.

He asserted that from its purposes and function the federal

[1] Georg Waitz: *Grundzüge der Politik*, 1862, p. 181. [2] Ibid., p. 182.

council was less an "organ than the censor of the collective state"—that is, less a representative organisation than a check.

And he concluded that it was "conceivable" in a republican state system "and perhaps difficult to avoid if a monarchical federal state is to be created," but "it is not necessary."[1]

His criticism of the federal council as an advisory body and censor in the collective state was a more or less adequate statement of its nature considered in the abstract; but the actual functioning of the federal council had often resulted in the overriding of the notion of the general function of the whole state in order to favour and protect state rights. His conclusion that the federal council "is not necessary" in the federal state is a significant remark, not only in the history of the German monarchical federal state, but also in that of the American and Swiss republican federal states.

This question was not only an historical problem but a present one. The question whether the federal state could or could not be carried on adequately without the federal council was not fully examined by Waitz, but the sufficiency of one chamber for the functioning of the federal state was a remarkable suggestion at that time (1862), especially as there was no foreshadowing of a single chamber in American federal discussions.

Probably Waitz was the only man in the history of German federalism who propounded this idea.

If we analyse his notion of state power, which was divisible, and the direct share and participation of the nation in every function of the state, whatever the diversity of the state powers might be, we find that the representation in a national assembly of a certain population and of certain areas might also result in the representation of the particular interests of certain districts.[2]

The judicial power of the collective state should be quite independent from the judicial courts of the individual states. The problem as to whether the power of the federal court should be derived from the power of the federal state itself, or should be shared by the individual states, was dealt with by him on the example of the North American federal judiciary, where the President, with the sanction of the senate, appointed all judicial officials.

The power of the federal court, therefore, was entirely based on the federal powers which were granted by the constitution and was quite independent of the state courts of the individual states. He quoted Tocqueville's phrase that "the union is in so singular

[1] Georg Waitz: *Grundzüge der Politik*, 1862, p. 182. [2] Cf. Vol. II, pp. 1108–1110.

a position that in relation to some matters it constitutes a people, and that in relation to all the rest it is a nonentity, but the inference to be drawn is that in the law relating to these matters the Union possesses all the rights of absolute sovereignty."[1]

Accordingly, when the law or any action of the states came in conflict with the law and actions of the federal state, justice could be obtained by reference to the federal courts which could declare the judgment of the state court to be valid or set aside the law as "null or void."

As the federal court possessed the power of decision in regard to its own competence, so the supreme court acted as the highest power of the federal authority and upheld its competence "over and against the individual states."

The division of powers could be determined only by the federal constitution, and was a matter which was entirely outside the province of the federal court, but conflicts between the states themselves or between the states and the people could be settled by the decisions of the federal courts.

In this service the federal court "should appear as an outside and independent Court of Appeal," even when it was appointed solely by the collective state.[2]

Though Waitz recognised the right and power of the federal court between and above the powers both of the individual and the federal states, and in consequence the "universal" independence of the court, yet in view of the co-ordination of the sovereignty and independence of the individual states with those of the collective state, the competence of the federal court must never extend beyond its own sphere of power and encroach on the power of the individual state, just as the latter should nowhere have the right to interfere with the activity of the former.

"The general domination" over the other state authorities, as in the case of the old German Empire, could, therefore, not be thought of as the test of the federal state.

Waitz then discussed the distribution of power which was theoretically due to "the twofold division of the state tasks" between the individual states and the collective state.

"The avowal of duties common to both state authorities cannot in theory be regarded as essential for the conception of the federal state"; but "it must be admitted that in practice the matter is of the greatest importance and cannot be overlooked in a scientific investigation."

[1] Tocqueville: *Democracy in America*, Vol. I, p. 143.
[2] Georg Waitz: *Grundzüge der Politik*, 1862, p. 184.

This distribution of the state functions was the question of how much of "what was of importance for state activity" belonged to the collective state or to the individual state.[1]

To him, as to other contemporaries, providing that this division gave an important and self-independent sphere of state activity to the collective and individual states respectively, it appeared to be conceived as "nothing more than the collectivity of foreign relations committed to the former and as much as possible all internal relations to the latter."[2]

In this argument the federal state appeared and acted as "a self-independent whole determined by itself," differing from the confederation which had foreign relationships based on active and passive *Gesandtschaftsrecht*, i.e. the right to send and receive envoys.[3]

On this general assumption he divided the affairs of the state into sets of activities. Foreign affairs, commercial affairs, transport, railways, shipping and canals and communications (postal service) and also universal rights, such as patents and copyright, must be essentially matters for the federal state, and all other internal affairs should remain within the competence of the individual states, including "what the state carries out because of the higher duty to promote the life of mankind in its sphere—church, sciences" and so forth. However, exceptions might be considered; as, for instance, the Swiss federal power undertook the direction of higher education, and the German exponents of the Frankfurt constitution, like Stahl, proposed that the Imperial federal power must be based on "the universal rule for many relations of political and national life."[4]

Waitz pointed out that it is necessary to the independence of the central authority in a federal state that it should have all the machinery requisite for the discharge of its tasks, and in this connection he discussed the position of its officials. The individual states should not be entrusted with the control of collective business and their officials should not as such be employed in it, for such a dual position can easily give rise to difficulties, as it might involve a dual allegiance.

Waitz recognised that the result of this principle might be an excessive number of officials and a difficulty in securing properly qualified service, but he did not regard these considerations as decisive, and the difficulty could be met by keeping the competence of the collective state within narrow limits. It should not

[1] Georg Waitz: *Grundzüge der Politik*, 1862, p. 186.
[2] Ibid., p. 186.   [3] Ibid., p. 187.   [4] Ibid., pp. 190–191.

extend to the offices of the ordinary administration nor to the judicial offices, and in respect of the technical services, such as the administration of the customs, excise, railways and posts there seemed to Waitz no need for any special precautions.

The officials concerned could, in their private lives, be on the same footing as the subjects of the individual states, and in political matters their special position should have no disadvantages.

Then he particularly dealt with the position of the military power for security within and without, and with general considerations as to the federal organisation.

He held that the collective state must have absolute control over military affairs, not only over the higher command, but also in general administration, even though the subordinate officers and the local military divisions would be under the control of the individual states.[1]

The naval power must undoubtedly be within the sphere of the collective state, for the protection of the nation and its commerce as a whole.

Finally, he emphasised the fact that the central power must have the financial means without which no government of to-day could carry out its duties, and must not be dependent on "the contributions of the individual states." The institution of the "contribution" conflicted with the nature of the federal state.

The federal state was not a union for a common purpose of the states, which had to unite for "the proportional contributions" to the cost arising therefrom, but was "to the nation, for a definite sphere of its activity, the institution in which the nation fulfils this part of its general duties, and the same considerations which make it necessary for the individual states to provide for their growing needs out of the means of the nation and from the whole of its capital must be taken into account."[2]

He concluded that, as the power of the federal state rested upon a direct relation to state affairs, so the federal state was to be considered as the complete organisation of the nation within a particular sphere of political action, determined by national unity and collectivity.

This collectivity or national unity must "not be a mere ideal," but should actually be the expression of state life.

The equal participation of every citizen in the common and particular interests covered by the dual state action, the direct relationship to the law and its observance by the citizens of the whole and of the individual states, were the main features

[1] Georg Waitz: *Grundzüge der Politik*, 1862, p. 194. [2] Ibid., p. 195.

of the federal state. The diversity of the rights and duties of citizens, and the different distribution of powers, could not be explained by law but only by reference to the actual facts.

From these assumptions he drew the conclusion that the monarchical federal state could be equally as effective as the republican one, if the hereditary authority in the individual states corresponded to hereditary monarchy in the collective state,[1] even though the lack of uniformity in the constitutions of the individual states, and their differences in size, presented great difficulty.

His criticism of federalism was entirely based on the American federalists, whereas from his historical survey of the German federal state his clear and definite solution of several federal problems was due to the modification of the German federal demand, for "the political life of Germany from its birth postulates monarchy and the freedom of the people, the unity of the nation and the plurality of its members."

Waitz's contribution to the federal state discussion had an outstanding influence on German federal ideas and opened the door to a discussion of the *Bundesstaat*, free from the traditional bias of the old German Empire.

§ 2

The federal theory of Waitz had become the fundamental maxim of German and Swiss federal ideas and remained so until a new doctrine of *Herrschaft* took the place of that of "divided sovereignty."

Ever since the Peace of Westphalia the German theory of federalism was evolving from the loose confederation to the federal state.

The idea of the federal state, both in practice and in theory, reached a stage of systematic discussion in political science after Waitz had put before the German thinkers his new conception, based on the system of the American federal state, in 1862.

The discussion of federalism between Waitz's school and the new school, which based federal principles on the *Herrschaft* theory, brought about in practice the formation of the North German union in 1866 and the establishment of the German federal empire in 1871, and in theory developed from the ideas of Robert von Mohl to those of Georg Meyer and to the theory

[1] Georg Waitz: *Grundzüge der Politik*, 1862, p. 215.

of Max von Seydel, and finally reached the epoch-making contribution of Paul Laband in 1876.

Nevertheless, the actual history of German federal ideas up till Hugo Preuss framed the present federal constitution in 1919 travelled, save in the exceptional case of Otto Gierke, on the road of the positive juristic interpretation of the federal organisation rather than that of the fundamental critical interpretation of federal theory.

A great jurist, Siegfried Brie, demonstrated that the new German system of unity in the theoretical discussion of the federal state had brought to light a new process of transformation that "has not yet led to a definite result, but may rather be considered a kind of fermentation or, taking various symptoms into account, may even be regarded as a process of decomposition."[1]

The followers of Waitz's doctrine, such as Hermann Schulze, C. F. von Gerber, H. Ahrens, R. von Mohl and H. von Treitschke, favoured in general the principle of the divided state authority, and the co-ordination of the individual and collective states in the federal state.

Adopting and repeating Waitz's theory of federalism, Hermann Schulze, in his *System des Deutschen Staatsrechts*, in 1865 developed the doctrine that in the federal state the individual states were not subordinated to the central authority, but that the sovereignty belonged to the collective state and to the individual states, equally and proportionally to each within its own sphere.[2]

Historically he agreed with the conception of the old German Empire as a federal state, but suggested that such a *Staatenstaat* or *Staatsreich* should not be formed by the combination of the feudal states, but was a general form of the union of the state.

He adhered strongly to Waitz's theory in all essential points, so that the newly founded constitution of the North German union could not induce him to make any modification of the ideas which he had previously expressed.

C. F. von Gerber, a great positivist jurist, on the other hand expressed the opinion that "the state authority in the German states is sovereign," but unfortunately did not say much about federalism in his work *Grundzüge eines Systems des deutschen Staatsrechts*, 1865. He drew between the confederation and the federal state the distinction that the former was a mere union of international relationships with a treaty-based organ; as he

---
[1] S. Brie: *Der Bundesstaat*, p. 155.
[2] H. Schulze: *System des Deutschen Staatsrechts*, Erster Band; *Einleitung in das deutsche Staatsrecht*, 1865, pp. 205–208.

said, "it emerges not as an act of a directly working government power, but only as the consequence of a treaty obligation of governments acting in the union"—and the latter was a union which possessed a state authority with the direct participation of the people within a definite sphere within which it maintained full activity.[1]

In the second edition, 1869, including a discussion of the *Norddeutsche Bund*, he referred to the theory of Waitz and pointed out, as the outstanding characteristic of the federal state, that it embodied the active state power based on the federal authority on the one hand and a " politically united people" on the other, and the limitation of the state authority to positively determined parts of the state life.[2]

On this general assumption the central power was to be sovereign but with a "fragmentary" state authority, whereas the supreme right remained to the particular state in an equally independent and "completely separate" sphere of activity. He differed from Waitz in a "few decisive motives" which he believed impossible to accept, especially the "entirely abstract principle" for the organisation of federal power.[3]

Differing from the positivist formal interpretation of the federal organization, given by Gerber and others, H. Ahrens criticised federalism from the point of view of legal philosophy—especially from the notion of *Naturrecht* and the fundamental principle of the relation of the state and association; he accepted Waitz's principle of the division of state authority.

He argued that "state" and "association" were "not identical and comprehensive conceptions," but were "partly within one another and partly outside one another," and must be comprehended "in a relative independence for the rightful appreciation and regulation of life."[4]

He pointed out as to the association theory that "all theories which do not explain the essential difference between states and associations, between that which can be carried out by the state authority, and in case of need by force, and that which must be put in the hands of private activity either for the sake of the preservation of true moral freedom or for all associated prosperity, will always be in a kind of wavering position which may easily

---

[1] F. von Gerber: *Grundzüge eines Systems des Deutschen Staatsrechts*, 1865, p. 24.
[2] Ibid., Zweite Auflage, 1869, Beilage IV, pp. 239–240, 244, "Der Norddeutsche Bund."   [3] Ibid., pp. 238–240, 244.
[4] H. Ahrens: *Naturrecht oder Philosophie des Rechts und des Staates*, 1870–1871, Vol. II, pp. 338–346.

turn in the wrong direction, and only sharply defined conceptions can determine the right boundaries."

He considered that the confederation was a union based on the relationship of the state authorities, whilst the federal state was "a national union" in which the people participated directly in the administration of the state power. Consequently, he acknowledged that sovereignty in the federal state must involve the equality of the federal and individual states within their own respective spheres of activity.[1]

His emphatic assertion of the mutual independence of the individual states from that of the collective state was not only derived from Waitz's federal doctrine of the division of duties of state life in the federal state, but also brought it into harmony with his fundamental theory of "the gradual development" (*Stufenfolge*) of the complete personalities, which comprised life in all its essential aspects, and particularly of the federal origin and organisation of the state.[2]

As he was not only a *Naturrecht* theorist, but also a legalist, his attitude towards federation was different from that of other jurists, and sought to explain the political organism not merely by positive legalism, but also by political reason, either rational or empirical, or from a subjective or objective basis of criticism.

Ahren's view of federalism, like Kantian *a priorism*, looked upon it as a political phenomenon which was equally compatible with a general association of human beings.

A great jurist, Robert von Mohl, made a wide investigation of federalism. This first comprehensive study of the federal idea is his early work, *Das Bundes-Staatsrecht der Vereinigten Staaten von Nord-Amerika*, in 1824.

Later his exhaustive study of the idea of the federal state in his work *Die Geschichte und Literatur der Staatswissenschaften*, in 1855, and the first edition of his *Encyklopädie der Staatswissenschaften*, in 1859, presented a twofold explanation influenced partly by the theory of a central authority to which the individual state should be "legally subordinated," and partly by a new theory of the division of the state power between the collective and the individual states.[3]

Nevertheless, in his second edition of the *Encyklopädie der*

---

[1] H. Ahrens: *Naturrecht oder Philosophie des Rechts und des Staates*, 1870–1871, Vol. II, pp. 342–343.
[2] Ibid., pp. 339–340.
[3] R. von Mohl: *Encyklopädie der Staatswissenschaften*, 1859, pp. 36–38, 110, 696–697.

Staatswissenschaften, in 1872, he advocated precisely Waitz's theory of the federal state.

The power of the federal state was based upon "the constitutional foundation," and was the expression of a moral personality, and did not rest on the collectivity of the member states. Its decision was based on independent legal right and was not a treaty agreement, but had "direct" and binding power over the individual.[1]

The competence of the state authority was actually and necessarily a limited activity, but not a common task of the legal states, because an essential part of the purpose of the state still remained "to the individual member states with self-independent law."[2]

The state authority in the federal state was co-ordinately divided into two spheres of constitutional function; each possessed their special organs and independent activity within their own sphere as "the active state authority"; the central power extended its right over the whole territory of the union, but the power of the member states was limited within their own respective territories. Therefore he asserted that the state authority for the member states rested "not on a limited, but on a divided sovereignty."[3]

Therefore, the content of the power of the federal state and its organisations depended on the legal constitution.

At the same time he recognised that the power of the central authority might consist partly of the right to take exclusive and direct action, and partly of the "right of supervision over certain activities." [4]

The demarcation between federal power and that of the individual states was not to be determined *a priori*, but by "the view of the purposes."

He, like other thinkers, held that the law of the federal power was directly binding on everyone belonging to the collectivity, and could enlarge the boundaries of its competence, according to essential necessity, without any co-operation by the legislation of the individual states. Nevertheless, the participation of the individual states in the federal government by means of the federal council seemed to him a matter of wisdom and justice, in securing harmony between the territorial principle and the principle of consolidation.[5]

His early works were a thorough advocacy of Waitz's theory,

---

[1] R. von Mohl: *Encyklopädie der Staatswissenschaften*, 1859, Zweite Ausgabe, 1872, p. 367.   [2] Ibid.
[3] Ibid.   [4] Ibid., p. 368.   [5] Ibid., pp. 373, note 2, 8.

on which he based his conception of the new German *Reichsrecht* in 1873.

At the same time H. von Treitschke, in his political and historical essays,[1] contended that the plan of uniting the German monarchies into a federal state would be possible, but likely to cause a great conflict.

The conflict of wills between the state and central authorities as to the determination and execution of the laws needed for its settlement a scientific doctrine as to the application of Waitz's solution—namely, the dual state authority in federalism. From his historical study of Germany and Italy he acknowledged that the practical impossibility of Waitz's application to Germany was due not to the invalidity of his theory, but to the plan for the restoration of the German federal state.

He thought that the more the many state activities and national unity were maintained, the wider would be the scope of the central power, and it must approach to the unitary state; but he regarded this development in Germany as the right one.

Professor Rüttimann, who made an extensive study of federalism in North America and Switzerland, adhered to the principle of Tocqueville that the central and state powers were independent of one another "to a certain degree," and that the Swiss federal union was less completely united than the North American federation.[2] But his later work, *Das nordamerikanische Bundesstaatsrecht*, published in 1867, more precisely expounded the principle of the federal state, not only advocating Tocqueville's view, but also Waitz's division of federal power.

He said that "the task of the state and the power necessary for the carrying out of that task are themselves divided between the collective state and the single states; each part moves with equal freedom in its own sphere as if the other part did not even exist"; and he added that the peculiarity of the federal state was that "the individual states are not subordinate to one another, but co-ordinate with the collective state, so that sovereignty may be attributed to individual states with as much right as to the collective state."

Yet this was not to be taken in an absolute sense, "for a certain supremacy of the whole over the parts is inevitable, without, however, the existence of a formal relationship as subjects."[3]

---

[1] H. von Treitschke: "Bundesstaat und Einheitsstaat," in *Historische und Politische Aufsatze*, 1865, pp. 445–595.

[2] Rüttimann: *Programm der eidgenossischen Polytechnischen Schule für das Schuljahr*, 1862.   [3] Ibid., *Das nordamerikanische Bundesstaatsrecht*, 1867, Sec. 54, p. 49.

Disciples of Waitz had exercised an outstanding influence on German federalism and caused it to be permeated by a new conception of the division of sovereignty and state activity between the authorities of the collective and individual states within their own boundaries, and of the direct relation of the federal power to the individual citizens of the states.

The key of their principle was the independence of the sovereign activity of two co-ordinate state bodies in the federal state. Against this theory there had still existed the conventional principles of the supremacy of the federal authority over the authorities of the individual states.

These schools of federal thought in Germany and Switzerland represented a contest between the constitutional jurists, who favoured the old federal conception, and those who adhered to a reasoned view of the division of the state power, and resulted in the setting-up of a new conception of federalism on the basis of the newly established North German union and the German federal empire in 1871.

In this transition period, H. A. Zachariä, in the second and third editions of his *Deutsche Staats- und Bundesrecht*, modified his early convictions as to the supreme power of the federal state over the powers of the individual state.

Adopting the orthodox federal principle along with the new theory of Waitz, he adjusted his view of the two essential characteristics, subjectively that the federal state with the state authority possessed the sovereign central power which was predominant over the individual state, and objectively that the federal state as well as the confederation rested on the separation of the federal affairs from the particular matters of the individual states.

Like other publicists, he divided unions of states into three different kinds: unions of different wholly sovereign states on the basis of international law; constitutional unions of many member states, i.e. with the member states united into a state body; and unions of a number of states for certain purposes, but otherwise remaining distinct and independent one from another.[1]

He laid down as the characteristic nature of the *Staatenbund* "the permanence of the absolute sovereignty of the individual states and their independence of one another," in so far as they are not restrained "by the right and obligation of the union determined by the treaty." The power of the union was not one assigned by the nature and unity of power of the state, but "a power of association" constituted by the treaty.[2] And the will

[1] H. A. Zachariä: *Deutsches Staats- und Bundesrecht*, 1865, p. 98.   [2] Ibid., p. 99.

of the union was built up by the wills of the individual states—i.e. by a representative assembly under the mandate of the individual states.

The German Empire, to which the previous thinkers adhered, was in a different category from the *Bundesstaat*, and also distinguished from an empire like the British Empire.

To him the *Staatenstaat* either arose in such a way that "for the individual members of the great state body, under the permanent recognition of the state authority extending over the whole, there developed politically independent inherent governing powers (such as in the early German Empire)"; or in such a way that the states which up to that time were sovereign, were "united by free treaty, or by an authority recognised by all, into a constitutional body; that is to say, under a governing power independent in its own sphere, into a constitutional community, whilst in all matters not assigned to this authority maintaining their independence as states."[1]

He classified the *Staatenstaat* as a kind of empire like the German union, which was different from a mere confederation of Switzerland or the American union of 1781.

His definition of the federal state was twofold. The one characteristic was that "the sovereign power within its own sphere of federal affairs is exercised by its own free will and armed with the necessary power which the federal state has in common with the state." The other was the self-government and independence of the individual states within their own sphere in so far as they did not override the interests and powers of the Empire or the federal state which the federal state had "in common with the confederation."

By the nature of the federal state the unity and force of the whole and also the freedom of the member state were harmonised by the characteristic organisation of the legislative and executive powers in the federal state, such as the representative system through "the presidential body" together with federal government and two-chamber representation of the people (*Volkshaus*) and of the states (*Staatenhaus*).

Like Bluntschli, Zachariä thought that the *Staatenstaat* and the *Bundesstaat* were transitional forms of the state between a confederation and a unitary state.[2]

Finally, it could not be decided *a priori* what should be within the scope of the federal state, and the distinction between the confederation and the federal state could not be made depen-

[1] H. A. Zachariä: *Deutsches Staats- und Bundesrecht*, 1865, p. 100.   [2] Ibid.

dent upon "the ambit of the material powers of the federal authority."

The difference between the confederation and the federal state was mainly due to the fact that the *Bundesstaat* must be a "state body," that is to say, that the federal power must be based on the public law as laid down in the federal constitution.[1]

The third category of unions was either real union or personal union.

His classification of the *Bund* was the prevailing conception in his day, and his characteristic assertion of federalism was the distinction between the confederation and the federal state which was not based upon differences in the distribution of power, but upon the kind of federal organ holding control and supervision over various general state activities.

His main modification of Waitz's doctrine was the assertion of the need for the *Staatenhaus* for the positive determination of the federal and state authority.

In the later editions of his *Deutsches Staats- und Bundesrecht*, he modified this. There was no difference between the conception of the federal state and that of the *Staatenstaat*.[2]

This conception of the federal state, according to his view, had two essential characteristics. The subjective importance which the federal state had in common with the state was that of being an independent central authority within its own sphere, and from the objective point of view the federal state, just as the confederation, should have control of the common federal affairs as distinct from the particular affairs of the individual states.

Since the independence of the central authority was composed of its independent authority as well as its indirect relation to the individuals, the freedom of the member state would be curtailed by the organisation of the central authority with unity and power of the whole, but the independence of the individual state, although mitigated by the representative system in the House of States, would only be guaranteed by the strict positive determination in the legal sphere of the federal and state authority.[3] Thus he advocated the increase of the competence of the *Norddeutscher Bund*.

Pözl, on the other hand, took the view of the subordination of the member states under the central authority,[4] but also adopted

[1] H. A. Zachariä: *Deutsches Staats- und Bundesrecht*, 1865, p. 103.
[2] Ibid. (2nd or 3rd editions), Sec. 25, II, Sec. 26, II. [3] Ibid., Sec. 27, I.
[4] Pözl: Article "Bundesstaat und Staatenbund," in *Deutsches Staats-Wörterbuch*, by Bluntschli und Brater, 1857, Vol. II, p. 285.

Waitz's idea of administrative relation to the central authority. He emphasised that the authority of the federal state—that of state power—must be exercised not only in respect of foreign affairs, as in confederations, which he designated as "social powers," but also must be extended to military and financial matters.[1]

Whilst the confederation had no relation to the subjects, the federal state had a "double relationship of subjects" who were the citizens of the individual states as well as of the collective state—that is, there was a direct relation of the federal power to the citizens.[2]

Heinrich Escher, a great Swiss publicist, in his remarkable work, *Handbuch der praktischen Politik*, published in 1863-1864, partly influenced by the preceding idea and partly by that of de Tocqueville, emphasised that the federal power in the federal state must be supreme, though he admitted the division of sovereignty between central and individual state authorities. He also strongly expounded the view, that, as the *Staatsgewalt* must be a federal power in direct relationship with the people and not with the member states, and as the federal power represented the whole nation and not the collectivity of states as such, it must have independent organs for the administration of common affairs, especially military, financial and customs matters, naturally directed by its own officials.[3]

Many works regarding *Staatsrecht* were successively published, and especially Zöpfl, Otto Mejer and Kaltenborn were distinguished for their theories of German *Staatsrecht*. In general they accepted the principle of the direct obligation of the subject of the individual state to the law of the central authority. Held, Vollgraff[4] and Trendelenburg took a different position.

Heinrich Zöpfl, in his work, *Grundsätze des allgemeinen und Deutschen Staatsrechts*, in the fifth edition, 1863, put forward a classification of the unions of states into the following categories: (1) *Staatenbund*; (2) *Bundesstaat*; (3) *Staatenstaat*; (4) "Personal Union; (5) "Real Union"; (6) "Incorporation."

Of these categories his definitions were not very different from those of other thinkers.[5] But as to the relationship between the *Bundestaat* and the *Staatenstaat*, he explained that there was no

---

[1] Pözl: Article "Bundesstaat und Staatenbund," in *Deutsches Staats-Wörterbuch*, by Bluntschli und Brater, 1857, Vol. II, p. 385. [2] Ibid., p. 386.
[3] Heinrich Escher: *Handbuch der praktischen Politik*, II, 1864, pp. 489-490.
[4] C. F. Vollgraffii: *De Confoederationibus sine et cum imperio*, 1859.
[5] Dr. H. Zöpfl: *Grundsätze des allgemeinen und Deutschen Staatsrechts*, 1855, I, pp. 109-115.

difference between them except with regard to their origin. The essential distinction was that the union of the collective state in the former case had its origin in treaty between the individual states, whereas the latter had its origin in some other manner as e.g. by "domination, feudal union, or devolution of a formerly existing unitary state."[1]

He pointed out one particular form of the union, namely, incorporation. In this category he gave the name of incorporation to those unions in which several states united together in such a manner that "besides the common law of hereditary succession only one and the same basic law is valid and together with the existence of a representative constitution there can be but one single form of representation."[2]

Zöpfl, like Zachariä and Pözl, did not adhere to the principle of the individual states under the central power, but asserted the principle that the collective state aims must be carried out exactly as in a unitary state.[3]

He thought that there could be no general rule with regard to the division of the activity and law of the state, but the independence of the central organs in the collective state and their direct relation to the people could be a possible characteristic of the federal state in contrast with the confederation.

Otto Mejer, however, in his *Einleitung in das Deutsche Staatsrecht*, in 1861, more clearly laid it down that if the central authority were raised to real sovereignty and if the confederated states remained independent only in those matters which did not come within the scope of the central authority, while they were subordinate in other matters to the central authority as if it were their own ruler, then the confederation was "transformed into a *Staatenstaat*, just as, on the contrary, a *Staatenstaat* can become a confederation by the emancipation of its parts."[4]

Yet he asserted the distinction between confederation and federal state to be that "the subject of the confederated states stands in the *Staatenstaat* directly under the will of the central authority as far as its competence extends, but in the confederation only so far as this will is adopted by the authorities of the individual states and made known to their subjects, and that resistance of the individual states to the central authority would

---

[1] H. Zöpfl: *Grundsätze des allgemeinen und Deutschen Staatsrechts*, 1855, I, pp. 108, 111.
[2] Ibid., p. 116.
[3] Ibid., 5. Auflage, 1863, Secs. 64, 65.
[4] Otto Mejer: *Einleitung in das Deutsche Staatsrecht*, 1861, p. 7.

be in the former case insurrection and in the latter breach of treaty."[1]

Carl von Kaltenborn, in his thorough-going work on federalism, expressed strongly the view that the federal state was "an organic unity," and not merely "a unity based on federal pact," and that the central authority was "a real analogy to the state power, although not really state power itself."

Therefore he emphasised that the sovereignty of the individual state was "essentially broken up" and gradually reduced to "a mere independence in provincial matters" and prevented from pursuing its own policy in internal as well as in foreign affairs.[2]

The citizens of the individual states were "directly subject to the laws of the central authority" and therefore there naturally arose a general civil law for all citizens of the federal state. He assumed consequently that "the resistance of the individual states to the central authority was not merely a breach of treaty, but was to be considered as insurrection."

Joseph Held expounded the definite view that the federal state embodied not an international legal character like the confederation, but a state nature.[3]

In his early work, *System des Verfassungsrechts*, he distinguished the *Staatenbund* and the *Bundesstaat* and the *Staatenstaat* from other forms of the union of the states such as alliance, by the fact that they were of a permanent nature. He drew a distinction between the first two forms, like Zöpfl,[4] in that the former was formed "through pact" and the latter by "another kind" of union of a number of states, which, however, had essentially a state form.

In the federal state the central authority was "an essentially state power" and in so far as it was legally formulated the full sovereignty of the federated states was broken up, and the independence of the federal state was firmly established.

Also, like Robert von Mohl, he endeavoured to base the conception of the union of states on empirical grounds, saying that the legal character of any so-called union of the states could be determined not "from the theory, but from the explicit decision

[1] Otto Mejer: *Einleitung in das Deutsche Staatsrecht*, 1861, p. 8.
[2] Carl von Kaltenborn: *Geschichte der Deutschen Bundesverhältnisse*, 1857, and *Einleitung in das constitutionelle Verfassungsrecht*, 1863, p. 159.—He, like Christian Wolff, attempted to prove that the international law, owing to its objective validity, represents a higher legal system over the states.
[3] Joseph Held: *System des Verfassungsrechts der monarchischen Staaten Deutschlands*, 1856–1857, I, pp. 392–395. [4] Ibid., pp. 390–497.

of the federal pact or concrete political activity."[1] Deducing from the actual facts of federal history and organisation, he set up a juristic definition, that, differing from the confederation which was nothing but a special system of state union possessing an international character, the federal state was a national union having the nature of "a state entity," and at the same time was "a transition from the confederation to a unitary state."[2]

He asserted that all the political activities of the union of the states, in so far as the union remained within its sphere, revolved around the full sovereignty "like planets round the sun."

From his conception of sovereignty as "unlimited" and "indivisible," there followed "freedom of the central authority in the federal state like the freedom of the confederated states in confederation."

Therefore, provided that a central authority in the federal state was a state power and could be a state within a state, he concluded that "the federal state in the strict sense of the word is not a union of states, but a state, the parts of which possess a certain degree of political independence which never becomes so great that these parts can themselves become states, because in that case the union would have to cease to be a state, and if that happened no federal state would exist any longer."[3]

In his later work, *Grundzüge des allgemeinen Staatsrechts*, in 1868, examining the forms of the state under the categories of monarchy, aristocracy and republic, he defined "the personal sovereignty" vis-à-vis "the popular sovereignty" (where the sanction of sovereignty "depended upon equal participation by the nation and aristocracy") and assumed that in the federal republic there must exist the *Staatenhaus* on the one hand, and the "House of Representatives" on the other, but "the carrying out of the resolution of the Congresses in the individual state is determined by the relationship between the single sovereignty and the unity."[4]

Then he developed his notion that when sovereignty was not juristically based on the nation, but on the exact limited aristocracy, and the representation of the remaining element was possible, this representation was "constitutional organisation" alone.

By the realization of the constitution the absolute power of veto must be granted to be the sovereign, and it "makes legally

---

[1] Joseph Held: *System des Verfassungsrechts der monarchischen Staaten Deutschlands*, 1856–1857, I, p. 393.   [2] Ibid., p. 394.   [3] Ibid., p. 395.
[4] Joseph Held: *Grundzüge des allgemeinen Staatsrechts*, 1868, p. 446.

a great difference whether the aristocracy is a part of the sovereign people or itself and alone sovereign."

Therefore he asserted that "the union of states is neither republican nor monarchical": the republican federal states were on a basis of divided sovereignty. But he rejected the division of sovereignty, by asserting that "no federal relationship which goes beyond the limits of an alliance can legally be exactly determined"[1]

From this point of view he formulated the rule that in so far as there was a possibility of the recognition of the majority principle in respect of general affairs, every union was to be included in the category of the federal state.[2]

Adolf Trendelenburg analysed federalism on his fundamental ethical principles in *Naturrecht auf dem Grunde der Ethik*, published in 1868, propounding "the ethical whole as organism," which he differentiated from the organism of Nature, and which was comprised of "the whole on the one hand" and "the part on the other."[3] The organic whole preceded that of its parts and the parts were created for the purpose of its existence; the opposite was not the case, namely, that the parts, independent before association, united together to form the whole by their own power.

Therefore, from the ethical standpoint there was need for some unique tie which would unite the individuals to the whole in such a way that, like the organs of the body, they had no will hostile to the will of the whole. The external tie was the force of the whole which, employing compulsion in the moral sense, makes even the fear, which it used to check the desires of the individual will, to subserve the purpose of the whole. Internally, the tie was that of the coalescing interests. And finally, the unified will of the whole and of the individuals had its basis in the ultimate resort in a common language, which made even the slightest feelings intelligible, and in a common sentiment.[4]

Therefore, for the whole and the individual, which had come near one another in their ideal determination, it was of great importance that "inasmuch as the elements of the ethical organism are individuals in a state of relative independence, its nature is in a still higher sense a systematic arrangement, as the existence of the organic already is in nature."

In the ethical association there was nothing that could not and

---

[1] Joseph Held: *Grundzüge des allgemeinen Staatsrechts*, 1868, pp. 447–448.
[2] Ibid., p. 463.
[3] A. Trendelenburg: *Naturrecht auf dem Grunde der Ethik*, 1868, p. 62.
[4] Ibid., p. 63.

should not be, at the same time, a part and a whole, a part for the purpose of a higher whole, and a whole in itself. On this assumption, ethical association in its development sought "combination and division to make easier and to improve the exchange and agreement of both functions."[1]

Starting from these fundamental maxims he examined the nature of the confederation and the federal state as state systems, laying it down that they were "expressions" of two different stages of permanent union of the states with one another. He assumed that "the *Staatenbund* consists of parts which are really independent, and which recognise the higher whole, the union, as a power above their will only in agreed directions," whereas "the federal state is formed of parts in closer unity, which only have their existence as a whole."[2]

The confederation depended upon the sovereign states and was a military and political union against foreign and domestic enemies, the chief motive being union against foreign aggression, and not "the affirmation of common legislation and common administration." On the other hand, the federal state was more firmly established in that "the collective consciousness of power became greater than the consciousness of power of the parts; further development takes place in such a way that the parts, the new states, arise only on the soil and through the protection of the whole, so that in this respect the whole is actually before the parts." Trendelenburg, like de Tocqueville and Waitz, strongly asserted the division of sovereignty in the federal state, "if the formation of the constitution in the parts, which are self-governing, was able to establish the law of the central authority by making individuals and not merely states responsible; and if states are willing to recognise themselves not as sovereign, but possessing a limited power—half sovereign."[3]

The federal state to him was based on the constitution by which, differing from confederation, the federal state was founded on "power"; and he contended that the latter possessed the object of unity and an ethical content in which "the subordination of the part under the whole," for the affairs and life of the whole, was required more precisely and exactly than in the confederation where it was only conditional, but both were based not only on the treaty, but also upon the united authority vis-à-vis foreign states.

He concludes that "in every federal law it will be a question

---
[1] A. Trendelenburg: *Naturrecht auf dem Grunde der Ethik*, 1868, p. 64.
[2] Ibid., pp. 584–585.　　　　　　　　　　　　　　　　[3] Ibid., p. 585.

of holding the balance between the law and power of the whole and the law and power of the parts and thus establishing important standards which shall do justice to both, but always consider the whole as above its parts."[1]

These arguments made a bridge between the theory of Waitz and that of Seydel.

The theoretic discussion as to German federalism was made concrete by the formation of the North German Union and the establishment of the German federal empire in 1871.

The contribution of Swiss contemporaries had no striking influence upon the development of federal ideas in Germany. J. Blumer proposed the co-ordination of sovereignty of the federal union with that of the individual state, but like de Tocqueville considered the former "only as exceptional" and assumed, like Snell, that the federal state was based on the constitution, but the confederation on the pact.[2]

And J. Dubs agreed theoretically with the co-ordination of the powers of the federal state and cantons, but said that practically the union must be given the power of acting effectively for the external as well as internal interests of common importance.[3]

Foreign federal ideas had influenced German thinking in the earlier stages of German federal development most noticeably in the time of Waitz, that is up to 1870.

The shift of German federal ideas from Waitz's theory to von Seydel's particularistic principle was a development corresponding to that from the proposal of the Frankfurt Imperial Constitution to the establishment of the German Empire.

The history of American federalism had shown the same process from the theory of the Federalists down to that of John Calhoun. Just as the various phases of the federal discussion during the period of development were a natural outcome of that development and the victory of Calhoun's particularism and with it the whole federal controversy was ended by the bloodshed of the Civil War, so the German federal principles of this period reproduced the American federal picture from 1789 up to 1866, and the controversy as to federal supremacy was ended by the victory of the Bismarckian policy in the two wars between Prussia and Austria in 1866, and with France in 1870.

The North German Union and the revised German federal

[1] A. Trendelenburg: *Naturrecht auf dem Grunde der Ethik*, 1868, p. 586.
[2] J. Blumer: *Handbuch des Schweizerischen Bundesstaatsrechts*, 1877.
[3] Dubs: *Zur Verständigung über die Bundesrevision*, 1871, pp. 112–113. *Das Öffentliche Recht des Schweizerischen Eidgenossenschaft*, 1878.

empire were, in their different ways, the product of political expediency directed to secure the unity of Germany under the hegemony of the Prussian kingdom.

The statesmanship of Bismarck had naturally as its main motive the setting up of a strong government in so far as federal unity could overcome the traditional prejudices of particularism.

§ 3

Just as in the United States the predominant tendency towards federalism found its expression chiefly in the commentaries on the American Constitution of 1787 such as those of Storey and Kent before the final verdict of the Civil War, so in Germany juristic thought was even more characteristically preponderant in the interpretation of the terms of the Imperial constitution of 1871.

The main problem in the federal discussions of those days was naturally as to whether divided sovereignty was valid or not, and whether the state authority should be subordinate to or co-ordinate with the central federal authority.

The controversy between G. Meyer and von Mohl on this problem led the way to the discussion as to whether the central authority in the federal state could extend the scope of its constitutional functions or if such an extension could only be made by agreement with the individual states.

The examination of Article 78 of the North German Constitution gave rise to two conflicting opinions as to the competence of the union, namely, the theory of the advocates of the *Kompetenz-Kompetenz* and the doctrines of Böhlau and G. Meyer, and the theory of constitutional supremacy put forward by von Mohl.

According to G. Meyer, Böhlau and H. A. Zachariä, it would be incompatible with the nature of the federal state if Article 78 of the federal constitution of the North German union had, as their opponents said, granted to the federal authority power to extend its constitutional competence. As soon as the federal authority was allowed to extend its competence and activity in any direction at its own discretion, then it became no longer a union or a federal state but a unitary state. The exponents of the competence of the North German union, on the principle of *Kompetenz-Kompetenz*, put forth the reasonable requirement that the federal authority, at present limited to certain common needs of the nation, might be allowed to extend according to time and circumstances.¹ They justified this power of extension of the North German union by pointing out its mingling of federal and unitary state characteristics.

After the German Empire was formed, G. Meyer, in agreement with Rönne's opinion,² admitted, firstly, the view that the unions of states must always have a limited competence;³ but the federal state, such as the North American and Swiss federal constitutions and the new German imperial constitution, could increase the scope of the law of the federal authority by means of an alteration of the constitution.

He further argued that whilst in America and Switzerland the supreme authority could not go beyond the powers given by the constitution, yet the imperial authority in the new German Empire had the power to extend its competence by means of a change of the constitution. Nevertheless, G. Meyer upheld the view that any conception of the federal state should be based on the same principle in so far as the seat of the sovereignty must be determined separately in each concrete political organization.⁴

Von Mohl contested the view of Böhlau, G. Meyer and L. Auerbach that the most complete authority was vested in the union as a whole. Von Mohl wrote: "How far this supreme federal authority actually extends is laid down when it is founded, and also in later decisions legally established—such supplementary decisions may consist in enlargements of the originally established limits or possibly in further limitations."⁵ Nevertheless, the conception of the federal state did not necessarily imply a definite and large amount of competence, but there was no doubt a sufficiently important amount required in order to warrant the designation of this federal authority as a state.

Not only did von Mohl adhere to the principle of Waitz, but also he endeavoured to seek the fundamental theory of the German federal state by a positive investigation of the actual facts and not by a categorical abstraction of a principle, saying that "scientific classification must not be a bed of Procrustes for the living reality."

In a word, from the fact that "a particular state form is, generally speaking, properly included in a scientific category,

¹ Böhlau: *Die Competenz-Competenz? Erörterungen zu Artikel 78 der Bundesverfassung des Norddeutschen Bundes*, 1869, pp. 42–43.
² Von Rönne: *Verfassungsrecht des Deutschen Reichs*, pp. 56–57.
³ G. Meyer: *Grundzüge des norddeutschen Bundesrechtes*, 1868, pp. 55–57.
⁴ G. Meyer: *Staatsrechtliche Erörterungen über die deutsche Reichsverfassung*, 1872, pp. 69–70, 82.
⁵ Von Mohl: *Das deutsche Reichsstaatsrecht*, 1873, p. 30.

we cannot with absolute certainty determine the validity in that case of any general principle applicable to the category, but we must take into account the special provisions and we must not leave out of consideration the superiority of the particular law over the general legal principles."[1]

This attitude of mind, although a juristic inclination was manifested in his works, led to his assertion of the permanent division of sovereignty as an essential of the federal state, not from a "determinate principle," but from "the practical need," assuming that "certainly a number of more or less important and far-reaching duties and claims have been set up; but in this case also there is lacking a general principle and a logical placing of the boundary line between central authority and the sovereignty of the individual states."[2]

Therefore the determination of the imperial constitution with regard to the care or prosperity of the German nation, or, in scientific terms, the prescriptions with regard to the police activity of the empire, have been no better.[3]

His argument was that a scientific division of the supreme rights of the empire was still quite impossible. The reason which he gave was that "on the one hand, many of the tasks, which are quite general for the empire and have been tacitly allotted to it, have not been taken in hand at all—and only then without doubt will the need for a division in individual matters appear—and, on the other hand, some of the limitations now imposed on the competence of the empire, e.g. with regard to legislation, must very soon prove to be untenable."[4]

The other debatable problem in the new German Empire was the distribution of powers. The constitution, though it might implicitly leave room for discussion, declared in some way or other definitely the extent of the direct authority of the federal law.[5]

But with regard to the exercise of the federal law controversy arose as to whether the central authority of the federal state might be carried out through a "compound system" or by direct administrative organs.

---

[1] Von Mohl: *Das deutsche Reichsstaatsrecht*, 1873, p. 3.
[2] Ibid., pp. 58–59.   [3] Ibid., p. 58.   [4] Ibid., p. 70.
[5] Article of the New German Imperial Constitution of 1871: "Within this confederate territory the Empire exercises the right of legislation according to the tenor of this Constitution, and with the effect that the Imperial laws take precedence of the laws of the states. The Imperial laws receive their binding power by their publication in the name of the Empire, which takes place by means of an Imperial Law Gazette."

The constitution had in view a twofold system of administration of the federal laws—namely, the direct exercise of governmental and administrative relations on the one hand and a supervisory or partial administration on the other.[1]

With this mixed system of administration, a diversity of opinions as to the federal authority was natural. Whilst Westerkamp and von Mohl favoured the direct authority of the federal state exercised by the federal officers, Holtzendorff and G. Meyer insisted that in these administrative relations the central authority might be dependent upon the individual state, and its independence was not essential to the conception of the federal state, but was "a mere matter of convenience."[2]

It must be noted that in these two different schools of thought, Mohl's school, which adhered to Waitz's theory, assumed the federal decentralisation of decision, but urged the federal centralisation of the administration, whereas Meyer's scheme asserted centralisation of decision and decentralisation of administration. There were other diversities of opinion as to the share of the individual states in the federal authority, especially in the German federal empire, owing to the exceptionally strong position of the Prussian Crown.

Not only the early exponents of the federal state, such as Hermann Schulze and H. A. Zachariä, but also Martitz, Gerber and G. Meyer, justified and insisted on the direct participation of the individual states in the working of the federal authority. For the German union, especially, in which many monarchical states were united into a federation, the council of states was an essential recognition of the particular political importance of monarchy.[3]

G. Meyer emphasised that the distinction between the federal state and the confederation rested on the "form in which the

[1] Article 36: "Collection and administration of duties and consumption taxes remain in the hands of each state of the Confederation."

Article 4, Sec. 7: "The organisation of the common protection of German commerce in foreign countries, of German vessels and their flags at sea, and the arrangement of a common Consular representation which is to be salaried by the Empire." While the commanding power of the navy rested entirely in the hands of the Empire, yet the contingent system applied to the Army.

[2] Holtzendorff: *Encyklopädie der Rechtswissenschaft*, Bd. I, pp. 640, 807. G. Meyer: *Norddeutschen Bundesrechtes*, pp. 19–22; *Staatsrechtl. Erört.*, pp. 19–20. Von Mohl: *Das deutsche Reichsstaatsrecht*, pp. 223, 196–198. G. B. Westerkamp: *Staatenbund und Bundesstaat*, in which he rejects the federal authority dependent on the individual state (pp. 63, 199).

[3] F. von Martitz: *Betrachtungen über die Verfassung des Norddeutschen Bundes*, 1868, pp. 69–71. Gerber: *Grundzüge des Deutschen Staatsrechts*, 2nd ed., p. 241.

federal power exercised its authority, not on the kind of "organisation," and added that "certainly it will not easily happen that a federal authority issues directly from the nation and yet only exists in relation to the state powers of the individual states; but the contrary is quite thinkable, that a federal authority, which does take its origin in the state powers of the individual states, should stand in direct relationship to the citizens of the states." Such a form of state would be a federal state, but the conclusions of earlier writers were against such a combination.[1]

According to G. Meyer, in the federal state "every part is actually a state to itself." The distinction between the federal state and other unions was that "in the confederation there is no collectivity, in the *Staatenreich* there are no members, in the federal state there must be both." He argued that the full exclusion of the individual state from the formation of the federal authority was "neither necessary through the nature of the federal state nor will be to any degree carried out practically,"[2] and contended that "the exclusion from state power of the individual state can take place still less in monarchies than elsewhere; in this case, where there are at the head hereditary rulers, who regard themselves as holders of the state power, jealousy for the preservation of the rights of sovereignty is much greater and the giving up of these is much more difficult."[3]

Therefore in general, when individual states were monarchies, there existed a greater leaning towards the formation of a confederation than towards that of a federal state; but if a federal state were formed, the authorities of the individual states would demand much more energetically a share in the formation of federal power than would be the case in republics.[4]

In opposition to the mandate conception of the federal authority Westerkamp and R. von Mohl adhered to Waitz's theory of the federal organisation.

Westerkamp advocated the same conclusion as to the need for the participation of the member states in the federal legislation and in the executive body, but he proposed the negative conclusion regarding the participation of the individual states on the rational ground that the union would absorb the competence of the individual states in so far as to allow certain action which might infringe on the independence of the individual state.

Von Mohl, in controversy with Martitz and G. Meyer, held the view that the central authority of the federal state was "the

---

[1] G. Meyer: *Grundzüge des norddeutschen Bundesrechtes*, p. 13.
[2] Ibid., p. 18.   [3] Ibid., p. 19.   [4] Ibid.

expression of a moral personality" and was not derived from the collectivity of the member states.

His criticism of the importance of the *Bundesrath* was characteristic. He argued that the assembly, or council formed of representatives of the governments of the member states, might be useful in co-operation with federal power, especially as providing for the participation of the princes of the member states of the monarchical federation in the federal government, as their delegation in that *Bundesrath* was "the highest wisdom of the federal organ."

In his *Deutsche Reichsstaatsrecht* he assumed that "no proof is necessary that in the federal state some institution is requisite to prevent the tendency to absolute unity obtaining the upper hand and the existing constitution coming to an end by the absorption of the individual states."[1]

His assertion as to the possibility of the incorporation of the individual states into the federal state was justified on the grounds that "such a threat may proceed both from the holder of the entire authority, out of ambition and desire for expansion, or from the mass of the population out of its desire for the advantages of a great state."[2]

But von Mohl assumed that this centralisation of the central authority could hardly be traced in the imperial constitution. On the principle of the representation of the federal elements a certain right of veto by the representatives of the members of the federation might be necessary, whether in republican or in monarchical federal states, such as the Senate in the North American union or the *Ständerath* in the German Empire; but even in this case "central government rules independently and exclusively in its own sphere."

Or it was imaginable that "in a court of justice the judgment in any actions might be overridden, on account of legislation which is contrary to the constitution, therefore itself invalid."[3]

Therefore if the rights, interests and wills of the individual states were represented in the imperial legislature, there would be a real security that the encroachment by the central power on the authority of the individual state would only take place by way of legislation.

If the interests and wills of the individual state were to be rightly represented in the imperial legislation, there should be no objection at all to their having special right to a share in the exercise of the federal government, but it must be admitted

[1] Von Mohl: *Das deutsche Reichsstaatsrecht*, p. 272.   [2] Ibid.   [3] Ibid., p. 273.

that this right of the individual state would not be justifiable if it infringed on that of the central authority. And also he admitted that in the monarchical federal state a monarchical head would be inevitable.

The discussions in the early German federal empire concentrated on the problem of the central authority in the federal state. According to G. Meyer, both in *Staatenbund* and *Bundesstaat* the federal authority had a dominating power over the member states, but the organisation of the federal authority made no difference to the character of these two kinds of union. There was no striking characteristic difference between *Staatenbund* and *Bundesstaat* except that in the federal state, law was enforced directly by the federal authority, whereas in the confederation it was done by the state authorities of the individual states.[1] Von Mohl argued that while this distinction was on the whole correct, it was only an external and logical consequence of the basic legal conception.[2] In his *Norddeutsches Bundesrecht*, Meyer established the limited competence of the central authority as the characteristic of the *Bundesstaat* as of every union, but he refused to give the *Bundesstaat* the name of "state," because a state must be able to determine independently its own sphere of activity.[3] In his later discussion Meyer thought that the individual states of the federal state were possibly not sovereign at all, since a higher authority could withdraw the rights still remaining to them. He would not admit the conception of the state as a sovereign community, but wished to substitute the conception of a political commonwealth.[4]

Another author, Auerbach, in his book *Das neue Deutsche Reich*, denied any characteristic differences between *Bundesstaat* and *Staatenbund* except in the nature of the limitation of independence of the individual states; in the case of *Staatenbund* there was a purely quantitative, in the case of *Bundesstaat* a quantitative-qualitative distinction.[5]

Joseph von Held, in his later work *Die Verfassung des Deutschen Reiches*, in 1872, put forward a new idea of federalism on a constitutional basis.

First of all he defined the German federal empire as "a constitutional union which in its external formation has arisen by

[1] G. Meyer: *Norddeutsches Bundesrecht*, pp. 11–12. *Staatsrechtliche Erörterungen*, p. 14.
[2] Mohl: *Deutsche Reichsstaatsrecht*, Sec. 11, II–IV.
[3] G. Meyer: *Norddeutsches Bundesrecht*, p. 24.
[4] G. Meyer: *Staatsrechtliche Erörterungen*, pp. 2–10.
[5] Auerbach: *Das neue Deutsche Reich*, 1871, pp. 90–92.

treaty—that is to say, the external form of its creation was not chance or force, but the externally free agreement of all German governments and all Germans or representatives of the people."[1]

He considered the treaty as a general association-form of life,[2] but the motive and purpose of the treaty of the federal union in its legal nature were differentiated from general "private or international relationships" and were based on "public law."[3]

Arguing from the legal character of this difference, he held that the German Empire was a constitutional union, based on the most complete form of law, and "has arisen by treaty between all subjects legally coming under the state will in Germany, who were counted as legal personalities," and was therefore neither a private nor an international relationship.[4]

The "constitutional union" was to him a form of the federal system which was different from the confederation or other form of union. From the nature of the constitution, this federal empire was a constitutional union having the "character of public law," and in so far as its constitutional nature extended, it must be, on the contrary, based on "the real individual determination of wills of all the direct and indirect members" and on the essential need for the empire.

Then he inquired what was the constitutional charter of the empire. In so far as the empire was based on "the constitutional competence" there existed, in the strict sense of the word, no states, and no sovereignty, within the empire.

One could not correctly say "within the limit of the German Empire," firstly because in one part of the empire, the so-called *Reichsland*, the constitution and the laws of the empire in general had not yet completely been established. Secondly, because for all members of the empire a certain equal measure of independence, together with external signs of their former sovereignty, was left by the imperial constitution itself.

Thirdly, to some individual states certain special rights were exceptionally granted, which, as compared with general rights of the German state, appeared as reserved rights.[5]

This incompleteness of the constitutional functions of the federal union was the outstanding feature of all *Staatenverbindungen*.

The first two matters were so obvious that any explanation was almost unnecessary, but the problem of reserved rights was the source of the main controversy as to the nature of the constitutional union. From the formation of the German union up to

[1] J. von Held: *Die Verfassung des Deutschen Reiches*, 1872, p. 1.
[2] Ibid., pp. 1–2.   [3] Ibid., p. 2.   [4] Ibid.   [5] Ibid., p. 7.

Held's day, in so far as the states claimed the sovereign character of their own right, the rights remaining to the individual Germanic states, the so-called "reserved rights," although they corresponded to the old conception, were entirely contradictory to the idea of the new German Empire. Held expressed the emphatic opinion that "a constitutional union or national union is only another expression for a unity with constitutional character, in contrast to an international union, or a legal unity in contrast to a private law (contractual) association."[1]

This constitutional union determined essentially the relationship between the empire and the individual states, and "not the special union treaties existing at the same time, which, indeed, unless there should be a return to the disintegration of Germany, must, in case of conflicts, yield to the former." But it was based on a constitutional unity which "can be nothing other than a unity with the common real legal character of a state, e.g. with the legal character of sovereignty, or the legal non-subordination of the higher legislation, jurisdiction and administration."[2]

He set up as the concrete definition of constitutional law that it was "that law through which all human beings in one of the territories are referred to a sovereign person, and according to which they must exist and behave themselves in a way that is suitable towards this person."

The constitution and all the functions of state life concentrated in a juristic state personality which was visualised as "a true collective person in the international system, in which the relationship between the parts of the territories and the whole state was a complete relationship between the nation and the individual members"—the whole is decisive for all the parts or members.[3]

This conception of the state as a coherent Hegelian unity led to his conclusion that "the constitutional law is therefore that law which assigns to each person his suitable and proper place and function in the community, but at the same time defines the limit where the legal sphere of the state ceases, and that of the private person begins."[4]

On this assumption he asserted that the conception of a so-called juristic person was not unknown to the constitutional law of the new German Empire, arguing that "the personality which is the subject of the competence based on the constitutional law newly founded by the German imperial constitution, is called the German Empire."[5] The particular relationship between "the

[1] J. von Held: *Die Verfassung des Deutschen Reiches*, 1872, p. 12.
[2] Ibid., p. 13.   [3] Ibid.   [4] Ibid.   [5] Ibid., p. 18.

emperor and the empire" was to him not an important problem but rather an historical reminiscence, and he thought that "at the present time, without a definite conception of sovereignty, emperor and empire itself must become not the central point, but the starting-point of a centrifugal movement which would lack force since the illusion of the absolutist hierarchy of earlier times had gone."[1]

Nevertheless, sovereignty was the main problem in "the monarchical federal state," and was the key to Germanic federalism.

Held propounded the view that "sovereignty is a natural and rational postulate of the state unity," and as to the relation of the federal state and member states he added that, "If sovereignty is a postulate based on the nature and reason of the state quality or organism, then its unity and indivisibility as regards content and competence appear as a postulate of sovereignty based on nature and reason, a postulate which justified absolutist centralisation just as little as it could be contended that an empire is called a constitutional union and its members themselves the states."[2]

Nevertheless, in the exercise of the single real law of the state power, a division and unity of function of the different factors might be possible, but the holder of the state authority must always be a unity, whether that authority be borne by a single person or a number of persons.

The distinction between possession and exercise of the state powers was the subject of much controversy.

Held observed that the present constitution of the empire, worked out over the long period since 1848 by Prussia, was a product of historical development and not formed by a systematic or doctrinaire exposition; it was the result of the energetic use of internal forces, in part their representation by eminent personalities, and with voluntary recognition by the individual states.[3]

Therefore, controversies as to the German constitution were mainly due to different understandings of the technical terminology or public law.

The main discussion was as to the division of sovereignty. Held believed that the division of sovereignty as regards contents and possession was "absolutely impossible." Whatever theory of divided sovereignty might be attempted, conflict between

[1] J. von Held: *Die Verfassung des Deutschen Reiches*, 1872, p. 19.
[2] Ibid.　　　　　　　　　　　　　　　　　　　　　　　　[3] Ibid., p. 20.

one part and the other would be the inevitable outcome, and would result in the subordination of the one part or the other; and therefore he argued that "the unity of sovereignty requires absolutely the totality of the essential rights which determine that sovereignty."[1]

Not only was the division of sovereignty impossible, but also a division of the content of sovereignty among its *Träger* was also "untenable."

He argued that the member states of the empire were to act, in so far as their activities were limited within the constitutional sphere, not as sovereigns, but in agreement with and subordinate to the laws of the empire; and under these supreme laws of the land the same political necessities might continue "to act as motive forces for further development of the empire as they had already compelled the substitution of the imperial constitution for earlier conditions."[2]

Held saw, further, that although the empire has appeared as something that has been allowed by the German states, owing to the treaty basis of the empire and its constitution, yet through the legal nature of the constitution of the empire "the sovereign rights of the individual states appeared as a concession granted by the empire."

He asserted that "at the present day the whole actually, legally and constitutionally is above all its parts and must therefore also determine the policy of the individual states, even in the enforcement of the rights which remain to them."[3]

He concluded that if the empire was really to remain a state organism, "as a partial state organism is either not a state organism at all or the partial is based on a fallacy," no essential supreme right and no competence of the state involved in it could be withdrawn from the empire as long as it lasted. If, on the other hand, the German states were really and permanently to remain states, then for the same reason no essential supreme right and no competence belonging to that right could, having regard to sovereignty, be regarded as belonging to the empire.

This criticism brought about the definition of the distinction between individual states and the constitutional union, or a union with constitutional character.

Thus Held characterised the German Empire as based on three things: unity, Prussianisation and the established independence of the German race.

[1] J. von Held: *Die Verfassung des Deutschen Reiches*, 1872, p. 24.
[2] Ibid., p 24.   [3] Ibid., p. 25.

His first principle was of great importance in the federal discussion.

For the purposes of that discussion he laid emphasis on: (1) the difference between the state which was characterised by the possession of absolute authority and the consolidation of all relationships, and the independent and decentralised states, and (2) the distinction between the state which was not called a federation but was a so-called consolidated state, and the federal state or confederation.

As to the first of these, there was no question as to the unity and integrity of sovereignty and the state. It was only a question —which was a possible one in any form of state—whether the administration of the state was or was not one which excluded self-government in the national and political divisions of the country and the participation of the people in the carrying out of legislation and control of the administration. Thus it was a question of the principle of government, in which in all circumstances the existence and maintenance of the state's unity are postulated.[1]

But the second difference evidently contained "a *petitio principii.*"

Every state, even the most unitary one, was a consolidated whole, and therefore the only question was out of what and in what manner it was consolidated.

If its formation was a natural one, and if its relationships to the whole were in accordance with that fact, the state would be more perfect in proportion as its parts were more closely united. Its progress depended on free union.

The opposite case was self-evident. The prosperity and progress of the German people depended neither on union nor disunion, but on whether and to what extent their needs and corresponding claims were satisfied.[2]

He examined the nature of the union and assigned to it a state character.

All so-called unions of states were therefore actually "stages" in the union or disunion of peoples—that is to say, "transitional stages" which could be put in precise constitutional forms.[3]

But the course which these developments took—in which owing to circumstances not only retrogressions, but also very long intervals of apparent immobility might occur—was "decisive, because all these developments must end in complete state unity—that is to say, a unity state, or in complete state disunity, i.e. in a number of really separate states."

[1] J. von Held: *Die Verfassung des Deutschen Reiches*, 1872, p. 28.
[2] Ibid., pp. 29–30.   [3] Ibid.

Thus he asserted that "it is natural that the making of state unity may just as little prevent the beginning of a new development in the direction of disunity as a most complete formation of a number of separate states may prevent the beginning of a further development towards unity."[1]

The question of Prussianisation was to him an essential one, since the constitution of the empire enacted in 1871 that Prussia rested on the establishment of the German Empire.[2]

The German Empire meant the present sphere of rule of the German nation, without being a perfect German national territory in the sense of the so-called principle of nationality.[3] With this foundation the new German Empire was based on the real supreme law. The supreme law appeared as "the essential real result of the state quality of a collectivity."[4] It followed:

(1) That it extended to all branches of human association in existence in so far as they entered the sphere of the state by external action, or were not entrusted to free individual determination, and that the state competence within its sphere in the quality of an essential sovereign must belong only to one state and to that state entirely.

(2) That this activity of the state could not be exercised without legally binding forms in the interest of the order, protection and claims of the whole.

Held's contribution to the theory of the German Empire in 1872 applied the federal ideal to the legal totality of the union in which the constitutional union possessed the state power, in opposition to the hitherto accepted doctrine of divided sovereignty as expounded by Waitz's school.

Along with the notion of sovereignty as indivisible and unlimited, Held presented the German federal empire as a constitutional juristic personality, and established as the basis of the federal state the principle that it was a constitutional union possessing a juristic personality, and thus clearly distinguished from the

---

[1] J. von Held: *Die Verfassung des Deutschen Reiches*, 1872, p. 30.   [2] Ibid., p. 34.
[3] Ibid., pp. 44–45.—"It does not therefore comprise all the lands in which the German population predominates, and therefore is not called the Empire of Germany, any more than the Emperor is called the Emperor of Germany, whereas in the lands and in the imperial territories belonging to the kingdom of Saxony and Prussia, it comprises various and in some places numerous non-German inhabitants such as Danes, French, Letts, Poles, Czechs, Wends and Walloons. That birth and language alone do not decide about nationality, is proved by our German-born and German-speaking socialists and ultramontanists, whose political views do not constitutionally speaking de-nationalise them."   [4] Ibid., pp. 47–48.

confederation which was dependent upon the possession of an international personality.

In the conditions resulting from the formation of the German federal state, Max von Seydel, a great Bavarian jurist, played the same part in German discussions of federalism as John C. Calhoun in the similar discussions in North America.

Seydel adhered to the fundamental theory of Calhoun, and quoted the famous phrase that "sovereignty is an entire thing; to divide it is to destroy it."

Criticising the various federal theories of his predecessors from Bluntschli to G. Meyer, Seydel proposed that the essential thing to determine the nature of a true federal state is a comprehension of the real character of the state.

The fundamental maxim of the state, which must be regarded as "uncontested," is that the state should rest on "land and people" as its basis, and on "unity of the whole and independence." And according to the general conception of the state it must be the highest form of human association.[1]

With this principle of the "perfect union" of the highest human society, he asserted that "the state is the association of the people of a land under the highest will." Like other German political thinkers, he assumed that "this will which rules the state must be the highest—that is, sovereign." It must be unitary and absolute because the existence of two highest wills vis-à-vis one another was conceptionally "impossible."

Accordingly the "right," which made this will valid and also the highest over the state, was called *Staatshoheit*—sovereignty.[2]

Sovereignty, therefore, was according to its internal nature "the exclusive right"—not "a sum of the enumerated rights," but the supreme law of the land. Therefore he concluded that sovereignty and state power were "indivisible."[3]

On these fundamental assumptions as to the state and sovereignty he totally rejected Waitz's theory of federalism. Such a conception of the federal state as postulated the possibility of division and limitation of the state power was "actually impossible," because it was entirely contradictory to the nature of the state.[4]

The criterion with which we must seek the true conception of the federal state should be based on its positive nature: "All these political formations which up till then used to be called

---

[1] Max von Seydel: *Commentar zur Verfassungs-Urkunde für das Deutsche Reich*, Second edition, 1897, p. 2.
[2] Ibid., p. 3.   [3] Ibid.   [4] Ibid., p. 4.

federal states (United States, the Swiss Unions, North German Union and German Empire) must be either simple states or confederations."[1]

As Calhoun preached the doctrine that the federal state was essentially of a confederated character, so Seydel declared that "the confederation is a permanent union of the states for the purpose of the common exercise of a special supreme right." Thus he stressed the fact that the permanent nature of confederation was its characteristic distinction from a mere alliance or the temporary union.

Seydel, however, differing from Calhoun's denial of any distinction between the confederation and the federal state, put forward the notion of the *Hoheitsrecht* as the test of the state form.

The sovereign right to be exercised in common could vary from case to case, but there could be no conceptional differences as to its method and object.

Therefore he assumed that "the state as such can be active both internally and externally." From the legal point of view the highest rights of the state were of two classes—external, or international rights, such as war and peace, or diplomatic rights, and internal, constitutional rights, such as those of legislation or administration.[2]

On this assumption he asserted that the confederation must be comprehensive, "not only for the common exercise of the external supreme rights, but also for the general exercise of the internal ones."[3]

Therefore he made a distinction between the two forms of the confederation, calling one the "international confederation" and the other "constitutional confederation."[4] But this difference was "not a distinction in nature, but in apparent form." In the international union the law was established and determined by the treaty between the states themselves. The other form of the union was a union for the common exercise of the constitutional supreme right, and he affirmed that "this union is to be operative also within the states, as within these only the will of the sovereign rules as law, so that it is necessary that the sovereign hands over by law to those allied with it the joint exercise of those supreme rights which are the object of the union; it is only by this means that the ruler can bind those belonging to the states to obedience

---

[1] Max von Seydel: *Commentar zur Verfassungs-Urkunde für das Deutsche Reich*, Second edition, 1897, p. 4.
[2] Ibid., p. 5.   [3] Ibid.   [4] Ibid.

to the federal authority, so that he makes this legally a power in the state which acts in its name."[1]

The constitutional union could only find its realisation "when the content of the federal pact between the states is made at the same time a law within the states."

A further distinction as to the form could be made according as the governments of the confederated states were "monarchy" or "democracy." Especially in these constitutional monarchies which were united by federal pact the federal system drew a sharp difference between the international and the constitutional confederation.

By the nature of the state function the external supreme right did not legally limit its power, while in the carrying-out of the internal supreme right the co-operation of the representatives of the people was enlisted.

Therefore, in the former, the common organ of government was only concerned with the federal affairs; whilst in the constitutional union the common organ or government was co-ordinate with a common representation of the people.[2]

This latter can suitably be designated a constitutional confederation, and of this kind the German Empire was an example.

He made the hypothetical assertion that the union would be "constitutionally a perpetual one," which was a main distinction between the federal pact and the treaty of alliance. He pointed out that "the unilateral secession of the member of the *Bund* only for the reason that the continuation of the federal relationship no longer corresponds to its real or theoretical interests" was to be regarded as not permitted, but held that "on the other hand the treaty-based dissolution of the union by the agreement of all the members may take place."[3]

Thus he, like Calhoun, came down to the doctrine of nullification and secession, namely, that as the individual states in the federation were not subordinate to the *Bund* but co-ordinate with one another on a treaty basis, so the federal power was not superior to the powers of the states, but was "the common state power of all and also of every state"—that is, the federal state rested on the treaty relationship; if this was broken, it was not "treason" but only a "breach of treaty."[4]

So he concluded that "the German union" was called "the

[1] Max von Seydel: *Commentar zur Verfassungs-Urkunde für das Deutsche Reich*, Second edition, 1897, p. 5.
[2] Ibid., p. 6. [3] Ibid., p. 33. [4] Ibid.

German Empire," but this designation was due not to "constitutional considerations, but entirely to historical traditions."[1]

German federal ideas from the early times down to 1872 were, in fact, implicit expositions either of the legal view of federalism or of the main foreign opinions as to foreign federal states. In particular the movement from Waitz's theory to Seydel's had been more or less in the same direction as the American discussion of federalism from the Federalists to Calhoun. And the difference between Held and Seydel was, in fact, nothing more than the difference between Story and Webster on the one hand and Calhoun on the other.

[1] Max von Seydel: *Commentar zur Verfassungs-Urkunde für das Deutsche Reich*, Second edition, 1897, p. 34.

CHAPTER III

DEVELOPMENT OF FEDERAL IDEAS FROM MAX SEYDEL TO SIEGFRIED BRIE

§ 1

The formation of the German Empire was an epoch in the development of federalism in Germany. Up to this time the discussion of the principle of the federal state had been either influenced by American federal ideas or confined to juristic theories which were quite foreign to actual German federalisation.

The North German union in 1866 in fact laid the foundation of the later German federal empire.

The political current towards the establishment of this federal state was, historically, strengthened by Bismarckian political expediency. The evolution of the new German federal state had taken a course different from that of the North American union. The former developed into the monarchical state, federated of various forms of states ranging from the free cities and feudal states to the monarchical kingdoms, and the latter had evolved entirely from a confederation of republican states.

The former was founded by an assembly of official representatives of the member states under the pressure of Prussian power, and the latter by a free convention of the representatives of the people of the member states.

Owing to the difference in the facts and conditions which led to the formation of the two federal states—the *Deutsches Reich* and the United States—the former was legislatively more centralised and administratively more decentralised than the latter, whereas the latter was legislatively more decentralised and executively more centralised than the former.

The characteristic differentiations between these two federations manifested the weakness of the federal mechanism as it functioned in the German federal empire in comparison with that of the United States.

Firstly, the variety of state forms in the federated states was a significant drawback in the German Empire, while the uniformity of republicanism in the member states of the United States was a great advantage in federal technique. The difference in the method of foundation of the federal state naturally brought about the fact that the German Empire had decentralised administration on the one hand and yet inclined to Prussianisation in the formation of the federal will on the other.

Secondly, the underlying forces which shaped the federal constitutions, although apparently differing in their mechanism, led, in both countries, to the evolution of that kind of political expedience which was manifested in the great political achievement of Hamilton and Madison in America in 1787 and of Bismarck in Germany in 1871.

No matter what political mechanism the United States and Germany might employ, the change from the merely ethical tie of a confederation to the legal structure of a federal state on the pretext of liberal democracy and the urgent need for national unity had resulted in an aristocratic domination over real and unfettered liberty.

As a result of the victory over Austria and the great triumph over Louis Napoleon, Prussian preponderance in the North German union led the South German states to accept the imperial constitution.

The people of Germany had no means whatever of access to real political power in the formation of the new federal empire.

The constitution of the German Empire in 1871 appeared as the supreme law of the German land, as a *Hoheitsrecht*, rather than as the treaty-based authority of the German people.

The federal idea now naturally entered on a new phase of development, on the basis of the imperial constitution. In this respect Albert Haenel was the first man to criticise the new federalism in a thoroughgoing manner as a *Herrschaft* state.

Max von Seydel threw a clear light on the notion of sovereignty, just as we have seen John Calhoun of South Carolina do in American federal history.

Seydel defined the state as "the collectivity of the people of a land united by a single highest will" and "this human collectivity must be ruled by a unitary highest will."[1]

He assumed "the will ruling over the state to be a conceptional requisite of the state, and from this it followed that this will must be also a right to will, a will that can be transformed into action." "And this supreme and unitary will with its powerful self-expression is the state authority" which possesses "the highest legal justification, namely, its logical necessity."[2] This state power is the highest power in the state and there is no other power

[1] Max von Seydel: *Staatsrechtliche und Politische Abhandlungen*, 1893, p. 5.
[2] Ibid., p. 6.

above or even equal to it. Therefore he concluded that this state power was sovereignty, which was "one and indivisible."

Criticising the previous conceptions of the federal state he held that "every state formation which one was bound to designate by the name of the federal state must be either a unitary state or confederation."

He inquired into three questions in order to demonstrate the confederated nature of the federal state.

Firstly, was the central power of the confederated state of Switzerland and the German Empire, according to their internal nature, the power of a single state, or was it the power of several confederated states? Secondly, who was the possessor, who was the executor of this power? And thirdly, in what relation did the power of the members stand to the whole?

He answered the first question, as regards Germany, by saying that: "The fact that one sovereign, the King of Prussia, takes a more prominent position in the union does not affect the nature of the union; that position is a concession, in accordance with the pact, in which the members took account of the actual position in respect of political power and the desire for a more effective means of enforcing the authority of the federation."[1]

Secondly, he said that although the emperor was constitutionally empowered to carry on war and make peace, yet the emperor as such was "not sovereign and not Emperor of Germany, but an organ of the union." Thirdly, the determination of the law by the *Reichstag* was binding on the delegates of every monarchical state.

Finally, whilst there was "a reciprocal union" between state membership and communal membership, they were quite independent—state membership and empire membership were "legally bound one to another" and, in fact, this latter relationship was "as close as that of a part is to the whole."[2]

On these assumptions the indivisibility of sovereignty was von Seydel's characteristic notion of the federal state in contrast with Waitz's conception of federalism. Therefore his idea of the confederated nature of the federal state was dependent on the union being an individual state with a single and indivisible sovereignty.

J. Held's constitutional federalism and G. Meyer's later notion of the absolute predominance of the federal state over the individual states were utterly contradictory to Seydel's definition of federalism, as being of the nature of *Staatenbund*.

[1] Max von Seydel: *Staatsrechtliche und Politische Abhandlungen*, 1893, p. 48.
[2] Ibid., p. 67.

Apart from the fact that their fundamental notion of sovereignty was based on a similar conception, their arguments turned simply on the verbal interpretation of the text of the constitution.

Nevertheless, although the effort so to interpret the constitution was the primary characteristic of these writers and the later positivist jurists, Albert Haenel was the first man to examine federalism closely and clearly from the standpoint of the principle of *Herrschaft*, in his work *Studien zum Deutschen Staatsrechte*, published in 1873. In order to protest against Seydel's notion of the federal state, Haenel first of all examined the principle of nullification and secession in the American federation, from the controversies between the Federalists and Jefferson to those between Webster–Lincoln and John Calhoun,[1] and concluded that the way to solve this problem was to make clear the relationship of authority between the central and the particular governments in the union on the basis of the legally valid notion of the sovereign power of the state.

The polemic of this argument was limited by a conception of federalism in which these relations were in general not dependent upon domination or subordination, but upon the co-ordination of the power of the twofold governments in respect of the source of authority, i.e. sovereignty; the whole controversy was as to its location. Against the view of Seydel, Haenel claimed for the individual state the right of secession from the union "in the case when the interpretation of the constitution by the processes provided for in that constitution appeared to it irreconcilable with the spirit of the union pact, but it must not remain in the union and still regard as null and void the decisions and regulations of the union authorities which it considers to conflict with the constitution."[2]

So the way to determine the juristic basis of the German Empire was naturally to search out the precise interpretation of the North German constitution which was the source of the German federal empire of 1871.

In order to formulate the constitutional doctrine his object was to investigate the historical development of these particular federal states with special regard to the contrast between *Kompetenz-Kompetenz* and the treaty-based constitutional power.[3]

He pointed out that for this purpose it was necessary to consider the introduction of the German imperial constitution, in its

---
[1] A. Haenel: *Studien zum Deutschen Staatsrechte*, 1873, pp. 1–26.
[2] Ibid., p. 27.   [3] Ibid., p. 28.

external relationship to the source of the constitution; the relation of the constitution to the pact; and the negotiations and final protocols relating to the constitutional pacts between the North German confederation and the South German states. A further and more fundamental part of the inquiry must be "the question as to the extent to which—whether as a whole or in important parts—the constitution of the empire could from any points of view be regarded as a treaty, and the legal relationships created by it as simply treaty relationships of the individual states between themselves and with the empire."[1]

In this historical exposition of the German federal state, Haenel, like Held, first of all considered the nature of the treaty which was the basis of the federal state.

He defined the treaty as "a general form of the origin, alteration, and dissolution of legal relationship by the agreement of the will of the several parties."[2] Its function as the "basic origin of legal relationship" was the first thing to be considered.

The question which came under inquiry was whether or not the conception of contract in private law—i.e. the obligatory nature of the contract—was applicable to that of the treaty in the sphere of public law.

Haenel thought that contract could be the juristic starting-point not only for the public law corporation subordinate to the state, but for the state itself. It did not form their legal basis or their only possible starting-point; the natural and moral necessity for the state and most public law corporations made any juristic starting-point, and contract in particular, possible only if particular prerequisites were fulfilled. But that such a starting-point was possible was shown by the foundation of the New England states, German colonisation by artificial communes, and the formation of diverse religious corporations; this was considered as beyond doubt by those who regarded the federal state as having the nature of a state. But normally and by their very nature the internal legal conditions of the state itself are entirely outside the scope of the contract. For the conception of contract is the "agreement of a number of independent wills, to which agreement there is given the power to determine juristically the relationship which is to prevail." That presupposes the equality of the parties *inter se*, but Haenel asserted that: "The state as the most comprehensive authority is entitled by its own will alone to regulate and decide all matters within the sphere of its rule; as such, and apart from its private law aspect

[1] A. Haenel: *Studien zum Deutschen Staatsrechte*, 1873, p. 31.   [2] Ibid.

as exchequer, it is never in the position of an equal among equals."[1]

In the relationship of the state to the subjects the contract, as a basis, and contractual relationships analogous to the legal relationships of private law, can exist only where the state has recognised the legal position of the subject as a right derived from its authority "by virtue of a particular legal system." Haenel assumed that on the whole the pact (treaty or contract) had the same status in the general system of international law as in private law, in that all the individual states are sovereign and equal. But it is the same mistake, as in private law, to regard the legal relationships founded on international pacts as exclusively treaty-based, i.e. as legal relationships analogous to the obligatory ones of private law, and differing therefrom only in that in private law a property interest prevails and in international law a political interest.[2]

The extreme case is the legal possibility of the absorption by treaty of one state into another, and the establishment thereby of a dominant relationship. At the other extreme—still outside of a mere treaty (contractual) relationship—is the transference of some particular governmental power from one state to another, to be not simply exercised by that other, but held by it of its own right. In between these two extremes is the relationship, based on treaty, which leaves one of the parties with only "semi-sovereignty," and also the legal possibility of a number of states uniting by treaty into a corporate union which establishes a relation of dominion and subordination between the collectivity and the individual member states.

With regard to the function of the contract or treaty to furnish the basis of legal relationships of diverse kinds it is possible to argue that it lays down, at the same time as for the legal relations to be established, the rules to determine the rights and duties of the parties. The resultant parallel between the provisions of the treaty or contract and laws has given rise to the opinion that the difference between them is not inherent, but only one of their external origin—that is to say, that treaty provisions are rules resulting from a treaty, and legal provisions are rules resulting from statute and law. To Haenel that opinion was mistaken, for he thought that from one point of view it could be argued that treaty provisions resulted from law. He distinguished in private law between "compulsory" and "optional" (*dispositive*) provisions, meaning by the latter term those which affect all

[1] A. Haenel: *Studien zum Deutschen Staatsrechte*, 1873, p. 33.   [2] Ibid., p. 34.

the spheres of human activity in which the will of the individual is unrestricted and are intended only to supplement private arrangements where incomplete, and elucidate them where they are insufficient or uncertain, and to do both these things not as rules controlling individual volition but rather as assisting it. That is to say, these "optional" laws formulate typical contract provisions, which in any case of doubt are assumed to have been intended by the contracting parties.[1]

There is the other case, where by the treaty (contract) between the parties a juristic person is set up. This juristic personality obtains its legal status vis-à-vis its members and third parties only by the fact that the former recognise the treaty provisions as being their own and as willed by them, and take them as guiding their domestic and external will and action.

The so-called basic treaties thereby obtain a scope and validity different from the treaty intentions and going beyond their legal force.

These *Grundverträge* are "statutes" or "laws"—"statutes" if their authority rests on a legal system superior to the juristic person, and "laws" if their authority rests on the rights and powers of the juristic person.[2]

Therefore he asserted that the legal form of origin could not be considered as bridging the gap between the treaty provisions on the one hand and statute and law on the other; there was an essential difference between them, and the difference in their legal form of origin does not really matter.

Statute and law are the rules formulated by the collectivity as such—they are the general will. Their legal validity is determined by "the existence and the extent of a relationship of authority which has gained legal acceptance, that relation of authority being one of domination and subordination, or organic union in a collectivity."

Treaty (or contractual) provisions, on the other hand, are rules decided upon by a number of individuals as such, agreeing together but in a position of complete legal equality. Their legal binding force can extend only to "those relations of life in which legal activity is allowed to the individual wills of individual persons as such."

No conclusion could therefore be drawn from the contractual origin as to the contractual nature of the resultant legal relation-

[1] A. Haenel: *Studien zum Deutschen Staatsrechte*, 1873, pp. 35–36.
[2] Ibid., pp. 36, 37.

ship and the rules determining it. It was unnatural for any system of law, private or international, to conceive of a contractual freedom of the parties which would have the character of a legal relationship different from a contractual one, and yet be contractual.

So Haenel reached the conclusion that in the federal discussion the problem of the contractual (treaty) nature of the German federal constitution and of the legal collectivity founded thereby could not be solved only by the preliminary inquiry whether its legal basis was a treaty or something else, but "by the determination of the essential characteristics of the political collectivity created by it." This raised the preliminary question of the nature of the federal state.

Haenel therefore next discussed the nature of the confederation and of the federal state. He first pointed out that despite the differences between monarchical and republican forms of government, and as to the competence of the federal and individual states and the organisation of the central power and its offices, there was a striking similarity between the political organisations of the United States of America, Switzerland and Germany. The difference between these federations was due to the fact that the particular political conditions of these three countries had differentiated the spheres of activity of the federal whole and the member states.

Haenel assumed that the foundation of the conception of the federal state, in the modern jural state, had been laid down by that "unequalled masterpiece of legal and political publication," the American *Federalist*, in 1787, which had founded in these three countries the federal states of to-day in contradistinction to the confederation.

According to the Federalists the main distinction between the federal state and the confederation was not the extent of the competence of the collectivity, but the fact that the confederation had relations only with the individual state, while the federal state developed a "relationship of authority" which directly affected the citizens and was furnished "with independent power and legal organs."

This fundamental conception of the Federalists had been almost unanimously adopted, though with some modifications, in the later literature, in the writings of J. S. Mill and Freeman in England, de Tocqueville and Laboulaye in France, Blumer and Rüttimann in Switzerland, and R. von Mohl, Pfizer and Waitz in Germany.

Haenel, however, was the first person to formulate the concrete idea of the confederation in Germany.

Denying the prevailing theory that the confederation is a mere treaty-based relationship of the individual states with one another, he asserted that all the three confederations named above were provided with "organs of will and activity" in which the formation of will within a determined sphere of competence did not take the form of treaty decisions of the individual states, i.e. "a treaty-based consolidation of the individual wills," but that of the "majority decision," i.e. the majority decision of congress in the United States, of the *Tagessatzung* in Switzerland, and of the *Bundesversammlung* in Germany.[1]

Only through this acknowledgment of the majority-based union was the confederation differentiated from a permanent alliance or from a simple treaty-formed relationship, or were associations such as the German customs union distinguished from the German union of 1815 or the Swiss confederation of 1798.

Accordingly, he asserted that in the confederation the competence assigned to the collectivity in the different spheres was not dependent upon "the sum of the individual states as such; but upon the collectivity as such."

In so far as the majority decision prevails and the "independent" legal sphere of the confederations extends, so far the individual states appear as members of a political collectivity and thereby the "relation of domination and subordination" comes into existence.

In regard to this collectivity the decision regarding the organisation and competence of the union and the resolutions of these organs themselves are not treaty-based decisions but are "constitution and laws"—"fundamental law and statutes," that is, in other words, "legally binding rules of the formation and activity of an organic whole."

Thus Haenel assumed that juristically the confederation was a "juristic person."[2]

Nevertheless, even though he cast the confederation in the mould of legal personality, he could not ignore the fundamental nature of the confederation, as it was, as "an international personality." Because the confederation was a legal person and, especially where it appeared as an international personality, it could take action without any direct reference to the individual states. It possessed exclusively international authority in regard

[1] A. Haenel: *Studien zum Deutschen Staatsrechte*, 1873, p. 41. [2] Ibid., p. 42.

to foreign affairs and declarations of war and peace. Even the Swiss confederation of 1815 allowed the cantons only very limited and strictly defined relations with foreign powers.[1]

Moreover, the members of the juristic person in the confederation were always "the individual states as such."

Therefore all direct relationship between the confederation and the subjects and officials of the individual states was excluded, and the laws of the confederation, even though formulated by itself, had to be exercised through the state powers in the names of the individual states.

At the same time, as the confederation was a legal person the sovereignty of the individual states is limited not only "by the treaty relationship but by that of domination and subordination," but sovereignty of the individual states in regard to their internal affairs is "absolutely unlimited."[2]

His assertion of sovereignty in this criticism showed clearly that he was a follower of G. Meyer and that he accepted a limited sovereignty with a distinction between internal and external sovereignty; the former was the essence of the state and its power, and the latter depended on the external distribution of the state powers determined by expediency as to their exercise.

Therefore in that sense the confederation is "an international corporation."

Nevertheless, the decisions which, from the point of view of the relations of the whole to the parts, form "the statutory constitution" and "the relationship of domination and subordination," are at the same time treaty decisions and the conditions of the treaty-based obligation of the individual states to recognise the union so formed and of the union thus qualified not merely by the treaty.[3]

According to this argument the confederation is, without doubt, although a "juristic person," also an "artificial collectivity" which can be dissolved again by agreement of the participants, although the fact that it is intended to be a permanent institution is shown by the exclusion of a unilateral right of secession. The fundamental laws of a confederation can be altered only by treaty-based consent of the members, but as a matter of fact it actually happened in concrete cases that the entry of new members was allowed by a kind of modified majority decision.

[1] A. Haenel: *Studien zum Deutschen Staatsrechte*, 1873, p. 42.
[2] Ibid., p. 43.   [3] Ibid., p. 45.

It followed, further, from this that the fundamental law could be interpreted and altered only by treaty. Therefore any attempt to enforce an alteration in the fundamental laws either directly or by majority decision can be regarded by the dissentients as "a breach of the treaty upon which the obligation to recognise the union rests, with all its international consequences."[1]

Comparing the confederation with the federal state Haenel asserted that they have two things in common. The one is that the federal state is also a "political unity and an international personality" only in its relations with foreign states; the second is that it presupposes a "political community" organised and carried out "in the manner of a state." It defines sharply its sphere of activity as compared with that of the individual states, and calls on the member states to co-operate in the formation of the will of the whole and regulates the behaviour of the individual states towards one another.

But the main characteristic of the federal state, in contrast with the confederation, is that the former makes a breach in the sovereignty of the federated states and places itself in "direct relationship" with the people of the states. The federal state claims that its decrees shall bind the people of the states directly and without the "intervention" of a sovereign act of the individual states. It assumes the right of direct execution of its orders either by means of its own organisation or by using the institutions of the individual states.

Finally, the federal state in its constitutional system "gives the citizens of the states a direct share in the formation of the will of the collectivity."[2]

Accordingly, in order to fulfil the common purposes of the federal state, it must obtain and exercise the necessary legal powers from the whole of the state authorities and use them as "constitutional supreme rights."

With regard to the relation of the federal state and its organs to the citizens Haenel emphatically asserted that the constitution of the federal state cannot be considered as treaty-based decisions or treaty-based relationships established thereby. Thus the federal state reveals itself "as having the complete nature of the state" and emerges from the legal system of international law as "a constitutional power."[3]

The question whether the federal state is based on constitutional power or on treaty-formed authority was the subject of

[1] A. Haenel: *Studien zum Deutschen Staatsrechte*, 1873, p. 46.
[2] Ibid.
[3] Ibid., p. 47.

controversy between Held and Seydel which Haenel criticised from the standpoint of his own theory of corporation. He set up the criterion, whether the treaty-obligatory relationship of the participants superseded the majority decision or the authority of the majority principle set up the legal entity of law.

Against the theory of the confederated nature of the federal state Haenel put forward the juristic personality and the conception of the state which was embodied in the nature of the federal state.

To him juristically the conceptions of Calhoun and Seydel were totally "impossible" of application to the German Empire and its constitution.

It was quite clear that "this application can only take place by taking the wording of the constitution in a wrong sense," by giving to all the decisions interpretations which could not legally be brought into effect, or (from the juristic standpoint) by transforming "actual phenomena" into "an empty illusion."[1]

On the contrary Haenel asserted that one would be justified in taking the wording of the imperial constitution in its strict sense, in rejecting distinctions legally inadequate, and in regarding the obvious intentions of the imperial constitution and therefore the external actual manifestation as a "juristic reality," if we determine to regard empire in its collectivity as a legal personality, in short "to recognise the empire within its legal sphere as constitutional power."[2]

Strong reasons of juristic technique would be necessary to force us to sacrifice this simple principle of legal relationship for other more subtle and complicated ones. And certainly the principles which had been regarded as conclusive would throw doubt on the fundamental conceptions of all public law.

The first is a legal conception of the nature of a juristic person which regards this as a fiction in order to set up a simple juristic construction of certain association relationships in the place of more complicated legal deductions. This construction was described as an abstract idea into which the method of juristic technique breathed "an artificial life" and was treated by that method as "something arbitrary" to which objective law assigned or refused its recognition for reasons of utility and convenience.

Haenel pointed out that this view was erroneous in two respects.

It was mistaken because it was "a misconception of the psychological and ethical nature of mankind as dependent for its development on community." And secondly, it was mistaken,

[1] A. Haenel: *Studien zum Deutschen Staatsrechte*, 1873, p. 57.   [2] Ibid.

because it misconceived the task of law, which should regulate the decisions of will of the community in regard to external affairs—a regulation which cannot exist if it denies and suppresses those effective expressions of will without which mankind and the communities of mankind cannot fulfil their highest and most essential ethical functions.[1]

On the other hand the "general will" as "something different from the individual will and the casually agreed sum of a number of individual wills" is "no fiction, no abstract or arbitrary idea," but "a powerful dominating fact."[2]

Haenel asserted that "it is a matter of psychology and ethics and of anthropology in the wider sense to adduce the proof that human nature possesses not only the ability, but also the need to determine for itself moral ideas or purposes of life, the possible realisation of which extends beyond the limits of individual capacity."[3]

These ideas or purposes of life are not subordinate to the individual will, but on the contrary dominate individual will and action.

They necessarily produce a "general will" which emerges "as the constant will of the collectivity" from "the sum of the variable individual wills." This collectivity is "a definite number of human beings united in their will."[4]

Haenel was bent on proving that every collectivity felt the impulse "to raise its ideal and abstract existence into reality." When once it was recognised that an individual or several individuals or sum of individuals in their more or less modified majority decisions possessed the "ability" to represent the "general will," when a "validity" was assigned to their will independent of the agreement of individual wills, then the collectivity obtained "organs of deliberation and action." The collectivity intervened externally in the relationship of will of its members, and constituted itself with regard to them a "deliberative and active personality vis-à-vis third parties."[5]

He emphatically stated that the law cannot act arbitrarily towards these actual phenomena. To him the state, summoned to carry out the law, might put the various collectivities within its association to the test with regard to their morality, competence, permanence and appropriateness of structure, or even for higher purposes suppress them. But in the theory of law a life purpose could not be recognised as justified and yet the collec-

[1] A. Haenel: *Studien zum Deutschen Staatsrechte*, 1873, p. 58. [2] Ibid.
[3] Ibid. [4] Ibid., p. 59. [5] Ibid.

tivity developed by its exertions be thought of as "a sum of individuals only outwardly united," and therefore "its existence denied as an independent power of will."[1]

Haenel asserted that the law could not find adequate expression "for the actual manifestation in any other manner than by admitting the collectivity organised for the fulfilment of will and action as the independent possessor of rights and duties."

The doctrine that jurisprudence could adopt an arbitrary interpretation in regard to these creations (*Bildungen*) was "a destruction of the life principle of jurisprudence and also of the principle of individual legal personality." For Haenel contended that "a general will" was that which was actually made manifest in the organs of a collectivity which determined and gave effect to the law, and this collectivity was a legal personality only by reason of its actual power of will.[2]

Therefore he drew the conclusion that neither an abstract idea nor the external aggregate of a number of individuals, but a "general will brought into life in its organs of deliberation and action," is "the natural basic foundation which the law is bound to recognise."[3] Such a "legal person" manifested itself in all the different branches of the legal system, in the spheres both of private and of public law. There is no reason why this should not equally apply to international law with regard to the relationship between state and state.

Haenel did not hesitate to observe that the state might attempt to achieve the highest purposes the accomplishment of which was beyond the power of an individual.

Starting from this fundamental principle he inquired whether the juristic personality belonging to the individual state could be ascribed to the *Bundesstaat* or the *Staatenbund*. There was no obstacle, arising from the nature of law and its technique, to the attribution of juristic personality to the federation or the confederation. It was a question of fact whether the German Empire, with its existing constitution, was a juristic person or not. He rejected the assumption that the German Empire in its totality could be taken as a treaty-decided or treaty-based relationship of the individual states with one another.

Therefore the views of Seydel formed a counter-movement to Haenel's *Herrschaft* theory.

Haenel followed the Aristotelean conception of the state to

[1] A. Haenel: *Studien zum Deutschen Staatsrechte*, 1873, p. 59.
[2] Ibid., p. 60. [3] Ibid.

the extent of believing that the state was a complete self-sufficing living association of the nation.

With the conception of the state as an ethical organic whole he contrasted the generally accepted view of the division of activities between the collective state and the member states.

This idea was in sharp contradiction to the conceptional characteristics of the state, whether termed "completeness, independence, self-sufficiency, sovereignty, unity, existence as the highest form of society, or as possessing the highest and supreme authority."

Calhoun's theory of the indivisibility of sovereignty was entirely unthinkable.[1]

Then he pointed out that there was still another alternative which found the conception of the state with its necessary attributes neither in one collectivity nor the other, nor simultaneously in both, but "only in their organic co-operation and combined functioning according to plan." According to this neither the individual state nor the collective state is really a state; they are "only political associations organised and acting like states. The only state is the federal state as the totality of both."[2]

Therefore the problem of the federal state, as a matter not only of practical politics, but also of scientific formulation, was whether "unity in the multiplicity" could be applied to the relationship of the collective state to the individual states, and whether thereby the requisite organic totality could be manifested in the federal state.

The unity of the state appears most clearly and crudely in the absolute monarchy; it becomes more ideal and abstract, and the result of a more complicated process, the closer the state approximates to the modern legal state. There the will of the state is established in general basic decisions which bind the sovereign itself; the members of the state have a part in the formation of that will; and the administration is decentralised in varying degrees among a number of officials and self-governing bodies.

The federal state uses even more "complicated machinery" in its co-ordination of the collective and the individual states.[3] It desires to uphold the independence of the individual states to such a degree that for the state tasks incumbent on them they maintain not only their independence of administration but also of legislation, of "final sanction and authority." He emphasised

[1] A. Haenel: *Studien zum Deutschen Staatsrechte*, 1873, pp. 62-63.
[2] Ibid., p. 63.   [3] Ibid., p. 65.

that the necessary unity must possess "an ideal and abstract character to the highest degree." The comprehensive and unifying power will be a "latent one," which can be "changed into actuality when it is a question of removing or obviating any disturbance of the organised collective functioning of the different powers of will working at the common task of the state."

Haenel next asserted that the unity of the federal state must be sought firstly in organisation, and secondly in the constitutional laws.

Firstly, the organisation, however varied its forms, allows the holders of the supreme power in the individual states to enter into a union as members holding the supreme power in the collective state or simply as sharers of that power.

Secondly, unity must be sought in the constitutional laws of the federal state in so far as they sharply divide and appropriately distribute those duties of the state which can be carried out only by an association supplementary to the individual states and those which are suited to and require individual treatment, and in so far as those duties impinge on the government of the individual states to the extent that is necessary to guarantee that essential agreement of the collective state and every member state in the conception of state duties without which systematic, mutual support for the attainment of the state purpose is quite "inconceivable."

Finally, he asserted that if this unity is not to be sought in vain "there must exist a law and power which not only safeguard this organisation and competence as a whole, but continue its development in accordance with the varying demands on the state and varying ideas as to the duties of the state and the means of carrying them out."

Then he concluded that in the nature of things these laws and powers could belong only to a collective state.[1]

By this he meant that even in regard to their own legislation and administration the individual states cannot be considered as quite independent or free of any connection with the collective state.

The relations between the two forms of state in the federal state are not simply those of co-ordination; the collective state is in the position of a "predominating power" in so far as it is called upon not only to fulfil the duties directly assigned to it as a member, but also to protect the whole of the federal state.[2]

Haenel also laid it down that the characteristic difference

[1] A. Haenel: *Studien zum Deutschen Staatsrechte*, 1873, p. 65. [2] Ibid., p. 66.

between the unitary and federal states does not lie in the limited scope of the sovereignty of the collective and individual states, but in a membership which is so loose that the individual states fulfil their state purposes in their own right and according to their own law, in so far as their activities are confined within the constitutional limits.[1]

His definition of the federal state and confederation was in the German federal theory a landmark known as *Herrschafts-Theorie*.

He remarked that in the federal state there existed the collective state on the one hand and the individual states on the other, and as a third the federal state itself, this last being the "co-ordination" of the collective and individual states in a full independence, and therefore "outwardly differentiated."

The collective state alone has simultaneously the duty of embodying the individual states as members of the whole and maintaining this membership permanently and continuously, and because it has these tasks, in addition to the direct discharge of the state duties assigned to it, Haenel asserted that "the collective state is not something different from the federal state, but is the federal state itself." He emphasised that under this conception the complete and essential characteristics of the state are to be found in the federal state alone.

§ 2

Paul Laband developed a federal theory based on a conception of positivist political jurisprudence in his epoch-making publication *Das Staatsrecht des Deutschen Reiches* in 1876.

He, like other contemporaries, accepted Gerber's positivistic formalism and emended his predecessor's principles for the purpose of their practical application, especially to the theory of federalism.

However authoritative Laband might be as a positivist jurist, it was difficult for him to extend the boundaries of formalistic public law and open the way for his new conception of legal technique.

He defined the state as "a juristic person," holding that "the state has independent supreme rights with regard to the carrying out of its activities and obligations and power of will"—that is,

[1] A. Haenel: *Studien zum Deutschen Staatsrechte*, 1873, p. 66.

the will of the state "is not the sum of the wills of its members, but a will independent of and above the wills of individuals."

His exposition of the state as the sovereign person to rule over its members paved the way to acceptance of Gerber's definition of sovereignty which was absolute, unlimited and indivisible internally, and limited and divisible by its will externally.

Laband set up the criterion of this highest sovereign power as a "power of self-determination" which could not legally be bound by decrees of any other powers.

Starting with this fundamental assertion as to the state Laband criticised the union of states.

His attitude towards federal union was, however, that of positivist formalism. Whatever different objects and organisations might exist in the unions of states, these unions must belong to one of two categories of legal conceptions; the "treaty-based or international" conception on the one hand, and the "corporative or constitutional" conception on the other; in other words, the former was based on "legal relationship" and the latter on "juristic personality."[1]

Using this federal criterion he analysed the German federal empire from its origin.

He argued that the German federal organisation was inaugurated by the ending of dualism in the German *Bund* by the Prussian declaration in the *Reichstag* on June 14, 1866, and the treaty of union of August 18, 1866, built on the international basis, and its relation to the federal constitution were of the greatest importance "for the common constitutional conception" of the North German union and the later German Empire.[2]

This August treaty of the North German union, which was contracted between Prussia and fifteen other North German states, laid down the obligations of the contracting parties, which were based on international duties and rights, and established the permanency of the union.

This *August-Bund* was to him entirely an international law basis for the establishment of the union, but in no respect was it the constitutional foundation of the North German union.[3]

Nevertheless, the successive proposals of the state, and the legal decisions of the *Reichstag* of the union,[4] led to divergent

---

[1] Paul Laband: *Das Staatsrecht des Deutschen Reiches*, 1876, Vol. I, p. 6; *Deutsches Reichsstaatsrecht*, 1919, pp. 16–17.
[2] Paul Laband: *Das Staatsrecht des Deutschen Reiches*, 1876, Vol. I, p. 17.
[3] Ibid., p. 19.   [4] Ibid., pp. 20–25.

opinions with regard to the legal basis of the North German union.

Max von Seydel, on the one hand, expounded the view that "the constitution in agreement with the North German *Reichstag*" had become equally the territorial law of all the confederated states, and the North German confederation constitution had become the "state law" of every federal state—nothing more and nothing less. Hence he drew the conclusion that all the laws issued on the basis of the federal constitution "derived their validity from the state constitutional laws, that is, were territorial laws."

Haenel, on the other hand, asserted that the content of the federal constitution was one that was quite impossible for the state constitutions; it presupposed a union of states whose organisation it prescribed, whereas a territorial law could regulate only matters falling within the scope of the territorial state, and not those which presuppose the existence of a number of states. The North German union and its constitution could not come into an actual and legal existence simply by means of a number of "particular laws," however identical in their terms, but was based on federal "organs of will and action" which had been anticipated in the federal constitution, agreed with the *Reichstag*, and adopted as "the highest legal expression of will."[1]

These views Laband criticised from his fundamental notion of law. He put forward the legal assertion that "in the modern sense of constitutional law the form of law is, as is well known, applicable not merely when a legal rule in a state is to be sanctioned, but also to every manifestation of the state will for which the agreement of the territorial head and the territorial representatives is necessary."[2]

The word "law" had a twofold meaning; a material one and a formal one.

The law in the formal sense is "a form of the manifestation of will of the state, no matter what its content may be."

The foundation of the North German union and the entry of the North German states into the union could not be considered "as the setting up of a rule of law or of a complexity of rules of law, but as an act, as a legal action of the North German states."[3] In other words, these states as persons capable of exercising will and action gave effect to a determination of will by the formation of the North German union.

[1] Paul Laband: *Das Staatsrecht des Deutschen Reiches*, 1876, Vol. I, p. 29.
[2] Ibid., p. 30. [3] Ibid.

Laband therefore asserted that the North German federal constitution was not an agreement of the laws of the individual states, and its sanction was not given for each state by the constitutional state authority, but the determination of each individual state to enter the union defined by this constitution was declared in the state by means of a territorial law.[1]

The North German *Bund*, therefore, could not exist without a determinate constitution, and moreover the sanction of this constitution could not be given by the *Bund* itself, but only by the decisions of the confederated states.

Thus the criterion of whether the federal union belonged to an international or a constitutional union depended on whether or not it maintained its form as a state.

Since the union was brought into being by the federated states, which preceded it and united together for this purpose, it followed that its constitution was not derived from itself, but from all the states which had a share in its formation.[2]

For the acceptance of the constitution of the North German union the sovereign of each state required the consent of the state representative assembly and it was essential that the state decision should be expressed in the form of law.

Then Laband examined the formation of the German Empire. The new German Empire was the outcome of the successive decisions taken by the treaties between the North German union and the several Southern German states during 1870, the Treaty of Versailles in November 1870, and the Treaty of Berlin of December 1870.[3]

By these treaties between the North German union and the Southern German states the formal relationship of the constitution was entirely changed, and the German union changed its name to that of "the German Empire," and the president of the union became the "German Emperor."

This transformation was of great importance for the juristic exposition of the federal system in Germany.

Laband observed that the Versailles Treaty of November 1870 was analogous to the Berlin Treaty of August 1886, and they were both entirely international in character and established reciprocal treaty-based rights and duties.

[1] Paul Laband: *Das Staatsrecht des Deutschen Reiches*, 1876, Vol. I, p. 31.
[2] Ibid., p. 33.
[3] Treaty between the North German Union and Baden and Hesse, November 15, 1870. Treaty between the North German Union and Würtemberg, November 25, 1870. Treaty between the North German Union and Bavaria, November 23, 1870. Treaty of Berlin, December 8, 1870.

But he made a distinction between this position and that which was created when the Southern German states entered the union as member states in January 1871.

This distinction was to him twofold. Firstly, even though there was no legal continuity between the old German Empire and the North German union, yet there existed a real legal continuity between the North German union and the new German Empire. And secondly, the August union did not settle a definite constitution, which the North German union was to have, but only the manner in which a constitution should be established for that union.

The "November Treaties" were founded on the constitution of the North German union and arranged for the extension of the union.

Therefore although the legal relationship between the North German *Bund* and the Southern German states rested on the same international treaty basis, yet the legal fulfilment of a treaty was transformed into the legal exercise of the power of the *Reich*, since its constitution came into being through the authority of the *Reichstag* on January 1, 1871.

Laband explained that the imperial constitution was transferred from the *Verfassungs-Redaktion* to the *Publikations-Gesetz*, which in its turn was replaced by the "formal validity of the imperial constitution of April 16, 1871."[1]

Laband endeavoured to test this German federal empire by his juristic conception of category and inquired whether the Empire was a state or a union of states for the common discharge of the state tasks. In regard to this he asserted, like Haenel, that the basic contrast between the state and the union of states is exactly the same as that in the sphere of private law between the juristic person and the association. Therefore the organisation, the indefinite duration, or the number of tasks obligatory on the *Reich* are not sufficient basis for the decision of this question.

The fulfilment of the same tasks and the same purposes in private law could be carried out in the legal form of either a juristic person or of an association, and also the internal structure of an association could approximate to the constitution of a juristic personality; and on the other hand, whilst this constitution could to a considerable extent take up elements from the association, the juristic person and the association were essentially so different from one another that the gulf could not be bridged.

Therefore Laband asserted that "in spite of all existing transi-

[1] Paul Laband: *Das Staatsrecht des Deutschen Reiches*, 1876, Vol. I, p. 50.

tional forms and compromises a state is never a confederation and a confederation is never a state, and there does not exist any political structure which is both simultaneously, since the one is the negation of the other."[1]

This contrast between a juristic person and *Sozietät* was that between the "legal subject" and the "legal relationship." The confederation is "a legal relationship between states"; the state is "an organised unity, a person" or legal subject. And at the same time it is self-evident that there are legal relationships between the state and its members, just as there are between the corporation of private law and its members.

Therefore, however extensive and important its state activities, every confederation is "in accordance with its juristic nature a creation not of constitutional law, but of international law"; whereas, however loosely its members may be united, the state cannot be governed by the principles of that law.

The legal basis of the confederation, as of the society, is the "treaty" or contract, but the legal principle of the state, just as that of the corporation of private law, is the constitution or statute.[2]

The nature of juristic personality involves independent legal capability which also entails an independent power of will. But the juristic person in private law is limited to the sphere of *Vermögensrecht* (property law), whereas the state as a legal personality maintains independent legal ability and independent power of will in the sphere of the public law—that is, of supreme rights.[3]

The juristic personality of the state is based on the fact that the state has independent powers for the purpose of carrying out its tasks and duties, and an independent authoritative will.

In the confederation the will of the union is only the expression of the common will of the members, even in cases where it has been arranged that the will of the majority shall be binding.[4] On the other hand, in the state, even in the consolidated state, the will of the state is distinct from that of its members and is not the sum of their wills, but an independent will even when the members are called on to co-operate in forming the "state will."

In the confederation the public supreme rights belong to the member states, even though they are to be exercised in common or on agreed lines—but in the state these supreme rights are not vested in the members, but in the state independently. Laband

[1] Paul Laband: *Das Staatsrecht des Deutschen Reiches*, 1876, Vol. I, p. 57.
[2] Ibid.   [3] Ibid.   [4] Ibid., p. 58.

asserted that the rights of the state are not "rights of members but right over members."[1]

This attitude towards the legal categorical conception was a leading characteristic of Laband's federalism. According to his conception of the state there existed only the *Staatenbund* on the one hand and the unitary state on the other. And of the unitary forms of the state there were two kinds, the unitary state and the consolidated state.[2]

In the former the highest power of the state—"the state authority"—extended directly over the territory belonging to the state and the people living in it. As people and land were directly subordinate to the supreme law of the state, the members of the state were "the single individuals," and as such were the object of the public law of the state, i.e. they were "subjects."

The consolidated state, on the other hand, differed in that it was a twofold organisation in which "firstly land and people are subordinate to a lower state authority, and next the states are subject to an upper state authority," which the Germans called *Reichsgewalt*.

Therefore the direct object of the supreme rights vested in the imperial authority was the states, and the states, as unities, as the juristic persons of the public law, were "the members," the subjects of the empire.

He asserted that by the very nature of the empire "the member state is master to those beneath it and subject to those above it."[3]

In this consolidated state it was possible, however, that in certain cases the *Reichsgewalt* could exercise its authority directly over the territory and individual subjects of the empire, and that in this way it could, through the authority of the individual states, affect directly land and people, the physical basis of every state. In certain cases the authority of member states could even be put aside, so that the citizens and territory became direct objects of the supreme rights of the state.[4]

Therefore he assumed that the nature of the consolidated state was not altered by the fact that its conception was not applied on lines rigidly laid down but that its fundamental characteristic was the principle that two or more state authorities were superimposed, so that the imperial authority had states for its subjects.

Laband held that the consolidated state could suitably be termed a *Staatenstaat*.[5]

[1] Paul Laband: *Das Staatsrecht des Deutschen Reiches*, 1876, Vol. I, p. 58.
[2] Ibid., p. 70.   [3] Ibid., p. 71.   [4] Ibid.   [5] Ibid.

He asserted that not every consolidated state was a federal state. The *Reichsgewalt* could be exempted from the state authority of the member states so that these were subjected to one of themselves or to a third party—this system resembled the subordination of the vassal states under a feudal lord, as in the old German Empire. Or the *Reichsgewalt* could be vested in "the collectivity of the individual states," considered as a unity.

What Laband designated as a federal state was one in which "the holders of the state authority of the member states regarded as a whole form a juristic personality of public law, and this legal personality is the subject of the supreme (and dominant) rights which are together comprised within the term federal authority." In this the individual states are not in any sense subordinate to others, but are united to establish a "collectivity of a higher order."

He asserted that the member states in the federal state were not constitutionally subordinate to a physical head different from themselves, but to "an ideal person of which they themselves are the essence."[1]

In the federal state every individual state is considered to be the object of the *Reichsgewalt*, but as a member of the juristic personality of the federal state, that is as legally participating in the government, it is also considered as a subject of the *Reichsgewalt*.

On this assumption Laband concluded that the participation of the individual state in the empire was not "a separate right as in the private law cases of the society or ownership," and the supreme rights of the empire did not belong either *pro diviso* or *pro indiviso* to the individual states, but the participation of the individual states was based exclusively on "their membership in the empire and their consequent rights to take a share and co-operate in the deliberations and activities of the empire."[2]

He asserted that this was "the juristic conception of the federal state" as exemplified in the constitution of the German Empire. On this fundamental assumption Laband pointed out in what respects his views, as just indicated, differed from the prevailing theory of the federal state.

First of all he attacked Waitz's theory of divided sovereignty. In this discussion he entirely favoured Seydel's conception of sovereignty and agreed with Held's assertion as to the "absolute impossibility" of the division of sovereignty. As sovereignty

[1] Paul Laband: *Das Staatsrecht des Deutschen Reiches*, 1876, Vol. I, p. 72.
[2] Ibid.

was in its nature indivisible and unlimited, so the question was whether the authority of the individual states in the carrying out of the state activities entrusted to them must conform to the standard set up by the authority of the collective state, or whether, on the contrary, the standard existing in the individual states formed a limitation on the exercise of the authority of the central state.

If a limitation were imposed on the authority of the individual state by an external will differing from its own, then its sovereignty was denied and it was no longer sovereign in the sphere of state activity assigned to it, since even in this sphere it felt either directly or indirectly the influence of central authority and was legally bound to obey it.

The real point at issue was the ownership of the supreme power—it belonged either to the central authority or to the member states—and which of the two was entitled to decide on the limits of competence of the other.

Laband, in this case, agreed entirely with Haenel that "division of sovereignty is not compatible with the nature of the federal state." In the confederation sovereignty belongs entirely to the individual states, but in the federal state entirely to the collective state.[1]

Secondly, according to Waitz the characteristic of the federal state was that it exercised its supreme rights not through the medium of the individual states but within its own sphere directly on the subjects.

Not only Waitz, but also nearly all thinkers, such as Gerber and even G. Meyer, had advocated the same principle, von Mohl and Holtzendorff being the only jurists who maintained that this direct authority was not in itself essential.

By the very nature of the federal state the relationship between the collective and the individual states was one not of co-ordination but rather of subordination. Laband thought it right for the federal state to be organised on the model of the unitary state, provided that the division of sovereignty was admitted and the federal state and the "unitary state" were both considered as "partial states."

In contrast to the confederation the federal state was a "state above individual states," a "sovereign political commonwealth" (*Gemeinwesen*) which had to carry out in accordance with its own will the "totality" of the state tasks and made use of the member states for this purpose. Then the significance of the

[1] Paul Laband: *Das Staatsrecht des Deutschen Reiches*, 1876, Vol. I, p. 75.

comparison between the federal state and the unitary state did not lie in their similarity but in their differences. The former was an international association relationship, whereas the latter was a state, i.e. a "juristic subject."

The legislation of the North German union and of the empire furnished numerous examples of the exercise by the federal authority of authoritative rights over the individual states. But Laband objected to Waitz's assumption as to the nature of the federal state and considered that "as long as the individual state retained the judicial power as an independent right" the penal code was a "standard" which the empire set up for the individual states.[1]

The individual states were responsible for the laws of the empire being carried out within their territories by the administrative officials and courts of justice, and as a rule there was no direct dependence of the officials on the central authority of the federal state, even in the territories controlled by the legislation of the empire.

It was clear that the federal laws were binding not only on the states as such but also on the subjects, but it did not follow that there was a direct subordination of the people to the federal authority and that single individuals within the sphere of the imperial legislation were "emancipated from the law of the individual states."

In the confederation there was no legislative authority for the union, and only the individual states could make laws; even if a federal decision was designated as a law it was really only an "agreement" which was to be shaped into law; whereas in the federal state the issue of the federal law was not a command to the individual states, but itself a rule with full legal sanction. In other words, the "federal law" was valid not only for the states, but also within the states, "because the states, with their lands and peoples, are subordinate to the central authority."

The federal law formed a part of the legal order not only of the whole, but also of its constituents—namely, the individual states. A promulgation of the federal law by the individual states would be inconsistent, because the law cannot be promulgated by the party for whom it was made.

Therefore Laband laid down that in the federal state the federal law binds directly the subjects of the individual states; but that it was quite wrong to conclude from this that the citizens of the individual states were freed from the state authority and

[1] Paul Laband: *Das Staatsrecht des Deutschen Reiches*, 1876, Vol. I, p. 79.

directly subordinated to the federal authority. He also asserted that the direct exercise of administration of law was not essential to the federal state, and it was simply a matter of choice whether the federal state carried out its administration and jurisdiction by itself or handed them over or delegated them to the individual states.[1]

Thirdly, he criticised the Waitzian doctrine of the federal state in which the individual states were excluded from the guidance of common affairs and the government was in no manner dependent on the individual states. He disagreed also with Waitz's idea that an assembly of delegates appointed by the individual states was a characteristic of the confederation sufficient in itself to differentiate it from the federal state.

This doctrinaire conception of the federal state Laband explained as being only a partial truth, because Waitz had taken the "species" for the "genus"—that is to say, had confused the federal state with the consolidated state.

The consolidated state, or *Staatenstaat*, required a state authority which stood above that of the individual states and consequently was different from the latter. Laband remarked that as the sovereignty could belong to different owners, either to the collectivity of the people or to a few persons or to a single person—that is to say, to either a democracy, aristocracy, or monarchy—the state authority in the *Staatenstaat* could belong either to the collectivity of the member states or to one of them.

He therefore concluded that for the genus, the consolidated state, a definite organisation was not actually essential; on the other hand, the species, the federal state, is conceptionally determined by a particular form of organisation—namely, by the participation of the member states in the formation of the collective will.[2]

Finally, Laband inquired into the conception of the federal state as an "organised and active political commonwealth" and into Haenel's view of the impossibility of the division of state duties between the federal and the individual state authorities, since he firmly believed that the "state was simply the federal state regarded as a totality comprising the collectivity and the member states."

Laband accepted this theory only if one regarded the state merely as an "objective institution." For the juristic development of the federal constitutional law the state must be considered as

[1] Paul Laband: *Das Staatsrecht des Deutschen Reiches*, Vol. I, 1876, p. 81.
[2] Ibid., p. 83.

"a subjective institution controlled by the laws." Comparing the federal state and the individual states as the subjects of the supreme law, both had important duties to fulfil towards their subjects and within their territories, and "regarded as separate spheres" were both states; nevertheless, the individual states were not sovereign but subordinate to the federal state. If, however, validity as a state was conceded to the individual state only as a "collective organisation," then the individual state appeared merely as an institution of the federal state, as a part of its organisation. In this latter case the difference between the federal state and the decentralised unitary state disappeared.

Laband emphatically asserted that the state as an institution for carrying out certain *Kulturaufgaben* was not completed by the co-operation of the federal state and the individual states; all the circles, communes and other self-governing bodies must be recognised as "members of the whole" and essential components of the "collective organism."

But the nature of the federal state was based on the fact that it allowed for members with separate individual existence as "states."[1]

Proceeding to the relationship of the empire to the individual states Laband asserted that starting from the principle of the state as a juristic personality the subject of the state authority must be "the state itself."

The juristic construction and scientific formation of the constitutional law by means of the personification of the state would lose its validity directly the monarch or the people or anyone else was accepted as the subject of state authority and consequently as the real sovereign.[2]

Similarly, the personality of the state as the subject of supreme rights would vanish if the state authority, which was "the essence of all these rights," were bestowed not on the state, "the organic community" itself, but on the princes or the parliaments or both together or anyone else who was a "subject different from the state itself." Thus applying this general principle to the German Empire, Laband deduced that the subject of the imperial authority could only be the empire itself, "as an independent ideal personality," whose basis was "the collectivity of the German individual states."

If the individual states carried out state duties in the manner of the state, then no reason existed for denying their recognition as states.

[1] Paul Laband: *Das Staatsrecht des Deutschen Reiches*, 1876, Vol. I, p. 84.
[2] Ibid., p. 86.

For a political recognition of the federal state as a form of associated organisation it was sufficient to regard the individual states as members of the collective organ; with regard to legal relations, it was "requisite that the federal state and individual state be considered as subjects of state rights and duties."

But Laband assumed that in the conception presented by Haenel it was not evident that the supreme rights belonging to the federal state are directly effective over individual states, that the federal state authority controls individual states when they are regarded as persons, gives them the standard of laws which legally determines their actions, and, as a rule by means of them and consequently indirectly, rules over the individual subjects of the states. Therefore he stated that of all the authors who up till now had tried to establish the conception of a federal state "Haenel has come nearest to the view here expressed."

The German Empire, by adopting the last principle, was "no monarchy," but—if the expression could be applied to a number of juristic persons—a democracy, that is to say, "the whole of the members of the empire, and not a *Kaiser*, were the possessors of sovereignty"; in other words, the German Empire was not a "juristic person of forty million members, but of twenty-five member states."

On this basis of individual state membership of the empire and participation in the federal authority it followed that the exercise of that membership was a "life activity of the state" and not a personal prerogative of the territorial lord. Laband assumed that the governments of the individual states in the exercise of their shares in the imperial authority could not be separated, but mutually represented the complete and living activity of the state. Therefore he asserted that "the government of the individual state, in accordance with its constitutional law, is politically and legally responsible for the manner in which it uses its membership of the empire."

He assumed that every juristic person required representation and organs capable of carrying out its will and action.

This *Träger* of the state authority was called sovereign, because he exercised the legal power belonging to the state conceived as a person, and in Laband's time this *Träger* of sovereignty could be either an individual, such as a monarch, or the collectivity of all the members of the state.

From this participation of the individual states in the federal authority there arose diversity of opinions as to the position of the individual states in respect of sovereignty.

Laband explained in what sense sovereignty could be attributed to the individual state.

The individual state, compared with the empire, was not sovereign, and since sovereignty was indivisible, it was not sovereign even "within its own sphere." But since the German individual states had a share in the federal authority over themselves they were not subordinate to an outside authority, but separately subordinate only to a "collectivity formed of themselves." Consequently the German states "as a collectivity" were "sovereign."

From this fundamental argument it was quite justifiable that the heads of the individual state should retain undiminished "their personal sovereignty" and also the constitutional and international rights of honour associated with it.

Therefore there could be no objection from the constitutional standpoint to designating the individual states as sovereign, provided that this was understood by reference to their share in the imperial authority and not to their position vis-à-vis the federal empire.[1]

So Laband asserted that from the nature of the federal state as "a public law corporation consisting of states," it followed that the member state had rights and duties.

The organisation of the juristic personality of the federal state was in itself the object of the objective legal order and created for its members subjective privileges: rights which were legally limited and protected; to these rights corresponded the public law rights and duties.

Laband summarised his views regarding the subordination of the individual states to the federal empire in the three following arguments:—

Firstly, he conceived that for the actual supreme rights the individual states were "put out of action," since the empire discharged both its legislative and administrative duties with its own officials and exercised its own rights independently and directly.

Secondly, he indicated that "in a wide sphere of the supreme rights of the empire" the individual states were "self-governing bodies."

He criticised the political meaning of self-government which Gneist was the first to develop.

He denied Gneist's definition of self-government as "an intermediate form between state and society," and as "an internal

[1] Paul Laband: *Das Staatsrecht des Deutschen Reiches*, 1876, Vol. I, p. 94.

legal administration of localities by honorary officials with payment of the costs by means of communal taxes." He also objected to the distinction between "magisterial self-government" and "economic self-administration (*Selbstverwaltung*)," because "the supreme right of the state will be operative in both spheres of administration."

He favoured Rösler's idea of self-government in which all self-government in the material sense was based upon the freedom of natural life and conscience, as well as on freedom of religion, science and art, and free decision and action must be retained in all circumstances in which they were regarded as an ethical necessity.

In order to determine the conception of self-government for the purposes of constitutional law he laid it down that self-government was "not an intermediate body between state and society, but one between state and subject."

Instead of the state carrying out its supreme rights directly, it delegated their execution to persons who were subordinate to it, but who had a "separate public legal sphere and a distinct existence."

Therefore self-government rested upon the self-limitation of the state, with regard to the exercise of its tasks and the enforcement of its magisterial supreme rights, to the establishment of standard norms (rules) and to the enforcement of their observance, whereas the application of these norms themselves was handed over to intermediary members.

At the same time Laband disagreed with the view that self-government was a manifestation of the free action of individuals.

In self-government, since the individual was the object of magisterial rights, it was not the natural freedom of the individuals which was active, but the "state authority" with "legal enforcement upon the individuals." On the other hand, it was not the state itself which carried out this enforcement, but the public law personality which was placed between the state and the individual and was used by the state to carry out its duties.

Agreeing with Stein's notion of self-government, Laband asserted that the natural basis of the self-governing body was exactly the same as that of the state—namely, a territorially limited sphere, with the citizens settled therein; and the legal source of its right was the sovereign supreme right of the state which had handed over or left to the self-governing body the independent management of juristic rights and duties.[1]

[1] Paul Laband: *Das Staatsrecht des Deutschen Reiches*, 1876, Vol. I, p. 103.

From his notion of self-government he conceived that the individual state in the federal empire was within its own sphere of activity an independent person (corporation) which carried out its administration under the sovereign legislation and supervision of the empire.

Thirdly, Laband asserted that besides the matters subordinate to the legislation and supervision of the empire, there existed a wide sphere of public law functions which remained to the individual states, such as the fixing of succession rights, electoral rights, the constitution of the civil service and so forth.

With regard to these affairs the individual states were not self-governing parts of the empire, but their position was a freer and more independent one since they were subordinate neither to the legislation nor to the supervision of the empire.

Thus the legal condition as to the relation of the individual states to the empire was that a sphere of state activity and power remained to the individual states in which they and not the empire were "the master." But it was equally incorrect to designate the individual states as sovereign in regard to the sphere of duties entrusted to them.

Laband explained that the distinction of these spheres from those in which the empire was competent, according to Article 4 of the imperial constitution, consisted only in the fact that "the individual states did not merely have self-government, but also set up the legal standards of the administration by determining the aims, purposes and means of the administration."

The chief characteristic difference between the sphere of competence belonging to the empire and that not belonging to it was that in the former the empire set up the "legal standard" of administration, and in the latter this was done by the individual states.

In this respect Laband assumed that in the latter sphere the individual states possessed the right of "self-legislation"—that is to say, "autonomy."

"Autonomy" was sometimes conceived to be the natural freedom of mankind to regulate its legal relations by the action of its will. But this conception, just as the misconception of self-government, was not a legal definition, but only an expression for the legally recognised faculty of will and action. Laband asserted that autonomy in the juristic sense is always a legislative power, but "in contrast to sovereignty."

The relation of the individual states to the federal empire was a subordinate one, partly as components of the empire, partly as self-governing bodies directly controlled by it, and partly as autonomous non-sovereign states.

Thus he explained the federal functions and relations in the federal state from the standpoint of the legal relationship of "membership right" and "individual right."[1]

On this assumption he recognised the existence of the individual state as a member of the federal state and as a "non-sovereign state."

The idea of the non-sovereign state was to him compatible with that of the member state,[2] which state as such, although not in the strictly legal sense, could be ordinarily designated "state."

He explained that when several hitherto independent states united together in such a manner as to have a higher authority over them, then they ceased to be sovereign, but they did not necessarily cease to be states.

If they still retained a very large proportion of the former state tasks and duties, and if they did not forfeit their political existence, the designation of "state" was left to them and the newly created higher authority was known by names such as *Bund* or *Reich*. Laband asserted that they were not only called states but actually were states, for they had not been degraded to the position of mere administrative districts of the *Bund*, but had remained "independent holders of very comprehensive and important supreme rights."[3]

Laband's exposition of federalism was legally so precise and explicit that his theory was of outstanding importance in Germany.

Philipp Zorn, professor of law at the University of Königsberg, published his work *Das Staatsrecht des Deutschen Reiches* in 1880 and laid down a theory of federalism based on Laband's formula.

Like other German thinkers, he started by formulating a conception of the state in order to define the consolidated state.

He held that "the state must juristically be conceived as a personality," since only in that way could one make the necessary presupposition of a "will of the state."[4]

He assumed that "the will of the personality of the state" was directed towards supremacy, quoting Savigny's dictum that "the state authority is will, is that of power," and he added that the nature of the state consisted in "the exercise of supreme rights."

[1] Paul Laband: *Das Staatsrecht des Deutschen Reiches*, 1876, Vol. I, p. 109.
[2] Ibid., pp. 62–63.   [3] Ibid., pp. 63–64.
[4] Philipp Zorn: *Das Staatsrecht des Deutschen Reiches*, 2nd Ed., 1895, Vol. I, p. 62.

So he declared that "the unlimited unity of collective supreme rights is sovereignty," and "sovereignty is the first and highest conceptional characteristic of the state."[1]

Zorn based his consideration of the nature of the state on the same reasoning as Laband, that "where there is no sovereignty, no state can exist"; and the only point on which he did not agree with Laband's theory was in dropping the idea of sovereignty as the essential conception of the state, whether emphasising, in adherence to the old theory, that it was the "first and highest characteristic of the state."

Nevertheless, in his definition of sovereignty he, like Laband, asserted that "sovereignty was the highest authority" over which no higher power existed, and could never be divided. Therefore sovereignty was "a unified conception" in both international and constitutional law. But like Laband he thought that it might be limited in its exercise internationally by means of treaty obligations between sovereign states, and internally by means of the formation of unions of states. He pointed out that "by this limitation the unity of sovereignty, regarded as necessary for the state, was not altered."

In the case of a number of independent states a limitation of sovereignty could be imposed only by treaty between state and state; such a treaty applied as a rule only to single sovereign rights.

But the conception of the federal state was indispensable, its logical justification was the scientific need of describing a particular form of state union in contrast to the simple unitary state.

In his general classification of the unions of states, a personal union was not a consolidated state, but two quite separate states under one head; a real union was by no means a "legal and precise conception," nor was an empire; a *Staatenstaat* was a federal state; and an alliance was a confederation.

Therefore he concentrated his study of the theory of the confederation and the federal state on the consolidated form of the state.

Like Laband, he asserted that the two conceptions, federal state and confederation, differed in that the former was "a state" and the latter was not; the former was "a unified personality," and the latter was a "union of many independent state personalities"; in the former the sovereignty was vested in the "central authority," and in the latter in the "individual

[1] Philipp Zorn: *Das Staatsrecht des Deutschen Reiches*, 2nd Ed., 1895, Vol. I, p. 63.

states"; the legal basis of the union in the former could be "law only" and in the latter "treaty only" the former was "a legal subject" and the latter was "a legal relationship"; the latter represented "a number of united but sovereign state authorities," and the former "a unitary but federally organised sovereign state authority."[1]

To Zorn in the confederation the members retained their sovereignty, but exercised it under a pact which imposed on them certain definite limitations, and no circumstance could alter the pact from being concluded as a "permanent" or "indissoluble" pact.[2]

The non-fulfilment or violation on the part of a member of the obligations undertaken by treaty would be sufficient justification for the dissolution of the relationship by all the others. Even if such a contingency were provided for in the federal pact, and courts appointed for settling difficulties of this kind, yet the decisions of the court would be based on the "treaty obligations."

Therefore he held definitely that the confederation was "no constitutional commonwealth," "no subject of state authority." It had "no authority as a state, but only particular delegated supreme rights."[3]

On this assumption the confederation was conceptionally no different from an alliance, because both had the same characteristics.

In the discussion of the federal state he, like Laband, admitted that the formation of the federal state out of states hitherto sovereign would be as a rule the result of treaty, but this was not always the case.

And this state treaty did not require the contracting parties to limit themselves in the exercise of sovereignty, but rather that the contracting parties should renounce their sovereignty in favour of a central authority, to be constituted in such a manner that they retained a large part of their sovereign rights, i.e. they received them back in order to exercise them.[4]

In the federal state the central authority limited its own legal exercise of sovereignty in favour of the individual states, whereas in the confederation the individual states limited by treaty their own sovereignty in favour of the central authority.

Therefore he emphasised the view that in the theory of the federal state "individual sovereignty" as such disappeared and

---

[1] Philipp Zorn: *Das Staatsrecht des Deutschen Reiches*, 2nd Ed., 1895. Vol, I, pp. 69–70.
[2] Ibid., p. 70.   [3] Ibid., p. 71.   [4] Ibid., pp. 71–72.

only continued to exist "constitutionally as a part of the joint sovereignty vested in the central authority."[1]

Directly the renunciation of individual sovereignty was made practical by the establishment of the central authority the pact ceased to have real legal validity and existed only as an historical fact, and the laws issued by the central authority became more and more authoritative.

Consequently, the individual state became a subject of a central authority and had to obey its laws, and therefore "the federal pact could not be dissolved, because it had ceased actually to exist."[2]

All disputes would be decided without appeal by the supreme court appointed by the central state authority and provided with every means of constitutional enforcement of its decisions.

From this general theory of the federal state he examined the German Empire as a federal state, and criticised every detailed function of the empire, and put before us a miniature of Laband's *Staatsrecht des Deutschen Reiches*.

Constantinus Bake, a Dutch jurist, published *Beschouwingen over den Statenbond en den Bondsstaat* in 1881. Although not a disciple of Zorn, he followed the same line of argument in regard to the federal theory, and also upheld the idea of indivisible and unlimited sovereignty as "a reasonable postulate for every state organisation."[3]

He emphatically declared that the federal state was alone sovereign, since it was a "state" whose limitation of sovereignty was determined by the application of the principle of *Kompetenz-Kompetenz*.[4]

He, like his contemporaries, drew the conclusion from his historical study of the federal theory that the individual states were to be regarded as provinces, and no longer as states, and their powers were subject to revision or amendment by the central federal authority.[5]

It is true that he considered the confederation purely as a treaty relationship, but he also adhered to the conception put forward by earlier publicists of an international personality belonging to the confederation as well as to the individual states.

As the basis of his theory of the sovereignty which was essential

---

[1] Philipp Zorn: *Das Staatsrecht des Deutschen Reiches*, 2nd Ed., 1895, Vol. I, p. 72.   [2] Ibid., p. 74.
[3] C. Bake: *Beschouwingen over den Statenbond en den Bondsstaat*, 1881, pp. 14–15.
[4] Ibid., pp. 172–176.   [5] Ibid., pp. 213–216.

for the conception of the state he discussed the nature of the federal state as compared with that of the confederation, without, however, contributing anything new.

The federal state as a state was "sovereign," whereas in the confederation, which was based on legal relationships, the individual states were sovereign; therefore confederation, in common with other unions of states, and especially with the alliance, had its formation in the bringing together of states which retained their sovereignty. The difference between alliance and confederation, according to Bake, was that the former was not permanent and indissoluble like the latter and that the confederation was "a juristic person founded on international law," whereas alliance had no juristic personality.

He pointed out that the characteristic of the confederation was that unanimity was essential for the amendment of the federal pact, because if the decision of the majority vote was valid, then the union would no longer be a confederation but a federal state.

The renunciation of the sovereignty of the individual states and the application of the *Kompetenz-Kompetenz* were the characteristics of the federal state as a state.

Bluntschli in his later works, *Das moderne Völkerrecht* and *Allgemeine Staatslehre*, and Schulze in his *Lehrbuch des deutschen Staatsrechts* in 1881, discussed the federal problem on almost the same lines as Bake. But a little later in the eighties Bluntschli modified his early acceptance of divided sovereignty and assumed a "relative sovereignty" in which the sovereignty of the federal state could be limited in extent, but not in content.

On the other hand he advocated the unity and indivisibility of sovereignty.[1] No modification or enlargement of his federal doctrine is manifest in his later works. Schulze also never abandoned Waitz's theory of the state and accepted the distinction between the national and the international union. The confederation was organised not as a national but as an international personality, whereas other unions, such as the alliance, which were dependent on the association treaty, had no international personality; the German union was internationally a single person.

His theory of federalism was better than that of Bluntschli, but since he failed to draw the logical deduction from actual conditions it had no special influence.

[1] Bluntschli: *Allgemeine Staatslehre* (*The Theory of the State*, Eng. Trans.), p. 506.

§ 3

The first great exposition of the theory of the union of states in Germany was the epoch-making publication of Georg Jellinek's *Die Lehre von den Staatenverbindungen* in 1882.

First of all Jellinek inquired into the validity of the theory of public law which had hitherto prevailed, and condemned not only the vague knowledge of public law, but also the inadequate conception of *Staatenverbindungen*, which had never been formed on a basis of scientific political theory. The formation of the North American federal state and the Swiss and German federal unions invalidated the previously existing theory of the unitary state.

He observed that the reason why science had not explained the actual phenomena satisfactorily was "the false or insufficient theories" which it used "as the basis of the investigation of the subject."[1]

Difference of opinion regarding a scientific object indicated uncertainty in principle and method, the cause of which was to be sought mostly in bad groundwork. The first step to acquiring an adequate conception of the state was to obtain an accurate knowledge of the principles and methods of constitutional and international law.

According to Jellinek legal philosophy was the source of inspiration for the scientific conception of the state. He emphatically asserted that from the days of *Naturrecht* down to his own time the conception of the state and the definition of its qualities and functions had been a matter of philosophical speculation.

His remarkable phrase that "the state formulated by legal philosophy is not a concrete actual state but an abstract state which has yet to come to realisation" was his starting-point for the formation of the theory of the state.

Accordingly, as a man could never form "his ideas quite independently from his environment," the so-called "standard or normal state" has many traces of the state as it exists, and is essentially only the actual state amplified and developed into a type. But as a whole the abstract state is not a being of this world, but "an ideal for judgment and often condemnation of the state in its actual condition." This was as much the case with the mechanical "contract state" which Hobbes and Rousseau put

[1] Georg Jellinek: *Die Lehre von den Staatenverbindungen*, 1882, p. 4.

forward as with "the organic state of the modern jurisprudence." Therefore he assumed that "the knowledge of the nature and the legal quality of the standard state" was the *Allgemeine Staatsrecht*.[1]

Accordingly, in order to attain to an adequate idea it must never ignore either the "ideal content" or the historical evolution. The consequence of the twofold origin of public law was that the abstract conception and the concrete manifestation of the state life frequently existed entirely aloof from one another, without perception of the necessity of bringing them into logical harmony.

Therefore he assumed that the ideal is a standard never to be entirely attained, which need not be coincident with reality, and the positive could and might deviate from the rules applicable to the "model state."[2]

Considering the diversities of opinions, not only as to theories of the unions of states, but as to theories of the state itself, Jellinek assumed that these conflicts were the inevitable result of the lack of a unitary doctrine of public law, that deduction from ideas and induction from phenomena took ways so different that their convergence became impossible.[3]

At the same time he recognised that another obstacle to the formation of the state theory was the mingling of politics with jurisprudence, because the state as subject and object of historical fact is to the state of jurisprudence as mankind in his natural and social life as a human being is to legal personality.

Thus he assumed that if anyone tried to determine legal principle by political expediency the whole legal basis of the nature of the state and of the relations of states would be destroyed.

The study of the public law in his day had quite moved away from the old intermingling of "politics and jurisprudence." The constitution was not simply "dead form" but a power developed to "vital power."

The evolution of international life upheld "the international law as an ideal need of actual power," and the formation of international institutions, such as River Commissions or the World Postal Union and so forth, was due not to the doctrinaire definition of law, but to "the reality of law." In the modern state of the public law sense there was ample justification for

---

[1] Georg Jellinek: *Die Lehre von den Staatenverbindungen*, 1882, p. 5. [2] Ibid., p. 6.
[3] Ibid., p. 7.—Contrasts of the notion of sovereignty between Montesquieu and Pufendorf and of the notion of federal conception between Mohl and Seydel were the proof of the lack of logical consideration of the public law.

the demand that constitutional and international laws must be treated as "purely juristic sciences." The reproach of scholasticism, which might be directed against such a procedure, was baseless, because life itself claims to teach us what there is of law in the state and between states.[1] The reproach would be justified only if the juristic method were able to encompass all sides of the nature of the state; that would be as untrue as the claim that private law could explain mankind in the totality of its being.

Law is "only one side of the state; to examine the state in all its scope and content would require the co-operation of almost all the sciences because the comprehensive examination of the most complicated of all social structures presupposes the knowledge of all the physical and psychological factors which have brought it into being, condition it and maintain it."

Nevertheless, within the theory of the state, and within political science, law can be assigned a position as clearly demarcated as possible. Still Jellinek reminded us that no mechanical line of demarcation could indicate the boundaries in view of the close interdependence of all the state's activities. But at the same time Jellinek did not contemplate the complete ignoring of politics. Consideration of their political importance will in many cases lead to a deeper understanding of the abstract principles of the public law, just as the economic and moral importance of the rules of private law first reveal their true value.

An entire isolation of the public law and the consequent wasting away of its theoretical and practical content was not Jellinek's aim; he stressed only the need of avoiding the confusion of the turbulent life of the particular state with the constant purpose and rule of law.

In order to avoid this error, he quoted Pütter's dictum that "the theoretical basis of state law, as soon as one treats it as a science, and if it is to deserve the name and be of use, is quite impossible without rightly determined and general basic rules."

Starting from this Jellinek argued for (i) the separation of politics from jurisprudence—not in the sense that the jurists deny the justification of the non-juristic method or demand that it be ignored, but that there be always a clear appreciation of the boundary between the juristic and other conceptions, and

---

[1] Georg Jellinek: *Die Lehre von den Staatenverbindungen*, 1882, pp. 9–10. Otto von Gierke: "Die Grundebegriffe des Staatsrechts und die neuesten Staatsrechtstheorien," published in the *Zeitschrift für die gesamte Staatswissenschaft* in 1874, reprinted in 1915, pp. 111–115.

(ii) within the field so defined, a clear juristic investigation of the legal ideas involved.¹

The juristic investigation can be successful only if all the phenomena coming under it are carefully examined and their common characteristics compared and consolidated.

The inductive method would be equally valid for the determination of the ideas of law as of all other ideas derived from experience. Only the complication of the state relationship and the fact that man himself with his enigmatic nature forms the "molecule of the state organisation" have given rise to the belief that it can be a subject of speculation but not of investigation.

The hypothetical speculation utilised for the formation of the state theory naturally resulted in "an intuitive induction, or rather an induction" which was not consciously such.²

Agreeing with Gneist's conception of the philosophy of the state Jellinek thought that every man regards the ideas and wishes derived from his own life as something common to all people and times.

Bodin's and Hobbes' views of absolute unlimited monarchy, Locke's and Montesquieu's ideal of English constitutionalism, Hegel's idealised Prussian kingdom, and Rotteck's and Welcker's French constitutionalism were their categorical imperative for their ideal state.

Disagreeing with these methods of intuitive induction as applied to the theory of the state Jellinek observed that if an actual phenomenon did not accord with these *a priori* definitions, it was regarded at best as being something *sui generis*, and generally as a freak whose existence must be accepted without affecting the validity of the general conception. For only "the type possesses real value and anything which does not have some traces of the type is not worth examining."³

Thus "with the conception of a state formation as an irregularity politics is given the task of clearing away the irregularity, so the actuality can at last correspond to the theoretical conception—the rationalism of the theory inexorably brings about rationalisation of the fact by itself, unhistorical thinking brings antihistorical action."⁴

Jellinek asserted that the consequences of judging concrete forms by "ideal types" were nowhere more clearly shown than in the theory of the union of states.

The prevailing conception of the state was only applicable

---
¹ Georg Jellinek: *Die Lehre von den Staatenverbindungen*, 1882, pp. 10, 11.
² Ibid., p. 11.   ³ Ibid., p. 12.   ⁴ Ibid.

to the unitary state, and was not adequately compatible with the various relationships of the consolidated state.

For the establishment of the fundamental theory of the union of states the conception of sovereignty was, according to Jellinek, the principal legal criterion to determine the validity of the various theories of federalism from Waitz down to von Mohl and Seydel.[1]

The object of the theory of *Staatenverbindungen* was therefore to lay down the fundamental doctrine of sovereignty which was the essential characteristic of the state conception.[2]

His positivist attitude towards the nature of the state and of federalism was entirely due to his empirical method as compared with former scholastic theories.

The categorical imperative of the conception of sovereignty was the categorical imperative indispensable in formulating the conception of state and federal theory, although up to the formation of this categorical imperative he employed the empirical method of the federal argument, yet as soon as he reached the marginal point of this cardinal theory he departed from the empirical method and turned to the method of juristic determination.

Sovereignty, however, had been recognised as a foundation of the juristic justification of the state since Bodin in 1576, and had taken the place of the older theory of the ethical basis of the state.

Nevertheless, Jellinek claimed that the political nature of sovereignty was constantly disputed because it theoretically depended some way or other upon the political parties in the state, yet on the other hand no agreement had ever been reached with regard to the juristic character of sovereignty since it depended on theoretical assertions.

The uncertainty which prevailed in the conception of sovereignty as based on constitutional or international law was the cause of the divergent views of the early American federal theorists.[3]

---

[1] Georg Jellinek: *Die Lehre von den Staatenverbindungen*, 1882, pp. 14, 15.
[2] Ibid., p. 16.
[3] Jellinek pointed out that Travers Twiss, in *The Law of Nations*, said that the states in the union are "all sovereign states" although they are not independent. According to Wheaton, in the *Elements of International Law*, and Halleck in *International Law*, in 1861, the international sovereignty of the separate states was destroyed, their domestic sovereignty retained. According to Ortolan in *Règles Internationales et Diplomatie de la mer*, and Vollgraff in *Wodurch unterscheiden sich Staaten-Bund, Bundesstaat und Einheitsstaat von einander?* the individual states

In order to make this conception of sovereignty clear, he analysed and criticised the hitherto prevailing theory of sovereignty.

First of all he examined that notion of sovereignty which conceived of the existence of certain state tasks as the criterion of sovereignty, or in other words conceived sovereignty as the sum of the individual state powers without any internal unity. These mistaken views were mostly advocated by international jurists; even Leibnitz adduced the right to make war and peace, ambassadorial rights and the right to conclude treaties as "the essence of sovereignty."

Jellinek pointed out that this view had entirely disregarded the fact that "it is legally possible for anyone to pledge himself not to exercise a right, without thereby surrendering that right."[1] And also, arguing from his fundamental thesis of the public law, he considered that, though politically the state could be deprived of one of the supreme rights by treaty, yet politics and jurisprudence were on quite a different basis. The delegation of certain sovereign rights by the holders of these to another did not necessarily make the latter sovereign; for instance, the rights of war and peace bestowed on the East India Company by British sovereignty did not make it a sovereign power.

He asserted that the mechanical definition of sovereignty as the sum of individual supreme rights was not only "theoretically incorrect" but also "untenable in practice."

According to many legal theorists, for the recognition of a state entity as a sovereign state not merely legal (*de jure*) but also a measure of actual (*de facto*) sovereignty was required.

Jellinek condemned this conception as incompatible with the fundamental nature of international law and as a violation of international legal principles. The first principle of international law was the recognition of the equality between states without regard to their size or political importance, since even some great powers might lack real freedom as compared with others.

The actual conditions were as important in the legal life of the state as in the life of individuals. Since the actions of a usurper might have legal effects on the state within and without, it might have no sovereignty at all. Tocqueville, in *De la Démocratie en Amérique*, and Rüttimann in *Das Nord-amerikanische Bundesstaatsrecht*, proposed the division of sovereignty. Calhoun asserted that the states in the union were possessors of sovereignty and proposed the theory of nullification and secession.

[1] Georg Jellinek: *Die Lehre von den Staatenverbindungen*, 1882, p. 20.

be required that for his recognition the *Träger* of sovereignty should always be the actual possessor of it. The juristic validity of the sovereignty could not be gauged by actual facts, but was the legal consequence of its existence and dependent only on the fact that it extended over a territory and the people therein and was recognised by the other powers as a member of the family of states. What means the state possessed for maintaining its position as a power was juristically quite irrelevant.

It was customary to speak of "constitutional and international sovereignty." By the former was understood the collectivity of the supreme rights of the state to be exercised over the territory and nation, and the latter meant the supreme rights belonging to one state as compared with other states. It was, however, an inexact terminology.

It was also asserted that sovereignty had a twofold character, firstly the quality of the state as the highest power and secondly as "independent power."[1] But logically these two meanings of sovereignty were complementary one to another.

Even G. Meyer's interpretation of this dogma failed to bring conviction since it was a *contradictio in adjecto*.[2]

Jellinek asserted that the state which depended on no other will but its own was "without limitation."

Even by treaty the state was subordinated only to its own will, for it was the state itself which bound itself by granting to other states international rights and only to such an extent as itself desired.

Therefore Jellinek asserted that constitutional and international sovereignty were not different but "one and the same." He added that because every state to which constitutional supreme power belonged was therefore internationally independent, what was called "international sovereignty" was only "the necessary reflex of the constitutional supreme authority towards outside powers."[3]

In the *Staatenbund*, where it was supposed that international sovereignty existed without constitutional sovereignty, there was really no independent power, but merely a "certain amount of delegated power entrusted to a 'common organ' of several states"; and, on the other hand, a political formation which was lacking

---

[1] Georg Jellinek: *Die Lehre von den Staatenverbindungen*, 1882, p. 22.
[2] Ibid., p. 23. G. Meyer: *Lehrbuch des deutschen Staatsrechtes*, 1878, Sec. 14, said that the constitutional sovereignty was not a limitation of the state activity, but the international sovereignty was independent of other power.
[3] Georg Jellinek: *Die Lehre von den Staatenverbindungen*, 1882, pp. 23, 24.

in international sovereignty could not possibly possess constitutional sovereignty.

He also disapproved of "depriving" the state as such of its sovereignty and attributing it to some element within the state, such as princes or people, or seeking it outside the state in an ethical or religious principle.

He assumed that these theories of sovereignty were merely "speculations" which placed material limitations on the state authority. The placing of the state sovereignty in the hands of princes or people or the dividing of sovereignty between the state and the *Träger* of the state authority was based on a "misconception of the nature of state personality."

This theory of the legal personality of the state Jellinek confronted with the empirical positivistic attitude, asserting that the state separated from "its constituent elements" was a phantasy, and nothing "actual," just as no personality could exist deprived of its "physical and psychological organs."

The state was only valid "through the organs" in which and through which it maintained "its existence."

The state could act only through its organs and be represented as a power only by means of them.

So he deduced that "the activity of the state organ is the activity of the state itself."[1]

Jellinek's view, which was in accordance with that of many of his contemporaries, was that all sovereignty was "state sovereignty" and as such within the competence of certain state organs, no matter what their composition might be. The only essential for the state is that "there shall exist some organ whose will is its will."[2]

Jellinek argued that the definition of sovereignty prevalent since the seventeenth century was incomplete since it was merely a negative one which did not explain the legal content of sovereignty and the manner in which its *suprema potestas* was expressed. And also the definition of sovereignty as a unity of state powers or as a unity of the state supreme rights was extremely vague, because it told us nothing about the nature of this unity.

Haenel had sought to give a clear legal conception of sovereignty. According to him the essence of sovereignty was that the competence of the state was not limited by any superior authority, but only by itself in the constitutional form of its will; briefly it was the legal power of the state over its competence.

[1] Georg Jellinek: *Die Lehre von den Staatenverbindungen*, 1882, p. 25.
[2] Ibid., p. 26.

This view was nearest to Jellinek's conception of sovereignty, but was not entirely adequate as it was based on the consideration that within the state no corporation and no individual could determine or enlarge its own competence independently but could do so only by means of the supreme power of the state which had to determine all competence, including its own. This view embraced only the constitutional relationship and left out of consideration that if a state had limited its own competence vis-à-vis other states by treaty, in that case a legal cause could relieve it from its obligations.

Jellinek asserted that internally the state was entirely free to withdraw any self-imposed limitation, but such was not the case in its international relations. Therefore the state was competent, i.e. free, but by concluding a treaty it became incompetent; that is to say, it was bound by the treaty which it had concluded. Consequently, to explain sovereignty as the legal power of the state over its competence was a denial of international law.

In order to obtain a satisfactory theory of sovereignty it was necessary for Jellinek to determine the juristic nature of state activity.

He did not enter into an attempt at the philosophical determination of the nature of the state, "because it was not the problem of the substance of the state" which he was considering, "but only the 'formal juristic' definition of its nature as a state power."

As the proper basis of the juristic consideration the state appeared to him to be in its nature a "state personality," i.e. "the established nation which is organised as a collective personality by a relationship of domination and subordination."

The state activity could be estimated from two points of view: from the object of the state power, and from the person subordinate to it. From this general assumption the state appeared as the highest power, and this dominant authority to rule (*imperare*) was "the essential content of the state function towards the subjects."[1]

The legal character of the *imperium* consisted in its absolute obligatory power over people.

Juristic obligation had a twofold nature: the obligation through one's will on the one hand and obligation through an outside will on the other.

The latter applied in the case of a subject who was legally subordinate to the *imperium*. In the last resort the subject was

[1] Georg Jellinek: *Die Lehre von den Staatenverbindungen*, 1882, p. 31.

subordinate in all his legal actions to the state will; that is to say, to a will other than his own. Therefore, assuming that every legal obligation must be "based on a principle of objective law, i.e. of the state will," Jellinek asserted that "entire obligation towards the state will, i.e. towards outside will, is the juristic characteristic of the subject."[1]

The second legal characteristic of the state function was due to the consideration of the state as subject of the state activities.

The state thus appeared in a twofold capacity, firstly in its relationship towards its subjects and secondly in its relations with other states.

The state, therefore, could only impose its will on its subjects as well as on foreign states when its own will was "legal guidance" and not of an arbitrary nature. It was only when the state recognised the statutes and decrees which it issued as binding also on itself, that "the confidence" in the state will was awakened which was the "foundation of legal life."[2]

With this legal basis the state will was directed not only towards those subordinate to its own power, but also towards itself by limiting its free activity by means of constitutional and administrative law.

The state could repeal the existing law but only in due legal form, so that even in altering the law the state was bound by legal formulae. In spite of this capacity of the state to alter all law, yet there was no real unlimited state will, i.e. "no formal free state will."

In the same way the state must establish standards for its activities in its external relationships, and recognise the principles which logically proceed from the nature of international relationship as binding on its own will.[3]

In international law it must give legal expression to its individual will in its relations with other states.

Therefore Jellinek asserted that all the actions of the state, both internal and external, contained an element of obligation on the state as subject, and "all law, in so far as it is public law, is also law to the state by which it is made." "To deny this principle" was "to deny the idea of the legal state." It followed that the state had legal validity only within its self-imposed legal limitations.

Starting from this dictum he asserted that "obligation to its own will is the legal characteristic of the state."[4]

Granting that the state was to be the highest power internally

[1] Georg Jellinek: *Die Lehre von den Staatenverbindungen*, 1882, p. 32.
[2] Ibid.   [3] Ibid., pp. 33, 34.   [4] Ibid., p. 34.

and an independent authority externally, the characteristic of self-imposed obligation was not sufficient to distinguish it, but it must also have the additional characteristics that no external will could legally be imposed on it and it could not be subordinated to any will other than its own.

Therefore he laid down the proposition that obligation solely to its own will is the juristic characteristic of the sovereign state.[1]

As to the fundamental nature of the sovereign state, he laid down his positivist conception of sovereignty that it was "the quality of the state by virtue of which the state can be legally bound only by its own will."[2]

On this fundamental quality of sovereignty and the nature of the state, Jellinek set up the juristic theory of federalism, and with this criterion of the conception of sovereignty he examined federal organs and systematised them according to the juristic forms which Paul Laband had laid down for the German federal empire on the basis of the self-limitation of the sovereign states.

The main problem of federalism to him was the relationship of authority between the collective and the individual states.

His attitude to this problem was determined by his conception of sovereignty—that is, whether sovereignty was the essential characteristic or not, or whether or not the state and the sovereign state were identical; in other words, the juristic justification of the "non-sovereign state."

According to the legal, philosophical and constitutional jurists, sovereignty was without doubt the necessary quality of the state; therefore the non-sovereign state was a *contradictio in adjecto*. Consequently, Seydel's view that the only possible state was a unitary state, and that confederation was the only possible type of a union of states, was logically derived from the prevailing conception of the state.

Nevertheless, Jellinek believed that the actual relationships between the member states and the federal state were scarcely compatible with the abstract conclusions formulated by Seydel.[3]

These contradictory theories gave rise to a diversity of views, from that of divided sovereignty down to Haenel's and Laband's theories of sovereignty, which in their turn gave way to a theoretical compromise with the actuality of political phenomena.

---

[1] Georg Jellinek: *Die Lehre von den Staatenverbindungen*, 1882, p. 34.   [2] Ibid.
[3] Ibid., pp. 37, 38.—"To refuse to the vassal state, to the member states in the federal state, a state character seems to distort actual circumstances into an abstract untenable theory, so that this is one of the cases when theory and fact cannot be reconciled."

Paul Laband was convinced that the prevailing conception of state rested on an incomplete induction; he thought that the identification of the state with the sovereign state was unjustified and that any political formation to which supreme rights inherently belonged possessed the characteristic of the state.

The older theorists of sovereignty, even Bodin, did not entirely omit to consider unions of states; Bodin recognised various grades of independence and of sovereign authority; Hertius mentioned *quasi regna* and Moser made use of the term "half-sovereignty."

The scientific discussion of sovereignty must allow the possibility of political formations to which sovereignty could not be ascribed, but which yet possessed "the essential characteristic which distinguished them from corporations subordinate to the state."

From the juristic standpoint "the possibility of obligation only through its own will" was the test of the state. Therefore, in order to ascertain whether a public law corporation was a state or subject to the state it must be determined whether it could establish its own law by its own will, or by means of its own supreme authority.

In the state it was not only the state authority that could establish legal principles, but other unions, such as self-governing bodies, might also be entrusted with the creation of laws.

Nevertheless, affairs regulated by these self-governing bodies were, in fact, affairs of the state, because their autonomy was entrusted to them, or recognised, by the state and the state used these bodies for its own purposes in certain definite spheres of state authority. The state thus created a secondary power, which was not in complete subordination to itself, but was yet subject to final supervision in all its functions.

The power of creating organic authorities with inherent rights and activities not subject to any control was "the special quality of the state." The state alone possessed "uncontrolled public law authority," which applied to the whole extent of state activity.

Jellinek therefore asserted that "when in any field of state activity a political formation is entitled to make binding laws in its own right, then that is a state in the juristic sense."[1]

In this assertion the theory of the division of sovereignty seemed to be reintroduced, for the non-sovereign state could be regarded as a proxy of the sovereignty. In order to solve this difficulty an exact definition of inherent competence was necessary. So Jellinek said that an inherent right was a right exercised only by its owner of his own will, and it was not essential that this inherent

[1] Georg Jellinek: *Die Lehre von den Staatenverbindungen*, 1882, p. 40.

right should originate in the personality of the possessor, or that it could not be taken away against his will.[1]

Jellinek argued that the nature of the inherent right was neither its origin nor its inalienability, but its special characteristic was that "he, to whom it belongs, is legally responsible to no one for its exercise"; and he added that "inherent right is legally an uncontrolled right."[2]

Applied to the public law corporation this meant that its inherent rights were rights which it could exercise independently of the control of a state.

Therefore he assumed that the nature of an inherent supreme right consists in this: that in a limited sphere of state activity a public law corporation is "entitled within that limited sphere to issue governing rules as the final authority, not subject to the control of a higher power."[3]

On this assumption as to the extent of the inherent power of the state in itself, such a public law corporation could legally be placed in the category of "a state," but such a state was "not sovereign" because the sphere of its activities did not depend upon its "own will" alone and because it was not and could not appear as an "independent state" in every respect, but only as a member of a higher sovereign whole.[4]

Then how could the non-sovereign state possess inherent rights over against the sovereign state? Obviously only by transfer or grant from it.

By the very nature of the sovereign state, whose inherent rights could be self-determined, it could grant state authority to a public law corporation which was yet subordinate to it.

Thus such a corporation became the holder of state power and could "use its supreme power over its own subjects," but it possessed it not as a "delegated" right but as a "derived" right.[5]

In this respect, even though the sovereign state could by virtue of its sovereignty alter its own *Kompetenz*, and take back again to itself a part of the state power entrusted to non-sovereign states, yet the conception of supreme powers inherent in non-sovereign states was not altered.[6]

In the federal organism the members of the federal state were non-sovereign states. Nevertheless, the historical facts had shown that the individual states of the German Empire were originally "sovereign communities"; but the power granted by the con-

[1] Georg Jellinek: *Die Lehre von den Staatenverbindungen*, 1882, p. 41.
[2] Ibid., p. 42.   [3] Ibid., pp. 43–44.   [4] Ibid., p. 44.
[5] Ibid.   [6] Ibid., p. 45.

stitution of the United States to congress for the formation of a new state of a certain population was another kind of historical process in the formation of the individual state.

What happened in the transformation of certain territories of the union into member states was conceptionally necessary in the formation of all non-sovereign states.

Jellinek therefore asserted that as "only through the will of the sovereign state could the non-sovereign state be formed," so "the sovereign state is conceptionally always primary, and the non-sovereign state is secondary."[1]

The transference of certain rights of sovereignty to other states to be exercised as their inherent rights was a frequent phenomenon in international law.

The state which by treaty received from another state legal authority over the territory and subjects of that other appeared in the exercise of that authority as independent, uncontrolled and irresponsible within the limits of the treaty.

The same process, which was applied to the relationship of one sovereign power to another, could be applied to the relationship between the state and one of its parts. If the state could separate from itself certain inherent rights by virtue of its own authority Jellinek asserted that "there becomes constitutionally possible that which undoubtedly already exists internationally."[2]

The transformation in the old German Empire of the unitary state into a consolidated state was the best historical example, in which the gradual separation of certain supreme powers from the empire and their transference to the "estates" of the empire for use in their own right could be clearly seen.

A confirmation of the doctrine that public law corporations which were provided with independent supreme rights derived from sovereign authority were states, and not merely associations subordinate to the state, was offered by international law. States alone were the subjects of international law.

Non-sovereign states, however, were "legal subjects" in the sense of international law, and those non-sovereign states which according to the federal constitution to which they were subordinate could not conclude any treaties between themselves or conduct diplomatic services, had, nevertheless, not completely lost their international existence.[3]

The public law corporation, which possessed state power as an inherent right, was able both internally and externally to appear

---

[1] Georg Jellinek: *Die Lehre von den Staatenverbindungen*, 1882, p. 46.
[2] Ibid., p. 47.   [3] Ibid., p. 49.

as the holder of those rights and duties which belonged to no other than "a state."

The internal connection of all activities of the state must be manifested in the relationship of the functions delegated by the sovereign authority as inherent rights, to those reserved to itself. Accordingly, any sharp division between these two kinds of state activity was impossible and would inevitably result in conflict between the sovereign and non-sovereign authorities.

Accordingly, Jellinek asserted that in the conflicts between these two authorities "the sovereign authority by its very nature asserts itself as the higher power."[1]

Finally, Jellinek inquired into the three main questions:—

Firstly, by what means can a state lose its sovereignty; how far can a state go in alienating its supreme rights and still appear as sovereign? Secondly, by what processes do non-sovereign states come into being? And finally, what distinguishes an international union of two states from a "constitutional union" in which there exists a relationship of domination and subordination?

To the first question the answer was an explanation of the real nature of sovereignty that "the delegation even of the most important supreme rights of a state did not deprive that state of its sovereignty."[2] As I have fully explained, no bounds could be set to the self-imposed limitation of the sovereignty of a state by its own will and authority.

Even when the state delegated to another sovereign state the supreme rights as inherent ones, the former did not give up its sovereignty, but only increased its self-limitation. The unity of sovereignty was in all cases preserved by the fact that the limitation of a sovereign state could only take place either in the way of treaty or by unilateral arrangement. In the latter case the state was not pledged to the other state at all; and the treaty bound the state only as long as it legally existed. As the limitation of ownership by substantive law did not take from that ownership its characteristic of absolute supremacy over a thing, so the alienation of sovereign right by treaty, however large an amount of the sovereign power was transferred to the other state, was not absolute.

The treaty, whatever its content might be, presupposed that the contracting party was "free," i.e. that its decision depended only on its own will.

Nevertheless, the state must beware of attempting to modify this

[1] Georg Jellinek: *Die Lehre von den Staatenverbindungen*, 1882, p. 52.
[2] Ibid., p. 53.

principle for the purposes of political expediency and thus rejecting "every standard of legal judgment of the circumstances."[1]

Jellinek asserted that juristically every state, so far and so long as it was bound only by treaty, and whatever its political situation thereunder might be, "must be regarded as a sovereign state," because sovereignty was, in fact, "the right of being able to pledge and be pledged by its own will."[2]

As the state remained sovereign despite the treaty, so the non-sovereign state could not be created by means of a treaty.[3] If the state lost its existence as a state entity by giving up its sovereignty in the treaty, it was legally impossible that it should continue to be a contracting party to the treaty, and at the same time because of the unity and indivisibility of sovereignty it could not be thought of as the *Träger* of supreme rights.

Then, was it true that the state could only either give up its sovereignty entirely and without reservation or not give it up at all?

Jellinek's answer to this second question was that the non-sovereign state could not be created by treaty, but only by the will of the sovereign state.

The sovereign state could only create the non-sovereign state "by providing one of its administrative areas with a self-governing body, subordinate to itself, with uncontrolled state power and supreme rights granted as inherent rights," and thus raising it to the status of a quasi-independent state.

On this assumption he asserted that "not the treaty of the independent states, but only the will of the sovereign state is the juristic basis of a constitutional union of states."[4]

The maxim at the basis of the discussion of the federal state was that if the treaty had preceded the formation of a union of states, the members of which were subordinated to the central power, this treaty could not be regarded "as the legal basis of the new constitutional and international existence."[5]

The answer to the third question was that if a state could be bound by an act of another state, which was able by its own right to impose an obligation on the former, then the state on which the obligation had been placed was "non-sovereign." But

---

[1] Georg Jellinek: *Die Lehre von den Staatenverbindungen*, 1882, p. 55.—"In the theory of the state servitude Heffter declares that the most extreme limitation is that the pledged state is not placed in complete dependence on the will of the contracting state, but is limited only in certain supreme power and can, therefore, still exist at least as a half-sovereign state, and he added in a note that this point is the most difficult one in the theory."
[2] Ibid.   [3] Ibid., p. 56.   [4] Ibid., p. 57.   [5] Ibid.

if the basis of the obligation of the state depended exclusively on its own will, which it enforced either itself or by means of another power, as the delegate of its will, then the state thus pledged was "a sovereign state."[1]

§ 4

Jellinek next proceeded to analyse and criticise the various forms of the union in the light of his legal positivism and put them into classes determined by his legal criterion of sovereignty with regard to the self-determination of inherent supreme rights.

According to his key to the theory of sovereignty he attempted to place unions into two categories: the unions of co-ordination and the unions of domination or subordination of the members; in other words, into international and constitutional unions.[2]

The divisions according to Jellinek could not be formed by such arrangement of the materials as would correspond to an *a priori* scheme, but only by such detailed investigation of materials as would make it clear into which category every form of union should be placed, and thus the two *Genera* together with their species could be compared with one another.[3]

Jellinek stated, however, that there was another point of view, according to which there was apparently a sharp division between the various unions of states.

The union of mere co-ordination of several states could be either one without any organs created by itself, and therefore without organisation, or it could possess organs created by itself and be in that case not merely "a mechanical co-ordination or coalition of states." He considered the former as non-organised unions and the latter as organised unions, and held that these were two groups into which all unions of states could be classified.[4] This empirical division of unions did not depend on "outward and unessential characteristics," but was based on "the sharp division of unions of states which rested on the nature of human association."[5] All human relationships required organisation for the attainment of the purposes of the association. Already in private law there was a great difference between a temporary relationship with reciprocal obligations and the corporation provided with organs for permanent purposes. The more

[1] Georg Jellinek: *Die Lehre von den Staatenverbindungen*, 1882, p. 57.
[2] Ibid., p. 58.   [3] Ibid.   [4] Ibid.   [5] Ibid., p. 59.

developed the organisation of the association, the more firmly was it welded together, the more assured its duration and the easier the accomplishment of its purposes.

This applied to the union of states in both international and constitutional relationships. Only an organisation can offer a guarantee of the attainment of the purposes of the union. Where no organisation of the union existed any relationships between the states were likely to degenerate, and the result would be either the dissolution of the union or the complete absorption of the politically weaker power by the stronger one.

Before investigating the unions of states themselves Jellinek considered those states which either possessed members that could be regarded politically, though not juristically, as having an existence of their own—these having been transformed from several separate states into unitary states—or which, without any legal union, yet appeared to be members of a union of states. There were the unitary states which either from the political-historical standpoint appeared as amalgamated states or were united to one another by the person of the holder of the state authority. When the states hitherto separate were united, they could be regarded from a juristic standpoint as a unified whole, and in the historical sense could be termed unions of states.

Therefore he asserted that "all the historical-political unions mentioned above could be properly contrasted with the unions possessing a juristic character."[1]

This comparative study displaced his positivistic investigation according to the empirical method and determined the final division of the unions on the basis of his juristic conception of sovereignty.

Jellinek considered, first of all, the historical political unions, which could not with legal justification accurately be termed *Staatenverbindungen*.

His attention was directed first, within this category, to the subject lands (*Nebenländer*) or colonies in their relations to the mother country.

The conception of the subject land was, no doubt, difficult to define in political theory, but Jellinek used the term to denote that part of a state union which played a politically subordinate part and had no share in the essential content of the life that centred in the main state.

Therefore a state with subject lands was not "a union of states"

[1] Georg Jellinek: *Die Lehre von den Staatenverbindungen*, 1882, p. 60.

in the juristic sense, but a "unitary state, the life of which, however, was not a unitary one."[1]

Among subject lands the colony occupied a prominent position. A colony, in the constitutional sense, was the settlement of inhabitants of the mother country in state territory hitherto uninhabited, or in foreign territory which by the fact of settlement was acquired by the native country of the colonists.

The ultimate fate of the colony depended on whether it was in close proximity to the mother country or far removed. Take as examples of the former the territories of the North American union which, having reached a certain population, were recognised by the mother country as member states of the federal union. On the other hand, in regard to colonies belonging to European states, the position was entirely reversed; as the colonies became more independent, their connection with the mother country became merely nominal or was ended by secession. This is what must inevitably happen in all cases when the European countries insist on treating their transatlantic possessions as subordinate provinces.

Even the highly self-governing Canada of the British Empire was under the *jus supremae inspectionis* as part of the empire. Therefore an empire such as the British Empire was "a unitary state" and not a "union of states."[2]

The second case considered by Jellinek was that of "incorporation."

What Jellinek meant by incorporation was that states could unite with one another: firstly, in such a manner that either one is completely subordinate to the other, i.e. that sovereignty is transferred to the other, or, secondly, in such a way that each of the states in question disappears as such and an entirely new state arises in its place.[3]

The former case belonged to the period of the formation and transformation of the state by dynastic politics, whereas the latter, with a few exceptions, was a creation of modern times, and appeared not as a union of states but as a completely new state formation, not "as the legal continuer" but as the "legal successor" of the former states. The older constitutional law used to bring into the theory of incorporation a number of scholastic distinctions which were derived partly from ecclesiastical law and particularly from the rules as to the union of bishoprics (*unio per suppressionem, per confusionem, per novationem*, and so on).

[1] Georg Jellinek: *Die Lehre von den Staatenverbindungen*, 1882, pp. 63, 64.
[2] Ibid., p. 68.   [3] Ibid.

Until the idea of the modern state had been firmly established, there was a certain justification for distinguishing between unions according as they were based on equal or unequal rights or on complete or incomplete corporation.

In the patrimonial and feudal states the principles of the public law, on the analogy of private law, were regarded as independent of the state, and the rights which were left to the corporations of "estates" after the absorption appeared accordingly as independent powers not derived from the newly formed state authority. In the modern national state, however, all authorities of public law are "derived from the state," and therefore different kinds of incorporations could not be juristically distinguished, however varied the historical processes of union and the political relations of the incorporated lands with the new state authority might be.

If the state entered into another state it entirely lost state quality. If, nevertheless, it was not governed in the same way as the other provinces of the state to which it now belonged, because its institutions were historically connected with those which it earlier possessed, this could only be considered as a right recognised and entrusted to it by the new state authority, as a far-reaching autonomy and self-administration which legally, although not historically, must be considered as something essentially new. Even when a state subordinated itself by treaty to another state in such a way that a certain measure of independence remained guaranteed to it, the granting of this independence was a unilateral state action and not a fulfilment of the treaty, because by complete subordination consequent on the fulfilment of the treaty, one of the contracting parties had disappeared and therefore there was no one who possessed a right derived from the treaty. It is possible for a state to pledge itself to a third power to allow the old institutions to continue in the incorporated territory or to grant new ones, but from this there arises only an obligation of international law towards the third power, and not towards the incorporated state.

The division of unions according to equal and unequal rights and from incomplete incorporations was, therefore, constitutionally not suitable in those cases where the state ceded its sovereignty to another. A state incorporated into another becomes part of that other, even if it keeps a large measure of autonomy.

The union of 1707 and that of 1800 incorporated Scotland and Ireland respectively into the English state, as was shown by the new designation of "Great Britain and Ireland"; constitutionally

England was a unitary state and Scotland and Ireland were only provinces of the empire.

As examples of the relatively great amount of independence left to newly acquired provinces might be taken the cases of Finland, acquired by Russia from Sweden in 1809, and of Poland, a part of which was incorporated in Russia during the years 1815 to 1832.[1]

As regards "real unions," Jellinek remarked that the use of that term for cases of incorporation was an incorrect expression of the historical fact that states previously entirely separate kept a distinct existence so long as the new unitary state allowed to its formerly independent members a large measure of autonomy. But juristically that fact was irrelevant. The decisive fact, legally, was that no component parts of the state in question should remain as "independent holders of supreme rights."

In the case of Austria-Hungary, by the constitution of 1867 the whole of the Austrian Crown lands together were legally a unitary state with an emperor, as the holder of the state authority, who was not merely a representative of the sum of the territorial princes.

To sum up: states or parts of states which had been incorporated into another lost their "state attribute" altogether, whatever position they might occupy in the new state.

The amount of independence left to them was to be regarded as a new creation, as autonomy granted and allowed to them by the dominant state authority. Since they were no longer states there could no longer be any legal connection between their present institutions and those formerly possessed by them.

However far-reaching the independence allowed to them, they could not again have the attribute of statehood, because they were subject to "the supervision of the ruling state," and therefore, at the most, were "self-governing bodies and not holders of the state supreme rights." The state so absorbed had become a province, and one could not speak of a union of states in the juristic sense because there was now no legal distinction between the original unitary state and that which had arisen by means of incorporation.

In regard to the act of incorporation, in so far as it was based on law at all it was always of an "international law nature," because it was concerned with the union of states hitherto separate, or of a state with a part of another state hitherto outside. Thus a

[1] Georg Jellinek: *Die Lehre von den Staatenverbindungen*, 1882, pp. 70–75.

constitutional relationship was founded by an act of international law.

The four principal methods of the formation of a complete union were as follows:—

>(I) Cession of a part of the state territory to another state;
>(II) Complete subordination of a conquered state;
>(III) Voluntary subjection of a state to another, e.g. by treaty;
>(IV) One-sided seizure of a foreign territory without previous state of war.

By means of one or other of these processes a state united with another on the basis of international, and not one of constitutional law, and such unions were neither unions nor federations in the legal sense of those terms.

The theory of the personal union (i.e. the union of a number of states under the same ruler), which had been somewhat obscured by the lack of a clear terminology, was considered, either in the historical or in the legal sense, generally to be quite a different form of union from the "real union."[1]

Jellinek conceived the personal union as differing from the real union in that it depended often only on the personal identity of a common ruler of two or more communities, and it did not matter whether this identity was only historically or also juristically relevant.

The consideration of historical and juristical possibilities, supported by actual facts, showed that there were, theoretically, four kinds of unions of states, which must be clearly differentiated:—

>(I) A state amalgamated of originally separate parts so that there had been a "plurality," and the union, therefore, was merely an historical fact; that is the case of the complete union.
>(II) A state possessing as members "non-sovereign" states; in this category the *Bundesstaat* must be placed.
>(III) A state consisting of an association depending on a mutually agreed will; to this class belonged the "real union."

---

[1] Georg Jellinek: *Die Lehre von den Staatenverbindungen*, 1882, p. 82.—He considered that "Real union means, according to many authors right up to the present day, a unitary state formed of originally independent states either alone or in association with what only legally can be maintained as a real state union."

(IV) Finally, whilst there was no legal bond between a number of states, the "physical holder of sovereignty was common to all for reasons which had nothing to do with mutual agreement."[1]

Only this final case could be called a "personal union."

Therefore Jellinek asserted that the personal union was not "a juristic, but an historical and political union of states which was legally a chance association of several states through the person of the ruler who legally consisted of as many personalities as there are states over which he ruled."[2]

Consequently, the personal union could only be comprised of monarchical states, and at the same time the states politically united by the common personality of the sovereign could not internationally pursue opposing aims. Therefore the personal union existed as an historical political union only so long as there was a physical ruler of both states by the right of election or the law of succession, and it could be ended only by such circumstances as death, abdication, dethronement or the dying out of the dynasty.

These three forms of union—the colony, the incorporation and the personal union—were historical and political unions, but not unions of states in the legal sense of the word; rather they were kinds of unitary decentralised states or accidental unions of two sovereign states under a single physical ruler.

Jellinek therefore claimed that the theory of the union in the legal sense was different from that of the historical-political union. Thus he differed from the earlier theorists only by his attempt to place the personal union in a separate category from all other legal unions.

Jellinek proceeded to divide unions having a juristic character into two classes: the non-organised union on the one hand and the "organised union" on the other.

First of all he inquired into the community (*Gemeinschaft*) of states and system of states (*Staatensystem*).

One of the first principles of scientific investigation, he remarked, was that the more a phenomenon could be isolated the more easily and completely could it be understood. It was by following this method of isolation that the astronomers first observed the course of planets and "Adam Smith considered economics as if developed entirely by the driving-force of self-interest."[3]

[1] Georg Jellinek: *Die Lehre von den Staatenverbindungen*, 1882, p. 84.
[2] Ibid., p. 85. [3] Ibid., p. 91.

However correct this procedure might be from the point of view of "method," yet the results could not claim any "scientific" but only "hypothetical" validity, since science must in the final instance comprehend phenomena as they really are—that is to say, "crossed, checked, influenced and altered by others."

This method of isolating subjects had, with few exceptions, been applied to political science from the time of Plato up to Jellinek's own day. The state had been regarded as if it were a unique genus, for, as it was considered to be "self-sufficing," it seemed to stand in a position completely independent of all others. But on this assumption a legal system which issued decrees binding states with one another was logically impossible, and international law seemed to be in contradiction with the nature of the state. But as actual facts showed, the authority and sovereignty of the state permitted between states unions of a legal character which were not incompatible with the nature of a state.

No state in this world was quite independent of other states, either politically, economically or socially; the existence and functions of the individual state were limited by the collectivity of other states.

It was quite unnecessary for science to deduce the possibility of unions, for these were obvious to all observers. It was the business rather of those who clung to the idea of the isolated state to explain the fact that a large part of the law which is operative in civilised states was based on state treaties, and that it was "the collectivity of states" which stamped a special mark on whole spheres of administration.

On this assumption he asserted that the self-sufficing state, unrestrained by any will, was merely an "abstract" formula, and that "the concrete state always appeared as a member of an association of states."

Jellinek held that association of states was "a fundamental fact in the state theory."[1] This meant that every state was "one among many," and therefore its existence was in essentials determined by the others, and, secondly, that as the state was "the highest form of human association organised as a ruling power," the state association was only "natural co-ordination, and not an organised relation of subordination and domination."[2] Just as individuals are limited by the existence of their fellow-men, so also was the state forced by the existence of other states to limit and discipline its own will.

The natural fact of the plurality of the states was altered by the

---

[1] Georg Jellinek: *Die Lehre von den Staatenverbindungen*, 1882, p. 93.   [2] Ibid.

fact that individual states were forced by their nature to associate with others, to join an association and, indeed, an association for common law. "Association could consist of relations between rational beings"; such relations were possible only when the will of one state was limited by itself in favour of another. When the self-limited will was a sovereign one, it made laws for itself, because all acts of the sovereign were legally creative.

This law proceeding from the nature of international relations, upheld by legal consciousness of the peoples, sanctioned by the sovereign will of states, was international law in the strict sense of the word. This international law comprised all the states in association with one another. By not recognising that law—that is, by refusing to associate with other states—any state would destroy itself. So Jellinek asserted that every state represented only "a fragment of mankind," and therefore required to be "supplemented."[1] He emphasised that "no nation could venture to assume the haughty Hegelian conception that the spirit of the universe had established his throne in it alone."[2]

The inexorable power of social and, above all, of economic conditions forced even the remotest community into intercourse with others.

On this assumption he laid down as the fundamental nature of the union that "the association of states, based on nature and rising by international law to a legal community, is the first and most comprehensive form of a union of states."[3]

That *civitas maxima* which endeavoured to absorb all the individual states into one world state for the salvation of mankind, could never be realised.

He urged in support of his argument that "as long as mankind actually lived and moved, it would require a plurality of states by whose mutual attraction and repulsion the progress in the life of the state was promoted and maintained."[4]

Within this community of states, state systems with common legal principles would develop "owing to geographical and historical proximity." The development of culture is bound up with the abandonment of state self-sufficiency; the more civilised a state becomes the more is it compelled to seek and utilise points of contact with other states—every new discovery and invention creates a new tie.[5]

---

[1] Georg Jellinek: *Die Lehre von den Staatenverbindungen*, 1882, p. 95.
[2] Ibid.   [3] Ibid., p. 96.   [4] Ibid.
[5] Ibid., pp. 96–98.—He mentioned the numerous commercial, navigation, post and telegraph conventions of the nineteenth century, and the growth of international law relating to war.

At the same time this association of states and the state systems included in it were not organised unions of states, for there did not exist any sovereign authority over the states which by its very nature would deprive the states of their sovereignty. A treaty-based organisation, which would unite the civilised nations or even unite European state systems into a kind of confederation, existed up to Jellinek's time only in the imagination of political theorists.

Every state by the mere fact of its existence entered the natural association of states by reason of the fact that it represented "an organised section of mankind." But in order to be received into a legal association, the recognition by other states was requisite, recognition being the act by means of which a state declared another to be "a legal personality."

The mutual recognition of legal personality required that one state entity should impose limits on its own freedom of action in favour of another, these limits being needed for the purposes of international law.

The self-limitations appeared to the state for whose benefit they were made simply as "concessions" or "subjective rights."[1]

The existence of the state was a natural fact, but recognition was a voluntary act of the states by which they changed that natural fact into a legal one. The nature of international law is thus shown to be a legal code based on the will of the states. A political community maintaining itself as a state may have a moral claim for recognition by other states, but it has no legal claim.

Thus it seems clear that although Jellinek adhered to positivism in his legal ideas, yet he did not refuse to admit the ethical validity of a state formation.

Jellinek assumed that the community of states was "a non-organised union of states" holding intercourse with one another, based on the fact of the plurality of states and raised by the fact of mutual recognition to the status of a legal community in which groups formed by closer communication and fuller development of law were marked off as "systems of states."[2] No state could free itself from the domination of international law "without losing its state quality." So Jellinek asserted that the *Staatengemeinschaft* was one of the pillars on which the state must rest in order that it might fulfil the functions imposed on it.

The recognition of one state by other states as a legal personality

[1] Georg Jellinek: *Die Lehre von den Staatenverbindungen*, 1882, p. 99.
[2] Ibid., p. 100.

was the prerequisite of legal intercourse between the states in question.

On this assumption "the legal form," in which states satisfied requirements extending beyond their own spheres, was the "Treaty," which is the meeting of several wills with regard to something desired and whereby the separate wills coalesce into "a single will with regard to their objective." Therefore Jellinek defined the treaty as "an agreement of wills."[1] Treaty was the only form by which a state could join with other states without losing its own independence, and the state which was bound only by treaty was and remained completely "sovereign," whatever the content of the obligations imposed on it by the treaty.

"The self-imposed restriction" of a state could be removed in favour of a higher claim on its will. For every act of that will is subject to the condition *rebus sic stantibus*. But clearly this principle may be abused if the state is to be sole judge in the last resort in its own affairs, and so Jellinek held that the final decision in case of conflict ought to be based on the synthesis of law and ethics "because only the state power which is upheld by ethical ideas will in the case of the sharpest conflicts grasp and carry out with certainty that which the conception of law requires."[2]

At the same time this special source of the state treaty as arising from the nature of the state had the consequence that everything done by a unanimous agreement of wills could be undone by a similarly unanimous agreement of all the parties to the treaty.

The principle that the treaty is the only possible form of union between two sovereign states was to Jellinek the foundation of every international union of states.

Therefore he asserted that "the general rules of state treaties also regulate all international unions," and no unions could escape from the rules of international law in regard to the origin, completion, permanency and termination of state pacts.[3]

Jellinek attached especial importance to the rule that all treaties between states can be dissolved by due legal process—a principle which he held to apply not only to treaties concluded for a limited period and which the parties had the right to denounce. Even when there was no expressed time or right of denunciation the treaty was not indissoluble, because no state will could be absolutely bound. Therefore in any conflict the pact must yield to the state, not the state to the pact.

[1] Georg Jellinek: *Die Lehre von den Staatenverbindungen*, 1882, p. 101.
[2] Ibid., p. 103.   [3] Ibid., pp. 101–102.

Since it was the highest duty of the state to maintain itself not only as a "stationary existing order," but also as a "motive force in the national life," in case of conflict the duty of fulfilling the treaty obligation must give way to the duty of self-preservation.

This applied to every commercial treaty as well as "the federal treaty" by means of which the confederation is constituted.[1] The federal pacts such as the North American confederation and the German Union Acts talked of "perpetual unions," but this phrase had juristically the same meaning as the phrase *paix et amitié à perpétuité* in a peace treaty.

Not even mutual discussion was necessary to destroy a treaty between states; because, as all its clauses were organically united, any breach of it by one of the contracting parties would dissolve the whole treaty.

As all treaties create unions of states, the various species of treaties are at the same time species of unions of states.

Criticising and rejecting various classifications of treaties as unsound in theory and unworkable in practice, he set up as his principle of division the kind and degree of the union produced by state treaties.[2]

The kinds of relationship of the states united by treaty were found by investigating the reasons for which one state made a pact with another. These reasons were of two kinds. Firstly, a treaty might be made in order to fulfil the duties imposed on the state by its own nature as the administrator of the common interest of its people. The state maintained and promoted the common interest of the nation "by its own free activity within the limitations imposed by its legal code." A state could utilise the capacity of its subjects by means of law, decrees and commands, but could bind foreign states to itself for the purposes of administration only by means of treaty. Jellinek designated the treaties of this kind as "administrative treaties,"[3] which included commercial, navigation, railway and consular treaties, and treaties relating to coinage, weights and measures, customs, postal services, copyrights and patents. In the second place the state could unite with another state in order to establish itself as "a power" and maintain its position vis-à-vis third parties and to strengthen itself both internally and externally.

Whereas the first kind of treaty was concerned only with the exercise of some particular function or the attainment of some

[1] Georg Jellinek: *Die Lehre von den Staatenverbindungen*, 1882, p. 103.
[2] Ibid., p. 105.   [3] Ibid., p. 106.

special objects, in the second kind the state was affected to its whole extent and even in its very existence.

If a state obtained or conceded a province by treaty, or entered a confederation, it would be affected in its whole extent by such treaties and its political position both within and without would be thereby conditioned. Those treaties which related to alliance, guarantee, protection or neutrality, and treaties of confederation, Jellinek called "political treaties."

It was difficult to draw a line between these two categories, because, all the activities of the state being organically connected, every act of the state must affect the whole of its relationships. The second division of treaties, that of degree, depended in the first place upon whether the "interests" of the contracting parties were opposed or harmonious.

In the former case conflicting interests might be satisfied by mutual obligations, as in commercial treaties or customs agreements by means of which the conflict between hitherto divergent interests was ended. These conventions, which produced "a reciprocal extension of the states," could really be described as "treaties in the more limited sense."[1]

When, on the other hand, the interests involved in the treaty coincided and there was no question of mutual satisfaction of need and solidarity was the sole basis of the treaty, then a treaty of quite a different character was produced. Since the bond between state and state was a closer and more intimate one than arose under a treaty of the former kind, this second subdivision of unions according to degree, determined by community of interests, would be more correctly called "a union" than a treaty. In this division there were two further subdivisions, the distinction between which was whether the carrying out of the union was left entirely to the agreed wills of the contracting states or there was set up by the treaty an organ in which the common will should find expression as a united will. This latter kind, which set up international organs, such as navigation commissions, postal unions and others for carrying out the agreed will of the allied states and to which the exercise of supreme rights for common purposes was entrusted, secured more permanent and more sure union than the former which lacked corresponding international organs.

Jellinek accordingly divided the second class of union by degree into the "non-organised" and "organised unions."[2] This

[1] Georg Jellinek: *Die Lehre von den Staatenverbindungen*, 1882, p. 107.
[2] Ibid., p. 108.

division of non-organised and organised unions in the legal sense was the first comprehensive demarcation of the forms of the union in German federal discussion. And though this division was open to criticism, yet it became more or less the standard division of unions of states.

Within the category of non-organised unions there were four kinds: (*a*) the "treaty-based occupation and administration of a state"; (*b*) the "alliance"; (*c*) "protection, guarantee and neutrality"; and (*d*) the *Staatenstaat*.

As regards the first of these it was "a frequent phenomenon of international life that a state granted to another state the exercise of administration over its territories." Examples of this were such "state servitudes" as rights of passage for military forces, garrison rights in certain fortresses and the functions of consular officers.

Further, it might happen that "a state for reasons of economy or convenience handed over to another state the partial or entire exercise of one branch of administration, or transferred jurisdiction in the higher instance to a foreign court; an example of the first was the administration of Norwegian foreign affairs by the Swedish Foreign Minister, and of the second the way in which an Austrian court acted as the final tribunal for Lichtenstein.

The control over Bosnia and Herzegovina, provinces of the Ottoman Empire, handed over by the treaty of Berlin in 1878 to Austria-Hungary for treaty-based occupation and administration, was due to the weakness of the Turkish administration,[1] and there were other examples, such as the relationship of Tunis to France and Malta to Great Britain.

Many forms and types of treaty-based occupation and administration were irregular in their nature and by no means compatible with the rigid legal conception of the state, because, as Jellinek emphasised, they were the product of a political situation which was not clear, and were provisional arrangements or relationships which later on would be shaped in a manner more favourable to the fuller freedom of activity of the administering state.

These administrative occupations, though somewhat unnatural, were yet instructive, because they showed that the actual facts of state life need not necessarily coincide with deductions drawn from the state conception, and that what *a priori* was regarded as unthinkable might nevertheless be the fact.

Jurists must endeavour to place these irregular relationships in their special legal category on account of the number of

[1] Georg Jellinek: *Die Lehre von den Staatenverbindungen*, 1882, p. 115.

questions involved, each of which would require a special individual decision.

The second form of unorganised union was the "alliance" which was "a union of two or more states for their common maintenance as powers"; its objects were essentially political, whether a hostile attitude towards third powers or the attainment of a peaceful purpose.

The alliance was unorganised and was based exclusively on the agreed wills of the contracting parties. International organs regulated "by time and purpose," as, e.g., in the case of a "collective guarantee," could be set up for certain limited objects. But the non-organised character of an alliance was not invalidated by the nature of these organs, which were quite transitory and subordinate.

Jellinek assumed that any kind of alliance, whether belligerent or peaceful, belonged to this category.[1]

The third form was a union arising either from the relationship of protection of one sovereign state by another, or the guarantee of a sovereign state by another, or the perpetual neutrality of one sovereign state protected and guaranteed by one or more states on the basis of international treaty.[2]

These three forms were to Jellinek "purely international relationships" which did not entail the subordination of one state to another.

To however large an extent the political activities of one state were limited by another it still remained sovereign. Therefore Jellinek assumed that all these forms of the union of states were "varieties of alliance" depending on treaty, and therefore not indissoluble.

Passing next to the *Staatenstaat* Jellinek pointed out that the modern conception of the relationship of citizens to the state was that they were directly responsible to the states to which they belonged, whereas in the mediaeval state the relationship between the subjects and the supreme feudal authority was mostly indirect and through the medium of their feudal lords (*Lehnsherrn*).

Jellinek asserted that this form of union of states in which the sovereign state exercised the supreme authority (*Hoheitsrechte*) which it retained not so much over individuals as over states, was not confined to the Middle Ages, and that in modern times there were state structures conditioned by the social organisation

[1] Georg Jellinek: *Die Lehre von den Staatenverbindungen*, 1882, pp. 121–126.
[2] Ibid., pp. 126–133.

of the empires concerned in such a way that there was no organic fusion of the individual parts.

In a state of this kind no organs existed in which the union between the ruling state and the subordinate states found expression. Neither was there any constitutionally based organisation of the relationship of subjects or of the subordinate states to the supreme authority.

In the *Staatenstaat*, as always the case in every non-organised state union, the bond uniting the parts to the whole was so loose that a centrifugal force was continually being exerted to drive them still farther apart, and this naturally tended towards the dissolution of the collective state.

When parts of a state were provided by it with inherent state authority—if they did not consequently appear as non-sovereign states—Jellinek distinguished two possibilities. Either all the state elements in the sovereign state were combined in a single unit or they were not.

This latter form was that of the union of states in which the subjects were subordinated to a state authority "through the medium of another," and there was no unity of all the elements of the state. No direct relationship between the sovereign power and the subjects existed. Those who were subjected to the sovereignty were not individuals but states, and the superior state appeared to the subjects of the subordinate states as an external power, because the subjects had no direct, but only indirect, contact with the sovereign authority and no voluntary expansion of the power of the subordinate state was permitted.

De jure the authority of the superior state was predominant over the state power of the subordinate one, but "the state power bestowed on the subordinate state in the form of privilege could not arbitrarily be withdrawn by the sovereign state."

Nevertheless, such a treaty-based relationship of public law nature was only a "mechanical" relationship between the member state and the whole state, and was incompatible with the fundamental nature of the unitary modern state. If a modern state creation such as the German Empire, imbued with the old conception of hereditary reserved rights, granted only certain rights, which could constitutionally be again withdrawn, this was a remnant of the old state conception which, like an "erratic block lying on a new stratum," was a proof that state life, like nature, does not always succeed in destroying and casting away altogether the remnants of vanished epochs.[1]

[1] Georg Jellinek: *Die Lehre von den Staatenverbindungen*, 1882, p. 142.

On this assumption he criticised earlier conceptions of the *Staatenstaat* as being either a unitary or a federal state.[1]

He definitely opposed the designation of the *Staatenstaat* being given to either of these, disagreed with von Mohl's description of it as a "feudal federal state," and accepted more readily J. Schulze's conception of it as a disjointed feudal state.[2]

The empire differed from a federal state in two important respects:—

(A) The subjects were subordinate to the imperial authority only indirectly through the intermediary of the territorial authority.

(B) In the institutions of the old empire there was nothing based on one of the chief essentials of a federal state authority— namely, member states and subjects.

The *Staatenstaat* was by its nature, therefore, not compatible with the essential character of the federal state.

§ 5

Jellinek next proceeded to discuss the second form of the *Staatenverbindungen*—namely, the organised unions; these he divided under the following heads: (*a*) the organised administrative union; (*b*) the confederation; (*c*) the real union; (*d*) the federal state.

First he defined the "union" (*Verein*) as the "form in which the state either extends its administrative activity beyond its boundaries or strengthens it within its territory by means of the powers of other states."[3]

The union was in his view distinguished from a mere administrative union by the facts that it possessed "independent organs," and its functions not only owed their existence "to the agreed will of the members," but also found expression "in its own organs."

Thus Jellinek asserted that the administrative union which maintained its own independent organs was an "organised administrative union," whilst one which had no central organs belonged to the non-organised class.[4]

The unity of administrative purpose which formed the basis of these unions made the union states into a common administrative area in regard to the common tasks to be accomplished.

[1] Georg Jellinek: *Die Lehre von den Staatenverbindungen*, 1882, p. 143.
[2] Ibid.   [3] Ibid., p. 158.   [4] Ibid., p. 159.

Thus the International Postal Treaty of 1874 made all treaty states into one immense postal territory in respect of the exchange of correspondence.[1]

He divided the organised administrative unions into two classes, according to whether the task of administration related to the sphere not only of its own states but of other states also, or its activity was confined to the sphere of its own states. In the first case the organs set up by the union had an international character, whilst in the second it was national organs which had to carry out essential state functions.

Thus the administrative unions, as he remarked, were divided into those which had "international objects" and those which had "state objects," and this difference of purpose was manifested by the different legal position occupied by the organs of the two kinds of union.[2]

The oldest kind of international administrative unions were those set up by treaties with regard to international rivers, which laid down the principles of free navigation.[3]

Taking the Rhine as an example of this, a central commission consisting of commissioners from the riparian states, each of which sent one representative, met every year at Mainz for the purpose of enforcing strict observance of the river regulations. Besides the central commission a second authority was created to supervise the carrying out of regulations, at the time when the central commission was not sitting. This permanent commission consisted of a head and three assistant inspectors.

The head inspector was originally appointed by the majority vote of the central commission, and the assistant inspectors by individual riparian states, and their duty was to act as an executive body to supervise the carrying out of the regulations and the policing of shipping. The chief inspector had therefore the right and duty to give instructions to the Custom Offices in this respect and work in conjunction with the other local authorities, and could also make proposals to the central commission. Similar commissions and inspectorships were set up later for the rivers Po and Pruth and for the lower Danube. But the European Commission of the Danube possessed much more power than the others since it was created for the collective interest of Europe and was therefore of an international character.

Jellinek added that these commissions issued shipping regulations and could impose penalties for infringement of their rules

[1] Georg Jellinek: *Die Lehre von den Staatenverbindungen*, 1882, p. 159.
[2] Ibid., p. 160.   [3] Ibid., pp. 160–161.

—penalties which the territorial authorities were bound to enforce.

And as they thus carried out acts of "international legislation" and functioned as courts of appeal in respect of offences arising within their sphere of operations they possessed the character of an "international judiciary"; and the union states also delegated to the common organ important state authority.

Other organised administrative unions, such as the International Postal Union of 1874 and the International Commission of Weights and Measures of 1875, were notable creations of the nineteenth century. The organs set up by the respective international treaties were the postal bureau at Berne and the bureau of weights and measures at Paris, and these were given certain limited powers of regulations and execution. Jellinek also foresaw the need for international sanitary organisation in the form of an administrative union for the prevention of the spread of infectious diseases.[1]

His argument as to the permanence of international administrative unions was based on empirical rather than on merely legal considerations.

Although these unions were nominally for a limited period, or the members were given the right of denunciation, it was obvious that, owing to the nature of the purposes for which they were formed, they would be perpetual, or alternatively that if they were dissolved unions with similar purposes would take their place.

The total destruction of the postal and telegraph unions, for example, was impossible, because of the common interests of civilised communities. This applied equally to the case of non-organised administrative unions, such as those for the protection of copyright and so forth.

As regards the legal position of the international officials of these permanent administrative unions Jellinek pointed out that they were not joint servants of the states of the unions but officers of the unions as such.[2]

This organisation of the administrative union was no doubt legally compatible with the federal structure. In this respect Jellinek's legal recognition of the organised administrative union was a deduction from the actuality of its structure and functions.

The second kind of state union was that which sought to fulfil the essential purposes of the individual states by means of

[1] Georg Jellinek: *Die Lehre von den Staatenverbindungen*, 1882, pp. 163–165.
[2] Ibid., p. 167.

common organs and institutions. But such unions were formed only between states which were either members of higher state creations, i.e. of a federal state, or were connected nationally and historically, or whose finances were insufficient to maintain their own organs.

The most organically complete form of an administrative union of this kind was the German *Zollverein* of 1867–1871 with its federal council and common legislation.

This *Zollverein* was not a "federal state but only a league of sovereign states." The unique feature of this union was that it had the right to legislate in customs matters; the individual states had to promulgate the decrees, but had no power to enforce them—an historical proof that the exercise of legislation by a league did not prove its possession of the state character.

It is particularly interesting to note that the majority principle prevailed in the *Zoll* parliament as in the federal council, so that the members of both these bodies were not so much representatives of the states which appointed them as of the "collectivity of union states."

Therefore Jellinek assumed that the common organs of this kind of state union were "not only the functionaries of the union as such," but were also "necessary factors in the organisation of the individual state." Whereas in the first kind of union international organs were created, in the second several state organisations were appointed as common to all.[1]

Then Jellinek put forward the definition that when several states united to form "a permanent political union," with standing organisations, which had at least as an object their "common defence," such a union was a "confederation."[2]

It differed from the alliance by the "establishment of permanent executive organs" for the carrying out of the purposes of the *Bund*, and from the merely administrative union by its "essential requisite of a political object." The confederation could include "purposes of internal state life," such as uniformity of legislation and administration, among the objects of the *Bund*, but all that was really essential was a union for "mutual protection and defence"—without that the political character of the confederations was lost.

It depended upon the will of the confederated states whether the joint action should be exercised in regard to internal as well as to external matters. However closely the confederated states might be united they were bound by treaty, "so that the

[1] Georg Jellinek: *Die Lehre von den Staatenverbindungen*, 1882, p. 172.   [2] Ibid.

confederated states were and remained sovereign." Therefore Jellinek asserted that "the confederation was limited only by the sovereignty of the confederated states."[1]

He remarked that the confusion of opinions which characterised the history of political theory in respect of the confederation, and particularly the difficulty of distinguishing the *Staatenbund* from other forms of state union, arose, firstly, from the confused conception of the theory of sovereignty and, secondly, from the tendency to confuse the unessential with the essential in such matters as the nature and form of the organisation of the federal power, the financial system for federal purposes, the relationship of the federal authority to the citizens of the states, the amendment of the federal pact either by the unanimous or by the majority vote, and the belief that in these things "the criterion of confederation" was to be found.[2]

Owing to this, the assertion had been made that there was no sharp distinction between "confederation and federal state," because in most points transitions from one form to another could very easily be made.

If, however, one fixed upon the essential characteristic which alone could give a clear insight into the nature of unions of states, namely, that of sovereignty, then all obstacles to the recognition of the true legal nature of the *Staatenbund* vanished, all ambiguity of conception was removed, and the confederation stood out as an independent creation clearly marked off from other unions.

He pointed out that the essential characteristics of the confederation, manifested by all its forms, were a purpose consisting at least of the protection of the federal territories, an organisation sufficient for the federal purpose, and the continuance of the sovereignty of the confederated states.[3]

It had often been stated that perpetuity was the prevailing characteristic of the confederation, since it was based on "a close national or historical association of the allied states." It differed from the alliance in that it was not dependent on every change of policy, and from the commercial treaty in that it was not concluded for a fixed term of years. It was true that the federal union might be termed a permanent one and the members of the union could renounce their right of secession. Nevertheless, even the "federal state" was by its nature not a permanent institution.

[1] Georg Jellinek: *Die Lehre von den Staatenverbindungen*, 1882, p. 172.
[2] Ibid., p. 173.   [3] Ibid., p. 174.

The "federal pact" itself could be concluded for a long but yet definite time limit without the union thus formed losing thereby its character of confederation, and the legal possibility of the dissolution by the unanimous will of all the participators in a union declared to be permanent could not be denied.

Moreover, as the confederated states were "sovereign" and the interpretation of a state treaty was according to international law vested in the parties to the treaty, it followed that the confederation must acquiesce in the withdrawal of any one of its member states if the latter's existence were threatened, or if in its judgment the federal authority exceeded its powers so that nothing was left for the individual state except submission to the union or secession from it.

Jellinek argued that nullification and secession, which were absolutely forbidden to the members of a unitary or federal state, followed "logically as a legal remedy from the nature of the confederation as a treaty-based institution."[1] For the sovereign state could be "bound neither unconditionally nor permanently."

The continuous sovereignty of the states made the confederation into a "shapeless unsatisfactory organ of state life"; the realisation of the purpose of the union was in actual fact left to the will of the confederated states.

The federal authority was not higher than the authority of the confederated states, nor was the latter subordinate to the former, but the federal authority consisted of "the supreme rights of the confederated states which had been handed over to it."[2]

In the confederation the state could exercise certain supreme rights only in association or agreement with others. But it did exercise these rights itself by delegating them to the common central organ, and the decisions of the central organ were therefore its own decisions, but nevertheless were in agreement with those of the other confederated states. The federal resolutions might indeed be carried by majority vote, but an out-voted state could have no grievance, since in the federal pact it had promised to conform to the will of the majority. Similarly, even if the execution of federal decisions was by the federal authorities, there could be no question of legal injustice. Nor was the creation of a federal court to decide disputes between the members incompatible with the sovereignty of the states, because the state which submitted to arbitration was not subordinating itself to an out-

---

[1] Georg Jellinek: *Die Lehre von den Staatenverbindungen*, 1882, p. 175.
[2] Ibid., p. 176.

side judgment, but merely entrusting a third party with the determination of the law. Thus a federal court in the confederation had a character of a permanent court of arbitration. Finally, it was quite possible for a supreme right to be entrusted to the central organ to exercise directly without the intermediary of the individual state authority.

With regard to the modern doctrine that the confederation exercised authority over the authorities of the confederated states, Jellinek regarded that opinion as destroying any possibility of distinguishing the confederation from the federal state by any essential characteristics.

He objected to the theory of domination over sovereign states on the ground that it was a contradiction in itself and impossible both in theory and in practice. He quoted in support of his view Madison's remark in the *Federalist* (No. XX), "a sovereignty over sovereigns, a government over governments, a legislation for community, as contradistinguished from individuals; as it is a solecism in theory, so in practice it is subversive of the order and ends of civil polity."

How it is possible that a treaty could be concluded in such a manner that it retained none of its essential characteristics—namely, its basis on the will of the contracting parties; how the decisions of the federal authority set up by the treaty could become dominating commands to the state authorities, were to Jellinek juristic riddles which the supporters of the theory had not even attempted to solve.

He held that the confederation was "a creation of international law." But international law recognised no "legal subjects other than states." Therefore he asserted that the confederation, which was not a state, "was consequently not a legal subject," but was rather, as Mohl and Laband had argued, a "legal relationship." It was not a juristic personality and never could be one.[1]

In this respect he argued that a juristical subject must, as its name implied, be a creation of "a state system of law," which "must stand above those by whose will it may be formed."

But "the legal system of international law, which had its legal sanction in the will of the states, could not possibly create a legal personality out of and above several state personalities."

The creation in a state of a juristic person by agreement between a number of individuals is made possible only by the fact that the state allows juristic personality to what has been

[1] Georg Jellinek: *Die Lehre von den Staatenverbindungen*, 1882, pp. 178, 179.

established by arrangements between the parties to the agreement, if the established legal rules have been observed.[1]

As the higher will of the state was the legal basis of the existence of the juristic person there was "no power above the confederation which could create that which to the combined wills of the individual states was impossible."[2]

As Laband assumed that the confederation was a "legal relationship" in contrast to the federal state which was a "juristic person of the public law," it was important to consider whether the juristic person was to be regarded as part of an international or a constitutional system of law. If the confederation is to be regarded as a legal relationship and not a legal subject, there is no explanation of the fact that a confederation appeared in external matters as a unity, not as "a sum of states," differing in this respect from an alliance in which the allied powers acted "as a number of international personalities."[3]

The reason Jellinek adduced for the differences between the confederation and the alliance was as follows:—

When states combined they remained "externally as separate powers, if their common policy did not contain a visible guarantee of permanency." If, however, the permanent uniformity of the external policy was "guaranteed by an organisation of the confederated states" which was to outlast any political changes, he asserted that "in the circumstances that permanent uniformity of action on the part of several members and internal unity regarded from without presented the same aspect, the collectivity of confederated states would be regarded as an international unity, and treated as a subject of international law."[4]

In the same way as the confederation and administrative union, the states of a real union, in spite of their mere association relationship, appeared as a unity when combined for united action in external affairs.[5]

Finally, the main characteristic of the confederation, arising from the principle of sovereignty, was a general presumption in favour of the competence of the individual states and against that of the confederation. In case of conflict the state, weighing the federal object against the highest particular purposes of the individual state, could take a decision as to its own competence, even against the final decree of the federal court, because so long as the state remained sovereign it could refuse acceptance of an arbitration award by virtue of its sovereignty.[6]

[1] Georg Jellinek: *Die Lehre von den Staatenverbindungen*, 1882, p. 179. [2] Ibid. [3] Ibid., p. 181. [4] Ibid., p. 182. [5] Ibid., p. 183. [6] Ibid., p. 184.

FEDERAL IDEAS FROM SEYDEL TO BRIE

Jellinek had already clearly shown that in the strictest sense of the word one could not speak of sovereignty of the union as such. Though before 1848 the ordinary expression used was "sovereign" German or "sovereign" Swiss confederation, the sovereignty thus assigned to the whole confederated state was not different from that of the individual states, but was "coincident with it, or rather it designated the authority derived from the sovereignty of the individual states, which was exercised in common in accordance with the federal pact."

To call a confederation "sovereign" was to use an inexact term to denote the fact that certain sovereign rights were exercised in common by the confederated states after preliminary agreement as to the mode of that exercise.[1]

Then Jellinek said that, of the two kinds of confederation, the first had hitherto almost exclusively been recognised and because of its historical manifestations had come to be regarded as the type. The Greek and mediaeval town unions, the United Netherlands, the Swiss confederation up to 1798 and then from 1815 to 1848, the North American union of 1778 to 1787, the confederation of the Rhine and the German confederation, belonged collectively and separately to this category.

Its characteristics were:—central organ consisting of a congress of envoys of the confederated states; voting in this congress according to instructions; need for unanimity as to changes in the federal pact; and the condition that laws and decrees made by the central authority became binding on the subjects and citizens only when promulgated by the individual governments.

In contrast to this form of confederation there was another which, however, had been developed only in theory; the first attempt to bring it into existence was destroyed by the Civil War in the United States of America.

The exponent of this second type of confederation was the American, John C. Calhoun, whose ideas had been developed by Max von Seydel in Germany. The confederation of the Southern states in North America during the Civil War was an attempt at the realisation of Calhoun's conception of federal government.[2]

Jellinek condemned the confederation theory of Calhoun as logically untenable. He explained that the application of Calhoun's idea to the new German Empire, which Max von Seydel had attempted with very little success, left out of consideration the great difference between the historical and social foundations

[1] Georg Jellinek: *Die Lehre von den Staatenverbindungen*, 1882, p. 184.
[2] Ibid., pp. 187–188.

of the German Empire, formed mainly of monarchical states whose princes for centuries had been subordinate to a common ruler, and those of the transatlantic federal state, built up on the ideas of popular sovereignty and the greatest possible autonomy of the member states. "Federal government," as theoretically developed by Calhoun, differed from "confederacy" in one important respect, although both were based on treaty. The central organ of the confederation of the first kind, as the American union in its origin, resembled a gathering of diplomatists to decide how a treaty between their respective sovereigns might be carried out, but left the carrying out of their decisions to the parties who had concluded the treaty. The federal government, on the other hand, possessed as its central organ an actual government affecting the citizens of the states directly and possessing power to legislate in addition to its own administration and judicature. This power, however, was not inherent in, but was delegated to, the central organ by the states, which retained some of their supreme rights; consequently state supreme rights were divided into two classes—"delegated and reserved powers."

The theory of the permanent possession of all supreme rights by the individual states in the confederation, though that was provided with a "federal government," was in complete harmony with American ideas of constitutional law. The holder of all supreme rights was the nation to which sovereignty inalienably belonged.

Jellinek declared that history had decided that the principles of Calhoun were "not applicable to the union, that not the states but the union decided through the supreme federal court as to the constitutionality of a law, and that consequently sovereignty was vested in the union and not in the individual states.[1]

Jellinek placed the real union in the category of organised unions. In contrast with the personal union—that is, the legally accidental union of several state powers under a single physical supreme personality—the real union, as a form of the juristic union of states, had been defined from the time of H. A. Zachariä as "the legally established union of a number of states under the same ruler."[2] That is to say, in the case of the real union emphasis was laid on "the constitutionality of the union," in that it was in accordance with a state law, founded by the law, coterminous with the law and terminated by the law.[3]

[1] Georg Jellinek: *Die Lehre von den Staatenverbindungen*, 1882, p. 194.
[2] Ibid., p. 197.   [3] Ibid., p. 198.

This conception had since been widened until to Jellinek the real union took its place "as a distinct constitutional form side by side with the federal state," both of them aiming at the "common discharge of common tasks." The "collectivity of organs" can transform itself into an actual unity, and there can thus be an imperceptible transition from the real union to the unitary states.

The essence of the fundamental law setting up a union of several states was that it embodied commands addressed to the personalities (individuals or associations) subordinated to the state power, whilst for personalities not so subordinated the law was capable only of having the "meaning of a unilateral declaration of will, without any binding power."[1] On this assumption Jellinek asserted that "a state cannot unite itself with another state simply by its own law," and a union of independent states could take place only through the agreement of the wills of both.[2]

Next, as to the nature of the real union. "Monarchical states can, without weakening their sovereignty, form a political organised union either of such a kind that the holders (*Träger*) of the sovereignty remain physically distinct, and therefore a special organ must be set up to give effect to the will of the union, or they can give expression to their political association by assigning the exercise (*Trägerschaft*) of their wills to one and the same person, who legally represents as many state authorities as there are states thus united."[3]

From the actual facts of the real unions of Sweden and Norway, and of Austria and Hungary after 1867, and the conclusions which the members of those unions had drawn as to their consequences, it was clear that in its purpose the real union is identical with a confederation.[4]

So Jellinek asserted that "the real union is therefore only a special case of the confederation" and "is that form of confederation which arises when two or more states that are independent of one another unite legally for common protection in such a manner that one and the same physical personality appears as the appointed holder of the state authority, and the states thus united remain entirely at liberty to extend the union to other fields of state activity if they so desire.[5]

Jellinek thus included the real union in the category of the *Staatenbund*, in which the member states are the holders of the sovereignty.

[1] Georg Jellinek: *Die Lehre von den Staatenverbindungen*, 1882, p. 198.
[2] Ibid., p. 199. [3] Ibid., p. 211. [4] Ibid., p. 214. [5] Ibid., p. 215.

§ 6

Then he proceeded to examine and define the federal state, which was the highest form of the union of states, and first of all sought to lay down some clear ideas as to the origin of the federal state.

However divergent the opinions as to the legal nature of the federal state, he assumed agreement on one point, namely, the "possibility of the consolidated state," and further that the federal authority was "a real independent state authority" and that the federal state therefore represented a creation not merely of international law but also of constitutional law.[1]

The actual facts to which he referred as the sources of federal theory were only those of three modern federal states—the North American union since 1787, the Swiss union since 1848 and the new German Empire, all of which had an independent central authority distinct from the authorities of the individual states.

Jellinek pointed out that in order to appreciate the peculiar nature of these three unions it is necessary to understand their origin, and so transfer the most difficult of all scientific problems, that of the formation of the state, from the sphere of abstract speculation to that of concrete fact.

The problem had been the subject of much discussion in the German Empire and in the American union—in the former as a matter of theory, but in the union for very practical reasons. In the union the two theories as to its origin—that is to say, as to its legal basis—were at the same time the postulates of two sets of party principles which were in sharp conflict.

One theory was that the federal constitution was a treaty between states; that the states retained their sovereignty with all its juristic consequences; they were superior to the union and therefore possessed the "inalienable right" of nullification or secession. This theory meant that the constitution was federal, not national; it existed for the sake of the peoples of the individual states, and not for the sake of a collective nation, which in fact did not exist. This was the doctrine of the "state rights" party—a doctrine originated by Jefferson, elaborated by Tucker and fully developed by Calhoun.

The other theory was that the constitution was not a treaty between the states, though it might be regarded as the result of

[1] Georg Jellinek: *Die Lehre von den Staatenverbindungen,* 1882, p. 253.

one; for once the treaty was concluded, it changed its nature and became "law." So far as the constitution extended, it created one people and one state; secession was not the exercise of an inherent right, but high treason; the laws of the union were the "supreme" laws, to which the laws of the individual states must give way. In this theory the constitution was not federal but national, and created not a "union," but a "state." This was the doctrine of the republicans, formulated in the *Federalist* by Hamilton, Madison and Jay, and defended by Daniel Webster in the contest with Calhoun.

The American conflict showed that the problem of the origin of the federal state was not merely a scholastic debating subject, but was politically of very great importance. Its interest is therefore two-fold, and equally great for political theory and for practical statesmanship.

As regards the first theory—that of the state rights party—Jellinek asserted that "this mechanical explanation of the birth of the federal state is simply logically impossible." An individual person can control only what lies within the sphere of its own will: a state can do as it pleases with its own powers, it can hand them over to another state, it can exercise them jointly with other states, but it cannot create another state personality distinct from its own. To Jellinek the most important basis of the state, the "organic element" by which and on which it is built up, is the nation:[1] but the nation cannot by its own will transform one state into another.

The "contract" or "treaty" theory was no doubt the result of the fallacious doctrine of *Naturrecht*, and the scientific overthrow of that doctrine carried with it the rejection of the treaty theory and finally freed constitutional law from the hackneyed and misleading examples of state formation by "contract," as for instance the formation of the New England states (on board the *Mayflower*) and of California.

So Jellinek asserted that "neither an individual nor a state can by a treaty with others create a nationality hitherto nonexistent." And he added that "the fact that a collectivity feels and knows itself to be a unity and gives expression to that unity, that it sets itself up as a collective personality, as a subject of will and action, this is the essential basis of the creation of the state, whatever may be the external circumstances and incidents that precede its creation."[2]

[1] Georg Jellinek: *Die Lehre von den Staatenverbindungen*, 1882, p. 256.
[2] Ibid., p. 257.

In the same way the theory that the constitution of a state rests upon a treaty basis is in direct conflict with the modern conception of public law. It is impossible to think of state authority as being set up originally by treaty, for the pact of subjection and of state regulation (*pactum subjectionis et ordinationis*) is incapable of forming a legal foundation of the state constitution. He contended that by its very nature a treaty cannot produce "any will which is higher than itself or an independent will on an equality with itself." But the existence of a state means that there has been created a personality endowed with a will higher than the wills of those who have created it. Unless that is the case there is nothing which makes the treaty permanent and unaffected by any change of mind of those who made it, and the treaty lasts only so long as it is compatible with the highest interests of the contracting parties—interests which are essentially "particularist."

Jellinek therefore held that the "association authority" (*Societätsgewalt*) thus established cannot have the main characteristic of a state authority; it cannot govern or command unconditionally, but is always dependent on the good will of the members of the association.[1] On this line of argument a treaty remains a treaty and cannot become a law.

Thus the theory of the *staatsrechtliche novatio* was open to all the criticisms directed against the atomist theory of the social contract, the chief of these being the logical impossibility of ascribing to the treaty-makers the obligation to carry it out in cases where the most important of their individual interests conflicted with those of the generality. The logical consequence of this doctrine had been deduced by Calhoun and subsequently by Seydel. It was that the federation is not a state but only a treaty relationship, its constitution is a sum of delegated powers and not itself an independent power.[2]

The fundamental postulate involved in the conception of the state—namely, that it is superior to any individual interest, and that consequently in the extreme limit every interest which conflicts with the purposes of the state must be sacrificed—clearly does not apply to a creation of such a kind, whether its constitution be in form a treaty or a law; its creators are not bound to sacrifice themselves for that which they have created, and each constituent state retains its own sovereign right, subject only to limitations imposed by its own will.

Another theory, which held that the federal state is the outcome

[1] Georg Jellinek: *Die Lehre von den Staatenverbindungen*, 1882, p. 258.   [2] Ibid.

of a treaty between its members, sought to demonstrate that the federal power is organic in its nature and protected against arbitrary dissolution—and thereby has the character of a state, by reference to various relationships in life, e.g. marriage, which indeed are entered into as the result of an agreement, but then develop a higher character peculiar to themselves and independent of that agreement. With this may be put the doctrine that the federal state is "a juristic person formed by member states, and possessing a collective will which is superior to the will of the contracting parties, and that therefore it does not necessarily follow from the treaty origin that the legal relationship remains simply that of a treaty."

Jellinek recognised that relationships resulting from agreements may be of a higher nature than those actually imposed by the agreements. But the existence and duration of that higher nature depend not at all upon the voluntary entry into the relationship, but either upon the organic absorption of the individual parties into a higher unity or upon the authority of a system of law which regards the creation of a juristic person as the legal consequence of the agreement and gives legal recognition to the relationships of superiority and subordination aimed at by the agreement. This second alternative is not possible in the case of states not previously associated, because international law does not recognise juristic persons, and because all the objections to the treaty origin of the state are equally obstacles to the possibility of the creation of a juristic person by states which are independent of one another. And even an organic relationship has no inherent stability, unless some higher power is legally entitled to restrain any party seeking to break away from the relationship. If the moral basis of a marriage ceases, the marriage no longer answers its purpose and continues only as a mere agreement, a compulsory civil law relationship. The state can declare such a marriage indissoluble, but then it exists not of itself but because of a higher will. This doctrine then gives no answer to the question: What is the legal security of the treaty-formed public corporation (which the federation is represented to be) against the arbitrary withdrawal of a member? We are faced again with the problem which no form of the treaty theory can solve: Whence does the treaty derive its binding power, even when it conflicts with the highest interests of the contracting parties, and what is the legal principle which prohibits secession in any circumstances?

Now the state is distinguished from all other forms of human association by the fact that none of its members has any absolute rights against it, and its sphere of authority does not depend on their good will. This unique quality of the state, its character of an organisation of a people, armed with supreme authority in order to maintain unity, is obscured and made unrecognisable if it is regarded as analogous to relationships which can arise only in a state and essentially with the co-operation of the state. Despite its far-reaching importance, in jurisprudence treaty or contract is and remains limited to the relations between the persons subordinate to the state and between states themselves.[1] It presupposes the existence of the state and cannot be its prerequisite.

Even if the Puritans when they set up the New England states had not made agreements among themselves and had not formally undertaken to form themselves into a state and obey the appointed authorities, the history of the English colonies in North America would have taken the same course. It was the need for expansion and for the solidarity of a handful of men in that terrible wilderness, combined with great religious fervour—that is to say, "organic driving forces"—that in this case as in all others first called the state into existence.

Therefore Jellinek asserted that all attempts to derive the establishment of the federal state from a compact of the member states must fail, because it is impossible to give a legal explanation of the formation of the state. "The state being the prerequisite of a system of law cannot be explained by a rule of law which depends upon the state for its sanction." Every juristic justification of the state was based on a *petitio principii*. The creation of states has been determined by no law other than that of "world history."[2]

He emphatically asserted also that in order to comprehend the creation of the federal state and its constitution, "it must not be regarded as an isolated phenomenon in the life of nations." The formation of the federal state had been the result of the same process as that of the national state.

Following this line of argument he held that "the federal state is one of the forms in which the modern state based on community of race or on some historical interdependence has manifested itself" and thus contrasted sharply with the dynastic formation of the mediaeval states.[3] In them the original territory of princes was enlarged by conquest, inheritance or exchange

---

[1] Georg Jellinek: *Die Lehre von den Staatenverbindungen*, 1882, pp. 260–261.
[2] Ibid., p. 262.   [3] Ibid.

and so forth, and formed by the ruler into a unified whole. To these processes the terms "incorporation," "cession," "conquest," "personal union," "real union" have been applied. The national states of modern times are the result of an entirely different process. National state formation is characterised by the fact that "a nation, that feels and knows itself to be a unity, gives expression to that unity by organising itself as a unit and consequently appears as a state." It is not the state that creates the nation, as in the states formed by dynastic policy or conquest, but a race, being a natural unit, already existing and working as a nation, strives to raise itself, by the process of state formation, from this merely natural condition of life to the status of legal existence as a national state. All national state-building arose from the fact that "race" and "nation" were not coterminous and that a race was either split up into a number of states or welded together mechanically into a nation with other elements not on a parity with it.[1]

In order to organise a nation into a state Jellinek held that two things were essential, the sweeping away of the old conditions on the one hand and a new creation on the other.

The old conditions could be overthrown either by "force"—revolution or war—or by "peaceful internal development," replacing the worn-out and unsuitable conditions by new ones better adapted to promote national well-being. This latter was "the path that has been taken in the creation of the federal state."[2]

Whilst in the first case the old state powers were entirely swept away, in the second case the new creation was brought about either with the co-operation of the legitimate powers hitherto existing, or at least without any violent attack upon them. But in both cases the result was something entirely new, not derived juristically from the former conditions. The process in every case is one of fact which can be described by an historical but not by a legal formula. Only when the state has been actually created can the jurist examine and interpret the forms in which that state manifests itself.

From the historical facts of the Swiss revision of the federal constitution, the summoning of the North American Convention of 1787, the North German Confederation Treaty of 1866 and the Versailles Treaty of 1870 between that body and the South German states, it appeared that these various agreements, recog-

[1] Georg Jellinek: *Die Lehre von den Staatenverbindungen*, 1882, pp. 263–264.
[2] Ibid., p. 264.

nised by international law, did not stand "in any juristic causal relationship with the federal states which arose later, but only set up reciprocal obligations between state authorities hitherto existent, obligations which the individual states, as such, had to undertake and discharge."

Then he inquired, What is a constitution? The creation of the national state is brought about by the establishment of a code or body of regulations governing the exercise of the various functions of the common life, and by the establishment of administrative organs to make effective that ability of the nation "to will and to do" which has hitherto been merely a national fact, but now becomes a legal right. The system so set up is called a constitution.[1]

The act of state formation is therefore identical with the act of the creation of the constitution, and consequently the state and the constitution are "inseparable" from one another, and the first constitution of the state is determined by the very nature of the state, and is "indeed the logical prerequisite of the state itself."[2]

On this assumption the state prior to the existence of its organs is an "unrealisable conception." The essential thing in the conception of the state is that it is an organisation, and a pre-organisation is a contradiction in terms, and the first organisation, that is the first constitution, is from the juristic standpoint not derivable from anything else.

This constitution, therefore, to Jellinek had "its basis in the existence of the state which is always something real," and he asserted that "the constitution of a newly arisen state is just as real and actual as the state itself."[3] Its existence is one of the assumptions from which the jurist has to start; it is only with the existence of the state and its original organisation that the field of the jurist's activity is opened to him. Jellinek's own jurisprudence was based on such a positivism, from which and through which he conceived the creation of the federal state as well as that of the national state.

He described the process of organisation as follows. In the case of the nation in which, because the government has been forcibly overthrown, there are no recognised state authorities, a provisional government is formed which convokes a constituent assembly. The constitution drafted by that assembly becomes the state constitution as soon as it is made operative—that is, as soon as

[1] Georg Jellinek: *Die Lehre von den Staatenverbindungen*, 1882, p. 265.
[2] Ibid., pp. 265–266.   [3] Ibid., p. 266.

the scheme of organisation prescribed by it is obeyed. Thus the draft of the constitution, which is in itself inorganic, is endowed with life and activity by the will of the nation, by the recognition accorded to it by the whole people.

The surest foundation of all law, namely, that it is rooted in the national consciousness, and is "sustained by the national spirit," appears as the direct sanction of the constitution, and so of the consolidation of the state and the development of the potential power of the state into a reality.

The same process as that described for the states which are the outcome of revolution takes place, though in a different way, in the national states which develop without any violent change in the old order. The state organs which summon the constituent conventions, commissions, etc., have the same relation to the state which is to be formed as the provisional governments in the revolutionary cases. They are the *de facto* governments of the state which is in process of formation, and the constitution evolved by the constituent assembly is its fundamental law.

As the modern state rests on this national consciousness, so the federal state has been developed on the same basis—that is to say, its formation is the outcome of a peaceful, and not of a revolutionary or violent, process. The mere working out of a constitution by a *de facto* government and parliament is not sufficient to bring the state into being. And obviously where a national state has been set up on the ruins of another there can be no relation of the new state to that which it has replaced. But where the old authorities still exist *de jure* the position is altogether different. The new state cannot come into existence, unless the old states assent to it and recognise its authority. Strictly, therefore, the federal state does not exist until the individual states included in the federal union give their sanction to the constitution of the union.[1] But the union may come into being even if formally approved only by a majority of the states intended to be included within it. And a state may become a member of the union without any express legal declaration to that effect and by the mere fact of submitting to the authority of the union. This was the case in the Swiss confederation in 1848 and in the North American union. In the German Empire, where the states had by treaty undertaken the reciprocal obligations to enter the union, the consideration of the federal constitution by the constitutional bodies of the individual states, which preceded the adoption of that constitution, was in order

[1] Georg Jellinek: *Die Lehre von den Staatenverbindungen*, 1882, pp. 269–270.

to determine if the new state was in accordance with the requirements of their various international obligations. The publication of the federal constitution in the individual states in the form of a state law was merely the solemn announcement by each state government of its decision to enter into the federal state. All state activity, whether in domestic or foreign affairs, can before the coming into operation of the constitution be carried on only by the old state authorities.[1]

The entry of a state into the federal state means exactly the same thing as the entry of an individual into an existing state—namely, subordination to the authority of the state of which one desires to become a member. Even though historically or politically it might be recalled that the relations had been originally determined by treaty, and though this could be shown particularly by the fact that the consent of the member states was necessary for any amendment of the constitution, yet juristically the only tenable principle is that the rights of the member states are possessed by them simply as members of the union. So Jellinek agreed that the foundation and corner-stone of the constitutional law of a federal state is Lincoln's dictum that "the states have their status in the union, and they have no other legal status."

In short, looking at the facts of history, Jellinek concluded that the nature of the process whereby the federal state is formed does not differ from the process of formation of the national state. Starting from this assumption he proceeded to examine the nature of the federal state.

When the state is being organised there are a number of possible courses which can be adopted. Firstly, if the state has the whole of its functions exercised directly by agents created by and dependent upon itself, so that nothing except those agents comes between itself and the individuals, then it is a "centralised unitary state."[2]

Secondly, in order to fulfil its purposes the state can make use of associations or bodies corporate already in existence as the result of historical development, or formed by itself, and do so either by requiring them to give effect to its own will or by allotting to them a sphere of independent activity subject only to general rules and a measure of supervision. This is the "decentralised unitary state."[3]

Thirdly, a state can entrust the carrying out of its tasks to

[1] Georg Jellinek: *Die Lehre von den Staatenverbindungen*, 1882, p. 271.
[2] Ibid., p. 276.   [3] Ibid., pp. 276–277.

associations or corporations which already exist or develop within it, and give up all control over the manner in which those bodies exercise the functions thus given to them; it can prevent them from going outside their allotted spheres, but abandon all supervision of their actions within those spheres. But a corporation which exercises state powers uncontrolled must be called a state. A state whose members possess uncontrolled powers—that is to say, have of their own right state authority—has, in fact, states subordinate to it. And if there is no organic relation between these members and the super-state, and the latter does not act directly upon the people, then the state has been broken up into a number of parts held together only artificially, and it becomes a *Staatenstaat*.[1] But if the state maintains a direct relationship with the people and surrenders only a part of its functions to the member states, such a state, with its relations to the member states determined by a constitution, is a "federal state."

Therefore Jellinek laid down as a definition that "a federal state is a state in which the sovereign power has by constitution divided the totality of the functions to be exercised within its sphere of power in such a manner that it reserves only a prescribed amount of those functions to b exercised by itself, and leaves the rest, without any control as to the determination of the governing principles or over the particular manner in which the functions are exercised, so long as the constitutional limitations are observed, to the non-sovereign member states which have been created by the grant to them, by the constitution, of state authority."[2]

As the sovereign state makes itself into a consolidated state in such a way as to create within itself a number of non-sovereign state authorities, so it gives to its people "a dual state qualification"; for in respect of the powers left to be exercised by the member states without control, the people are made subject to a non-sovereign state authority. In the federal state, therefore, the people are subjected firstly to the power of the central state, and, secondly, to the power of the member state in respect of the latter's particular functions, i.e. "a dual state allegiance" is set up; the inhabitants of the federal state are subjects of that state and of a member state also.

If the opinion be correct that the federal state by its constitution creates the member states, it logically follows that "allegiance to the federal state is the primary matter and alle-

[1] Georg Jellinek: *Die Lehre von den Staatenverbindungen*, 1882, p. 278. [2] Ibid.

giance to the member states takes only a secondary place," and that just as it is the federal state which first confers on its members a state nature, so it subordinates its subjects or citizens to the non-sovereign authority by the same act as that by which it calls that authority into being.[1]

The process of admission of an alien into the union must therefore be that he becomes first a subject or citizen of the federal state and then of a member state. But actually this logical conclusion is drawn only in the case of the North American union. There one becomes a citizen of one of the member states only after one has been admitted as a citizen of the union. On the other hand, by the constitutions of Switzerland and the German Empire it is laid down that citizenship of a canton or state carries with it Swiss or German citizenship. But in the German Empire it was possible to be a subject of the empire without being a subject of a state; the people of Alsace-Lorraine were subjects of the empire (*Reichsangehörige*) without being subjects of any individual member state (*Landesangehörige*), whereas on the contrary member state allegiance (*Landesangehörigkeit*) without empire allegiance (*Reichsangehörigkeit*) was inconceivable.[2]

The fact of the organisation of a state in federal form may be due to either one of two sets of historical facts. The state may have been a centralised or decentralised unitary state (as defined above) and found itself compelled to grant to its parts autonomous powers, either because it could not enforce its authority upon provinces with a tradition of independence, or because of the nature of its constitution. Jellinek pointed out that, if the proposals of the federalist party in Austria were realised, the Austrian Empire would be an example of this process.[3]

Or the federal state may be the incorporation into a single state of a people previously divided into a number of states, but incorporation in such a way that the former state authorities are not entirely swept away, but allowed to continue within prescribed limits, as in the three existing federal states (U.S.A., Switzerland, Germany). In these there is historical continuity between the states which formerly were sovereign and are now non-sovereign; but, nevertheless, the power of these non-sovereign states must be regarded legally as something entirely new—otherwise we come back to divided sovereignty, the treaty origin of the federal state, in a word, to the whole Waitzian theory of

[1] Georg Jellinek: *Die Lehre von den Staatenverbindungen*, 1882, p. 279.
[2] Ibid., pp. 279–280.   [3] Ibid., p. 280.

the federal state and all its inherent contradictions. Thus the process of creating a federal state of this kind is juristically exactly the same as that of the confirmation by the new sovereign power of the provincial constitution of territory transferred to it, as, for instance, the maintenance under Russian rule of the constitution of Finland.

The member state, as soon as it is subjected to the federal state, takes over all the rights and duties which are assigned to it, receiving them from the sovereign state, and thereby becomes the legal heir of that sovereign power which it formerly possessed. Consequently it takes over, for example, all its previous financial liabilities, and as a non-sovereign state enters into all its previous international relations, so far as they are not modified or terminated by its subordination to the federal power.

If it be necessary from the legal standpoint to regard the member states as created by the federal constitution, and to maintain the "state" nature of the federation and the unity of sovereignty, it becomes impossible to sustain Laband's explanation of the federal state which regarded it as a juristic person made up of the member states.

Laband unfortunately derived his theory only from the case of the German Empire; it was in no way applicable to the other federal states. Apart from the fact that the doctrine is untenable in theory, it means in practice that the federal state is not the realisation of the national state, for it is not the nation but states which have created the state.

In his later works Laband substantially modified his earlier views, as he recognised that in respect of the activities carried on by the empire directly the member states (*Länder*) had ceased to function, and thereby admitted the direct subjection of the peoples of the member states to the empire.

This direct exercise of the federal authority over the whole people first gives to the federal state the possibility of an organic life. When the state authority acts directly upon the people, the state can function without disturbance, for against a few recalcitrant individuals the state's power is overwhelming. But when it has to deal not with its physical subjects but with collective persons, then the enforcement of its commands largely depends upon the good will of those persons, for the coercion of a state is not so certain or so easy as the coercion of individuals.

Jellinek, like the American federalists, admitted that even if there were a strong central authority the mechanical operation of such an indirect rule would result in constant friction and conflict. The essential nature of the state as a personality striving for the fullest possible independence would manifest itself by attempts on the part of the member states to confine their subjection to the over-state within the narrowest possible limits, and we should have the spectacle of a *Staatenstaat* kept in being only by artificial means.

In a state which represents only the theoretic unity of a number of states, delegations from the parliaments of the member states can serve adequately as the constitutional means of giving the people a share in the formation of the state will. But if the federal state is to be an organism, if there is to be direct contact between the state authority and the nation, there must be a parliament directly elected by the people, and representative therefore not of the particular states in which they happen to be elected, but of the whole state community.

So Jellinek pointed out that in all federal states there were parliaments directly elected, and thereby, as Zorn said of the German *Reichstag*, the idea of national unity was most clearly expressed with all its implications. The federal council or senate provided for the representation of the member states.[1]

Jellinek proceeded next to examine the division of powers between the central and member states. He observed first that, in opposition to Waitz's requirement of an absolute demarcation between the powers of the central and state authorities, it had recently been urged that the federal authority must be so organised as to give the member states a share in the making and exercise of the general will. The federation is not simply a national state, it is also a federal state; it is not only a state, it is a union.

To Laband, who regarded the federal state authority as theoretically the unification of the authorities of the member states, the participation of those states in the formation of the federal will is a necessary deduction from his conception of federalism. But on the assumption that the federal state is created not by the states but by the nation, Jellinek held that there is no compelling reason why the central authority should be a unity formed of the state authorities.[2] Indeed, if a state character be ascribed to the federal authority, then from the purely legal standpoint it does not matter how the will of the federal state is formed and made effective. The method by which the will of the state is formed, though of very great political and ethical

[1] Georg Jellinek: *Die Lehre von den Staatenverbindungen*, 1882, p. 284.
[2] Ibid., p. 285.

importance, is, when considered from the strictly legal point of view, a matter of concern only so far as the organs by which the national will is formed and exercised are prescribed by rules of law and their modes of operation are legally determined.[1]

Jellinek pointed out that the process of the formation of the will was impossible of juristic conception. In all states the laws are the outcome not of individual wills, but of a union of wills expressed by various persons and bodies, as for example in an absolutist state the government with its legislative commissions, in constitutional states the legislatures whose decisions are approved by the princes, and in a republic the organs entrusted by the people in accordance with the constitution with the task of expressing the national will.

Therefore juristically the law can be considered not as "the will of the individual persons and associations which have made it, but only as the unitary will of the state." And the stages by which the law has reached the statute book are juridically of no importance.

These various stages from the introduction of a bill to its enactment are in fact to the jurist merely internal concerns of the person that is the state, comparable with the mental processes of an individual which lead up to decision and action, and however great may be their effect upon the final determination and the manner of its exercise, they have no juridical importance.

Any bill, as it passes through its preliminary stages, is to the minds of jurists only "internal preliminaries of the state personality" and legally of no importance, however great the influence of those stages on the formation of will and manner of execution. Psychologically, decision and will appear as an indivisible act which is different from all the preceding psychical processes of every kind. But if the will of the state must juridically be a series of indivisible acts of a unitary person, then it is only from the politico-ethical standpoint that the participation of a number in the formation of the state will is conceivable. If a number of individuals are called upon to be the "holder of the state will" the state will is still not the sum of the individual wills but the will of a personality differing from all those individuals; that is to say, "the will of the collectivity of the holders of the state power."[2]

Consequently, a division of sovereignty of this nature could

[1] Georg Jellinek: *Die Lehre von den Staatenverbindungen*, 1882, p. 285.
[2] Ibid., p. 286.

be postulated only in an ethical and political sense. As regards allowing the co-operation of the member states in the determination of the state will and the exercise of the state power, Jellinek recognised that this may well be a matter of political importance, but he did not regard it as having any particular influence on the character of the state.

Just as it is of no importance to the conception of monarchy whether the monarch is an absolute one or has imposed constitutional restrictions upon himself, and as monarchy and republic are both comprised within the conception of the state, so it does not matter in the conception of the federal state in what way its will, different from the wills of its members and superior to those wills, comes into being. And Jellinek added that the federal state, so organised that the member states are given a definite share in the activities of the state, is only one species of the genus "Federal State."[1] Nevertheless, this participation of the member states in the federal power, though juridically quite unnecessary, is politically of the greatest significance. Jellinek pointed out that the health of the state life depends on the utilisation for the purposes of the state of all the influences at work among the people, otherwise there is the danger that they may become antagonistic to the state. Like Tocqueville, he held that just as "political wisdom" made it advisable for the state not to antagonise any social class, so it would be foolish for the state to ignore and fail to utilise the political corporations existing in its midst and possessing a good deal of autonomy.[2] Similarly, the amount of the participation to be allowed by the federal state to its member states is a question not of juristic logic but of political expediency, to be determined by the particular circumstances of each case.

To Jellinek the federal organisation of the power of the federal state was not an essential characteristic of such a state. But nevertheless it is so expedient, and it is so likely that in every federal state constitution the federal idea will be given some scope, that the attribution to the member states of some influence upon the central government—an influence which cannot be precisely defined and must depend on the particular conditions —may be regarded as inherent in the conception of the federal state.

In the same way it is not possible to lay down any general rules as to the field of activity which the central government should reserve to itself or its modes of operation. One thing only

[1] Georg Jellinek: *Die Lehre von den Staatenverbindungen*, 1882, p. 287.   [2] Ibid.

is necessary; if the federal state is to be organised as a "state" it must discharge "the necessary functions of state life—legislation, government, administration and judicature." But as to the precise extent and mode of discharge of these functions there is a wide field of choice. A federal system can exist in every form of the state; it can be monarchical, as in the German imperial constitution of 1849; or power may be in the hands of a number of persons, as in the German Empire; or the whole people may be recognised as the repository of power, as in the United States and Switzerland. Its centre of gravity may be in the member states, in the sense that their activities are the rule and those of the central government the exception; or alternatively all important functions may be assigned to the central government and the member states have only to fill up the gaps. And in the discharge of its own administrative duties the federal state can avoid making use of the member states and act for the most part through its own agents (as in the United States), or it can make use of the member states (as in the German Empire and Switzerland).

As every state formation is "the product of historical, social and political conditions," and therefore possesses "a particular individual character" as well as the general characteristics of a state, so every federal state has its own peculiarities in respect of form and distribution of powers. But whatever that distribution may be, the character of the federal state as a sovereign state is maintained by the fact that the sovereign rights, even those made over to the member states, are vested in the federal state, and the member states are non-sovereign, because their sphere of action (though they may be subject to no control within that sphere) is assigned to them by the federal constitution.

Passing next to consider the difference between the confederation and the federal state, Jellinek rejected the theory that this results from any difference between their spheres of action, or from a difference in purpose (the confederation being concerned only with external affairs, whilst the federal state concerns itself with internal matters also). He asserted that the differences in the legal structure of associations of states are the results not of differences of purpose but of differences as to the legal basis.

An association based on a treaty, however complete the centralisation may be, does not evoke a state; the constitutional position of the member states towards the federal power, however great the limitations imposed on the central power, does not give to the association the character of a league of independent states.

So Jellinek concluded that in a confederation the sovereignty of the member states is limited only by that of the central authority, whereas in the federal state the sovereignty of the central power is limited only by that of the member states.

The only three essential matters in the conception of the federal state are "the sovereignty of the central power, the direct subordination of the people to that power, and the existence of the member states."[1]

The sovereignty of the federal power has the consequence that all matters affecting the life of the whole body corporate must be assigned exclusively to the central government—such matters are the making of peace and war, and the conclusion of treaties other than those of a purely administrative kind.

The fact that it is convenient for the federal state to prescribe at the outset in the constitution only its own sphere of operations, and the powers it intends to exercise, has given the impression that the powers not so reserved to the central authority are possessed by the member states of their own right, and has strengthened the popular idea that the federal state is the result of a treaty, and that its constitution can be altered only by treaty. Hence also the idea, widely spread through the literature of federation and finding apparent support in the 10th Amendment of the United States constitution and Article 3 of the Swiss constitution, that in all doubtful cases the assumption is against the federation and in favour of the member states. But this is a complete mistake; the doctrine is legally untenable and impossible in practice.

As disputes as to the respective spheres of the federal government and the member states are certain to arise, some provision must be made for their settlement, and from the nature of the federal state it follows that only the federal state can decide—a court of arbitration is impossible. So in the American union the interpretation of the constitution rests with the supreme court, in the Swiss federation (since the last revision of the constitution) with the federal court, and in the German Empire with the federal council (*Reichsrath*).

Calhoun, on the other hand, was strongly opposed to this right of the supreme court to annul acts of the member states, a right which he denounced as "usurpation," because of his

[1] Georg Jellinek: *Die Lehre von den Staatenverbindungen*, 1882, p. 291.

doctrine of state sovereignty. To Jellinek the theory of Calhoun was untenable as part of any conception of the federal state.[1]

And secondly, just as the federal state is entitled to decide its competence within the existing constitution, so it alone has the legal right to alter that constitution. As the original constitution is a law of the federal state, and not a treaty, so a change in it can be made only by federal legislation. If we admit that a change in the public law relations between the federal state and one of its members can be made only by a treaty, we must accept *in integrum* the doctrine of dual sovereignty, and recognise that the division of the functions of the state into two separate and unrelated parts is not incompatible with the nature of the state.

Treaty or contract is the form appropriate to arrangements between equals; but where their legal relationship is that of superiority and inferiority, the relations of life are determined not by treaty or contract, but by "command and obedience." If, then, we try to mark out a sphere within which the federal state and a member state are to be on an equal footing, the resultant division of state functions means the division and ultimate destruction of the very idea of the state. So Jellinek contended that it is only when the federal state definitely and by a law abandons the right to deal with a particular matter, and that matter is constitutionally within the competence of the member state—only then can there be formed a treaty relationship between the federal state and its member. But such cases must obviously be exceptional and very limited in range.[2]

Amendments of the constitution become necessary because of the life of the state. The right to amend the constitution is therefore a deduction from the idea of the state. But if the life of a state is dependent upon the good will of its members, that state is not a sovereign state, for "sovereignty" implies independence.

Therefore Jellinek concluded that "where the competence of the union can be changed only through the unanimous will of the members expressed in a pact (*Vertrag*), there is no federal state and no state at all, but there exists only a social power (*Socialgewalt*) equipped with delegated power which can be withdrawn at any time."[3]

From the nature of sovereignty it follows that its supreme powers include the right to determine the method by which the

---
[1] Georg Jellinek: *Die Lehre von den Staatenverbindungen*, 1882, pp. 293–294.
[2] Ibid., p. 295.   [3] Ibid., p. 296.

functions of the state, in all the various phases of the life of the state, shall be carried out. The sovereign power can discharge its tasks by the agency of relatively independent bodies and leave them uncontrolled. But it must always be within its power, if the principle of sovereignty is to be maintained, to determine by its own organs the scope of the direct activities of those bodies. So Jellinek concluded that in the federal state the constitution can be amended by the appropriate organs just as in the unified state it can be amended by legislation.[1]

The negation of the conception of the federal state is not made entirely untenable by the fact that complete unanimity as to an amendment of the constitution is not required. It is true that in the United States three-quarters of the states, in Switzerland a majority of the cantons, in Germany a three-quarter majority in the federal council, must assent. But by the constitution of the Southern states of America, which formed not a federal state but a confederation, and maintained the complete sovereignty of the associated states, unanimity was not necessary for change in the basic agreement.[2]

Finally, in the light of these considerations Jellinek inquired into the essential difference between the confederation and the federal state. Theoretically the distinction was easily formulated; in the latter the sovereignty vests in the union, whilst in the former it vests in the member states.[3] But in any case of doubt the practical test is whether the member states have or have not the right of secession.

The conviction that the member state is subordinate to the federal state, and therefore has not the right to break away from the national body, is a firmly established legal deduction. But Jellinek laid emphasis on the fact that whilst constitutional law must be firmly based on the principles of jurisprudence, its consideration cannot proceed on absolute and *a priori* lines, but must be influenced consciously or unconsciously by political opinions as to the nature and purpose of the state, and the facts of a particular state structure. Recognition of the federal state and of a particular federal state as being in the nature of a true state is based on the political assumption that such a state will be found to be the realisation of a national sentiment or some historical necessity.

Thus Haenel and Laband's conception of the federal state was, in fact, based on the idea that the empire was the national

---
[1] Georg Jellinek: *Die Lehre von den Staatenverbindungen*, 1882, p. 296.
[2] Ibid., p. 297.   [3] Ibid., p. 298.

state of the German people, and the national sentiment was so strong amongst the representatives of the science of jurisprudence that no defender was found among them for the theory of the "constitutional confederation," even in the modified form propounded by Seydel.

Jellinek observed that in the United States the result of the Civil War, whilst it had not entirely reduced the defenders of state rights to silence, had at least stifled their voices and moderated their claims; but before the war it would have been almost impossible to obtain a decision in favour of either party from an impartial tribunal guided by purely legal considerations, because all legal discussion started with some particular view as to the nature of the union, and the conclusion was therefore a foregone one.

It is only when we examine the historical development of a nation and realise the dangers to the national life that arise from particularism that, if a nation has been raised above the level of a mere association of governments, we can with assurance find the realisation of the national state in the form of a federal authority armed with powers acting directly upon the people, ascribe to that state the essentials of the sovereign state, and consequently declare any dissolution of the union either by agreement or by secession of the member states to be legally impossible. But such a formal juristic criterion as maintains that a particularistic conception of the federal state is *a priori* untenable, was certainly not applicable to the examples of that state which existed when Jellinek wrote, as he recognised; and certainly the criterion is not the possibility of the defeat of a minority of the member states by the majority on amendments of the constitution.

With respect to an organised union of states there are two possibilities; either the union is "itself a state" or it is based on "treaty."[1]

Consequently, when the position is looked at from the juristic standpoint, only two conclusions are possible, and these are drawn from two directly antagonistic sets of political opinions; the choice lies between a national state, with members possessed of a measure of autonomy, and associated individual states with interests which will always be particularist and therefore dangerous to the nation.

If the existence of a treaty basis for the federal state be accepted, it is necessary to impose some limit on the extent to

[1] Georg Jellinek: *Die Lehre von den Staatenverbindungen*, 1882, p. 300.

which it can of its own authority extend its sphere of activity—that is to say, it is necessary to deny the sovereignty of the federal state. On the other hand, if the federal state is regarded "as a state and as a nation organised into a sovereign collective personality," then the restrictions on its sphere of activity are only those imposed by itself. Every sovereign state can, if it serves its purpose, exercise its authority directly throughout the whole life of the community, but every state must recognise that there are spheres within which it must give its subjects liberty of action.

In every modern legal state these limitations exist, but they are "not absolute"; they must cease to operate if the higher purposes of the state so require, or they can and must diminish, for an entirely unlimited authority (which, in fact, has never existed even in the most despotic state) is altogether incompatible with the modern theory of the state.

There must therefore be a constitutional limitation of the will of every state, based upon law, whose task it is to further all the purposes of national life, and at the same time the possibility of determining, independently of any outside power, the manner in which it will carry out its tasks and the ambit of its authority. But however great the need for self-limitation may be, no part of the life of its members is in principle excepted from its authority, and therefore, whilst in the idea of the state there is implied the existence of some general limitation to state activity, there is no precise indication of the extent of that limitation.[1] So the federal state may constitutionally require the assent of a member state to the withdrawal of a right which the member state has hitherto enjoyed, but even so it is only by the will of the federal state that this restriction is imposed upon itself.

If the only limits of the competence of the federal state are those which are self-imposed, and are even then not absolute, the membership rights of the constituent states are also subject to its will. Admittedly an attempt has been made to impose a formal limit, at least in so far as the state may make changes in or withdraw the rights of its members without their unanimous consent, only so long as all the member states are treated equally. But Jellinek pointed out this is by no means a juristic deduction from the federal concept. The principle of equality of rights is a "material," but not a "formal" principle of law.[2]

[1] Georg Jellinek: *Die Lehre von den Staatenverbindungen*, 1882, p. 301.
[2] Ibid., p. 302.

The equal share of the member states in the amendment of the constitution, and the impossibility of withdrawing from one or more of them against their wills the independent exercise of government authority, is a limitation upon the competence of the federal state only in so far as it is imposed by the federal constitution. Thus in the constitution of the United States the rights which cannot be withdrawn from the member states without their consent are expressly enumerated, but where such constitutional provisions do not exist the principle of the equality of rights of the member states has merely a moral sanction, though a sanction so strong that it is practically equivalent to a constitutional obligation. But in the observance of this equality of rights between the member states the limitations imposed upon the federal state are not limitations of principle which must be observed in any amendment of the constitution, and all attempts to define such limitations are due to a confusion between the politically unlikely and the legally impossible. A limitation in respect of constitutional changes exists only in so far as the constitution itself imposes an exception, but even so that constitutional exception is not absolute. The withdrawal of a member state from the federal union was to Jellinek not permissible, not because such withdrawal would be in conflict with the treaty-based permanence of the federal state, but because the modern state is indivisible.

If any provision in the constitution were to mean a *Noli me tangere* for the state wills, the state must, in cases of extreme conflict, yield to the provisions of the constitution—and this is out of harmony with the idea of the sovereign state as the supreme organisation of a nation. Only in so far as the state is in a position to adapt its constitution to meet political, social, legal, economic and ethical needs is it able to fulfil its purpose and maintain itself and the community. Every sovereign state must, therefore, possess the capacity of altering the constitution and adopting any appropriate form. Otherwise circumstances may arise in which it will be driven to do so by means of a revolution or a breach of the constitution. A sovereign state is not bound down to a particular form—monarchical or republican; Aristotle's dictum that a change of form means a change of nature is not valid for the modern thinker. On the contrary the admissibility of a *lex in perpetuum valitura* must be rejected as directly antagonistic to the state. No form of state has at any time a *character indelibilis*, but depends on such conditions as are compatible with the continuance of the state.

Far-reaching constitutional changes are made only in cases of absolute necessity. The member states are therefore no more subjected to arbitrary action on the part of the federal state, because the latter has the power of altering the constitution, than are the citizens of a state to arbitrary action to restrict their civil rights on the part of the state, even though in that case also the action may be constitutional. The acceptance of the principle that the member state exists only at the pleasure of the federal state, only means that in the last resort, if, within the sphere of the federal state, the interests of any "person" conflict with its own, the federal state as the higher power must decide. To deny the legal possibility of transforming the federal state into a unified state by constitutional processes involves the denial to the federal state of its sovereign and therefore state character, for the federal state cannot be a true state if it is not sovereign.[1]

The third essential of the federal idea, side by side with that of the direct and sovereign rule of the central power, is the presence of members organised as states and equipped with authority. And just as it is impossible to lay down precise legal principles as to the organisation and scope of the federal authority, so it is equally impossible to formulate principles as to the organisation of these member states. It is a matter of fact in each particular case.[2] It can only be said in general terms that those functions which by the very nature of the federal state belong to the central authority, the right to make peace and war, are withdrawn entirely from the member states, and their right to make international treaties is restricted to administrative agreements only.

Similarly, the extent to which the federal authority may influence the organisation of the states cannot be laid down in a general formula. The fact that the form of organisation of the member states is prescribed by the federal constitution does not conflict with the idea of the statehood of the members, so long as they are given a sufficient measure of freedom within that form of organisation. The rules of international law are applicable to the member states in so far as concerns their state character. Therefore, unless expressly forbidden by the constitution, they can send and receive envoys and conclude treaties in respect of the matters within their spheres—but only with states which are recognised by the federal state and are in friendly relations with it. Any provisions of such treaties which

[1] Georg Jellinek: *Die Lehre von den Staatenverbindungen*, 1882, p. 306.   [2] Ibid.

conflict with the federal constitution are invalid; and, further, as the non-sovereign state can be bound by the acts of the sovereign state, any provision of such treaties as conflict with those of a treaty subsequently made by the federal state are *ipso facto* annulled.

Just as it is not contrary to the nature of the federal states to allow the member states a certain restricted amount of freedom in foreign affairs—though that is politically by no means advisable—so the member states can make arrangements between themselves in respect of matters within their competence, so far as there is no constitutional prohibition. They can send and receive envoys to and from one another and make agreements between themselves, and these agreements, unless the contrary is expressly stipulated, are subject to the rules of international law, and not of the general law of the federation. But disputes between the member states of the federal state can only be settled, like those between the members of a confederation, by peaceful means. But there is this difference: in the confederation the tribunal cannot be more than a court of arbitration, whereas in the federal state there must be a court able to enforce the decision, for the ordinary means of ultimate settlement of disputes between states—that is war—is excluded, both because it would conflict with the state character of the federation and for the technical reason that the right of making war is reserved to the federal authority. So the judicial decision in cases of disputes between member states is vested in the federal state itself.

The status of the member states is shown by the fact that if they neglect to fulfil their constitutional obligations the federal state cannot take civil or criminal proceedings against their subjects or citizens, but can enforce fulfilment only by the procedure of international law—that is, by warlike measures which, however, are not of the nature of an international war, but constitute "federal execution." And even if the federal constitution does not provide for such action, it nevertheless results from the very nature of the case.[1] Its purpose is simply and solely to re-establish the constitutional position.

As long as the member states possess uncontrollable state powers, the character of the federal state remains unaltered. But as it is not possible to prescribe in a formula of general validity the extent of the liberty which must be given to the member states if they are to keep their character, the antithesis

[1] Georg Jellinek: *Die Lehre von den Staatenverbindungen*, 1882, p. 310.

between the federal state and the unified state is by no means so clear—for both are comprised within the "state" category—as is that between the federal state and the confederation, which differ from one another *toto genere*.[1]

If the member states of the union retain the whole of their rights so that the division of authority is not altered, and there is set up constitutionally a control or even the possibility of such a control of their acts by the central power, then such a state formation would differ in no respect "from a decentralised unitary state."

In many South American republics attempts were made to adopt the system of the United States. In Venezuela, of which the official title is the United States of Venezuela, there were a number of "states" each with its own legislature, but as the Venezuelan Congress could annul any act of the local legislatures, so, in spite of its name, Venezuela was simply a decentralised unitary state.

If in any present-day federal state a similar rule were adopted, that state would become a unitary state, even though the spheres of activity of the members were largely increased, and the application of the idea of sovereignty would be historically justified, but of no legal significance. By a simple clause in the constitution, giving to the central authority the *jus supremae inspectionis*, the federal state can be turned into a decentralised unitary state.[2] An examination of the constitutional relation of the British possessions to the mother country (as things were in 1882) showed how very far self-government can go without the unitary character of the state being affected. But it would be a mistake to describe the federal state as certainly a unitary state in the making. The opinion that the transformation of the federal state into the unitary state is inevitable was, in Jellinek's opinion, warranted only where the federal state is "dynamic," and consequently represents only a stage in national development. But this is not required either theoretically or historically.

Finally, though the central authority in the federal state hands over a number of the powers and duties of the state to the member states to be exercised by them independently, and so creates a number of non-sovereign states, the sum total of the tasks which the state is called upon to undertake cannot be discharged by the federal authority alone or by the state authorities alone. Co-operation is necessary if the objects of the state

[1] Georg Jellinek: *Die Lehre von den Staatenverbindungen*, 1882, p. 311.
[2] Ibid., p. 312.

are to be attained. In this higher sense, which goes beyond mere juristic considerations, it is right to say that in the philosophy of history "the totality of the federal and member states represents the state."[1] Even in the unitary state all the purposes of the state are not served solely by the state authority; they are served also by the various associations having a status recognised by public law, though those associations act at the instigation of the state and under its supervision. In this case also, Jellinek said, "the completed state is the highest union of the state authority and the self-governing bodies."[2]

But the juristic basis of this higher conception is the recognition of the sovereignty of the union as indivisible; in spite of the assignment of uncontrollable state powers to the members, all rights of the sovereign state are in principle maintained. And so Jellinek concluded that if the nature of sovereignty be rightly understood, it is possible to ascribe to the members a state character of the kind elaborated by him in his treatise, and in harmony with the actual facts to recognise that in the federation the members are not only politically, but also juristically something more than communal organisations of a high order.

Finally, Jellinek remarked that the federal state ends the list of associations of states which he had set out to examine: other categories which had occasionally been suggested, for example the *Bundesreich* and the *Staatenreich*, cannot be regarded as distinct juristic conceptions; they are names of definite political institutions coming under the legal types already examined by him.

In a final summing up, Jellinek observed that a comprehensive survey of the various relationships between states reveals the existence of a number of associations based on international law which conform to a common type in that they are unions based on agreement or treaty, but differ very greatly in respect of scope and political character. But among all these diversities it is the sovereignty of the members which offers the soundest basis for the legal definition of their nature from the standpoint of international law.

Whilst the forms of associations of states based on international law are numerous, those based on constitutional law are very few. In associations based on international law the highest conception common to all is that of the compact or treaty between states, but associations based on constitutional law must be included in the category of states, they are manifestations of the

[1] Georg Jellinek: *Die Lehre von den Staatenverbindungen*, 1882, p. 313.   [2] Ibid.

state which as composite states can be set side by side with simple states as two species of one and the same genus. The guiding principle in the case of these constitutional associations is the non-sovereign status of the members.

The associations based on international law include the confederation and the real union, which is only a variation of the former; these are organised political alliances intended to be permanent.

There are only two forms of the composite or consolidated (*zusammengesetzte*) state; the *Staatenstaat*, in which the individual citizen is only indirectly subject to the sovereign power, and the federal state (*Bundesstaat*), in which the people are directly subject to the authority of the central power. Only the federal state is in accord with the organic nature of the modern state.[1]

In this comprehensive survey Jellinek developed a theory as to associations of states which influenced not only German but also all federal theory, and gave especially a great impetus to American federal ideas in the last decade of the nineteenth century and also in the present century, such as the theory of Willoughby and his school.

His analysis of the federal idea was not only a juristic one, but involved an examination of the actual forms of associations of states as they had previously existed and as they existed in his time.

The "administrative union" could hardly be placed in the category of unions of states in 1882, but it might be justifiable in our own time since the establishment of the League of Nations, and if the alliance or personal union were placed in the class of *Staatenverbindungen*.

The main significance of Jellinek's federal theory was his treatment of the federal state.

He defined the federal state as a state in the juristic sense, but criticised and analysed it on a purely empirical basis, and endeavoured to set up a theory of the federal state and to justify his juristic conception without being biased by legal *a priorism*.

His struggle between the empirical idea and formal legal positivism in the formation of his theory of the federal state was far more significant than in the case of any other thinker in Germany.

[1] Georg Jellinek: *Die Lehre von den Staatenverbindungen*, 1882, p. 316.

§ 7

The criticism made in Dr. Heinrich Rosin's famous essay on *Souveränetät, Staat, Gemeinde, Selbstverwaltung* [1] on Jellinek's theory that the juristic characteristic of the sovereign state is its "exclusive obligation by its own will" was the outstanding attack on the prevailing conception of sovereignty.

Jellinek had demonstrated the inadequacy of Haenel's inductive theory of sovereignty as being *Kompetenz-Kompetenz*, though it had been adopted by Liebe and Zorn, by directing attention to actual formations of constitutional law in which (as, for example, in the case of the relations of a suzerain to a vassal state) the sovereign power had not the legal right, vis-à-vis the subordinated collectivity, to determine its competence by itself.[2] Now his own theory was subjected to equally searching criticism.

Jellinek had defined sovereignty as "that quality of a state by reason of which it can be bound only by its own will"; and from this he deduced the categories of "supreme and independent power," of the "indivisibility" and "permanence" of sovereignty, and the conclusion that "within the limits imposed on it by its very nature" the sovereign state "can determine its own competence."

Rosin pointed out that Jellinek's line of reasoning was as follows. Legal obligation can be of one of two kinds: obligation by own will and obligation by external will. The characteristic of the subject is that he is bound exclusively by the state will—that is, by an external will. On the other hand, the state, and only the state, imposes obligations upon itself, both internally by means of the rules of constitutional and administrative law, and externally in international intercourse and treaty. And, in order that the state may be the supreme power, to the quality of obligation by its own will there must be added that of freedom from obligation by any other will.

Rosin held that Jellinek was frequently wrong both in the general line of his argument and in his conclusions. It is not true that the characteristic of the subject is his exclusive obligation by the state will; in the sphere of private law he binds himself and only himself; his will is the source of his obligation and not the legal system of the state, which indeed may not have been made applicable to the case. "The legal system, or the state

[1] Heinrich Rosin: *Souveränetät, Staat, Gemeinde, Selbstverwaltung*, in *Annalen des deutschen Reichs*, 1883.   [2] Ibid., p. 265.

which has set it up, is rather only the potentiality by force of which the will of the individual is the source of his obligation and has this as a legal consequence.[1] In the sphere of international law the treaty-making state appears to be bound by international law, and so must lose the characteristic of sovereignty which Jellinek had postulated. Rosin pointed out that Jellinek himself had been driven to admit this similarity of international and private law agreements, and had written, in his discussion of the confederation as a treaty relationship: "Even if the carrying out of a federal decision should have to be enforced by federal execution, it is its own will which the state encounters, just as in the case of those who do not carry out a private law contract it is their own will to which effect is given in the enforcement of the fulfilment of the contract."[2]

Rosin next proceeded to discuss the question of sovereignty. As a preliminary he observed that a theory, of law or anything else, is simply an abstract generalising of a series of concrete phenomena, by means of a common characteristic. As to the starting-point of this generalising there are two possibilities: there is the inductive method of starting with the phenomena and seeking the theory, and there is the deductive method of starting with a theory which is regarded as established, and testing a series of phenomena by it, to see if they do or do not come within it. To Rosin the first alternative was in this case impracticable, because a survey of the literature showed the absence of any agreement as to the collectivities of which sovereignty could be predicated. So the second alternative must be adopted, and one must start from the characteristics (however indefinite) of sovereignty, and arrive at some conclusions which should enable a decision to be quickly taken as to whether a particular collectivity is or is not sovereign. "The solution of this problem is the solution of the question as to the theory of sovereignty in the sense of present-day science."[3]

Ever since Bodin had written of the *puissance souveraine* of the state, the conception of sovereignty as a *summa potestas*, a highest or supreme power, had been generally accepted. It was necessary therefore to consider the two conceptions of "power (*Macht*)" and "highest, supreme."

As regards the first, our only basis for further deductions is that we are concerned with a conception of law. This means

[1] Heinrich Rosin: *Souveränetät, Staat, Gemeinde, Selbstverwaltung*, in *Annalen des deutschen Reichs*, 1883, p. 266.
[2] Ibid., p. 266, note 3.   [3] Ibid., pp. 267–268.

that actual power conditions are not the determinant of the conception of sovereignty, but that only "legal" power is involved. As law is the limitation of the will power of personalities, so legal power is the concrete content of the will of a personality whose will is the determinant of the wills of others.

Secondly, the category of "highest" means that in the superiority and subordination of a series of beings one stands on the highest level. It is therefore a relative category; it means that on the one hand the "highest" being has no other being above it, and on the other hand that it stands higher than other beings to which the adjective "highest" can for that reason not be given. The consideration of this relation downwards gives us at once the content of the negation of this conception.[1] But by itself this conception of "highest" gives no further guidance, and in particular it tells us nothing as to the nature of this "highest" being; it denotes a relation but no more, and we must seek for knowledge of the nature of this highest being not in its characteristic of "highest," but elsewhere. Equally the conception of "highest" tells us nothing as to the nature of the beings which are "not highest."

The combination of the two categories in their existing form had the result, Rosin thought, that the conception of sovereignty related to the superiority and subordination of legal personalities.[2] The question therefore is, What is the nature of superiority and subordination, and what is the nature of the equality (*Gleichheit*) of personalities? If the will power of one personality over another is the ability to determine the will of the latter according to the content of one's own will, this can be so only because the will power of the determining personality has its legal basis in the will of the determined personality. Determination by an external will which is based on my own will is in fact determination by my own will, and retains equality of personality. On the other hand, this equality is excluded and a relation of superiority and subordination set up so soon as a personality is determinable by another, whose will has its legal source in itself and not in the will of the determined personality. The nature of the legal superiority and subordination of personalities, or in other words the domination of one personality over another, lies in this, that the former finds in itself the legal basis for its determination of the latter, and is entitled to determine the will of the latter "of its own power."[3]

[1] Heinrich Rosin: *Souveränetät, Staat, Gemeinde, Selbstverwaltung*, in *Annalen des deutschen Reichs*, 1883, p. 268.   [2] Ibid., p. 269.   [3] Ibid.

From the relation of the sovereign personality upward and downward certain conclusions emerge:—

1. There is the positive conception of sovereignty as "that legal position of a personality by virtue of which it cannot on the basis of the existing law be legally determined by the will of any other personality," or, putting it affirmatively, "as exclusive determinability by own will." From this and what has been previously said it follows that the attribution of sovereignty to a personality is possible even when that personality is determined by an external will, if the latter has its source in the will of the determinable personality. (Later Rosin argued that the union of wills of the member states of a federal state has not its legal basis in the wills of those states, but presents a relation of domination which has deprived the individual states of their sovereignty.) On the other hand, he contended that the conclusion by the state of an agreement in the sphere of private law or of international law, and the obligations resulting therefrom, do not rob the sovereign state of its sovereignty, any more than the obligation of a private person puts the latter in the power of his creditor. Even in the sphere of constitutional law the state does not lose its sovereignty by imposing obligations on itself, e.g. as a landowner or industrialist to pay the communal taxes. The state remains sovereign, even if it takes upon itself an irrevocable obligation, as was shown, Rosin thought, by the relation of the Turkish Empire to its vassal states in view of their guaranteed legal status.[1]

2. From the relation of the sovereign personality to those below it there arises the negative conception of non-sovereignty. That personality is non-sovereign which can be determined by an external will of its own power, i.e. an external will the legal source of whose strength lies in itself. And in regard to this Rosin asserted that determinability by an external will in any one single respect puts an end to sovereignty. "There is only the direct antithesis of sovereignty and non-sovereignty—there is no such thing as half, incomplete, divided sovereignty; the choice lies between exclusive or non-exclusive determinability by own will."[2] However much a being determinable in one point of its personality by an external will or subject in one part of its personality to external rule may be legally independent otherwise of any foreign influence, it cannot retain its sovereignty, even partially.

[1] Heinrich Rosin: *Souveränetät, Staat, Gemeinde, Selbstverwaltung*, in *Annalen des deutschen Reichs*, 1883, p. 270.   [2] Ibid.

Rosin proceeded to apply these conceptions to the concrete position in the German Empire, and reached the following conclusions:—

1. The *Reich* was sovereign, because in the whole ambit of its personality it could be determined only by itself. The individual states had a constitutional share in the formation of the *Reich* will, but (like members of a corporation) only as members and organs of the *Reich*, not as independent personalities. The will when formed was the will of the *Reich*, not of the states; the right of the latter is that of internal participation in the forming of the will, not that of determining the will from outside.

2. The individual states were non-sovereign, because under the constitution they were to a very large extent determinable by the *Reich*. First, as regards the scope of their personality, the *Reich* had (under the *Kompetenz-Kompetenz* clause of the constitution) the legal right by its own legislation, i.e. by its own will, to limit the sphere of activity of the individual states. And secondly, the *Reich* could encroach even upon the sphere of activity so left to the states, in that imperial legislation took precedence over state law (should there be any conflict), and the decisions of the tribunals of the states in cases arising under imperial laws and the administration of those laws needed the concurrence of the legislative will of the *Reich*.

From this Rosin concluded that the *Kompetenz-Kompetenz* vested in the empire by the constitution was neither the exclusive source nor the exclusive characteristic of the non-sovereignty of the individual states. It was one particular way in which the domination of the *Reich* over the states, and the determination of the latter by the will of the *Reich* of its own power, found expression. It could vanish, without the individual states being any more sovereign. That was not because, if conflict proved inevitable, the *Reich* would in any event decide as to the demarcation of powers between itself and the states, for in such a case the *Reich*, like an independent court, called upon to decide the issue, would have to decide not according to its own will but in accordance with the law, it would not be entitled to make a new demarcation, but only to make clear the existing one. But the states would not be any more sovereign than before, if the *Kompetenz-Kompetenz* of the *Reich* disappeared, because, even if the scope of the activity of their wills were externally guaranteed against the empire, yet internally they would experience directly or indirectly the sovereign power of the *Reich* in all their spheres of activity, owing to the number of matters subject constitutionally to the legislation and supervision of the *Reich*, and the impossibility of a mechanical separation of state activities into two independent parts.

From the fact, as he regarded it, that neither the conception of sovereignty nor that of non-sovereignty gives any indication of the nature of the entities of which those qualities are predicated, Rosin argued that certain conclusions drawn by various writers, including Jellinek, from the ideas hitherto accepted, were untenable.

(*a*) The conception of sovereignty gives no indication as to whether and how far the personality characterised as sovereign is a state, and the personality not so characterised is not. Certainly, to avoid mistakes, the sovereign collectivity can be called state, and the non-sovereign something else. But this is simply a matter of nomenclature and has no value if it conflicts with customary usage.

(*b*) For the determination of the sphere of activity (the competence) of a sovereign personality the conception of sovereignty offers a basis only in so far as it makes it certain that that sphere cannot be legally limited by the will of another personality. Beyond that it does not help. For in the first place the sovereign personality can determine, i.e. can limit itself in favour of another personality; and in the second place the sphere of action of a personality extends beyond its own will, and like this will is dependent on the personality's objective existence, on the powers which are naturally inherent in it, or in the case of arbitrary creation have been brought into it by the will of its constituents. And in the last resort it is not the will of the constituents which expresses constantly its authority over the newly arisen collective personality, in the sense of a prohibition of any widening of competence, but it is rather the collective personality itself that brings this restriction into being, and this is not permanently derived from outside, but is inherent in its very nature.

Applying these conclusions to the German Empire, Rosin concluded that the sovereignty of the empire would not have suffered if the *Kompetenz-Kompetenz* had not been conferred on it by Article 78 of the constitution.

This conclusion was strongly supported by the consideration that even in the case assumed, though the empire lacked *Kompetenz-Kompetenz*, the individual states would not possess it because they were not entitled to widen their sphere of activity at the expense of the empire; so that the advocates of *Kompetenz-Kompetenz* as the characteristic of sovereignty would be unable to find it either in the empire or the states. The states had the constitutional right to extend their activity by increasing their tasks within their allotted spheres so long as the demarcation between them and the empire was maintained. So Rosin repeated the conclusion that competence and *Kompetenz-Kompetenz* are entirely independent of the conceptions of sovereignty and non-sovereignty, and are prescribed by the nature of the personality concerned.[1]

(*c*) That which is true of the sphere of activity of the sovereign and non-sovereign personalities applies equally to the question of the scope and content of their rights. The conception of sovereignty gives us no help in this respect. Rosin disagreed in this regard with Jellinek and Zorn, and declared that "it is an obvious mistake to deduce from the fact that a particular personality has nothing above itself, and on the contrary is higher than another (i.e. has authority over that other), that this latter cannot be in its turn higher than others, than other personalities subordinate to it, and have in its own right authority over them."[2]

In this respect Rosin represented the new school of thought. He disagreed with Laband, Jellinek and Zorn, and agreed with Gierke in rejecting the criterion of "own right" as the basic distinction between state and commune.

Passing next to discuss the question whether sovereignty is an essential quality of the state, he pointed out that in ordinary speech and in constitutional documents the term "state" was applied to the vassal states of Turkey and the members of the North American union and the German Empire, although it was generally agreed that these had not the quality of sovereignty. So the inquiry as to the possibility of non-sovereign states is really an attempt to justify a mode of speech, and the question, "Is sovereignty an essential characteristic of the state?" is really a question as to the justification of a popular terminology.[3]

In the reciprocal spheres of activity of the German Empire and the states there were three points to which Rosin directed attention, (*a*) the fact that the demarcation of the competences of the empire and the states was made by the constitution, i.e. by an act of will of the former; (*b*) the fact that merely quantitative comparison of the scope of competences and rights belonging to empire and states respectively did not point to any essential difference between the legal personalities of the empire and

[1] Heinrich Rosin: *Souvernänetät, Staat, Gemeinde, Selbstverwaltung*, in *Annalen des deutschen Reichs*, 1883, p. 273. [2] Ibid. [3] Ibid., p. 274.

states respectively; (c) the fact that a comparison of the content of the competences of the empire and states respectively led to the same negative result; and (d) the fact that the rights possessed by the empire and the states respectively for the purpose of carrying out their tasks were alike and indeed indistinguishable.[1]

Rosin also thought that Jellinek was mistaken in holding, with the American Cooley, that the distinctive nature of "own right" lies in its freedom from control, holding that liability to control in the exercise of a right does not prevent that right from being one's own.[2]

Rosin then went on to point out that the idea that sovereignty is not an essential characteristic of the state, and that consequently non-sovereign states are possible, had been criticised as destroying the distinction between "state" and commune.

1. He held that "the individual state can lack sovereignty, without thereby losing its character of a state, but it can also be sovereign; the commune can never be sovereign, it is by its very conception a non-sovereign collectivity, but this quality does not constitute the whole nature vis-à-vis the state, but is rather simply a consequence of the relations between them."[3]

2. The criterion of determinability or control is of no greater utility if applied by itself to the contrast between state and commune. As sovereignty is freedom from control by an external will, obviously a commune uncontrolled in the whole scope of its personality is sovereign therein, and consequently a state. On the other hand, the existence of control in the case of any collectivity only shows that it is non-sovereign: it does not show if it is a state or only a commune.

Rosin held that not only theory but actual facts contradicted Jellinek's dictum that only the state, even the non-sovereign state, has "uncontrollable public power"; and did this both positively and negatively. On the one hand in the case of non-sovereign states there is a sphere of activity within which they are subject to the will of the sovereign state; and on the other hand both the commune and the non-sovereign state have spheres, of whatever extent, within which their wills are uncontrolled. "The *jus supremae inspectionis*, especially in relation to the commune, in the sense which Jellinek seems to give to it, namely that every decision of the commune can be confirmed, annulled or amended, may in its indefiniteness and indefinability be

---

[1] Heinrich Rosin: *Souveränetät, Staat, Gemeinde, Selbstverwaltung,* in *Annalen des deutschen Reichs,* 1883, pp. 275–276.
[2] Ibid., p. 277.
[3] Ibid., p. 284.

appropriate to the 'police' state, which regards the commune at best as a state institution acting under a sort of guardianship, but is at the present time not appropriate to the legal state (*Rechtsstaat*), which alone can afford the basis of juristic consideration, and which ascribes to the commune an independent personality."[1]

So Rosin asserted that Jellinek's categorical imperative could not furnish any fundamental distinction between state and commune, and least of all between the non-sovereign state and commune.

He proceeded to discuss the contention that the commune has no "supreme rights" (*Hoheitsrechte*) of its own, and that these belong solely to the state. He pointed out that this means that the rights which the commune exercises over its members are exercised not in its own name, but as the representative of the state. But that raises the question, "What is the test as to whether a right is exercised by a person in his own name or in that of another?" That is, it raises the question of the nature of the legal subject, which he agreed with Windscheid is one of remarkable difficulty.[2]

The generally prevailing idea was that the commune was distinguished from the mere state administrative district by the possession of legal personality. Rosin agreed with Gierke that "whilst the state administrative district forms only a geographical division of the state, the commune is a corporation of the public law, a public law personality."

Personality, he held, is legal subjectivity; "person" is "a being that is a subject of law or whose capacity of being a subject of law is recognised by the legal system." Law, in the subjective sense, Rosin had described as legal will power, or more precisely as a permissibility of will (*Wollendürfen*) derived from the law, that will being determinant of the wills of other personalities. The operation of law is therefore the activity of will corresponding to the permissibility of will, so far as that is determinant to other personalities.[3] It follows from this that a subject of law is that being that can "will" the content of the law, and Rosin held that the commune can do this, and no conclusion can be drawn therefrom as to whether in so doing it exercises its own right or that of the state.

Next Rosin pointed out that, "as is well known, Ihering has

[1] Heinrich Rosin: *Souveränetät, Staat, Gemeinde, Selbstverwaltung*, in *Annalen des deutschen Reichs*, 1883, p. 285.
[2] Ibid., p. 286. [3] Ibid., pp. 286–287.

attempted to base the conception of subjective law not on will but on 'interest,' according to which the law defines interest as that which is legally protected, i.e. by the right of action, and therewith sets up as subjects of law the 'destinaries' of the law, that is, those whose rights are protected by it." Rosin agreed with the criticism that "not all legally protected interests represent actual rights," and consequently Ihering's conception was necessarily inadequate in its application to the sphere of administrative law, but nevertheless he fully accepted the idea underlying Ihering's theory. That idea was that law does not create rights in the subjective sense for their own sake, but in order to satisfy the needs and interests of personalities, or, in other words, rights are for the person who possesses them not ends in themselves, but means to ends. Subjective law cannot be defined except in relation to the interest of a personality; the mere permissibility of willing does not exhaust the conception. But Rosin thought that Ihering went too far in assuming that to every law there corresponds a definite, individual interest as its constant basis; this parallelism of interests and laws did not, he held, exist either in thesis or hypothesis, in the past or in the present; a law can serve to-day for the satisfaction of one particular interest and to-morrow of another, and be useful to one person for one purpose and to another person for another. The one thing common to all manifestations of law, in the subjective sense, is its relation to the collective interest, the life purpose of its subject, and not to this or that particular interest of the subject.[1]

If the personality is a being to which the law ascribes a life purpose of its own, then the relation of the law (in the objective sense) to the life purpose of the personalities differs according to whether it is concerned with the personality of the individual or with the collective entities superior to the individual and taking a great variety of forms.[2]

Although the doctrine of purpose contains an inherent error, Rosin boldly applied it to the theory of the state and of federation, and used it as the test of the demarcation between commune and state, and between the individual state and the collective state in the federal state. As regards the first of these distinctions he laid down the following propositions:—

1. To ascribe to the commune the attributes of a public law personality means the assumption that the law recognises that

[1] Heinrich Rosin: *Souveränetät, Staat, Gemeinde, Selbstverwaltung*, in *Annalen des deutschen Reichs*, 1883, p. 288.   [2] Ibid., p. 289.

the commune has a life purpose of its own, for the realisation of which it exercises its own power to will. It is the existence of this purpose which distinguishes the commune from the merely geographical state administrative district, though it may coincide with it in area.

2. To ascribe on the one hand to the commune a personality and life purpose of its own, even in the sphere of public law, and at the same time assume that these same supreme rights are exercised only in the name of the state, is a direct contradiction.

3. The real distinction between the commune and the state therefore lies, logically, in the difference of their purposes. "The commune is the organism of the collectivity, the state is the organism of the national collectivity."[1] Whilst the satisfaction of the communal needs resulting from the facts of living close together and the propinquity of holdings of land is the purpose of the local commune, it is the task of the state to secure the national interests of the whole people, that is, those which it has as a natural collectivity. Admittedly in individual cases the collective view of a people as to the demarcation between local and national interests may change, and with it the content of the two conceptions, but this does not affect the basic difference between them. But within their respective spheres commune and state have each the totality of the common purposes, except in so far as some of the communal tasks may be transferred to some higher body made up of a group of communes, and some of the state tasks may be transferred to a collective state. And he asserted that, subject to that limitation, the commune as well as the state has *Kompetenz-Kompetenz*, i.e. the capacity of gradually working out the potential totality of its purposes.[2]

So Rosin arrived at the juristic conclusion that with due regard to their equality of status and their distinctiveness the state can be defined as the public law collective personality for the realisation of national collective purposes, and the commune as the public law non-sovereign collective personality for the satisfaction of local collective interests within the state.[3]

It was on the assumptions which have thus been outlined that Rosin set out his own ideas of the federal state and its relation to the decentralised unitary state and the confederation. He held that the conception of the federal state is determined,

[1] Heinrich Rosin: *Souveränetät, Staat, Gemeinde, Selbstverwaltung*, in *Annalen des deutschen Reichs*, 1883, p. 291.   [2] Ibid., p. 292.   [3] Ibid.

positively and negatively, solely by two factors—one being the abstract factor of its public law personality, and the other its individualisation as a result of the purposes of the federal state. And that state he defined as "a state in which the state tasks are looked after partly by the sovereign collective state and partly within it by a series of member states comprised within and subject to it."[1] From this definition he drew the conclusions that[2]:—

(i) The federal state differs from the confederation in that it has a legal personality. The confederation is a treaty-based relationship between sovereign states for the common fulfilment of state tasks; "the federal state is a collective personality, standing above individual states which have by that fact been deprived of their sovereignty, and charged with a part of the state tasks as an independent life purpose of its own."[3]

(ii) The federal state and the decentralised unitary state not belonging to a federal state are on the same footing, in that each has a public law sovereign personality. The difference between them is only that the former carries out what are at any time regarded as national tasks, not alone, but in conjunction with the member states.

(iii) The member state of a federal state conceptionally resembles the commune of a decentralised unitary state in that both have a public law non-sovereign personality: the difference between them is that the former alone is a state, because it has tasks which, in the conception of the law (which is the expression of national consciousness), are regarded as tasks of the state, whilst the life purpose of the commune is limited to the discharge of local tasks.

(iv) The member state stands on the same footing as the federal state of which it forms part, both in the abstract as a personality and in its nature as a state; it differs from it in being subordinate to it, a fact which deprives it of sovereignty. But Rosin, differing from previous theories, held that "sovereignty in the federal state is not divided, rather is it vested solely in the collective state: it is the state purposes which are divided and with them the state tasks resulting therefrom."[4] And so as to federal technique he argued that because the sovereign authority (*Herrschaft*) belongs to the union alone, the result is that the division of the state tasks is not a mechanical severance, but an organic division of functions.[5]

[1] Heinrich Rosin: *Souveränetät, Staat, Gemeinde, Selbstverwaltung*, in *Annalen des deutschen Reichs*, 1883, p. 302.   [2] Ibid.
[3] Ibid.   [4] Ibid.   [5] Ibid., pp. 302–303.

Rosin therefore held that "state personality and state purpose, and the domination and subordination of state personalities arising from the division of the state purpose between the collective state and a series of member states, make up the whole conception of the federal state."[1] These alone mark it off from other structures: the introduction of any other factor only indicates differences between federal states within the federal conception itself. This is in his opinion particularly true of the following factors:—

(a) The way in which the federal state is formed. It may have its basis in an historico-political development apart from any legal normativeness: but it may also have it in a constituent act of will of the states to be united in it. This constituent act is not a treaty; it is rather, as in the case of the setting up of the juristic person of private law, an act of will of a number of persons joining together which establishes their common wills as a unity and thereby calls into being a new person dominant over them. Rosin said: "Although the individual will, which, in the collective will, is a co-operative cause of the setting up of the collective will, it is not a cause of its existence; once called into being the organism of the collective state exists of itself and of its own will."[2] So the constitution of the federal state is not a treaty between the states, but the will of their unity.

(b) The system of the direct and indirect operation of the federal will upon the subjects. The delimitation of the spheres within which the federal will binds the subjects directly or only through the intermediary of the rule of the member states can differ from one actual federal state to another. Rosin disagreed with Laband's dogma of the indirect subordination of the subjects in the federal state as a necessary consequence of its special formation by the will of the individual states, and held that the relation of the subjects to the collective state may well be the basis of the rule of the subjects by the collective state, but does not necessarily indicate the way in which that rule is in fact exercised.[3]

(c) The organisation of the state authority in the federal state. It may be, as in the German Empire, that the association (*genossenschaftlich*) character manifests itself by the fact that the collective state presents itself to the individual states as the holder of the federal state power. But that is only a particular form of the federal state, and Rosin agreed with Jellinek that it may

[1] Heinrich Rosin: *Souveränetät, Staat, Gemeinde, Selbstverwaltung*, in *Annalen des deutschen Reichs*, 1883, p. 303. [2] Ibid. [3] Ibid., pp. 303–304.

be that the member states are used only as electoral districts for a council of estates sharing in legislation and administration (as in Switzerland), or they are given their respective shares in the creation of a senate entitled to participate in legislation and administration.[1]

(d) Lastly, the "competence." The only thing essential to the federal state is that there shall be some division between it and the individual states of the competence to discharge the tasks of the state; the nature of that division, in detail, is conceptionally irrelevant.

Rosin certainly represented a new school of thought among legal theorists and jurists. His federalism has as a matter of fact no relevance to the organic theory, though he agreed with Gierke's conception of the state as a public law corporation.[2] His great contribution to the discussion is his complete elimination of sovereignty from the theoretical justification of the federal state; its main weakness, as Preuss has pointed out, the application of Ihering's theory of "purpose" to the division of state authority.

The basis of his federal idea was the graphic picture which he presented of the federal states, the American union, the Swiss federation and the German union, illuminated by his juristic notion of the conception of the state and sovereignty.

Whether his attitude of psychological positivistic jurisprudence was acceptable or not, his attempt to formulate the theory of federalism was on the basis of something more than juristic *a priorism*; it started with an empirical study, in method and in principle, and was completed by his own formal positivist legal philosophy.

§ 8

Four years after Georg Jellinek had published his outstanding work, Siegfried Brie, a great jurist, made a striking contribution to the German federal discussion in his work *Theorie der Staatenverbindungen*, issued in 1886.

His earlier work, *Der Bundesstaat*, published in 1875, was certainly one of the most significant expositions of the history of the theory of the federal state, and had been the first theoretical

---
[1] Heinrich Rosin: *Souveränetät, Staat, Gemeinde, Selbstverwaltung*, in *Annalen des deutschen Reichs*, 1883, p. 304.
[2] Heinrich Rosin: *Das Recht der Öffentlichen Genossenschaft*, 1886.

study of German federal ideas. His descriptive analysis of the theory of the federal state in Germany gave a great impetus to the development of those ideas.

But even more than his earlier historical work the publication of Brie's *Theorie der Staatenverbindungen* exercised an immense influence on German federal theory, especially because of the contrast which it presented to Jellinek's characteristic contribution to the theory of the union of states on the basis of empirical positivism.

First of all Brie asserted that any theory of associations of states must naturally start from the elements of every such union, i.e. from the "state."[1] But he did not think it necessary to attempt to elucidate the whole idea and nature of the state, or examine the legal nature of the state in all its aspects; and examination must be limited to those characteristic features of the idea of the state which are of real importance to the legal form of the various kinds of associations of states; and these are the features which distinguish the state from all other forms of human association. The features which must be taken into account are "the purpose of the state and the competence and supremacy of the state authority."

The conception of the state is twofold; there is the idealistic conception on the one hand and the empirical on the other.

The general theory of the state or the general idea of constitutional law seemed to him unable to formulate the conception of the state "directly from experience," and could answer adequately the question as to the kinds of human association which have a state character only by reference to "the idea of the state"; that is to say, those historical formations which claim to be a realisation, even if only partial, of the idea that the state must be recognised and described by science as "states."

Therefore he laid it down that only "the idea of the state provides a general rational standard for the appreciation of the diverse manifestations of the life of states, and especially of the mutual relationships between them."[2]

But, on the other hand, the idea of the state must not be simply an arbitrary conception, and cannot be derived wholly or mainly from the inner consciousness of the individual; it must be derived from the rational needs of human beings, as these have been manifested by collective historical experience, and it must be checked by comparison with the actual forms in which the idea has found expression.

[1] S. Brie: *Theorie der Staatenverbindungen*, 1886, p. 4.   [2] Ibid., p. 5.

The definition of the conception of the state on an empirical basis can be limited to definite times and peoples; but it can also be generalised, at least as regards all the states known to history.

The distinction between the ideal and empirical conceptions of the state arises from the fact that the former covers also those historical manifestations which embodied a "modification of the idea of the state."[1] Such variations from the ideal type of the state result generally from some overpowering rational need in each particular case, but may also in some instances be regarded as unwarranted anomalies, that is, as malformations. But Brie emphasised the rule that, if any organisation is to be characterised as a state, "the essential kernel of the idea of the state" must be the determinant of its nature.

Therefore he laid down the definition that "the state is in principle a commonwealth of human beings formed for the purpose of assisting the promotion of all reasonable interests of its members in the present and in the future."[2]

On this basis the essential thing in the conception of the state is "the all-sided and enlarging nature of the state purpose," and it is this characteristic which distinguishes the state from all other forms of human association.

In order that human life may be as complete as possible, and may take a form corresponding as fully and harmoniously as possible with the requirements of reason, it is necessary to supplement individual self-determination and initiative, and the further provision made by the co-operation of a number of individuals for the most varied interests of persons and groups of persons, by an association which, having a united will, can safeguard and care for every reasonable interest which cannot in any other way be sufficiently provided for.

The purpose of the state determines its material sphere or competence. The community whose task it is to serve, or to be in a position to serve, all reasonable interests of its members must have the right to extend its operations into all fields of human activity. Brie therefore asserted that "the universality of competence must correspond to the universality of purpose."[3]

But, on the other hand, as the task of the state is to supplement individual effort, the competence of the state need not extend at all times to everything; rather it is reasonable for the freedom of individuals or certain corporations to be protected against

[1] S. Brie: *Theorie der Staatenverbindungen*, 1886, p. 5.
[2] Ibid.
[3] Ibid., p. 6.

the arbitrary government of the state by legal rules. So Brie asserted that it was sufficient if the state were entitled at any time to adjust its competence according to need—that is, to have the so-called *Kompetenz-Kompetenz*.

From the nature of the state purpose it follows that the will of the state in every relation must be superior to the individual wills of the members, and to the collective wills of the corporations existing for special purposes. Without such superiority the state would not be able to give adequate legal protection—that is, to safeguard the reasonable interests of individual members or corporations against the arbitrary or relatively unreasonable encroachment of other members or corporations.[1]

By reason not of the characteristic purpose of the state, but of its quality as a collectivity, there arises "the need of a legal establishment and a legal organisation." The obligation resting upon those subjected to the state to recognise the existence of a superior common will and of a definite holder of that will must be based on "a rule of objective law." That rule may be established by treaty (compact), by customary law or by statute law.

On this basis Brie inquired into and discussed the theory of the *Staatenverbindungen*.

To him the existing states were simply more or less imperfect embodiments of the idea of the state. Thus Brie took as the first test of the state quality of an organisation the purpose of the organisation, and drew from this certain deductions as to the sphere of the state authority and its relation to all other authorities. But he pointed out that another opinion, strongly held by some modern legists, sought to find the requisite test in some presupposed unique quality possessed by the state power. He proceeded to examine the various doctrines, and began with that which regarded sovereignty as the essential characteristic of the state—the doctrine which had been expounded by Jellinek.

By origin and customary use the term "sovereignty" means the supremacy of an authority within its own sphere; it means on the negative side that within that sphere the authority is not subject to any will other than its own, and on the positive side that within that sphere all other wills are subject to its will; but it does not define the sphere. It is certain that in order to fulfil its purpose the authority of the state must extend to all fields of human activity and be superior to the authority of any special corporations which exist among its members, and so

[1] S. Brie: *Theorie der Staatenverbindungen*, 1886, p. 7.

reason demands that the state and the state alone shall be sovereign in all things. But this has no historical validity. And in any event it applies only to the relation between the state and individuals and non-state corporations; it lays down nothing as to the relations of states to one another.

The question whether or how far the subordination of one state to the will of another state or of a community formed of a number of member states is permissible cannot be answered by reference to any special distinction between the purpose of the state and the purposes of the non-state communities. The question, like all other questions relating to the state, can be answered only by reference to the primary characteristic of the state, namely, its purpose; but in this case the decisive consideration is the relation of the purpose of the state to the purpose of each particular kind of association into which states enter.

Therefore Brie assumed that the sovereignty of the state could not form the foundation of the theory of the union of states, but only a careful analysis of unions could show "whether or not sovereignty is an essential quality of the individual concrete states" even from the ideal standpoint. He concluded that this question must be answered in the negative and that, moreover, often on historical grounds, in opposition to the state idea, the sovereignty of some actual state has been taken away or modified by its subordination to the authority of some other state.[1]

Brie also disagreed with another widely spread theory which did not consider the quality of the state authority as the chief factor in the conception of the state, but regarded power or rule (*Herrschaft*) as the essence of the state, so that the state differs from other collective bodies only in that it has power over its members. This theory is closely associated with the ideas that at least the power of legislation is vested solely in the state, and that the power possessed by a subject is the result of delegation by the state.

The essence of every legal relation of authority is the subordination of the dependent "part" in respect of its individual rights. Not only is the "part" bound to do, or to abstain from doing, certain things, but its independence is positively diminished and thereby its equality before the law, at least vis-à-vis the holder of power. But an authority of this kind does not belong only to the state; no collective body can properly fulfil its purpose if it has not the right to give directions, positive or negative, to its members. Although at the present time the autonomy of most

[1] S. Brie: *Theorie der Staatenverbindungen*, 1886, p. 10.

corporations is very limited, it still exists to a certain extent and was at other periods much more extensive; in many states to-day the churches have within their own sphere the right of independent legislation. And if a corporation by its very nature needs to have authority over its members and to legislate for them, there is no ground for assuming that that authority must be delegated from the state and is vested only in the state. So Brie, like Rosin, held that every "person" has by its nature its own specific purpose, and it is in accordance with the "supplementary" purpose of the state to recognise the peculiar purposes and the peculiar rights of bodies corporate; and he therefore rejected the *Herrschaft* theory.

Brie recognised that his opinion that the nature of its purpose is the distinguishing characteristic of the state would have to be abandoned if the doctrine (propounded by Gierke and others) were shown to be valid, namely, that other corporations and collectivities have the same comprehensive purposes and sphere of activity as the state.

According to that doctrine the state is a member of a wider category of political communities comprising the state and those communes (local communes and groups of communes) which, like the state, are directly concerned in the promotion of the common good.[1]

Brie admitted that the state and the commune differ from other corporations in this respect, that they have a territorial basis, and further that only a body corporate which rules over a territory inhabited mainly by its own members can promote the development of human society in all respects. And among these communes those which have a comprehensive purpose (the so-called "political" communes) are in their nature closely akin to the state. But in fact the communal interests are not entirely coincident with the purposes of human life, and consequently the task of the political commune is not coincident with that of the state.

The object of the communes is determined primarily by their territorial relationship. The political commune, whether it be the local commune (*Ortsgemeinde*), circle (*Kreis*) or provincial union is concerned with the promotion of those interests which are common to the residents in one and the same area. These include economic and cultural interests (education of children and the provision of hospitals). On the other hand, defence against foreign enemies, legislation, the judicial system and church

[1] S. Brie: *Theorie der Staatenverbindungen*, 1886, p. 13.

matters are not properly to be included among the tasks of the (so-called) political commune.

It is true that history furnishes examples of a wide extension of the scope of communes, but this does not affect the nature of the communes so long as their tasks and competence are not in principle regarded as unrestricted; a commune whose purpose is theoretically as comprehensive as that of the state is itself a state. Frequently, in modern political life, the scope of activity of the commune is extended by the state entrusting to it the exercise of certain functions; this has the "advantage" that the exercise of these functions is adapted to the particular needs of the commune. But the purposes in respect of which the commune is then active remain state purposes, the delegated powers remain in substance state powers, and (as Gierke also held) the conceptional difference between state and commune is not affected.

In order to answer the question—which is an inevitable preliminary to discussion of the theory of state combinations, namely, what organisations can be regarded as states?—it is of the utmost importance to distinguish not only between states and other corporations (communes) with a territorial basis, but also between the state and the territorial divisions of the state. In theory such a division (e.g. the province) is distinguished from the state as well as from the commune in a number of respects: it has no legal personality, no rights and duties, no purposes, no organs, no membership, of its own; but in practice it may be very difficult to determine if a particular organisation is a state or a province. This is especially the case if territories which were formerly separate states are combined under one ruler, or if and so long as it is not clearly settled if the authority entrusted with the exercise of the state power in the territory in question is to be regarded as the holder of that power.

So far in his discussion of the theory and nature of the state Brie had considered only the individual state, and had touched on the coexistence of a number of states only so far as was necessary to distinguish in principle the state from other collectivities, or from the mere division of the state. He now laid down the proposition that "the existence of a number of states side by side with one another" is the necessary condition precedent of the existence of unions of states.[1]

The recognition of this fact is not sufficient to give a complete understanding of these unions of states, but the reasons why there are, and must be, a number of states are of vital importance.

[1] S. Brie: *Theorie der Staatenverbindungen*, 1886, p. 17.

And moreover, to evaluate the unions properly it is necessary to understand how and why the spheres, in which the wills of the various states are operative, are separated from one another not only because of the differing state allegiances of individuals but also in actual space.[1]

The bringing together of all mankind into a single state—the "world state," in the form of the federal state of Bluntschli's ideal—is impracticable because it is impossible from one centre to watch over all the interests which need state assistance and to direct all the requisite action. But national differences are also an obstacle to the world state, and it is these which provide the national bases for the division of mankind among a number of states. So Brie asserted that "only in the national state does the idea of the state, like the idea of nationality," attain its full development.[2]

Owing to a great variety of causes the nation and the state may not be coextensive; the population of a state may be drawn from a number of nations, or sections of a nation may constitute separate states. In the latter case, however, effect can be given to the principle of nationality by setting up at the side of, or (better) above, the parts a collective national state.

Next Brie pointed out that the coexistence of a number of states involves a limitation of the scope of the power of the individual state in respect of both persons and place.

Firstly, the power of the state extends only over its members, and this power, like the membership, would be in general exclusive vis-à-vis other states; for he assumed that membership of, and subordination to, a number of collective bodies (*Gemeinwesen*), each of which covered or could cover the whole field of human activity, would be "irrational."

Similarly, the power of the state is restricted to a defined territory, and in this respect again it is normally exclusive in relation to other states. This territorial supremacy (*Gebietshoheit*) narrows the circle of the subjects of a particular state and also restricts the extent to which the power of the state can be exercised vis-à-vis its members. But whilst the states have thus entirely separate spheres of authority, both personal and territorial, many relationships between the coexisting states are inevitable or at least reasonably expedient, and extend the tasks and functions of the individual states. There is the risk that owing to the encroachment of a state upon the interests or legal rights of another state, conflicts of will may arise. Again, states are brought into contact

[1] S. Brie: *Theorie der Staatenverbindungen*, 1886, p. 17.   [2] Ibid., p. 18.

by the economic relations between their members, who may appeal to their respective states for assistance or protection. And finally a state may find it necessary, in order to carry out its tasks, to invoke the help of other states, and frequently a number of states have to combine for their common interests.

In order that these relations between states may accord with reason, they must, like the relations between individuals, be governed by rules of law.[1] It is the object of these rules to limit the will of the individual states in accordance with the reasonable common interests of all the participant states. Such a limitation does not conflict with the conception of the state, so long as the limitations are not such as to deprive the subject of essential state characteristics.

There is in the nature of the state nothing which in principle prevents the legal limitation of the will of the state over against other states. The constitution of a state contains limitations upon the will of the state in respect to its members, but the substance of these limitations is dependent upon the will of the state itself. Brie, like Jellinek, although in the different sense of the *Kompetenz-Kompetenz*, asserted that the state could at any moment "modify its own constitution according to its own judgment, so long as in doing so it follows the legally prescribed procedure."[2]

But it is different with the legal obligations of the states to one another; in regard to these the will of the individual state cannot itself as a rule decide as to the continuance of the legal limitations placed upon it, because its will "cannot be decisive for the other states standing in legal relations with it, at least in so far as they are on an equality with it, or even superior to it."[3] Brie emphasised that such a form of legal limitation of the state will is not in conflict with the conception of the state, because neither the universality of the state purpose nor that of the state authority is affected by the fact that in the exercise of that authority the state has to observe legal restrictions (whether in foreign or in domestic affairs) which cannot be set aside merely at its own pleasure.[4] Any other conclusion can be drawn only from a quite untenable theory of sovereignty. Even if sovereignty, defined as complete independence of any higher will, be regarded as an essential characteristic of the state, legal relationships between the states and such reciprocal obligations as do not involve the subordination of one state to another, or of several to a collective power, are not thereby logically excluded. And as, in accordance with the theory

---

[1] S. Brie: *Theorie der Staatenverbindungen*, 1886, p. 20.
[2] Ibid., p. 21.   [3] Ibid.   [4] Ibid., p. 22.

elaborated by Brie, subordination to a higher power is compatible with the theory of the state, the individual state can in relation to other states be subject to such legal restrictions as in their origin or continuance presuppose a will superior to the individual state.[1]

The legal regulation of the mutual relations of states need not and should not be of such a kind as to take away from the legally limited community its state quality. It would be logically a contradiction to assume legal relations between states if those concerned, or a part of them, were lacking in the characteristic qualities of a state. And if the union as such is not of the nature of a state, then there would be no statehood for the members of the legally associated or at least legally restricted communities, whereas the associated life of mankind in states must be regarded as a general necessity based on reason.

Brie held that the division of the obligations and functions of the state between different independent communities would be incompatible with the comprehensiveness of purpose and authority which is an essential part of the conception of the state. Particular functions of a state can be withdrawn from it in favour of other states, so long as the principle of comprehensiveness is maintained, since in that event the conceptional difference between the state and non-state communities is maintained in substance, although the idea of the state is to some extent modified by the absence of some supreme powers.[2]

Thus Brie's legal-political philosophy was based on his own legal idea of the state and the rejection of Jellinek's theory of the state; the former emphasised that the idea of the state is based on "universality of purpose and authority," whereas the latter insisted on sovereignty as the essential quality of the state.

Starting with these premises, Brie held that every friendly relationship between states could be called a union of states, but in the legal sense a union of states is any friendly "relationship between states which is governed by rules of law." The legal conception of state union covers also those relations between states which result from the establishment of positive law affecting them all equally.

History shows that legal unions of states have been very numerous and diverse. They have differed especially in respect of their purposes, or of their duration, or of the legal position of the member states to one another "or to a higher collective personality."

[1] S. Brie: *Theorie der Staatenverbindungen*, 1886, p. 22. [2] Ibid., p. 23.

Thus he divided unions of states into the three following principal classes, according to their juristic construction: Firstly, unions of states without any subordination of the members. Secondly, unions of states in which members are in the relationship of superiority and subordination to one another. Thirdly, unions of states in which members are on an equality among themselves, but are subordinate to a higher collective power, which collective power may itself have the character of a state authority.[1]

In the first case the member states retain "absolute sovereignty"; in the second the subordinated states lack sovereignty or their sovereignty is only relative; in the third case this lack of sovereignty or possession of only relative sovereignty applies to all the associated states.

"Unilateral dependent relationships" are essentially the result of unilateral interests of the superior or subordinate states; in the former case the superior state exercises rule (*Herrschaft*), in the latter it exercises a protectorate.

Among the unions of states based on the principle of equality the most important are communities which accord with the principles of international law and associations of states.

The former are based on the existence of a body of common positive law, on the existence of a complex of legal rules governing the mutual relations of a number of independent states. The associations of states exist to promote the common interests of a number of states by the co-operative action of their members. If these common interests are of long duration and a joint organisation is set up to deal with them, this organisation can, broadly speaking, be called a union of states (*Staatenverein*). Such a union may be of several kinds. It may have no "personality" distinct from its members, and its executive (organ) is then only a joint executive of the associated states. A collective organisation of this kind may be confined to the provision of a subordinate executive (instances of this are the administrative union and unions for the administration of justice); or the supreme authority may be a joint one (as in the real union).[2]

There is an important distinction between this union of states with only a common executive and the union of states which has itself a collective personality and if necessary its own executive quite separate from the executives of the individual states.

Such a union formed by a number of states, and in so far as the member states take an actual share in its formation, is commonly

[1] S. Brie: *Theorie der Staatenverbindungen*, 1886, p. 25. [2] Ibid., p. 26.

FEDERAL IDEAS FROM SEYDEL TO BRIE

called a *Bund* and is either a confederation or a federal state. The first is a mere *Bund*; the second is both a *Bund* and a state.[1]

Thus, while other state associations or unions of states depend on the juristic structure of the international community, and do not differ from one another in any important respect, the unions (*Bunde*) which are composed of states are the highest category of the unions of states, those in which "the co-ordinate member states are subordinate to a collective (federal) authority".[2]

With this categorical division and subdivision of the unions of states, Brie made an elaborate exposition of the legal character of the various forms of union.

In the first place he examined the unilateral relations of superiority and subordination between states. These differ greatly according to whether they are based on the interest of the superior or of the dependent state—a fact which determines their legal form.[3]

From this point of view he drew a distinction between the rule of one state over another, and the protectorate exercised by one state over another; a modified form of the latter is "suzerainty." It frequently happens that a state is strong enough to impose its rule upon a weaker state with the object of compelling, and in such a way as to compel, that state to serve the purposes of the superior state. Such a rule has an inherent tendency to become unrestricted. But it can—so far as law is concerned—be limited to particular matters, so that in respect of all other matters the ruled state retains its sovereignty. But although the rule of the superior state, if it is unlimited in scope, is of the nature of state authority, one essential feature of such power will be lacking so long and so far as the ruling state is not entitled to act directly upon the individual members of the subordinate states.[4]

The case is quite different with the protective power, which in the first instance at least is based not on the interests of the superior state, but on those of the subordinate state. In this case the latter has legally "a relative—but restricted—sovereignty."[5]

This relationship of one-sided superiority and subordination between states is in most cases based on "treaty."[6]

This unilateral relation between states, involving the dependence of one of them, appeared to Brie to be both in its nature and results in direct conflict with the true conception of the state; and he regarded the unnaturalness of this relation as the reason for attempts to conceal it under a fine-sounding name, such as

[1] S. Brie: *Theorie der Staatenverbindungen*, 1886, p. 26. [2] Ibid.
[3] Ibid., p. 30.   [4] Ibid., p. 31.   [5] Ibid., pp. 31–32.   [6] Ibid., p. 34.

"protectorate," which, of course, does not modify its essential character. Moreover, he asserted that although the subordination of one state to the protectorate of another does not in itself conflict with the idea of the state, so long as the protectorate is based primarily on the interests of the protected state, there is no guarantee that the protecting state will not in some cases act in its own interests alone.

And lastly, as in the feudal system the vassal subordination was "modified" by the notion of the private law equality of the lord and his vassals, so also the suzerainty of one state over another is less defensible than the protectorate when judged by the true theory of the state. And it is not in accordance with the *raison d'être* of the state for its power to be regarded as not originating from itself, but derived from outside.

Brie next examined the principle of the state relationships based on equality.

Differing from the one-sided dependent relation, the common legal characteristic of these relationships is that within the sphere of the association of states it is not the will of one of the associated states that is legally decisive as to the mutual relations of the states, but only their agreed wills or a higher will equally binding upon all.

The first and most pressing need of this kind of union is a law (*Recht*) determining the common objectives and mutual relations of the states, and a body of legal rules which will prevent the arbitrary encroachment of one state upon the legal sphere or reasonable interests of another state, and so prevent any disturbance of the common welfare.

This regulation of peaceful intercourse between independent states is known as "international law"; the union in which independent states are associated with one another by virtue of their equality under international law is called the "international community."[1]

This international community is legally differentiated from the union of states mainly by "the negative character (both as to purpose and content) of the legal rules of which it consists."

The members of this international community are not dependent on one another or subordinate to any superior authority; but it is possible for states which are subordinated to other states, or to a higher collective will, to serve as members of the international community in all relations not so subordinated and to be subjects of international law.[2]

[1] S. Brie: *Theorie der Staatenverbindungen*, 1886, p. 39. [2] Ibid.

The actual rules which make up the body of international law have been developed out of customary law or out of the pact (state treaty or international treaty). A legislative central authority for this purpose is entirely incompatible with the nature of the international community which depends upon the principle of the sovereignty of the individual states.

If a large number of states make up the international community, international law will be based chiefly upon customary law, for whilst it is very difficult to get a number of states to agree unanimously upon limitations of their freedom of action in regard to their mutual relations, the realisation of a common reasonable need is much more likely to lead to the acceptance of a definite legal rule as to those relations. This internationally accepted validity of a principle of law may result from the joint operation of treaty and custom, a principle embodied in a treaty being adopted by other states not parties to the treaty.

Therefore Brie asserted that the international community was based on nothing but "the voluntary process of customary law."[1]

He proceeded to point out that within the international community, which embraces a large number of states, there naturally form themselves a number of "special" unions, similar or closely allied to the international community and therefore governed primarily by the rules of international law. The members are subject to the general obligations of international law, and also to special legal obligations appropriate to the particular purposes of these "special" unions.

Under "special international unions" in the wider sense, he included all those unions of states which, like the international community, are based on the principle of the "personal" equality of the associated states without any subordination to a higher common authority.

The narrower sense of the term comprises only those unions which lack not merely a collective personality and collective organs, but any common organisation at all.[2] It was to these special international unions that he next devoted his attention.

These special unions are due partly to a common need felt by a number of states which are independent of one another—a need which is not wholly or sufficiently satisfied by general international law—and partly to special requirements felt by the members in their mutual relations.

As a rule the international special union is based either on "customary law" or "treaty"; but in contrast with what has

[1] S. Brie: *Theorie der Staatenverbindungen*, 1886, p. 41.   [2] Ibid., p. 46.

been said as the origin of international law and the international community, the treaty origin is in this case of dominant importance.

Brie pointed out that in so far as the special obligations and corresponding rights of independent states towards one another cannot be directly founded on customary law or treaty-based legal principles, but require for their formation a special act of will, they can usually only be the result of a bilateral legal arrangement, or compact, between the parties to be given rights and to undertake obligations. For as in international relationships mutually independent wills are in face of one another, normally any legal gain can be made only by consent of the state on which thereby special obligations are imposed and with the co-operation of the will of the state to which the right is to accrue.

Numerous attempts have been made by theorists to classify international special treaties according to their subject-matter or legal operation. This classification relates chiefly to the inferior kinds of international unions of states. In making it, the first test to be applied is whether there is under consideration a community in the sense of objective law, or a legal union based on the co-relation of subjective law and the corresponding obligation, or a combination of both forms.

The international special legal relationships differ according as they are based on unilateral or bilateral subjective special rights and corresponding obligations, and in the second case a further important differentiation can be made among the bilateral rights and obligations in respect of their subject-matter. But for both kinds of legal classification the diverse interest relations are the main test.[1]

An international union between two or more states may be of such a nature that only one party has rights and the other has obligations. This situation may arise when a state simply makes use of its greater strength to obtain from another state concessions serving its unilateral interests, or it may be due to other practical considerations. But between the private law subordination of a state and the unilateral special obligation there are important differences in respect of both the subject-matter and the operation of the obligation.

In the first case the obligations of the subordinate state are determined entirely by the arbitrary decision of the superior state; in the second case they are determined once for all by the act (treaty, compact or other arrangement) which establishes

[1] S. Brie: *Theorie der Staatenverbindungen*, 1886, p. 49.

the relations on which the obligations are imposed, and the status of the state on which the obligation is imposed is not affected by its subordination to a higher will. All that happens is that it becomes bound to observe certain legally imposed restrictions upon the exercise of certain specific rights of government. So that a "servitude" under international law (*völkerrechtliche Dienstbarkeit*) is not incompatible with complete sovereignty.[1]

On the other hand, the bilateral powers and obligations of an international special union are based normally on bilateral interests, which may be particular or common.

If the interests of the two parties to the union are not common, the natural legal result is an "exchange" of obligations, i.e. one party undertakes obligations in return for the assumption by the other party of certain other obligations. If the particular interests differ in kind, the rights and duties of the two parties will also differ in kind. If on the other hand the particular interests of the two parties agree in substance, the rights and duties of the two parties will be identical in kind, and there will be a reciprocal legal undertaking of obligations essentially of the same nature. As in this case the most obvious fact is a contractual relation between the parties, mutually independent states are much more ready to agree to such limitations of their legal freedom of action.

There is, however, frequently a community of interests between two or more states, so that the promotion of its own interests by one state in a particular direction may be to the advantage of the other states also. Such community of interests may be due to very diverse physical or historical circumstances, especially geographical propinquity, racial kinship, balance of power, common social conditions, or constant intercourse of the subjects or citizens of the two states.

It may be that this community of interests will not lead to the formation of any legal tie, because the separate activities of the individual states suffice to satisfy the common needs or because the interested states content themselves with the—from the legal standpoint—accidental similarity of their action. But in very many cases something more is required and, in particular, if there is a need for express co-operation, this can be secured only by some definite arrangement legally binding upon the parties to it. In this way there arises out of the state community of interests (*Interessengemeinschaft*) the union for direct action, governed by definite legal rules.

[1] S. Brie: *Theorie der Staatenverbindungen*, 1886, p. 50.

Brie defined the association of states as the legal union of coequal states for the fulfilment of a common purpose by active co-operation. Its essential characteristic is "the legal obligation of the members to work actively for one and the same common purpose."[1] To this positive obligation other obligations of a negative kind may be attached, or they may arise out of the purpose of the association, but their absence does not matter in theory.

Subject to the general conception of the association of states the legal methods of bringing about common action may be very different. The necessary action may be taken by the separate co-ordinate organs of the individual states; or organs common to the states may be legally established to serve the common purposes; or out of the associated states there may be formed for the common purpose a commonwealth with organs of its own.

In the first place there exists what Brie called an "unorganised state association" or "state community in the narrower sense"; in the second case there is what he designated a "state community with common organ" or "organised state association"; in the third case there is what he called a "state community" or (having regard to its normal type) a "union" (*Bund*).[2]

The first and second forms could, in contrast to the state community, be classed together as "state associations in the wider sense" or "state associations without collective personality." The second and third forms, in contrast to the unorganised state association, or state association in the narrower sense, could be classed together as "organised associations of states" which are in essentials identical with "unions of states."

Discussing first the "unorganised state associations" Brie pointed out that in respect of legal structure they belong to the class of international special unions with bilateral rights and duties of the members.[3] As such an unorganised association can hardly arise except from a contract or treaty, it is in all respects analogous to the *Societas* of Roman private law.

So Brie cleared the way for the consideration of the organised state association, or in other words of the union of states.

[1] S. Brie: *Theorie der Staatenverbindungen*, 1886, p. 52.
[2] Ibid., p. 53.   [3] Ibid.

§ 9

The union of states was defined by Brie as "a permanent organised legal union of coequal states for the fulfilment of a permanent common purpose by joint and positive action," or, more shortly, "a permanent organised association of states."[1]

The union is only one kind of state association, but differs from all other institutions falling within the same general category by the necessity for the coexistence of two closely related and historically very rarely isolated characteristics; firstly, the permanency of the union, and secondly, the establishment of a common or collective organisation, over the individual states, to fulfil the common purposes. On the other hand, the precise manner of creation of the particular organisation is not important.

Brie considered a third characteristic—"natural origin"—unessential, and many jurists agreed with him. There was no sufficient reason when using the expression *Verein* for thinking only of the single act of foundation by union of wills, and not rather of the permanent union of persons, or of the powers, in the *Verein*.

As a legal characteristic of the association of states duration must be regarded as only of minor importance. The requirement of duration has only this importance, that the association and co-operation of the members, for the purposes prescribed, must continue for a long period, either definitely fixed, or if unfixed, likely to be long.[2]

An association of states, intended to last, can exist although the constituent states are entirely separate in respect of organisation; but in the great majority of cases some organisation is set up to assure or facilitate the joint working. In theory it is sufficient if an organisation is set up which belongs technically not solely to each particular state, but rather to all the states together. From the juristic standpoint the decisive consideration is whether the organisation remains based on the association principle or there is set up a collective person distinct from the individual states.

In the first case there is only a "common" or "collective" organisation, whilst in the second case there arises from the collectivity of the individual states a higher collective will, possessing its own organs for the fulfilment of the common purpose.

[1] S. Brie: *Theorie der Staatenverbindungen*, 1886, p. 56. [2] Ibid., p. 57.

The collective state union takes naturally two different forms, according as the common organ is legally the supreme organ of all the federated states or has no such legal status.

The first category—in the only form in which, in practice, it presents itself, namely, that of a common monarch—is usually designated a "real union"; the second is of importance mainly as community of administrative and judicial organs subordinated to the head of the state.

Before examining in detail the various kinds of unions of states, with community of organs, Brie considered briefly certain forms of association not only theoretically possible, but actually manifested in history, which seem to resemble these particular unions. Such are the cases in which one and the same person chances to be the ruler of a number of states, or ambassador or consul for a number of states; the cases in which some of the functions of a number of states are entrusted to a common organ, without there being any co-operation of the state governments; the cases in which a state in special cases and for its own convenience entrusts particular matters to the authorities or courts of another state; and the cases in which a quite temporary association of states establishes some common organisation for the better attainment of the temporary purposes (e.g. the allies in a war). But all these Brie dismissed as not in fact falling within the category.

In an association of states the legally established common organ is frequently a subordinate organ. Such an association exists where the constituent states have each a special supreme ruler or supreme will-organ, but are yet materially bound to let their common functions be discharged wholly or partly by the same physical person or persons, without that person or persons being regarded as the organ of a collective personality superior to the individual states.[1]

As history shows, the common state purposes for which an association of states with common subordinate organs has been formed are very diverse, but this kind of association has been of practical importance chiefly for the common exercise of international commercial functions or for the common administration of justice; but for permanently effective mutual defence such an association appears much too loose.

There is no inherent reason why, in such an association of states, the subjects of the associated states should not be directly bound by the orders of the common organs, for the individual

---

[1] S. Brie: *Theorie der Staatenverbindungen*, 1886, p. 62.

state imposes obligations on its subjects by the commands of an organ of which it makes use in common with other states just as much as when it makes use of an organ of its own.

The most natural method of forming a common indirect organ, at least for the most important affairs of the association, is for it to consist of joint deliberating, or even deciding, delegations of the governments of all the member states. Sometimes the common functions have been entrusted to the administration of one of the member states; frequently a standing administrative organ has been set up, which is legally the agent of each of the states; and sometimes the method adopted, when decisions of far-reaching importance are involved, has been that of periodical or occasional congresses or conferences of plenipotentiaries, as in the cases of the German *Zollverein* and the International Postal Union.

Finally Brie pointed out that associations of this kind have characteristics which juristically give them outwardly the character of a corporation. There is, for example, generally an idea of permanence of association and purpose. There are frequently provisions as to the admission of new members, or even as to the continuance of the union although individual members withdraw. There are common organs for common purposes, sometimes permanent, sometimes subject to reappointment; in numerous cases these organs are entitled to act on a majority decision. But it would be wrong to regard associations which have all these characteristics as being therefore collectivities. Such associations are really analogous to the numerous associations known to private law, which by their nature are akin to societies (*Gesellschaften*) but individually present modifications of the fundamental principles on which societies are based. To determine the corporation character of a particular association of states it is necessary to know if majority decisions of the organ of the association are permitted, and if the decisions of that organ need to be ratified by the highest authorities in the individual states.

Passing next to the real union Brie defined this as "a union of states with a legally collective head of the state and particularly a monarchical head of the state."[1] The collectivity of the supreme state organ of will had up to his time been manifest only among monarchical states and could scarcely be brought into practice in states with a republican form of government.

The limitations of the real union to monarchies were justified from the rational-historical point of view and by the juristic sense

[1] S. Brie: *Theorie der Staatenverbindungen*, 1886, p. 69.

of the obligation of the members of the state union. The legal collectivity of the personal representative of monarchy was based only on the relations of co-ordinate states and of equal legal obligations.

But in the conception of the real union the essential problem was the right of secession.

As the real union was a permanent state union, owing to its specific nature, the right of secession was not permitted to any individual state at its own pleasure, but on the other hand a dissolution could be carried out by "the agreed will of all the individual states."[1]

Then Brie criticised the main forms of federalism under the category of "state commonwealths" (unions).[2]

Since for the further promotion of the permanent common interests of the several states a union of the kind just discussed, namely, the real union, was frequently insufficient, therefore a collective higher will with its own organs was needed to hold its own against the diverging wills of the individual states and be superior to them within the ambit of the purposes of the union.[3] This need for corporative consolidation would make itself felt if a large number of the individual states in the union had a share in the common interests and if these interests were of decisive importance for the existence of the states.

He put forward as a supplementary axiom that the idea of state was "by no means incompatible with dependence on a superior common will," because it was not "a purpose unconnected with the member states," but, on the contrary, one needing fulfilment which was "the object of the state-commonwealth."

But the will, which was superior in all its aspects to all other common and individual wills and was provided with authority higher than theirs, had the "natural tendency" to consider itself independent of any subordination. As a rule this tendency could be overcome only by the participation of the peoples of the individual states "and by a federal organisation of the common will."

In this form of state Brie remarked that every state commonwealth by its very nature was established on "a more or less national basis and had legally the characteristics of a union."[4] By a "union" he meant "a commonwealth consisting of a consolidation of states" in which all the member states had a legal right of participation in the formation of the common will.[5]

[1] S. Brie: *Theorie der Staatenverbindungen*, 1886, pp. 71–72.
[2] Ibid., p. 79.   [3] Ibid.   [4] Ibid., p. 80.   [5] Ibid.

Finally, the method of formation of the state commonwealth was quite immaterial to the conception of union. Certainly most unions of states had been established by treaty, but in many cases state unions formed by other methods had also been termed "unions," and consequently there was no essential difference between the legal nature of a union of states provided with "collective personality" and that of an organisation of the kind just described.

Apparently to Brie it did not suffice for the conception of the union that the common will should be exercised exclusively by the collectivity; rather it was essential that all the states united in the commonwealth should be permitted to have a share in its constitution through the agency of their own organs, especially in matters affecting them all in common.

The kind of organisation characteristic of the "union" was frequently designated "federative" and Brie himself used the term in that sense, but the expressions "federative" and "confederation" were used with quite different meanings.[1]

All known commonwealths of states (*Staatengemeinwesen*) had given effect to the federative principle.

Brie put forward the federal notion that historically every state obliged to recognise a higher authority over itself had the "natural desire" to exercise at least a co-operative influence in the formation of this common will in order to have indirect control in matters concerning itself which had been withdrawn from its direct sphere of determination.

It is in accordance with the principle of the personal equality of the members of the union that, just as in the association of states the members all take an active part in matters of common concern, so in the collectivity of states they all take an active part in collective affairs. The reasons which in the case of other collectivities make a limitation of the right of participation in the representation of the whole necessary or advisable do not apply in this case: the appointed organs of the wills of each state must be regarded as having that intelligence and moral purpose which appear necessary for their participation in the formation of the collective will. The joint operation of the wills of the individual states in collective affairs thus manifests itself as the outcome of the union of their capabilities—and without it conflicts between the individual states and the central authority would be much more likely to arise. But Brie admitted that "complete equality of the legal influence of the states upon the conduct of

[1] S. Brie: *Theorie der Staatenverbindungen*, 1886, p. 81.

collective affairs is not a necessary consequence of the federal idea."[1]

He pointed out that in particular some modifications of the equality of voting rights might result from differences in the strength of the various states; and there might be some functions of the federal authority for which a unitary direction, entrusted to a single state, or to an organ of a single state, may be requisite.[2]

And finally, "if the union is to possess a true state character, then in the formation of the collective organ other factors, and not merely the individual states, must be taken into account."[3]

Both the ways in which effect has been given to the actual idea of federation and the whole legal form of collectivities of states have historically been very diverse. The most complete distinction is, however, that between the confederation (*Staatenbund*) and the federal state (*Bundesstaat*), and this distinction is based primarily upon a difference of purpose.[4]

Then Brie proceeded to examine the legal nature of the confederation. He defined it as "a union of states possessing a legal personality of its own, and its own federally-formed organisation," or, more shortly, a "federal collectivity composed of a number of states."[5]

As typical forms of confederation, he mentioned the United Netherlands of 1579–1795; the North American Confederation of 1778–1789; the Swiss Confederation of 1815–1848; and the German Union of 1815–1866.

Brie laid down four conditions as being fundamental characteristics of a confederation.

First, the confederation is "not a mere legal relationship, but a commonwealth or legal subject, not only in relation to an outside state, but also in relation to its own member states."[6]

The confederation, whose activity is chiefly in respect of foreign affairs, is a person in international law. As the political unity of the confederated common powers, the confederation as an international personality required international recognition, and although the majority decision was usually accepted in the federal congress in regard to foreign affairs, yet by the very nature of its treaty-based union no ratification on the part of the highest representative organs of the individual states was necessary.

Secondly, with regard to the connection between the external legal position and internal legal relations of a personal union, the "federal assembly," composed of delegates of all the con-

[1] S. Brie: *Theorie der Staatenverbindungen*, 1886, p. 82.   [2] Ibid.
[3] Ibid., p. 83.   [4] Ibid.   [5] Ibid.   [6] Ibid., p. 84.

federated states, was used as the general instrument in regulating federal matters. The decisions of the federal assembly were as a rule carried by majority vote, and even those member states which were in opposition were definitely pledged to obey those decisions.

Thus within the sphere of federal competence there did appear without doubt subordination of the will of individual states to the majority will. Such a complete recognition of the majority principle, according to Brie, was a strong argument in favour of the corporative character of a union of persons, whereas the natures of a corporation and of a confederation were historically incompatible with one another.[1]

Thirdly, the confederation was a collectivity but not a "state creation," because it lacked not only the comprehensive purpose and the comprehensive competence, but also "the personal basis of the state."[2]

The purpose of the confederation was limited to certain definite aspects of the general state purpose, and there corresponded to these a specialised competence limited to a definitely marked-out sphere of authority, and especially to federal protection against foreign aggression.

In addition to the limitation just mentioned, the union did not even possess the right of extending its sphere of competence by majority decision; for such extension the unanimous consent of all the members of the union was indispensable.

Brie held that a collectivity whose competence was limited to certain functions could not claim to have the character of a state.[3] The confederation was therefore "a commonwealth composed of states, a union of states provided with collective personality."[4] The confederation was based upon the collectivity of the confederated states and its members were the individual states belonging to it. It was not a community of individuals, but it was a community of member states as "active participants in its organisation," and consequently it had no direct relation to the citizens of the member states.

Lastly, the confederation not only lacked the character of a state, but since it possessed as a collective personality only to a small extent a position higher than its members, it actually approximated to an organised state association.[5]

Although the sovereignty of the member states was limited, yet legally that sovereignty was given the utmost possible validity.

[1] S. Brie: *Theorie der Staatenverbindungen*, 1886, p. 86.   [2] Ibid., p. 88.
[3] Ibid., p. 89.   [4] Ibid.   [5] Ibid., p. 91.

The confederation had then to Brie two essential characteristics—recognition of the sovereignty of the confederated members on the one hand, and on the other limited purpose and competence.[1]

Despite the corporate nature of the confederation, this form of association of states is neither very effective nor very stable. As the confederation, by its very definition and nature, must rule states but is dependent for its effectiveness upon the goodwill of at least the great majority of those states and can promote the collective good only by sacrificing their individual interests, its effectiveness must be limited; and the more in its structure and organisation the independence of the member states is maintained, the less is it able to act effectively. On the other hand, for defence against aggression, the primary purpose of confederation, a strong concentration of purpose and strength is essential. But a confederation even moderately adequate to that task has never existed and probably never will exist. The confederation is entirely incapable of satisfying permanently the needs of a national collectivity—and yet history shows that even so loose a federate collectivity is only practical where either the peoples of a number of states are held together by a common nationality or a nation is beginning to develop out of a number of groups of people. Historically the confederation therefore appears as the precursor of a closer union corresponding to the natural needs of a nation, that is, of a federal state.[2]

Scarcely any problem has occupied the attention of German political scientists so much as that of the theory and nature of that form of union which is appropriately called the federal state.

First Brie defined the federal state as being "at once union and state." Conceptionally, it is on the one side a collectivity made up of states and federally organised, and on the other hand a collectivity made up of human beings with a purpose and scope embracing in principle all the purposes of human life.

Therefore the conception of the federal state was, to him, not based partly on that of the union and partly on that of the state, but combined in itself "all the essential characteristics of the union and of the state"; that is, these two groups of characteristics are not merely externally associated, but are made into one composite whole, in which they reciprocally "condition and limit each other." Consequently the full and complete federal state is not in one

[1] S. Brie: *Theorie der Staatenverbindungen*, 1886, pp. 94–95.   [2] Ibid.

respect a union and in another respect a state, but in all respects manifests this characteristic dual nature.[1]

This dual nature distinguished it conceptionally on the one hand from the confederation which is a union but not a state, and on the other hand from the unitary state, which cannot be at the same time a union.

On this basis the characteristic of the federal state is that each of its members is, like the whole, an actual state, with a purpose and sphere of its own which in principle includes all forms of human activity.

Holding these views as to the theoretical basis and general legal character of the federal state, Brie found himself to be in disagreement with most previous writers on the subject, and especially with those who had written since the creation of the German Empire. He disagreed with those who (like Treitschke) denied state character to the members of the federation or (like Haenel and Gierke) regarded the whole and the members as parts of a single state. He disagreed with writers like Laband, G. Meyer, Jellinek and Rosin, who, whilst asserting the state character of the federal state as a whole and also of its parts, failed to recognise the need either for direct relations between the federal authority and the people, or for the comprehensiveness of that authority (at least in principle), or ascribed a state character to the states on insufficient grounds. The more recent discussions of the federal theory seemed to him mistaken in their treatment of the federal organisation principle, either treating it as unimportant in relation to federal theory, or else giving it a unilateral importance incompatible with the dual nature of the federal state. Brie remarked that the true theory had in the main been set out before 1848 in the writings of Pfizer and Welcker, but had been pushed into the background by the doctrines of Tocqueville and Waitz as to the division of powers in the federal state—doctrines which in their turn have failed to withstand scientific criticism.

Brie next pointed out that every theory of the federal state was deduced and formulated from the positive legal material found in the legal instruments and especially the constitutions of three federal states—the North American union, the Swiss federation after its revisions of 1848 and 1874, and the new German Empire.

The fact that two of these were republican and one monarchical, and that in the latter one particular state exercised a dominant influence, gave rise to differences between the constitutions of the three federal states, which in his opinion threw much light

[1] S. Brie: *Theorie der Staatenverbindungen*, 1886, p. 96.

on the question of the possibilities of variations and indeed anomalies in the practical working out of the federal theory.

First of all, he asserted that for the federal state, as for every collective person, the purpose for which it exists is the chief factor in determining its nature.

If it be assumed that the federal collectivity has the nature of a state, then the purpose of the federal state is necessarily identical with the purpose of the state generally; that is, it seeks to promote all those interests of the human beings united within it which are in need of its assistance. If, on the other hand, the federal state is regarded merely as a union of states, then its purpose is simply a comprehensive extension of the constituent states. But these two theories of purpose are in no way incompatible; it is simply that their combination emphasises the subsidiary character resulting from intelligent correlation of functions and the unavoidable limitations upon the universality of the state purpose.[1]

In the federal state the fulfilment of state obligations rests in the first instance with the member states and the collective state is called upon to give effect to the state purpose only so far as this cannot be adequately satisfied by the member states. It is, therefore, by this universality that the purpose of the federal state is differentiated from that of the confederation, which is limited to the promotion of certain definite interests, and also from that of the unitary state in that the latter is alone charged with the fulfilment of the purpose of the state, whereas the federal state is called on to supplement comprehensively the activity of its members in carrying out the state purpose.

Whilst the fundamental laws of the old German Empire, in which a federal organisation had developed out of a unitary state, did not expressly lay down the tasks of that organisation, modern federal states formed by the voluntary coming together of the individual states have adopted constitutions in which the purposes of federation are definitely prescribed. Amongst these purposes there are always three principal ones, which are identical with the three principal purposes of the state, namely, "defence against external attack, legal protection at home, and care for the welfare of the people."[2] But although "the all-sidedness of the purpose of the federal state" received express constitutional recognition, yet the provisions contained in the constitutions as to the purposes of the three federal states do not emphasise the principle that those purposes are supplementary to the purposes of the states. Nevertheless, that ideal lies at the basis of the con-

[1] S. Brie: *Theorie der Staatenverbindungen*, 1886, p. 100.   [2] Ibid.

stitutions. This is made indisputably clear by the provisions as to the competence of the central power, and particularly by the detailed statements of its powers and duties. Actually, the juristic importance of this doctrine—that the collective state is supplementary or subsidiary to the individual states—lies in the delimitation of their respective spheres.[1]

Brie recognised that the proposition that in the federal state both the whole and the parts are states was valid only if both the central authority and the separate state authorities had, at least in principle, competence in respect of the whole of human life, and had this in their own right.[2] But the difficult problem of the necessary division of powers was only very inadequately solved, according to Brie, in the old German Empire; he thought, however, that in the later federal states an easy and certain solution had been found.

In the old empire the power of the territorial rulers had resulted from the agglomeration of private law rights and state powers transferred from the empire, and had developed gradually into an authority based on its own right and theoretically covering and ruling all the inhabitants of each territory. This process was substantially completed by the Peace of Westphalia; thereafter the empire (i.e. the Kaiser) had exclusive authority only in very few and unimportant matters. But in theory the imperial power continued to possess that *plenitudo potestatis* which was previously inherent in it. There was no systematic legal demarcation of powers. It is true that the intervention of the head of the empire in the internal affairs of the territories was almost entirely forbidden, partly by general rules, partly by the grant of privileges; but the all-embracing competence of imperial legislation was limited only by a very vague reservation of *jura singulorum*. In fact, the legislative action of the empire was paralysed.

In modern federal states, on the other hand, there is a clear statement of the functions of the central power as well as of the central organs; and there is a constitutional recognition of the right of the central power to extend its scope by the amendment of the constitution. With few exceptions the mass of prerogative powers remain vested in the member states.[3]

Modern federal states were formed in place of the previous confederate unions and by the free agreement of the future member states. The competence of the collectivity, therefore, was naturally limited to the needs of the unity at that time, and the

[1] S. Brie: *Theorie der Staatenverbindungen*, 1886, p. 101.
[2] Ibid.
[3] Ibid., p. 103.

most natural way of giving effect to that idea seemed to be to impose positive limits to the sphere of the central power, following the example of the confederation. In this way the character of the federal state was legally defined as that of a collectivity made up of states, like a confederation, and its functions were marked as being subsidiary to those of the individual states which had the primary responsibility for realising the purposes of the state within the scope of their authority.

At the same time a positive limitation of the competence of the central authority would be incompatible with the state nature of the federal state, unless there were secured to the collectivity in the federal state the possibility of extending the scope of that competence by amendment of the constitution—by a procedure more elaborate than that of ordinary legislation. Only by that means could the fundamental principle of comprehensiveness of scope be legally established side by side with that of the supplementary nature of the federal powers. Otherwise the federal state would not possess the dual nature Brie had previously predicated of it, and would remain on the same level as the confederation. For this reason Brie asserted that the so-called *Kompetenz-Kompetenz* was conceptionally a necessity for the federal state,[1] though it was incompatible with the nature of the confederation.

In the case of the new German imperial constitution, which followed on the constitution of the North German union, this right of extension of scope was given very definitely to the collective state, for the introduction of changes of the constitution was entrusted to the ordinary legislative authority of the collective state. The federal constitutions of the United States of America and Switzerland differed from this in that in the former proposals for changes must be approved by a three-fourths majority of the states, and in Switzerland must be approved by a majority both of the electors and of the cantons. But in neither case does this mean that constitutional changes are not within the legal right of the collective state, but that for this purpose alone the organisation of the collective state differs somewhat from its organisation for the discharge of its constitutional functions.

On the other hand, the deduction to be made from the theory of federalism must be somewhat modified when the German imperial constitution (Article 78) makes the whole or partial withdrawal of certain rights from the individual states dependent

[1] S. Brie: *Theorie der Staatenverbindungen*, 1886, p. 104.

upon the consent of those states. And it is an anomaly, only ascribable to the especial importance of Prussia in the German Empire, that Prussia could by itself veto any amendment of the constitution and thereby prevent any extension of the imperial power.

As the member states handed over to the collective state only certain definite powers, they retained their former state authority, apart from these transferred powers. This principle is expressly recognised in the constitutions of the two republican federal states, and it also applied to the individual states in the German Empire. This marks the far-reaching difference between collectivities of this kind and communal corporations. The fact that the sphere of the individual states in modern federations is theoretically unlimited gives them legally the character of states, however many functions may be withdrawn from them.

But it does not necessarily follow that all the various subject matters placed under the authority of the central power are completely withdrawn from the member states. Frequently the collective interest does not require the central authority to have more than an influence upon some department of state activity; it may, for example, be necessary for the central authority to lay down general rules applicable to a particular matter throughout the federation without centralising the actual administration of those rules.[1]

The Swiss federal constitution, and to a great extent the German federal empire, applied this consideration, whereas the North American constitution defined and limited the sphere of activity of the federal authority and entrusted to the federal authority the exercise of the federal laws.

Nevertheless, however desirable it may be that federal authority should deal with general interests and the individual states with their particular interests, yet actually in the three leading federal constitutions of Brie's time the federal authority permitted its component states in most matters to exercise competence concurrently with itself.

Brie assumed that, although the collective state fully maintained the complete direction of foreign affairs, the member states still retained to a greater or less extent their international personality.[2]

Therefore to him the sphere of competence belonging exclusively to the federal authority in the modern federal state was a comparatively small one.

[1] S. Brie: *Theorie der Staatenverbindungen*, 1886, p. 107. [2] Ibid.

The withdrawal of certain supreme rights from the individual states entailed the modification of the state idea; nevertheless, Brie considered that this modification "appeared to be compatible with the empirical conception of the state." This exposition of his modification some way or other of the *a priorism* in the state idea paved the way for the introduction of the empirical idea into his juristic conception of the state.

His explanation of this idea was that when the member states formed a combination into a commonwealth higher than themselves, "the supreme rights which remained to them did not lose the character of inherent rights," although they could be "withdrawn" or "diminished" by the higher collective will and could be exercised only by means of delegation on the part of the collectivity, and could accordingly be regarded as belonging to the individual states by virtue of their exercise.[1]

As Ludolph Hugo recognised, if the territorial authority in the earlier German Empire, although historically derived from the imperial authority, was not juristically based upon a delegation from the imperial authority, this view must apply even more certainly to the authority of the members in the modern federal state, since in the latter the historical process was quite the reverse.

Then Brie argued that conformably with the dual character the federal state must have a twofold personal basis.

In its quality of union it consisted legally of states; as a state it was legally composed of people. Therefore its members were not only individual states but also individual people, although technically the term "members" applied only to the former.

Thus Brie disagreed with the earlier theory of the federal state, that the individual states had an existence apart from the collectivity, but held that there existed "a close reciprocity" between them and the collective state, which reciprocity appeared "in the legal subordination of the individual states to the legal decision of the central authority as well as in their co-operation in the formation of the central will."[2]

The subordination of the individual states to the federal authority in confederation was even more intensified in the "federal state union" (*bundesstaatliche Vereinigung*). In the federal state the central authority maintained direct command over the people, but frequently it so acted as to limit the will of the individual states in the common interest of the whole, or made the individual states serve the interests of the collective state. And he pointed out that the will of the collective state "must

[1] S. Brie: *Theorie der Staatenverbindungen*, 1886, p. 108.   [2] Ibid., p. 109.

take precedence over that of the individual state in every case of conflict between them."[1]

As in the old German Empire the subordination of the individual state to the empire was recognised, so in the modern federal state the subjection of the separate state authorities to the central power of the collective state was shown in the following ways:—

Firstly, inasmuch as certain supreme rights of the individual states were withdrawn or limited by the federal constitution, the central authority had to exercise vigilance "that these constitutional decisions were not violated by the individual states." The "right of supervision" over the individual states was granted to the imperial authority in the German Empire, and the Swiss federal constitution of 1874 assumed the right of supervision over the exercise of the supreme rights possessed by the cantons.

Secondly, the modern federal state obtained the greater part of its resources from the individual states. The proportional contribution of the individual states was only of secondary importance, but the practical impossibility of refusing each individual state the control of its own forces and the equal impossibility of the existence of separate armies for the federal state and for each member state led to the system of military contingents.[2]

Thirdly, the orders issued by the collective state within its competence took precedence over those of the individual states. This fundamental principle was clearly expressed in the constitutions of North America and the German Empire, and applied equally to the Swiss confederation.[3]

Fourthly, any dispute in regard to the competence of the central authority and of the individual states was settled in the three modern federal states by an organ of the collective state.[4]

Lastly, the power of the central authority to enlarge its own competence stressed the subordination of the individual states.

Owing to the subordinate position of the individual states under the central state, the former might be termed "real but non-sovereign states." An exception to this was made by those German states which within a limited sphere possessed certain reserved rights which were inalienable except by their own consent. The Prussian state even managed to retain its sovereignty, because "any extension of the imperial competence beyond the previous constitutional limits needs the consent of Prussia."[5]

Following Brie's method of argument it seems that an *a priori*

[1] S. Brie: *Theorie der Staatenverbindungen*, 1886, p. 109.   [2] Ibid., p. 111.
[3] Ibid.   [4] Ibid.   [5] Ibid., p. 112.

formula in political-legal criticism had to be employed admitting, however, of certain exceptions when the examination of the political system rests on an empirical basis.

Thus the individual states were "not only passive but also active members of the collective state," that is to say, they had not only "obligations of membership but also rights of membership."

By the constitution of the modern federal state the individual states had a recognised legal claim to protection by the collective state against foreign aggression, and the constitutions of both the republican federal states also granted to the individual states the right to federal assistance in cases of internal disturbance.

But, above all, the individual states by virtue of their federal character exercised a legal influence on the formation of the collective will, and in German phraseology were actually *Mitträger des Gesamtwillens*.

The federal state was then based not only on the individual state, as the confederation was, but also "on the nation as a whole"; and it stood in direct legal relationship with the subjects of the individual states.[1]

The right of entering into direct connection with individuals was necessary for the federal state, since it would be impossible for it to carry out its comprehensive duties if its legal influence affected only the states.[2]

Therefore in the federal state there was a twofold "civil right" for the individuals who were citizens of an individual state and at the same time of the collective state.

So Brie explained that the relationship between membership of the collective state and membership of individual states could be regulated in various ways, no one particular way being solely or specially in accord with the nature of the federal state. Either, as in the German Empire or Swiss federation, membership of the federal state can be bound up with membership of the individual state so that the former is gained or lost with the latter, or conversely, as in the United States, citizenship of an individual state is merely consequential on federal citizenship.

Further, the individual subjects or citizens have, both naturally and in accordance with the laws of actual federal states, duties as well as rights in relation to the whole body.

The central authority does not always need to make a direct use of its legal power over individuals; it may employ the states as intermediaries; the old German Empire did so to such an extent that its direct action upon the people was scarcely apparent.

[1] S. Brie: *Theorie der Staatenverbindungen*, 1886, p. 113.   [2] Ibid.

But naturally the laws made by the collective state must be directly binding upon the individuals and must be promulgated by the organs of the collective state, for otherwise it might suffer from delay or neglect of publication by the individual states. So in the three modern federal states there is publication of enactments by the central authority, and thereby they become binding upon the respective subjects or citizens. And further, in order that the collective state can overcome any opposition by the states and see that the burdens laid upon the subjects or citizens of the member states for common purposes are evenly distributed, the collective state must be able to call directly upon the individuals for contributions and services. So in the modern federal states the central authority has the right of taxation (limited in Switzerland to certain indirect taxes) and in all three cases there is an obligation of military service.

There is no general rule, derivable from the nature of the federal state, as to the extent to which rights of citizenship, in particular rights of liberty, are to be safeguarded for individuals by the collective state; the republican federal states have, in fact, gone further in this respect than the old and new German Empire. But, above all, an active participation of individuals in the operations of the collective state makes itself recognised as a requirement arising out of the very nature of the federal state, so far only as there are the other rational presuppositions for constitutional representative institutions. The dual nature of the federal state must find expression in its organisation. The institutions of all the federal states considered by Brie meet this requirement. They differ mainly in the mode of formation of the holders of the federal authority. He admitted that no general and decisive rule as to this could be drawn from the nature of the federal state.

A necessary consequence of the nature of the federal state is that the individual states have a decisive influence on the conduct of the collective affairs. The application of the federative principle must differ more or less between the federal state and the confederation, because of the smaller regard paid in the former to the sovereignty of the individual states, but the consequential differences of organisation are of an unimportant kind, and are of no particular note for the conception of the two forms of union.

Brie pointed out that a distinction of principle between the organisation of the federal state and that of the confederation was based on the fact that the "state quality" of the former must receive recognition in its form of organisation. It is conceivable that in the federal state an organ formed from the collectivity of individual states could be called upon to discharge the tasks of the central authority, without the intervention of other organs, just as in the unified state the state organisation can be based on subordinate corporations or communes. But then the characteristic dual nature of the federal state would not find expression—that is, there would be only an incomplete realisation of the idea of the federal state—and in practice a federal state dependent for the formation and exercise of the central will upon the co-operation of the individual states would give to the individualist interests and aims of the latter a validity which might be seriously inimical to the fulfilment of its own purposes.

Brie laid it down that the expression of both the state (unitary) and federal ideas was not merely permissible owing to the dual nature of the federal state, but was an absolute requisite, and however diverse the ways in which effect can be given to this in the organisation of the federal state, a unitary representative body—representative, that is, of the people—appears to be by far the best way of expressing the state nature of the federal state and the underlying national unity.

The nature and powers and duties of the various organs of the federal state will be determined by the same kind of considerations as make different kinds of organs for different tasks necessary or advisable in the individual state. Generally, for obvious reasons, the organs of the federal state will be on the same lines as those of the member states.

Brie remarked that the factors to which he had thus drawn attention had influenced the constitutions of modern federal states, and even that of the old German Empire, although in that the popular element was lacking. In the organisation of the old German Empire the federal principle was predominant. At the head of that collectivity was a monarch, the expression of the state character of that empire. But the exercise of the power of the emperor was dependent in a great measure upon the will of the estates of the empire, for not only was the "Kaiser" elected by some of the most powerful of the territorial lords, but he could not make a law or issue any important imperial rescript without the preliminary consent of the imperial diet, which thereby possessed in fact an *imperium* conjointly with the emperor. This imperial assembly was, however, formed on a purely federal basis; it consisted of envoys sent by the majority of the individual state authorities and strictly bound by their instructions.

The peoples of the empire had constitutionally no share whatever in the conduct of its affairs. There was a certain harmony between the institutions of the empire and those of the territorial states, inasmuch as (at any rate until the eighteenth century) the majority of the territorial rulers were restricted by the estates in the same way as the emperor was restricted by the estates of the empire.

Brie admitted that the organisation of the new German Empire was in many respects parallel to that of the old Empire, but nevertheless held that a real federal state had been devised more completely and more in accordance with political requirements, and more effect had been given to the federal principle, inasmuch as the supreme authority was for most purposes vested in a "college," namely the federal council,[1] composed of plenipotentiaries of the several states, appointed by the governments of those states and provided with definite instructions; the distribution of votes was the same as in the old German confederation, but as compared with that institution there was less regard for state particularism and complete recognition of the principle of majority decisions (except for changes in the constitution and a Prussian veto in certain cases).

But apart from this the balance of the federal and unitary principles appeared to be conserved in the organisation of the empire which was given a twofold representation, namely, in the person of the emperor and in the *Reichstag*.[2]

Some very important functions of the federal authority, particularly those requiring "unitary and energetic direction," were excepted from the fundamentally comprehensive competence of the federal council and handed over permanently to the emperor as an independent organ of the empire.[3]

The necessary unity in the exercise of the federal authority was secured by the fact that the emperor possessed very great influence in the federal council because of the large Prussian membership and his constitutional prerogatives, and by the fact that co-operation of the emperor and the federal council was in many cases a constitutional requirement. The permanent unity of the imperial dignity with the Prussian kingship was not inherent in the nature of the federal state, but Brie, like Laband, held that it was not in conflict with it, because the imperial power was vested in "the head of the Prussian state, not as such but as a constitutional organ of the empire."[4]

[1] S. Brie: *Theorie der Staatenverbindungen*, 1886, p. 119.
[2] Ibid., p. 120.   [3] Ibid., p. 121.   [4] Ibid.

And he added that by the side of these two supreme organs entrusted with the exercise of the imperial authority, there was another body with more limited functions and charged chiefly with co-operation in legislation and supervision of the imperial administration, namely, the *Reichstag*, the collective representation of the German people.[1]

The form of the new German Empire differed from that of the majority of the member states in that the former had not a monarchical head, but the emperor had, in fact, a quasi-monarchical position, and the legal position of the *Reichstag* was analogous to that of the parliaments of the member states.

In contrast to the German Empire, Brie next considered the organisation of the two republican federal states, the North American Union and the Swiss Federation. In both, the dual nature of the federal state was closely associated with the bicameral system.

In both federal states an assembly was the highest authority, and in each case the assembly was made up of two parts—one directly elected by all the citizens (the house of representatives and national council respectively) and the other composed of representatives of the separate states or cantons (senate and federal council),[2] in the United States for legislation and certain important acts of government, and in Switzerland for the general exercise of the federal power.

The federal council was composed in both cases of equal numbers of members from each federated state, who voted not on instructions from that state but according to their individual judgment. As a rule, the governments of the separate states had no direct influence on the actions of the central authority; nevertheless, the numerical equality of representation in the upper house in each case did emphasise the federal principle; and these two facts are explained by the constitutions of the separate states with their democratic and representative bases.

In the separate states the people or their representatives are more easily satisfied than is a monarch with an indirect influence on the conduct of federal affairs, and on the other hand the populations of the larger states find in representation according to population in the elected chamber an adequate offset to the disregard in the other chamber of differences in size and power. In Brie's opinion the Swiss federal council resembled more closely the council of a confederation than did the American senate, and was therefore more akin to the German federal

---

[1] S. Brie: *Theorie der Staatenverbindungen*, 1882, p. 121.   [2] Ibid., p. 122.

council. For the manner of appointment of the members and the periods of office are decided entirely by the cantons, whereas in the United States these matters were expressly determined by the federal constitution.

With regard to the executive, the North American federal state was more unitary than the Swiss federation, since in America the executive was independent of the legislature and was entrusted to an individual "President," subject to the concurrence of the senate in the exercise of some important functions. In Switzerland, on the other hand, the executive is exercised by a college—the federal council—chosen by the federal assembly and subordinate to it.

Besides the function of the general organs of the central authority, "direct action of the individual cantons" or of the nation as a whole was constitutionally provided for in matters affecting the whole union, both in the Swiss and the North American unions, though in the latter it was limited to constitutional amendments.

There existed a striking similarity between the organisation of the collective state and that of the individual states in North America, the legislation in both cases being entrusted to two chambers. The Swiss cantons had a similar organisation with a democratic basis and differed from the collective organisation in having only the single chamber system.[1]

The constitutions of both these federal states determined that the organisation of the individual states must remain on the same basis (republican) as that of the collective state, and the American federal constitution guaranteed the republican, i.e. democratic, state form to its member states.

Arising from the discussions about the organisations of the then existing federal states, Brie asserted that it was impossible to postulate a uniform mode of forming the "holders" of the central authority.

In the early German Empire the emperor "as monarch of the collective state" was undoubtedly the "holder" of collective authority. The dispute as to whether the "estates of the empire and towns possessing feudal rights were or were not" joint holders of the central authority with the emperor, Brie decided in the negative.

But of the new German Empire he definitely asserted that the highest exercise of the imperial authority belonged in general to the federal council.

[1] S. Brie: *Theorie der Staatenverbindungen*, 1886, p. 125.

As the members of the federal council could only express the wills of the heads of the individual states in imperial affairs, "the collectivity of the heads of the individual states" must legally be considered as the "holder" of the imperial authority. The question whether the emperor was the direct organ of the empire or the representative of the collectivity of the governments of the individual states was one "not easy to solve"; but Brie gave the preference to the former view.[1]

He considered that the *Reichstag* had as small a share of imperial supremacy over the German nation as a whole, as the *Landtage* in the several states had of supremacy over their own citizens.[2]

Nevertheless, in the republican Swiss federal state, based on a democratic representative system, he admitted that the collective Swiss people, as the collectivity of the active citizens, and the collectivity of the cantons appeared together as *Träger* of the federal authority. This view was confirmed especially by the fact that any decisions as to constitutional amendments were made jointly by "the direct participation of the collective nation and of the cantons." In the United States of America the holder of federal authority held a practically analogous position. Consequently, both the Swiss and the North American nations might be designated in their collectivity and their state membership as *Träger* of the authority of the collective state.

On this assumption as to the dual nature of the federal state, the structure of the *Träger* of central authority consisted of "a combination of a unitary and a federal factor" as in the Swiss or American republican federal states. And even if, in the formation of the *Träger* of the central authority, little regard is paid to one of these factors, the examples of the old and new German Empire show that in some other way it can be given equivalent expression —and even preponderating expression.

Consequently Brie, unlike Jellinek and others, asserted that "the question of the manner in which the *Träger* of the central authority is formed has no decisive importance, in principle, in respect of the nature of the federal state."[3]

Next Brie laid it down that, in accordance with the dual nature of the federal state, a difference, legal and historical, of origin was both theoretically possible and a demonstrable fact. Historically the federal state came into being either by division or by union. It arose either out of a unitary state, whose parts acquired the status of states without the abolition of the previously existing

[1]. S. Brie: *Theorie der Staatenverbindungen*, 1886, p. 127.
[2] Ibid.   [3] Ibid., p. 128.

state within which they had been comprised; or out of a number of states, hitherto not united in any form of state, which were brought together into a higher form of state organisation, even one directly affecting their subjects and citizens, but without losing their own state individualities.

But in each case, in order that the collective state should give effect to the federal idea, the effective legal co-operation of the individual states in the formation of the collective will must be secured.

An example of the first kind is furnished by the old German Empire, which acquired the character—though admittedly only in part—of a federal state by the formation within it of separate states. The second way—the union of states previously associated only in a confederation—is illustrated by the three modern federal states, the German Empire and the Swiss and North American federations.

Brie held that these historical differences of origin corresponded with differences in the legal bases of the existence and constitution of the federal states.

Whilst by process of customary law (*Gewohnheitsrecht*) a unitary state can transform itself into a federal state or a number of states can develop together to a federal state, the creation of a federal state by law is possible only by the unitary state conferring on its parts the status of member states, and, on the other hand, the only way in which a federal state can be set up by a pact is for a number of hitherto more or less sovereign states to create by agreement a federal state and become members thereof. It is true that a pact does not by itself bring a federal state into being; that happens, and the federal state attains to the power of thought and action only when the pact is carried out. But, even so, the pact is much more than a necessary preliminary to the legal formation of the federal state and the validity of its first constitution; it is the fundamental "law" from which the federal state derives its legal existence and the federal constitution its binding authority over the individual states.

In consequence of the dual nature of the federal state a sympathetic attitude, and in some cases the active co-operation, of the people is required to bring the federal state into being. The individual subjects or citizens of the member states become subjects or citizens of the collective state and under its constitution incur obligations and acquire rights, not directly from the pact pursuant to which that state is set up, but under territorial laws confirming the provisions of that pact and duly promulgated.[1] Thus the federal state, so formed by the agreement of the future members, acquires—in accordance with its legal character as a corporation—a personality independent of the individual wills of the member states and a will of its own superior to theirs.[2] In relation to the individual subjects and citizens the federal constitution is not simply a territorial law, but a law regulating the life of a higher state unity and superior to the territorial laws. Juristically it does not matter if later on the federal state gives its constitution the form of a statute; and there is no difference as to legal validity between the constitution as originally determined by the pact and later modifications of it made by the constitutional statute.[3]

If these propositions are sound, the question as to how existing federal states and their constitutions came into being is only of minor importance and does not materially affect the legal nature of the federal state.

In conclusion, Brie laid down the proposition that the natural purpose of the federal state, as a state, is to satisfy the political needs arising from a national common existence; and that, on the other hand, the division of a nation into a number of separate states appears, when the parts of the nation dwell side by side, to be justified in reason and history only if, by reason of original differences of settlement or as the result of later developments, there are marked and lasting differences in their interests and outlook. But where there are these natural prerequisites for unity and plurality the federal system offers the best possible solution of the difficult dual problem.

The particular interests of the various parts are assured of the fullest consideration by the maintenance of the individual state authorities based on their own inherent rights and in principle covering all the activities of human life; and, on the other hand, the action of the collective state can satisfy completely the need for unified direction and system.

The necessary harmony between the parts and between the parts and the whole is assured partly by the subordination of the individual states to the central power and partly by the participation of the parts in the formation of the collective will.

History had already shown that many states of very diverse extent and powers could carry out "a beneficial working in and with such a union," and that the permanence and prosperity of a federal union were not dependent upon the adoption of any

[1] S. Brie: *Theorie der Staatenverbindungen*, 1886, p. 130.
[2] Ibid.   [3] Ibid., p. 131.

one state form. Brie concluded, therefore, that the federal state is not one definite state form, but must vary according to time and circumstance. He himself started his examination of the union of states from the basis of the legal criterion of the idea of the state —the comprehensiveness of the state purpose; but his conclusion as to the federal state was reached by the empirical method.

His last word was as to the comparison between the federal state and the decentralised unitary state.

In the federal state not only is the decentralisation of state functions carried to the furthest point compatible with the conception of the state, but the idea of the state is given very exceptional form, inasmuch as the supplementary nature of the scope and purpose of the state, which in other cases applies only to the relations of the state with individuals and non-state communities, here applies also to the relations between states themselves. And, on the other hand, the idea of the association of states is most completely realised in the federal state, for there the union of states itself attains to the dignity of a state.[1]

His conception of the federal state in this discussion was more or less the theoretical assertion of the federal state in general, but his theory weighed the idealistic principle in the balance of the unitary and federal scale. On the basis of the nature of the federal state he set up the legal assumption of the dual nature of the state.

Compared with Jellinek's theory of the union of states, Brie put forward his theory far more legally and rigidly than the former, who based the juristic survey on empirical grounds.

These two jurists made an outstanding study of federalism in Germany and the theory of the union of states in general, and gave a great impetus to the development of the federal idea not only in Germany, but also in America and Switzerland and in other countries.

§ 10

Besides these three outstanding expositions of federal theory by Laband, Jellinek and Brie, G. Meyer expounded the doctrine of the union of states based on his conception of *Herrschaft* more emphatically in his later work, *Lehrbuch des deutschen Staatsrechts* published in 1878 (sixth edition by G. Anschütz in 1905), than in his earlier works.

[1] S. Brie: *Theorie der Staatenverbindungen*, 1886, p. 135.

He began with the notion of the *Gemeinwesen*, that is, the union of a number of men with "an organisation and will to which the individual members are subordinate."[1]

Its sphere of activity can be either a limited one, as in the cases of a church or an economic association, or an unlimited one, as in the case of a "political commonwealth" with its dual basis first racial and then territorial. This conception of the political commonwealth involves three essentials: (*a*) the existence of a human community, i.e. an organised plurality of men; (*b*) a territorial basis; (*c*) an unlimited scope of activity.[2] And in Meyer's view "political commonwealths" include states, communal associations forming parts of states (in Germany communes, circles, districts and provinces) and unions of states in which a number of states are combined into a single higher unit.

A political organisation can be of so simple a kind that in any given territory only one single political commonwealth exists, and the state and the commune coincide. But the position is rarely so simple; generally, the political organisation is much more complicated. There is a series of political commonwealths which stand in a relationship of superiority and subordination to one another, and thereby are united in a political collectivity. The sphere of activity of this political collectivity is unlimited; the individual political commonwealths of which it is composed have only limited spheres. There are, however, a remarkable number of ways in which political tasks can be divided between the individual commonwealths; consequently, the most diverse forms of political organisation are possible. But for modern states there are two outstanding forms—the unitary state and the union of states.[3]

In the ancient world the state attained its highest development in the city state; the state was the sole political organisation. Consequently, neither the political philosophers nor the Roman legists had any reason to distinguish between the state and other political commonwealths; and even when in the later Roman Empire there developed a distinction between *imperium* and *municipium* the latter was regarded as an artificial creation, deriving its rights from the former. In the Middle Ages the jurists applied the Roman conception of the state to the empire, but they recognised that between the empire and the individuals there were intermediate associations which possessed governmental powers and in which a communal life developed. So they worked out

---
[1] Georg Meyer: *Lehrbuch des deutschen Staatsrechts*, ed. by G. Anschütz, 1905, p. 3.
[2] Ibid.   [3] Ibid., p. 4.

the idea of the "commonwealths" (*Gemeinwesen*) in the sense of state law: these differed from the empire in that they were subject to it; whereas the empire had no superior. With the practical cessation of the empire after the end of the Middle Ages the conception of the state was applied to the kingdoms and territories hitherto regarded as parts of the empire. To these and their rulers was ascribed that supreme power which had previously belonged only to the empire and emperor. Despite the centralising tendencies of the sixteenth to the eighteenth centuries, the existence of intermediate associations was recognised, and the distinction between these and the state was found in the sovereignty inherent in the latter. But in the latest period there came into being the federal constitutions of the United States, Switzerland and the German Empire, in which a number of states were formed into a larger political union and subjected to its authority. These states were then non-sovereign because they lacked that quality which had been regarded as the essential characteristic of the state.

So Meyer was forced to consider whether sovereignty is in fact "a necessary ingredient of the conception of the state," and in this connection he set out the *Herrschaft* theory.

If sovereignty be deemed essential to the idea of the state there are two possibilities. Either the term "state" is applied to the individual states in a federation and sovereignty is ascribed to them—in that case the federation cannot possess authority (*Herrschaft*) over them, and so must be regarded merely as a treaty relationship in accordance with international law; or, alternatively, it must be assumed that the federation is sovereign, that is, is itself the state, and in that case the individual states are regarded simply as provinces, that is, as communal bodies. But in Meyer's opinion neither of these theories was in accordance with the facts. For the federations mentioned above unquestionably possess authority over their constituent states, whilst, on the other hand, these same states have certain qualities in common with sovereign states, and there are wide differences between the constituent states in a federation and the communes in a unitary state.

So to Meyer sovereignty was not an essential part of the idea of the state; there are sovereign states and non-sovereign states. It became necessary to find some other line of demarcation between the state and the commune. This he found in the difference of the legal position (status) of the two kinds of communities—the difference is a juristic one and not merely an historico-political one. But Meyer admitted that as to the nature of this distinction there was great difference of opinion. He himself found the distinction to lie in the fact that the authority of the state over the communes is legally unrestricted, whereas the authority of the federation over the constituent states is legally restricted, and the states have what the communes do not possess, namely, a twofold autonomy, that is, power to carry out certain political tasks independently, that is, in accordance with their own laws, and power to regulate their own organisation independently, that is, again by their own legislation.

Therefore Meyer asserted that the term "states" means all those political collectivities which have the power to discharge their political tasks independently, that is, in accordance with their own laws and to regulate their constitutions independently, by means of their own laws.[1] And these "states" he divided into sovereign (unitary) states, that is, those not subject to any superior power, and non-sovereign states, those subject to the limited authority of a higher political union.

Proceeding to discuss the unitary state, he defined the state as "a human community based on a defined territory" bringing the members united in it into a higher unity and subordinating them to its authority (*Herrschaft*).

The state has often been described as an organism, but that description has only a comparative value; its importance is chiefly that it contradicts the older and erroneous doctrines which regarded the state as a piece of mechanism, as a contractual association of individuals, or as something artificial. For the juristic interpretation of the state the idea of organism has no utility.

From the juristic standpoint the state is described as a person —that is, a legal personality in public law. The rights of government (*Herrschaftsrechte*) over the subjects belong to the state as a political commonwealth, and not to the ruler; the ruler appears only as the agent of the state. This idea of the state as a legal personality, entirely independent of the person of the particular ruler, was clearly expressed by the political philosophers of classical antiquity. But the characteristic of mediaeval doctrines of the state and public law was to treat all legal relationships as personal relationships between individuals, and so the ruler came to be regarded not as the agent of the state, but as a personal lord, between whom and his subjects there existed a series of rights and

[1] Georg Meyer: *Lehrbuch des deutschen Staatsrechts*, ed. by G. Anschütz, 1905, p. 10.

obligations. On the other hand, the mediaeval Italian doctrine held firmly under classical influence to the idea of the state as an independent personality, and after the sixteenth century there was a general reversion to that idea—although even in the nineteenth century the mediaeval German conception still found some defenders.

The activity of the state finds expression mainly in the work of government (*Ausübung von Herrschaftsrechten*), but not solely in that, for there are many activities in which the state is not a ruler of, but is on an equality with, other legal persons. That is particularly the case in international relations, but within the state itself there may develop many activities which the state encourages but does not order or direct.

As the state is a "conceptional abstraction," there must be physical persons (individuals or bodies of individuals) entrusted with the exercise of the powers of the state. These are called by Meyer the state organs (*Organe*).

This exercise of the powers of government can be entrusted either to a single organ (as, for instance, the monarchy in an absolute monarchy or an assembly of the whole body of citizens in a pure democracy) or to a number of organs working together in accordance with constitutional rules (as in a constitutional monarchy or a democracy with representative institutions).

There is a further conception to be noticed, that of the *Träger* of the state power, a term applied to the person or persons possessing the state authority in their own right. The holder of the state power can exercise the rights of government either directly or by another person acting in his name. This idea of the bearer of the state power is not a consequence of the unity and indivisibility of the state power, for the conceptional unity of the state power does not exclude its exercise by a plurality of organs.[1]

Meyer defined "sovereignty" as "independence of any higher power" and as the quality possessed by the state as the supreme governing commonwealth. It involves two things: (*a*) the state's freedom from the rule of any other commonwealth, and (*b*) the subordination to the state of all persons and corporations existent in its territory. The former is the external aspect of sovereignty expressed in constitutional law. The sovereignty of the state is incompatible with any limitation by a higher will, but it is not incompatible with limitation by its own will, e.g. by the undertaking of contractual obligations towards other states.[2] The unitary

[1] Georg Meyer: *Lehrbuch des deutschen Staatsrechts*, ed. by G. Anschütz, 1905, pp. 15–18.   [2] Ibid., pp. 19–23.

state is always sovereign; in form it is unrestricted, that is to say, omnipotent. But there are practical limitations, determined by the nature of the state purpose, and realised by an intelligent state leadership. And the unitary state has an unlimited scope for its activities. It has only to decide what political tasks it will undertake itself and what it will leave to the communal bodies subordinate to it. That is, it possesses the so-called *Kompetenz-Kompetenz*. But, like Brie and Rosin, Meyer held that *Kompetenz-Kompetenz* was not the whole nature of sovereignty; to him it was possible to conceive of sovereignty within a limited sphere and without *Kompetenz-Kompetenz*. For a commonwealth to possess sovereignty it is, he maintained, only necessary that its powers cannot be taken away without its consent.

Sovereignty as the quality of a person or a plurality of persons meant then to Meyer the legal position in the state of that person who appears as the *Träger* of the state power (the sovereign). The power of that sovereign is supreme in the state, but it is not necessarily unlimited; in the exercise of the rights of government the sovereign can be bound to follow a prescribed procedure and to co-operate with other organs.

To the discussion of the form and functions of the unitary state Meyer contributed nothing new.

In the examination of unions of states (*Staatenverbindungen*) he started by distinguishing between the wider and the narrower meanings of that term.

In the wider sense, the term "unions of states" comprises all unions of a number of states, and therefore includes those which are such merely in international law, and alliances, and unions resulting from the fact that there is one and the same monarch in several states (personal unions, e.g. England and Hanover, and real unions, e.g. Sweden and Norway).[1] In the narrower sense "union of states" means the union of a number of states into one larger commonwealth. In these there is a higher power, superior to the individual constituent states. But that power is not unlimited, but is subject to constitutional limitations.[2] The authority (*Herrschaft*) over the associated states can be either possessed by one of them (then the relation is one of suzerainty), or it can be vested in a power constituted from the collectivity of the associated commonwealths, and the resultant union of states is a federation —including within that term the confederation, which differs from the federation in that its authority is only over states,

[1] Georg Meyer: *Lehrbuch des deutschen Staatsrechts*, ed. by G. Anschütz, 1905, p. 38.   [2] Ibid., p. 39.

whilst that of the federation extends directly to the subjects and citizens.[1]

In contradiction to the prevalent view as to the confederation, Meyer defined it as being that form of federal relationship in which the federal authority is exercisable only over the individual states, and he held that the confederation is not merely "a treaty relation, but a legal subject of public law."[2] It can enter into legal relations with other legal persons, with both foreign states and private persons; but it possesses authority only over states. And from this he drew the conclusion that the confederation is not only a subject in international and private law, but also a subject in constitutional law. Applying the private law analogies of *societas* and *universitas* to the sphere of the public law, he pointed out that an alliance could correspond to the conception of the *societas* and that every federal relation is a *universitas*.[3]

As the federal authority in a confederation possesses no direct authority over the citizens of the individual states, which are alone members of the confederation, it can exercise its *Herrschaftsrecht* only by the intermediary of the state powers of the individual states. Therefore the confederation can legislate; but it cannot do more than make the laws; for them to be binding it is essential that they shall be carried out by the individual states. So the federal authority can act directly in foreign affairs where it has to deal only with foreign states, but not in domestic matters, which would involve it in immediate relations with individuals; it may have jurisdiction in disputes between the states, but it may not have jurisdiction in respect of individuals.

The confederation has a limited competence which is formulated precisely in the fundamental law or the federal pact. For the enlargement of this competence there are two possibilities: either the consent of all the confederated states is necessary (and this is more appropriate to the nature of the confederation), or—differing in this from the exponents of the *Korporation* theory—a decision of the federal authority is sufficient. The first alternative has, in fact, always been the case.

Contrary to the prevailing view, Meyer asserted that the individual states in the confederation are "not sovereign"[4] since they are subject to the federal authority within the sphere of the federal competence and must obey its orders; but in relation to their own subjects and citizens they retain their full authority. Their sovereignty is limited externally, not internally.

[1] Georg Meyer: *Lehrbuch des deutschen Staatsrechts*, ed. by G. Anschütz, 1905, p. 41.   [2] Ibid.   [3] Ibid., p. 41 (Note).   [4] Ibid., p. 42.

Finally, Meyer laid it down that the confederation possessed organs just as the unitary state. He considered the "actions of these organs" as actions of the union itself. And even where—as is generally the case—the federal power is vested in the representatives of the individual states, he would not ascribe to the federal decision the character of agreements or compacts, as he held that for these unanimity is necessary, whereas in the confederation a majority vote is decisive.[1]

Meyer's doctrine that the constituent states of a confederation are non-sovereign remained peculiar to himself; his theory that the decisions of the confederation are not compacts or agreements was in conflict with the opinions of those who, like Laband, regarded the confederation as simply a treaty relationship.

In contrast to the confederation Meyer defined the federal state as "that relationship of union in which the federal authority exercises its *Herrschaftsrecht* directly over the individual subjects." It is "a legal subject of public law" like the confederation. It can enter into legal relations with other legal subjects; but possesses *Herrschaftsrecht* over its members and has its own organs, whose wills and acts are its own wills and acts.[2]

Therefore the difference between federal state and confederation lies in the manner in which the union exercises its rights of government. On these two different conceptions had been based the constitution of the United States of America, and the constitutions of Germany and of Switzerland before 1848. The former set up the federal state; the two latter constitutions set up the confederation, and the nationalist movements of Germany and Switzerland had been directed towards transforming their confederations into federal states. The essential difference between them was that the Swiss and German unions ruled over states, while the American union ruled directly over the subjects of the individual states. So Meyer reiterated that this is the one criterion —the essential distinction—between confederation and federal state. Every federal relationship, in which the federal power has direct rule over the individual subjects or citizens of the states, is "a federal state."

Therefore the federal authority in the federal state possesses competence not only in the sphere of external administration, but also in the domestic spheres of legislation, administration and judicature.[3] And the federal laws are made binding by their simple publication by the federal state.

[1] Georg Meyer: *Lehrbuch des deutschen Staatsrechts*, ed. by G. Anschütz, 1905, p. 42. [2] Ibid., p. 43. [3] Ibid., p. 45.

In the federal state there is a division of political tasks between the union and the individual states, but the precise nature of the division seemed to Meyer of no importance.

According to his theory of *Herrschaft*, as he stated it, the union and the individual states are not independent and equal commonwealths, but are rather the individual state members of a greater political union, and are subordinate to the authority of the union within the sphere of federal competence just as provinces and communes are subordinate to the state. The federal authority is entitled to make laws which the individual states are bound to obey. And not only does the federal authority possess its own organs to enforce the laws, but it can make use of the organs of the individual states to enforce its orders, just as the unitary state uses the organs of the local governments for that purpose.[1]

The participation of the state powers of the individual state in the formation of the federal authority is by no means in conflict with the nature of the federal state, for it is of the nature of the federal state that the federal authority shall be formed by, and based on, the collectivity of the state authorities of the individual state.

The unlimited sphere of activity possessed by the state is not possessed in the federal state by either the states or the union; both are restricted. In order to extend the competence two courses are possible. It can be done either by a decision of the federal authority or by the agreement of the individual states. Actually the first is the general rule, taking the form of a change in the constitution.

So to Meyer the states in the federal state are "not sovereign."[2] The federal authority is superior to the individual states, and the latter no longer possess complete state authority and power over their subjects and citizens. The subordination of the individual state to the federal power is limited to the sphere of the federal competence, but may be extended so far as the federal authority can of its own right enlarge its competence. Only if an extension of the federal authority must be assented to by all the states—of which there is at present no instance—is it possible, in Meyer's opinion, to ascribe to the states a limited sovereignty. But, with this exception, in the federal state sovereignty is vested in the union.

Lastly, Meyer pointed out that the federal state, like the individual state, can come into being in a number of ways. Of these

[1] Georg Meyer: *Lehrbuch des deutschen Staatsrechts*, ed. by G. Anschütz, 1905, p. 46. [2] Ibid., p. 48.

two are important. It may result from the breaking up of a unitary state or from the joining together of a number of wholly independent states, or of states hitherto joined in a confederation.

G. Meyer thus boldly rejected the dominant idea of federalism in this analysis of the nature of the *Staatenbund* and of the *Bundesstaat*.

Considering the individual states in the federal state as well as in the confederation, he placed them in the same rank as local organisations, such as communal unions, and only differentiated them from local political institutions in respect of the extent to which they can exercise independent authority.

He totally rejected Laband's conception of the confederation, and regarded it as in the same category as the federal state.

Federalism, according to his theory of *Herrschaft*, was not any particular political technique, but rather a kind of political mechanism concerned with the relations between the central and local governments.

G. Meyer's federal theory, based on the *Herrschaft* principle, stood with that of Albert Haenel as one school of thought in federal discussion in Germany, with Laband's, Jellinek's and Brie's theory of federalism as the other.

From 1871 down to 1900 the German theory of federalism was fully developed by the successive publications of a number of outstanding works. G. Meyer and Haenel's *Herrschaft* federalism, Laband's formal positivistic federalism, Jellinek's empirical positivistic federalism and Brie's juristic ideal federalism laid the foundations of the theory of the federal state in Germany.

Along with these principles of federalism the famous work of Otto Gierke, *Das deutsche Genossenschaftsrecht*, published in 1868, gave a new impetus to the creation of the new federalism in Germany.

In this development the new German federal ideas made great progress, partly through Triepel and Anschütz, and partly through Gierke and Preuss, and paved the way for a new formation of the federal republic in 1919.

INDEX

Achaean League, 21–23
Adams, John, 47
Ahrens, H., on federalism, 387, 388
Albany, plan of Union, 130
Althusius, Johannes, on federalism, 27–30, 207, 328
Amphictyonic Council, 21
Aristotle, definition of the State, 22
Asquith and Oxford, Lord (H. H.), rejection of Imperial Federation, 264
Auerbach, L., on federalism, 407
Austin, John, on federalism, 143–145, 282; ——, on right of Secession, 148; ——, on sovereignty, 144
Australia, Convention of Colonies of, 256; ——, federal development, 251–263; ——, federation, compared with that of Canada, 259–263; ——, self-government granted, 253
Australian Commonwealth Federation Act, 258

Bake, C., on federalism, 453
Barker, Ernest, on the State, 315
Bartolus, on federation, 25
Bassermann, 362
Beaconsfield, Lord, on Imperial federation, 238
Beard, C., on federalism, 200–202
Behr, W. J., on federalism, 347
Bentham, Jeremy, on Colonial emancipation, 221; ——, on federalism, 277–282; ——, political views, 124
Berg, G. H. von, on federalism, 346
Besold, C., on federalism, 30
Blumer, J., 400
Bluntschli, J. C., on Lieber, 128; ——, on federalism, 363–367, 454
Bodin, Jean, on federalism, 26
Böhlau, H., on federalism, 401–402
Brie, S., on federalism, 196, 386, 538–579; ——, on Theory of State, 539–541
British Empire, colonial conferences, 232, 237, 241, 252, 256; ——, colonial development, 43, 44, 212, 228; ——, devolution conference, 266; ——, federalism, 207–323; ——, imperial conference, 264, 273; ——, Imperial Federation League, 241, 242, 251; ——, Round Table Conference, 274

British Empire, United Empire Trade League, 241; see also India and names of Colonies
British N. America Act, 1867, 232
Brown, Sir George, 252
Brownson, O., on sovereignty, 145
Bryce, James, on federalism, 162–176, 297
Bundesstaat: see Federal State
Buol-Schauenstein, on the German Union, 349
Burgess, J. W., on federalism, 156–159; ——, on sovereignty, 156
Burke, Edmund, on British American colonies, 217–220; ——, policy, 218 and fn.

Calhoun, J., on nullification right, 116; ——, political views of, 84, 97, 105–117, 495, 496, 498, 514; ——, on sovereignty, 111, 116
Canada, federal development, 221–235; ——, federation compared with that of Australia, 259–263
Carnarvon, Earl of, Canadian federation supported, 232–234
Casmannus, Otto, on federalism, 30
"Centurion," federal scheme of, 241
Chamberlain, J., on Australian Federation, 258, 259
Chase, Chief Justice (U.S.), 182
Cicero, 131
Cole, G. D. H., on a guild state, 268, 315, 318
Commune, characteristics of, 532–536, 543
Confederation, compared with Federal State: see Federal State
Cotton, John, 44
Croly, 200

Dante, 24
Davis, Jefferson, 123
Davis, N. D., federal scheme, 242
Dewey, J., 200
Dibbs, Sir G., 257
Dicey, A. V., on Imperial federalism, 298; ——, on federalism, 304–312
Disraeli, B., on imperial federation, 238
Dubs, J., 400
Duffy, C. G., report on Australian federal union, 255
Durham, Lord, Canadian administration, 223–226

Eddy, C. W., on federalism, 238
Elgin, Lord, Canadian administration, 226
Engelbert, 24
England, Reform Act, 124; ——, Union with Scotland, 208; ——,
Escher, Heinrich, on federalism, 394

Federal Council of Australia Act, 256
Federalism, American, 42–204; ——, British, 207–323; ——, early types, 21–25; ——, German, 327–588; ——, Greek, 21, 22, 207, 327
Federalists, The, 50–71
Federal State compared with Confederation, 155, 349, 361, 365, 388, 407, 426, 428, 453, 536, 560-562
Feudalism compared with federalism, 327
Fichte, J. G., State theory of, 333
Figgis, A. J., 315
Filmer, Sir R., advocacy of divine right of Kings, 42
Finer, H., 269, 270
Ford, H. J., 200
Forster, W. E., on Federation, 241
Frankfurt, parliament, 337
Franklin, Benjamin, drafting of Albany plan of Union, 130
Frederick the Great, 331, 332
Freeman, Edward A., on federalism, 290–297, 235
Fries, J. F., on federalism, 350

Gagern, Friedrich von, on German Union, 349, 353–355
Genossenschafstheorie, 313, 315, 322, 336, 338, 588
Gerber, C. F. von, on federalism, 386
German Empire, contrast with U.S. federalism, 418; ——, confederation replaced by federalism, 362; ——, extension of authority claim, 401; ——, federalism, 327–588; ——, imperial laws' authority, 403 fn.; ——, Zollverein, 490
Gierke, O., on federalism, 25, 313
Gladstone, on imperial federalism, 251
Goodnow, F. J., 200, 202
Greece, federal idea, 21, 22, 207, 327
Green, T. H., on Rousseau's federalism, 38 fn., 161; ——, on Kant, 333
Grey, Earl, Australian administration of, 254; ——, Canadian administration of, 226
Griffith, S., plan of Confederation of Australian Colonies, 256
Grotius, Hugo, on federalism, 31 329,

Häberlin, K. F., 344
Haenel, A., on federalism, 421–434, 436, 516; ——, on sovereignty, 427, 462
Haldane, Lord, on Imperial federalism, 252
Hamilton, A., federal ideas, 47, 50–57, 62, 72, 84
Harrington, J., on democracy, 42
Heeren, A. L., on German Union, 349
Hegel, G. W. F., state theory of, 124, 334, 336
Held, J., on federalism, 396–398, 407–414, 420
Herrschaftstheorie, 385, 421, 431, 434, 542–543, 581–588
Hobbes, T., political views, 34
Hobson, S. G., 315
Hoenonius, P. H., on federalism, 30
Holy Roman Empire, 330
Hooker, Thomas, 45
Howe, J., 235
Hugo, Ludolph, on federalism, 31, 329, 340–342
Hume, D., ideal of a perfect commonwealth, 211, 213; ——, on U.S.A., 213 fn.; ——, philosophy of, 34
Hurd, J. C., on federalism, 150–154, 282; ——, on sovereignty, 151

Ihering, R., theory of state, 533, 534
India, federalism proposed, 274–276
International administration, 488

Jackson, Andrew, democratic principles, 86; ——, nullification doctrine, 97
James, William, pragmatic theory of, 200, 315
Jameson, J. A., on federalism, 154
Jay, John, political views of, 51
Jefferson, T., on federalism, 72–85, 97; ——, on right of secession, 82
Jellinek, G., on federalism, 192, 197, 455–525; ——, on the non-sovereign state, 467–471; on right of secession, 519; ——, on sovereignty, 459–471
Jenkins, E., on imperial federation, 236, 237
Jews, federation of tribes, 21
Judson, H., 203

Kaltenborn, C. von, on federalism, 396
Kant, I., philosophy of, 332, 336; ——, on International federalism, 40

INDEX

Kelsey, S. W., scheme of federation, 239
Kennedy, W. P. M., Quotations from "The Constitution of Canada," 226 fn., 227 fn.
Kent, James, on federalism, 98
Klüber, J. L., on German Union, 349
Kompetenz-Kompetenz, 401, 421, 453–454, 525, 529–531, 535, 541, 566, 584
Laband, P., on federalism, 196, 434–450, 509, 516; ——, on sovereignty, 441, 447
Labillière, F. P. de, on Imperial federalism, 243, 245–251
Laski, H. J. on federalism, 203, 321–322; ——, political views, 269, 317–323; ——, on sovereignty, 317–318
Leist, 344
Lieber, Francis, on federalism, 124, 129–143; ——, on right of secession, 137; on sovereignty, 135–141
Lincoln, Abraham, elected President, 122; ——, on right of secession, 123
Lippman, W., 200
Locke, John, political views, 34, 42; ——, on federalism, 211
Lowell, A. L., on federalism, 190

Mably, Abbé de, on Greek federalism, 22
MacDonald, J. A. Murray, on federation, 227, 229, 230, 271; ——, on Devolution, 266, 267
Madison, James, on federalism, 52, 54, 55, 57, 58, 59, 62; ——, on right of secession, 101
Maitland, F. W., on association, 313–315
Marshall, Chief Justice (U.S.), 97
Martitz, F., 404, 405
Mejer, Otto, on federalism, 395
Merriam, C. E., on federalism, 199
Meyer, G., on federalism, 402, 405, 407, 579–588; ——, on sovereignty, 581–587
Mill, James, 221
Mill, John Stuart, on federalism, 285–289
Mohl, R. von, on federalism, 385, 386, 388, 402, 406
Montesquieu, C. de, influence on founders of U.S.A., 47; ——, political views, 35, 36, 345

Monzambano, Severinus de: *see* Pufendorf
Morley, John, on Imperial federalism, 243–245; ——, quotation from life of Edmund Burke, 218
Moser, J. J., 343

Napoleon, 331, 332
Netherlands, Confederation of the, 328
New Zealand, responsible government granted, 254

Oppenheimer, F. von, 264

Paine, Thomas, 46
Parkes, Sir H., scheme for federation of Australian states, 256
Penn, William, followers of, 45
Penty, A. J., 315
Pfizer, P. A., on federalism, 355
Pfyffer, Kasimir, 360
Political Pluralism, 312–233
Polybius, 23, 327
Pomeroy, J. N., on federalism, 149
Pound, Roscoe, 200
Powell, Governor, on British federalism, 213
Pözl, on federalism, 393
Pragmatism, Wm. James's system of, 200; *see* Vol. II, Conclusion
Preuss, Hugo, 386
Prussia, growth of, 330–332
Pufendorf, S. von, on federalism, 31–33, 329, 342
Puritans, in American colonies, 44
Pütter, Johann S., on federalism, 343

Quakers, Society of, 44, 45

Radowitz, J. von, on federalism, 368, 377
Rawle, W., on federalism, 103; ——, on right of secession, 105
Reformation, political effects, 330
Rheinbund, The, 331, 345, 348
River navigation, administration, 488
Rock, J. S., 182
Rogers, Sir R., 237
Roman Empire, government of, 24
Rönne, von, on federalism, 402
Rosin, H., on federalism, 526–529; ——, state theory, 196, 525–538
Round Table Conference (1930), 274
Rousseau, Jean-Jacques, on federalism, 36–40
Royal Colonial Institute, foundation of, 238

Russell, Lord, Canadian administration, 226
Rüttimann, Prof., on federalism, 390

Schulze, Hermann, on federalism, 386, 454
Secession, Right of, 82, 100, 101, 103, 105, 119, 123, 137, 148, 296, 498, 519
Seeley, J. R., support of federalism, 243
Senate, Waitz's argument on, 380–381
Seydel, Max von, on federalism and sovereignty, 414–417, 419, 436, 495
Sidgwick, Henry, on federalism, 298–304
Smith, Adam, on British American colonies, 213–217
Smith, Goldwin, 235, 236, 237
Snell, Ludwig, on federalism, 361
South Africa, federation, 263
South Carolina, declaration of independence, 122, 123
Sovereignty, theories of, 25, 111, 116, 118, 135–141, 144, 149, 151, 154, 156, 317, 427, 441–447, 451, 459–471, 526–529, 581–587; ——, theory of divided, of Bluntschli, 454; of Jefferson, 75; of Madison, 101; of Waitz, 370–371, 375; of Welcker, 358
Spalding, T. A., on devolution, 265
Spinoza, 345
Staatenbund: see Confederation
Stahl, J., on federalism, 367
Stettler, F., 361–362
Story, J., on federalism, 99–100; ——, on sovereignty, 98
Strabo, 23, 327
Swiss Federal States, formation, 328, 329, 352; ——, revision of constitution, 360–362
Sydenham, Lord, Canadian administration, 226
Sydney, Algernon, democratic ideas, 42

Taney, Chief Justice (U.S.), 122, 181
Thompson, W., 203
Tiffany, J., 149
Tittmann, F. W., 350–352
Tocqueville, A. de, on federalism, 86–96, 329, 339
Treitschke, H. von, on federalism, 386, 390
Trendelenburg, A., on federalism, 398–400

Troxler, I., on federalism, 361
Tucker, H. St. George, on federalism, 103

United Kingdom, formation of, 208
United States, civil war, 123, 141; ——, Declaration of Independence, 46–49, 131; ——, Declaration of Rights, 72, 131; ——, economic development, 179–182; ——, federalism, 21, 42–204; ——, federalism contrasted with that of Germany, 418; ——, House of Representatives, 65; ——, decision of the supreme court, 181–184; ——, nullification doctrine, 97 fn., 116, 119, 120; ——, President, method of election, 63; ——, railway development, 141; ——, secession, right of: *see* Secession; ——, Senate, 65

Vogel, Sir Julius, 235
Vollgraff, C. F., 394

Waitz, Georg, on federalism, 329, 369–385
Ward, Sir Joseph, demands for Imperial Federation, 264
Webb, Mr. and Mrs. Sidney, Socialistic Commonwealth scheme, 267, 268 fn.
Webster, D., on nullification right, 119, 120; ——, on Constitution of U.S., 117–121; ——, on secession, right of, 119; ——, on sovereignty, 118
Welcker, Carl, on federalism, 356–359, 377
Williams, Roger, on Church and State, 44
Willoughby, W. W., on federalism, 191–200
Wilson, Woodrow, on federalism, 184–189
Wolff, C., 345
Woolsey, T. D., on federalism, 155

Young, Sir F. E., on Imperial Federation, 239

Zachariä, H. A., on federalism, 367, 391–393
Zachariä, K. S., on federalism, 346
Zöpfl, H., on federalism, 394
Zorn, P., on federalism, 450–453; ——, on sovereignty, 451